COMPUTER SCIENCE

COMPUTER SCIENCE

A Breadth-First Approach with C

John Impagliazzo
Paul Nagin

Hofstra University
Hempstead, New York

John Wiley & Sons
New York   Chichester   Brisbane   Toronto   Singapore

ACQUISITIONS EDITOR   Steven Elliot
MARKETING MANAGER   Susan Elbe
SENIOR PRODUCTION EDITOR   Nancy Prinz
COVER DESIGNER   Dawn L. Stanley
INTERIOR DESIGN   Levavi & Levavi
COVER ART   Otherworld Artyfax
MANUFACTURING MANAGER   Susan Stetzer
ILLUSTRATION COORDINATOR   Rosa Bryant

This book was set in ITC Garamond Light by Publication Services and printed and bound by R. R. Donnelley & Sons, Crawfordsville. The cover was printed by Phoenix.

Library of Congress Cataloging-in-Publication Data
Impagliazzo, John.
    Computer science : a breadth-first approach with C / by John
Impagliazzo and Paul Nagin.
        p.   cm.
    Includes bibliographical references and index.
    ISBN 0–471–58552–1 (paper)
    1. Computer science.   2. C (Computer program language)   I. Nagin,
Paul A.   II. Title.
QA76.I423   1994
004––dc20   94-33250
                                                                              CIP

Printed in the United States of America

10 9 8 7 6 5 4 3 2

Preface

The computing sciences are in their infancy. Although electronic computing machines have been in existence since the 1930s, this area of study was not formalized until the late 1960s when the Association for Computing Machinery (ACM) published its first curriculum recommendations for four-year programs in computer science. "Curriculum '68—Recommendations for Academic Programs in Computer Science"[1] encouraged the study of discrete mathematics and calculus and proposed a set of computing courses. "Curriculum '78—Recommendations for the Undergraduate Program in Computer Science"[2] updated the previous recommendations of 1968 in response to the rapidly changing field of computing. In 1984 and 1985 ACM published "Recommended Curriculum for CS1"[3] and "Recommended Curriculum for CS2,"[4] which encouraged use of data structures and software design and implementation in the early stages of a computer science curriculum.

The curricula recommendations in the computing sciences were becoming reactive rather than proactive as educators responded to the needs of a changing computing profession. In the late 1980s a special task force was created to address this issue. It published the "Report of the ACM Task Force on the Core of Computer Science,"[5] also called the "Denning Report." The report established topic areas that define the discipline this way:

> *The discipline of computing is the systematic study of algorithmic processes that describe and transform information: their theory, analysis, design, efficiency, implementation, and application. The fundamental question underlying all of computing is, "What can be (efficiently) automated?"*

A more general definition of computer science from the Denning Report incorporates the paradigms of *theory* (mathematical approach), *abstraction*

[1]ACM Curriculum Committee on Computer Science. "Curriculum '68—Recommendations for Academic Programs in Computer Science." *Communications of the ACM, 11,* 3 (March 1968), 151–197.

[2]ACM Curriculum Committee on Computer Science. "Curriculum '78—Recommendations for the Undergraduate Program in Computer Science." *Communications of the ACM, 22,* 3 (March 1979), 147–166.

[3]Koffman, Elliot B., et al. "Recommended Curriculum for CS1: 1984." *Communications of the ACM, 27,* 10 (October 1984), 998–1001.

[4]Koffman, Elliot B., et al. "Recommended Curriculum for CS2: 1984." *Communications of the ACM, 28,* 8, (August 1985), 815–818.

[5]Denning, Peter, et al. "Report of the ACM Task Force on the Core of Computer Science." ACM Press, New York, 1988. Also known as the "Denning Report." Reprinted in part in *Communications of the ACM, 32,* 1 (January 1989), and in *Computer* (February 1989).

(experimental approach), and *design* (engineering approach) within the following nine topic areas:

Algorithms and data structures

Programming languages

Architecture

Numerical and symbolic computing

Operating systems

Software methodology and engineering

Database and information retrieval

Artificial intelligence and robotics

Human-computer communication

The report also encouraged sensitivity to the social context of computing.

Previous curriculum recommendations promoted *depth* in the beginning stages of the curriculum through the early study of and concentration on programming. The Denning Report suggests *breadth* in the study of computing as a whole in the first stages of the discipline coupled with laboratory experiences, similar to the study of biology, chemistry, and physics.

The ACM and the Computer Society of the Institute for Electrical and Electronic Engineers (IEEE-CS) embraced the Denning Report. In 1991 both societies jointly published "Computing Curricula 1991,"[6] which serve a variety of computing programs. These recommendations do not prescribe courses for study. Instead they decompose the nine topic areas into knowledge units that can be arranged for an individual program of study. Such a program should consist of the nine topic areas and reflect one or more of the paradigms of theory, abstraction, and design. Many of these concepts are also reflected in other ACM publications such as *Computing Curricula Guidelines for Associate Degree Programs*[7] and the *Model High School Computer Science Curriculum.*[8]

GOALS OF THIS TEXT

This text arose from the emerging demand for an introductory, broad-range, or *breadth-first* book on computer science. We believe that using the breadth-first

---

[6]Tucker, Allen B., et al. "Computing Curricula 1991—Report of the ACM/IEEE-Computer Society Joint Curriculum Task Force," ACM Press, New York, 1991. Reprinted in summary in *Communications of the ACM* (June 1991), 68–84.

[7]ACM Two-Year College Computing Curricula Task Force. "Computing Curricula Guidelines for Associate Degree Programs—Computing Sciences," ACM Press, New York, 1993.

[8]ACM Task Force of the Pre-College Committee. "ACM Model High School Computer Science Curriculum," ACM Press, New York, 1993.

approach will not interfere with the remainder of the typical undergraduate computer science curriculum. Rather it should increase class motivation since students will have an overall sense of the field instead of merely a narrow-band knowledge of programming.

Breadth-First versus Depth-First   The traditional, depth-first approach to teaching computer science generally consists of a two- or three-semester exposure to a particular procedural language like C with emphasis on syntax, algorithm design, and data structures. Other topics in computer science are generally ignored. This *programming approach* reinforces the misconception that computer science is the study of programming syntax and applications. Although it is true that programmers do (mostly) programming, computer scientists deal with *computing*, using programming as a tool with which to explore and develop ideas.

The breadth-first approach, on the other hand, gives exposure to the essential elements of computing. Selected topics include: machine architecture, algorithms, data communications, complexity theory, database design, artificial intelligence, information retrieval, and software engineering. Programming is integrated throughout the topics as a tool for exploring these aspects of the field. Depth of knowledge is relegated to other courses taken in the remaining years of undergraduate and graduate study.

We believe that students should be exposed to the various aspects of computing early in their education and sample the breadth of the discipline so that they will have a clearer understanding of what the field comprises. It is for this reason that we adhere to the principles promoted in the "Denning Report" and in "Computing Curricula 1991."

Use of the C Language   A number of programming languages are used in industrial and scientific computing environments. Although most programming languages have their partisans, C apparently meets the needs of scientists and programmers working in a range of applications. Indeed, many observers agree that C is evolving into a *de facto* language of choice. Some academic institutions require their students to study languages that are not generally prominent or useful in the commercial area. These languages have their own special advantages; however, it is our belief that students should have an early exposure to a language that has both pedagogical soundness and practical benefit.

It is our strong belief and experience that if C is introduced early in the discipline, students can achieve initial success. The remaining years of undergraduate study provide ample time to master the C language, resulting in a versatile and highly marketable tool for their developing careers.

Although not specifically mandated in either of the two previously mentioned reports, we have chosen to incorporate the C programming language because it is both instructive and of practical use in the marketplace. The breadth-first approach coupled with the increasing prevalence of the C language stimulated the development of this text.

NOTE TO THE PROFESSOR

Philosophy   For many instructors, teaching a breadth-first course in computer science is a novelty. The range of topics may even seem intimidating, especially when they are intended for an audience of first-year majors. Experience has shown us, however, that students gravitate to the breadth topics of computer science, which stimulate new ideas for them and generate meaningful discussions.

We do not mean to teach beginning students all of computer science or all the intricacies of the C language in a one-year course. It is more important to let students sample areas of the discipline in small doses and develop a basic understanding of C. Some topics are taken to a greater level of detail to give instructors more flexibility in the presentation of the material. This detail can be omitted without loss of continuity.

Implementation   The material in the text is designed for first-year undergraduate majors and minors in computer science for presentation over two semesters. Accelerated programs can also use the text for a one-semester course. Upon completion, students will have developed a broad foundational knowledge of the principal elements in the science of computing and a working knowledge of C.

The following table provides suggested coverage for a one-year sequence with three possible tracks. The A-track is the most complete, needing full coverage

CHAPTER	SECTIONS A-TRACK	SECTIONS B-TRACK	SECTIONS C-TRACK
1	1, 2, 3	1, 2, 3	1, 2, 3
2	1, 2	1, 2	1, 2
3	1, 2, 3	1, 2, 3	1, 2, 3
4	1, 2, 3	1, 2	1
5	1, 2, 3	1, 2, 3	1, 2, 3
6	1, 2	1, 2	1
7	1, 2, 3, 4	1, 2, 3	1, 2, 3
8	1, 2	1, 2*	1
9	1, 2	1, 2	1, 2
10	1, 2	1, 2	1
11	1, 2, 3	1, 2, 3	1, 2, 3*
12	1, 2	1	1
13	1, 2, 3	1, 2	1, 2*
14	1, 2	1, 2	1
15	1, 2	1, 2*	1
16	1, 2	1, 2*	1
17	1, 2, 3*	1, 2*	1
18	1, 2	1*, 2	2*
19	1, 2	1, 2*	1
Required sections	46	36	29

with one optional section. The B-track offers more flexibility, with 11 sections that are optional. The C-track is the minimum necessary coverage for a breadth-first approach. Asterisks (*) show optional sections. All tracks ensure sufficient coverage of programming methodology and design.

Students completing this text will have gained a general understanding of the significant topic areas of study in the field of computer science. In addition, they will have a substantial preparation in C programming. We believe that the integrated breadth-first approach gives students a strong foundation in the subject and the skills to become knowledgeable and effective computer scientists. This knowledge will be a solid platform on which students can build a career in computing.

SUPPLEMENTS

The following materials are available to accompany the text.

1. An instructor's manual with suggested lesson plans and solutions to most exercises.
2. A computer disk for instructors containing program samples and suggested questions for examinations.

ACKNOWLEDGMENTS

We wish to acknowledge the contributions made to the manuscript by our students, colleagues, reviewers, and editors. We thank the many students who participated in the class testing of the material and in particular Alan P. Baker, Andrew Botwinick, Richard N. Gruenfelder, Jeanette R. Sones, David J. Stecher, and Frank P. Tufano for their assistance in developing and testing some of the programs. A special thanks to our Hofstra colleagues, Thomas B. Steel, Jr. and Olga Salizkiy, for their comments and suggestions in the early stages of manuscript development.

The reviewers of the manuscript made fine suggestions that were incorporated in this text. We extend our heartfelt thanks to:

Lillian Cassel
Villanova University

Marsha Moroh
College of Staten Island

Karl J. Klee
Jamestown Community College

Vaidy S. Sunderam
Emory University

Ann Ford
University of Michigan

Robert D. Campbell
Manatee Community College

John D. McGregor
Clemson University

Eleanor Quinlan
Ohio State University

Linda Werner
University of California: Santa Cruz

Clifford Shaffer
Virginia Tech

Ken Collier
Northern Arizona University

Elizabeth Adams
Richard Stockton College

Maria Petrie
Florida Atlantic University

Dennis J. Frailey
Southern Methodist University

Our work was made easier because of their comments and contributions. To these professionals we are most grateful.

We also wish to thank those associated with John Wiley & Sons. We are much appreciative of the support given by our publisher, Wayne Anderson, our executive editor, Charity Robey, and by Nancy Prinz, Dawn Stanley, Susan Elbe, and Lisa Passmore. A very special thanks to our development editor Judith Goode for her insightful comments and her meticulous professional skill. We are most grateful to our editor, Steven Elliot, for his many hours of personal dedication to this work.

Last but not least, we would like to thank our families for their untiring support.

To the Student

You are probably beginning this course with some exposure to computers and introductory programming. This exposure can manifest itself in many forms, from casual self-taught knowledge to formal courses. Additionally, you are expected to have experienced rudimentary problem solving through the study of high school mathematics and science.

It would be beneficial for you to study discrete mathematics concurrently with this book. That branch of mathematics presents many concepts such as sets, logic, graphs, and recursion that are essential to your understanding of computing. Although some introductory discrete mathematics is included in the book, we believe that these concepts are important enough for you to study them in depth in a separate setting.

PEDAGOGICAL FEATURES OF THE TEXT

The text contains the following pedagogical features to help you learn and apply basic concepts.

Chapter Opener   Each chapter begins with a *photograph* related to the theme of the chapter. The chapter opener contains two features: *Learning Goals* and *Chapter Activity*. *Learning Goals* are a series of statements that highlight what you learn from the chapter. *Chapter Activity* is some endeavor or problem that you should be able to do after completing the chapter. This is intended as a "sneak preview" of the level of the material and provides a framework for the rest of the chapter.

Section Activities   Each section contains activities to engage the reader. These include:

> **Perspective**—*short vignettes with historical perspectives and curiosities, social and ethical issues, mathematical reminders, programming tips, human–computer communication issues, and other topics of interest. These exposures add different views of the subject and raise the social conciousness of those entering the profession.*

> **Before You Go On**—*short, on-the-spot exercises whose solution can be drawn from the text immediately preceding them.*

Exercises   Each section ends with a set of exercises of increasing difficulty in a variety of formats. The exercises are arranged as follows.

*A **Concept Check*** *consisting of 12 short questions grouped into true-false, multiple choice, and fill-in formats. Answers to these questions can be easily extracted from the text.*

The *Concept Check* is followed by three sets of open-ended questions of increasing difficulty.

Set A questions *are relatively easy and all students should be able to find the right answers with a minimum of effort.*

Set B questions *are moderate to challenging, occasionally needing substantial time and effort.*

Set C questions *often include laboratory exercises to be done using the computer. The suggested laboratory activities in Set C are designed to motivate and engage you in closed as well as open laboratory activities.*

Answers to many of these exercises are given after the appendixes.

The appendixes include library references to the C language, escape sequences, keywords, operators, ASCII and EBCDIC character codes, and a derivation of Simpson's rule. An index is also supplied.

ACTIVE LEARNING

Computer science can only be mastered by active participation on the part of the student. This means carefully reading the material, doing as many of the exercises as possible, participating in classroom discussions, and dedicating sufficient time to prepare and properly execute computer programs. There are no shortcuts.

Computer science is filled with thorny technical and theoretical issues needing analytical, nonintuitive thinking. Many of the real-world problems currently under investigation may take years or decades to solve, if ever! This new and rich area of study needs patience and perseverance. Try not to get too frustrated if things do not fall into place the first time you encounter them. Be persistent and ask questions. Become an active student!

JOHN IMPAGLIAZZO
PAUL NAGIN

1995 January

Brief Contents

Contents

Introduction to Computing Systems

ENIAC—First large-scale general-purpose electronic digital computer (1946).

After completing this chapter you should be able to do the following:

Learning Goals

- Describe the field of computer science
- Describe the nine areas of computing
- Apply computing to its social context
- Name some end-user applications
- Define the computing terms in this section
- Describe the components of a computer system
- Distinguish between input, output, and peripheral devices
- Be familiar with data storage media, types of operating systems, and communications networks
- Describe some of the highlights in the evolution of computing
- Explain the principles underlying the von Neumann machine and concepts of processing that differ from von Neumann's
- Be aware of the ethical concerns of computing professionals
- Suggest future trends in computing

Chapter Activity

The use of windows in computing has flourished over the last 10 years, although windowing was developed in the 1960s. Research this topic and write an essay with at least three references describing the origins and the development of this interactive computer tool. Include specific examples in your presentation.

1.1   A PANORAMA OF COMPUTER SCIENCE

Introduction

In today's world it is hard to escape computers. Just look around you. Computers seem to be everywhere. Television, appliances, alarm systems, reservation systems, inventory and payroll processors, bar code scanners, medical instruments, word processors, spacecraft, automobiles, and airplanes are just a few areas where you will find computers. So what is a computer?

A computer is an electronic machine that can process information according to a set of instructions. In essence, information called **data** is provided as **input** to a computer (*information* and *data* are often used interchangeably). The data are **processed** by the computer and new data called **output** are then generated. For example, consider a computer that produces a payroll. The input might consist of an employee's name, rate of pay, and hours worked. The computer processes these data by computing the gross pay, subtracting deductions such as taxes, and calculating the net pay. The output consists of a paycheck and an update of the computer accounting ledgers. Figure 1.1–1 is a block diagram of the input–process–output functions of a computer.

Computers typically fall into two categories: general-purpose computers and special-purpose computers. **General-purpose computers** are designed to perform a variety of functions using software programs. The same machine can be used as a word processor, an accounting ledger, an information organizer, or a graphic illustrator. On the other hand, **special-purpose computers** are designed for a single purpose only, such as the control mechanism in alarm systems, automobiles, and telephones. Special-purpose computers are often transparent to the user, whereas general-purpose computers are visible in the home, school, or workplace.

1.1.1 The Elements of Computing

The elements of the nine general areas of computing listed in the preface are covered next. A look at these elements puts in perspective the studies you are about to pursue.

The topic of algorithms is elementary to computing. Loosely defined, an **algorithm** is a finite sequence of steps that solves a problem. A step-by-step recipe to bake a pie is an example of an algorithm. In computing, algorithms provide a foundation for the most common methods of problem solving. For example, you might use a computer to sort a random list of 500 names. To do this, you design an algorithm and apply it to the list of names so that at the conclusion of the algorithm, the list is sorted.

Input   Process   Output

Figure 1.1–1   Block diagram of a computer

The list itself is organized in a particular way. Schemes used to organize data are called **data structures**. There may be more than one way to organize data and some ways may be more efficient than others. Data structures and their applications (discussed in Chapters 7 and 11) are important to the study of computing.

To **implement** an algorithm means to code it in a programming language so that it can run on a computer. A **programming language** is a formal artificial language with a set of rules (grammar) that describes how the elements of the language are used together (syntax). A programming language must be unambiguous so that a computer can understand its meaning.

An algorithm written in a programming language is a **program**, a sequence of instructions that tells the computer what to do. Programs convert the language code written by the programmer into machine language. There are many programming languages with a variety of purposes. Some of these are FORTRAN, BASIC, Prolog, LISP, Pascal, and C. We explore aspects of the C language throughout this book.

A program needs a physical machine on which to execute (run) an algorithm. The internal structure of a computer that allows data to interact with a program is called **computer architecture**. Computers have physical and nonphysical parts. The physical parts of a computer are called **hardware**; the nonphysical parts are called **software**. Software is generally considered to be programs, but not all programs are considered software. Some programs are embedded in hardware and are called **firmware**.

A key element of software used with general-purpose computers is the operating system that connects the hardware with the user. An **operating system** is actually a group of programs that manages the operation of a computer. Some well-known operating systems include UNIX®, originally from AT&T Bell Laboratories, MS-DOS® from Microsoft Corporation, VMS from Digital Equipment Corporation (DEC), and OS/2 from International Business Machines (IBM). Operating systems control processes such as printing, the input and output of information, and file access.

A computer can be used in a number of ways. Historically, computers served as *number crunchers* because they could do calculations rapidly. This application, called **numerical computing**, uses computers to solve mathematical, scientific, and engineering problems. By contrast, **symbolic processing** deals with non-numeric information. Examples include file processing, as in merging two mailing lists; string processing, as in using a word processor; and data management, as in a computerized library catalog. In this context a **file** is a set of data organized so it can be stored as a single entity and a **string** is an ordered collection of symbols. Computer scientists look for new algorithms and processes to do numerical and nonnumerical computing more effectively and efficiently.

One area of computer information processing that combines numeric and nonnumeric information is database management. A **database** is a collection of different types of information organized to facilitate data retrieval and manipulation. A **database management system (DBMS)** is a software program that allows us to store and retrieve, restructure, analyze, and synthesize information.

We can think of a program as solving a problem by a sequence of steps implemented in a programming language. Few if any commercial programs are short: They often have thousands or millions of lines of code. Programs for the special-purpose computers that operate automobiles contain more than 50,000 lines of code. The onboard computers in spacecraft are controlled by programs with more than 20,000,000 lines of code. The fact that no single person can program millions of lines of code has led to an area of computing called **software engineering (SE)**. Software engineering includes the assessment, design, implementation, testing, and maintenance of large-scale computer programs. This is a growing area of computing with a promising future.

Another area of computing, **artificial intelligence (AI)**, attempts to replicate intelligent behavior with computers that act as "thinking" machines. Artificial intelligence includes **robotics**, the science of programmable motion machines called **robots**. Robots are increasingly popular in manufacturing and assembly-line processes for building appliances, computer components, and automobiles. Other branches of artificial intelligence include the study of speech and image recognition. Some computer scientists believe that the future of computers lies in artificial intelligence.

Computers would be of little use if they did not communicate with people. Two facets of communication are data communications and human–computer communication. **Data communications** is the transfer of information between computer devices or computer-related devices. It includes data transmission, networks, satellites, and other local-area and wide-area transmission and reception of information. Increasingly popular are the **local area network (LAN)** and the **wide area network (WAN)**, communications channels connecting computing devices for short (local) or long (wide-area) geographic distances. Two networked computers in different parts of the world can now exchange information with ease.

Finally, the widespread use of computers motivated computer professionals to consider how people use or interact with computers. This area of computing, called **human–computer communication** or the **user interface**, is concerned with human factors and designs that enable people and computing machines to interact more effectively. Operating systems that include a **graphical user interface (GUI)** with icons and other visual aids have contributed to friendlier human–computer communication.

1.1.2 The Social Context of Computing

Computers affect almost all people living in modern society. Some suggest that we live in a time of information revolution analogous to the agricultural and industrial revolutions of past centuries. With the computerization of business, industry, and government agencies comes the responsibility to balance the needs of factories and offices with the needs of people. For example, the conversion to a computerized assembly line from one operated by people may cause great hardship to those displaced by the change.

With the acceptance of an information revolution comes a difference in attitude toward information itself. Information is now both a resource and a commodity. As a *resource*, information can be used to create new markets and add value to existing goods and products. As a *commodity*, it is a valued possession that can be bought or sold much like stocks or bonds. For example, a department store can use a computerized mailing list as a resource to mail information to its customers. It can also use the list as a commodity by selling it to a credit card company.

The use of a new technology can also bring abuse, and the use of computers in the information age is no exception. For example, should the health and financial records of individuals be made public? Should common business data be shared among competitors? Our immediate reaction is probably negative in both cases. But the problem is that computers allow information stored in one location to be easily transferred, intentionally or otherwise, to another location. Thus, the privacy and confidentiality of information are threatened by the use of computers.

To offset the possible invasion of information privacy, computers often include various methods of **protection** for preserving the integrity of information. One protection method is to make information accessible only to authorized individuals. Another is to develop a communications system with an encryption program that makes information intelligible only to the people authorized to have it.

The ease of access computers afford to people who know how to use them and the lack of scruples on the part of some users have led to a significant increase in computer crime. Theft of money and software, for example, accounts for approximately 60 percent of **computer crime**. Intentional damage to software, alteration of information, theft of services, and trespassing account for the remaining 40 percent. The amount of money lost through computer crime each year is not known but some estimates are in the tens of billions of dollars. Theft of hardware such as computers and computer chips is a minor problem relative to the theft and damage of information.

Destruction and alteration of information are more subtle crimes than copying software. Two forms of these crimes use computer viruses and worms. A computer

virus is a segment of code that attaches itself to application programs or to other executable system components and repeatedly replicates itself. A **worm** is a program that destroys information but does not replicate like a virus. [3] Viruses and worms are designed to cause mischief and harm. The federal government takes all forms of computer crime seriously and can prosecute individuals and organizations for committing such crimes.

> **PERSPECTIVE**
>
> The ACM and other computing societies have created codes of ethics to raise the awareness of the computing profession. These codes emphasize the obligations of professionals to society, employers, clients, and colleagues. There are severe penalties for violating regional and federal laws related to computer crime.

1.1.3 End-User Applications

There are two kinds of software: systems and applications. **Systems software** is software needed to operate a computer. System software includes operating systems and programming languages. In contrast to systems software, **applications software** enables the user to do a particular task on the computer and is usually supplied by software vendors to satisfy consumer needs. Popular applications include word processing, desktop publishing, spreadsheets, databases, graphics, integrated software packages, and communications.

One of the most popular software products is the word processor. A **word processor** is an applications program that is used to compose a written document and to revise, print, and store the document. Word processors offer sophisticated functions such as the ability to move blocks of text, use a spell checker and thesaurus, and design graphics. In addition to composing a document, you may need to add special features such as graphics so that the finished product looks like a professionally typeset document. In this case an applications program that does **desktop publishing** is better suited. The use of a high-resolution printer often makes it hard to distinguish between a document produced using a desktop publishing program and one that was professionally typeset.

Databases (discussed in Section 1.1.1) are essential tools for businesses and public and private organizations, and database applications software is used for this purpose. A database management system consolidates information and makes it available to a group of people. Applications of databases seem unbounded, from the simple telephone directory to the complex federal social security system. The question of what information should be accessible and to whom (discussed in Section 1.1.2) is especially relevant to database applications software.

Another popular end-user applications program is the spreadsheet. A **spreadsheet program** models the way accountants solve financial problems. Based on ledgers consisting of rows and columns, these programs are used for preparing documents such as balance sheets and operating budgets. Spreadsheets are also used for mathematics, science, engineering, and personal finance, which gives such programs a more universal appeal.

The sophistication of even the simplest computers today has popularized **computer graphics**, software applications used to draw images on a computer screen. Computer graphics programs can be integrated with other software to create vivid and realistic images.

Communications software is becoming standard for computers because it allows access to networks. Also standard is **integrated applications software** that combines two or more programs into a single program. Word processing, database, and spreadsheet programs are combined. This means that the user has to learn only one system with uniform commands and functions.

Many of the most intriguing new applications of computers are in the area of **virtual reality (VR)**. With this multimedia technology, three-dimensional (three-d) images combined with stereo sound are presented to the user via electronic goggles and gloves. The net effect is the illusion of being inside an artificially generated world. Within the goggles, the computer presents slightly different views of the same scene, projected onto tiny liquid-crystal screens. The human visual system fuses these two images to create a three-d world whose immediacy can be quite compelling. By altering your gaze and turning your head, you can see different views. At the same time, you can use a *data glove* to manipulate objects. The stereo sound adds another dimension, further immersing you in this strange new world.

The potential applications of this technology are dizzying. An early and ongoing use of VR is flight simulation for pilots-in-training learning how to take off, land, and fly an airplane. Busy executives can hone their golf skills by using a special VR screen that displays a chosen golf course. When a ball is shot at the screen, the VR software takes over and projects its trajectory onto the virtual course. Someday surgeons might learn new techniques while operating on virtual patients. The potential even exists for two or more viewers to interact on the same virtual landscape from anywhere on earth, connected via a high-speed network!

On a more sobering note, although a great potential for VR exists, the state of the art is somewhat restricted and leaves much to the imagination of the participant. The primary limitation today is computer speed. Creating realistic three-dimensional objects requires billions or trillions of calculations. Animating these objects in real time is beyond the capability of today's supercomputers.

EXERCISES 1.1

Concept Check

Answer statements 1 through 4 with true *or* false.

1. Data are information.
2. A file is used to store organized data.
3. The term *human–computer communication* describes the way information is channeled over networks.
4. Copying licensed software is an example of computer crime.

For statements 5 through 8 choose the answer that best completes the statement.

5. Computers designed to perform a variety of functions are called
   a. personal computers
   b. supercomputers
   c. general-purpose computers
   d. special-purpose computers
6. Which of the following is not considered a topic of the computing sciences?
   a. electronic wiring
   b. architecture
   c. databases
   d. artificial intelligence
7. A team approach for the development of large-scale computer programs is called
   a. the breadth-first approach
   b. computer science
   c. software engineering
   d. human–computer communication
8. A communications channel over short geographic distances is called
   a. human–computer communication
   b. a LAN
   c. a database management system
   d. firmware

For statements 9 through 12 fill in the blanks with the right word.

9. The area of _____ in computing combines the elements of motion and color to form an integrated image.
10. A(n) _____ is a program that models an accounting ledger sheet.
11. The guarding of computer information and programs from misuse or abuse is called _____.
12. MS-DOS is an example of a(n) _____.

Set A

Write a short essay for each of the following.

13. Refer to the preface and describe how the Denning Report was different from other curriculum recommendations.
14. Refer to the preface and describe the difference between a breadth-first and a depth-first approach to learning a science.
15. List the nine topic areas of computer science.
16. Explain how information can be both a resource and a commodity.
17. Describe how theft and destruction of information contribute to computer crime.
18. Describe what might be pros and cons of integrated applications software.
19. How would you describe virtual reality?

Set B

20. Computer graphics is an important area of computing. Why do you think it is not listed in the nine topic areas of computer science in the preface?

21. Programming is an important part of computing. Why do you think it is not listed in the nine topic areas of computer science in the preface?
22. Why can software be considered part of computer architecture?
23. An operating system can be considered the heart of a general-purpose computer. Why do you think an operating system is of little or no significance to a special-purpose computer?
24. Name some of the activities of software engineering.
25. The LAN and the WAN are both examples of communications networks. Describe an appropriate scenario for using each.
26. Computer viruses and worms contribute to information destruction. Explain the difference between them.
27. Almost all computer crime is a federal crime. Why do you think that is so?
28. Describe some of the pros and cons surrounding the use of virtual reality in the medical profession.

Set C

29. Research the topic of information protection and computer security. Write a short essay on this subject.
30. Research the topic of computer ethics. Write a short essay on this subject.

1.2   COMPUTER HARDWARE AND SOFTWARE

Introduction

In Section 1.1 we survey computer science and discuss its current form. Computer science includes the topics of algorithms and data structures, programming languages, architecture, numerical and symbolic computing, operating systems, software methodology and engineering, database and information retrieval, artificial intelligence and robotics, and human–computer communication. The social and ethical context of computing is also introduced. Now we investigate some of the details of computing systems.

1.2.1 Preliminaries

Computers fall into two basic categories: analog and digital. An **analog computer** processes information directly from devices that produce continuously measurable quantities. Such devices include electrical circuits, motors and generators, and scaled meters such as volt meters and mercury thermometers. A **digital computer** processes information from discrete off and on states. The difference between these two machines is in the words *continuous* and *discrete*. Because of their ability to quickly detect discrete off and on states, the majority of computers in the world are digital computers.

The discrete off and on states used by digital computers are represented by binary digits called **bits**. We arbitrarily use the number **0** to represent an off state and the number **1** to represent an on state. The numbers 0 and 1 are the values

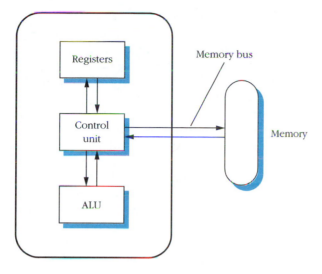

Central processing unit

Figure 1.2–1   A CPU with memory

used to represent states in a digital computer and to form a **binary system**. Both numerical and nonnumerical data can be represented by a **string** (sequence) of 0s and 1s. For example,

0110011101001101

is such a string. Thus digital computers are ideal for manipulating and processing digital information and for processing symbols.

A **computer system** is the integration of physical entities called **hardware** and nonphysical entities called **software**. Hardware consists of the physical components of the machine, including the central processing unit, memory, and peripheral input and output devices. The **central processing unit (CPU)** interprets and executes instructions given to it, controls the flow of input, output, and storage, and does logical and arithmetic operations. The **control unit (CU)**, a part of the CPU, retrieves instructions from memory and executes them. Logical and arithmetic operations are done in another part of the CPU called the **arithmetic logic unit (ALU)**. Between any two parts of the CPU is a pathway called a **bus** that allows the transfer of binary information between them. The CPU also contains **registers**. These are high-speed storage areas where instructions are executed. The CPU is connected by buses to a component called **memory** or **primary storage** that stores programs and other data waiting to be processed. Figure 1.2–1 shows a CPU and the primary storage area.

1.2.2 Peripheral Input and Output Devices

A computer device that is not part of the central processing unit and its primary storage area is called a **peripheral device**. Some peripheral devices (such as keyboards) perform strictly input, some (such as printers) strictly output, and others (such as diskettes) both. Let's consider output, the transfer of computer information to humans or other machines. Output takes the form of machine-readable data, text, images, or sound. **Machine-readable data** are in the form of bits and can be written or read by a computer. **Text** consists of symbols such as numbers and letters. **Images** include visible output such as pictures, line drawings, and graphics. **Sound** consists of audible output such as voice or music. Text, images, and sound require the interaction of people and machines.

Two categories of output devices are soft copy and hard copy. **Soft copy** is the display of output on a surface that cannot be physically transported. Voice devices and **monitors** (video displays) are examples of soft copy output. **Hard copy** is the display of output on a medium that can be physically transported. Printers, camera image copiers, and plotters are examples of hard copy output devices. Printers fall into two categories: impact printers and nonimpact printers. **Impact printers**, like typewriters, have a mechanism that strikes a medium such as paper, whereas **nonimpact printers** do not have a striking mechanism. Dot-matrix and belt printers are examples of impact printers. Laser, inkjet, and thermal printers are examples of nonimpact printers.

Input is the transfer of information from people or machines to computers. Many devices are used for input. An obvious input device is the **keyboard**, which consists of alphabetic, numeric, and special-symbol keys like typewriter keys. When you press a key on the keyboard, a signal is sent to the computer identifying the letter, number, or symbol. Another input device is the **mouse**, which is used as a pointing device on a computer screen. Other input devices include **optical character recognizers (OCR)** used to capture images or text, **magnetic ink character recognizers (MICR)** used to process bank checks, **bar code scanners**, which read the bar-shaped codes found on many consumer products, **sensors** used in pacemakers, and **speech recognizers** used to input data directly from voice.

Some devices are used for both input and output, such as diskettes (also called floppy disks) and hard disks. A **diskette** is made of plastic and is coated with magnetic material. These disks are either flexible or firm, and placed in a suitable casing. Common diskette sizes are 3.5 and 5.25 inches. A **hard disk** is made of rigid metal coated with a magnetic material. Both diskettes and hard disks are used to store data. **Disk drives** are hardware units consisting of motors that spin the disks and have accompanying sensing devices with read/write heads.

The storage capacity of diskettes and hard disks is measured in bytes. A **byte** is the smallest addressable memory unit. Each byte contains a certain number of bits. Depending on the standard that is used, a byte can contain from 1 to many bits. For most computers the standard is 8 bits per byte. Thus 2 bytes equal 16 bits and 4 bytes equal 32 bits. Figure 1.2–2 shows a typical arrangement of bits in bytes.

0 0 1 1 0 0 1 0 1 1 1 0 0 1 0 1 0 0 0 1 0 0 0 1 1 0

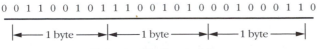

Figure 1.2–2   Bytes in relation to bits

A single bit can have 2 values: 0   1

2 bits can have 4 values: 0 0   1 0
                                        0 1   1 1

3 bits can have 8 values: 0 0 0   1 0 0
                                      0 0 1   1 0 1
                                      0 1 0   1 1 0
                                      0 1 1   1 1 1

Four bits can have 16 values; 5 bits 32 values, and so on. In general, if s is the number of values and n is the number of bits, the total number of distinct values is

$$s = 2^n$$

Table 1.2–1 shows the number of values for various numbers of bits expressed in powers of 2.

1 kilobyte (KB) is $1024 = 2^{10}$ bytes and **1 megabyte (MB)** is $1,048,576 = 2^{20}$ bytes. The prefix *kilo* means thousand and *mega* means million. In computer terms these prefixes approximate their general meaning.

The storage capacity of diskettes is more conveniently measured in kilobytes or megabytes than in bytes. Diskettes usually store data on both sides of the two-sided plastic disk and are called **double-sided (DS)**. Diskettes are format-ted into **tracks** (circular rings) and **sectors** (wedges) for storing information. Figure 1.2–3 is a simplified drawing of how diskettes are formatted; note that a typical diskette is divided into 40 to 1024 tracks and hundreds or thousands of sectors. For example, on MS-DOS-based machines, 5.25-inch diskettes are formatted for three capacities: low density at 360 KB, double density at 720 KB, and high density at 1.2 MB. Likewise, 3.5-inch diskettes are formatted for three capacities: low density at 720 KB, high density at 1.44 MB, and ultrahigh density at 2.88 MB.

Hard disks store information in the same way as diskettes. They are usually stacked so that several surfaces are mechanically available to the **read/write heads** in the disk drive for reading and writing data. As the surfaces rotate, data can be stored or retrieved from any surface at any given time. When disks are stacked, format tracks are lined up on each surface to form imaginary **cylin-ders** and sectors are lined up to form imaginary **wedges**, as shown in Figure 1.2–4.

Table 1.2–1   Powers of 2

n	2^n	s
1	2^1	2
3	2^3	8
4	2^4	16
84	2^8	256
10	2^{10}	1,024
12	2^{12}	4,096
16	2^{16}	65,536
20	2^{20}	1,048,576

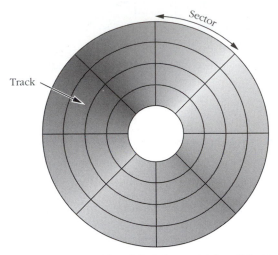

Figure 1.2–3 Simplified format of a diskette: four tracks, eight sectors

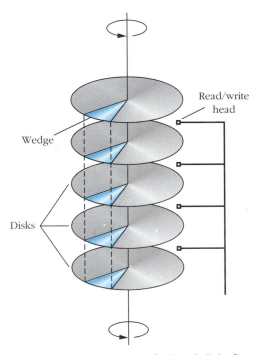

Figure 1.2–4 Format of a hard disk: five disks, four read/write heads

Table 1.2–2 Comparison of Spatial Units of Measure

UNIT	SYMBOL	POWER OF 2	VALUE
Byte		2^0	1
Kilobyte	KB	2^{10}	1,024
Megabyte	MB	2^{20}	1,048,576
Gigabyte	GB	2^{30}	1,073,741,824
Terabyte	TB	2^{40}	1,099,511,627,776

Figure 1.2–5 Communication between two modems

In addition to the mechanical availability of the many surfaces they provide, their higher storage density for data enables hard disks to store vast amounts of information, from 10 MB to more than 1 **gigabyte (GB)**—more than 1 billion bytes. Table 1.2–2 shows a comparison of spatial units of measure used in relation to computer storage capacities.

Input/output devices also include terminals. A **terminal** is a single-purpose device, usually with a keyboard and a monitor, that receives and transmits data in a computer system. Terminals do not have their own CPU or disk drives and have to be connected to a mainframe or other computer. Sometimes a computer acts as a terminal through a terminal-emulation program.

A **modem** (modulator-demodulator) is a communications link that allows digital information from computers to be sent and received over ordinary analog telephone lines. (See Section 8.1.3.) When sending, a modem converts digital information to analog information. When receiving, it converts analog information to digital information. This enables computers (each connected to its own modem) to communicate with other computers at remote locations for the cost of a telephone call. Figure 1.2–5 shows this mode of communicating among computers by modem.

1.2.3 More on Hardware Basics

As we said earlier, hardware is the physical components of the computer. In the CPU are registers for temporary storage, an ALU where operations take place, and a control unit to manage data flow. The CPU is connected to **primary storage** or **memory** for storing programs and data. This storage area, called **random-access memory (RAM)**, can have information written to it or read from it. RAM is organized into small memory areas or **cells**, each containing a fixed number of bits. Each cell has an address and adjoins another cell. (See Figure 1.2–6.) The

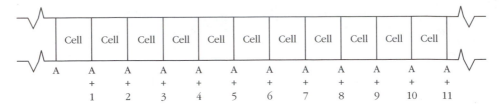

A = Address

Figure 1.2–6 How RAM is organized

word *random* means that it takes the same time to access any address in RAM. The size of RAM can be measured in kilobytes or megabytes, although megabytes is the prevalent measure now. Typical RAM sizes range from 1 MB to 64 MB.

Sometimes, permanent memory is embedded in a computer and can be read from but not written to or altered. This is called **read-only memory (ROM)**. One use of ROM is to hold the instructions that **boot** (start up) and prepare a computer for use. An application of ROM includes the hardwired programs that can be accessed without software, such as video game computers in an arcade. Another application of ROM is the read-only optical storage technology that uses a **compact disk (CD)** called a **CD-ROM**. Databases, for example, are often stored on CD-ROMs.

Primary storage (RAM) is volatile, and information stored in RAM disappears when a computer loses its power. In addition to primary storage, computers have external memory or **secondary storage**, the part of a computer where programs and data are stored when not in use. Secondary storage commonly uses hard disks, although other media such as magnetic tape can be used. **Magnetic tape** is much like ordinary audio tape that is treated with a magnetic film to record digital information. A single magnetic tape cassette can hold up to 250 MB of information. Secondary tape storage saves information in a **sequential** manner, one item after another. To access a specific information item, it is often necessary to start at the beginning of the tape and search through it until the item is found. Because of the inefficiency of sequential access, secondary disk storage is used that permits the random access of information.

One way to measure a computer's performance is by its processing speed: clock speed and instruction speed. A **clock** is an electronic circuit that generates pulses used to synchronize events in the computer's CPU. The rate at which it generates pulses is its **clock speed**. Clock speeds vary based on the processor. A typical clock speed for a modern high-speed computer is about 120,000,000 pulses per second, described as 120,000,000 H (hertz) or 120 MH (megahertz).

Instruction speed measures the number of machine instructions processed in a second. This value is more important than clock speed because it measures what the computer can actually do. For modern computers this speed is measured in millions of instructions per second **(MIPS)**, and a rating of 100 MIPS is not unusual. Table 1.2–3 shows some of the temporal units of measure used to describe the time it takes to process a single instruction. The symbol μ (the Greek letter mu) represents millionths. It should not be long before nanoseconds and picoseconds become ordinary speeds for processing a single computer instruction.

Table 1.2–3 Temporal Units of Measure

UNIT	SYMBOL	POWER OF 10	DECIMAL VALUE
Second	s	10^0	1.0
Millisecond	ms	10^{-3}	0.001
Microsecond	μs	10^{-6}	0.000001
Nanosecond	ns	10^{-9}	0.000000001
Picosecond	ps	10^{-12}	0.000000000001

Computers can be classified according to their storage capacity, clock speed, instruction speed, and cost, although it is hard to make clear distinctions. Four computer classifications are personal computers, minicomputers, mainframe computers, and supercomputers. A **personal computer (PC)**, also called a **microcomputer**, is one whose CPU is contained on a single chip. A personal computer is generally found in a home or office and is a single-user, general-purpose computer. A **mainframe computer** provides high storage capacity with high-speed processing and is likely to be found in commercial establishments where large quantities of data are processed. Mainframe computers are generally multiuser machines and provide a base for gateways with PCs on LANs. A **minicomputer** is a middle-range machine between a mainframe and a microcomputer. **Supercomputers** have very large storage capacities and operate at the highest possible speeds. Most supercomputers contain multiple CPUs and are sometimes called **parallel computers**. Multiple CPUs process many instructions simultaneously (in parallel), thereby speeding up the overall performance of the machine. Supercomputers are generally found in technical areas where high-speed processing is needed using large quantities of numerical data such as in weather forecasting or a space-vehicle control system.

Computer speeds and storage capacities of personal and mainframe computers appear to be converging. With processors now on a chip, cost and the needs of the user seem to be the factors that will distinguish personal computers from other classifications in the future.

1.2.4 Software Basics

The two major software components of a computer system are the operating system and applications programs. As mentioned in Section 1.1, operating systems manage the operation and control of a computer system. This includes the management of resources such as input/output (I/O) devices, secondary storage, and other devices needed for the system to work. Operating systems can also implement computer security by allowing access only to authorized persons.

Operating systems used on computers in the late 1950s did not allow human interaction while a job was being processed and only one job could be processed at a time. This was called **batch processing**. Although batch processing had its merits, demand arose for **interactive processing** in which the computer could respond to users while in a processing state. By the mid-1960s interactive processing became accessible to most users and it remains an important feature

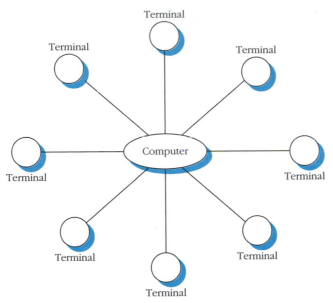

Figure 1.2–7   A typical multiuser system

in many computer systems. In some systems, data processing keeps pace with the task at hand so that the results produced by the process are part of the transaction. This is called a **real-time system**. One example is an airplane guidance system.

The expense of hardware in the 1960s motivated the development of **multiuser systems** in which several users could run the same computer at the same time. These **time-sharing systems** allowed the processing capabilities of the CPU to be partitioned into slices of time and shared by multiple users. Typically, a multiuser system consisted of one main computer connected to terminals. Figure 1.2–7 is a sketch for such a system. Today, some multiuser systems are being replaced by PCs on a LAN. Note that a multiuser system is not the same as a multitasking system: A **multitasking system** does more than one task on the same computer at the same time and is often a feature of multiuser systems.

1.2.5 Communications Basics

Over the past 20 years personal computers have surpassed some early mainframes in performance. Personal computers are now networked so that they can interact with other computers while still running independently as stand-alone computers.

When computers are connected to a network or to a peripheral device, they are **interfaced** with hardware or software so that they can interact with the network or device. The interface is made at an addressed location, called a **port**, where information is exchanged in serial or parallel form. **Serial** exchanges are made one bit at a time whereas **parallel** exchanges are made on all bits of a byte simultaneously. The bus used to connect peripheral devices to a computer is a **cable**.

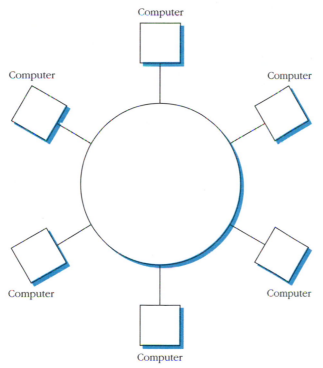

Figure 1.2–8 Ring network

Networks offer a communications path between computers; they can be LANs or WANs. A network's **topology** is the configuration of its components. A closed-loop channel is called a **ring topology** or **ring network** (see Figure 1.2–8). A central unit with a separate channel to each satellite unit is called a **star network** (see Figure 1.2–9). In a ring network each unit is a control unit, with the advantage that if one of its units fails, the network still functions. A star network has the advantage of needing only one control unit, but if the control unit fails, the whole network fails.

To prevent network failure a **distributed topology**, or distributed network, can reroute a transmission to reach its destination (see Figure 1.2–10). There are several ways for A to communicate with B. The path through point X is the shortest, but failure at point X does not impede the transmission because it can be routed through points Y and Z. Distributed networks are becoming extremely popular, especially for networks that cover large geographic distances.

EXERCISES 1.2

Concept Check

Answer statements 1 through 4 with true *or* false.

1. An enumeration system that uses only zeros and ones is a binary system.
2. A gigabyte is approximately 1 trillion bytes.
3. A ROM is a memory device that cannot be altered by the user.

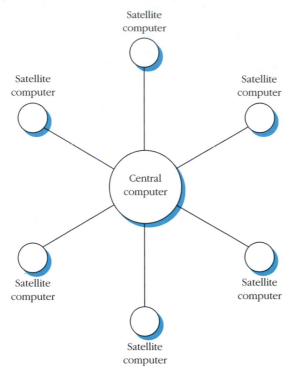

Figure 1.2–9   Star network

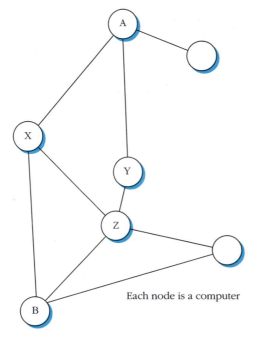

Figure 1.2–10   Distributed network

4. A computer rated at 66 MIPS means that its clock sends 66 million pulses each second.

For statements 5 through 8 choose the answer that best completes the statement.

5. A computer that processes continuous information from devices is called
    a. a digital computer
    b. a microcomputer
    c. a computer system
    d. an analog computer
6. A 1-MB computer storage area contains
    a. 1,000,000 bytes
    b. 1,000 bytes
    c. 1,048,576 bytes
    d. 1,024 bytes
7. A secondary sequential storage device that can store up to 75,000,000 bytes of memory is most likely
    a. a diskette
    b. a magnetic tape
    c. a ROM
    d. a modem
8. General-purpose microcomputers are most often found
    a. in robots
    b. in schools
    c. on assembly lines
    d. in space ships

For statements 9 through 12 fill in the blanks with the right word.

9. A distributed network combines the topologies of _____ and _____ networks.
10. The convention that a byte consists of 8 bits means that 1 byte can achieve as many as _____ states.
11. The _____ are high-speed temporary storage areas of the central processing unit.
12. Output displayed on a monitor or presented by audio is categorized as _____.

Set A
Write a short essay for each of the following.
13. Explain the difference between a digital computer and an analog computer.
14. The CPU is the workhorse of any computer. What are its parts and how do they interact with each other?
15. Consider the words *kilometer* and *kilobyte*. The prefix *kilo* has two different meanings. Explain.
16. For future computers, the time it takes to do a task is expected to be measured in nanoseconds or even picoseconds. What does this mean?
17. Describe a real-time system and where it might be used.
18. General-purpose computers usually have both serial and parallel ports. Explain the difference between the two.

Set B

19. Suppose you are told that each memory cell of a digital computer can assume 100 different states. What is faulty about this claim?
20. Two computers must communicate with each other. Is a modem always necessary? Describe conditions when a modem may be needed and when it may not be needed.
21. Explain the difference between ROM and RAM.
22. Computer A is a 50-MH machine. Computer B is a 66-MH machine. Explain why computer B may not be the faster machine.
23. Some say that mainframe computers may be machines of the past. Provide some pros and cons with respect to this claim.
24. Describe why a multitasking computer system is not the same as a multiuser computer system.

Set C

25. One definition of a hacker is a person who accesses a computer without authorization. Research this word and write a short essay on how a person becomes a hacker.
26. A terminal is not a computer. Research this word and write a short essay on the advantages and disadvantages of terminals on a computer system.
27. One sector of one track of a hard disk can store 4 KB. Given that the disk is formatted to have 96 tracks with 13 sectors and there are 12 surfaces to the disk, calculate the storage capacity of the disk.
28. Write a short essay on the possible computer activities involved when a bar code scanner is used in a supermarket. Consider possibilities beyond the price of individual items.
29. Sometimes programs are embedded in hardware and are called firmware. Research this word and write a short essay on how firmware is used.

1.3 COMPUTING PERSPECTIVES

Introduction

Before we go further in the study of computing, it is useful to see how computing evolved to its present state, to consider recent advances, and to look forward to what the future might bring. Certain past events and concepts, some of which were mentioned in Section 1.2, form the foundation of computing as we know it today. Some of those events and concepts are discussed next.

1.3.1 Evolution of Computer Hardware and Software

Calculating machines have existed for millennia. The first known calculating machine is the **abacus**, a hand-held device made of beads strung on cords that can be used for addition, subtraction, and even multiplication and division. The abacus has probably been used for more than 4,000 years and is still used in

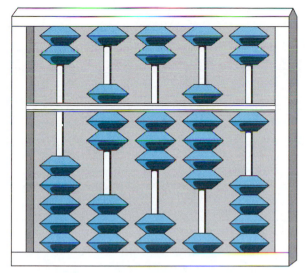

Figure 1.3–1   A simple abacus

many parts of Asia and some parts of eastern Europe. Figure 1.3–1 is a sketch of a simple abacus representing the number 7,391.

The **first mechanical calculator** was invented in 1623 by Wilhelm Schickard. This machine could do limited multiplication and division using logarithms. In 1642 Blaise Pascal invented the first **automatic mechanical calculator**, called the **Pascaline**. This machine could do limited addition and subtraction but was not used commercially. The **punched block**, invented in 1804 by Joseph-Marie Jacquard, was used in his silk loom business to make patterned fabrics automatically. The punched-block was the forerunner of what we now call programming.

Charles Babbage invented a machine called the **difference engine** in 1822, which mechanically calculated mathematical tables. In 1833 he invented a machine called the **analytical engine**, a general-purpose calculating device. He never finished the analytical engine, but his friend, Augusta Ada, the Countess of Lovelace and daughter of the English poet Lord Byron, is often credited with being the first programmer because she conceptualized the analytical engine as a mechanical computer. Unfortunately, the analytical engine received neither commercial support nor success. In 1854 George Boole created an algebra based on logic, known today as **Boolean algebra**, the mathematical foundation of computing. The efforts of Babbage, Ada, Boole, and others influenced the development of electronic computing machines a century later.

PERSPECTIVE

The world's first computer program may have been a pamphlet called *Rule of Computation on the Abacus*, written by the mathematician Gerbert (c. 940–1003), who later became Pope Sylvester II. This would make Gerbert, not Ada, the first programmer and Latin the first programming language.

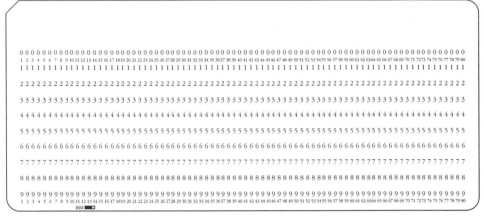

Figure 1.3–2   An IBM punched card

In 1886 Herman Hollerith used the idea of Jacquard's punched block to create **punched cards**. These cards were used to tabulate data for the 1890 U.S. census. Figure 1.3–2 shows an example of a punched card made of thin cardboard or heavy paper with coded holes punched in designated columns. These cards were passed over electrical brushes. Electrical contact was made where holes were present; no electrical contact was made where holes were not present. Hollerith's punched cards represent data through bit values 1 (contact) and 0 (no contact). The cards reduced the time needed to tabulate the census by more than 50 percent and set the stage for what was to come in the next century. Hollerith later became a cofounder of IBM.

In the mid 1930s John Atanasoff of Iowa State University invented the first primitive **electronic computer**, which used binary arithmetic and electronic memory. Other pioneers were Konrad Zuse of Germany, George Stibbitz of Bell Laboratories, and Howard Aiken of Harvard University.

Before 1945 computers were electromechanical devices made of vacuum tubes and electrical relays. In 1945 John von Neumann developed a version of the Electronic Discrete Variable Automatic Computer **(EDVAC)** at the Institute of Advanced Studies (IAS) of Princeton University. Often called the **IAS machine**, it was the first to use the idea of a **stored program**: The computer would first store and then execute programs. Von Neumann's invention was so clever that he is called the father of modern computing. The first large-scale computer using the stored-program concept was the Electronic Delay Storage Automatic Calculator **(EDSAC)** developed by Maurice Wilkes at Cambridge University in 1949. Most computers today are considered **von Neumann machines** because they use the stored-program concept and an architecture similar to his original machine.

Computers of the late 1940s and the early 1950s used **vacuum tubes** rather than electromechanical relays as switching devices. The first large-scale electronic digital computer was the Electronic Numerical Integrator and Calculator **(ENIAC)**, developed by Presper Eckert and John Mauchly in 1946, and contained more than 18,000 vacuum tubes. Vacuum tubes made computers faster and more efficient and spawned what we now call the first generation of computer hardware.

In 1951 the first commercial computer, the Universal Automatic Computer I (**UNIVAC I**), was designed by Eckert and Mauchly of Remington Rand. Also, International Business Machines (IBM) produced its first commercial stored-program computer in 1952, the **IBM 701**. The invention of the **transistor** in 1947 at Bell Laboratories by John Bardeen, Walter Brattain, and William Shockley, however, led to smaller computers. In 1954 the first transistorized computer, the **TRADIC**, was developed at Bell Laboratories. This launched what we now call the second generation of computer hardware.

Before 1953, programming was done in **machine language**—a collection of simple instructions intended for a particular machine and recognized by its CPU. Machine language was and still is difficult to use because it is written in binary (bits) form. This difficulty led to the invention of **assembly languages**, which consist of symbolic codes in one-to-one correspondence with a particular machine language. A sample of a machine language and the corresponding assembly language is shown in Figure 1.3–3. Assembly language made programming

```
MACHINE LANGUAGE                              IBM 360/370
   REPRESENTED                                 ASSEMBLY
 IN HEXADECIMAL                                 LANGUAGE
90 EC D0 0C         19              STM     14,12,12(13)
05 C0               20              BALR    12,0
                    21              USING   *,12
50 D0 C4 DE         22              ST      13,SAVE+4
41 D0 C4 DA         23              LA      13,SAVE
                    24     *
                    25     * OPEN INPUT AND OUTPUT FILES
                    26     *
                    27              OPEN    (SYSIN,(INPUT))
                    33              OPEN    (SYSPRNT,(OUTPUT))

                    39     * DOS   ******
                    40     *        OPEN   SYSIN
                    41     *        OPEN   SYSPRNT
                    42     **************

                    43     *
                    44     * INITIALIZE DISTRIBUTION COUNTERS
                    45     *
41 50 C1 32         46              LA      5,DISTR
58 60 C1 06         47              L       6,N
58 70 C4 52         48              L       7,=F'0'
50 75 00 00         49     INIT     ST      7,0(5)
41 55 00 04         50              LA      5,4(5)
46 60 C0 2C         51              BCT     6,INIT
                    52     *
```

Figure 1.3–3   Machine and assembly languages

computers easier. It was first used commercially in 1953 for the IBM 701 computer. The use of machine language marked the beginning of the first generation of computer software and the use of assembly language marked the beginning of the second.

Even with assembly language, however, programming was not easy. Efforts were made to create a **high-level language** not specific to a machine that had an English-like code and would be accessible to individuals other than computer specialists. IBM and the UNIVAC company piloted this effort. The first widely used high-level programming language was **FORTRAN** (Formula Translating System). FORTRAN was designed in 1954 at IBM under the direction of John Backus and was implemented in 1957. FORTRAN became very popular, especially among engineers, scientists, and mathematicians.

Other languages soon emerged for different applications, notably LISP in 1958 from John McCarthy at MIT and COBOL in 1959 from a committee that was influenced by Grace Murray Hopper. **LISP** (List Processing) became useful for problems in artificial intelligence. **COBOL** (Common Business Oriented Language) was designed for payroll, accounting, inventory, and other similar applications. Because of its commercial appeal, COBOL became one of the more popular computer languages. The development of languages such as FORTRAN, LISP, and COBOL heralded the third generation of computer software.

In 1959 the first integrated circuit was developed at Texas Instruments by Robert Noyce. An **integrated circuit (IC)** consists of a group of interrelated electronic circuits packaged in a single highly compact structure. Figure 1.3–4 is a sketch of a small IC magnified approximately 100 times. Starting in 1965 most computers were designed using ICs, making them smaller, faster, and cheaper. ICs were the basis for the third generation of computer hardware.

The early 1960s saw many new efforts in computing. Digital Equipment Corporation (DEC) produced its first commercial mini computer, the **PDP-1**, in 1960 to compete with the massive and expensive mainframes. IBM produced its **7090** in 1961, Burroughs its **6500** in 1962, and IBM launched its popular **360**

Figure 1.3–4   Sketch of Intel 4004 integrated circuit

Table 1.3–1 Generations of Computer Hardware

GENERATION	TIME PERIOD	PRINCIPAL EVENTS
0	1642–1945	Mechanical caculators
1	1945–1955	Vacuum tubes
2	1955–1965	Transistors
3	1965–1971	Integrated circuits
4	1971–present	Computer chips

series in 1964. In 1964 the **PL/I** language was created by IBM, and John Kemeny and Thomas Kurtz invented **BASIC** (Beginner's All-Purpose Symbolic Instruction Code). BASIC is best known for its friendly interactive features, especially on multiuser systems.

The late 1960s and the early 1970s brought new breakthroughs in computing. **Virtual reality** was first demonstrated in 1965, the **mouse** was invented in 1965, and the **diskette** was developed in 1970. But it was the invention of the **4004** chip by Intel in 1971 that caused a revolution in the computer industry. The **chip**, a highly dense IC processor, put the power of a large-scale computer in a very small area—less than 2 inches by 2 inches—reducing the size and cost of computers while increasing their efficiency. By the late 1970s small microcomputers (personal computers) began to appear, including the Commodore PET, the Radio Shack TRS80, and the Apple II. The chips that made the new computers possible marked the beginning of the fourth generation of computer hardware. Also, the development of the **supercomputer** by Seymour Cray in 1972 set a new level of computing power.

By 1980 Intel had developed its **80186** 16-bit CPU, an improvement over its **8086** and **8088** CPUs of 1978, and Motorola launched its 32-bit CPU, the **68000**, an improvement over its **6800** CPU of 1975. IBM personal computers (**IBM-PCs**) appeared in 1981, using Intel chips and Microsoft's MS-DOS operating system. **Compact disc (CD)** technology appeared in 1982 and Microsoft developed the **Windows** environment in 1983. By 1984 Apple® introduced **Macintosh®** computers, using the Motorola 68000 chip, that featured windows and icons that made these computers easier to use. In 1987 IBM launched the **PS/2** series of computers, using its **OS/2** operating system. Soon after, Motorola developed the **68040** chip and in 1993 Intel launched the **Pentium** chip.

The evolution of hardware and software is summarized in the two tables that follow. Table 1.3–1 shows the generations of computer hardware and Table 1.3–2 shows the generations of computer software. Note that the time periods are approximate and that generation 0 precedes the era of electronic computers.

Table 1.3–2 Generations of Computer Software

GENERATION	TIME PERIOD	PRINCIPAL EVENTS
1	1945–present	Machine languages
2	1953–present	Assembly languages
3	1957–present	High-level languages

Today we hear about **fourth-generation**, report-generating languages often used with databases and **fifth-generation** languages used with logic programming. Both are discussed further in Chapter 14.

1.3.2 von Neumann and Non–von Neumann Architectures

As mentioned earlier, one of the great contributions of John von Neumann to computing was the concept of the stored program. Before 1945 computers could do calculations on data but the instructions for manipulating the data were stored in **hardwired programs** built with electric wires. Developing hardwired programs was tedious and time-consuming, even for simple programs.

The **stored program** uses a single memory area to store both data and program instructions. The data are manipulated by the instructions to produce the desired results. This computer design is the basis for the traditional general-purpose computer and is called a **von Neumann computer**, as described in Section 1.3.1. The key is that instructions and data coexist in the same RAM, making it possible to modify instructions by using other instructions. A von Neumann machine fetches an instruction from memory, decodes the instruction, and then executes it. When the action on an instruction is complete, the next instruction follows the same fetch–decode–execute sequence until a stop occurs, as shown in Figure 1.3–5. The von Neumann computer is called a **single-instruction stream–single-data stream (SISD)** computer.

One way to use an SISD computer is by **pipelining**: fetching, decoding, and executing instructions at different time intervals. Suppose instruction #1 is fetched. While it is decoded, instruction #2 is fetched. While instruction #1 is executing, instruction #2 is decoded and instruction #3 is fetched. This completes the cycle for instruction #1. While instruction #2 is executed, instruction #3 is decoded and instruction #4 is fetched. The process continues until all the instructions are executed. Figure 1.3–6 shows the process of pipelining.

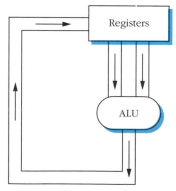

Figure 1.3–5   A simple von Neumann computer

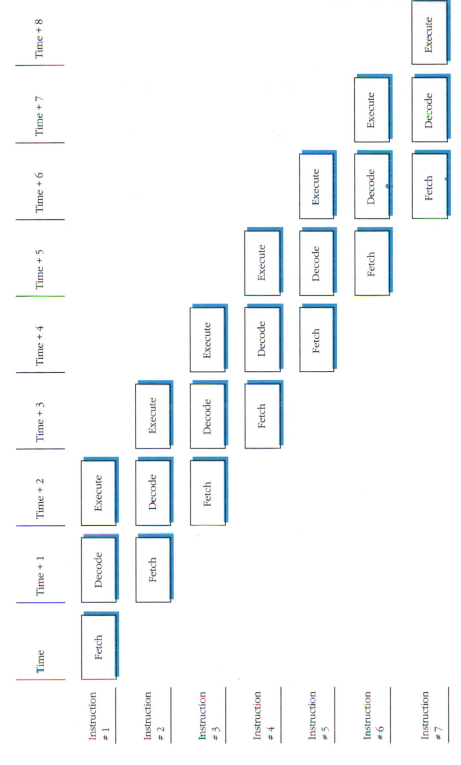

Figure 1.3–6 Example of pipelining

29

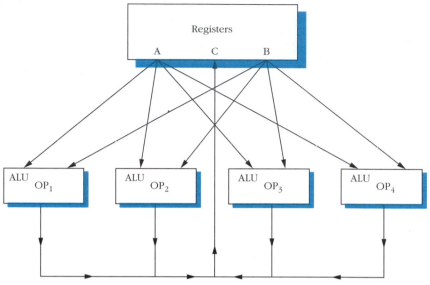

Figure 1.3–7 A parallel-processing computer showing C←A op B

Not all computers are the von Neumann SISD type. Another approach involves processing information in parallel. A **parallel-processing** computer, for example, uses two or more processors in parallel. Each of these processors can execute instructions simultaneously with the others. Suppose a parallel computer has four processors, each doing one of four operations (addition, subtraction, multiplication, and division), as shown in Figure 1.3–7. The four processors share the same memory, the same control unit, and the four arithmetic tasks.

Another version of a parallel computer is the **array processor**, in which each processor has its own memory but all the processors share the same control unit. This is called **single-instruction stream–multiple-data stream (SIMD)**. Array processors are usually in a grid formation of rows and columns, and work well for matrix applications. Figure 1.3–8 shows this design.

Sometimes, individual CPUs are used in parallel and may or may not share a common memory. This is a **multiple-instruction stream–multiple-data stream (MIMD)** computer, or a **multiprocessor** (shown in Figure 1.3–9). Well-known computers of this type are the Cray supercomputer, with a shared memory, and the Connection Machine by Thinking Machines, without a shared memory.

The typical computer today is a **complex instruction-set computer (CISC)**, meaning that many machine instructions are provided to make a computer operative. An important quest among computer professionals, however, is to build the most efficient machine possible. One strategy involves using only a small subset of the instructions of a CISC machine, which is possible because most programs are based on a few machine instructions. By optimizing hardware

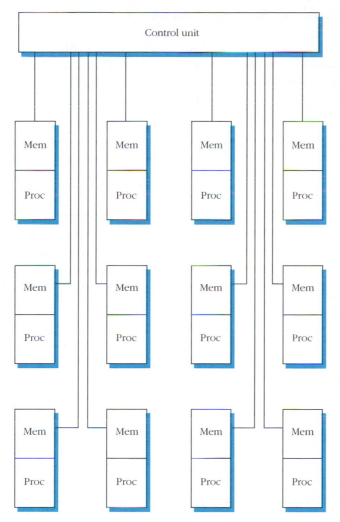

3 × 4 array: each unit has local memory and a processor
with shared control

Figure 1.3–8　Example of an array processor

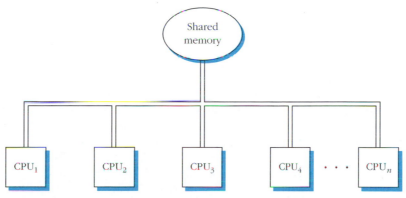

Figure 1.3–9　A simple multiprocessor

and software on a simpler set of instructions, these **reduced instruction-set computers (RISC)** can achieve greater speed and efficiency. John Cocke of IBM pioneered RISC architecture in 1975 and in 1980 IBM launched its **801 computer**, the first RISC machine.

1.3.3 Professional Roles

Several job classifications have emerged in the computing industry. **Programmers** write or modify computer programs. **Computer scientists** serve as hardware and software specialists and are well-versed in the elements of computing (see Section 1.1). These people have a responsibility to society. They must be aware of the manner in which the products they develop affect other individuals and disciplines.

The **user interface** (computer–human communication) has become a major factor in how computers are designed. Software should be **user friendly** so that the interaction between the person and the machine does not become frustrating. **Ergonomics**—the ways in which people interact physically with objects in their environment—affects the design of work areas, furniture, and the computers themselves to ensure that people work comfortably and safely. Indeed, the computer industry's awareness of the issue of people and machines has resulted in the development of a "friendly" **graphical user interface (GUI)** in software products and in a better hardware design by manufacturers.

1.3.4 The Future of Computing

What will the computing world be 5, 10, or 20 years from now? Most people agree that computing is still in its infancy. In the late 1970s the Japanese launched a government-sponsored initiative for a fifth-generation computer based on logic software that was to revolutionize the way computers are used. These computers were supposed to have massively parallel structures and to achieve computation speeds measured in teraflops (10^{12} floating-point operations per second). After two decades Japan abandoned this project because of its slow progress.

However, many of the desired features of a fifth-generation computer are already with us. Voice, pen, and pointers may soon make keyboards optional. Artificial intelligence, the fifth-generation mechanism, is now used in a variety of machines (such as washing machines and automobiles), for robots, for vision processing, for speech recognition, and even for natural-language processing. Global networks and information highways are in daily use.

Computer scientists continue their efforts to design a computer that will match the capabilities of humans. Computers are expected to possess extensive problem-solving capabilities and be intelligent partners with people. The next generation may include machines that are optically or molecularly based, with revolutionary effects on hardware design and structure. We should expect great strides in networking that allows interaction between home computers throughout the world (and maybe beyond).

The next decade should be an exciting time for computer designers and computer users and a challenging experience for everyone.

EXERCISES 1.3

Concept Check

Answer statements 1 through 4 with true *or* false.

1. The mouse was first used as an input device in the 1980s.
2. The first high-level programming language was FORTRAN.
3. Most computers today are von Neumann machines.
4. Computers based on RISC architecture work according to a probabilistic design.

For statements 5 through 8 choose the answer that best completes the statement.

5. The first calculating device was the
    a. calculator
    b. computer
    c. abacus
    d. slide rule
6. Second generation computer hardware is best known for the use of
    a. vacuum tubes
    b. chips
    c. integrated circuits
    d. transistors
7. The first commercial computer was the
    a. EDSAC
    b. TRADIC
    c. UNIVAC
    d. IBM 701
8. Pipelining is an example of
    a. array processing
    b. parallel processing
    c. a von Neumann architecture
    d. multiprocessing

For statements 9 through 12 fill in the blanks with the right word.

9. A language whose codes are in a one-to-one correspondence with machine language is called _____.
10. The area of mathematics on which computers are based is called _____.
11. The first programming language that made computers widely accessible was _____.
12. High-level programming generally characterizes the _____ generation of computer software.

Set A

Write a short essay for each of the following.

13. Explain the importance of assembly-language programming, especially in the early days of computing.

14. Why do you think each of the software generations overlaps with the one before it?

15. Parallel processing can be done in several ways. Name three versions of parallel processing and show how they differ from each other.

16. Explain how a computer might work without the use of the stored-program concept.

Set B

17. Review the definitions of an integrated circuit and a chip. Describe the difference between them.

18. Computer scientists often complain of the inadequacies of COBOL as a programming language, yet the language is still very popular. Research this claim and explain the apparent discrepancy.

19. Describe some of the roles of a computing professional.

20. Some say that one day computers will make humans useless. Why might this be false?

21. Why do you think supercomputers are called by that name even though personal computers today have surpassed the performance of the early versions of such machines?

22. Suggest reasons why the von Neumann architecture for computers has remained dominant for more than half a century.

23. Japan's fifth-generation project never achieved its promise. Research this topic and suggest some reasons for this disappointment.

24. Explain why computer scientists are not programmers.

Set C

25. Research the properties of a compact disc and explain the difference between it and a diskette.

26. Research the topic of Babbage's analytical engine. Picture yourself in the year 1830 working on this machine. Write a short essay on how you might program this machine.

27. Research the transistor. Describe why it is considered a major breakthrough in physics, electronics, and computing.

28. Write a short essay identifying some problems in artificial intelligence and explaining why they are difficult to solve.

ENDNOTES

1. Oz, E. "Ethics for the Information Age." *Business and Educational Technologies* (1994), p. 31.
2. Oz, E. "Ethics for the Information Age." *Business and Educational Technologies* (1994), pp. 75–77.
3. McAfee, J. and Haynes, C. *Computer Viruses, Worms, Data Diddlers, Killer Programs, and Other Threats to Your System.* St. Martin's Press, New York (1989).

2 Problem-Solving Concepts

The Thinker by Auguste Rodin.

After completing this chapter you should be able to do the following:

Learning Goals

- Solve simple problems analytically
- Solve simple problems using an algorithm and pseudocode
- Write a formal statement from a given problem description
- Apply the tools for algorithm development: sequence, selection, and repetition
- Verify an algorithm using desk checking
- Incorporate prettyprinting into an algorithm
- Draw a hierarchy chart
- Solve a problem using a top-down design strategy
- Compare the top-down strategy to the bottom-up strategy

Chapter Activity

A software firm needs to modify a payroll algorithm to reflect the conditions of a new employment contract. The original conditions were as follows:

1. Gross pay is calculated as hours $\times$ rate, with no provision for overtime.
2. Federal tax is specified in a three-tier fashion for weekly pay:

gross under $400	federal tax rate = 15%
gross between $400 and $1600	federal tax rate = 25%
gross over $1600	federal tax rate = 33%

3. Social security is fixed at 5.5 percent of gross weekly income under $1600

These relationships are expressed in the following algorithm.

Step 1: INPUT employee record (wage rate, hours worked)

Step 2: gross = hours $\times$ rate

Step 3: IF gross < 400
      tax = 0.15 $\times$ gross
    ELSE IF gross $\geq$ 400 AND gross $\leq$ 1600
      tax = 0.15 $\times$ 400 + 0.25 $\times$ (gross − 400)
    ELSE
      tax = 0.15 $\times$ 400 + 0.25 $\times$ 1200 + 0.33 $\times$ (gross − 1600)

Step 4: IF gross < 1600
      social security = 0.055 $\times$ gross

ELSE
social security = 0.055×1600

Step 5: net pay = gross − tax − social security

Step 6: OUTPUT net pay

Step 7: STOP

Under the new contract the following conditions were changed or added:

1. Overtime is calculated for time spent over 42 hours.
2. The overtime rate is 1.4 times the normal rate of pay.
3. Medical insurance costs (5 percent of gross) are to be shared equally by employer and employee.

Write an algorithm that incorporates these new provisions. The algorithm should be designed to process all the employee paychecks in the company, not just one employee paycheck. The number of employees is specified as an additional input.

2.1   THE ANALYTIC APPROACH

Introduction

On any given day most people are faced with a myriad of situations that demand their attention and force them to think of appropriate actions to take. Some of these scenarios might be "What should I wear today?" or "Whom do I have to call and whom should I try to avoid?" or "An accident is ahead. What detour should I take?"

Depending on your point of view, each of the above situations can be problematic. That is, you need problem-solving skills to resolve them. Most such problems are solved without much serious thought. Although some problems, especially those involving human emotions, are indeed intractable, illogical, or irrational, many problems are solvable. You may not know the best route to take to work but surely there is some route that will get you there. You may not know the solution to your physics homework but you know there is an answer. These problems are solvable but you need a systematic approach to find a reasonably good answer in a reasonable amount of time. For now we will concentrate on simple kinds of problems, those that appear to have a rational solution.

2.1.1 Problem-Solving Approaches

We begin on a somewhat disheartening note: There is no perfect method to solve all problems. Moreover, none of the methods illustrated in this chapter are completely mechanical; that is, there is still no problem-solving computer to which we could simply describe a given problem and wait for it to churn out the solution. This is the realm of artificial intelligence, which uses computers to simulate human behavior. Unfortunately, the extreme complexity of artificial intelligence problems makes progress much slower than hoped (see Chapter 19).

Problem solving is a creative act and cannot be completely explained. Still, we can use certain accepted procedures to structure our thinking and help us solve problems. Many methods of problem solving exist, but three kinds are prominent. The first is the **analytic method** used in mathematics and physics, which is discussed below. The second is the **algorithmic method** used by programmers and prevalent in computing. This is discussed in Section 2.2. The third is the **software engineering method** discussed in Chapter 10.

PERSPECTIVE

Analytic problem solving has been a tool since the relationship among the sides of a right triangle was discovered more than 2500 years ago. Algorithmic problem solving began at about the same time as the area and circumference of a circle were discovered by using inscribed polygons with an increasing number of sides. Software engineering by formal definition is of recent vintage. The principles of software engineering, however, such as top-down design, have been in use since people first began to build complex structures such as the Parthenon and the pyramids thousands of years ago.

Each method has four basic components: problem, reasoning, solution, and test. *Problem* presents the situation that requires a solution. *Reasoning* implies a true comprehension of the problem (a cursory impression of it is not enough). *Solution* is the process we develop to solve the problem, which may include insight and constructive skills. *Test* is the checking process we use to confirm that the solution is correct. Testing is always necessary in problem solving because valid methods can sometimes lead to invalid results.

2.1.2 The Analytic Approach

The analytic approach is probably the most familiar: It is what we use to solve algebra, chemistry, and physics problems. After reading over a word or story problem several times, we try to solve it. First we isolate the given quantities, then we determine what is to be solved, then we apply formulas, then we may do mathematical operations such as factoring and dividing, and finally we get an answer. If we are diligent, we check the answer, often by substituting it back into the original formula. Let's illustrate this method with a few simple examples.

EXAMPLE 2.1–1

Problem
Six identical computers are bought. The total cost is $14,627.30, which includes $340.00 for shipping and a sales tax of $724.00. Find the cost of an individual computer, excluding shipping and taxes.

Reasoning
To find the cost of one computer, first find the total cost of all six computers. This is the total cost less the shipping and tax.

Solution
Let x be the cost of one computer. Then the cost of six computers is $6x$. The net cost of the six computers is the total cost less shipping and tax. In this case

net cost = total cost − shipping − tax

where

$$\text{computer cost} \cdot (6) = \text{net cost}$$
$$6x = \text{net cost}$$

Because

net cost = total cost − shipping − tax

then

$$\text{net cost} = \$14,627.30 - \$340.00 - \$724.00$$
$$= \$13,563.30$$

so

$$\text{computer cost} \cdot (6) = \$13,563.30$$

or

$$6x = \$13,563.30$$
$$x = \$13,563.30/6$$

so

$$x = \$2260.55$$

Test
A single computer costs $2260.55. To check that the answer is right, substitute the value 2260.55 for x in the original equation. That is,

$$6x + \text{shipping} + \text{tax} = \text{total cost}$$

So

$$6(2260.55) + 340.00 + 724.00 = 14,627.30$$
$$14,627.30 = 14,627.30$$

The next example of the analytic method is a problem in descriptive statistics: finding the mean of a set of data.

EXAMPLE 2.1–2

Problem
Find a formula to calculate the mean (the arithmetic average) of five numbers.

Reasoning
The problem involves calculating the sum of five arbitrary numbers and then dividing by 5 to yield the mean value.

Solution
Choose symbols for the five numbers—in this case a, b, c, d, and e. The first task is to find the sum of the numbers. Using the word SUM, this can be written as

$$\text{SUM} = a + b + c + d + e$$

Next let MEAN be the symbol for the mean. This mean is calculated as

$$\text{MEAN} = \text{SUM}/5$$

Test
The problem is to find a formula for the mean of 5 numbers. As a test case, substitute actual values for the symbols a, b, c, d, and e. For example:

$$\text{SUM} = 5 + 7 + 11 + 12 + 15$$

$$\text{SUM} = 50$$

Then substitute for SUM and calculate the mean as

$$\text{MEAN} = 50/5$$

$$\text{MEAN} = 10$$

This suggests that the definition and formulation for the mean are plausible for this situation. ●

2.1.3 Unsolvable Problems

Analytic problem solving has roots in mathematics, physics, engineering, chemistry, and a host of other areas of science and technology. We do not intend to address these areas here but only to show that computer scientists need to be aware of the analytic method.

Some problems can not be solved analytically even with the most sophisticated technique. For example, mathematicians have proven that no analytic method can find the roots of a simple fifth-degree polynomial equation of the form

$$ax^5 + bx^4 + cx^3 + dx^2 + ex + f = 0$$

for arbitrary real-number coefficients when f is not zero. Likewise, there are numerous problems in the sciences and mathematics for which analytic solutions are not possible. Computers are often used to solve such problems and sometimes the approximate answers that result are accurate enough to be accepted as solutions.

BEFORE YOU GO ON

QUERY: The fifth-degree polynomial $x^5 - 1 = 0$ can be factored as $(x - 1)(x^4 + x^3 + x^2 + x + 1) = 0$, leading to one answer of $x = 1$ that is easily verifiable. This does not contradict the previous claim that fifth-degree polynomials have no general analytic solution. Why?

RESPONSE: The claim is a general statement and refers to fifth-degree polynomials that have arbitrary coefficients. The equation $x^5 - 1 = 0$ happens to be a specific solvable case where $a = 1, b = c = d = e = 0$, and $f = -1$.

EXERCISES 2.1

Concept Check
Answer statements 1 through 4 with true *or* false.
1. All problems have solutions.
2. Understanding a problem is usually easy.
3. The analytic method of problem solving can be used to solve most real-world problems.
4. Testing an answer to a problem is not necessary.

For statements 5 through 8 choose the answer that best completes the statement.
5. The phases of analytic problem solving are
   a. understanding and reflection
   b. solution and verification
   c. problem, reasoning, solution, and test
   d. none of the above

6. The steps to analytic problem solving are
   a. those that must be followed strictly
   b. not unique
   c. useful to many problem-solving situations
   d. unique
7. The quadratic equation $x^2 - 2x - 15 = 0$
   a. has only $x = 5$ as a solution
   b. has no solution
   c. has only $x = -3$ as a solution
   d. has both $x = -3$ and $x = 5$ as solutions
8. Which problems in science and mathematics can analytic problem solving solve?
   a. all physics problems
   b. few problems
   c. all engineering problems
   d. no problem

For statements 9 through 12 fill in the blanks with the right word.
9. Eight identical computers cost at least $24,000.00. Therefore, each computer costs _____.
10. The four phases of analytic problem solving are _____, _____, _____, and _____.
11. The solution to a problem is _____ unique.
12. When solving problems we should not expect to always find a _____.

Set A
Solve each of the following problems using the analytic method by showing that you understand the problem, know how to solve the problem, and tested the solution.
13. Computer chips are bought in lots of 100. A company buys 65 lots of a given chip and pays $130,000.00 for the total shipment. Find the cost of each chip.
14. A company employs 1,200 people. At least 73 people will be terminated. Approximately what percentage of the employees will lose their jobs?
15. A company makes three different types of computer printers: low-, medium-, and high-quality. Low-quality printers sell for $255.00, medium-quality printers sell for $634.00, and high-quality printers sell for $1279.00. If in one week 12 low-quality, 19 medium-quality, and 14 high-quality printers were sold, find the gross revenue generated for these sales for the week.
16. The product of two positive consecutive integers is 506. Find the two integers.
17. Two cables have a total cost of $12.00. The difference in the cost is $2.00. Find the cost of each cable.
18. The product of two numbers is 96 and their sum is 20. Find the two numbers.

Set B

Solve each of the following problems using the analytic method by showing that you understand the problem, know how to solve the problem, and tested the solution.

19. A company has a $195,000.00 budget to install 25 identical personal computers for its staff. Renovation and furniture for the these computers cost at least $45,000.00. Find the highest cost of the most affordable computer the company can buy.

20. A school needs 12 identical computers for a laboratory to be housed in a classroom. Carpeting and furniture for the classroom is budgeted at $6,000.00. If the total budget is $90,000.00, find the highest cost of the most affordable computer the school can buy.

21. A software package needs a total of 6 MB of RAM. Base memory for the existing hardware is 512 KB with no extended memory. Adding RAM chips will extend the memory to accommodate the software. If each RAM chip has a capacity of 256 KB, find the number of chips to be used for extended memory.

22. Because of a new network hookup, a computer will be modified so it can act as a file server to the network. The computer's hard disk capacity must be at least twice the capacity of the sum of all the other hard disk capacities of the computers on the network. Each computer on the network has a 230-MB hard disk and there are 18 computers on the network. Find the minimum capacity of the hard disk for the server.

23. Explain the importance of the test phase of problem solving.

24. Find the mean of the numbers 3.2, 5.6, 3.9, 8.1, 7.3, 2.9, and 5.2.

25. Find the solution to $x^2 - 5x - 36 = 0$.

26. Find the solution to $x - y = 4$ and $2x + y = 7$.

2.2   THE ALGORITHMIC APPROACH

Introduction

Section 2.1 discusses analytic problem solving used in mathematics and the sciences. With that approach, specific knowledge, techniques, and skills are applied to a problem and lead to a solution. What follows is an alternative approach called the **algorithmic method**, in which a finite set of well-defined steps is used to solve a problem.

2.2.1 Algorithms

Algorithms are not unique to the computational sciences. An algorithm is a recipe, a sequence of steps that leads from a starting point to a finished product. When we bake a cake, for example, the starting point is assembling the ingredients. The algorithm is the cake recipe in the cookbook we are using. We

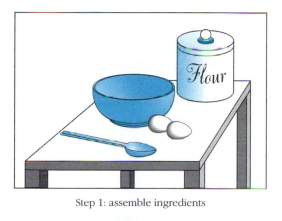

Step 1: assemble ingredients

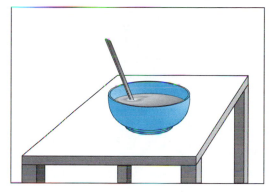

Step 2: mix

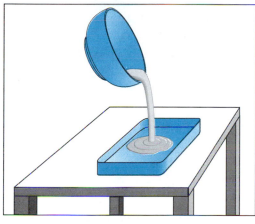

Step 3: pour

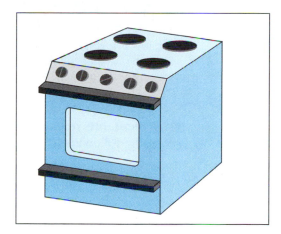

Step 4: bake

Figure 2.2–1　**Steps for baking a cake**

assume that if we follow the recipe exactly, the finished product will be a cake that fits the description of the cake in the cookbook (see Figure 2.2–1).

This algorithm describes the solution to the problem of baking a cake but it also describes the solution to problems of a similar type. Using the same algorithm and simply changing some of the ingredients, we can produce many kinds of cakes.

In the language of computer science, the ingredients are the **input parameters** and the finished cake is the **output parameter**. In a cookbook, the input is precisely quantified as 6 eggs, $1/2$ cup of sugar, 1 teaspoon of salt, etc. The output is also precisely quantified: a 12-inch, double-layer, chocolate truffle cake. In mathematical terms, we might say that an algorithm **maps**—supplies directions—from the input parameters to the derived output parameters. Of course, not all problems need input; the problem of determining whether the number 1127983 is prime does not need input, for example.

From a computational perspective a true algorithm is a **mechanical** procedure. That is, for a given set of inputs an algorithm should produce an exactly reproducible output (a clone). For this to happen, there must be ground rules (some might say disclaimers) to ensure the desired consequences. A formal definition of an algorithm is as follows.

An **algorithm** is a sequence of executable instructions with these properties:

1. There is no ambiguity in any instruction.
2. There is no ambiguity about which instruction is to be executed next.
3. The description of the algorithm is finite.
4. Execution of the algorithm concludes after a finite number of steps.

PERSPECTIVE

The word *algorithm* is believed to be a variation of the word *algorism* and the Greek word *arithmos*, meaning number. The word *algorism* describes the art of computation using the Arabic numerals 0 through 9 and reflects the name of the ninth-century Arabic mathematician al-Kh(u)warizmi.

An **executable instruction** is one that can be carried out. For example, consider the following get-rich-quick scheme:

Step 1: Get $1,000.

Step 2: Go to a commodities broker.

Step 3: Get a copy of tomorrow's newspaper and write down the closing values of today's commodities.

Step 4: Buy or sell options on those commodities appropriately.

Step 5: Take the profits and return to Step 2.

This is not an algorithm for two reasons. First, Step 3 is not executable in the known universe. Second, although the specification itself consists of a finite number of steps, its realization (or running) calls for an unlimited number of repetitions of some of those steps. The sequence from Step 2 to Step 5 and back to Step 2 again is called an *infinite loop* because these steps are repeated continuously without termination. Such a situation is a clear violation of Part 4 of the algorithm definition.

Consider the instructions.

Step 1: Make a list of the odd positive integers.

Step 2: Compute their sum.

Step 3: Compute their average.

Step 4: Print the average.

This is not an algorithm either because only Step 4 is executable. At Step 1 it is impossible to make an infinite list of numbers. At Step 2 it is impossible to compute an unbounded infinite sum. At Step 3 division by infinity is not possible.

Notice that the inability to execute Step 1 is not just the inconvenience of having to write down billions and trillions of numbers, for this task could be assigned to a computer and a high-speed printer. Rather, this is a theoretical impossibility: No matter how fast the computer is, no matter how much paper is put into the printer, no matter how much time we allocate to the process, it just can't be done. Some problems are like this and sometimes it is easy to tell from the nature of the problem that it can't be solved.

More often, however, it is not so easy to tell whether a given problem or a given step of a problem is executable. Some mathematicians and computer scientists choose to deal with this in a formal way. For them it is important to be able to categorize a problem as computable or noncomputable. Moreover, as discussed in Chapter 18, some problems, though finite, are just not worth trying to compute because computing them would take such an inordinate amount of time that they might as well be infinite.

PERSPECTIVE

Computer games and, in particular, computer chess are examples of computerized problem solving in the area of artificial intelligence. You might think that this is simply a matter of programming the computer to memorize all the possible chess games. Then, as a game develops, the computer could look into its vast memory and pull out the best response to any given move. This exhaustive technique would work except for one catch: There are approximately 10^{160} (1 followed by 160 zeros) games of chess. Compare that with the number of molecules in the known universe, 10^{80}. So if every molecule in the universe were a supercomputer capable of looking up a new chess move every trillionth of a second, it would still take thousands of times the age of the universe to complete one game!

Algorithmic solutions are not unique and are not restricted to mathematical problems. For example, a description of arriving at a location for an early morning class can be complicated depending on the level of detail. Some intermediate steps might include waking up to an alarm clock, having breakfast, driving to school, parking your car, and taking a seat. Surely there could have been many other steps. Whatever algorithm is used to arrive to class is not unique: There may be hundreds of algorithms to solve the same problem.

2.2.2 Phases of Algorithmic Problem Solving

Algorithmic problem solving has four phases: problem, reasoning, solution, and test. *Problem* presents the situation that requires a solution. *Reasoning* means to read and reread the problem statement until it makes sense to you. This may involve discussions with other people such as classmates, teachers, and colleagues to help clarify the key issues and develop a design strategy. In this phase of algorithmic problem solving, the focus is on generating a formal statement to summarize your understanding of the problem. In the **formal statement** you restate the problem so that it answers three questions: the **input** needed, the **output** to be produced, and the **process** to be performed. Notice that the formal statement describes what has to happen, not how to do it.

In the *solution* phase of algorithmic problem solving, you design the solution and write the algorithm. Note that any set of instructions that meets the four criteria in the definition of an algorithm can be considered an algorithm. In computer science, however, an algorithm generally implies sequence, selection, and repetition. That is, an algorithm is usually written as a step-by-step procedure (**sequence**) in which choices can be made where necessary (**selection**), and all or part of the process can be repeated (**repetition**). You will learn how to combine these components effectively as you progress in the study of computer science.

The fourth phase of algorithmic problem solving is the *test* phase. Although in practice it is often impossible, full testing of an algorithm is desirable to confirm that the algorithm truly solved the problem for which it was designed. Hand verification, sometimes called **desk checking**, is useful for short algorithms. Desk checking means you "play computer" and apply a set of test data to the algorithm. This should reveal logic flaws and allow you to rethink the solution and make corrections.

2.2.3 Sequence

An algorithm is based on the notion of **sequence**, which is the ordering of instructions. When we write an algorithm we use the convention of numbering the steps. This is both for reference and to stress that there is a specific order to the algorithm that becomes significant when the algorithm is put to use. Unless stated to the contrary, it is assumed that Step n cannot be started until Step $n - 1$ is completed. Consider the following.

EXAMPLE 2.2–1

Problem

A **trapezoid** is a four-sided geometric figure (quadrilateral) in which two sides, called the bases, are parallel. The area of a trapezoid is given as one-half the product of the height and the sum of the lengths of the two bases, base1 and base2. Symbolically,

$$A = (\text{base1} + \text{base2})h/2$$

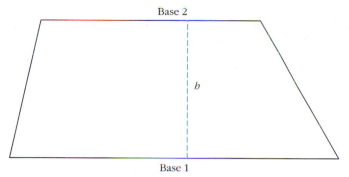

Figure 2.2–2   Trapezoid of height *h*

The height *h* is the distance between the two parallel lines. (See Figure 2.2–2.) Develop an algorithm that calculates and prints the area of a trapezoid when the values of the bases and height are given as input.

Reasoning

This is a simple geometry problem involving the calculation of the area of a special quadrilateral. We begin by restating the problem as a formal statement.

Formal statement: trapezoid problem

Input: base1, base2, height

Output: area

Process: area = (base1 + base2) $\times$ height / 2

Solution

The algorithm picks up where the formal statement left off by describing how to get from the input to the output and make the computation. Here is a possible solution.

Step 1: INPUT base1

Step 2: INPUT base2

Step 3: INPUT height

Step 4: basesum = base1 + base2

Step 5: area = basesum $\times$ height / 2

Step 6: OUTPUT area

Step 7: STOP

Test

Desk check that this sequence of steps is an algorithm whose execution solves the intended problem. Try the reasonable values.

base1 = 10

base2 = 20

height = 15

then

basesum = 10 + 20 = 30

and

area = 30 × 15/2

= 225   •

You can see that the sequence of steps is critical because it does not make sense to compute the area of the trapezoid (Step 5) until the basesum has been calculated (Step 4). Similarly, the area cannot be output until it has been calculated.

Note that we capitalize the words *INPUT, OUTPUT,* and *STOP* as part of an algorithm language that is sometimes called **pseudocode** because of its resemblance to high-level programming languages. Also, note that the words *base1, base2, height, basesum,* and *area* are in lowercase. These words are not part of the pseudocode but are arbitrarily chosen to represent the data manipulated by the algorithm.

Mathematically, *base1, base2,* etc., represent the names of **variables** because their values can change depending on the actions taken in response to the algorithm. In programming they are called **identifiers** or **variable identifiers** because they serve to identify, by name, the memory locations in the computer where the corresponding data are stored. Although the names chosen are arbitrary, as a matter of style it is better to choose names that are **mnemonic**—that is, suggest what the name means.

BEFORE YOU GO ON

QUERY: Some students with experience in the BASIC programming language tend to use single-letter variable names when writing algorithms. Which is easier to understand, the algorithm in Example 2.2–1 or the following:

Step 1:   INPUT x

Step 2:   INPUT q

Step 3:   INPUT t

Step 4: $r = x + q$

(continued)

Step 5: $m = r \times t/2$
Step 6:   OUTPUT m
Step 7:   STOP

RESPONSE: The mnemonic representation of identifiers in Example 2.2–1 is easier to understand. Furthermore, mnemonic identifiers help to create self-documenting algorithms, which describe the procedure called for by the algorithm.

2.2.4 Selection

Another tool for writing algorithms is selection. **Selection** is the choice of alternate paths (branches) depending on a contingency that may arise in the logical flow of the algorithm. The ability (and necessity) to allow for contingencies is also the biggest source of problems with algorithms. When writing an algorithm, you must think ahead to all possible conditions that might occur and include steps for appropriate action. This is hard to do and explains why computer software sometimes has latent problems called **bugs**.

PERSPECTIVE

The word *bug* in computing was first used in the 1940s when an insect was found inside a mechanical relay in a computer. Grace Murray Hopper, a pioneering computer scientist, is said to have declared that a bug had caused the program to malfunction. It is still not clear if that insect really caused the problem, but program bugs and their removal (debugging) remain with us today.

EXAMPLE 2.2–2

Problem
A person who travels between Kansas City and Toronto needs an algorithm that accepts a number representing either a Fahrenheit or a Celsius temperature scale and converts it to the other scale.

Reasoning
To solve this you need to know the formulas for converting from Fahrenheit to Celsius and from Celsius to Fahrenheit.

Formal statement:	temperature conversion problem
Input:	scale (Fahrenheit or Celsius), temperature
Output:	converted temperature
Process:	CelsTemp = 5/9 (FahrenTemp − 32)
	FahrenTemp = 9/5 CelsTemp + 32

Solution

The algorithm must make a selection based on the user's input values and take an appropriate action. The action is contingent on the value of *scale*, which is unknown at the time the algorithm is being written. Therefore, one scale or the other must be anticipated and processed.

Step 1: INPUT scale

Step 2: INPUT temperature

Step 3: IF scale == 'f'
$\qquad$ newTemp = 5/9 × (temperature − 32)
$\quad$ ELSE
$\qquad$ newTemp = 9/5 × temperature + 32

Step 4: OUTPUT newTemp

Step 5: STOP

Test

You can easily check this algorithm by trying various values for temperatures such as 212 Fahrenheit and 100 Celsius, which are equivalent. •

Step 3 of Example 2.2–2 introduces the new pseudocode **IF ... ELSE**, which is a **selection structure**. This can be read as "*IF* it is true that the scale equals f (Fahrenheit), then convert the input temperature to Celsius, otherwise (*ELSE*) convert it to Fahrenheit." Note that Step 3 uses a double equal sign in the expression *scale* == *f*, which has a different meaning from the single equal sign in the statement *newTemp = 5/9 × (temperature− 32)*. The first is a logical equality, meaning that a test is being performed, whereas the second is an assignment of the calculation on the right side of the equal sign to the identifier on the left. A detailed explanation of this is given in Chapters 3, 4, and 5.

Notice that we have introduced **prettyprinting** to show an indentation in the algorithm. In Step 3 of the algorithm of Example 2.2–2, statements that are affected by the *IF* statement are indented from the **structure heading** to show that they form the **body** of the selection structure. Through prettyprinting, it should be visually apparent that Step 4 of Example 2.2–2 is *not* affected by the selection and is to be performed after the structure has terminated regardless of which branch was taken at Step 3.

EXAMPLE 2.2–3

Problem

Assume that a salesperson is paid a commission based on the number of sales made during the week. The salesperson is paid a commission of $8 per sale for less than the established quota of 15 sales, $12 per sale if the quota is reached, and $16 per sale if the quota is exceeded. Write an algorithm to find the salesperson's commission.

Reasoning

The problem is to compute a commission based on a pay rate and number of sales made. The pay rate is specified in three tiers based on the sales and the preset quota.

Formal statement:	sales commission problem
Input:	number of sales
Output:	commission
Process:	commission = rate × number of sales
	where rate is determined as:
	$ 8/sale for fewer than 15 sales
	$12/sale for exactly 15 sales
	$16/sale for more than 15 sales

Solution

This problem requires multiple selection based on the input value of *sales,* which is unknown at the time the algorithm is being written.

Step 1: INPUT sales

Step 2: IF sales < quota
             rate = 8
         ELSE IF sales == quota
             rate = 12
         ELSE
             rate = 16

Step 3: commission = rate × sales

Step 4: OUTPUT commission

Step 5: STOP

Test

To check this algorithm you must verify that it can handle all the specified cases. Do this by trying values that are below the quota, above the quota, and at the quota.   ●

Step 2 of Example 2.2–3 introduces **multiple selection** and can be read as "*IF* the sales are less than the quota, then the rate = 8; otherwise if the sales equal the quota, then the rate = 12; otherwise by default the rate = 16." This structure can be extended indefinitely by repeated use of *ELSE IF.*

Notice that in Example 2.2–3 the pay rate must be determined before the commission can be computed (in sequence) even though in the formal statement it appears that the commission is computed first! Also notice that the last *ELSE* of the multiple *IF* becomes the default or catchall case that is considered if none of the other possibilities is true. Finally, notice that for any given run, only one path (one value for rate) can be chosen. This structure is sometimes called **mutual exclusion** because choosing one path excludes all the remaining ones.

As problems become more complex, testing also becomes more complex. Which values are appropriate to test? At a minimum the testing should include numbers that drive each possible branch of the test at Step 2. What happens if the number −6 is input? This algorithm generates a commission of $−48! What if the number 10,000 is input? The algorithm would pay the salesperson $160,000. (Not bad for a week's work.)

Input errors are seldom deliberate. Presumably no one would intentionally enter the number −6 because it is impossible to make a negative number of sales. On the other hand, entering 10,000 doesn't sound bad. As shown later in this section, one of the rules of program development is that all input should be tested to ensure that it is reasonable within the boundaries of the problem. Here it seems reasonable that the number of sales must be at least 0 unless returns are included in the commission scheme. What should the upper bound be? 100? 1,000? There is no easy answer because whatever number you choose is arbitrary. More information would be needed about this particular problem to set an appropriate upper bound.

2.2.5 Repetition

The third tool used in the development of an algorithm is called **repetition,** or **looping**, which provides for repeated execution of part of the algorithm. An obvious deficiency in Example 2.2–3 is its inability to handle more than one salesperson. You could replicate Steps 1 through 4 for each salesperson. Then you have the clerical chore of writing these four steps over and over, especially for a large sales staff, and the problem of hiring and firing. There may be 20 salespeople at one time and 50 at another. It seems unreasonable to have to expand and shrink an algorithm depending on the business cycle! One way to deal with this problem is shown next.

EXAMPLE 2.2–4

Problem
Reconsider the problem in Example 2.2–3 but allow for an entire sales staff.

Reasoning
This is essentially the same problem as Example 2.2–3 with the addition of a looping structure. The looping structure processes the data for each salesperson. The input is adjusted to include the number of salespeople to be paid.

Formal statement: sales commission problem (2)

Input: number of salespeople
                         number of sales for each salesperson

Output: commission for each salesperson

Process: commission = rate × number of sales
                         where rate is determined as:
                         $ 8/sale for < 15 sales
                         $12/sale for = 15 sales
                         $16/sale for > 15 sales

Solution

A loop is used to repeatedly read the data for each salesperson and compute the associated commission. The word *LOOP* here means that the following sequence of steps (2a to 2d in this case) is to be repeated for a specific number of iterations (numSalespeople in this case).

Step 1: INPUT numSalespeople

Step 2: LOOP numSalespeople times
      a. INPUT sales
      b. IF sales < quota
          rate = 8
        ELSE IF sales == quota
          rate = 12
        ELSE
          rate = 16
      c. commission = rate × sales
      d. OUTPUT commission

Step 3: STOP

Test

You can test this algorithm by desk checking; that is, by trying different values for sales (above, below, and at the quota) and calculating the results. •

BEFORE YOU GO ON

QUERY: Why are Steps 2a to 2d indented?

RESPONSE: As with the selection structure, prettyprinting is used to visually distinguish the loop heading from its body, making it clear that Step 3 is not affected by the loop and is performed after the loop has finished.

The algorithm in Example 2.2–4 assumes that the number of salespeople currently on the payroll is known. The loop construction is only appropriate if the number of iterations can be predetermined as it is here. For many situations, however, this is not possible and a more flexible looping structure is needed, as we see in the next example.

2.2.6 Conditional Looping

This second, more flexible loop continues for an indeterminate number of repetitions as long as a particular condition is valid. This is useful when the number of repetitions cannot be specified ahead of time.

Consider a problem that arises in programming: checking the input for errors. From the previous examples, what if the input value for *sales* is unreasonable—for example, −6 or 10,000? The algorithm has to respond to such a contingency with a special action. One possibility, shown below, would be to include a decision statement that says "*IF* the input value is out of range, *THEN* inform the user of his/her mistake and stop the processing." For the moment assume that an appropriate range has been specified and that input values must lie between a minimum value, called *minsales*, and a maximum value, called *maxsales*. The algorithm can be rewritten as

Step 1: INPUT numSalespeople

Step 2: LOOP numSalespeople times
      a. INPUT sales
      b. IF sales > maxsales OR sales < minsales
          1.   OUTPUT error message
          2.   STOP
      c. IF sales < quota
          rate = 8
        ELSE IF sales == quota
          rate = 12
        ELSE
          rate = 16
      d. commission = rate × sales
      e. OUTPUT commission

Step 3: STOP

This solution prevents the program from making a ridiculous calculation but it introduces two new problems. First, it is not **user-friendly** because it does not give the user the chance to reinput the value. It simply alerts the user to the mistake and then stops.

The second problem is more subtle because it is a function of the design of the algorithm. When you design an algorithm (or program) it is important to build the logic so that it is simple, clear, and easy to follow. A principle of **structured programming** is that there should be one way to enter an algorithm and one way to exit. The **one-in, one-out** design is easier to follow, easier to debug, and easier to maintain. But the word *STOP* at Step 2.b.2 and at Step 3 means that there are now two possible exits from the overall process.

A second possible solution to the problem of verifying the sales value is to include a decision statement that says "*IF* the input value is out of range, *THEN* inform the user and ask for a new value." This is shown in the algorithm excerpt:

    b. IF sales > maxsales OR sales < minsales
        1. OUTPUT error message
        2. INPUT sales

This solution answers the two criticisms raised above but leaves open the possibility of a second mistaken value for *sales* (or a third, a fourth, etc.). As shown next, the best solution uses an error-checking loop structure.

EXAMPLE 2.2–5

Problem
Reconsider the sales problem of Example 2.2–4 but allow for unlimited error checking on the sales value.

Reasoning
The problem is essentially the same as in Example 2.2–4 except that after the *sales* value has been input, a checking loop is included to catch a user mistake.

Solution

Step 1: INPUT numSalespeople

Step 2: LOOP numSalespeople times
    a. INPUT sales
    b. WHILE sales > maxsales OR sales < minsales
        1. OUTPUT error message
        2. INPUT sales
    c. IF sales < quota
        rate = 8
      ELSE IF sales == quota
        rate = 12
      ELSE
        rate = 16
    d. commission = rate × sales
    e. OUTPUT commission

Step 3: STOP

Test

Now choose unreasonable as well as reasonable values to test the revised algorithm.   •

The new Step 2.b checks the *sales* value to determine whether it is out of range. If it is, the algorithm outputs an error message and asks for additional input. The algorithm is then automatically reexecuted from the beginning, including the error checking. The pseudocode word **WHILE** means "As long as this condition remains true, continue to perform the following sequence of steps (the **body of the loop**)." Now the process of entering unreasonable values can go on indefinitely—that is, until the input is indeed valid.

How can we resolve the problem of not knowing the number of salespeople in advance? A simple solution is to substitute another WHILE loop within the WHILE loop in Step 1, as shown next.

Step 1: WHILE more salespeople to process
        a. INPUT sales
        b. WHILE sales > maxsales OR sales < minsales
            1.   OUTPUT error message
            2.   INPUT sales
        c. IF sales < quota
            rate = 8
        ELSE IF sales == quota
            rate = 12
        ELSE
            rate = 16
        d. commission = rate $\times$ sales
        e. OUTPUT commission

Step 2: STOP

Notice the WHILE within a WHILE (Steps 1 and 1.b). This is called **nesting** or **nested loops** and is perfectly acceptable logic. The inner loop is simply one more step to be processed in the course of processing the body of the outer loop.

Table 2.2–1   Elements of an Algorithmic Language

LANGUAGE ELEMENT	MEANING	EXAMPLE
INPUT	Accept data from the user.	INPUT radius
OUTPUT	Send results to the user.	OUTPUT area
=	Assign the calculation on the right side to the variable on the left side.	area = pi × radius × radius
STOP	End the algorithm.	STOP

IF ELSE	If the condition is true, execute the sequence of statements that follows; otherwise execute the second sequence of statements.	IF hours ≤ 40
		  a. gross = wage × hours
		  b. OUTPUT gross
		
		ELSE
		  a. gross = wage × 40 + overtime_pay
		  b. OUTPUT gross

LOOP	Repeatedly execute a sequence of statements for a specific number of times.	LOOP numstudents times
		  a. INPUT gr1, gr2
		  b. OUTPUT (gr1+gr2) / 2

WHILE	Test the condition before entering the loop and repeatedly execute a sequence of statements as long as the loop condition is true.	WHILE classSize < 0
		  a. OUTPUT "Error in class size"
		  b. INPUT classSize

Table 2.2–1 summarizes the algorithm language that we have learned about in this chapter. It is interesting that relatively few words are enough to describe any computable process.

EXERCISES 2.2

Concept Check

Answer statements 1 through 4 with true *or* false.

1. Through the use of sophisticated computer techniques, problem solving has become somewhat routine.
2. Algorithms are used only in the computational sciences.
3. The formal statement details how to get the solution.
4. Mutual exclusion occurs when only one branch of a multiple-selection statement is executed.

For statements 5 through 8 choose the answer that best completes the statement.

5. The phases for writing algorithms are
   a. problem, reasoning, solution, and test
   b. sequence, selection, and repetition
   c. formal statement, program, and desk check
   d. dependent on the nature of the problem to be solved

6. Prettyprinting means
   a. the use of high-resolution printers for program output
   b. the proper use of the tools for writing algorithms
   c. the use of indentation when writing selection and repetition structures
   d. the use of structured problem solving
7. Multiple selection with repeated applications of IF . . . ELSE is
   a. not a good problem-solving technique because the logic is too complicated to follow
   b. useful in problem verification
   c. an alternative form of looping
   d. sometimes called *mutual exclusion*
8. As defined in the text, the pseudocode word *LOOP* means
   a. to repeat a section of an algorithm an indeterminate number of times
   b. to repeat a section of an algorithm a preset number of times
   c. to test for a condition and to repeat if the condition is true
   d. to test for a condition and to repeat if the condition is false

For statements 9 through 12 fill in the blanks with the right word.
9. An algorithm can be viewed as a mapping from a set of _____ to a set of _____.
10. A(n) _____ is a step-by-step procedure that, given the same input, should always produce the same output.
11. A formal statement contains specifications for the _____, the _____, and the _____.
12. One of the principles of structured programming is called _____ design.

Set A

Write algorithms for each of the following problems.
13. Given an input value for the length of the side, write an algorithm to find the area of a square.
14. Write an algorithm to output the square and the cube of the input value.
15. Rewrite Questions 13 and 14 but allow the user to input repeatedly, up to 10 different values (use a loop).
16. The area of a circle is $A = \pi r^2$. Write an algorithm to find this area for a single input radius r.
17. Write an algorithm to compute the volume of a sphere ($4/3 \pi r^3$). The algorithm should check to make sure that the input value for the radius is greater than 0.
18. Redo Question 17 but allow the user to repeatedly enter values for the the radius of the sphere and stop if the radius is less than or equal to zero.

Set B

19. The monthly payment on a mortgage is calculated according to the formula
$$M = (P \times i \times (1 + i)^n)/((1 + i)^n - 1)$$

where P represents the principal

         i represents the monthly interest (= yearly rate / 12)

         n represents the number of payments (= #years $\times$ 12)

Write an algorithm that inputs values for the principal, yearly interest rate, and term in years and outputs the corresponding monthly payment. The algorithm should allow many runs.

20. Revise the algorithm from Question 19 to allow for input checking. Assume the following bank-imposed limitations on borrowing.

INPUT PARAMETER	MINIMUM VALUE	MAXIMUM VALUE
Principal	$50,000	$500,000
Yearly interest	5%	15%
Term in years	10	40

21. Use multiple selection to calculate simple interest on a loan if the rate is 6 percent when the time is less than or equal to 1 year, 7 percent when the time is between 1 and 6 years, and 8 percent when the time is greater than or equal to 6 years.

22. Repeat Question 21 to accommodate an 8% rate range for times between 6 and 10 years inclusive, and a 9% rate range when time is greater than 10 years.

23. Write an algorithm to generate the squares of the first 10 positive integers i for $1 \le i \le 10$.

24. Repeat Question 23 and generate the squares and cubes of the first 100 positive integers.

25. A manufacturing firm sells low-grade, medium-grade, and high-grade printers. Low-grade printers sell for $200, medium-grade for $500, and high-grade for $1,300. If commissions are set at 6 percent for all printers, write an algorithm to calculate total sales and total commissions if the number of sales for each grade of printer is 2,500, 1,200, and 800, respectively.

26. Write an algorithm to print the multiplication table from 0 through 12 of the numbers 1 through 10.

Set C

27. Suppose a person's salary is the sum of his or her base pay plus the commission earned on sales. The base pay is calculated at a rate of $5.25 per hour for time less than or equal to 40 hours and time-and-a-half for all time exceeding 40 hours. Let the commission on sales be described by the information from Example 2.2–3. Write an algorithm to calculate the salary for all sales people in a company.

3 Elements of the C Language

Cleveland Stadium, the old home of the Cleveland Indians.

After completing this chapter you should be able to do the following:

Learning Goals

- Explain the history of the C language
- Write a simple program in C
- Write a short, professional-looking program in C
- Name and distinguish C's basic data types
- Explain the naming conventions for C identifiers
- Use constants and variables correctly
- Use `scanf` and `printf` correctly
- Explain the operator-precedence scheme in C
- Evaluate integer and mixed-mode arithmetic correctly
- Write statements containing compound-assignment operators
- Use the increment and decrement operators

Chapter Activity

A construction firm is designing a building facade with many arbitrary steel plates. Each plate is a donut-shaped ring with a uniform thickness but with varied measurements for inner and outer radii. Design a software module to calculate the inner and outer circumference, area, and volume of a single circular plate when the thickness, and the external and internal diameters are given. The following information is known:

$$\text{circumference} = \pi \times \text{diameter}$$

$$\text{radius} = \text{diameter}/2$$

$$\text{area (circle)} = \pi \times \text{radius} \times \text{radius} = \pi \times \text{radius}^2$$

$$\text{area (donut)} = \text{outer area} - \text{inner area}$$

$$\text{volume} = \text{area} \times \text{thickness}$$

Write a program to compute the measurements for a single donut.

3.1 BACKGROUND AND STRUCTURE OF C

Introduction

This section introduces the C language and some elementary programming concepts, beginning with a short history of the evolution of the language. For a more thorough history of C and other programming languages, see Chapter 14.

3.1.1 History of C

C evolved from two earlier languages: BCPL (Basic Combined Programming Language) and B. BCPL was developed in 1967 by Martin Richards of Cambridge University as a language for writing operating systems software and compilers. In 1970 Ken Thompson of Bell Laboratories developed the B language, based on BCPL, to implement the first UNIX operating system. C, developed in 1972 by Dennis Ritchie of Bell Laboratories, is an outgrowth of B and provides a combination of the features of a structured high-level language and those of a low-level assembly language.

Both BCPL and B were typeless languages: They did not distinguish, for instance, between integer and decimal values. The typical data type in these languages was based on machine organization with abundant use of **memory address** arithmetic. That is, instead of referring to data symbolically through variable names, programmers had to specify particular memory addresses for data storage and retrieval. The C language was a result of the way software developers used the basic ideas of structured programming. These ideas include explicit data typing, which means that all variables must be given a specific data type from a set of predefined choices; control structures without GOTOs, such as the IF . . . ELSE and the WHILE loop covered in the last chapter; and block-structured programming allowing easier program design and debugging.

The rapid expansion of C for various **platforms** (computer systems) led to many similar but often incompatible variations. This was a serious problem for software developers who needed to create **portable code** that could be used on different machines. In 1983 a subcommittee was formed by the American National Standards Institute (ANSI) Committee on Computers and Information Processing to "provide an unambiguous and machine-independent definition of the language." In 1989 the ANSI C standard was approved.

C is traditionally called the **development language** of the UNIX operating system: the language used to write the operating system. Today, however, ANSI C is a mature general-purpose language available on many machines and for many operating systems. It is becoming a common industrial programming language, and many software packages from major software vendors are written in C. These include operating systems as well as word processing, database management, and graphics software.

3.1.2 A Simple Program in C

Program 3.1–1 shows the structure of an elementary C program. Ignore the strange punctuation and look over the program to get a general sense of what is going on.

PROGRAM 3.1–1

```
/*      Area of a circle                                       */
/*      This program computes the area of a circle with a particular radius  */

#include  <stdio.h>
main ( )
{
    float   radius, area;
    radius = 10;
    area = 3.14159 * radius * radius;
    printf ( "The area = %f", area );
    return ( 0 );
}
```

Commentary on Program 3.1–1

1. The first two lines of the program are called **comment** lines and serve to document, in plain English, the purpose of the program. Each group of comments begins with the symbol /* and ends with */. Comment lines are not executable (not translated by C) and cannot be embedded in other comments.

BEFORE YOU GO ON

Query: Does C process comments?

RESPONSE: C ignores all comments. Comments are for the benefit of the reader of the program (you or another programmer). In the process of converting the program to executable machine code, C ignores all text between the beginning and ending comment markers.

2. The next line is an instruction to the C **preprocessor**. The preprocessor scans a C program before it is compiled into machine code and makes certain changes to the program. In this case the instruction says to include the "standard input/output header" file. This file in turn contains instructions that enable the program to perform basic input and output operations (see Appendix A–1). Because all meaningful programs perform at least one input or output operation, this line should be included in every C program.

Query: How would you characterize a program that includes no input? No output?

RESPONSE: A program that does not include any input from the outside is legitimate but it always generates the *same* results. A program that does not include any output is useless!

3. C programs are collections of **functions** designed to perform a specific task and return a computed result. At a minimum, all C programs must specify one function called **main**, followed by a left and a right parenthesis.
4. The left brace **{** marks the beginning of the function **body**. Notice that there is a corresponding right brace **}** at the end of **main**, marking the end of the function body. In this case the right brace also happens to be at the end of the overall program. The statements between the two braces specify the exact actions that are to be performed.
5. The next line is a **declaration** (as opposed to an *executable* statement) and serves as an informative message to the C compiler. The statement shows that the program uses some variables called **radius** and **area**, and that the data associated with these variables is of the **float** type, which stands for **floating-point numbers**—real numbers with a decimal point. The effect of this statement is to allocate memory cells for the specified variables.
6. The next line is called an **assignment**. Its purpose is to give the **radius** variable a particular value. In C the **=** sign means *is assigned to* (for example, **radius** is assigned the value 10) and does *not* mean mathematical equality.
7. Another assignment is used to give **area** (πr^2) the value of **3.14159 * radius * radius**. Notice the use of the ***** to mean multiplication. C does not provide an operator for exponentiation, so there is no symbol for it. (Exponents are handled with a built-in function called **pow**, which is discussed later.)
8. The **printf** function is accessible through the standard C input/output header file (**stdio.h**). It allows data to be output to the standard output device, usually the screen. **printf** consists of two parts: a control string (enclosed in double quotes) and a list of variables. In this case the control string includes text characters (**"The area ="**) and a **format specifier**, **%f** (floating-point number). The **%f** is a placeholder and shows that a floating-point value is to be included at this location in the output. Because **area** is listed after the control string, its value will be substituted for the **%f** and then output to the screen.

Query: What would the following statement output?
```
printf ( "The area = area" );
```

RESPONSE: Output: `The area = area`
Textual information enclosed in the double quotes is output literally. The symbol `%f` as it appears in sample program 3.1–1 is not treated as text but means that the numeric value of a variable is to be output. The `%` symbol means that the characters that follow it are format-control characters.

9. Functions generally end with **return**, the purpose of which is to pass back the value computed by the function. In this case returning a value of 0 means that **main** has successfully completed processing.

   Notice that each statement of a C program ends with a semicolon.

PERSPECTIVE

You will begin to appreciate that C programs can be difficult to read. As with English prose, it is important to follow rules of style that have evolved over the years to help you understand C programs. These rules are explained as we progress in the study of the language.

3.1.3 A High-Quality C Program

Although Program 3.1–1 is a correct solution to the problem, it lacks finesse. Serious programmers are concerned with more than just getting the right answer. For them, writing a C program is a task with at least three goals: The finished program must be correct, readable, and modifiable. These are explained in Chapter 10 but for now let's concentrate on the easiest of the three goals, readability. **Readability** includes the visual layout of the program *(prettyprinting)*, the incorporation of adequate documentation (instead of a mere comment or two), and the use of mnemonic (meaningful) names.

Query: Readability is for whose benefit? The user's?

RESPONSE: Readability is for the benefit of another programmer who might be reading the program to modify it. It also helps the original programmer in debugging or modifying the program. It is not meant for the benefit of the user because users may not be programmers. Also, software bought by users is rarely in human-readable form and is usually supplied in machine-readable form (binary).

Consider the following revision of the area of a circle program.

P R O G R A M   3 . 1 – 2

```
/***************************************************************************
 * Title:        area of a circle    (revisited)                          *
 * Filename:     area2.c                                                  *
 *                                                                        *
 * Description:  Program to compute the area of a circle. This program reads *
 *               a value representing the radius of a circle.  It then    *
 *               computes the corresponding  area using "area equals pi r *
 *               squared"  The area is then output.                       *
 *                                                                        *
 * Input:        radius                                                   *
 * Output:       area                                                     *
 * Process:      area = pi * radius * radius                              *
 *                                                                        *
 * Written by:   ...                                    Date: ...         *
 ***************************************************************************/

#include    <stdio.h>
#include    <math.h>

main (  )
{
   const  float  PI = 3.14159;

   float radius, area;

   printf ( "\nInput a value for radius: " );             /* Prompt */
   scanf  ( "%f", &radius );                               /* User input */

   area  =  PI *  pow ( radius, 2 );                       /* Process */
                                                           /* Output result */
   printf ( "\nFor a radius of %6.2f the area = %6.2f", radius, area );

   return ( 0 );
}
```

Commentary on Program 3.1–2

1. *Program documentation:* The comments have been expanded significantly and are now properly termed **documentation,** meaning a written description of the process. Documentation is an absolute necessity when writing programs

and must be carefully thought out even though it is irrelevant to the C compiler. Here it is composed of the following: a box to visually isolate the documentation from the rest of the program, a title, the C filename containing the program, a statement of purpose, and the formal statement (see Chapter 2) followed by the author and the date. Although there are no universally accepted rules of documentation, the above model is reasonably effective and is used throughout this book.

In addition to documentation at the beginning of a program, it is often necessary to place individual comment lines within the program. These **inline comments** should be used whenever a statement or group of statements might be unclear to another reader, or simply to delineate the various sections of the program.

2. *Library files:* Besides `stdio.h`, this program references the `math.h` file, which provides access to a range of built-in mathematical functions (see Appendix A–2). Here the `pow` (power) function is used to square the value of `radius`. A reference to `pow( x, y )` is equivalent to x^y. (A list of other library files and associated functions is found in Appendix A.)

> ## PERSPECTIVE
>
> Header files such as `stdio.h` and `math.h` generally contain definitions of useful constants and functions. These definitions are grouped into a particular header file based on the similarity of their purpose. For example, `stdio.h` contains definitions needed by input/output operations and `math.h` contains definitions needed by mathematical functions such as sin, cos, and log. The functions to perform these tasks are in **run-time libraries** (collections of prewritten, precompiled software) that must be linked with the program before its execution.

3. *Constants:* `const` allows programmers to set up their own named **constants**— symbols whose values do not change in the program. Here the word `PI` is associated with the constant value of 3.14159. Notice that the assignment statement for `area` now refers to `PI`. As discussed later, using a named constant communicates more information than simply inserting a number into the program. By convention, named constants are generally capitalized to distinguish them from variables.

4. *Variables:* The value for `radius` is no longer predetermined by the programmer as it was in Program 3.1–1 but is obtained from the user through the `scanf` function. Although this feature does not improve the clarity of the program, it is more user-friendly because the user can now compute the area of any circle. The resulting program is also more versatile.

5. *Input prompts:* The `printf` statement before `scanf` is an **input prompt** that tells the user what to do next. As a rule, all statements requesting input from the keyboard should be preceded by a prompting message.

Notice the `\n` control symbol in the `printf` control string. This tells the program to skip to the beginning of a new line in the output. The backslash `\` means that an escape character follows. In this case the `\n` stands for *newline,* which causes the computer to start a new line at this point. (A table of escape characters is found in Appendix B.)

The `scanf` function causes data to be read from the standard input device (usually the keyboard) into the variables specified. The programmer must include a **format string** that shows what type of data is to be read, such as `%f` for floating-point data, and the names of the variables needed to store the input values. The `radius` variable is preceded by the ampersand `&` or **address-of** operator. As we explain later, `scanf` needs to know the memory address of each listed variable.

6. *Readable output:* The final `printf` has been altered to enhance the appearance of the output. First, notice that the output reflects (**echoes**) the original input value. This aids the user of the program in understanding the meaning of the results. Second, in the original program the value for the `area` variable is displayed with a long string of digits to the right of the decimal point. In this program the `%f` format specifies the desired precision of the output. The `%6.2f` format means that a field of at least six print positions is to be output, with exactly two of the six occurring to the right of the decimal point (the decimal point counts as one of the six). Assuming that the input value for radius is the number 10, the unformatted output would be

```
For a radius of 10.00000 the area = 314.158997
```

The formatted output is more readable:

```
For a radius of 10.00 the area = 314.16
```

PERSPECTIVE

Notice that in the output the answer is rounded off to the specified precision.

C always provides enough space for as many digits as there are to the left of the decimal point. Thus, if `area` equals 98765.3278, the output with the `%6.2f` format appears as 98765.33. C pads to the left (provides leading blanks) if the integer portion of the number doesn't need all the spaces provided. Therefore, if `area` equals 1.23 it is output as `xx1.23`, with each *x* representing a blank space on the output line.

BEFORE YOU GO ON

Query: Because `PI` was specified as 3.14159 and `radius` was input as 10, why is the unformatted output 314.158997 instead of 314.159?

RESPONSE: When a floating-point number such as 3.14159 is converted to binary for storage on a digital computer, there is often a slight conversion error. Here the number was apparently represented internally as 3.14158997.

7. *Spacing:* Finally, notice the use of prettyprinting to visually enhance the program. Blank lines are used to isolate logically related areas of the program, as blank lines are used to separate paragraphs in a written document. Accordingly, the `printf` (prompt) and `scanf` functions are shown as a pair of related statements and are enclosed by blank lines. Spacing within a line spreads out the various components of a statement and lines up related components of succeeding statements (for example, the opening parentheses of the `printf` and `scanf` pair are lined up). Spaces are placed around all operators (for instance, `+ - * / =`) before and after parentheses and after commas.

EXERCISES 3.1

Concept Check
Answer statements 1 through 4 with true *or* false.
1. C evolved from the languages A and B.
2. C offers the advantage of being a typeless language.
3. Documentation is necessary for the C compiler.
4. C programs must contain a function called `main`.

For statements 5 through 8 choose the answer that best completes the statement.
5. `#include <stdio.h>` means
   a. include a studio package for high-resolution graphics work
   b. include a file that enables input/output operations
   c. nothing because it is an optional statement of a C program
   d. improves the readability of the program
6. The inclusion of `main ( )`
   a. is not really necessary but good style
   b. is necessary but not very good style
   c. is necessary and is conventional style
   d. was not discussed in this section
7. Readability is enhanced by
   a. improving the output of the program
   b. the use of short variable names
   c. prettyprinting, documentation, and carefully chosen names
   d. including the standard input/output header file
8. Serious C programmers are
   a. mainly concerned with getting the right answer
   b. highly overpaid
   c. concerned with correctness, readability, and modifiability
   d. wary of rules of style because they lengthen the program

For statements 9 through 12 fill in the blanks with the right word or phrase.
9. `printf` is a _____.
10. C statements are terminated with a _____.

11. Readability is for the benefit of the _____.
12. `const` is used to create _____.

Set A

13. Write a `printf` statement to display the message "C is fun."
14. Write an assignment statement to give `class_size` the value 25.
15. Declare a floating-point variable called `volume`.
16. Write a comment statement for a program that solves the trapezoid problem from Example 2.2–1.
17. Write a `printf` statement to display the value of the temperature from the temperature problem in Example 2.2–2.
18. Write a `scanf` statement to read in the value of the number of sales from the sales commission problem in Example 2.2–3.

Set B

19. Write a program to output:

> The heart has its reasons
> which reason knows nothing of.
> —by Blaise Pascal

20. Convert the algorithm from the trapezoid problem in Example 2.2–1 to a C program.
21. Write a program to compute the area of a square, given an input value for the length of the side.
22. Write a program to compute a person's gross pay based on input values for their wage rate and number of hours worked during the week.
23. Write a program to convert inches to centimeters. There are 2.54 centimeters per inch.
24. Write a program to compute a bowling average based on total scores from a person's last eight games.
25. Using the math library, write a program to compute the absolute value and the square root of an input value.

Set C

26. Implement Program 3.1–2 (area of a circle). Test the program by running it repeatedly, using a variety of values for the radius.
27. Implement on the computer any of the Set B problems.
28. Write a program that inputs two numbers and outputs their quotient. Observe what happens if the second number is 0 (called a **run-time error**).
29. Write a program to compute the volume of a sphere ($\frac{4}{3}\pi r^3$) based on an input value for the radius.
30. Write a program to convert miles to kilometers.

3.2   DATA TYPES, VARIABLES, AND INPUT/OUTPUT

Introduction

This section explores the data types that can be used in a C program, the use of variables and symbolic constants, and the use of input and output.

When we write computer programs, we must distinguish between the different types of data that are used in different situations. Some data are integral (have no fractional part), such as the number of students in a class or the number of questions on a test. Other data, such as the area of a circle, the cost of a gallon of gasoline, the distance between circuit lines etched into a silicon chip, and the positioning of a laser surgical device controller for microscopic surgery, include decimal points and fractional parts. Still other data are nonnumeric, such as character data as in a word processing program document.

A **data type** is a set of values and a set of operations defined for those values. A standard data type is one that is predefined by the language. Four standard data types are recognized by C: **int** (integer), **float** (floating-point), **double** (double-precision), and **char** (character data). Each of these is discussed in the next subsection and again in Section 3.3.

3.2.1 int Data Type

The **int** data type represents **integer** values, meaning any positive or negative number, or zero, without a decimal point. When such values appear in a program they are called **integer literals** or simply **integers**. Examples of valid integer literals are

    2   −26   1234   +72   −9872

An integer literal consists of an optional plus or minus sign followed by a series of digits and cannot contain any other characters. Commas, decimal points, or special symbols such as the dollar sign or **e** for exponential notation are not allowed.

BEFORE YOU GO ON

Query: Which of the following are not valid integer literals?

    17   987.332 $2,523   77,234   24997   + 3.1

RESPONSE: 987.332   (decimal point)
             $2,523   ($ and comma)
             77,234   (comma)
             +3.1   (decimal point)

Each computer has a range of the largest and smallest integers that can be used in a program. These limits depend on how much storage the compiler allocates for an integer. On a typical personal computer an integer is represented with 2 bytes

(16 bits) giving a decimal range of $-32,768$ to $+32,767$. On mini- and mainframe computers an integer can be allocated 4 bytes (32 bits), giving a decimal range of $-2,147,483,648$ to $+2,147,483,647$.

3.2.2 float and double Data Types

The **float** data type represents **floating-point** values, meaning any signed or unsigned number having a decimal point. Examples of valid **float** literals are

2. -26.23 1234.111 $+72.0$ $-9872.$

A **float** literal consists of an optional plus or minus sign followed by a series of digits and must include a decimal point. It cannot contain commas or special symbols such as the dollar sign but can include the letter **e**, as we see later in this subsection. **float** literals can be single- or double-precision (4 or 8 bytes, typically, although this varies with the system). The **default**—the assigned data type when one is not specified—is **double** (double-precision), which is typically twice the number of bytes as **float** (although the exact specification depends on the compiler).

float and **double** literals can be written in exponential or scientific notation if needed by using the letter **e** (or **E**) followed by an exponent representing a power of 10:

123000.0 can be written as 1.23e5

0.000123 can be written as 1.23e–4

The number following the **e** indicates the number of places to move the decimal point to give the standard decimal value. The decimal point is moved to the right if the number after the **e** is positive and moved to the left if the number after the **e** is negative.

<table>
<tr><td>**BEFORE YOU GO ON**</td><td>Query: Which of the following are not valid **double** literals?

23   647.122332 $5,322 $-765l$ -2497
$+3.1$ $723.OO   123.0e03   314159e–3</td></tr>
<tr><td></td><td>RESPONSE: 23   (no decimal point)
$5,322   ($ and comma and no decimal point)
$-765l$ (no decimal point, letter "l" instead of number "1")
$723.OO   ($ included, "OO" as two characters, not as two numbers "00")
314159e–3 (no decimal point)</td></tr>
</table>

3.2.3 char Data Type

C also recognizes nonnumeric character data. A **char** literal is any valid ASCII or EBCDIC character (depending on the coding scheme used on the particular computer) enclosed in single quotes. Examples of **char** literals are

'z' '<' 'X' '3' '[' '!' 'Z'

Query: Which of the following are not valid `char` literals?

'z' 'zz' "zz" '0' z ' '

RESPONSE: 'zz'   (2 characters)

"zz"   (double quotation marks and 2 characters)

z   (no quotation marks)

3.2.4 Naming Conventions

Programs generally do not directly manipulate literal values but deal with **variables** and **symbolic constants**. A **variable**, such as `radius` and `area` in Program 3.1–2, is a named memory location where numbers and characters can be stored. With a **symbolic constant**, such as `PI` in Program 3.1–2, the data in this memory location are prevented from changing.

According to the ANSI C standards, any entity that has a name associated with it (an identifier), whether it is a variable, symbolic constant, or a function name, must obey certain rules:

A name must start with a letter or (rarely) an underscore (_).

A name can contain letters, digits, or underscores (_).

A name cannot contain blanks, commas, or any other special characters.

A name cannot consist of more than 31 characters.

A name must conform to case sensitivity (C differentiates between uppercase and lowercase alphabetical characters).

A name cannot be a C **keyword;** that is, a word that is part of the C language itself (see Table 3.2–1).

(See Appendix C for examples of selected keywords and their usage.)

Table 3.2–1   C Keywords Arranged by Usage

DATA TYPE		CONTROL FLOW		STORAGE CLASS
char	signed	break	for	auto
const	sizeof	case	if	extern
double	struct	continue	goto	register
enum	typedef	default	return	static
float	union	do	switch	volatile
int	unsigned	else	while	
long	void			
short				

Query: Which of the following are not valid identifier names?

x   c3p0   3p0   _abc   −abc   radius   void   next$time

RESPONSE: 3p0   (begins with a number)
           −abc   (uses a minus sign instead of an underscore)
           void   (is a C keyword)
           next$time   (uses a dollar sign)

3.2.5 Symbolic Constants

A **symbolic constant** is a programmer-defined name with its associated data. It differs from a variable in that its value can be determined only by the programmer (not by the user as through the `scanf` function) and its value cannot be changed during the run of the program; that is, it cannot appear on the left side of an assignment. Symbolic constants are usually specified at the beginning of a program, often before `main`, although they are also allowed to appear after the opening brace { of `main`. As shown later, programs usually contain functions other than just `main`. With multifunction programs, constants to be used in a particular function can be put after the opening brace of the function.

Consider a program that makes extensive use of π. We could use the literal constant 3.14159 throughout, but there are several compelling reasons not to. First, there is the possibility of a typographical error on one of the occurrences of the number. Second, if it later becomes important to change the degree of precision, we have to find all occurrences of 3.14159 and replace them with, say, 3.141592653589793. Finally, it is usually more informative to use a name rather than a "mystery" number whose value may have no meaning to the reader and may get confused with other unrelated numbers.

PERSPECTIVE

A good rule of style is to use symbolic constants whenever it is reasonable to do so. You should avoid the use of numbers within the body of a function. As with all names, symbolic constants should be mnemonic.

C provides two techniques for creating symbolic constants. The first, as shown in Program 3.1–2, uses `const`. We specify the keyword `const`, then the data type of the constant, then its symbolic name, and finally an assignment of its given value. Examples using `const` are as follows:

```
const float PI        = 3.14159;
const int   YEAR_LENGTH = 12;
const char  ANSWER    = 'Y';
```

For stylistic reasons, we use the convention of writing constants in uppercase. This distinguishes them from variables (see the next subsection), which are usually written in lowercase.

The second technique for creating constants, the only method that was available before ANSI C, is through the `#define` preprocessor directive. The `#define` directive has an effect similar to `const`, although the syntax is slightly different. Examples of preprocessed defined constants are as follows:

```
#define   ANSWER            'Y'
#define   PI                3.14159
#define   RADIUS            27
#define   DAYS_OF_WEEK      "Mo Tu We Th Fr Sa Su"
#define   FIRST_PROGRAMMER  "Ada Lovelace"
#define   TRUE              1
#define   FALSE             0
#define   POLLUTION         FALSE
#define   CIRCUMFERENCE     2 * PI * RADIUS
```

Unlike `const`, which is a true C-language element, `#define` is a preprocessor directive and is handled differently. Before compilation, the preprocessor removes all references to the symbols created by `#define` and replaces them with their designated values. That is why no equal sign or semicolon is associated with them: An equal sign or a semicolon would become part of the value of the constant!

Notice that in the last two examples a constant is defined in terms of other constants that have already been defined, and can even include the use of arithmetic expressions.

PERSPECTIVE

`const` and `#define` are subtly different. `const` is a qualifier used in a declaration that tells the compiler to limit the context into which the associated identifier can be placed. For instance, if a `const` identifier were to appear on the left side of an assignment, the compiler would generate a syntax error. Similarly, a `const` is precluded from use with the increment or decrement operators (see Section 3.3.5). `#define` enables us to use a symbolic name instead of literal value, but the name is removed during preprocessing and replaced with the literal value.

3.2.6 Variables

A **variable** is a programmer-defined identifier whose associated data value is expected to change during the program. All variables must have a name and a data type. To enhance the program's clarity, the name should be mnemonic. The data type should be chosen carefully because it determines how the computer internally represents the associated data. If the situation calls for integer data, such as the number of pages in a book or the number of characters in a word, use the `int` data type. If the situation calls for decimal precision, such as the volume of a sphere, use the `float` data type. For extra precision in floating-point numbers (at the expense of using more memory and increased computation time), use the **double** data type. Finally, for processing character data, use the **char** data type.

Examples of variable names and their data types as they might be declared at the beginning of a function are as follows:

```
int     class_size, num_questions;
float   fahrenheit, celsius, area_of_a_circle;
double  distance_to_sin, size_of_nucleus;
char    response;
```

If wanted, variables can be given an initial value in their declaration, as in:

```
int   total  = 0;
char  answer = 'Y';
```

3.2.7 Input and Output

Several different functions are available in most implementations of C for input and output (I/O). For now we concentrate on the two that we have used in previous programming examples, **scanf** and **printf**.

The **scanf** and **printf** I/O functions are called **formatted functions** because we must specify formatting codes that instruct the compiler how to interpret the various values of incoming or outgoing data. The syntax for both functions is similar and consists of two parts: a control string (also called a format string) enclosed in double quotation marks followed by a comma, and then a list of variable names. There are some subtle technical differences, however, that we discuss next.

Consider the input statement

```
scanf( "%f%d", &radius, &length);
```

In the case of **scanf**, the control string describes how the compiler is to interpret the *incoming* data. The control string consists of a series of **control codes** and **format codes** that are usually separated by spaces (for readability). When present, control codes such as \n (new line) or \t (tab) determine the spacing of the input. Because **scanf** can input data successfully regardless of the spacing, control codes are generally omitted. We discuss their use later in the context of **printf**.

Format codes such as %f, %d, and %c are always included with **scanf** and determine how the input is interpreted. These codes are associated, in order, with the list of variable names that follows the control string. In the example shown earlier, the first number that the user enters is interpreted as a floating-point value, %f, and is stored at the address of the floating-point variable called **radius**. The second number is interpreted as an integer value, %d, and is stored at the address of the integer variable called **length**.

As explained in Chapter 9, **scanf** needs the memory addresses of the listed variables in which to store the incoming data. Because **radius** and **length** are the *names* of variables, not their addresses, you have to specify where these variables reside. This is done through the address-of operator &, which is prefixed to each variable in the **scanf** variable list.

The `scanf` function allows the use of many other format codes, notably `%c` for **character** (`char`) and `%lf` for **long floating-point** (`double`), as needed. Although `%i` can also be used to denote an integer, for historical reasons most programmers use `%d`.

Output is formatted with the `printf` function, whose syntax is similar to `scanf`. Consider the segment

```
income  = 30000;
printf( "\nFor an income of $%d \nthe tax = $%8.2f\n",income, income * 0.33);
```

As with using `scanf`, using `printf` entails the specification of a control string that must be enclosed in double quotes, followed by a list of variables, constants, and arithmetic expressions.

Let's analyze the control string. The control character `\n` tells the computer to skip to a new line. `\n` can appear anywhere and as often as wanted within the control string. The characters `For an income of $` are output literally. The format code `%d` means that the value of an integer variable should be output. Because this is the first format code, the computer takes the first variable listed, `income`, and outputs its value. Next, the control character `\n` causes a line to be skipped before outputting the literal characters `the tax = $`.

Finally, the `%8.2f` format code causes the value of the next floating-point quantity to be output. Here the arithmetic expression `income*0.33` is computed and then output. Because the format specifies `8.2` as the degree of precision, the result is displayed this way: The notation `8.2` denotes a field width of eight total digits, two of which are to the right of the decimal point. If this is not enough space, the field is expanded but the decimal portion is still restricted to two digits. The actual output would be:

```
For an income of  $30000
the tax  =  $ 9900.00
```

Program 3.2–1 incorporates many of the concepts just discussed. Make sure you fully understand it.

PROGRAM 3.2-1

```
/*****************************************************************************
 *  Title:        average of 5 numbers                                      *
 *  Filename:     average.c                                                  *
 *                                                                          *
 *  Description:  Program to compute the mean of 5 numbers. This program    *
 *                inputs 5 numbers and computes the sum.  It then outputs    *
 *                the sum and mean.                                         *
 *                                                                          *
 *  Input:        5 numbers                                                 *
 *  Output:       sum, mean                                                 *
 *  Process:      mean  =  sum / 5                                          *
 *                                                                          *
 *  Written by: ...                                            Date: ...    *
 *****************************************************************************/
```

```
#include <stdio.h>

main ( )
{

  const int SIZE = 5;

  int     num1, num2, num3, num4, num5;
  float sum;                /* need decimal precision when calculating the mean */

  printf (  "\nPlease input five numbers:  " );
  scanf (  "%d %d %d %d %d",    &num1,  &num2,  &num3,  &num4,  &num5 );

  sum    =  num1 + num2 + num3 + num4 + num5;

  printf (  "\nThe following data was input: %d %d %d %d %d",
                                  num1, num2, num3, num4, num5 );
  printf (  "\nThe sum of the data  = %10.2f",   sum );
  printf (  "\nThe mean of the data = %10.2f",   sum / SIZE );

  return ( 0 );
}
```

BEFORE **YOU** **GO ON**	Query: This program does not explicitly calculate the mean but uses the `printf` function to make the calculation. How would you change the program to create a variable called `mean` and then incorporate `mean` into the calculations? RESPONSE: 1. Declare **mean** as a **float** variable. 2. Insert an assignment after the statement `sum = ...` as follows: `mean = sum/SIZE;`. 3. In the final **printf** output **mean** instead of **sum/SIZE**.

EXERCISES 3.2

Concept Check

Answer statements 1 through 4 with true *or* false.
1. The cost of gasoline is typically represented as integer data.
2. C accepts only three data types: **int**, **float**, and **char**.
3. **float** data can include an optional dollar sign.
4. **double** data can contain strings of characters.

For statements 5 through 8 choose the answer that best completes the statement.

5. `char` literal values
   a. must be enclosed in double quotes
   b. must be enclosed in single quotes
   c. can be enclosed in either single or double quotes
   d. does not need to be enclosed in quotes

6. `int` literal values
   a. can include an optional comma to improve readability
   b. can include an optional dollar sign when representing money
   c. can include an optional plus or minus sign
   d. can consist only of digits

7. Symbolic constants
   a. must appear in capital letters
   b. are frowned on by serious programmers
   c. enhance the readability of a program
   d. can include keywords

8. Variables
   a. are created using the `#define` directive
   b. are floating-point by default
   c. should have simple names
   d. can be defined as having any C data type

For statements 9 through 12 fill in the blanks with the right word.

9. On a personal computer an integer is usually represented with
   _____ bytes.

10. Names can be composed of _____ , _____ ,
    or _____ .

11. Names can not contain _____ characters.

12. `#define` is called a _____ directive.

Set A

Write C statements for each of the following problems.

13. Declare a variable to represent the volume of a sphere.

14. Declare a variable to represent the answer to a true/false question. Assume that true has a value of 1 and false has a value of 0.

15. Write an input statement to read the variable in Question 13.

16. Write an output statement to write the variable in Question 14.

17. Create two constants, one representing the base and the other representing the height of a parallelogram.

18. Create a constant called AREA whose value is derived from the constants in Question 17.

Set B

19. Write a program to output individual characters such as *a* and *x* using both the `%c` and the `%d` formats. What is the meaning of the output?

20. Why is the ampersand used with variables in the `scanf` function?

21. Write a program to compute the area of a triangle using the base and the altitude as symbolic constants (*area = base × height*/2).
22. Write a program to compute the area of a triangle when the values for the base and the height are provided by the user.
23. Why does **printf** not use ampersands for its variable identifiers?

Set C

24. Implement Program 3.2–1 (the average of 5 numbers) using a variety of values for the numbers in each execution.
25. Change Program 3.2–1 so that it finds the average of 10 numbers.
26. Write a program to output the square and the cube of an input integer value. What happens when the input value is greater than 100? Greater than 1,000? What kind of problem occurs? What can be done to rectify it?
27. The distance, *s*, that a free-falling object travels is determined by the expression $s = gt^2/2$, where *g* is the gravitational constant equal to 32 feet per second per second. Write a program to calculate *s* for any time *t*.

3.3   ARITHMETIC IN C

Introduction

The previous section defines some of the data types you can process in C. This section explores how C performs arithmetic and logic operations.

3.3.1 Operator Precedence

Consider the expression

$$5 + 3 \times 2 + 12/6$$

What does it equal? On a simple calculator it might equal 4.6666 because

$$5 + 3 = 8$$
$$8 \times 2 = 16$$
$$16 + 12 = 28$$
$$28/6 = 4.666666$$

Algebraically, however, it equals 13 because

$$3 \times 2 = 6$$
$$12/6 = 2$$
$$5 + 6 = 11$$
$$11 + 2 = 13$$

According to the rules of arithmetic, an implied hierarchy in the original expression gives multiplication and division precedence over addition and subtraction and they are done first (from right to left). The use of parentheses, of course, can change the meaning of the expression.

BEFORE YOU GO ON	**Query: What is the value of the following expression?**
	$(((5 + 3) \times 2) + 12)/6$
	_____
	RESPONSE: 4.666666. In this case the calculator is correct. With embedded or nested parentheses, evaluation proceeds from the inside out.

Table 3.3–1 shows the operator-precedence scheme for simple arithmetic operators as used in C. C has a rich set of operators, only some of which are shown in the table. (Appendix D provides a complete listing.)

The rules can be summarized as

1. Expressions or portions of expressions with parentheses are evaluated first. In the case of nested or embedded parenthetic expressions (parentheses within parentheses), the innermost expression is evaluated first. As shown in Table 3.3–1, using parentheses allows you to completely override the default precedence scheme.
2. Multiplication, division, and modulo operations are done next. The modulo operator % returns the remainder of integer-by-integer division. (This is discussed in Subsection 3.3.2.) All of these operators are at the same level. If an expression contains more than one of these, however, evaluation proceeds from left to right. Note that parentheses cannot be used to imply multiplication as in standard algebra. In C the expression (1 + 3)(17 − 4) is invalid. The correct C expression is (1 + 3) * (17 − 4).
3. Addition and subtraction, which are also at the same level, are done next. Again, when more than one addition or subtraction is present, expressions are evaluated from left to right.

Table 3.3–1 Operator Precedence in C

LEVEL	SYMBOL	MEANING	ORDER
1	( )	Parenthetic expression	Inside to outside
2	* / %	Multiplication Division Modulo (remainder)	Left to right
3	+ −	Addition Subtraction	Left to right

Evaluation from left to right (or right to left) is called the **associativity of an operator**. All the operators shown in the rules above associate from left to right. Other operators to be discussed later, such as the assignment operator =, associate from right to left.

3.3.2 Integer Arithmetic

For the most part, arithmetic in C is straightforward:

$6 + 3$ evaluates to 9

$6 - 3$ evaluates to 3

$6 * 3$ evaluates to 18

$6/3$ evaluates to 2

But there are a few catches. First, because C distinguishes integers from floating-point and double-precision values (whether as data or variables), it also distinguishes the results of arithmetic operations involving integers and either floating-point or double-precision numbers. In particular, *operations involving only integers yield only integer results*. This means that just as $6/3$ evaluates to 2, $7/3$ also evaluates to 2. Because 7 and 3 are both integers, C keeps only the integer portion of the result, truncating any fractional part.

BEFORE YOU GO ON	Query: What is the value of $999/1000$?
	RESPONSE: Even though 0.999 is almost 1, C disregards the noninteger portion of the division, leaving 0 as the answer.

Sometimes you may want to get the remainder of integer-to-integer division. In this case you can use the modulo operator %:

7 / 3 ⟶ 2
7 % 3 ⟶ 1

As you were taught in elementary school, 7 divided by 3 has a quotient of 2 with a remainder of 1.

What about 8 % 2? Because 2 is a divisor of 8, the modulo operator returns 0. How about 2 % 8? 2 divided by 8 is 0 with a remainder of 2, so the modulo operator returns 2.

BEFORE YOU GO ON	Query: Assume that x and y are integer variables and assume that x is less than y. What is the value of x % y?
	RESPONSE: Under these conditions, the modulo operator returns the value of x no matter what value x is.

The modulo operator has an interesting use in that it can help determine the **parity** (oddness or evenness) of a number. Consider the following:

```
6 % 2 ──→  0
7 % 2 ──→  1
8 % 2 ──→  0
9 % 2 ──→  1
```

That is, **x % 2** is either 0 or 1 depending on the parity of **x**. Now verify this for other values. And one final comment: The modulo operator is defined only for integer constants or variables. The expressions

```
7.0 % 3     and     7 % 3.0
```

are treated as syntax errors by C.

3.3.3 Mixed-Mode Arithmetic

Calculations get more complicated when an arithmetic expression mixes data types. With mixed expressions, C uses a data type hierarchy whose rules dictate that double precision dominates floating-point, which in turn dominates integer. The highest mode of any data or variable determines the mode of the operation. For example,

999 / 1000 is 0 (integer to integer)

999.0 / 1000 is 0.999 (double dominates integer)

999 / 1000.0 is 0.999 (double dominates integer)

By default, all *constants* having a decimal point are stored as double precision. In the expression $999.0/1000$, the constant 999.0 is the dominant mode and C coerces (converts) the 1000 to double precision for the purpose of doing the calculation. Consider

$$20.0/3 * 20/3$$

C evaluates this as follows.

1. The leftmost division is processed first because it is the leftmost of 3 equal-level operations.
2. Because 20.0 is by default double-precision, C coerces 3 to become 3.0 and then does the division, yielding a quotient of 6.666666.
3. The next operation is multiplication. What is the dominant mode? The multiplication uses the result of the previous division, which is a double-precision constant times the integer value 20. The 20 is therefore coerced to 20.0 and the operation yields 133.33333.
4. The last operation is division. Again the dominant mode is double-precision. The 3 becomes 3.0 and the final result is 44.444443.

Now change the problem slightly:

$$20/3 * 20.0/3$$

C evaluates this as follows.

1. The highest-level operation is again the first division.
2. Because 20 and 3 are both integers, their quotient is also an integer, namely 6.
3. The next operation is multiplication. What is the dominant mode? The multiplication uses the result of the previous division, which is an integer, times the double-precision constant 20.0. The 6 therefore becomes 6.0 and the operation yields 120.000.
4. The last operation is division. Again the dominant mode is double-precision. The 3 is coerced to 3.0 and the final result is 40.0.

BEFORE YOU GO ON

Query: What is the value of $20.0/3 + 20/3$?

RESPONSE: The expression is evaluated in the order

$$20.0/3 \longrightarrow 6.666666$$
$$20/3 \longrightarrow 6$$
$$6.66666 + 6 \longrightarrow 12.666666$$

Consider one other problem associated with floating-point and double-precision arithmetic. Algebraically, the expression $7.0/3.0 \times 3.0$ is equal to 7, but on some computers it does not exactly equal 7 but rather 6.999999. This is an example of the **finiteness** of storing data on digital computers: there is no exact representation of the quotient of 7.0 / 3.0 and multiplying by 3.0 can not undo the effects of finite precision. A certain amount of accuracy is lost. This is much worse if all of the numbers are integers because in C, $7/3 \times 3$ equals 6.

3.3.4 Assignment Statements

All of these problems are outside the context of an actual program. What happens when variable assignments are involved? First, recall that the assignment operator = means "is assigned to." The left side of the = is always a variable whose address specifies where to store the data on the right side. Therefore, assignment precludes such statements as

```
x + 3  =  y * 17;      /*  NOT a legal C statement !!!  */
```

The left side can be only a variable, not an arithmetic expression, not even one that includes only variables.

Next consider the effect of the assignment operator on the arithmetic expression

```
float x;
x =   7 / 3;
```

You might think that **x** would equal 2.333333 because **x** is itself a floating-point variable. But unlike the arithmetic operators shown in Table 3.3–1, the assignment operator associates *from right to left*. In addition, **=** has a lower precedence than **/**. Therefore, the expression on the right side is evaluated first and the resulting value is assigned to the variable on the left. The right side contains an integer-integer division that evaluates to 2. Next, the value 2 is assigned to the floating-point variable **x**, meaning that the 2 must be coerced to floating-point. So **x** is given the value 2.0.

Next consider the reverse situation:

```
int   x;
x  =  7.0 / 3.0;
```

In this case the double-precision result 2.333333 is truncated for representation as an integer, 2, which is assigned to **x**.

BEFORE YOU GO ON

Query: What is the output of the following program fragment?

```
int    x;
float  y;
y   =  19 / 4;
x   =  y * 4;
printf ( "y = %3.1f,   x = %d", y, x );
```

RESPONSE: y = 4.0, x = 16

Because assignment (**=**) is an operator in C, multiple assignments are possible in a single statement. For example, to assign three integer variables the same value as in

```
a = 10;
b = 10;
c = 10;
```

you could substitute the single program line

```
a = b = c = 10;
```

in their place. Recall that **=** associates from right to left. In the above assignment, **c** is first given the value **10**, which becomes the value of the expression at that point. Next, **b** is given the value **10**, which then becomes the value of the expression. Finally, **a** is assigned the value **10**.

BEFORE YOU GO ON

Query: What is the output of the following?

```
int    a, b, c;
a  =  2;
```

(continued)

```
b  =   3;
c  =   4;
a  =  b  =  c  =  5;
printf (  "%d %d %d",  a,  b,  c );
```

RESPONSE: The output is 5 5 5

BEFORE YOU GO ON

Query: Multiple assignment seems like a good idea because one line of code is better than three. Is this correct?

RESPONSE: In programming, brevity is not necessarily a virtue. Clarity is, however, and programmers should use shorthand features such as multiple assignment sparingly.

Another C convenience (which should also be used carefully) is the so-called **compound assignment**. Suppose you wanted to multiply the value of a variable by 15. One way would be to include a statement such as

```
x  =  x * 15;
```

Although algebraically this is meaningless (except when x is 0), it is a perfectly reasonable use of the assignment operator. Recall that C evaluates this in *two* steps: The right-side expression is calculated first, and then C stores the result at the address of the variable on the left. A one-step shortcut that produces the same result is

```
x   *=   15;
```

Keep in mind that the variable on the left is applied to the *entire* expression on the right; that is,

```
x   *=   15 + y;
```

is equivalent to

```
x   =   x * (15 + y);
```

not x = x * 15 + y;. Compound assignment can be used with other arithmetic operators such as -, +, /, and %.

BEFORE YOU GO ON

Query: What are the final values of *x*, *y*, and *z*?

```
x  =  y  =  z  =  10;
x     +=    15;
y     -=    15;
z     %=     3;
```

RESPONSE: $x = 25$, $y = -5$, $z = 1$

3.3.5 Increment and Decrement Operators

A common activity in programming is to create a variable that acts as a counter. The job of a **counter** is to repeatedly add (count up) or subtract (count down) a fixed value (usually 1) from a variable. Counters are most commonly found where looping takes place. A **counting loop** is a sequence of statements executed repeatedly until the counter variable reaches its limiting value. If the counting is to proceed in steps of +1, a C operator called the **increment operator**, **++**, can be used. For counting in steps of −1, C provides a decrement operator, **−−**.

Consider

```
x  =   3;
x  =   x + 1;
printf (  "\nX = %d",  x  );
```

The output would be **X = 4**. This same code could be written more compactly as

```
x  =   3;
x++;
printf (  "\nX = %d",  x  );
```

or even

```
x  =   5;
x--  ;
printf (  "\nX = %d",  x  );
```

The increment and decrement operators are more compact (and more efficient to execute) than the equivalent compound-assignment operators but are restricted to cases of adding or subtracting 1.

It can be confusing when the increment or decrement operators are used in a larger expression, as

```
x  =   0;
printf (  "%d",   x++  +  4 );
printf (  "%d",   x  );
```

In this case the first output is 4 and the second is 1. When the increment (or decrement) operator is placed after the variable, the operator is said to be in its *postfix* (as opposed to *prefix*) form. With **postfix**, the corresponding variable is not changed until *after* the expression is evaluated. With **prefix**, the variable is changed *before* it is used in the expression. Therefore, at the time of the first output, **x** is still 0. It is only after the statement has executed that **x** is incremented, thus yielding 1 for the second output.

Finally, avoid

```
x  =   10;
y  =   ++x  +  x;
```

What is the value of **y**? 20? 21? 22? It turns out that the value of **y** is **compiler-dependent**. On some compilers it equals 21 and on others it equals 22. The problem is the way C evaluates addition: Which **x** is processed first? If the left-most **x** is processed first, then the expression equals 11 + 11 = 22, but the compiler might process the rightmost **x** first, yielding 11 + 10 = 21. Stay clear of this trap.

BEFORE YOU GO ON	Query: Subtract 1 from a variable **x** in four different ways.
	RESPONSE: assignment: x = x − 1;
	compound assignment: x −= 1;
	decrement (postfix): x−− ;
	(prefix): −−x ;

3.3.6 Type Casting

C provides an additional mechanism for changing the evaluation of a given arithmetic expression, called the type cast. Type casting allows you to change the data type of an expression. Consider the following:

```
float f;
f  =  (int) (2.5 * 4.3);          /* f = 10.0 */
```

The type cast (**int**) tells C to interpret the result of **2.5 * 4.3** as the integer 10, not 10.75. Because **f** is a **float,** its stored value is 10.0. Note that any data type can be used as a type cast simply by putting it in parentheses before a given expression. The expression can involve constants or variables, as in

```
int x, y;
y = 10;
x = (float) (y) / 4 * 10;            /* x = 25 */
```

PERSPECTIVE

Type casting a variable applies to that expression only; it does not permanently alter the data type of the variable.

Without the type cast, **x** would be 20 because $10/4 = 2$ and $2 \times 10 = 20$. Note that the type cast applies to the *result* of the expression that follows it. Therefore, the following yields a different value for **x**.

```
int x, y;
y = 10;
x = (float) (y / 4) * 10;          /* x = 20 */
```

C first performs the operation **y/4**. The result, 2, is cast to a **float** and multiplied by 10, yielding a result of 20.0. The **float** value 20.0 is then converted to the integer value 20 for storage in the variable **x**. (Type casting is further discussed in Chapter 13.)

EXERCISES 3.3

Concept Check

Answer statements 1 through 4 with true *or* false.

1. In C, the expression **14 + 13 * 3 + 27 / 3**   has a value of 36.
2. In C, the expression **(((14 + 13) * 3) + 27) / 3**   has a value of 36.
3. In C, the modulo operator **%** takes precedence over division.
4. In C, **999999/1000000**   equals .999999.

For statements 5 through 8 choose the answer that best completes the statement.

5. Arithmetic expressions in C
   a. are evaluated in about the same way as on a simple $5 calculator
   b. are evaluated according to precedence and associativity rules
   c. are evaluated from left to right
   d. are evaluated from right to left
6. What is the value of **133 % 24**?
   a. 5
   b. 13
   c. 5.54
   d. 5.541666
7. What is the value of **3 + 4 % 6 / 2 + 5**?
   a. 5
   b. 9
   c. 6
   d. 10
8. What is the value of **x**   after **x = y = 4; x *= 3 + y;**   is executed?
   a. 7
   b. 28
   c. 11
   d. 16

For statements 9 through 12 fill in the blanks with the right word.

9. In the evaluation of arithmetic expressions, the operator with _____ is performed first.
10. With regard to data types, _____ has higher precedence than _____.
11. The result of dividing an integer by an integer is an _____.
12. The modulo operator is defined only for the _____ data type.

Set A
What is the output in each case?
13. printf ("%d", 3 * 17 - 189 / 18);
14. printf ("%f", 193 / 19 / pow(3.0,2.0));
15. printf ("%d", -4 + 23 * 2) / 3);
16. printf ("%f", 3 * 17 - 189.0 / 18.0);
17. printf ("%f", 193.0 / 19.0 / pow(3.0,2.0));
18. printf ("%d", (37 + 15 % 4) / (5 * 5));

Set B
What is the output in each case?
19. printf ("%d", (int) (3.2 * 4) / 3);
20. printf ("%d", 5 % 2 + 14 / 3 - 6);
21. printf ("%d", 5 + 2 * (3 + 7));
22. printf ("%d", 3 + (4 % (6 / 2)) + 5);
23. printf ("%d", 12 / 5 * 3);
24. printf ("%d", 6 * 5 / 10 * 2 + 10);
25. printf ("%4.2f", (float) (6 * 5) / (10 * 2) + 10);
26. printf ("%d", (6 * 5) / (10 * 2 + 10));
27. printf ("%d", (6 * 5) / (10 * (2 + 10)));

Set C
28. x = -1; printf ("%d\n", ++x + 1);
29. x = -1; printf ("%d\n", x++ + 1);
30. What are the values of **x**, **y**, and **z** after the following statements have executed?

```
int x, y, z;

x = y = z = 10;

x += 15;
y -= 15;
z *= 5;
x /= 5;
z %= 4;
```

Computer Logic and Architecture 4

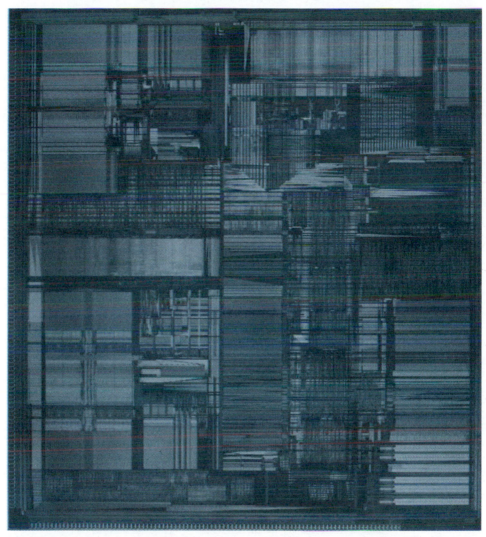

Intel Pentium Processor (1994) contains 3.3 million transistors running at 100 megahertz.

After completing this chapter you should be able to do the following:

Learning Goals

- Find character equivalences in both ASCII and EBCDIC codes
- Convert any number from binary, octal, or hexadecimal to decimal
- Convert any decimal number to binary, octal, or hexadecimal
- Add, subtract, and multiply any two binary numbers
- Apply the truth tables for NOT, AND, OR, and XOR
- Construct elementary digital circuits using logic gates
- Convert Boolean functions to truth tables and to logical circuits
- Determine whether two digital circuits are equivalent
- Apply the C language equivalents of Boolean logic and relational operators
- Construct floating-point numbers in both single- and double-precision
- Determine the precision and accuracy of numbers

Chapter Activity

A computer hardware engineering firm receives an order to produce a simple logic unit that forms the AND and XOR of the contents of two 3-bit registers. The entries to the registers are in 3-bit binary form. Design a hardware device that meets these specifications. Figure 4.0–1 shows one way to do this.

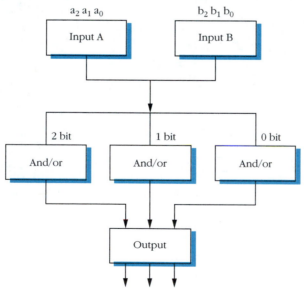

Figure 4.0–1   ANDing or ORing two, 3-bit registers

4.1 NUMBER SYSTEMS

Introduction

The central processing unit (CPU) is the hardware component that handles a computer's primary functions, including the control of data flow, logical operations, and arithmetic operations. The operating system (OS) is the software component that tells the CPU what to do. In both cases the information to be processed, such as programs and other data, is represented by patterns of 0s and 1s. For arithmetic and logic operations, these patterns are usually interpreted as binary numbers or binary strings. For peripheral communications, such as between the keyboard and primary memory, the binary patterns represent a special code. So to understand either hardware or software, we must first understand the number system on which binary codes are based.

4.1.1 Binary Codes: ASCII and EBCDIC

Information codes have been used for thousands of years, whether by patterns of smoke signals, beats of a drum, flashes of sunlight, or patterns of dots and dashes in Morse code. The same idea holds for computers. Information is transmitted from one point to another by patterns of **bits.** Mathematically, these bits are represented by 0s and 1s. The 6-bit pattern 010011 is different from the pattern 011010.

When information is transmitted to or from a peripheral device (hardware other than the CPU), a special coding procedure is used. In the early days of computing, each manufacturer developed its own information code. For example, when punched cards were used, patterns of holes in columns represented certain characters, as shown in Figure 4.1–1. However, this varying assignment of patterns to convey information created complications for both the user and the manufacturer, and standardization became a necessity.

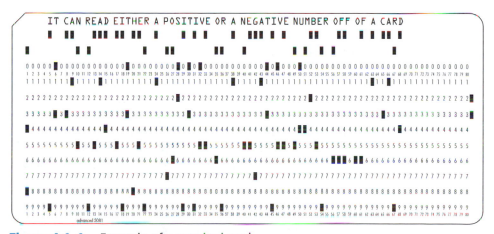

Figure 4.1–1   Example of a punched card

01000001	A	01100001	a			
01000010	B	01100010	b			
01000011	C	01100011	c			
01000100	D	01100100	d			
01000101	E	01100101	e			
01000110	F	01100110	f			
01000111	G	01100111	g			
01001000	H	01101000	h			
01001001	I	01101001	i	00110000	0
01001010	J	01101010	j	00110001	1
01001011	K	01101011	k	00110010	2
01001100	L	01101100	l	00110011	3
01001101	M	01101101	m	00110100	4
01001110	N	01101110	n	00110101	5
01001111	O	01101111	o	00110110	6
01010000	P	01110000	p	00110111	7
01010001	Q	01110001	q	00111000	8
01010010	R	01110010	r	00111001	9
01010011	S	01110011	s			
01010100	T	01110100	t			
01010101	U	01110101	u			
01010110	V	01110110	v			
01010111	W	01110111	w			
01011000	X	01111000	x			
01011001	Y	01111001	y			
01011010	Z	01111010	z			

Figure 4.1–2   Some ASCII characters

Computer manufacturers still develop their own coding schemes, but only for special purposes. The general practice in the United States is to use one of two standardized codes. One is the American Standard Code for Information Interchange (**ASCII,** pronounced *ask-ee*). The other is the Extended Binary Coded Decimal Interchange Code (**EBCDIC,** pronounced *eb-se-dik*). EBCDIC is typically used in IBM mainframes and some Unisys mainframes, whereas ASCII is the standard for most mini- and personal computers.

Figure 4.1–2 shows selected characters with their corresponding bit patterns based on the 7-bit ASCII code. Notice that each pattern has 8 bits, which allow for 256 different patterns. The remaining 128 patterns are used mainly for special characters such as Greek letters and mathematical symbols. (Appendix E shows 128 ASCII characters.)

Query: Why does an 8-bit code generate 256 distinct patterns?

RESPONSE: Because each bit has two possibilities, 0 and 1, n bits can generate 2^n patterns. That is, a 1-bit code has $2^1 = 2$ possibilities, a 3-bit code has $2^3 = 8$ possibilities, and an 8-bit code has $2^8 = 256$ possibilities.

EXAMPLE 4.1–1

Problem

Using the 8-bit ASCII code, write the bit pattern for the word *Cat*.

Solution

According to the table of ASCII characters in Figure 4.1–2, the code for the uppercase letter C is 01010100, the code for the letter a is 01100001, and the code for the letter t is 01110100. Thus, the bit pattern for the word Cat is 010101000110000101110100. •

EBCDIC is an 8-bit code providing 256 possible characters. It evolved from the early Binary Coded Decimal (BCD) code, which is almost extinct now. Some common EBCDIC characters are shown in Figure 4.1–3. (A complete set of EBCDIC characters is shown in Appendix E.)

EXAMPLE 4.1–2

Problem

Given the bit pattern 110101001001011010010100, find its representation in EBCDIC code.

Solution

Because the EBCDIC code provides for 8-bit patterns, the given pattern of 24 bits is partitioned into three segments as

11010100   10010110   10010100

The first pattern corresponds to the uppercase letter M, the second pattern corresponds to the lowercase letter o, and the third pattern corresponds to the lowercase letter m. The original pattern is the EBCDIC code for *Mom*. Notice the different patterns for uppercase and lowercase representations for the letters M and m. •

4.1.2 Positional Notation

Patterns of bits are not restricted to characters: They can represent many things. One interpretation for a pattern of bits is a binary integer.

10000001	a	11000001	A			
10000010	b	11000010	B			
10000011	c	11000011	C			
10000100	d	11000100	D			
10000101	e	11000101	E			
10000110	f	11000110	F			
10000111	g	11000111	G			
10001000	h	11001000	H			
10001001	i	11001001	I			
				11110000	0	
10010001	j	11010001	J	11110001	1	
10010010	k	11010010	K	11110010	2	
10010011	l	11010011	L	11110011	3	
10010100	m	11010100	M	11110100	4	
10010101	n	11010101	N	11110101	5	
10010110	o	11010110	O	11110110	6	
10010111	p	11010111	P	11110111	7	
10011000	q	11011000	Q	11111000	8	
10011001	r	11011001	R	11111001	9	
10100010	s	11100010	S			
10100011	t	11100011	T			
10100100	u	11100100	U			
10100101	v	11100101	V			
10100110	w	11100110	W			
10100111	x	11100111	X			
10101000	y	11101000	Y			
10101001	z	11101001	Z			

Figure 4.1–3 Some EBCDIC characters

Before investigating binary numbers, let's consider the decimal (base-10) number 4,362. This is read

four thousand three hundred sixty-two

and means

4,000 plus 300 plus 60 plus 2

or

4,000 + 300 + 60 + 2

This sum can be rewritten in terms of the base (10) as

$$4 * 10^3 + 3 * 10^2 + 6 * 10^1 + 2 * 10^0$$

Therefore, the number 4 is in the 1000s position, the number 3 is in the 100s position, the number 6 is in the 10s position, and the number 2 is in the units position. Recall that any nonzero real number raised to the zero exponent is always equal to 1. (Real numbers are further discussed in Section 4.3.1.) That is, $x^0 = 1$ whenever $x \neq 0$.

BEFORE YOU GO ON

Query: Find the place value of each digit in the base-10 number 74,629.

RESPONSE: The 9 is in the units position, the 2 is in the 10s position, the 6 is in the 100s position, the 4 is in the 1000s position, and the 7 is in the 10,000s position.

Each digit in the base-10 number corresponds to a position value that is a power of 10.

PERSPECTIVE

The Arabic method of enumeration, also called the Hindu–Arabic system, was developed more than 1,200 years ago and replaced the older system that was based on Roman numerals. This newer system introduced positional notation and place value. The numerals 0 through 9 as we now use them are Arabic numerals. For example, the Roman number DCCXLVIII is written in Arabic as 748.

4.1.3 Binary to Decimal Conversion

Positional notation can be used with numbers in any base. The value (weight) associated with each position is the number of symbols used in the system—the base of the system—raised to a power. For example, in base-8 (octal) there are eight digits, usually written as 0, 1, 2,...6, 7. The values of the five rightmost positions are 8^4, 8^3, 8^2, 8^1, 8^0. In base 16 (hexadecimal) there are 16 digits. Traditionally, we use the 10 decimal digits 0, 1, 2,...9 and append six additional symbols—A, B, C,...F—to denote the hexadecimal digits. Table 4.1–1 shows number representation in four different bases: binary, octal, decimal, and hexadecimal.

BEFORE YOU GO ON

Query: A base-4 number is written as 34201. Is this possible?

RESPONSE: No. The digits 0, 1, 2, and 3 are the only allowable digits in base-4.

Table 4.1–1   Number Representations

BINARY	OCTAL	DECIMAL	HEXADECIMAL
00000	00	00	00
00001	01	01	01
00010	02	02	02
00011	03	03	03
00100	04	04	04
00101	05	05	05
00110	06	06	06
00111	07	07	07
01000	10	08	08
01001	11	09	09
01010	12	10	0A
01011	13	11	0B
01100	14	12	0C
01101	15	13	0D
01110	16	14	0E
01111	17	15	0F
10000	20	16	10
10001	21	17	11
10010	22	18	12
10011	23	19	13
10100	24	20	14

Numbers represented in binary are easily converted to other bases that are powers of 2, such as base-4, -8, or -16. To convert binary to base-4, partition the binary number from right to left into groups of 2 bits and then interpret each group. To convert binary to base-8, partition the binary number from right to left into groups of 3 bits. To convert binary to base-16, partition the binary number from right to left into groups of 4 bits. For example, consider the binary number

010110100010111110101011

To convert this to base-4, partition the bits into groups of 2 bits from the lowest-order bit (the right) and interpret each group:

Base-2:   01   01   10   10   00   10   11   11   01   01   11

Base-4:   1   1   2   2   0   2   3   3   1   1   3

To convert to base-8, partition into groups of 3 bits from the lowest-order bit (the right):

Base-2:   0   101   101   000   101   111   010   111

Base-8:   0   5   5   0   5   7   2   7

To convert to base-16, partition into groups of 4 bits from the lowest-order bit:

Base- 2:   01   0110   1000   1011   1101   0111
Base-16:   1   6   8   B   D   7

Query: Convert the binary number 1011010001001101110 to octal.

_____

RESPONSE: Partition the binary number from right to left into patterns of 3 bits: 1 011 010 001 001 101 110. The conversion to base-8 is 1321156.

EXAMPLE 4.1–3

Problem
Find the decimal representation of the octal number 375.

Reasoning
In this case the number corresponds to the expansion

$$3 * 8^2 + 7 * 8^1 + 5 * 8^0$$

Solution
The previous expression can be rewritten as

$$3(64) + 7(8) + 5(1)$$
$$= 192 + 56 \ + 5$$
$$= 253 \text{ (base-10)}$$

Test
Use a desk check of the arithmetic to verify the answer.   ●

A decimal representation of a binary number is found by using a base-2 expansion of the binary number. For instance, the binary (base-2) number 1011 corresponds to

$$1 * 2^3 + 0 * 2^2 + 1 * 2^1 + 1 * 2^0$$

and can be rewritten as

$$1(8) + 0(4) + 1(2) + 1(1)$$
$$= \ \ 8 + 0 \ \ + 2 \ \ + 1$$
$$= 11 \text{ (base-10)}$$

EXAMPLE 4.1–4

Problem
Find the decimal representation of the binary number 101101.

Reasoning
The binary number is written in powers of 2 as

$$1*2^5 + 0*2^4 + 1*2^3 + 1*2^2 + 0*2^1 + 1*2^0$$

Solution
The previous expression can be rewritten as

$$1(32) + 0(16) + 1(8) + 1(4) + 0(2) + 1(1)$$
$$= \quad 32 + 0 \quad + 8 \quad + 4 \quad + 0 \quad + 1$$
$$= 45 \text{ (base-10)}$$

Test
Use a desk check of the arithmetic to verify the answer.

BEFORE YOU GO ON

Query: The output from a computer reveals the number 1000. How would you interpret this?

RESPONSE: It is not clear whether the number is in base-10, base-2, or some other base. In base-10 the value is 1000; in base-2 the value is 8.

Another way to convert a binary number to decimal is to make a table of three rows with enough columns to accommodate the binary number. The entries in the first row are the binary bits. The entries in the second row contain the powers of 2 starting with 2^0 in the right-most cell and proceeding in ascending order from right to left. The entries in the third row are the product of each bit with its corresponding power of 2. The solution (conversion) consists of the sum of the entries in the third row. For the binary number 100101, the table of values is as follows.

Binary number	1	0	0	1	0	1	
Place value	$2^5 = 32$	$2^4 = 16$	$2^3 = 8$	$2^2 = 4$	$2^1 = 2$	$2^0 = 1$	decimal equivalence
Value = row1 * row2	32	0	0	4	0	1	sum = 37

The sum of the entries in the third row is 37, which is the binary number converted into decimal.

BEFORE YOU GO ON

Query: Why isn't 2^0 equal to 0?

RESPONSE: The number 0 can be written as the difference between a number and itself, or $n - n$. Write 2^0 as 2^{n-n} and then, by the laws of exponents, write 2^{n-n} as $2^n/2^n$, which equals 1, not 0. Another way is $2 = 2^1 = 2^{1+0} = 2^1 * 2^0$, in which $2^0 = 1$.

EXAMPLE 4.1–5

Problem
Convert the hexadecimal number 3E4AC to decimal.

Reasoning
Applying the "table approach" as we did earlier, enter powers of 16 in the middle row and enter the respective hexadecimal digits above in the first row. Compute the result by finding the products for each place value and then finding their sum.

Solution
Recall that hexadecimal E equals decimal 14, hexadecimal A equals decimal 10, and hexadecimal C equals decimal 12. The table of values changes as follows.

Hexadecimal number	3	E	4	A	C	
Place value	$16^4 = 65536$	$16^3 = 4096$	$16^2 = 256$	$16^1 = 16$	$16^0 = 1$	decimal equivalence
Value = row1 * row2	196608	57344	1024	160	12	sum = 255148

The sum of the elements in the last row gives a result of 255,148.

Test
To verify the result, recompute the elements of the table.   •

4.1.4 Decimal to Binary Conversion

It is important to know how to convert a binary number to decimal and it is equally important to know how to convert a decimal number to binary. Consider the decimal number 43. Which powers of 2 can be added to produce the number 43? Consider all the powers of 2 not exceeding 43: 2^0, 2^1, 2^2, 2^3, 2^4, and $2^5 = 32$. (We have to stop at 2^5 since $2^6 = 64$, which is greater than 43.) Now do the conversion observing this rule: Each of these powers of 2 can be in the sum once at most and if the power of 2 is in the sum, set that bit position to 1; otherwise set it to 0. And now the question is, which positions need to be "turned on" (set to 1)?

One way to answer this question is to use a bit table as we did earlier, but in reverse. That is, we can put the decimal place values on top and then solve for the bits. Start by placing a 1 in the most significant bit position, in this case the 32s position. Doing so leaves $43 - 32 = 11$ to be converted. Because 16 does not fit into 11, its position is set to 0. The largest power of 2 that *does* fit into 11 is 8, so turn on the bit in the 8s position. This leaves $11 - 8 = 3$ to be converted. Now set the 2s position bit on, leaving 1. Finally, set the 1s position bit to 1. Thus the number 43 in decimal converts to 101011 in binary. This procedure is summarized in the following table.

32	16	8	4	2	1
2^5	2^4	2^3	2^2	2^1	2^0
1	0	1	0	1	1

We can formalize this process of converting a decimal number to a binary number by means of an algorithm. Notice that the succession of decreasing powers of 2 is equivalent to successive division by 2. That is, $32/2 = 16$, $16/2 = 8$, and so on. This reasoning sets the foundation for an algorithm that works for all conversions from positive decimal integers to any positive integer base, as shown in the following examples.

EXAMPLE 4.1–6

Problem
Convert the number 43 (base-10) to a binary number.

Reasoning
The algorithm has to follow the same reasoning we used in the conversion where we divided the original number (43) by 2, leaving a quotient and remainder (0 or 1), and repeated the process until the quotient was 0.

Solution
Use the following algorithm:

```
2 |  43
2 |  21   with remainder = 1     43/2 = 21 with remainder = 1
2 |  10   with remainder = 1     21/2 = 10 with remainder = 1
2 |   5   with remainder = 0     10/2 = 5 with remainder = 0
2 |   2   with remainder = 1      5/2 = 2 with remainder = 1
2 |   1   with remainder = 0      2/2 = 1 with remainder = 0
      0   with remainder = 1      1/2 = 0 with remainder = 1
```

Reading the remainders in *reverse* gives the result

1 0 1 0 1 1 (base-2)

Test
When we use the place values for base-2, this binary number becomes

$$1 * 2^5 + 0 * 2^4 + 1 * 2^3 + 0 * 2^2 + 1 * 2^1 + 1 * 2^0$$

and this becomes

$$32 + 0 + 8 + 0 + 2 + 1 = 43$$

The result here is the same as the one we found earlier with a table of cells. ●

BEFORE YOU GO ON

Query: In Example 4.1–6, the equation 21/2 = 10 appears to be faulty because 21/2 = 10.5, not 10. What does this mean?

RESPONSE: The purpose of the operation is *integer division* rather than the division of real numbers. Integer division yields an integer result (the quotient) and truncates the remainder.

EXAMPLE 4.1–7

Problem
Convert the number 155 (base 10) to a base-8 number.

Reasoning
The algorithm for this problem is the same as the one we used in Example 4.1–6. We do successive divisions by 8 and record the remainders after each division until the quotient is 0.

Solution
Use the following algorithm:

$$8 \mid \underline{\quad 155 \quad}$$
$$8 \mid \underline{\quad 19 \quad} \text{ with remainder } = 3 \qquad 155/8 = 19 \text{ with remainder } = 3$$
$$8 \mid \underline{\quad 2 \quad} \text{ with remainder } = 3 \qquad 19/8 = 2 \text{ with remainder } = 3$$
$$0 \text{ with remainder } = 2 \qquad 2/8 = 0 \text{ with remainder } = 2$$

Reading the remainders in *reverse* leads to this result:

2   3   3   (*base*–8)

Test
When we use the place values for base-2, this binary number becomes

$$2*8^2 + 3*8^1 + 3*8^0$$

and this becomes

128 + 24 + 3 = 155   •

The algorithms we have just discussed can be used to convert an integer from any integer base-m to another integer base-n. This is shown in the following example.

EXAMPLE 4.1–8

Problem
Convert the number 246 (base-7) to a number in base-5.

Reasoning

Neither base-7 nor base-5 is a power of 2 so the use of binary is not necessary. However, because we already know how to do arithmetic in base-10, we can first convert the number from base-7 to base-10 and then convert the number from base-10 to base-5.

Solution

The number 246 (base-7) means

$$2*7^2 + 4*7^1 + 6*7^0$$

and this becomes

$$2*(49) + 4*(7) + 6*(1) = 98 + 28 + 6$$
$$= 132 \quad \text{(base-10)}$$

To convert 132 (base-10) to a base-5 number, proceed with the algorithm by successively dividing by 5 and finding the remainders. In this case,

```
5 |  132
5 |   26  with remainder  = 2    132/5 = 26 with remainder  = 2
5 |    5  with remainder  = 1     26/5 =  5 with remainder  = 1
5 |    1  with remainder  = 0      5/5 =  1 with remainder  = 0
       0  with remainder  = 1      1/5 =  0 with remainder  = 1
```

Reading the remainders in *reverse* leads to this result:

1   0   1   2   (base-5)

Test

When we use the place values for base-5, this base-5 number becomes

$$1*5^3 + 0*5^2 + 1*5^1 + 2*5^0$$

and then becomes

$$125 + 0 + 5 + 2 = 132 \quad (\textit{base-}10)$$

Successive divisions by 7 produce remainders that result in the original base-7 number.   •

4.1.5 Negative Numbers in Twos Complement Form

Binary numbers can be negative as well as positive. There are several ways to formulate their representation and one of these is called the **twos complement** of the number.

Before we look at this method, consider a decimal (base-10) integer such as 347. The **nines complement** of this number is formed by exchanging each digit in the number with a new integer so that for each place value, the new integer plus the given integer equals 9—that is, the nines complement of 347 is 652 because 347 + 652 = 999. The tens complement is 1 more than the nines complement of the number. So the tens complement of 347 is 653.

Notice that the sum is restricted to only 3 digits, as in 347 + 653 = 000, supporting the fact that sum of a number and its negation equals 0. With this restriction, the tens complement of an integer can be considered the negative of that integer—that is, if we accept the premise that

$$347 + 653 = 000$$

then it follows that

$$347 + 653 - 653 = 000 - 653$$

or

$$347 = -653$$

Thus, when restricted to the same number of digits as it was in the original number, the tens complement is a representation of the negative of that number.

BEFORE YOU GO ON

Query: Find the negation of 82 in tens complement form.

RESPONSE: The nines complement of 82 is 17. The tens complement (negative) of 82 is 18. (Note that 100 − 82 = 18.)

What we observed about decimal numbers holds for binary numbers too. To form the negative of a binary number, first find its **ones complement** and then add 1 to it. This forms the twos complement. When we restrict the number of bits formed through this process, we can show that the twos complement is indeed the negative of the original number.

What is the ones complement? It is the number x that when added to y gives 1. So the ones complement of 0 is 1 and of 1 is 0! Applying this technique bit by bit tells us that the ones complement is formed simply by inverting all the bits: 0101 becomes 1010, for example. The **twos complement** of a number is the ones complement plus 1. And the twos complement of 0101 is 1011. When a number is added to its twos complement for a finite bit field, the result is always 0. For example, for a finite field of 4 bits

```
    0101
+   1011
    0000   (restricted to 4 bits)
```

By analogy to the decimal example above, we can therefore interpret 1011 as the negative of 0101.

But why use twos complement? If the lead bit is the signature (sign bit) of the number, why not simply use 1101 for −5 (prefix a 1 to the binary 101) rather than the twos complement 1011? The answer is that when we design the logic for addition in computer architecture, we can use the twos complement to make the same logic also do subtraction. This saves space in the computer and cost to the manufacturer.

<table>
<tr><td>

BEFORE
YOU
GO ON

</td><td>

Query: What is the twos complement negative of 001101 ?

RESPONSE: The ones complement of 001101 is 110010. The twos complement negative is 110011.

</td></tr>
</table>

The catch is: How do we distinguish a positive number from a negative one? Because all data on a computer are stored as patterns of 0s and 1s, we can not assume that negative values will be prefixed with a special symbol such as a minus sign. Instead, we adopt the convention that in a machine using twos complement notation, the leading bit of any binary integer represents the negative place value associated with that bit. In this case, a leading 1 would signify a negative number and a leading 0 a positive number. Thus, positive integers always have a leading 0. The decimal integer +6 is stored as 0110 and not 110. To find the twos complement (negative) of decimal +6 do the following steps:

1. Represent +6 in binary as: 0110
2. Take the ones complement: 1001
3. Add 1 to form the twos complement: 1010

To check this, add the two 4-bit binary numbers:

$$
\begin{array}{r}
0110 \\
+\quad \underline{1010} \\
1\ 0000
\end{array}
$$

We ignore the carry of 1 because it is not included in the 4 bits. So $(+6)+(-6) = 0$. (For more on twos complement numbers, see Section 3 of this chapter.)

4.1.6 Addition and Multiplication

Addition in base-2 is similar to addition in base-10 except that it is much simpler. Because there are only two digits, 0 and 1, the addition tables for binary arithmetic are very short. Binary multiplication is also simple compared to multiplication in base-10. Figure 4.1–4 shows these operations. Note that 0 multiplied by any bit (0 or 1) is always 0. Multiplication by 1 just repeats (echoes) the other bit pattern.

BIT ADDENDS	SUM	BIT MULTIPLIERS	PRODUCT
0 0	0	0 0	0
0 1	1	0 1	0
1 0	1	1 0	0
1 1	10	1 1	1

Figure 4.1–4   Addition and multiplication tables

BEFORE YOU GO ON

Query: Given the binary number $B = 10010110$, what are $B * 0$ and $B * 1$?

_____

RESPONSE:

$10010110 * 0 = 00000000$
$10010110 * 1 = 10010110$

Addition in base-2 is almost as easy. It can also be expressed as $0 + 0 = 0$, $0 + 1 = 1$, $1 + 0 = 1$, and $1 + 1 = 0$ with a carry of 1. We write this as 10 (base-2). The two addends and the resulting sum must have the same number of bits.

BEFORE YOU GO ON

Query: What is the sum of 0011 and 0010 ?

_____

RESPONSE: Align the two numbers according to place value and then add their respective place values. This results in

```
  0011
+ 0010
  0101
```

EXAMPLE 4.1–9

Problem
Find the sum of the two 12-bit addends 000110101110 and 010101101010.

Reasoning
We evaluate the sum of these two binary numbers by doing binary addition for respective place values and using a carry wherever needed.

CARRY	ADDENDS	SUM
0	0 0	0
0	0 1	1
0	1 0	1
0	1 1	10
1	0 0	1
1	0 1	10
1	1 0	10
1	1 1	11

Figure 4.1–5   Addition with carry

Solution
Begin by aligning the two numbers according to place value as follows and then do the binary addition. The carry digit is placed above the respective place value when it equals 1.

$$
\begin{array}{r}
1111\ \ 111 \quad \leftarrow \text{carry} \\
000110101110 \\
+\ 010101101010 \\
\hline
011100011000
\end{array}
$$

Test
Check the result of each place value using the addition table in Figure 4.1–5. Remember the carry bit when it is present. Alternatively, convert each addend to decimal, sum the two addends in decimal, then reconvert to binary.   ●

To multiply two numbers in base-10, treat each digit of the multiplier as a power of 10. This causes a shift to the left, as shown in the following example.

EXAMPLE 4.1–10

Problem
In base-10, find the product of 2845 by 649.

Reasoning
Multiply by 649 means multiply by 9, then by 40, and then by 600. Then add these three results.

Solution

Traditional		Meaning
2845		2845
649		649
25605	multiply by 9	25605
11380	multiply by 40	113800
17070	multiply by 600	1707000
1846405		1846405

Test
To verify this result, use a calculator. ●

Binary multiplication is similar to multiplication in base-10. In base-2 each digit of the multiplier is treated as a power of 2. This causes a shift to the left, as shown in Example 4.1–11. We treat each bit in the multiplier as its respective place value when we evaluate a product. For fixed-length representation of numbers, the number of bits in each factor must be the same. The number of bits in the product is double the number of bits in a factor.

EXAMPLE 4.1–11

Problem
Find the binary product of the 7-bit numbers 0100110 and 0001101.

Reasoning
Treat 0001101 as the multiplier. The low-order (right-most) bit (2^0) value is 1, the 2's bit (2^1) value is 0, the 4's bit (2^2) value is 100, and the 8's bit (2^3) value is 1000.

Solution
Set each number with matched place values and do ordinary binary multiplication followed by binary addition:

```
              0 1 0 0 1 1 0
          ×   0 0 0 1 1 0 1
              0 1 0 0 1 1 0
            0 0 0 0 0 0 0 0
          0 1 0 0 1 1 0 0 0
          0 1 0 0 1 1 0 0 0
        0 0 0 0 0 0 0 0 0 0 0
        0 0 0 0 0 0 0 0 0 0 0 0
        0 0 0 0 0 0 0 0 0 0 0 0 0
        0 0 0 0 1 1 1 1 0 1 1 1 0
```

The product is the 14-bit number 00000111101110.

Test
The binary number 0100110 can be represented by the decimal number 38 and the binary number 0001101 can be represented by the decimal number 13. Using base-10 multiplication, $38 \times 13 = 494$, which is represented in binary as 00000111101110. ●

BEFORE YOU GO ON

Query: What is the product of 0101 and 011 ?

RESPONSE: In binary, the product of 0101 and 0011 is 00001111.

4.1.7 Subtraction and Division

The tens complement can also be used for subtraction of one integer from a second integer, since subtraction is the addition of the negation of the second number. For example, $8 - 2 = 8 + (-2) = 6$. As with tens complement addition, subtraction must be performed within a fixed number of digits. Note that division is just repeated subtraction, so it is a convenience rather than a mathematical necessity. (Division is explored further in Section 4.3.3.)

BEFORE YOU GO ON	Query: Use tens complement to evaluate $8 - 2$ with a fixed length of one digit. RESPONSE: The nines complement of 2 is 7. The tens complement of 2 is 8. Adding $8 + 8$ results in 6, to one digit.

EXAMPLE 4.1–12

Problem
Find the result of $5{,}823 - 37$ using the tens complement.

Reasoning
We do subtraction by forming the addition of the minuend and the negative of the subtrahend. The operation is valid only if it is done within a preset number of place values.

Solution
First represent 37 as 0037 because the larger number has four digits. The nines complement of 0037 is 9962. The tens complement of 0037 is 9963. Then

$$5{,}823 - 37 = 5{,}823 + (-37)$$
$$= 5{,}823 + (-0037)$$
$$= 5{,}823 + 9963$$
$$= 5{,}786$$

Notice that the carry of 1 into the fifth place-value position was ignored because the numbers are restricted to four digits.

Test
You can use ordinary subtraction to verify that 37 subtracted from 5,823 is 5,786.

    The process is similar in binary. Recall that we get the twos complement of a binary number by inverting all bits and then adding 1. That is, for two binary numbers a and b, the difference $a - b$ is found by finding the twos complement of b and adding the result to a. Also recall that as in base-10, the process has significance only if the representation of a number is restricted to a preset number of place values, as shown in the following example.

EXAMPLE 4.1–13

Problem

Using twos complement form, subtract the binary number 0110110 from the number 001001011101. (Assume that there is 12-bit representation for the numbers.)

Reasoning

Because each number is represented in 12 bits, we can rewrite the problem as

$$001001011101$$
$$-\ \underline{000000110110}$$

or, equivalently,

$$001001011101$$
$$+\ \underline{(-000000110110)}$$

Solution

Rewrite the second addend (negative binary) in twos complement form. Its ones complement is 111111001001 and its twos complement is 111111001010. Therefore, the difference is representable as the sum of

$$001001011101$$
$$+\ \underline{111111001010}$$

and this results in

$$\text{lost bit} \longrightarrow 1 \qquad 001000100111$$

Test

The binary result 001000100111 represents the decimal number 551. This is the result of subtracting 000000110110 (54 base-10) from 001001011101 (605 base-10).

•

BEFORE YOU GO ON

Query: Find the result of 011001 − 0101.

RESPONSE: Convert the 4-bit number 0101 to a 6-bit number. The twos complement of 000101 is 111011. The result of the the subtraction is 010100.

BEFORE YOU GO ON

Query: The bit string 111010 in binary represents −6 (base-10). Show that this is true.

RESPONSE: Find its twos complement by inverting the bits and adding 1. The ones complement is 000101. The twos complement is 000110. Note that 000110 converts to +6 (base-10).

EXERCISES 4.1

Concept Check

Answer statements 1 through 4 with true *or* false.

1. EBCDIC is typically used on personal computers.
2. A string of six bits produces 64 distinct bit patterns.
3. The decimal value of the binary string 0110101 is 46.
4. The expression ABC9FDEGC5E can be interpreted as a hexadecimal expression.

For statements 5 through 8 choose the answer that best completes the statement.

5. The place value of a digit in a number is determined by
   a. the base of the number
   b. the physical location of the digit in the number
   c. answers (a) and (b) above
   d. natural means
6. The nines complement of 537 is
   a. 735
   b. 375
   c. 573
   d. 462
7. The binary sum of 0011011 and 0001111 is
   a. 0110100
   b. 0101010
   c. 0011010
   d. 0100100
8. The binary product of 01101110 and 00000111 is
   a. 0000100100010010
   b. 0000001011011010
   c. 0000010100010110
   d. 0000001100000010

For statements 9 through 12 fill in the blanks with the right word.

9. For a twos complement representation of a binary number, the leftmost bit equal to 1 signifies that the number is _____.
10. To convert from binary to octal, the bits are grouped into sets of three bits starting from the _____.
11. A character code that has become standard for most personal computers is the _____ code.
12. The binary representation in twos-complement form of the decimal number 99 is _____.

Set A

Solve each of the following problems.

13. Find the tens complement of 1356.
14. Find the tens complement of 4793.

15. Find the twos complement of 100010111010.
16. Find the twos complement of 011011001011.
17. Convert the binary number 01011101 to decimal.
18. Convert the binary number 01101011 to decimal.
19. Convert the decimal number 2573 to binary.
20. Convert the decimal number 3927 to binary.
21. Multiply 001000101011 and 000000101101 in binary.
22. Multiply 010010011010 and 000000110011 in binary.
23. Subtract 000101101101 from 011010011011.
24. Subtract 000011010110 from 010100101101.

Set B

25. Use the 8-bit ASCII code to convert the word *Happy* to binary.
26. Find the tens complement of the number 3976428.
27. For the binary number 00101001101101010101110101010101, find its twos complement.
28. Subtract the decimal number 3956742 from 8392743 using the tens complement.
29. Given binary numbers $A = 0011011101011101$ and $B = 0101101110111011$, find $A - B$.
30. For the numbers in Question 23, find $B - A$.
31. Using EBCDIC, convert the word *Georgia* to hexadecimal.
32. Convert the octal number 36271504 to decimal.
33. Convert the hexadecimal number A7D2F4E to decimal.

Set C

34. Add the hexadecimal numbers D3F2 and 3A7C and give the answer in decimal. (Suggestion: convert first to binary, then back to hexadecimal.)
35. Devise a scheme to do binary integer division. A 4-bit binary integer in twos complement form (the divisor) divides another 4-bit binary integer in twos complement form (the dividend). (Hint: Put the dividend in an 8-bit register.)

4.2   LOGIC AND COMPUTERS

Introduction

Section 4.1 introduced the binary number system and simple binary arithmetic. Since numbers are represented by patterns of 0s and 1s in binary, this system applies to many problems that are based on the concept of 0 and 1. Some examples are no or yes problems, false or true problems, and debit or credit problems; all of which can be translated into binary patterns. Mathematical logic is the area of computing where binary patterns and the problems they represent play a significant role.

4.2.1 Logic and Binary Systems

Logic in its philosophical setting can be traced back thousands of years, from Socrates to Aquinas to present-day legal debates. The quest for truth has led to thousands of works encompassing the full range of human thought—in theology, mathematics, science, and other fields. Logic is central to computers and the computing sciences. No computer can run effectively unless its operations are based on logic. And logic is the basis of both elementary hardware circuits and sophisticated communications devices.

What is logic? **Logic** is the process of reasoning; it can be inductive or deductive. **Inductive reasoning** makes specific observations general. For example, the sun has risen today, therefore the sun will rise tomorrow. **Deductive reasoning** makes general observations specific. For example, *All flowers are beautiful* is a general statement. If we accept it as truth, we can also acknowledge that because all flowers are beautiful and a rose is a flower, then a rose is beautiful.

Without engaging in a discourse on philosophical logic, we can agree that the principle is whether there *is no* truth or whether there *is* truth, which for computers is equivalent to a binary status of 0 or 1, respectively. By convention 0 means false and 1 means true. A statement's truth (or falsity) is illustrated in the following example.

EXAMPLE 4.2–1

Problem
Find the values of x that make the statement $x^2 - 1 = 0$ true and the values of x that make the statement false.

Reasoning
It is not clear if the statement is ever true and we need to determine which values of x will make the statement true. Maybe no value, maybe one value, or maybe more than one value make the statement true. For example, if $x = 3$ then the statement is not true.

Solution
By ordinary algebraic techniques $x^2 - 1 = 0$ can be rewritten as

$$x^2 = 1$$

from which we see that one answer is $x = +1$. Another answer is $x = -1$. These values of x make the statement true. Any other values make the statement false. Thus the statement is either false or true depending on the value of x.

Test
Substitution in the original equation shows that

$$(+1)^2 - 1 = 0 \text{ and } (-1)^2 - 1 = 0$$

So $x = 1$ and $x = -1$ solve the equation and make it true. All other numbers make it false. ●

As we saw in Example 4.2–1, some numbers make the statement true, namely, +1 and −1. Any number other than these makes the statement false. For example, $(-3)^2 - 1 = 8$, which is not 0, so −3 makes the statement false.

BEFORE YOU GO ON

Query: A claim is made that the equation $x^2 - 16 = 0$ is true only for $x = 4$. Is this correct?

_____

RESPONSE: No. The equation has *two* solutions: $x = 4$ and $x = -4$.

4.2.2 Truth Tables: NOT, AND, OR, XOR

The discussion that follows shows how to use some elementary statements and combine them with other statements. First, consider the concept of negation. We assume that if a given statement is true, then its negation or **logical complement** is not true and is therefore false. We can formalize this concept as shown in Figure 4.2–1. To do this we assume that **negation** is Boolean and that it has only one of two values: false or true. If a statement is not false, then it is true, and if a statement is not true, then it is false. Negations are represented in computing by the word **NOT.**

PERSPECTIVE

In 1854 the British mathematician George Boole developed an algebra of logic. His theory was based on three operators: *not, and,* and *or.* This work was important at that time because it expressed logic in mathematical formulas that could be manipulated and possibly simplified. Today this theory, called *Boolean algebra,* is the basis for the design of logic circuits.

There are also some non-Boolean schools of thought about logical processes. Suppose we assume that a statement is true. The negative of the statement need not necessarily be false. This is commonly called **fuzzy logic.** For example, the negation of *The iron is not hot* may imply other states such as warm or cool. (The ramifications of fuzzy logic are discussed in Chapter 19.)

Languages (human or computer) and their grammar provide for the use of compound statements. Compound statements in English use conjunction or

STATEMENT	NEGATION
p	NOT **p**
0	1
1	0

Figure 4.2–1   Boolean negation

STATEMENTS		CONJUNCTION	STATEMENTS		DISJUNCTION
p	*q*	*p* AND *q*	*p*	*q*	*p* OR *q*
0	0	0	0	0	0
0	1	0	0	1	1
1	0	0	1	0	1
1	1	1	1	1	1

Figure 4.2–2   Conjunction and disjunction

disjunction. In English, the word *and* is conjunctive and the word *or* is disjunctive. A **conjunction** of two statements is true only when both statements are true; otherwise it is false. Conjunctions are represented in computing as **AND.** An **inclusive disjunction** of two statements is false only when both statements are false; otherwise, it is true. Disjunctions (inclusive) are represented in computing as **OR.** The tables in Figure 4.2–2 illustrate truth for both conjunctive and inclusive disjunctive statements.

EXAMPLE 4.2–2

Problem
Given two statements: *It is not hot* and *It is raining,* find the negation of each statement and form their conjunction and disjunction.

Reasoning
Each statement can be either false or true depending on the actual weather conditions. The logical operations of negation, conjunction, and disjunction can be explained in the following statements.

Solution
We would resolve the questions this way:

Negation of 1.:	*It is hot* (derived from *It is not true that it is not hot*)
Negation of 2.:	*It is not raining* (derived from *It is not true that it is raining*)
Conjunction of 1. and 2.:	*It is not hot and it is raining*
Disjunction of 1. and 2.:	*It is not hot or it is raining*

Test
These answers are correct according to the definitions of negation, conjunction, and disjunction.   •

The word *or* in English has two different meanings. Consider the following compound sentence.

  Steve will eat or watch a movie.

The implication here is that if the statement is true, Steve will eat, watch a movie, or perhaps eat *and* watch a movie. This is because with the disjunctive operator

| STATEMENTS | DISJUNCTION |
p q	p XOR q
0 0	0
0 1	1
1 0	1
1 1	0

Figure 4.2–3   The exclusive OR

the only way the statement could not be true is if both parts of the compound (eating, watching a movie) are false. Both acts are possible so the disjunction is inclusive.

Sometimes disjunction is intended but the possibility of doing both acts in a compound sentence is excluded. No single word in English expresses this concept, but we can rephrase the sentence to read

Steve will either eat or watch a movie.

The *either...or* suggests the exclusion of both events and tells us that one or the other event will happen but not *both*. The result is an **exclusive or,** represented in computing as **XOR.** This means that the disjunction is false when its two parts are both true or both false, otherwise the disjunction is true. The formal structure of the *exclusive or* operator, shown in Figure 4.2–3, is an important part of computer logic.

| **BEFORE YOU GO ON** | Query: Let U and V be two simple statements. The compound statement U OR V is created. U and V cannot both be true. Is this correct? |

RESPONSE: No. The interpretation would only be correct if the compound statement were *U XOR V.*

4.2.3 Logic Gates

The logical operations of NOT, AND, OR, and XOR are illustrated by schematic diagrams called **logic gates.** Each gate has at least one *input line* (sometimes called an *input lead*). A **NOT gate** or **inverter** shows the negation operation, which simply reverses bits. A NOT gate can have only one input line because negation is a unary operation. A conjunction is represented by an **AND gate,** which must have at least two input lines. An inclusive disjunction is represented by an **OR gate,** which must have at least two input lines. An exclusive disjunction is represented by an **XOR gate,** which is restricted to two input lines. Figure 4.2–4 shows the four logic gates.

The reason each logic gate has only one output line is that it shows the single result of a logical operation. By contrast, AND and OR gates can have any finite number of inputs because AND is true only if all of its components are true,

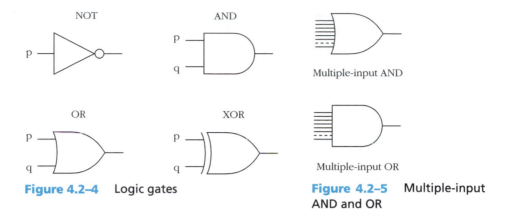

Figure 4.2–4   Logic gates

Figure 4.2–5   Multiple-input AND and OR

whereas OR is false only if all of its components are false. Therefore, AND and OR gates can look like those shown in Figure 4.2–5.

BEFORE YOU GO ON

Query: Suppose a pseudo-XOR gate has three input lines. Explain what this would mean.

RESPONSE: We can interpret an XOR gate with three inputs this way: the output is 1 (true) only when there is exactly one 1 at the input lines; otherwise it is 0 (false). That is, 100 or 010 or 001 produces a 1 output; all other combinations are 0.

4.2.4 Logic Functions Using Gates

One or more gates can be combined to make a **logic circuit,** also called a **Boolean circuit.** For instance, the input to an OR gate could be the output of a NOT gate, an XOR gate, and an AND gate, as shown in Figure 4.2–6. For example, let

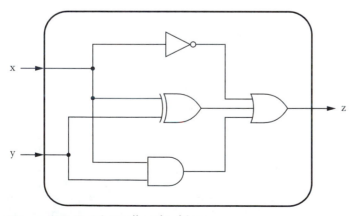

Figure 4.2–6   A small-scale chip

x and y be inputs to this logic circuit. Input x is connected to the input of the NOT gate and to one of the inputs to each of the AND and OR gates. Input y is connected to the other inputs of the AND and XOR gates. We can enclose this assemblage of gates and their connections in a rectangle to make an invented entity that may or may not have immediate practical use. We call this entity a chip. (The word *chip* is usually reserved for logic circuits with more than 1,000 gates.)

> ### PERSPECTIVE
>
> In the early days of computing, circuit boards were wired by hand to make a computer work. Breadboards, as they were called, were two feet by three feet and could hold 20 logic gates. Today a chip the size of a dime can hold millions of gates. Some computer scientists predict that in the near future chips will hold billions of gates.

And what does this chip do? Let's find out. Represent the output of this chip by a symbol, say z. Then the output of the chip is a function of x and y, which can be written symbolically as

$$z = f(x, y)$$

The function $f(x, y)$ is a **Boolean function** because its output values (the output of the OR gate) and its input values are all binary. In the design for the chip shown in Figure 4.2–6, the function is an inclusive disjunction of three inputs: the inversion (negation) of x, the exclusive disjunction of x with y, and the conjunction of x and y. Symbolically, this is written as

$$z = f(x, y) = (\text{NOT } x) \quad \text{OR} \quad (x \text{ XOR } y) \quad \text{OR} \quad (x \text{ AND } y)$$

Just as we can construct a Boolean function from a chip, so we can construct a chip from a Boolean function, as shown in the following example.

EXAMPLE 4.2–3

Problem
Given the Boolean function

$$f(u, v, w) = (u \text{ OR } v) \quad \text{AND} \quad (\text{NOT}(v \text{ XOR } w))$$

draw the corresponding logic circuit or chip.

Reasoning
The three input values for this function are: u, v, and w. The function is a conjunction of two other Boolean components: the disjunction $u \text{ OR } v$ and the negation of an exclusive disjunction $\text{NOT}(v \text{ XOR } w)$.

Solution
Draw a rectangle to display the proposed logic circuit. Show on this rectangle the three input values u, v, and w and the single output value, which we can

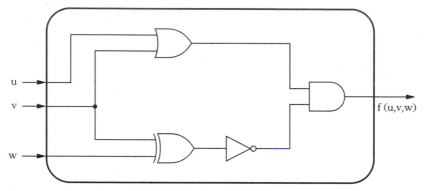

Figure 4.2–7 Logic circuit for $f(u, v, w) = (u \text{ OR } v) \text{ AND } (\text{NOT } (v \text{ XOR } w))$

arbitrarily call z. At the output, draw an AND gate with two input lines. One line is attached to an OR gate, the other to a NOT gate. An XOR gate is attached to the input of the NOT gate. Now attach to the OR gate its respective input values u and v and attach to the XOR gate its respective input values v and w. This logic circuit (chip) is shown in Figure 4.2–7.

Test
Using the process we just described, you can reconstruct the Boolean function from the chip design. Try it!   •

4.2.5 Equivalent Circuits

Sometimes we express one logic circuit in terms of another. Consider a logic circuit with one NOT gate connected to another NOT gate. When the input is 0, the first NOT gate inverts the 0 to a 1 and the second NOT gate inverts the 1 back to a 0. Likewise, when the input is 1, the first NOT gate inverts the 1 to a 0 and the second NOT gate inverts the 0 back to a 1. This is the equivalent of a single-input, single-output circuit with no gate at all. The two logic circuits are shown in Figure 4.2–8.

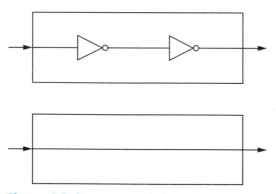

Figure 4.2–8 Two equivalent logic circuits

ANTECEDENT	CONSEQUENT	CONDITIONAL
p	*q*	IF *p* THEN *q*
0	0	1
0	1	1
1	0	0
1	1	1

Figure 4.2–9   The conditional

There are techniques for reconstructing a given logic circuit to form another one, called an **equivalent circuit** or an **equivalence.** This is done to simplify the circuit and has both theoretical and practical importance. Several of these equivalences are appropriate for this discussion.

Consider the conditional sentence:

If Carol passes the course, then she will graduate.

The sentence has two components. The *if* part is called the **antecedent** and the *then* part is called the **consequent.** The consequent is the necessary result when the antecedent is true, and when the antecedent is false, the consequent can be either true or false. For the conditional statement to be true, graduation is necessary should Carol pass the course, but not passing the course means that she either may or may not graduate. That is, the conditional is always true when the antecedent is false.

Yet a conditional sentence such as this one is often misinterpreted as *If the antecedent is not true, then the consequent is not true.* This error leads to legal disputes and quarrels in daily life. (Figure 4.2–9 shows the truth table for IF . . . THEN statements.)

BEFORE YOU GO ON	**Query:** What does the following conditional sentence mean? *If Kate gets a car loan, then she will buy the Chevy.* **RESPONSE:** This sentence in a legal contract can get buyers into trouble because it addresses only what will happen if they get the loan. If Kate gets the loan, she must buy the Chevy; if she does not get the loan, she may or may not have to buy the Chevy.

A stronger way to express conditional statements is with the biconditional. This prevents the vagueness accompanying a false antecedent. With the biconditional, if the antecedent is true, then the consequent is true, and if the consequent is true, then the antecedent is true. We write this symbolically as:

A iff *C*   which means   *A* if and only if *C*

For example, *I will pick you up if and only if it is raining* means *If it is raining, then I will pick you up, and if I pick you up, then it is raining.* Figure 4.2–10 shows the truth table for the biconditional.

STATEMENTS		BICONDITIONAL
p	*q*	*p* IFF *q*
0	0	1
0	1	0
1	0	0
1	1	1

Figure 4.2–10   The biconditional

BEFORE YOU GO ON

Query: If we say that the biconditional has the same truth as the exclusive OR, is this correct?

_____

RESPONSE: Not quite. The biconditional is in fact equivalent to the inverse (negation) of the exclusive OR.

BEFORE YOU GO ON

Query: Why is the negation of the biconditional an exclusive OR ?

_____

RESPONSE: The standard output pattern for a biconditional is

   1, 0, 0, 1

whereas the standard output pattern for the exclusive OR is

   0, 1, 1, 0

The patterns are inversions of each other.

EXAMPLE 4.2–4

Problem
Draw the logic circuit for the biconditional.

Reasoning
We can see from Figures 4.2–3 and 4.2–10 that the exclusive OR and the biconditional are each other's inverse.

Solution
Draw a logic circuit for an exclusive OR. Then put a NOT gate at the output of the exclusive OR to produce the result shown in Figure 4.2–11.

Test
Check the four input possibilities (00, 01, 10, 11) to verify that the logic circuit corresponds to the biconditional.   ●

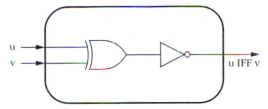

NOT (u XOR v) equivalent to u IFF v

Figure 4.2–11 Logic circuit for the biconditional

Because the biconditional is related to the exclusive OR, is the ordinary conditional related to another operation? Perhaps. Suppose the conditional is represented by the statement

IF x THEN y

where x is the antecedent and y is the consequent. Now consider the inclusive disjunction of

(NOT x) OR y

The truth tables for each of these statements are

x	y	IF x THEN y		x	y	NOT x		NOT x OR y
0	0	1		0	0	1		1
0	1	1		0	1	1		1
1	0	0		1	0	0		0
1	1	1		1	1	0		1

Notice that for the same input patterns, IF x THEN y and NOT x OR y produce the same output patterns. Thus the two expressions are equivalent.

EXAMPLE 4.2–5

Problem
Draw a logic circuit that is the equivalent of the conditional.

Reasoning
Because an IF...THEN gate does not exist, we must use the equivalent circuit using a disjunction to get the right result.

Solution
Draw the logic circuit with two inputs u and v and one output, and an OR gate to provide the inclusive disjunction. Connect the v input to one line of the OR gate and invert the u input before connecting it to the OR gate. The result is shown in Figure 4.2–12.

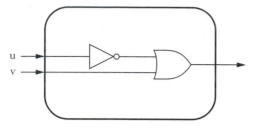

(NOT u) OR v equivalent to IF u THEN v

Figure 4.2–12   Logic circuit for the conditional

Test
Check the four input possibilities individually to verify that the logic circuit corresponds to the conditional IF . . . THEN.   •

4.2.6 Relational and Logical Operators in C

Let's now integrate our understanding of logic with our knowledge of C. C provides several relational and logical operators that can be used to compare two or more quantities. These operators are generally used in the context of decision-making statements (covered in Chapter 5). For now, we will concentrate on the use of the operators themselves.

Expressions used to compare two quantities are called relational expressions and can involve constants or variables of any data type. A relational expression consists of two operands and an intervening relational operator. Table 4.2–1 lists the relational operators in C and shows examples of their use. Note that spaces are not allowed between the symbols comprising a compound operator such as `<=`, `>=`, `==`, and `!=`.

BEFORE YOU GO ON	Query: Which of the following are not valid relational expressions in C? `15 > 3,` `size =< 20,` `time ! = 24, whole > sum_of_parts`

RESPONSE: `size =< 20`   should be   `size <= 20`
                 `time ! = 24`   should be   `time != 24`
                                     (C does not allow spaces within an operator)

Table 4.2–1   Relational Operators in C

OPERATOR SYMBOL	INTERPRETATION	EXAMPLE
<	less than	`weeks < 53`
>	greater than	`overtime > 40`
<=	less than or equal	`reg_hours  <= 3.75`
>=	greater than or equal	`salary  >= 3.75`
==	equal	`class  == 25`
!=	not equal	`answer  != 'y'`

Logically, relational expressions can be false or true, but in C they evaluate numerically either to 0 (false) or 1 (true). Although relational expressions can appear in several contexts in a C program, we usually see them in decision and looping statements, or in assignments and output statements, as shown next.

```
printf ( "%d", 12 > 15);
```

outputs 0 and

```
done  =  ( answer == 'y' );            /* parentheses added for clarity */
```

assigns the value 1 to **done** whenever the variable **answer** has the value **'y'**. The variable **done** is otherwise assigned 0. Notice the use of = and ==.

BEFORE YOU GO ON

Query: What is the difference between = and ==?

RESPONSE: = means *is assigned to* and causes the variable on the left to change its value. == means *is equivalent to* and does not cause any change in either operand.

C allows the comparison of both character data and numeric data. The results depend on the ASCII or EBCDIC values of the characters involved. For instance, all of the following relational expressions are false (evaluate to 0):

```
'd' <= 'c'      'R' == 'w'
'M' == 'm'      '1' > '1'
```

and all of the following are true (evaluate to 1):

```
'a' < 'e'      'd' <= 'd'
's' > 'p'      'q' >= 'q'
'x' != 'z'     'y' == 'y'
```

In addition to the relational operators, C also provides three logical operators,

```
&&   meaning   AND
||   meaning   OR
```

and

```
!    meaning   NOT
```

that can be used with relational expressions to form **compound relations.** (Note that in C XOR is only provided as a bitwise operator.) For instance, the following expressions are all true for teenagers:

```
age > 12  &&  age < 20
age >= 13  &&  age <= 19
age > 12  &&  age <= 19
```

And the following expresses a possible college admission requirement that the applicant's GPA be above 2.5 or the results of the applicant's SAT be above 625.

    gpa > 2.5 || sat_score > 625

Combining ANDs and ORs can be tricky. How should we interpret the following?

    gpa > 2.5 || sat_score > 625   && age > 16

Interpretation #1:

a. **gpa** > 2.5, or
b. both **sat_score** > 625 and **age** > 16

That is, if *either* condition *a* or condition *b* is true, a 14-year-old with a GPA of 2.6 can be admitted.
Interpretation #2:

a.   **gpa** > 2.5 or **sat_score** > 625, and
b.   **age** > 16

In this case *both* conditions must be met for admission so anyone 16 or under cannot be admitted.

The right interpretation is based on this **operator hierarchy** and **precedence** for logical operators:

    NOT before *AND* before *OR*

That is, negations precede conjunctions precede disjunctions. In C this can be expressed as

    !   before   &&   before ||

In addition, the relational operators <,   <=,   >, and >= have higher precedence than the relational operators == or !=. Also, all relational operators have precedence over the logical operators !,   &&, and ||.

For our example, the first interpretation is correct as far as C is concerned but probably incorrect as far as the admissions office is concerned. As in arithmetic operations, parentheses are used for clarity or to override the hierarchy. The right expression is:

    (gpa > 2.5 || sat_score > 625) && age > 16

(See Appendix D for the hierarchy and precedence of operators.)

Query: The following C-like pseudocode statement is made:

IF ((x > 1) && (x < 0)) THEN 7==6

Why is this wrong?

_____

RESPONSE: For any value of x the antecedent is false. The consequent, therefore, can be true or false. In this case 7==6 is false. The problem here is that the antecedent can never be true so the use of the conditional is moot.

An interesting aspect of negations, conjunctions, and disjunctions is the logical equivalences called DeMorgan's Laws. These laws for Boolean expressions p and q in C notation are:

Law A: !(p || q)   is equivalent to   !p && !q

Law B: !(p && q)   is equivalent to   !p || !q

Law A says that the negation of a disjunction of two statements is equivalent to the conjunction of the negation of the two statements. Law B says that the negation of a conjunction of two statements is equivalent to the disjunction of the negation of the two statements. DeMorgan's Laws can often simplify Boolean expressions, as shown in the following example.

EXAMPLE 4.2–6

Problem
Find the negation of the conditional IF x > y THEN z == 4 and draw the equivalent logic circuit.

Reasoning
Represent the antecedent x > y by the symbol p and the consequent z == 4 by the symbol q. The statement simplifies to IF p THEN q. Use C notation for logical operators and recall that IF p THEN q is equivalent to !p || q.

Solution
The given problem is !p || q. Its negation is !(!p || q). By DeMorgan's Law A

  !(!p || q)   becomes   !(!p) && !q

Because !(!p) is p, the statement reduces to p && !q. In the original problem the statement becomes x > y AND z != 4.

Test
Check that !(!p) is indeed p and that DeMorgan's Law has been followed. The logic circuit is shown in Figure 4.2–13.   ●

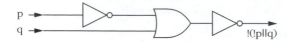

Figure 4.2–13

EXERCISES 4.2

Concept Check

Answer statements 1 through 4 with true *or* false.

1. A disjunction requires all input expressions to be true for the output to be true.
2. For a conditional statement, the consequent is true only when the antecedent is true.
3. An AND gate should be used to detect whether at least one input value is 0.
4. In C the symbol || means an exclusive OR.

For statements 5 through 8 choose the answer that best completes the statement.

5. The statement *The disk is full if and only if error message #296 is indicated* is an example of a
   a. conditional
   b. conjunctive disjunction
   c. biconditional
   d. conjunction
6. In C the expression 3 < 4 && x > y
   a. has the value 1 for all **y**
   b. is an illegal expression
   c. has the value 0 for all **x**
   d. has the value 0 for only some values of **x** and **y**
7. A conditional logic circuit
   a. has a natural gate function
   b. must be constructed as a disjunction
   c. must be constructed as a conjunction
   d. must be constructed from an exclusive OR gate
8. A mode of reasoning that starts from general principles and forms a specific conclusion is called
   a. inductive reasoning
   b. nonsense
   c. Boolean logic
   d. deductive reasoning

For statements 9 through 12 fill in the blanks with the right word.

9. A _____ is a compound statement that is true only when all of its components are true.

10. A relation in which all input values are binary and the output is binary is called a _____.

11. An XOR gate is _____ of a biconditional gate.

12. Two different Boolean expressions are said to be _____ if they have the same truth table.

Set A

Find the output for each of the following statements.

13. `printf ( "%d", (7 + 3) > 10 );`
14. `printf ( "%d", ( (3 > 7) || (3 <= 7) ) && (7 != 10) );`
15. `printf ( "%d", !( 1 * 4 == 5 ) );`
16. `printf ( "%d", (18 < 16) || (7 − 2 == 5) );`
17. `printf ( "%d", (18 < 16) && (7 − 2 == 5) );`
18. `printf ( "%d", ( (2 + 8) <= 11) && (17 * 2 == 34) );`

Set B

19. Find the output of the Boolean function $f(x, y) = $ NOT x XOR y using the standard input on two variables (00, 01, 10, 11).

20. A Boolean function is defined by $g(u, v, w) = (u$ AND $v)$ OR NOT w. Find the output using the standard input on three variables (000, 001, 010, 011, 100, 101, 110, 111).

21. Using only AND and NOT gates, design an equivalent circuit for an OR gate.

22. Using only OR and NOT gates, design an equivalent circuit for an AND gate.

23. Find the Boolean function $g(x, y)$ if $g(0, 0) = 1$, $g(0, 1) = 0$, $g(1, 0) = 1$, and $g(1, 1) = 0$.

24. Draw the logic circuit for the function described in Question 23.

25. Construct the truth table for the Boolean function f defined as $f(x, y, z) = $ (NOT x OR NOT z) AND NOT$(x$ OR $y)$.

26. Draw the logic circuit for the Boolean function in Question 25.

27. One of DeMorgan's Laws is that the negation of a conjunction is the disjunction of the negations. This can be written symbolically as NOT$(x$ AND $y) = $ NOT x OR NOT y for logical statements x and y. Draw the equivalent logic circuits for each side of the equation and construct their corresponding truth tables.

28. Another of DeMorgan's Laws is that the negation of a disjunction is the conjunction of the negations. This can be written symbolically as NOT$(x$ OR $y) = $ NOT x AND NOT y for logical statements x and y. Draw the equivalent logic circuits for each side of the equation and construct their corresponding truth tables.

Find the output for questions 29 through 34.

29. `printf ( "%d", !(12 > 8 − 2 ) );`
30. `printf ( "%d", (32 − 6 == 24) && ( !( ( (3 + 12) / 4) == 4) ) );`

31. `printf ( "%d", ( (6 * 4) + 18) == (18 + 6 * 4) );`
32. `printf ( "%d", ( ( (15 * 3) − 2) < 100) || (25 < 100) );`
33. `printf ( "%d", ( (9 − 6) + 2 * 11) <= (16 / 4 − 3) );`
34. `printf ( "%d", ! ( ( (10 + 2 * 4) >6) && (11 >(7 + 12) / 4) ));`

Set C

35. Use ordinary electronic materials (battery, wire, lamp, switches) to illustrate the meaning of a negation.
36. Use ordinary electronic materials (battery, wire, lamp, switches) to illustrate the meaning of a conjunction.
37. Use ordinary electronic materials (battery, wire, lamp, switches) to illustrate the meaning of a disjunction.
38. Write a C program to simulate any given Boolean function by generating its truth table.

4.3   MACHINE REPRESENTATION OF NUMBERS

Introduction

Computers are sometimes called **number crunchers** because they can do arithmetic calculations at incredible speeds. But numbers stored and processed by computers are not always accurately represented. For example, it is impossible to have an exact representation of 4/3 or π when they are stored in binary on a computer. Each of these numbers is an *infinite decimal* that a computer can only approximate to a finite number of decimal places. In the discussion that follows we consider the limitations of a computer and treat numbers in the context of these limitations.

4.3.1 Integers and Real Numbers

Numbers in computers are stored in memory areas of a finite length. We call these memory areas **registers.** The standard register length for many of today's personal computers and mainframes is 32 bits. Integers are generally represented in twos complement form. For example, the decimal integer +278 is represented as

00000000 00000000 00000001 00010110

and the decimal −278 is represented as

11111111 11111111 11111110 11101010

The spacing after every 8 bits enhances readability. It also conforms to an industry standard that 8 bits are grouped to form 1 byte.

BEFORE YOU GO ON

Query: What is the decimal equivalent for the following twos complement integer?

11111111 11111111 11111111 11011001

RESPONSE: Recognize that this is a negative number because its leading bit is 1. To find its decimal value, first invert the bits and then add 1, yielding 00000000 00000000 00000000 00100111. This can be converted to decimal 39. Thus, the original pattern was 39.

Integers can be represented without errors if they are in the acceptable range for the machine. For 32 bits the range for an integer N is

$$-2^{31} \le N \le 2^{31} - 1$$

BEFORE YOU GO ON

Query: Suppose a register has only 4 bits. What is the range for an integer?

RESPONSE:
$-2^3 \le N \le 2^3 - 1$ or $-8 \le N \le +7$

A **real number** in a mathematical sense is an infinite decimal. All integers, rational numbers (fractions, repeating decimals), and irrational numbers (nonrepeating decimals) are examples of real numbers. The following shows that an integer can be represented as a real number.

EXAMPLE 4.3–1

Problem
Given the real numbers 17, 22/7, and π, find their decimal equivalent.

Reasoning
In each case the number is an infinite decimal that can not be completely expressed.

Solution
The decimal equivalent for 17 is 17.000000000000000000... The decimal equivalent for 22/7 can be found by dividing the denominator into the numerator, which yields 3.142857142857142857... The decimal equivalent for π is 3.141592653589793... to 15 decimal places.

Test
The decimal equivalent for 22/7 can be found by ordinary division, has a repeating decimal pattern of ...142857..., and is a rational number. The decimal value of

π has no repeating pattern and is irrational. Notice that the *decimal* equivalent of the integer 17 has a repeating pattern of all 0s. •

PERSPECTIVE

The search for the ratio of the circumference of a circle to its diameter has been a challenge for thousands of years. This ratio, designated by the Greek letter π, is believed to be an irrational number (a nonrepeating decimal) that is approximately equal to 3.14. Current calculations on supercomputers to billions of places have shown no repetitive pattern. To 40 decimal places,

π = 3.14159 26535 89793 23846 26433 83279 50288 41972...

4.3.2 Floating-Point Numbers

A computer can not store a real number as an infinite decimal or as an infinite binary number. These numbers are represented as **floating-point** numbers that are **truncated** (chopped-off) real numbers. One difference between floating-point numbers used by computer scientists and pure real numbers used by mathematicians is that floating-point numbers have a different representation from real numbers. So, how are floating-point numbers stored?

Every floating-point number has three parts: a signature, a mantissa, and a characteristic. The **signature** (also called *sign*) indicates whether the number is positive or negative. The **mantissa** is the body of the number and denotes the number of bits or place values used to represent the number. The **characteristic** denotes the power of a base (such as base-2 or base-10) used to multiply the mantissa, usually expressed in a special coded form. Floating-point representation is much like scientific notation, a system of notation using exponentiation (discussed in Section 3.2).

EXAMPLE 4.3–2

Problem
Write the numbers $-593{,}462$ and 0.0000000359 in scientific notation.

Reasoning
In each case the number should be represented as a decimal (fractional) value with a nonzero lead digit times a power of 10.

Solution
The number $-593{,}462$ is represented as $-0.593462 * 10^6$. The number 0.0000000359 is represented as $0.359 * 10^{-7}$.

Test
Multiply each mantissa by the related power of 10 to find the original numbers. •

1	1000010	10010011110101111000010

Signature   Characteristic   Mantissa

Figure 4.3–1

In a computer numbers are represented in binary rather than in decimal, or in bits rather than in digits. There is no single accepted representation for floating-point numbers: the method varies among computer manufacturers. Attempts have been made to standardize representation such as the IEEE Floating-Point Standard 754 established in 1985. In this discussion we take a generic approach to floating-point representation with the following assumptions.

1. A floating-point register consists of 32 bits.
2. The lead bit denotes the signature: 0 for a positive or zero value and 1 for a negative value.
3. The 24 right-most bits denote the mantissa of the number.
4. The remaining 7 bits between the signature and mantissa denote a binary integer in absolute form called the **characteristic** that is used to calculate the **exponent** of a predefined base called the **radix.**

Figure 4.3–1 shows a generic register that reflects these assumptions in the bit pattern 11000010   10010011   11010111   11000010.

From the bit pattern in Figure 4.3–1, it is immediately clear that the floating-point number is negative because the lead bit is 1. The characteristic consists of the next 7 bits, 1000010, and needs interpretation. The method used to find the exponent of the radix is called **excess 2^{n-1}**, in which the characteristic (a binary integer in absolute form) represents the exponent by more than the excess of 2^{n-1}. For example, a 3-bit binary integer in absolute form ranges from 000 to 111 with decimal equivalents of 0 to +7, respectively. The excess is $2^{3-1} = 4$. The numbers being represented (the exponent) range from -4 (for 000) to +3 (for 111). In general, an n-bit binary integer in absolute form ranges from 0 to $2^n - 1$. The range of the excessed numbers is from -2^{n-1} to $+2^{n-1} - 1$. We use this convention for the exponent of the floating-point number, as shown in the following example.

EXAMPLE 4.3–3

Problem
Given the characteristic 110010 in excess form, find the value of the exponent.

Reasoning
Because there are six bits, the excess is $2^{6-1} = 2^5 = 32$, which means that the characteristic exceeds the exponent by 32.

Solution

The characteristic 110010 is the decimal equivalent of 50. In excess 32, the characteristic 50 is 32 more than the exponent so the exponent is 18.

Test

Test to see if 18 + 32 does indeed lead to the original string of 110010.   ●

In Figure 4.3–1, the 7-bit characteristic 1000010 in absolute form implies an excess of $2^{7-1} = 64$. The 7-bit characteristic is +66, which exceeds the exponent by 64. Thus the exponent is $66 - 64 = 2$.

The mantissa in Figure 4.3–1 is the 24-bit string

10010011   11010111   11000010

One way to treat this is with each bit as a place value for a power of 2. The interpretation for the first 8 bits would be

$$1 * 2^{-1} + 0 * 2^{-2} + 0 * 2^{-3} + 1 * 2^{-4} + 0 * 2^{-5} + 0 * 2^{-6} + 1 * 2^{-7} + 1 * 2^{-8}$$

and we could write

$._2 10010011$

where $._2$ is a **binary point,** meaning that the binary value to the right of the binary point is a fraction.

Because for 24 bits the process could be tedious, another way to treat the mantissa is in hexadecimal form where the interpretation for the 24 bits is six groupings, each containing 4 bits

1001   0011   1101   0111   1100   0010

represented in hexadecimal as

9   3   D   7   C   2

so the 24-bit mantissa is interpreted as

$$9 * 16^{-1} + 3 * 16^{-2} + D * 16^{-3} + 7 * 16^{-4} + C * 16^{-5} + 2 * 16^{-6}$$

We could write this as

$._h 93D7C2$

where $._h$ is a **hexadecimal point,** meaning that the hexadecimal value to the right of the hexadecimal point is a fraction.

Because of the hexadecimal grouping it is convenient to choose a radix of 16 rather than two or another value. (16^2 is more convenient for calculations than 2^8.) Continuing with the 32-bit number, the correct interpretation, with the exponent equal to +2, would be

$$-[9*16^{-1} + 3*16^{-2} + D*16^{-3} + 7*16^{-4} + C*16^{-5} + 2*16^{-6}]*16^{+2}$$
$$= -[9*16^{+1} + 3*16^0 + D*16^{-1} + 7*16^{-2} + C*16^{-3} + 2*16^{-4}]$$
$$= -[9*16^{+1} + 3*16^0 + 13*16^{-1} + 7*16^{-2} + 12*16^{-3} + 2*16^{-4}]$$
$$= -[144 + 3 + 0.8125 + 0.02734375 + 0.002929687 + 0.000030517]$$
$$= -[147 + 0.842803954]$$
$$= -147.842803954$$

EXAMPLE 4.3–4

Problem

A floating-point register contains the hexadecimal number BECA4DAB. Find its value in base-10.

Reasoning

Assume a conventional representation of the number with radix 16. The lead bit is the signature, the next 7 bits contain the characteristic in excess 64, and the remaining 24 bits contain the mantissa. The bit representation of the number is

$$1 \quad 0111110 \quad 1100 \quad 1010 \quad 0100 \quad 1101 \quad 1010 \quad 1011$$

where the lead bit equals 1, the 7-bit characteristic in excess form is +62, and the remaining 24 bits for the mantissa are as indicated.

Solution

The number is negative. The exponent is calculated as $+62 - 64 = -2$. The mantissa is represented by the hexadecimal pattern of CA4DAB, where each hexadecimal digit corresponds to its respective place value. The number can be written as

$$-[C*16^{-1} + A*16^{-2} + 4*16^{-3} + D*16^{-4} + A*16^{-5} + B*16^{-6}]*16^{-2}$$
$$= -[C*16^{-3} + A*16^{-4} + 4*16^{-5} + D*16^{-6} + A*16^{-7} + B*16^{-8}]$$
$$= -[C*16^5 + A*16^4 + 4*16^3 + D*16^2 + A*16^1 + B*16^0]*16^{-8}$$
$$= -[12*1048576 + 10*65536 + 4*4096 + 13*256 + 10*16 + 11*(1)]*16^{-8}$$
$$= -[12582912 + 655360 + 16384 + 3328 + 160 + 11]*16^{-8}$$
$$= -[13258155]*16^{-8}$$
$$= -[13258155]*(1/4294967296)$$
$$= -0.003086904$$

Test

To verify the result, convert this number to hexadecimal with the proper exponent representation. ●

4.3.3 Precision and Accuracy

The use of floating-point numbers always causes a real number to be truncated. The **precision** of the number is the number of place values used to represent that number. In the conventional representation, a real number is 32 bits, although some computers have 36-, 48-, or 60-bit words. In the conventional representation of floating-point numbers, called **single precision,** the mantissa allows for 24-bit precision. This is equivalent to 6 hexadecimal-digit precision, which is approximately 7-digit precision for decimal numbers.

BEFORE YOU GO ON

Query: Why do conventional floating-point numbers allow up to 7-digit precision for decimal numbers?

———

RESPONSE: The lowest-order bit has a place value of 2^{-24}, which can be viewed as $2^{-12} * 2^{-12} = (1/4096) * (1/4096) = 1/16{,}777{,}216$ or approximately 10^{-7}.

Precision is different from accuracy. **Accuracy** means the number of place values for which a floating-point number *approximates* a real number. For example, consider the real number π again. If π is approximated by 3.1, the approximation is accurate to two decimal places (place values). If the approximation is 3.14159, the approximation is accurate to six decimal place values. In each case the floating-point precision is seven decimal places or 24 bits. An approximating number can be precise but highly inaccurate. Likewise, an approximating number can be accurate but not precise. Accuracy is far more important than precision.

BEFORE YOU GO ON

Query: The following assignment to the single-precision (`float`) variable **x** appears in a C program

    x = 3.846357353556598562;

Why is this unreasonable?

———

RESPONSE: Because single-precision numbers are precise to only seven decimal places.

We can consider floating-point numbers as **double precision** or 64 bits. In C the double-precision numbers are typed as `double`. The construction is the same: a signature, a characteristic, and a mantissa. Because of the extra available bits we sometimes extend the characteristic to 11 bits, thereby allowing 52 bits for the mantissa. Figure 4.3–2 shows a typical double-precision number. Note that with this configuration 13 hexadecimal digits are used for the mantissa, which is one more than twice as many as for single-precision numbers.

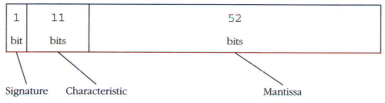

Signature   Characteristic   Mantissa

Figure 4.3–2

The finite nature of floating-point numbers can cause errors when the natural boundaries of the floating-point number are exceeded. Consider single-precision numbers. The largest exponent occurs when the characteristic is 1111111, corresponding to an exponent of +63. So the largest positive number is represented as

0   1111111   1111111111111111111111111

and is approximately equal to $+16^{63}$, which is approximately equal to $+10^{76}$.

BEFORE YOU GO ON

Query: Why is 16^{63} approximately equal to 10^{76}?

RESPONSE: One way to show this is with logarithms. Using common (base-10) logarithms, $\log 16^{63} = 63 \log 16 = 63 * 1.204 = 75.852$ and $\log 10^{76} = 76 \log 10 = 76 * 1 = 76$. A calculator shows that $16^{63} \approx 7.2 * 10^{75}$, which is almost as large as 10^{76}.

Likewise, the most negative single-precision number is

1   1111111   1111111111111111111111111

and is approximately equal to -10^{76}. Any number greater than $+10^{76}$ or less than -10^{76} causes an **overflow error.**

The smallest positive number that can be represented in single precision is theoretically

0   0000000   0000000000000000000000001

It shows a lead bit of 0, and a characteristic of 0 that represents an exponent of -64. However, computers usually **normalize** numbers so that the lead hexadecimal digit of the mantissa is not 0. From a practical standpoint, with radix 16 the smallest positive number is represented by

0   0000000   0001000000000000000000000

This means that

$$+(16^{0-64}) * (1 * 16^{-1})$$

or $+16^{-65}$, which is approximately 10^{-78}.

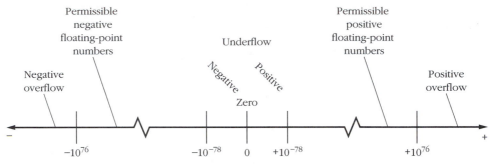

Figure 4.3–3   Ranges of overflow and underflow

BEFORE
YOU
GO ON

Query: What is the approximate value of the single-precision negative number closest to 0?

RESPONSE:
-16^{-65}

Any number that is not 0 but is in the range of -10^{-78} to $+10^{-78}$ causes an **underflow error.** Underflow and overflow errors occur because there is no machine representation of the number to be expressed. This can cause a program to terminate. Figure 4.3–3 shows the "safe" ranges for single-precision numbers and the ranges that cause overflow and underflow errors.

PERSPECTIVE

The representation of 0 in floating-point form presents a problem because any exponent of a radix multiplied by 0 is 0. An accepted convention is to represent 0 by the single-precision representation of

0   0000000   00000000   00000000   00000000   00000000

4.3.4 Machine and Program Considerations

After reading Section 4.3.3 you may be cautious about trusting a computer to handle numeric tasks. But precision and accuracy depend on the system you use, both its hardware and its software. This is why we have to test a computer for precision and accuracy before we do numeric computations. (See the Set C exercises in Section 3 of Chapter 5 for laboratory experiments with a sample program to do such testing. We recommend that you do the tests when you finish studying that chapter.)

EXERCISES 4.3

Concept Check

Answer statements 1 through 4 with true *or* false.

1. Integers in hardware are represented in the same way as floating-point numbers in hardware.
2. Floating-point numbers are always represented by 32 bits.
3. Excess 2^{n-1} is a process to estimate floating-point values beyond their range of definition.
4. The implied base of a floating-point number is called an exponent.

For statements 5 through 8 choose the answer that best completes the statement.

5. A floating-point number represented in hardware does not have one of the following components:
   a. binary point
   b. mantissa
   c. characteristic
   d. signature
6. Calculation of an integer in excess 16 means that the number has
   a. 16 bits
   b. 4 bits
   c. 5 bits
   d. 3 bits
7. Approximating a quantity within a given number of place values is called
   a. estimation
   b. accuracy
   c. precision
   d. averaging
8. An 8-bit integer in twos complement form has a range of
   a. 0 through 7
   b. −8 through 7
   c. −128 through 127
   d. 0 through 256

For statements 9 through 12 fill in the blanks with the right word.

9. The number of place values used to represent a floating-point number is called the _____ of the number.
10. The _____ of a floating-point number determines whether the number is positive or negative.
11. The _____ determines the exponent of a floating-point number.
12. In general a floating-point number that has 64 bits is called _____.

Set A

Solve each of the following problems.

13. Convert the bit pattern 10010100101011100110110110111111 to hexadecimal.
14. A floating-point number is represented as CEAF3DE4 in hexadecimal. Find the signature and the exponent.
15. A double-precision floating-point number has a hexadecimal representation of D4E3ACDE5F240FEA. Find the signature and the exponent.
16. A 6-bit mantissa has the bit pattern 100110 for radix 4. If the exponent is 3, what positive number does it represent?
17. Express π to 1-, 2-, 3-, 4-decimal place values.
18. Suppose a floating-point register has only 12 bits. If the characteristic has five bits, find the bit precision of the mantissa.

Set B

19. Calculate the decimal value of the floating-point number represented by a 7-bit characteristic with radix 16 that has the hexadecimal representation of C3DF4E.
20. Calculate the decimal value of the floating-point number represented by a 7-bit characteristic with radix 2 and with 00101011010110 as its binary representation.
21. A binary integer in twos complement form is represented as 11010111. What is the number?
22. Explain why it is unreasonable to use excess 2^k for a k-bit string.
23. A floating-point register has the hexadecimal contents of BDC40000. Find the decimal equivalent.
24. A double-precision floating-point register has the hexadecimal contents of C04A0C0000000000. Find the decimal equivalent.

Set C

25. In C we can find the size in bytes of a data type by using the C function **sizeof**. Write a C program to find the size of different numeric and character types such as **char**, **int**, **long int**, **float**, and **double**.
26. Research IEEE Floating-Point Standard 754. Write a short essay on that standard for both **float** and **double** type values.
27. The following floating-point numbers are put in 32-bit floating-point registers. Write the hexadecimal equivalent of these numbers using IEEE Standard 754.
    a. $3.72 * 10^{+3}$
    b. $8.47 * 10^{-5}$
    c. $9.31 * 10^{-8}$
    d. $4.95 * 10^{+4}$

Functions and Control Structures

Looping at highway intersection M-3 and M-25 in Staines, South of England.

After completing this chapter you should be able to do the following:

Learning Goals

- Explain what a function is and be able to write one
- Write a function with arguments and a return value
- Incorporate one-way selection structures into a program
- Explain the meaning of structured programming
- Incorporate two-way selection structures into a program
- Explain mutual exclusion
- Incorporate multiple selection using a ladder structure
- Incorporate multiple selection using a switch statement
- Distinguish looping from selection
- Use a `while` loop for conditional looping with pretesting
- Use a `do...while` loop for conditional looping with posttesting
- Use a `for` loop for iterative looping

Chapter Activity

Write a program a professor can use to post the results of a recent examination. The input is the letter grade for each student in any order. The results are counted and output in two forms. The first output summarizes the number of A's, B's, C's, D's, and F's. The second output is displayed in a bar graph like the one in Figure 5.0–1.

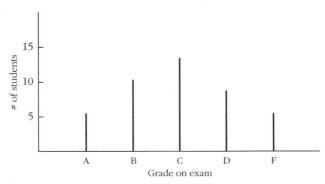

Figure 5.0–1

5.1 FUNCTIONS

Introduction

As your skills develop you can expect to be writing or cowriting relatively large and complex programs. Chapter 10, on software engineering, explores some of the techniques for designing and implementing such programs. In this section we look at one of those techniques: modularity.

A **modular** program is designed in small segments. Instead of writing one large program to solve a particular problem, the careful programmer breaks the problem down into a series of modules, each designed to do a specific task. C facilitates this modular approach through the use of functions. Computer scientists argue over the principles of software design but they agree that functions make programs easier to design, read, debug, and maintain.

You have already written at least one function, `main`, and you have used library functions such as `printf`, `scanf`, and `pow` in the programs you wrote earlier. A **function** is a program segment that is self-contained and performs a specific task. Functions are sometimes called **miniprograms** for the following reasons. First, functions can have inputs and outputs and can process information. Next, functions are usually short, typically less than a page of code, for ease of writing and debugging. Finally, functions are mostly independent of each other, just as one program is independent of another program. Most of the activities in a function are hidden from the rest of the program.

5.1.1 Writing Functions

As a first step, let's write a function that generates a set of instructions to users of Program 3.1–2 from Section 3.1.

PROGRAM 5.1–1

```
/***************************************************************************
*   Title:       area of a circle   (revisited)                          *
*   Filename:    area3.c                                                  *
*                                                                         *
*   Description: Program to compute the area of a circle. This program    *
*                reads a value representing the radius of a circle.  It   *
*                then computes the corresponding area using: "area equals *
*                pi r squared."  The area is then output.                 *
*                                                                         *
*   Input:       radius                                                   *
*   Output:      area                                                     *
*   Process:     area = pi * radius * radius                              *
*                                                                         *
*   Written by:  ...                                        Date: ...     *
***************************************************************************/
```

```c
#include   <stdio.h>
#include   <math.h>

void   instruct_user ( void );                          /* Function prototype */

main ( )
{
   const  float PI = 3.14159;

   float  radius, area;

   instruct_user ( );                                   /* Function call */

   printf (  "\nInput a value for radius: " );          /* Input */
   scanf ( "%f", &radius );

   area = PI * pow ( radius, 2 );                        /* Process */

                                                         /* Output */
   printf (  "\nFor a radius of %6.2f, the area  = %6.2f", radius, area );

   return ( 0 );
}                                                        /* End of main */



void   instruct_user ( void )                            /* Function header */
{
   printf ( "\nThis program allows you to compute the area of a circle."  );
   printf ( "\nThe user must supply a value for the radius and the program" );
   printf ( "\nwill compute the corresponding area (pi * radius squared)." );
   printf ( "\nBe sure to input a value greater than 0!!!!"                );
}                                                /* End of instruct_user */
```

The `instruct_user` function is **called** or **invoked** from `main`. The left and right parentheses are included to indicate that this is a function call and not just the name of a variable. The computer transfers control from the **caller** (the calling function) to the called function and executes whatever statements are specified. On completion of these statements, control is **returned** to the caller. In this case `main` calls `instruct_user`, the statements in `instruct_user` are processed, and control returns to `main`.

You may have seen the following statement before the beginning of `main`:

```c
void instruct_user ( void );                 /* Function prototype */
```

As indicated in the comment and explained in subsection 5.1.3, this is the **prototype** for the function. The prototype informs the compiler that a function is going to be called and what its form will be.

The `instruct_user` function is listed after the closing brace of `main`. It begins with a *header* that specifies the following.

1. data type of the function
2. name of the function
3. parameter list enclosed in parentheses

Let's analyze the header of `instruct_user`. The *data type* of a function refers to the value that is computed and returned to the caller. This function does not compute anything that `main` needs to know about; it only prints to the user. Its data type is listed as `void`, meaning that it does not return the results of any computation. The name of the function is arbitrary but like any name it should be mnemonic. Finally, the *parameter list* is a list of variable names used to store any data that might be passed to the function from the caller. Because `instruct_user` does not need any information from `main`, no variables are listed. The `void` keyword is used a second time but now it means that there are no parameters.

Like `main`, the body of a function consists of an opening and closing brace with any C statements between the braces. Although it is not shown here, functions may contain variable declarations, do assignments, and even call other functions.

The execution of `instruct_user` produces a printout of a series of messages. Once the last instruction has executed, control of the program automatically returns to the caller `main` and processing continues from there.

5.1.2 Functions with Arguments

It would not be useful if all functions were as independent of each other as `main` and `instruct_user`. Note that `instruct_user` does not contribute anything to the logic of `main`; it simply sends an informative message to the user. Most functions depend on other functions to some extent. For instance, it does not make sense to call the `pow` (**raise to the power**) function without specifying values for the base and the exponent. Moreover, `pow` is not useful unless it sends back the result of the computation. Therefore, we might say that `pow` depends on the caller to provide it with the two values (for the base and the exponent, respectively). Similarly, the caller depends on `pow` to return a meaningful result. These dependencies are sometimes called the **interface** or **communications channel** between the caller and the called function.

Sending data to a function is called **passing arguments**—that is, sending variables, constants, or expressions whose values are needed by the function. The arguments are the input data that the function needs to compute its result. This result is then returned for use by the caller.

Query: Analyze the statement `x = pow ( y, z );`

RESPONSE: The `pow` library function takes two input arguments, in this case `y` and `z`, representing the base and exponent, respectively. `pow` computes y^z and returns this as the value of the function. The return value is then assigned to the variable `x`.

Let's try writing a function that receives data when it is called. (This is shown in Program 5.1–2.) A short function is used to calculate the net pay of an employee, based on values for the wage rate and hours worked. These values are passed as arguments to a function called `calc_net_pay`. The function then computes the net pay (gross less deductions) and returns the computed value to `main`.

PROGRAM 5.1–2

```
/******************************************************************************
*  Title:       payroll                                                      *
*  Filename:    payroll.c                                                     *
*                                                                            *
*  Description: Compute the net pay for an employee, based on values         *
*               for the wage rate and number of hours worked.                *
*                                                                            *
*  Input:       wage rate, hours worked                                      *
*  Output:      net pay                                                       *
*  Process:     net pay = gross - deductions                                 *
*                  where deductions include federal tax and social security. *
*                                                                            *
*                                                                            *
*  Written by:  ...                                            Date: ...     *
******************************************************************************/

#include   <stdio.h>

float  calc_net_pay ( float wage, int hours );        /* Function prototype */

main ( )
{
  float   wage, net_pay;
  int     hours;

  printf ( "\nPayroll calculations.\nThis program determines net pay " );
  printf ( "based on wage and hours worked.\n\n" );

  printf ( "\nInput the wage rate and number of hours worked:" );/* User prompt */
  scanf ( "%f  %d", &wage, &hours );                        /* User input */
```

```
    net_pay  =  calc_net_pay ( wage, hours );                /* Function call */


                                                              /* Output results */
  printf ( "\nFor a wage of $%8.2f and %d hours worked ", wage, hours );
  printf ( "\nThe net pay = $%8.2f",  net_pay );

  return ( 0 );
}                                                             /* End of main */



/****************************************************************************
*  Function name:       calc_net_pay                                        *
*  Description:         Compute the net pay based on wage rate and          *
*                       hours worked and take deductions for federal tax and *
*                       social security.                                    *
*                                                                           *
*  Input parameters:  wage, hours                                           *
*  Output parameters: none                                                  *
*  Return value:       net_pay                                              *
****************************************************************************/

float   calc_net_pay ( float wage, int hours )            /*  Function header */
{
    float gross_pay, fed_tax, soc_security, net_pay;        /*  Function body */

    const float   FED_TAX_RATE = 0.28;
    const float   SOC_SEC_RATE = 0.055;

    gross_pay    = wage * hours;
    fed_tax      = FED_TAX_RATE * gross_pay;
    soc_security = SOC_SEC_RATE * gross_pay;
    net_pay      = gross_pay - ( fed_tax + soc_security );

    return ( net_pay );
}                                                           /*  End of calc_net_pay */
```

The `calc_net_pay` function is called from `main` and given two arguments: `wage` and `hours`. As with the previous example (`instruct_user`), once it is called, control is transferred to the function itself and processing continues from there. When control is transferred to `calc_net_pay`, the current values of the arguments are assigned, in order, to their counterparts listed in the function header.

Once inside the function, the arguments are called **parameters**. Each parameter receives its initial value from the corresponding argument. Figure 5.1–1

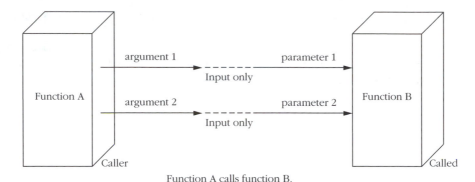

Function A calls function B.

Figure 5.1–1 Arguments and parameters

illustrates the relationship between arguments and parameters. Notice that the documentation of `calc_net_pay` refers to **output parameters**. Output parameters provide a second method (the first is `return`) for a function to communicate results back to the calling function. (We discuss output parameters more fully in Sections 7.2 and 9.2. Functions, arguments, and parameters are covered in depth in Chapter 9.)

Notice that the `FED_TAX_RATE` and `SOC_SEC_RATE` constants are declared within `calc_net_pay`. Because these values are relevant only to the function and not to `main`, they are declared there and are appropriately called **local constants**. Similarly, the variables `gross_pay`, `fed_tax`, `soc_security` and `net_pay` are called **local variables**. (Local and nonlocal variables and constants are covered in Chapter 9.)

In this example, the `wage` and `hours` argument names are the same as the corresponding parameter names. This is not a C requirement and in fact we sometimes have to use different names, as for widely used utility functions such as `pow` and `scanf`. Because for these functions we have no way of knowing what argument names will be used on any given call, we make the parameter names different from the argument names.

PERSPECTIVE

When the names of the arguments in the call are different from the names of the parameters in the function, the same function can be called in different ways. For example, all of the following are legitimate calls to `calc_net_pay`.

```
net_pay = calc_net_pay ( 5.0,  40   );
net_pay = calc_net_pay ( wage, 35   );
net_pay = calc_net_pay ( 7.5,  hours );
net_pay = calc_net_pay ( x,    y    );
```
(continued)

Regardless of the variables or constants used to call the function, there is still only one function, calc_net_pay, with the wage and hours parameters. The names of the calling arguments do not matter as long as they logically correspond to the parameters in the function header.

The parameters are listed in the function header along with their respective data types. In addition, the function itself is preceded by a data type, in this case float. Recall that the data type specified in the function header determines the data type of its return value net_pay. After the header, the function body begins with a left brace and ends with a closing right brace.

As before, any C statements can be between the braces. Definitions of other functions, however, cannot appear in the body of a given function. This means that you cannot nest function definitions in C. Functions can call other functions, but all function definitions must be listed sequentially in the program.

The statements in the body of calc_net_pay calculate the net pay just as they might if these same statements had been written in **main**, but you supply a **return** statement and a single value to be returned to the caller when that function has finished. The return value is critical because it is the only way the function can return data directly to the caller. (Chapter 9 explores a method for *indirectly* returning more than one value from a function.)

BEFORE YOU GO ON

Query: What happens if the calc_net_pay function is given negative values for either wage or hours?

RESPONSE: The function calculates the net pay—even if this produces a negative paycheck! As shown later in this chapter and in Chapter 2, this is why you have to make sure that any data the user enters to a program are checked to see that they are reasonable.

Notice the use of documentation at the beginning of the calc_net_pay function. This is important in high-quality programs and has a use similar to the documentation for **main**. Here you supply the function name, a brief description of the function's purpose, the input parameters, the output parameters, and the return value. In this way the documentation summarizes the communications between the caller and the function itself. In-line comments should also be used to clarify the activities performed within the function.

5.1.3 Function Prototypes

The **function prototype** is needed for all ANSI C programs and declares the function interface. The prototype is basically the same as the function header: It lists the function's data type, the name, and the list of parameters with their respective data types. The prototype ensures that the arguments from the function call match the parameters in the function header. For instance, a prototype enables conversion of an integer argument in the function call to a `float` parameter in the function itself. Likewise, a syntax error can be issued if an attempt is made to call a function with three arguments when the prototype indicates that there are only two parameters.

PERSPECTIVE

The names of the parameters do not have to be mentioned in a prototype, only their data types. We list the names here for consistency as they appear in the function header. The best way to write the prototype is to use a text editor and make a copy of the header (don't forget to put a semicolon at the end of the prototype). Doing so ensures that the header and prototype match exactly.

The placement of the prototype determines the accessibility of the function to other functions. Placing a prototype **globally** (outside a function) allows any other function to call it. Placing it **locally** (inside a function) allows only that function to call it. In the programs we just discussed and throughout this text, the prototypes are placed globally, allowing any function to access any other function. Doing so also reduces some of the clutter from `main`.

EXERCISES 5.1

Concept Check

Answer statements 1 through 4 with true *or* false.
1. The function header and the function call have identical syntax.
2. Functions are called miniprograms because they are usually short and have input, output, and computations.
3. Arguments and the corresponding parameters are sometimes called the interface.
4. Function prototypes are no longer needed.

For statements 5 through 8 choose the answer that best completes the statement.
5. Each parameter receives its initial value
   a. in the function body
   b. from a corresponding argument in the function call
   c. from a `#define` or `const` statement in the function
   d. from a set of assignment statements in the calling function
6. According to the principles of software design, functions
   a. should compute at least two results to be worth the overhead
   b. should be short and compute one result
   c. should be as long as necessary but compute one result
   d. are not really necessary for good software design

7. A function prototype
   a. is an outline of the purpose of the function
   b. is the same as the function header
   c. is the same as the function call
   d. is not necessary in ANSI C
8. Arguments and their corresponding parameters
   a. must have the same names
   b. are independent of each other
   c. should logically represent the same information
   d. are usually not needed in C programs

For statements 9 through 12 fill in the blanks with the right word.

9. The use of _____ parameters and a _____ value creates an interface between two functions.
10. The arguments are listed in the _____.
11. The parameters and their data types are listed in both the _____ and the _____.
12. Use the _____ data type when the function does not return a value.

Set A

13. C includes a function called **sqrt** that returns the square root of its parameter. Write the prototype for **sqrt** assuming that the parameter has a **double** data type and the function returns a **double** value.
14. Assuming that its parameters are the **double** data type, write a function header for the **pow** power function.
15. Modify the call to **calc_net_pay** to include an additional argument representing overtime hours worked. Write the revised prototype.
16. Show several different function calls for Exercises 13 through 15.

Set B

Solve each of the following problems.

17. Rewrite Program 5.1–2, expanding the instructions to the user (for example, tell the user to enter reasonable values and that the net pay reflects deductions for federal tax and social security). Put the instructions in a function.
18. Write a function that returns the mean of its six input parameters.
19. Write a function that converts the input parameter representing degrees Fahrenheit to its Celsius equivalent. Return the converted temperature.

Set C

20. Implement on the computer any of the Set B problems.

5.2 SELECTION STRUCTURES

Introduction

Recall that the algorithmic structure of selection is discussed in Section 2.2.4 and that Section 4.2.6 covers the construction of relational and logical expressions whose value can be interpreted as true or false. Next, we explore the application of these expressions to program decision making.

5.2.1 One-Way Selection Using the if Statement

Section 2.2.4 develops the pseudocode for the IF selection statement. This enables an algorithm to selectively execute a group of statements depending on a contingency that might or might not arise. We can use the same capability with slightly different syntax by means of the `if` statement:

Syntax: if (expression)
           statement

For example, to print the word `Overtime!` when the hours are greater than 40, we would write

```
if ( hours > 40 )
    printf ( "Overtime!\n" );
```

As in the pseudocode version, the *expression* acts as a kind of gate: If the *expression* is true, then the *statement* is executed; otherwise the statement is ignored.

PERSPECTIVE

In C the *true* state is any value other than 0. In the `if` statement that follows, `printf` executes for any value of `x` other than 0.

```
if ( x )
    printf ( "So, this is the truth!\n" );
```

The `if` statement can be visualized using a **structured flowchart,** as shown in Figure 5.2–1.

A box around the flowchart shows that this is a **structured** operation. One entrance is at *A* and one exit is at *B*. There is no other way to get to the statement except through the gate.

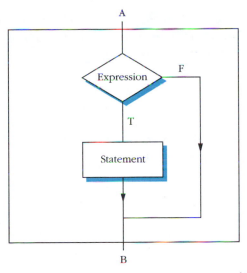

Figure 5.2–1 if statement structured flowchart

BEFORE YOU GO ON	Query: Why is it important to write well-structured programs?
	RESPONSE: The use of structured programming helps to design and debug a program because it limits the accessibility of a particular statement. When analyzing an if statement, the person debugging the program knows that if the statement executes, that can only mean that the expression was true. Conversely, if the expression is true, then the statement executes.

| BEFORE YOU GO ON | Query: The following is supposed to cause an action whenever x is greater than y.

    `if ( x > y ) then`
        `printf ( "x is greater than y" );`

Why is this wrong?

RESPONSE: Unlike other languages, in C the if statement does not use the then keyword. |

| BEFORE YOU GO ON | Query: The following is supposed to cause an action whenever x is equal to y.

    `if ( x = y )`
        `printf ( "x equals y" );`

Is there anything wrong with this?

RESPONSE: This is a common mistake in C. The expression mistakenly uses the assignment operator = instead of a relational operator ==. The effect is to assign the value of y to x.

                                       (continued) |

> The expression then takes on the value of the assignment. If **y** happens to be 0, the assignment makes **x** equal 0. Because 0 is interpreted as *false*, the `printf` statement cannot execute even though **x** does in fact equal **y**!

Note that in C a statement can be simple (one statement) or **compound**. A compound statement is one or more statements surrounded by left and right braces. A compound statement can be used wherever a simple statement can be used. The semicolon is not needed after the closing brace of a compound statement. For example, consider the following problem.

EXAMPLE 5.2–1

Problem

The current luxury tax on cars is 10 percent but the tax is applied only to the portion of the sales price over $30,000. Write a program to calculate the tax for a given sales price.

Reasoning

This problem needs one input representing the sales price of the car. The decision has to be made in the program as to whether the luxury tax is appropriate. If so, the amount of the price over $30,000 is calculated and this is the amount to be taxed.

Formal statement

      Input: cost of car
      Output: tax, if any
      Process: tax = 10% of cost over $30,000

Solution

Algorithm
      Step 1:   INPUT cost
      Step 2:   IF cost > $30,000
                   a. tax = (cost − $30,000) * tax_rate
                   b. OUTPUT tax
      Step 3:   STOP

PROGRAM 5.2–1

```
/*******************************************************************************
*  Title:      luxury tax calculation                                         *
*  Filename:   luxury.c                                                        *
*                                                                             *
*  Description: Compute the applicable luxury tax on a vehicle.                *
*                                                                             *
```

```
*  Input:       cost of car                                                    *
*  Output:      tax                                                            *
*  Process:     tax = 10% of cost in excess of $30,000                         *
*                                                                              *
*  Written by:  ...                              Date: ...                     *
***************************************************************************/

#include  <stdio.h>

main (  )
{
  const float CUT_OFF    = 30000;
  const float TAX_RATE   = 0.1;

  float cost, tax;

  printf ( "\nLuxury tax computer...Enter cost of car: " );
  scanf ( "%f",  &cost );

  if ( cost > CUT_OFF ) {
      tax =  ( cost - CUT_OFF ) * TAX_RATE;
      printf ( "\nFor a car costing $%8.2f, a luxury tax of $%8.2f is due.", cost, tax );
  }

  printf ( "\nThank you for helping the economy." );

  return ( 0 );
}
```

Test

A test consists of inputting at least three values—one smaller than $30,000, one equal to $30,000, and one larger than $30,000—and checking that the correct values are output. •

Notice the use of prettyprinting to separate the statements that make up the if body from the if control expression itself. Indenting these statements three spaces is one of the simplest and most effective ways to improve a program's readability.

5.2.2 Two-Way Selection Using the if...else Statement

The second form of the if statement allows for two-way selection and follows the same general format as the pseudocode IF...ELSE statement:

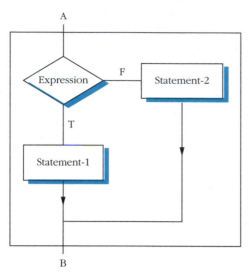

Figure 5.2–2 `if...else` statement structured flowchart

Syntax: if (expression)
                statement 1
            else
                statement 2

For example, to find the larger of two variables you can use an `if...else` statement:

```
if ( x > y )
        max = x;                        /* NOTE: semicolon required here! */
else
        max = y;
```

As with the one-way `if`, statement 1 executes only if the expression is true. The two-way `if` provides a second alternative listed after the keyword `else`. As before, we can make statement 1 and statement 2 either single or compound by placing braces appropriately. The two-way `if` is diagramed in Figure 5.2–2.

The Figure 5.2–2 flowchart shows **mutual exclusion** or **exclusive or** because exactly one branch executes depending on how the expression is evaluated. The following example explains two-way selection.

EXAMPLE 5.2–2

Problem

Write a program to compute an employee's gross pay based on the wage rate and number of hours worked. Allow for overtime wages of 1.5 times the normal rate for all overtime hours worked.

Reasoning

The difficulty here is the overtime. Regular time is assumed to be 40 hours, whereas overtime is assumed to be hours over 40. This leads to

Formal statement

Input:	wage, hours	
Output:	gross	
Process:	gross = wage * hours + overtime (if any)	

Solution

Algorithm

Step 1: INPUT wage, hours
Step 2: IF hours ≤ regular_hours
      gross = wage * hours
    ELSE
      a. overtime_hours = hours − regular_hours
      b. overtime_pay = overtime_hours * overtime_rate
      c. gross = wage * regular_hours + overtime_pay
Step 3: OUTPUT gross
Step 4: STOP

Step 2 uses a function to compute the gross pay.

PROGRAM 5.2-2

```
/*****************************************************************************
*  Title:      payroll calculation                                         *
*  Filename:   payroll.c                                                    *
*                                                                          *
*  Description: Compute a person's gross pay including overtime.           *
*                                                                          *
*  Input:      wage, hours                                                 *
*  Output:     gross pay                                                   *
*  Process:    gross pay  =  wage * hours  +  overtime                     *
*                                                                          *
*  Written by:  ...                              Date: ...                 *
*****************************************************************************/

#include <stdio.h>

float  calc_gross_pay  ( float wage,  int hours );          /* Prototype */

main ( )
{
   float  wage, gross_pay;
   int    hours;
```

```
    printf ( "\n\nPayroll...Enter wage rate and hours worked: " );
    scanf ( "%f %d",    &wage,    &hours );

    gross_pay = calc_gross_pay ( wage, hours );          /* Function call */
                                                         /* Output results */
    printf ( "\nFor a wage of $%8.2f and %d hours worked ", wage, hours );
    printf ( "\nThe gross pay = $%8.2f",   gross_pay );


    return ( 0 );
}                                                        /* End of main */



/*****************************************************************************
 * Function name:     calc_gross_pay                                         *
 * Description:       Compute the gross pay, including overtime.             *
 *                                                                          *
 * Input parameters:  wage, hours                                           *
 * Output parameters: none                                                   *
 * Return value:      gross pay                                             *
 *****************************************************************************/

float calc_gross_pay ( float  wage,  int  hours )
{
    const int   REG_HOURS     = 40;
    const float OVERTIME_RATE = 1.5;

    float  gross_pay, overtime_hours, overtime_pay;

    if ( hours  <=  REG_HOURS )
        gross_pay  =  wage * hours;

    else {
        overtime_hours  =  hours  -  REG_HOURS;
        overtime_pay    =  wage * overtime_hours * OVERTIME_RATE;
        gross_pay       =  wage * REG_HOURS  +  overtime_pay;
    }

    return ( gross_pay );
}                                               /* End of calc_gross_pay */
```

Test

Test this program by running it with at least three values for hours: <40, =40, >40. Keep in mind that this program computes the gross pay even if the values for **wage** and **hours** are impossible—for example, −10 hours/week, 500 hours/week, $−5/hour, or $100,000/hour—or almost impossible! A high-quality program would check these values before calculating **gross_pay**.

5.2.3 Multiple Selection Using the if Ladder

Sometimes you must test more than two conditions. For example, a program designed to accept input from a **menu** must allow for multiple input possibilities from the user. (See Figure 5.2–3.)

We can handle this with the **ladder** structure, which is a series of nested `if...else` statements. A ladder used to convert a month number to a month name is

```
printf ( "Input month number: " );
scanf  ( "%d", &month );

if ( month == 1 )
     printf ( "January" );
else if ( month == 2 )
     printf ( "February" );
else if ( month == 3 )
     printf ( "March" );
else if ( month == 4 )
     printf ( "April" );
else if ( month == 5 )
     printf ( "May" );
else if ( month == 6 )
     printf ( "June" );
else if ( month == 7 )
     printf ( "July" );
else if ( month == 8 )
     printf ( "August" );
else if ( month == 9 )
     printf ( "September" );
else if ( month == 10 )
     printf ( "October" );
else if ( month == 11 )
     printf ( "November" );
else if ( month == 12 )
     printf ( "December" );
else
     printf ( "Error in month number!!!!" );
```

```
    Menu Program
1)  Word Processing
2)  Spreadsheet
3)  Database
4)  Programming in C
5)  Quit
Please indicate your selection:
```

Figure 5.2–3   Menu program screen display

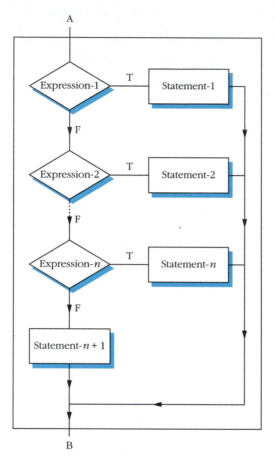

Figure 5.2–4   Ladder structure

The ladder is diagrammed in Figure 5.2–4. Notice that this structure is a further example of mutual exclusion in that only one path executes. When a true path is found, the corresponding statement or compound statement executes and the program skips over the rest of the structure. Thus, the evaluation is **short circuited** as soon as one of the expressions is found to be true. The final **else**, although not necessary, is often included as a default case and executes only if none of the expressions is true.

BEFORE YOU GO ON

Query: What is the difference between the ladder in Figure 5.2–4 and the series of one-way if statements shown next:

```
if ( expression 1 )
    statement 1


if ( expression 2 )
    statement 2
```

(continued)

> ```
>                 ...
>         if ( expression n )
>             statement n
> ```
> _____
>
> RESPONSE: The one-way `if` series is not as efficient as the ladder and does not show mutual exclusion because more than one statement can execute. In fact, all the expressions could be true, so each `if` statement has to be checked to determine its logical value.

As a final example of the ladder, let's convert the sales commission problem from Example 2.2–3 into C using a function to find the appropriate pay rate.

P R O G R A M   5 . 2 – 3

```c
/*******************************************************************************
 *  Title:       sales commission                                             *
 *  Filename:    sales.c                                                       *
 *                                                                            *
 *  Description: Compute a sales commission based on the number of sales.      *
 *                                                                            *
 *  Input:       # sales                                                       *
 *  Output:      commission                                                    *
 *  Process:     commission = #sales * rate                                    *
 *                    where rate varies with # sales                           *
 *                                                                            *
 *  Written by:  ...                                    Date: ...             *
 *******************************************************************************/

#include   <stdio.h>

int   find_rate ( int  num_sales );                        /*  Prototype */

main ( )
{
  int    num_sales, rate, commission;

  printf ( "\n\nSales commission...Input number of sales this week: " );
  scanf ( "%d",   &num_sales );                            /* User input */

  rate  =  find_rate ( num_sales );                        /*  Function call */

  commission  =  num_sales * rate;                         /* Compute commission */

  printf ( "\nFor sales of %d, the commission = $%d", num_sales, commission );

  return ( 0 );
}                                                          /*  End of main */
```

```
/***************************************************************************
 *  Function name:      find_rate                                          *
 *  Description:        Find the pay rate, according to the # of sales     *
 *                      made.                                              *
 *                                                                         *
 *  Input parameters:   num_sales                                          *
 *  Output parameters:  none                                              *
 *  Return value:       rate                                              *
 ***************************************************************************/

int     find_rate ( int num_sales )
{
    const int QUOTA      = 15;
    const int LOW_RATE   =  8;
    const int AVE_RATE   = 12;
    const int HI_RATE    = 16;

    int     rate;

    if ( num_sales < QUOTA )
        rate  =  LOW_RATE;

    else if (  num_sales  ==  QUOTA )
        rate  =  AVE_RATE;

    else
        rate  =  HI_RATE;

    return ( rate );
}                                                    /*  End of find_rate */
```

Note that the ladder is not a new syntactic component but an accepted programming convention that we can interpret through prettyprinting. The ladder for selecting month names could be written

```
if ( month == 1 )
    printf ( "January" );
else
    if ( month == 2 )
        printf ( "February" );
    else
        if ( month == 3 )
            printf ( "March" );
        else
            if ( month == 4 )
                printf ( "April" );
```

```
else
   if ( month == 5 )
       printf ( "May" );
   else
      if ( month == 6 )
          printf ( "June" );
      else
         if ( month == 7 )
             printf ( "July" );
         else
            if ( month == 8 )
                printf ( "August" );
            else
               if ( month == 9 )
                   printf ( "September" );
               else
                  if ( month == 10 )
                      printf ( "October" );
                  else
                     if ( month == 11 )
                         printf ( "November" );
                     else
                        if ( month == 12 )
                            printf ( "December" );
                        else
                            printf ( "Error in month number!!!!" );
```

This ladder is harder to read than the first, so the left-justified (rather than nested) construction is adopted in this text.

5.2.4 Multiple Selection Using the switch Statement

We can use the `if...else` ladder whenever multiple mutual exclusion is needed. The expressions that make up the ladder have no restrictions and can include any data type and any kind of arithmetic or logical operation. Sometimes we may want to test the value of a single integer variable or expression that can only produce a small set of outcomes, as in a program that offers the user a menu of choices (Figure 5.2–3). In this case, we can use the cleaner `switch` statement to handle multiple mutual exclusion:

Syntax: switch (expression) {
             case value 1:   statement 1
             case value 2:   statement 2
                . . .
             case value n: statement n
             default: statement x
         }

For example, a menu can have a choice of one of several programming applications. Using the `switch` statement we would write

```
switch ( choice ) {
    case 1:  printf ( "Word Processing" );
             break;                    /*  Needed to prevent C from  */
                                       /*  "falling through" to the   */
                                              /*  next case selection  */
    case 2:  printf ( "Spreadsheet" );
             break;

    case 3:  printf ( "DataBase" );
             break;

    case 4:  printf ( "Program in C" );
             break;

    case 5:  printf ( "Quit" );
             break;

    default: printf ( "Error");
}
```

The `switch` keyword causes the program to evaluate the associated expression. Note that the expression must produce an integer value or else a compiler error results. Variables of `char` data type are stored as integers and are acceptable in a `switch` expression.

In the `switch` statement the `case` keyword is used to label each value that is compared to the value produced by the `switch` expression. A match is sought between the value of the `switch` expression and in turn each `case` value. If a match is found, all of the statements execute that are associated with the `case` value. If no match is found, the whole `switch` statement is ignored. An optional `default` case value is allowed whose associated statements execute if no previous match is found. If the `default` label is included it usually comes after all other `case` labels. Note that braces are *not* needed around statements following a `case` label.

A match means that no further testing of `case` labels is done. Instead, all the remaining statements in the body of the `switch` statement execute until either the end of the entire `switch` statement is reached or an optional `break` statement is reached. The `break` statement, which can be used in any C control structure, terminates the structure. It is usually put at the end of each `case` statement group. Unlike most languages, such as Pascal, C requires a `break` statement to prevent the program from "falling through" to the succeeding `case` labels. Consider the following.

```
scanf ( "%d",   &invalue );
switch ( invalue ) {
    case -1:  printf ( "\nInput value = -1" );
              break;
    case 0:   printf ( "\nInput value = 0" );
              break;
    case 1:
    case 2:
    case 3:
    case 4:   printf ( "\nInput value between 1 - 4" );
              break;
    default:  printf ( "\nInput value <-1 or > 4" );
}
```

In this example there are three expected case values: -1, 0, and 1 through 4. The absence of a **break** statement for case values 1, 2, and 3 means that if any of those numbers happens to be the value of **invalue**, the program falls through to case value 4 and executes the statements there, ending with **break**. Any other input value is caught by the **default** label, which does not need a **break** statement if it is listed last (many programmers insert one for consistency).

Note that the use of **break** violates the **one way in and one way out** principle of structured programming. We take the position that the **switch** statement is the only C construction in which it is acceptable, even necessary, to use **break**. As a final example consider the following program, written first with an **if...else** ladder, then with a **switch** statement. The program inputs a letter representing a color name and outputs its color complement, as though from a color wheel. For instance, an input of **R(ed)** generates an output of **Green.** A **void** function (one without a return value) is used to output the color complement for any given color choice.

PROGRAM 5.2–4

```
/*******************************************************************************
 * Title:        color complements (ladder version)                          *
 * Filename:     color1.c                                                     *
 *                                                                            *
 * Description:  Input a color and output its complement.                     *
 *                                                                            *
 * Input:        color value                                                  *
 * Output:       color complement value                                       *
 * Process:      determine complement of input color                         *
 *                                                                            *
 * Written by:   ...                              Date: ...                   *
 *******************************************************************************/

#include <stdio.h>

void show_complement ( char choice );                        /* Prototype */
```

```
main ( )
{
  char    choice;

  printf ( "\nThis program will determine the color complement of your choice\n" );
  printf ( "\nInput a color choice: (B)lue, (G)reen, (O)range, (P)urple, (R)ed >" );
  scanf  ( "%c",  &choice );

  printf ( "\nThe complement of your color is:" );

  show_complement ( choice );                                    /*  Function call  */

  return ( 0 );
}                                                                /*  End of main  */



/****************************************************************************************
 *  Function name:       show_complement                                              *
 *  Description:         Display the complement of the input color choice.            *
 *                                                                                    *
 *  Input parameters:  choice of color                                                *
 *  Output parameters: none                                                           *
 *  Return value:       none                                                          *
 ****************************************************************************************/

void    show_complement ( char choice )
{
  if      ( choice == 'B'  ||  choice == 'b' )
      printf ( "Orange" );

  else if ( choice == 'G'  ||  choice == 'g' )
      printf ( "Red" );

  else if ( choice == 'O'  ||  choice == 'o' )
      printf ( "Blue" );

  else if ( choice == 'P'  ||  choice == 'p' )
      printf ( "Yellow" );

  else if ( choice == 'R'  ||  choice == 'r' )
      printf ( "Green" );

  else
      printf ( "\nError in color choice!!" );
}                                                    /*  End of  show_complement  */
```

Program 5.2–5 illustrates the solution using a `switch` statement.

PROGRAM 5.2–5

```
/*******************************************************************************
 *  Title:           color complements  (switch version)                      *
 *  Filename:        color2.c                                                  *
 *                                                                             *
 *  Description:     Input a color and output its complement.                  *
 *                                                                             *
 *  Input:           color value                                              *
 *  Output:          color complement value                                   *
 *  Process:         output complement of input color                         *
 *                                                                             *
 *  Written by:      ...                              Date: ...                *
 *******************************************************************************/

#include  <stdio.h>

void  show_complement ( char  choice );                        /* Prototype */

main ( )
{
  char   choice;

  printf ( "\nThis program will determine the color complement of your choice\n" );
  printf ( "\nInput a color choice: (B)lue, (G)reen, (O)range, (P)urple, (R)ed >" );
  scanf ( "%c", &choice );

  printf ( "\nThe complement of your color is:" );

  show_complement (  choice );                                 /* Function call */

  return ( 0 );
}                                                              /* End of main */




/*******************************************************************************
 *  Function name:    show_complement                                          *
 *  Description:      Display the complement of the input color choice.         *
 *                                                                             *
 *  Input parameters: choice of color                                          *
 *  Output parameters: none                                                    *
 *  Return value:     none                                                     *
 *******************************************************************************/
```

```
void  show_complement ( char  choice )
{
   switch ( choice )  {

      case 'B':
      case 'b': printf (  "Orange"  );break;

      case 'G':
      case 'g': printf (  "Red" );break;

      case 'O':
      case 'o': printf (  "Blue" );break;

      case 'P':
      case 'p': printf (  "Yellow" );break;

      case 'R':
      case 'r': printf (  "Green" );break;

      default : printf (  "\nError in choice!!" );
   }
}                                          /*  End of  show_complement  */
```

Although it is more complicated to learn, use of a **switch** can result in simpler code than the equivalent ladder.

EXERCISES 5.2

Concept Check

Answer statements 1 through 4 with true *or* false.
1. All expressions in C, logical and arithmetic, evaluate to numeric values.
2. The **if...then** statement is used for one-way selection in C.
3. Structured programming allows total access to individual statements.
4. The ladder structure facilitates testing by mutual exclusion.

For statements 5 through 8 choose the answer that best completes the statement.
5. Structured programming
    a. is hard to follow but worthwhile
    b. calls for **one way in, one way out** structures
    c. makes debugging difficult
    d. relies heavily on **goto** statements
6. The statement **if (x = 0) printf ("X = 0");**
    a. is incorrect syntax
    b. is correct syntax, but **X = 0** will never print
    c. causes a run-time error
    d. has no effect on the program

7. Two-way selection in C
   a. is not possible
   b. is acceptable but poor style
   c. cannot be used directly but can be simulated by a series of `if...else` statements
   d. allows mutual exclusion
8. The C `switch` statement
   a. can always be used as a substitute for the more clumsy ladder structure
   b. can be used only with an `if...else` statement
   c. is most useful when testing a variable having a limited range of possibilities
   d. all of the above

For statements 9 through 12 fill in the blanks with the right word.

9. When evaluating a ladder structure, the program stops testing after the first true expression is found. This is called _____.
10. The _____ statement behaves like the logical operator XOR.
11. The _____ statement can sometimes be used as an alternative to the ladder structure.
12. The _____ statement is used to exit from a control structure.

Set A

Solve each of the following problems by writing a function in C.

13. Output the appropriate messages depending on whether the variable `answer` has a value of T or F.
14. Output the appropriate messages depending on whether the value of a variable is odd or even. (Hint: compute the value of the variable modulo two.)
15. Output the appropriate messages depending on whether the value of a character variable is in the first half of the alphabet (A–M) or in the second half (N–Z).

Set B

Solve each of the following problems by writing a function in C.

16. Input an integer. Output the appropriate messages depending on whether the number is positive, negative, or zero.
17. Input a character. Output the appropriate messages depending on whether the character is a vowel or a consonant.
18. Write a `switch` statement that outputs messages indicating what day has been numerically input (for example, 1 → Monday, 2 → Tuesday...).
19. Write a function that returns a 0 if parameter 2 is a multiple of parameter 1. Otherwise return a 1. Hint: Use the `%` (modulo) operator.
20. Write the `isdigit` function to return a 1 if the character parameter is in the range of '0' to '9'. Otherwise return a 0.

Set C

21. Implement on the computer any of the Set A or Set B problems.

5.3 LOOPING STRUCTURES

Introduction

Now we come to the last of the three tools needed to convert algorithms to programs: looping structures. Recall from Section 2.2.5 that a **looping structure** enables repeating an algorithm or program segment. Recall also the two kinds of loops: conditional and iterative. The conditional loops provided in C are the `while` and `do` statements, and the iterative loop is the `for` statement.

5.3.1 Conditional Looping Using the while Statement

A **conditional loop,** sometimes called an **indefinite loop,** is one whose continued execution depends on the value of a logical expression. The syntax of the `while` statement takes the form

```
while (expression)
    statement
```

In other words, as long as the expression is true, the statement continues to execute. More specifically, the *expression* is evaluated and if it is false (evaluates to 0), the structure is skipped. If the expression is true (evaluates to non-0), the statement executes. The statement can be simple or compound enclosed in braces. Once the statement executes, control is automatically returned to the expression, which is then reevaluated. If it is false, the loop is terminated; otherwise the entire structure is repeated. This is diagrammed in Figure 5.3–1.

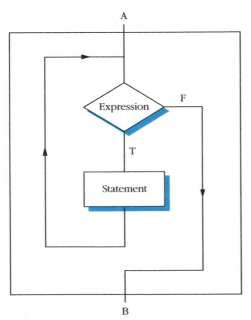

Figure 5.3–1   `while` statement structured flowchart

Consider the example

```
while ( number != 999 ) {
    printf ( "\nInput value = %d", number );
    scanf ( "%d", &number );
}
```

As long as the user does not type 999, this loop continues to output the input value (**echo** the input) and request another input value. You may wonder what is output for `number` on the first entry into the loop. Because `number` is not given a specific value before the loop, its value is indeterminate!

Query: What happens if by chance the value of `number` is 999 before the loop?

RESPONSE: The loop is ignored because the expression is false the first time it is entered.

Query: What happens when this loop executes:

```
x = 0;
while ( x < 100 ); x++;
```

RESPONSE: It is an infinite loop! The erroneous semicolon after the `while` expression is interpreted by C as the loop body. Because `x` does not change in the loop, the `while` expression is always true.

The example we just discussed illustrates an important rule for `while` loops: the variable tested in the expression should be **primed** or **initialized** before entry into the loop. So the example should have been written

```
printf ( "\nInput a number, 999 to stop." );
scanf ( "%d", &number );

while ( number != 999) {
    printf ( "\nInput value = %d", number );
    scanf ( "%d", &number );
}
```

This means that the input statements must be programmed twice but it is a necessary overhead for the `while` loop. A second rule for `while` loops is that the variable whose value is tested within the expression must be changed somewhere in the loop body. Consider the example

```
printf ( "\nInput a number, 999 to stop" );
scanf ( "%d", &number );
```

```
while ( number != 999)   {                        /* Infinite loop! */
   printf ( "\nInput value = %d", number );
   printf ( "\nValue squared = %d", number*number );
}
```

Here **number** is initialized outside the loop but never changed inside the loop body. Notice that the second **printf** statement does not change the *stored* value of **number**; it simply squares it for output purposes. If the user does not enter 999 before the **while** statement, the loop executes indefinitely. This is called an **infinite loop** and can be stopped only by pressing a special control sequence on the keyboard (for example, **break** or **control-Y**) that is unique to each computer system. Stopping a program in this fashion is called a **nongraceful exit!**

The **while** loop is useful when the number of repetitions is not known in advance. A typical application is input testing. Recall that one principle of structured programming is to check every incoming value for validity. If any value is out of range, alert the user and allow reentry of the data. You could use an **if** statement, as in the following example, in which a value is entered that represents the radius of a circle.

```
printf ( "\nInput a positive value for the radius" );
scanf  ( "%f", &radius );

if ( radius <= 0 ) {
   printf ( "\nError in radius...Re-enter >" );
   scanf  ( "%f", &radius );
}
```

The last example does not allow for a second or third mistake. You cannot know in advance how many tries it will take for the user to follow the instructions! For this reason, a **while** loop is preferable, as shown in the following program segment.

```
printf ( "\nInput a positive value for the radius" );
scanf  ( "%f", &radius );

while ( radius <= 0 ) {
   printf ( "\nError in radius...Re-enter >" );
   scanf  ( "%f", &radius );
}
```

Notice that the loop body might never execute: It is simply there as a guard to protect the program from faulty data.

5.3.2 Conditional Looping Using the do...while Statement

One of the features of the **while** statement is **pretesting**—testing the expression *before* the loop body is entered. As we saw in the previous example, pretesting

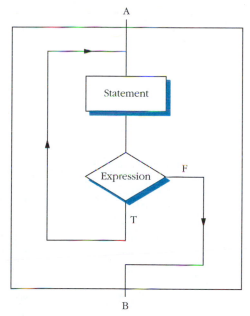

Figure 5.3–2 do statement structured flowchart

implies that the loop might not be executed even once. Sometimes, however, it is better to test the expression *after* the loop body is allowed to execute. This is called **posttesting.** The posttest conditional loop in C is a `do...while` loop:

Syntax: do
                statement
            while (expression)

For example, we could print a list of numbers from 21 to 99 using the C code:

```
int x = 21;
do
    printf ( "X = %d", x++ );
while ( x < 100 );
```

The statement can be a simple or compound statement enclosed in braces. The `do...while` statement is diagrammed in Figure 5.3–2.

The following program segment shows an application of the `do...while` statement in which continued execution depends on the user entering a Y or an N in response to a question.

```
do {
    printf ( "\nInput a number: " );
    scanf ( "%f",   &number );
    printf ( "\nNumber squared = %8.2f",   number * number);
```

```
        fflush ( stdin );                        /*  Must clear the input buffer  */
                                                 /*  before reading a char  */
        printf ( "\nDo you want to continue (Y/N)?   " );
        scanf ( "%c",   &answer );


    }  while ( answer == 'Y' || answer == 'y' );
```

Notice that the disjunctive expression after **while** allows for both uppercase and lowercase responses.

<table>
<tr>
<td>

BEFORE
YOU
GO ON

</td>
<td>

Query: What does the **fflush (stdin)** statement mean in the previous program segment?

RESPONSE: When **scanf** is used to input data, the input is stored in a temporary memory area called a **buffer.** The buffer contains all the data entered by the user, including the carriage return. When reading numbers, **scanf** removes numeric data from the buffer and puts it in appropriate variable locations but ignores the carriage return (treats it as a space). But when **scanf** reads character data, the carriage return appears as a legitimate character. By "flushing" the standard input buffer using **fflush (stdin)**, you can remove any leftover carriage returns and make the buffer safe to read from. Call this function whenever character data is about to be input with **scanf**.

</td>
</tr>
</table>

Note that a **while** statement could have been used above but, as shown in the following segment, it might be annoying to the user.

```
        printf ( "\nDo you want to continue (Y/N)?" );
        scanf ( "%c",   &answer );


        while (  answer == 'Y'    ||    answer == 'y' )    {

            printf (  "\nInput a number >" );
            scanf (  "%f",   &number );

            printf (  "\nNumber squared = %8.2f", number*number );

            fflush ( stdin );
            printf (  "\nDo you want to continue (Y/N)?" );
            scanf (  "%c",   &answer );
        }
```

As you can see, this segment asks whether to continue a program that the user just started! Some programmers prefer the following technique to keep using the **while** statement.

```
        answer = 'Y';

        while ( answer == 'Y'    ||    answer == 'y' ) {
```

```
            printf (  "\nInput a number >" );
            scanf (  "%f",    &number );

            printf (  "\nNumber squared = %8.2f",    number*number );

            fflush ( stdin );
            printf (  "\nDo you want to continue (Y/N)?" );
            scanf (  "%c",    &answer );
        }
```

The segment we just looked at simulates a **do...while** statement by forcing the loop body to execute at least once. However, we find it more reasonable to use the language features as they were intended and choose the **do...while** statement.

5.3.3 Iterative Looping Using the for Statement

The most powerful looping statement in C is the **for** statement, which we generally use when a *counter* is needed. Many programming situations call for a loop that executes for a specific number of repetitions (iterations), each one counted as it completes. When all the iterations have completed, the loop automatically finishes. This is the design of the **for** statement. The syntax of **for** is more complicated than for other loops because it includes a parameter as an automatic counting facility:

Syntax: for (expression 1; expression 2; expression 3)
                statement

For example, you can use the following C code to print the numbers from 0 through 9.

```
        for ( count = 0; count < 10; count++ )
            printf ( "%d  ", count );
```

This is diagrammed in Figure 5.3–3.

Let's analyze the syntax of the **for** loop using the output of the last example: 0 1 2 3 4 5 6 7 8 9. The first expression in the **for** loop initializes one or more variables. In this case a single variable, **count**, is given the value 0 before the first execution of the loop. Next, the logical expression **count < 10** is evaluated. If the result is true, the loop body executes. In this example a single statement outputs the value of **count**. You can substitute a compound statement enclosed in braces.

After the loop body executes, the third expression, **count++** in this example, increments the value of **count** by 1. The cycle is then repeated (excluding the initialization) until expression 2, when next tested, becomes false. This happens when **count** is incremented to 10. At that point, the loop finishes and control passes to the statement that follows the loop body.

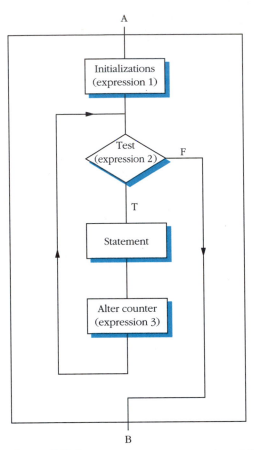

Figure 5.3–3   for statement structured flowchart

Note that the comma operator (,) can be used to create more complex expressions than shown above. That is, the following loop is like the last example.

```
for ( count = 0, max = 10;   count < max;  count++ )
      printf ( "%d ", count );
```

Here **count** is initialized to 0 and **max** to 10 by separating the two initialization expressions with a comma.

Let's consider some variations. Suppose we want to print the odd integers from 11 through 21. The program segment would look like this:

```
for ( count = 11;   count <= 21;   count = count + 2  )
      printf ( "%d ",   count );
```

This time **count** is initialized to 11 and the expression has been changed to check for **count <= 21**. Because we want counting by 2, we substitute an assignment for the increment operator.

BEFORE
YOU
GO ON

Query: How would you use a compound assignment operator to count by 2?

RESPONSE: `for ( count = 11; count <= 21; count += 2 )`

BEFORE
YOU
GO ON

Query: Write a `for` loop that counts backwards from 100 to 0 by 10.

RESPONSE: `for ( count = 100; count >= 0; count -= 10 )`

Each component of the `for` loop control structure is optional but the semi-colons are needed. For example, the following program segment is valid C syntax.

```
count = 0;
for ( ;  count < 100; )   {
  printf ( "%d ", count );
  count++;
}
```

Notice that we have just reinvented the `while` statement! Some programmers use the `for` loop to handle all looping tasks because it encompasses both the `while` and the `do...while` statements. Stylistically, however, it is better to use the language as it is intended in order to maximize the readability and efficiency of the code.

BEFORE
YOU
GO ON

Query: How do you decide which loop to use??

RESPONSE: Use a `while` or `do...while` loop for conditional looping that does not involve counting. Choose `do...while` over `while` if the loop must execute at least once. Use the `for` loop for iterative looping that does involve counting but may also involve testing.

Although all the components of the `for` loop control structure are optional, avoid omitting expression 2 because it causes an infinite loop, as in the following.

```
for ( count = 1;  ;  count++ )
```

For readability, we always include all three components of the `for` control structure. It is easier to understand the overall process when the expressions are conveniently localized instead of distributed throughout the loop.

PERSPECTIVE

Looping structures were used in the early days of programming in machine language and in assembly language. In the late 1950s the first structured loop, the `DO` loop, appeared in the FORTRAN language. Current versions of FORTRAN include a statement called `DO...ENDDO`, which is like the `for` loop in C.

5.3.4 Nested Loops

Sometimes you need to place a loop inside another loop. This is called **nesting** and is often used with table or matrix processing (as shown in Chapter 7). A simple use of nesting is the following.

EXAMPLE 5.3–1

Problem

Output a multiplication table for numbers in an arbitrary range.

Reasoning

The problem calls for the output of a table whose values equal the product of the row and column labels. For instance, for the values from 4 to 7 the corresponding output might look like the following.

	4	5	6	7
4	16	20	24	28
5	20	25	30	35
6	24	30	36	42
7	28	35	42	49

The formal statement for this problem is as follows.

   Input: low end of range, high end of range
  Output: multiplication table for the specified range
  Process: product of all pairs of values within the range

Solution

Algorithm
    Step 1:   INPUT low, high
    Step 2:   OUTPUT table header
    Step 3:   LOOP row: low TO high
            a. LOOP column: low TO high
                i. OUTPUT row * column

Notice that we have changed the pseudocode LOOP to include a counter variable and a range specification for that variable.

PROGRAM 5.3–1

```
/*******************************************************************************
*   Title:        multiplication tables                                       *
*   Filename:     mult.c                                                      *
*                                                                            *
```

```
*    Description:   Compute a multiplication table for a pair of      *
*                   input values.                                     *
*                                                                     *
*    Input:         low end and high end of range                     *
*    Output:        multiplication table                              *
*    Process:       all products within specified range               *
*                                                                     *
*    Written by:    ...                             Date: ...          *
*********************************************************************/

#include <stdio.h>

void  put_heading ( int  low,   int  high );                /*  Prototypes  */
void  make_table  ( int  low,   int  high );

main ( )
{
   int  low, high;

   printf (  "\nEnter low end and high end of range: " );
   scanf  (  "%d %d",   &low,  &high );                    /* User input  */

   put_heading ( low, high );                    /* output the table heading  */
   make_table  ( low, high );                /* compute and output the table  */

   return ( 0 );
}                                                          /*  End of main  */


/***********************************************************************
*    Function name:      put_heading                                  *
*    Description:        Output the heading for the multiplication    *
*                        table.                                       *
*                                                                     *
*    Input parameters:   low, high   (limits of table)                *
*    Output parameters:  none                                         *
*    Return value:       none                                         *
***********************************************************************/

void put_heading ( int low, int high )
{
   int column;

   printf (  "\n\n\n   " );                        /*  Output column heading  */
   for ( column = low;  column <= high;  column++ )
      printf (  "%3d",   column );
```

```
    printf ( "\n\n   " );                              /* Underline heading */
    for ( column = low;  column <= high;  column++ )
        printf ( "---" );
    printf ( "\n" );
}                                                     /*  End of put_heading */



/********************************************************************************
 *   Function name:      make_table                                           *
 *   Description:        Compute and output a multiplication table.           *
 *                                                                            *
 *   Input parameters:   low, high (limits of table)                          *
 *   Output parameters:  none                                                 *
 *   Return value:       none                                                 *
 ********************************************************************************/

void make_table ( int low, int high )
{
   int row, column;

   for ( row = low; row <= high; row++ ) {            /*  Output the row number */

       printf ( "%3d |", row );

       for ( column = low; column <= high; column++)  /*  Output row products  */

           printf ( "%3d", row * column );

       printf ( "\n" );
   }
}                                                     /*  End of make_table */
```

Test

Test this program by entering values such as 4 and 7 for **low** and **high**. What happens to the output when you enter a wide range? What happens if you enter the higher number first? How would you deal with this situation and still produce readable output?   ●

Next, consider a second, slightly more complicated example of nested loops.

EXAMPLE 5.3–2

Problem

The combined effect of wind and temperature on the human body can be severe, particularly in cold climates. The relative effect of the combination is called the

wind-chill factor. The wind-chill factor can be computed using the following equations formulated by meteorologists.

Factor1 $= 0.447 *$ wind speed

Factor2 $= (10.45 + 10 * \text{sqrt(factor1)} - \text{factor1}) * (33.0 - \text{temperature})$

Windchill $= 33.0 - (\text{factor2}/22.034)$

Write a program to output a wind-chill chart for a range of user-determined Celsius temperatures and wind speeds. Regardless of the input ranges, the output should be in 10-degree temperature increments and 5-mph wind speed increments. The user should be able to run as many charts as wanted.

Sample interaction:

Input range of temperatures: −50–20
Input range of wind speeds: 5–30

TEMPERATURE	WIND SPEED	WIND CHILL
−50	5	−54.26
−50	10	−69.17
−50	15	−78.65
−50	20	−85.32
−50	25	−90.19
−50	30	−93.79
−40	5	−43.75
−40	10	−56.86
. . .		

Do you want to continue (Y/N)? N
Thank you for using this program!

Reasoning

The program needs a doubly nested **for** loop to iterate through all the values of temperatures and wind speeds. In addition, the program needs a **do...while** loop to allow for repeated runs of the program. The situation calls for a triply nested looping structure, as shown in the algorithm.

Formal statement:

Input: range of temperatures, range of wind speeds
Output: wind-chill factor chart corresponding to the input
Process: wind-chill using formulas in the problem description

Solution
Algorithm:
    Step 1:   LOOP for all user requests
                a. INPUT low-temp, high-temp, low-speed, high-speed
                b. LOOP temp: low-temp TO high-temp STEP 10

> 1. LOOP speed: low-speed TO high-speed STEP 5
>   a. factor1 = .447 * speed
>   b. factor2 = (10.45 + 10 * sqrt(factor1) − factor1) *
>   (33.0 − temp)
>   c. windchill = 33.0 − (factor2 / 22.034)
>   d. OUTPUT temp, speed, windchill
> c. OUTPUT request for more runs
> d. INPUT user response
>
> Step 2: STOP

Notice the further modification of the LOOP pseudocode to include an explicit increment (STEP) for the counter variable.

PROGRAM 5.3-2

```
/*************************************************************************
*    Title:        wind-chill factor calculation                        *
*    Filename:     windchil.c                                           *
*                                                                       *
*    Description:  Compute a wind-chill factor table for a range of wind speeds and *
*                  temperatures.                                        *
*                                                                       *
*    Input:        windspeed range  and  temperature range             *
*    Output:       wind-chill factor table                             *
*    Process:      windchill = 33.0 − (factor2 / 22.034)               *
*                  factor2   = (10.45 + 10*sqrt(factor1) − factor1) (33.0 − temp) *
*                  factor1   =  0.447 * windspeed                       *
*                                                                       *
*    Written by:   ...                        Date: ...                 *
*************************************************************************/

#include <stdio.h>
#include <ctype.h>
#include <math.h>
                                                         /* Prototype */
void calc_windchill ( int low_temp, int high_temp, int low_speed, int high_speed );

main ( )
{
   int  low_temp,  high_temp,  low_speed,  high_speed;
   char response;

   do  {

      printf ( "\n\nEnter low end and high end of temperature range: " );
      scanf ( "%d %d",   &low_temp, &high_temp );                /* User input */
```

```
        printf (   "\n\nEnter low end and high end of wind speed range : " );
        scanf  (   "%d %d",   &low_speed,  &high_speed );                        /* User input */

                                                          /* compute and output the table  */
        calc_windchill (  low_temp,  high_temp,  low_speed,  high_speed );

        fflush (  stdin );
        printf (   "\n\n\nDo you want to continue (Y/N)?"  );
        scanf  (   "%c",  &response );

    }  while (  toupper ( response )  ==  'Y'  );

    printf (  "\n\nThank you for using this program!" );

    return ( 0 );
}                                                          /*  End of main  */
```

```
/*************************************************************************************
*    Function name:       calc_windchill                                            *
*                                                                                   *
*    Description:         Compute and output the wind-chill table.                  *
*                                                                                   *
*    Input parameters:    low_temp, high_temp, low_speed, high_speed (limits of table) *
*    Output parameters:   none                                                      *
*    Return value:        none                                                      *
*************************************************************************************/

void calc_windchill ( int low_temp, int high_temp, int low_speed, int high_speed )
{
    const int TEMP_INCR  =  10;
    const int SPEED_INCR =   5;

    int   temp,  speed;
    float factor1,  factor2,  windchill;

    printf (  "\n\n\nTemperature      Windspeed      Wind-chill" );

    for (  temp = low_temp;   temp <= high_temp;   temp += TEMP_INCR )

       for ( speed = low_speed; speed <= high_speed; speed += SPEED_INCR ) {

          factor1   = 0.447 * speed;
          factor2   = ( 10.45 + 10.0 * pow ( factor1, 0.5) - factor1 ) * (33.0 - temp );
          windchill = 33.0  -  ( factor2 / 22.034);
```

```
      printf (  "\n %2d     %2d      %.2f",    temp, speed, windchill );
   }
}                                                /*  End of calc_windchill  */
```

Test

Test this program by entering values for the temperature range and the wind speed range. Note that the **toupper** function is accessible through the header file **ctype.h** and converts lowercase characters to their uppercase equivalents. (See Appendix A-3 for a list of related functions.) •

EXERCISES 5.3

Concept Check

Answer statements 1 through 4 with true *or* false.
1. The **while** statement uses posttesting.
2. The **for** statement is the least powerful of all three looping structures.
3. Conditional looping is only possible with the **do...while** statement.
4. The **if** statement and the **while** statement can be used interchangeably.

For statements 5 through 8 choose the answer that best completes the statement.
5. Assuming **x** does not equal 0, the statement **while (x == 0) printf ("X=0");**
   a. is an infinite loop
   b. will never output
   c. causes a syntax error
   d. will output once
6. Assuming **x** does not equal 0, the statement **do printf ("X=0"); while (x==0);**
   a. is an infinite loop
   b. will never output
   c. causes a syntax error
   d. will output once
7. The statement **for (x = 0; x < 1; x++) printf ("X=0");**
   a. is an infinite loop
   b. will never output
   c. causes a syntax error
   d. will output once
8. The statement **for (x = 0; x <= -1; x++) printf ("X= 0");**
   a. is an infinite loop
   b. will never output
   c. causes a syntax error
   d. will output once

For statements 9 through 12 fill in the blanks with the right answer.
9. The _____ loop is generally used with a counter.
10. Conditional looping is also called _____ looping.

11. The **for** loop counter variables should not be of the _____ type or of the _____ type. They should only be of the _____ type.

12. The _____ loop uses posttesting.

Set A

Find all errors (syntax or logic) in each of the following program segments. The programs attempt to print the integers from 1 through 100.

13.
```
x = 1;
while (  x < 100 );
printf (  "X = %d", x );
x++;
```

14.
```
num = 100;
while ( num > 1 );
printf (  "Number = %d",  num );
num++;
```

15.
```
for (  x = 1;  x <= 100;  x++ )   {
    printf (  "X = %d",  x );
    x++;
}
```

16.
```
x = 1;
do
    printf (  "X = %d",  x );
    x++;
while ( x <= 100 );
```

17.
```
x =  0;
do {
    printf (  "X = %d",  x );
    x++;
} while ( x < 100 );
```

18.
```
for (  x = 1;  x <= 100;  )
    printf (  "X = %d",  x );
    x++;
```

Set B

19. What does the following program output?

```
#include <stdio.h>
main ( )
{
   int i, j, k;
   k = 0;
   for ( i = 1;  i <= 30;  i++ )
       for ( j = 1;  j <= 20;  j++ )
           if ( j % 3  ==  0 )   k++;
   printf (  "\nk = %d",  k );
   return ( 0 );
}
```

20. Write a program to sum the even integers from 1 to 100 using a **for** loop. Output the sum.
21. Ask the user for two numbers representing the low-end and high-end values of a range. Compute and output the sum of all the numbers in the range.
22. Write a function to compute and return **n factorial** defined as

$$n! = (n*(n-1)*(n-2)*\cdots*2*1).$$

Set C

23. Program 5.3–3 shows some of the concepts explored in this chapter. Enter the program into your computer and observe the results. Note that the program behaves differently depending on the computer and the compiler you choose. If possible, run the program on two different computers and compare the results. Implement each of the eight modules *individually* to test the limits of your computer.
    a. Execute test #1
    b. Execute test #2
    c. Execute test #3
    d. Execute test #4
    e. Execute test #5
    f. Execute test #6
    g. Execute test #7
    h. Execute test #8
    i. Execute test #9

PROGRAM 5.3-3

```
/***************************************************************************
*    Title:        machine representation of numbers                      *
*    Filename:     numbrep.c                                              *
*                                                                         *
*    Description:  Test the limits of   int,   float,   and   double.     *
*                                                                         *
```

```
*    Input:         none                                                  *
*    Output:        results of various arithmetic tests                   *
*    Process:       computations of very large and very small numbers     *
*                                                                         *
*    Written by    ...                                     Date: ...      *
**************************************************************************

#include <stdio.h>
#include <math.h>


main ( )
{
int      i, j;
long int  long_i;
float     x,  y;
double    double_x;


   printf (  "\n\n\nTest#1:  Compute 2^i using int type" );
   for (  j = 2,  i = 2;   i <= 16;   i++ )   {
       j = pow ( 2.0, i );
       printf (  "\ni=%d   2^i=%d",   i, j );
   }


   printf (  "\n\n\nTest#2:  Compute 2^i using long int type" );
   for (  long_i = 2,  i = 2;  i<=32;  i++ )   {
       long_i = pow ( 2.0, i );
       printf (  "\ni =%d   2^i=%ld", i, long_i );
   }


   printf ( "\n\n\nTest#3:  Compute 2^i using float type"  );
   for ( x = 2, i = 2; i <= 128; i++ ) {
       x = pow( 2.0, i );
       printf ( "\ni=%d   2^i=%f", i, x );
   }


   printf ( "\n\n\nTest#4:  Compute 2^i using double type" );
   for ( double_x = 2, i = 2;  i <= 1024; i++ ) {
       double_x = pow( 2.0, i );
       printf ( "\ni=%d   2^i=%f", i, double_x );
   }
```

```
printf ( "\n\n\nTest#5:  Compute 1/(2^i) using float type" );
for ( i = 2; i <= 150; i++ ) {
    x = 1.0 / pow ( 2.0, i );
    printf ( "\ni=%d    1/2^i=%e", i, x );
}


printf ( "\n\n\nTest#6:  Compute 1/(2^i) using double type" );
for ( i = 2; i <= 1024; i++ ) {
    double_x = 1.0 / pow ( 2.0, i );
    printf ( "\ni=%d    1/2^i=%e", i, double_x );
}


printf ( "\n\n\nTest#7:  Divide by 0" );
i = 5 / 0;
printf ( "\ni=%d", i );
i = 5;
j = 0;
printf ( "\ni/j=%d", i/j );


printf ( "\n\n\nTest#8:  Comparison of two floating point values" );
y = 8.0001;
x = 8.0001 / 3 ;
x *= 3;
if ( x == y )
    printf (   "\n x=y" );
else
    printf (   "\nx =%e  \ny =%e", x, y );


printf ( "\n\n\nTest#9:  Behavior of floating point values" );
for ( x = 0.0; x <= 11.0; x += 0.1 )
    printf (   "%f \n", x );

return ( 0 );
}
```

Operating Systems

6

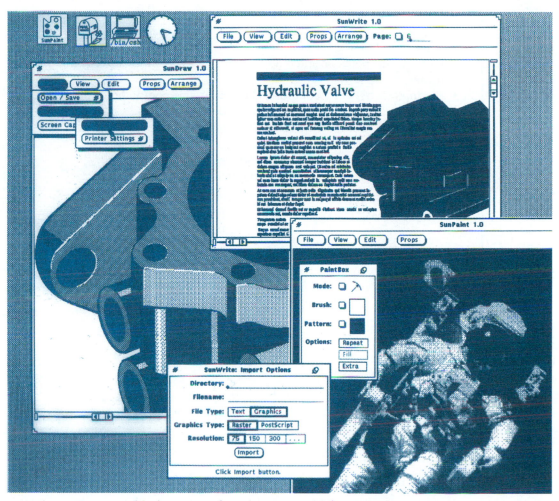

Sun Microsystems graphical user interface showing multiple application windows.

After completing this chapter you should be able to do the following:

Learning Goals

- Understand a model for a single-user operating system
- Understand a model for a multiuser operating system
- Understand time cycles for time-shared systems
- Distinguish between preemptive and nonpreemptive scheduling algorithms
- Distinguish between computer protection and computer security
- Distinguish between an editor and a debugger
- Understand models showing the flow from source modules to executable code
- Understand models for paging and its use in virtual memory
- Understand and use part of a paging algorithm

Chapter Activity

A computer has 16 MB of RAM. The operating system is designed to partition the memory into 128 page frames. Write an *algorithm* to execute paging between physical and virtual memory for any applications software of arbitrary size. Assume that the system is limited to a single user. Figure 6.0–1 shows a model for the page table needed to do the paging.

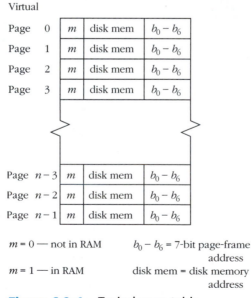

Virtual

Page	0	m	disk mem	$b_0 - b_6$
Page	1	m	disk mem	$b_0 - b_6$
Page	2	m	disk mem	$b_0 - b_6$
Page	3	m	disk mem	$b_0 - b_6$

Page	$n-3$	m	disk mem	$b_0 - b_6$
Page	$n-2$	m	disk mem	$b_0 - b_6$
Page	$n-1$	m	disk mem	$b_0 - b_6$

$m = 0$ — not in RAM $b_0 - b_6$ = 7-bit page-frame address

$m = 1$ — in RAM disk mem = disk memory address

Figure 6.0–1 Typical page table

6.1 WINDOWS TO HARDWARE

Introduction

In the early days, computers consisted solely of hardware components like those discussed in Chapter 4, and programs were wired by hand as we learned in Chapter 1. Users at that time were hardware programmers and computers were out of reach for the ordinary applications user. Hardware programmable by machine language was an improvement but the ordinary user still had no access to such systems.

We saw in Section 1.1.1 that a software program was needed to make addressing simpler; make input/output cleaner; simplify job, file, and task management; and manage the overall resources of a computer. This was a description of an **operating system** linking applications software and hardware.

Operating systems added efficiency to computing. Many stages of the computing cycle were still done manually such as mounting data media (punched cards or magnetic tape), scheduling jobs, monitoring time use, controlling access to the single computer, and managing resources. This made job turnaround time long (often hours or days), inefficient, and costly. Modern operating systems have reduced typical turnaround time to minutes and seconds, making computers more efficient and usable.

6.1.1 The System Executive

Imagine an operating system as the "orchestrator and conductor" of the hardware and software in a computer system. For example, the operating system controls the input and output peripherals and manages the loading of software programs into RAM. Because the operating system is responsible for the access to and transfer of applications data and systems data among the components that make a computer a working system, it is sometimes called the **system executive.** Figure 6.1–1 shows a typical computer system under the operating system's control.

The operating system serves several purposes related to applications programs. To begin with, it establishes a command-processor interface enabling the user to communicate with the computer. The interface varies from system to system. For example, on a computer running UNIX or a PC running DOS, the user enters command words such as *dir* for a list of directory files or *print* to send a file to the printer. If the command is not recognized, a message to that effect is displayed. If the command is recognized, the operating system performs the activity ordered by the user. On the other hand, operating systems such as Windows/NT™ and Apple Macintosh rely on pictures, called **icons,** rather than command words. The icons show operations visually—for example, with the image of a printer to represent the print operation or the image of a file cabinet to represent a collection of files.

On a multiuser system, once the user has communicated the intention of running a job, the operating system arranges for its execution through a **scheduler.** The scheduler ensures that the files needed by the job are accessible and that the resources such as memory and file space needed by the computer are available. When the scheduler has finished its work, another software component of the operating system called the **dispatcher** gives control of the central processing unit (CPU) to the job. Figure 6.1–2 shows a typical sequence

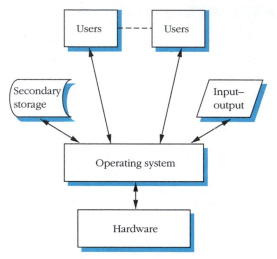

Figure 6.1–1 The operating system as system executive

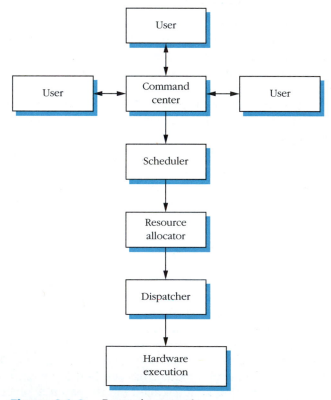

Figure 6.1–2 Events in execution

of events in the execution of a job. (Double arrows indicate a two-way interaction.) The operating system also acts as a **resource allocator** for both hardware and software by managing memory space, file storage space, use of the CPU, and input/output devices, and by making choices about which requests for resources are satisfied and in what order.

6.1.2 Time Sharing

As we saw in Section 1.2.5, **batch processing** collected and ran all the jobs together that needed the same resources. For example, FORTRAN programs were batched so that the FORTRAN compiler could be loaded once and used repeatedly. Because no interaction was possible between the user and the computer, the process that was running had to be temporarily stopped so that the computer operator could, for instance, load a tape or do any other task requested by the user. Figure 6.1–3 is a diagram of a typical batch process with possible operator intervention.

The obvious need to transfer the computer operator's interactive role to the system itself led to more sophisticated operating systems and **interactive processing,** shown in Figure 6.1–4. Next came **multiuser systems** and **time sharing** in which the CPU alternates between several jobs while appearing to process them at the same time, shown in Figure 6.1–5. (See Section 1.2.5.)

As a simple illustration let's specify a time cycle of 1 second to be shared by a number of users. Suppose there are four users each executing a different job on the same computer. Each job would share 1/4 of a second (0.25 seconds) during

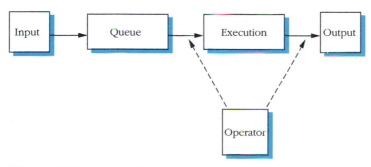

Figure 6.1–3 Batch processing

Figure   6.1–4 Interactive real-time processing

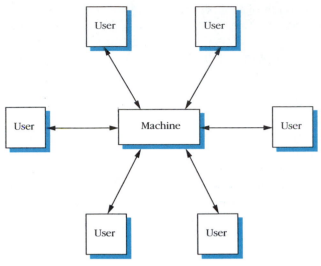

Figure 6.1–5   Multiuser system

each cycle of computer time. Example 6.1–1 shows time sharing in the course of a time cycle.

EXAMPLE 6.1–1

Problem
Consider the time cycle for a computer to be 0.001 of a second. This time is shared among n jobs. If 10 percent of the time cycle is reserved for data transfer, find the actual amount of computer time that is allocated for each job within each time cycle. Do this for both $n = 5$ and $n = 20$. Assume that the time allocated to each job is enough to execute an instruction completely.

Reasoning
We solve this problem by the analytic method. Assume that each job has the same allotted time, say T, which includes the 10 percent overhead for data transfer.

Solution
The actual CPU time is 90 percent of T; for n jobs,

$$T = 0.001/n \quad \text{second}$$

Therefore, for $n = 5$,

$$T = 0.001/5 = 10 * 10^{-4}/5$$
$$= 2 * 10^{-4}$$
$$= 0.0002 \quad \text{second}$$

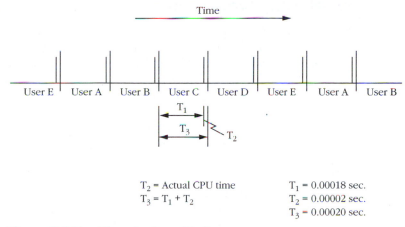

T_2 = Actual CPU time T_1 = 0.00018 sec.
$T_3 = T_1 + T_2$ T_2 = 0.00002 sec.
                              T_3 = 0.00020 sec.

Figure 6.1–6   Time sharing with five users

Likewise, for $n = 20$,

$$T = 0.001/20 = 100 * 10^{-5}/20$$
$$= 5 * 10^{-5}$$
$$= 0.00005 \text{ second}$$

Because there is a 10 percent overhead gap for data transfer, the actual computer time is calculated as 90 percent of T for each value of n. These values are 0.00018 of a second and 0.000045 of a second, respectively. Figure 6.1–6 shows how time sharing is done when $n = 5$.

Test
It is easily shown for each case that multiplication of T by the value for n results in the given time cycle of 0.001 of a second.   •

BEFORE YOU GO ON

Query: A computer system runs 12 computer terminals simultaneously with a time cycle of 0.06 of a second. What is the time allocated for each user in a time cycle? Assume no overhead.

RESPONSE: $T = (0.06)/12 = 0.005$ of a second.

Multiuser time-shared systems were a response to the high cost of single computers in the 1960s. The low cost of single computers in the 1990s has put them in greater demand. This flip-flop in events is the result of the mass availability of today's personal computers, the increased demand for computer networking, and the efficiency and usability of modern operating systems.

6.1.3 Scheduling Algorithms

Before discussing scheduling algorithms, let's consider how the CPU handles jobs. One way is to let a job monopolize the CPU until it is completely finished. This is not always efficient because the CPU may have to be idle until a non-CPU task such as retrieving data from a hard disk is done.

Suppose two jobs, *A* and *B*, need execution. Suppose *A* is in execution and needs an I/O access. The operating system can release *A* from the CPU to do its I/O task and let *B* use the CPU until it is released by the operating system. *A* is then allowed to continue. These periods of CPU use are called **CPU burst times** and can be used to increase the efficiency of scheduling the two jobs. Figure 6.1–7 shows some burst times.

A **scheduling algorithm** determines access to the CPU. One well-known scheduling algorithm is **first-in-first-out (FIFO)**, also called first-come-first-served (FCFS). Although such schemes seem "fair" they can also be inefficient. If a long job precedes shorter ones on a queue (waiting line), the shorter jobs must wait until the long job is finished.

One way to make scheduling more efficient is with **priority,** a scheme that gives one application precedence over another. An example of a priority scheme found at some universities is as follows:

Student programs have lower priority than faculty programs.
Faculty programs have lower priority than administrative programs.

A rationale for this priority scheme, for example, is that faculty members and student aides might never get paid if administrative payroll programs did not have a higher priority. Regardless of the rationale for a priority scheme, priorities should be fair so that all users of the computer system have reasonable opportunity for access.

Another scheduling algorithm uses the **shortest-job-first (SJF)** priority scheme in which the job with the shortest use of its current CPU burst time goes first on the next scheduled burst time. In this case, a long job may have to wait much longer than it would have using the FIFO scheduling algorithm. However, because it can potentially process more jobs the SJF protocol optimizes job waiting time.

The problem with SJF is estimating the amount of CPU burst time needed by a job in its *next* CPU burst, based on the time used in the *current* and *past* CPU burst times. One way to do this is by using a predictive formula such as

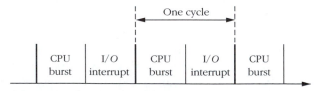

Figure 6.1–7 Simple example of CPU bursts

the **exponential average** as follows. Let $T(n)$ represent the predicted CPU burst time at the nth burst based on actual history, where $T(0)$ is the initial prediction. Let $t(n)$ be the actual CPU burst time at the nth burst. If p is a weighting parameter between recent and past history, then we can write

$$T(n + 1) = pt(n) + (1 - p)T(n)$$

where $0 \le p \le 1$. That is, the predicted CPU burst time at the *next* CPU burst can be a weighted average of the current actual and predicted CPU burst times. A rough segment of C code to form a table for permissible values of T using the exponential average is as follows.

```
scanf  ( "%f %d", &param, &max_num_burst);
                                        /* Value of weight and maximum limit */
scanf  ("%f",&time_predicted);                      /* Initial condition */
printf ("The weighting parameter is %f",param);      /* Echo parameter */

for ( index = 0; index <= max_num_burst; index++)   {
    printf ( "Enter the value for t when index = %d: ", index);
    scanf  ( "%f", time_actual);
    printf ( "%9.3f %9.3f %9.3f", index, time_actual, time_predicted);
    time_predicted  =  param * time_actual  +  (1.0 - param) * time_predicted;
            /* time_predicted  on left is the new value of  time_predicted */
}
```

BEFORE YOU GO ON

Query: Suppose $p = 0.5$—that is, equal weights. How could the predicted burst time formula be rewritten?

RESPONSE: $T(n + 1) = (t(n) + T(n))/2$

Scheduling algorithms are classified as preemptive or nonpreemptive. **Nonpreemptive** algorithms do not allow a job to be stopped once its CPU burst starts. **Preemptive** algorithms allow a job to be stopped either because it has used up an allocated amount of time or because a higher-priority job has arrived.

Consider the following situation. Job A with medium priority has control of the CPU. Job B arrives with low priority so it must wait until A releases control of the CPU by either terminating or by issuing an input/output request. Job C arrives with high priority. Based on a preemptive scheduling algorithm, C preempts or *bumps* A off the CPU and initiates execution. Depending on the number of waiting jobs and their preemptive priorities, it is theoretically possible that a job like B may never complete execution.

6.1.4 Protection and Security

In single-user systems, the operating system is not as complicated as in multiuser systems. The reason is obvious: There is no concern for multiple users' jobs while the computer is running. Still, it is possible for single-user computers to execute multiple jobs concurrently (called **multitasking**) and for the operating system to keep these jobs from interfering with each other. Allocation of resources for single-user systems is relatively simple and computers are safeguarded from malfunction caused by the software or the user.

With multiuser systems comes the necessity of protecting not only the integrity of the system but also each user's information from infringement by other users. **Protection** of a computer system implies that the hardware and software that control access to internal-resource information is available only to designated users. Protection is the *method,* or *how,* the system is guarded. The *measure* of protection, called **security,** describes *who* has the right of access to the protection.

As we saw in Section 1.1.2, destruction and theft of computer information have made protection and security important issues in recent years. Allowing access only to users with passwords (access codes) is one method of protecting the system. However, passwords are not foolproof and they have to be changed frequently. They can also be found out accidentally or guessed when a user imprudently chooses the name of a close relative or Social Security number as a password. Passwords can also be found intentionally (perhaps criminally) by means of cracker programs.

BEFORE YOU GO ON

Query: When asked to give a password for his computer account, Sam chooses the name of his girlfriend. This is unwise. Why?

RESPONSE: People who know Sam may not necessarily be his friends. But they may easily guess that the password could be his girlfriend's name.

With the prevalence of computer networks today, computer protection and security become ever more important. Some people try to break computer protection for the sport of it, others with criminal intent such as theft of information. Indeed the loss of assets by computer theft amounts to billions of dollars each year, as was stated in Section 1.1.2.

PERSPECTIVE

In 1984 the American Bar Association reported that the annual cost of computer crime exceeds $10 billion. This excludes theft by copying software, which is difficult to document. [1]

EXERCISES 6.1

Concept Check
Answer statements 1 through 4 with true *or* false.
1. A computer operating system is part of the computer hardware.
2. Nonpreemptive algorithms are of little use in scheduling.
3. Interactive processing is limited to single-user systems.
4. Burst time is the time it takes for a computer to access I/O.

For statements 5 through 8 choose the answer that best completes the statement.
5. A preemptive algorithm
   a. overrides the operating system
   b. sets the conditions of priority
   c. allocates resources according to priorities
   d. is executed before other algorithms
6. Computer security
   a. is a device that controls access to a computer
   b. controls which individuals have a right of access to protected information
   c. denotes how computers are protected
   d. denotes the safety of computers
7. One of the simplest of the scheduling algorithms is
   a. the shortest-job-first method
   b. the first-come-first-served method
   c. the class of nonpreemptive algorithms
   d. an algorithm using exponential average
8. A system that allows for the use of one computer by more than one user is called
   a. a time-sharing system
   b. an interactive system
   c. a multiuser system
   d. a real-time system

For statements 9 through 12 fill in the blanks with the right word.
9. The process of _____ is useful in multiuser systems.
10. The appropriation of computer and I/O time is controlled by the _____ of the operating system.
11. The ability of a user to intervene with a program during execution is called _____.
12. Assignment of CPU time is controlled by the _____ of the operating system.

Set A
13. A computer's burst time is 6 milliseconds. If a maximum of eight user terminals can be used on the system, find the maximum time allocated to each user.
14. Give three reasons why an operating system is called a *system executive*.

15. Describe two priority schemes for accessing a CPU.
16. An operating system performs many functions like scheduling and managing memory space. Using those discussed in this section, represent the functions as layers in which the CPU is the lowest layer.
17. Explain how preemptive scheduling can result in a situation where a program is never executed.
18. Explain the difference between computer protection and computer security.

Set B
19. What is exponential averaging?
20. Interpret a calculated burst time when the weighting parameter is 0.
21. Interpret a calculated burst time when the weighting parameter is unity.
22. Calculate the predicted burst time if the estimated time and the actual time are both 2.7 μs and the weighting parameter is 0.5.
23. Calculate the predicted burst time if the estimated time and the actual time are both 8.4 μs and the weighting parameter is 0.25.
24. Calculate the predicted burst time if the estimated time and the actual time are both 0.96 μs and the weighting parameter is 0.75.
25. Research the exponential averaging of burst times and discuss the reason for its name.

Set C
26. Write a C program for a nonpreemptive algorithm to process jobs on a first-come-first-served basis.
27. Write a C program to apportion an arbitrary time cycle for n users with a variable overhead factor. See Example 6.1–1.
28. Write a C program that executes the algorithm for a shortest-job-first scheme using exponential averaging.
29. Write a C program that executes the algorithm for calculating the exponential average of burst times for various initial times and weighting parameters.

6.2   SYSTEM TOOLS AND VIRTUAL MEMORY

Introduction

Operating systems offer tools to help you develop applications. These tools include the use of a text editor for writing software and the capability for loading machine code into memory.

Let's look at these tools. Editors and debuggers make program development easier. Linkers and loaders allow machine language to execute in the hardware, enabling a program to run. Virtual memory combines the capacities of primary and secondary storage devices, enabling you to write programs without concern for the limits of primary memory.

6.2.1 Editors and Debuggers

A **text editor** is a software utility program that allows you to create, add, delete, and change textual documents. (Software utility programs are supplied by the operating system to add to the efficiency of a computer system.) Text editors suited to programming have features such as auto indenting for prettyprinting. Some text editors include a check for balanced braces { } around a block of C code. Most operating systems accommodate programs written on external editors. Editors embedded in operating systems allow you to make changes to programs directly on the system without returning to external environments.

Most operating systems also support a **debugger** program to find logic errors in executable code. The debugger offers tools like *breakpoints* to predefine a series of temporary stop locations at chosen instructions. As each breakpoint is reached in a program, the debugger temporarily stops the action while the programmer queries the values of any variables being tracked. Debuggers can also *single-step* through a program, temporarily stopping after each instruction has completely executed and displaying whatever information you have requested. The way to avoid logical errors, of course, is to not make them in the first place: Careful algorithm design and implementation are the best weapons for this.

6.2.2 Assemblers, Compilers, and Interpreters

When a program is written in a high-level language like C, it is written in a context and style that you as a programmer can recognize. For example, the C segment

```
scanf ( "%f %f", &x, &y );
z = x + y;
printf ( "The sum is %f", z );
```

is recognizable by all C programmers and even some who are not familiar with C. The computer hardware, however, does not understand this language. Thus by a **high-level** language we mean one that is understood by a programmer and by a **low-level** language we mean one that is understood by a computer. Computers understand only the low-level **machine language,** whose instructions are based on patterns of bits.

So how does a language such as C get converted to a machine language? This is the job of assemblers and compilers, generically called **translators,** which are software programs that often accompany operating systems. The information written in the original language (by the programmer) is called the **source module** and the source module translated into machine language is called the **object module.** Figure 6.2–1 illustrates this concept.

Figure 6.2–1   Source-to-object translator

Computer languages take different forms. As we saw in Section 1.3.1, the most rudimentary is **assembly language** in which each assembly instruction generates one instruction in the machine language. An **assembler** is one of the translators—a software program that translates assembly statements into machine code. A segment of an assembly language program looks like this:

```
PROG    LOAD     REG7,0
LOOP    LOAD     REG4,X
        ADD      REG4,Y
        STORE    REG4,Z
        ADD      REG7,1
        COMPARE  REG7,6
        BRNOTEQ  LOOP
```

Each statement in assembly language corresponds to an equivalent statement in machine language. The segment creates a loop that loads the contents at a location symbolized by X into register 4 and adds to register 4 the contents at location Y. The sum in register 4 is stored at location Z. The loop control uses register 7, which is initialized to 0 and incremented by 1 until six loop cycles are completed. As an exercise, try writing the segment in C.

BEFORE YOU GO ON

Query: With reference to the assembly segment, a student believes that because the contents of register 7 are compared to the value 6 and that 1 is added before the comparison, the loop has five passes rather than six. Why is this wrong?

RESPONSE: Register 7 is initialized with zero and the branch to location LOOP is on "not equal." Only after the sixth pass is the branch to LOOP ignored.

A **compiler** is software that allows you to write programs by using a well-defined code, checks them for **syntax** errors, and translates them to machine language. High-level instructions usually translate into more than one machine instruction. An operating system almost always works with compilers for different programming languages, provided the compiler is designed for that particular operating system. For example, an operating system can work with a different compiler for each of the C, Pascal, and Ada languages. Figure 6.2–2 shows the execution sequence of a compiler.

When a program is compiled, object code is created. If any change is made in the program, it has to be compiled again and a new object module created,

Source module → Compiler → Object module

One line ——————→ Many lines

Figure 6.2–2 Compiler conversion sequence

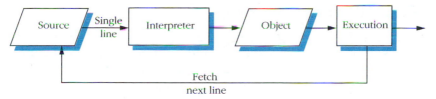

Figure 6.2–3 Interpreter conversion sequence

an inefficient process if frequent minor changes are made to large programs. Therefore, instead of translating an entire source program into machine language, you can interpret it rather than compile it using a software program called an **interpreter** to execute one instruction of source code at a time. Figure 6.2–3 shows the execution sequence of an interpreter. Note that if a program is to run repeatedly, a compiler is preferable to an interpreter because it produces nearly optimal machine code. Compiled programs are also faster and more efficient to run than interpreted ones.

6.2.3 Linkers and Loaders

When source code is translated into object code, it is probably not ready for immediate execution: It may need other machine code to execute properly. This code can be information from input and output routines, system library functions, external subprograms created by the user, and other system needs. All the parts of a source program are assembled by a software utility program called a **linker.** Linkers organize the various code modules and generate an integrated machine language object called a **load module.** The load module is what goes into the memory of the computer.

The load module is put into memory by another software utility program called a **loader.** For single-user, single-process systems the loading process is straightforward. For multiuser systems the loading process is more complicated because the loader must ensure that the portion of the program that is put into memory fits into its allotted memory space. The details of this are best left for a more advanced text. Figure 6.2–4 shows the phases in the loading process.

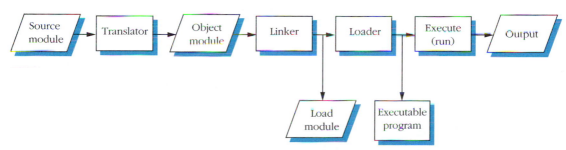

Figure 6.2–4 Multiphase sequence from source to execution

6.2.4 Virtual Memory

You may think that the whole program must be in memory for it to execute. However, object code may be too large for primary memory because it can include such things as external subroutines and system library functions. In response to this problem computer scientists have sought ways to execute programs without having the whole program in physical memory.

One way is to detach **logical memory,** the memory space needed by the *program,* from **physical memory,** the actual memory space of the *computer.* This detachment, called **virtual memory,** extends the apparent size of a computer's primary storage (RAM) by using part of the computer's secondary storage (hard disk) as an extension of RAM. Remember that virtual memory does not exist in reality; physical memory does. When using virtual memory, you are not concerned with memory allocation of your program.

6.2.5 Pages and Page Frames

One way to use virtual memory is to put parts of logical memory into physical memory as needed. A formula for doing this is the following. Let physical memory (RAM) be of size M. Let it be partitioned into r equal parts, each of size M/r. Each of these partitions is called a **page frame** of *physical memory.* Assume that logical memory is partitioned into p parts, each of size s. Each of these parts is called a **page** of *logical memory.* The size of each page *must equal* the size of a page frame—that is, $s = M/r$. The number of pages in logical memory must be large enough to hold the program. If L is the size of a program the product of the number of pages times the size of each page must be greater than or equal to the program size—that is, $ps \geq L$. Because $s = M/r$, it is also true that $pM/r \geq L$.

EXAMPLE 6.2–1

Problem
Suppose physical memory is 256 KB and is partitioned into eight page frames. If logical memory is 5 MB, find the number of pages needed in virtual memory.

Reasoning
The size of physical memory is $M = 256$ KB. The number of memory partitions is $r = 8$. The size of a page frame must equal the size of a page.

Solution
The size of a page frame is $M/r = 256\ \text{KB}/8 = 32$ KB. So the size of each page s must also be 32 KB. The amount of logical memory is $L = 5$ MB. Before continuing, we must convert MB into KB to preserve the units of the equality. In this case,

$$5\ \text{MB} = 5 * 2^{20} = 5 * 2^{10} * 2^{10} = (5 * 2^{10}) * 2^{10} = 5,120 * 2^{10}$$
$$= 5,120\ \text{KB}$$

The size of a page is $s = 32$ KB and the size of logical memory is $L = 5,120$ KB. Because $ps \geq L$, we find the number of pages needed by

$p \geq L/s$

$p \geq 5,120 \text{ KB}/32 \text{ KB}$

$p \geq 5,120/32$

$p \geq 160$

That is, 160 pages in logical memory are needed.

Test
There are 160 pages each of 32 KB, making the total size of logical memory equal $160 * 32$ KB $= 5,120$ KB $= 5$ MB.   ●

Virtual memory is produced by **paging,** which is the swapping of pages into page frames as needed for executing the program. In this way, paging is used to put the logical information into physical memory. Again, for the swapping to work properly the size of a page must equal the size of a page frame or $s = M/r$. The size of a page frame is usually a power of 2.

BEFORE YOU GO ON

Query: Physical memory of 4 MB is partitioned into 256 page frames. Assuming that all memory is free, find the number of pages a program can consume without paging.

RESPONSE: Page frame size is $M/r = 4$ MB$/256 = 4,096$ KB$/256 = 16$ KB. Therefore page size $s = 16$ KB. To prevent paging, logical memory size L can not exceed physical memory size M. Thus the number of logical pages p can not be more than 256.

Program size is not related to page size. A program spreads over as many pages as is needed. Figure 6.2–5 shows the relationship between virtual and physical memory when physical memory is 8 KB partitioned into four pages of 2 KB each. Suppose a program is large enough to need a logical memory of 32 KB. A **page table** in RAM keeps an accounting of which pages from logical memory are in frames of physical memory. The addresses in the page table parallel those of the pages in logical memory. Each unit of the page table consists of at least three items: the page frame reference, which is a single bit to show if the page is actually in memory; the address of the page frame where the page is stored; and the address of the secondary memory location (usually a hard disk) where the page is located.

Typically, at least one page is loaded into a page frame and execution begins. While executing, the program may demand access to the address of an instruction in another page that is not yet in memory. If the instruction address is valid but is in a page (in logical memory)—not in physical memory—an operating system interruption (a change in control usually caused by I/O activity) results. This

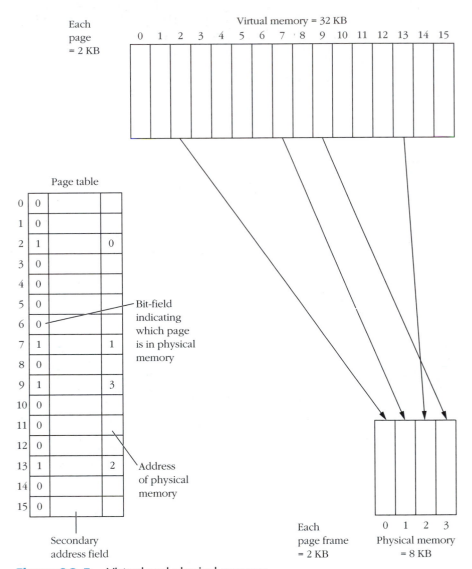

Figure 6.2–5 Virtual and physical memory

interruption, called a **page fault,** forces the operating system to search for the next logical page and put it into physical memory. A typical algorithmic sequence might be as follows.

Step 0. Get address of instruction
Step 1. If address is not valid
terminate program

Else
    a. Access PageTable in RAM
    b. Determine page (virtual memory)
    c. Determine from PageTable if page is in memory
    d. If page is in memory
        1. Execute or terminate program
        2. Find next instruction
    Else interrupt occurs
        1. Give control to operating system
          e. Find page in secondary memory
          f. Retrieve page from secondary memory
          g. Transfer page contents to page frame in physical memory
          h. Update PageTable
        2. Find next instruction
Step 2.   Repeat at Step 0

Be aware that if a page fault occurs, the process again begins at Step 0 and the whole routine must be repeated for effective execution.

BEFORE YOU GO ON

Query: A program segment calculates products of numbers and stores the result at the symbolic location ANSWER. Suppose a page fault occurs when the results are stored to ANSWER. What would happen?

RESPONSE: The page from secondary memory must be brought into a page frame of primary memory and the page table updated. Then the data could be stored.

6.2.6 Other Considerations with Virtual Memory

There are many factors to consider with virtual memory. For example, when a page is put in a page frame of primary memory, how efficient is the process? A measure for demand paging is its access time (AT), the weighted average of the time it takes to handle a page fault (FT) as described in Algorithm 6.1–1, and the time it takes to access memory (MT). This can be described as

$$AT = p * FT + (1 - p) * MT$$

where p is the probability of a page fault and $0.0 \leq p \leq 1.0$. Memory access time depends largely on the architecture of the computer and page fault time depends on both hardware and software characteristics. If there is no possibility of page faults, $p = 0$ and the access time, or AT, equals the memory access time, or MT, as expected. However, a high probability of page faults, approximately $p = 1$, implies that access time, or AT, is approximately equal to the page fault time, or FT—again as expected.

EXAMPLE 6.2–2

Problem

The time needed to process a page fault is approximately 3 ms and the time needed to access memory is approximately 150 ns. Write a C program segment to calculate the access time for demand paging for probability p.

Reasoning

One interpretation of this problem is to allow the user to input a value for p and have the program calculate the access time. To do this the program includes a data filter that prevents the user from using an improper value for p. Also note that the time units must be uniform; time measured in μs appears to be a balanced compromise. The time 3 ms equals 3,000 μs; the time 150 ns equals 0.150 μs.

Solution

A rough program segment to calculate the access time is as follows.

```
#define FAULT_TIME   3000.0
#define MEM_TIME       0.150

scanf (  "%f",   &prob );
while  ( prob > 1.0  ||  prob <0.0 )        /*  While entered probability  */
   scanf (  "%f",  &prob );                 /*  not in range  */

access_time   = prob * FAULT_TIME  +  ( 1.0 - prob ) * MEM_TIME

printf (  "\nFor  p = %9.3f,   fault time = %9.3f  and
          memory time = %f,  \n", prob,  FAULT_TIME,  MEM_TIME  );
printf (  "\n the access time is %9.3f.",   access_time  );
```

Test

Execution of this program is included in the exercises at the end of this section.

Virtual memory also presents the problem of **thrashing,** or high paging activity. Thrashing is related to page size, memory access time, and hardware and software design. One response is to make the size of a page frame small because small pages do not waste space. For example, if a page is 4 KB, a program of 3 KB wastes only 1 KB of memory. Yet small pages have the disadvantage of causing many more page faults than large pages.

Large pages cause fewer page faults but have too much memory for small programs. For example, if a page is 32 KB, a program that is 3 KB wastes 29 KB of memory. Also, when a page fault does occur a large page carries the overhead of transferring more bytes than a smaller page. Ideally the operating system adjusts the page size for each application (or applications) at any given time during use, a goal that is still difficult to reach.

When a program does not use the full contents of a page, **fragmentation** results. On the average, one half-page remains empty per process. For example, a page of 32 KB on the average wastes 16 KB of space per process, whereas a page of 4 KB on the average wastes 2 KB of space per process. Small pages do minimize fragmentation, but at the cost of more page faults. Designers of operating systems are well aware of this tradeoff.

The greatest problem with thrashing is underuse of the CPU. The time spent on swapping pages from secondary memory into page frames can leave the CPU in a waiting state that is wasteful and costly, or it can prompt another process to be scheduled. Different approaches can be taken to minimize thrashing, but their discussion belongs in a more advanced text on operating systems.

6.2.7 Large-Scale and Personal Computers

As we saw in Chapter 1, in the early days operating systems were nonexistent and the functions that are now automatic were then handled by programmers. As computers became more sophisticated and compilers more common, these functions were taken over by operating system software.

A prominent operating system of the late 1950s, the **Atlas,** was developed in England at the University of Manchester and used what were then innovative features such as spooling, demand paging for memory management, and a cache memory. **Spooling** is holding information in a buffer (temporary memory storage) until an output device is available to use it. **Caching** is the use of a high-speed memory area to hold information temporarily, usually between working registers and main memory.

Section 1.3.1 traced the generations of computer hardware and software from the earliest computing devices through the crucial period in the 1960s. This was when IBM developed the **OS/360** operating system for its 360 mainframes, which evolved into the **VM** (virtual machine) operating system. The 1970s saw DEC introduce the **VMS** (virtual memory system) operating system for its **PDP** series of minicomputers, which later became the DEC/VAX series. The PDP series using VMS was streamlined compared to the OS/360.

Most of the early 8-bit PCs of the 1970s used the **CP/M** (control program for microprocessors) operating system that featured simple commands for the ordinary user and avoided the complexities of multiuser systems. CP/M was displaced by **MS-DOS** (Microsoft disk operating system), prevalent on modern 16- and 32-bit, IBM-compatible PCs in the 1980s. In 1984 Apple launched its new **Macintosh** operating system.

Today's PCs are based on **windowing,** which is the integrated use of icons, pull-down menus, and graphics. Some popular environments include **Windows 3.1**™ and **Windows/NT**™ from Microsoft, and **Macintosh/7.0** from Apple. These computers with their efficient operating systems exceed the performance of mainframe computers of the 1960s.

With the goal of a universal time-sharing operating system, Bell Laboratories developed **UNIX**®. This system first appeared in 1969 and is now available for both large-scale computers and microcomputers. UNIX, which is written in C, uses the positive features of many operating systems in a way that is transparent to the user. Key features of UNIX are portability (the ability to transfer from one system to another) and power. Its popularity is based on its interactive use and the fact that it was made available at little or no cost to many colleges and universities. UNIX may become the operating system of choice for computer professionals. Many **workstations**—PCs with high primary and secondary memory capacities, high-speed CPU and bus rates, and high-resolution graphics—have windowed interfaces that run under UNIX.

EXERCISES 6.2

Concept Check

Answer statements 1 through 4 by with true *or* false.

1. Loaders are used to install source code in a computer.
2. CP/M stands for computer products and manufacturers.
3. The size of virtual memory is bounded by the size of physical memory.
4. The size of a page frame must be the same as the size of a page.

For statements 5 through 8 choose the answer that best completes the statement.

5. A utility that connects the components of a program together is called a(n)
   a. editor
   b. loader
   c. linker
   d. assembler
6. In virtual memory the component that keeps an accounting of the pages present in memory is
   a. the operating system
   b. the page table
   c. the interpreter
   d. the loader
7. The time it takes to execute demand paging is a function of
   a. the size of memory
   b. the operating system
   c. the capacity of the hard drive
   d. the time needed for page faults and memory access
8. Personal computers of the 1990s
   a. equal the capacity of mainframes of the 1960s
   b. probably exceed the capacity of mainframes of the 1960s
   c. have modest graphic capabilities
   d. are limited to 16 MB RAM

For statements 9 through 12 fill in the blanks with the right word.

9. A high-speed memory area is called a _____.
10. Paging is the swapping of _____ into
    _____.

11. A utility program that helps programmers write software is called a
_____.

12. The conversion of source code into machine code is called
_____.

Set A

13. A program is under development. Explain the advantages in using (a) an interpreter rather than a compiler and (b) a compiler rather than an interpreter.
14. Memory is 512 KB and is partitioned into 2048 page frames. Find the size of each frame.
15. There are 8,192 pages, each of 16 KB. Find the total logical memory in megabytes.
16. Explain the meaning of virtual memory when programs are always smaller than physical memory.
17. Explain what happens when a program is larger than physical memory.
18. Explain why the size of a page must equal the size of a page frame.

Set B

19. A computer takes 2 μs to access memory. If the probability of a page fault is zero, calculate the access time for demand paging.
20. Find the size of a page if physical memory of 16 MB is partitioned into 4,096 parts.
21. Use the result from Question 20 to calculate the approximate size of a program if it consumes 35 pages.
22. For a probability of a page fault equaling 0.32, calculate the access time for demand paging if memory access takes 12 μs and a page fault takes 0.4 ms.
23. Repeat Question 22 with $p = 0.84$.
24. Research some of the features of the VM and the VMS operating systems. Compare and contrast these two systems.
25. Research some of the features of UNIX and cite some advantages and disadvantages of UNIX compared to VM and VMS.
26. Research some of the features of the Windows/NT and Macintosh 7.0 operating systems. Compare and contrast these two systems.

Set C

27. Implement the algorithm in Example 6.2–2.
28. Complete the solution and testing of the problem in Example 6.2–2 by using the algorithm given in that example.

ENDNOTE

1. Oz, Effy. *Ethics for the Information Age*. Business and Educational Technologies (1994), pp. 75–77.

7 Arrays

Arrays of similar homes, Levittown, New York.

After completing this chapter you should be able to do the following:

Learning Goals

- Create a multidimensional array of any C-defined data type
- Initialize an array to any desired values of the appropriate type
- Do arithmetic operations using arrays
- Implement a bar graph using arrays
- Pass a whole array or an array element to a function
- Define an output parameter of a function
- Construct strings using arrays
- Use library functions for elementary string and character processing

Chapter Activity

One simple technique used to encode a string is called *alphabetic substitution* and it is one of many forms of data encryption. By means of this technique, each letter of the alphabet is exchanged for a different letter in the encrypted string. Reversing the process brings the encrypted string back to its original value. Write a program to input a string and output its encrypted value. The program should also decode the string.

7.1 OVERVIEW OF ARRAYS

Introduction

Consider this simple problem: Input 50 numbers, compute the mean, and output any of the input numbers that are above the mean. Because there are many numbers to input it is not practical to associate a unique variable with each input value. Instead, the data must be read in the context of a loop. Here is a possible pseudocode solution:

Step 1: sum = 0
Step 2: LOOP 50 times
      a. INPUT number
      b. sum = sum + number
Step 3: mean = sum / 50
Step 4: ? ? ?

How do we continue beyond this point? If we want to output the values above the mean, we need access to the original data again. However, the only data item still accessible is the last number read in; the previous 49 numbers have been overwritten in memory.

We could ask for the data to be reinput, as in the following pseudocode segment.

Step 4: LOOP 50 times
      a. INPUT number
      b. IF number > mean
          1. OUTPUT number

This solves the problem but in a program the duplication of input would annoy the user. What we need is to keep the data as they are input. Then the program can refer to all or part of the data as often as necessary. The way to do this is with an array.

7.1.1 Array Basics

A one-dimensional (1D) **array,** sometimes called a **vector** or **contiguous list,** is a collection of memory locations, all of which have the same data type and can be accessed by a single variable name. When an array is allocated, the computer finds contiguous memory locations, that is, without gaps between array elements. An array is called a **data structure** (as opposed to a *simple* variable) because it can access (store and retrieve) more than one data item using a single variable name.

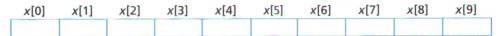

Figure 7.1–1 10-element array called **x**

Query: The simple variable **x** can take on different values, such as 5 or 13. Why is **x** not called a data structure?

RESPONSE: The value of any simple variable such as we have been using up to now can change over time. Yet at any given time, only one value can be associated with a simple (unstructured) variable: There is a one-to-one correspondence between its name and its current value. By contrast, a structured variable has a one-to-many correspondence between its name and its current values.

You can access individual elements in an array by supplying an **index** or **subscript** after the name of the array variable. In the past, computers did not display subscripts (literally, below the line script such as "x_3") so many languages use brackets or parentheses to denote an array index. C uses square brackets. For example, if **x** is an array then **x[3]** refers to the element in **x** whose index is 3. This is read **x** *sub 3* for **x** subscript 3.

Although our discussion is limited to 1D arrays, 2D, 3D, or higher-dimensional arrays are also allowed in C. In each case two or more subscripts are needed to specify an individual element. (These structures are discussed in Section 7.3.)

We create storage for arrays by including the size of the array (the number of elements) after the name and data type. For example, `int x[10]` declares an array with storage space for 10 integers (see Figure 7.1–1). *Note that in C, array elements are always numbered from 0 to (size − 1).* That is, the first element of **x** is **x[0]** and the last is **x[9]** for an array of 10 integers. This sometimes confusing style of subscripting, called **zero-based indexing,** has to do with the method by which C accesses array elements (discussed later in this chapter).

Arrays follow the same naming rules as simple variables (discussed in Section 3.2.4). As with simple variables, array data can be associated with any valid data type.

Query: If an array is declared as `float x[10]`, does that mean that the subscripts are also floating point?

RESPONSE: No! The data type of an array is the *kind* of data that can be stored in the individual cells of the array. The subscript of any array is *always* an integer in the range of 0 to (array size − 1).

There are two restrictions in the use of arrays. First, you have to specify the amount of storage for a declared array at compile time (before execution). Therefore, an array must have a fixed (nonvariable) size. (A mechanism for variable-length arrays is discussed in Chapter 13.) Second, the data type of an array applies uniformly to all the elements and for this reason, an array is called a **homogeneous** data structure. As shown in Chapter 11, other data structures are **heterogeneous:** They can hold any number of different data types.

<table>
<tr><td>

BEFORE YOU GO ON

</td><td>

Query: A problem calls for a list of numbers to be input. The user decides how many numbers, as shown below.

```
int    size, biglist [ size ];
printf ( "\nInput size of the list" );
scanf  ( "%d", &size );
```

What's wrong with this program segment?

_____

RESPONSE: The size of a declared array must be a constant. Because the value of **size** is not fixed at compile time, the array is not described correctly and the declaration generates a syntax error. We have to estimate a reasonable maximum size for the array and use that number in the array declaration.

</td></tr>
</table>

7.1.2 Using Arrays

Here are some more examples of using arrays:

C CODE	**EFFECT**
`float rainfall [12];`	Creates an array called **rainfall**, which has 12 floating-point memory cells indexed 0 through 11
`rainfall [3] = 2.5;`	Sets cell 3 in rainfall to 2.5

`if ( rainfall[3] > rainfall[11] )`
`    printf ( "More rain in April`
`              than in December" );`
	Compares two elements of rainfall and takes an action

`for ( i = 0; i < YEARLENGTH; i++ )` `    scanf ( "%d", &rainfall[ i ] );`	Uses a **for** loop to read values into the array

Notice that in all cases the array reference must have a well-defined subscript, that is, any constant, variable, or arithmetic expression within the bounds of the array. It does not make sense, for example, to refer to **rainfall [15]** or **rainfall [−2]** or **rainfall [i]** unless **i** happens to be within the range 0 through 11. It is perfectly acceptable to refer to **rainfall [3*2]** or **rainfall [i*2]** as long as **i*2** evaluates to a number within the bounds of the array.

Query: What happens if an array is referenced outside of its bounds?

RESPONSE: Out-of-bounds references are allowed but they are not checked and the results are unpredictable! As the programmer you are responsible for ensuring that all arrays are correctly referenced.

In the example at the beginning of this section, the problem was to compute the mean of a set of numbers and output the numbers greater than the mean. The solution consists of storing the input data in an array, computing the mean of the array values, and outputting the data that is above the mean. Program 7.1–1 shows the solution in C code.

PROGRAM 7.1–1

```
/*********************************************************************
 * Title:        values above mean                                  *
 * Filename:     overmean.c                                         *
 *                                                                  *
 * Description: Determine which numbers are greater than the mean of a data set.*
 *                                                                  *
 * Input:        size of list and the data set                     *
 * Output:       numbers greater than the mean                     *
 * Process:      mean = sum of all data / size                     *
 *               output any number if it is greater than the mean  *
 *                                                                  *
 * Written by:   ...                                Date: ...       *
 *********************************************************************/

#include <stdio.h>

main ( )
{
   int   index;
   float list [ 50 ], sum = 0, mean;

   printf (  "\nInput a list of 50 numbers>\n" );
   for ( index = 0;   index < 50;   index++ )           /* Input the numbers */
      scanf ( "%f",   &list [ index ] );

   for ( index = 0;   index < 50;   index++ )           /* Compute the sum */
      sum += list [ index ];
   mean = sum / 50;                                     /* Compute the mean */

   printf (  "\n\nThe items which are greater than the mean are:\n" );
```

```
    for ( index = 0;   index < 50;   index++ )        /* Output the numbers */
        if ( list [ index ] > mean )                  /* above the mean */
            printf ( "\n%.2f",   list [ index ] );


    return ( 0 );
}
```

Array processing is often found in the context of a **for** loop. This is because programs tend to perform a given action on all the array elements, not just one or two of them. As we saw in Program 7.1–1, the **for** loop control variable is a simple way to subscript. You can set the **index** loop variable to run through all the subscripts of a particular array (from 0 to 49, in Program 7.1–1) and then use it as the subscript of the array in the body of the loop—for example, **list [index]**. Note that the array data are always available to use or reuse during the execution of the program.

<table>
<tr><td>**BEFORE YOU GO ON**</td><td>**Query: How can you change array data?**

RESPONSE: As with simple variables, you can change array data with an input statement such as **scanf** or with an assignment statement as in **list [3] = 7;** As the programmer you must be sure to supply a well-defined subscript for the array.</td></tr>
</table>

Arrays are powerful. When you use a variable for the subscript, the code needed to access an array is *independent* of the size of the array. To read in and later make reference to, say, 10 pieces of data without using arrays, you would need to identify 10 variables such as

```
scanf (  "%d%d%d%d%d%d%d%d%d%d",  &a, &b, &c, &d, &e, &f, &g, &h, &i, &j );
```

and then to find the sum of these data:

```
    sum = a + b + c + d + e + f + g + h + i + j;
```

If this is unwieldy, can you imagine what the sum calculation would be if there were 100 variables? Assuming that you have declared the array as **int list [100];** the input is simply

```
        for ( index = 0;   index < 100;   index++ )
            scanf ( "%d",   &list [ index ] );
```

and the summation reduces to

```
        for ( index = 0;   index < 100;   index++ )
            sum  += list [ index ];
```

Now let's consider another problem in array processing, this one simulating vector subtraction using arrays.

Array A $\quad$ | ^{0} 10 | ^{1} 21 | ^{2} 13 | ^{3} 17 | ^{4} 19 |

Array B $\quad$ | ^{0} 19 | ^{1} 44 | ^{2} 72 | ^{3} 3 | ^{4} 0 |

Array C $\quad$ | ^{0} 9 | ^{1} 23 | ^{2} 59 | ^{3} −14 | ^{4} −19 |

$C[i] = B[i] - A[i]$

Figure 7.1–2 $\quad$ Array subtraction

EXAMPLE 7.1–1

Problem

Create three arrays. Read data into the first two of them. Subtract each element in the first array from the corresponding element in the second array. Store the differences in the third array. Print all the arrays. The relationships between the arrays are shown in Figure 7.1–2.

Reasoning

Our intuitive understanding of the problem is *difference = second − first*. However, we can not do whole-array operations in C: Array references almost always have a subscript. The only way is to **traverse** the array, element by element, and compute the differences. You can do this with a **for** loop.

Formal Statement:
Input: $\quad$ first array, second array
Output: $\quad$ difference array, first array, second array
Process: $\quad$ difference[i] = second[i] − first[i] for all i in the range of the arrays

Solution

The pseudocode for the problem is as follows.

1. LOOP all array elements
         INPUT first[i]
2. LOOP all array elements
         INPUT second[i]
3. LOOP all array elements
         difference[i] = second[i] − first[i]
4. LOOP all array elements
         OUTPUT first[i], second[i], difference[i]
5. STOP

The C code for the problem is shown in Program 7.1–2.

P R O G R A M   7 . 1 – 2

```
/*****************************************************************************
* Title:        vector subtraction                                         *
* Filename:     vector.c                                                    *
*                                                                          *
* Description: Compute the difference between two arrays and store the      *
*              result in a third array.                                     *
*                                                                          *
* Input:        values for two arrays                                       *
* Output:       computed difference between the input array values          *
* Process:      difference [ i ] = first [ i ]  -  second [ i ]             *
*                                                                          *
* Written by:  ...                                       Date: ...          *
*****************************************************************************/

#include <stdio.h>

#define  MAX_SIZE 5

main ( )
{

   int    first [ MAX_SIZE ],  second [ MAX_SIZE ],  diff [ MAX_SIZE ],  i;

   printf (  "\nEnter %d data items for first array",  MAX_SIZE  );
   for (  i = 0;   i < MAX_SIZE;   i++ )                    /* Input first array */
      scanf (  "%d",   &first [ i ]  );

   printf (  "\nEnter %d data items for second array", MAX_SIZE  );
   for (  i = 0;   i < MAX_SIZE;   i++ )                    /* Input second array */
      scanf (  "%d",   &second [ i ]  );

   for (  i = 0;   i < MAX_SIZE;   i++ )               /* Compute the differences */
      diff [ i ]  =  second [ i ]  -  first [ i ];

   printf (  "\n\nOutput the arrays:"  );
   for (  i = 0;   i < MAX_SIZE;   i++ )                    /* Output the arrays */
      printf (  "\n%5d %5d %5d", first [ i ], second [ i ], diff [ i ]  );

 return ( 0 );
}
```

Test

You can easily test this program by entering data for each of the two arrays and checking the output. •

Notice that **MAX_SIZE** could have been set to any value, not just the number 5. Is there a technique that would let the *user* decide the size of a declared array? As we said earlier, the array size must be fixed at compile time. However, the array does not have to be filled with data. You could set **MAX_SIZE**, for instance, to 100. Then you could prompt the user to supply the *working size* of the array—or the portion of the array to be filled with data. The revised vector subtraction program is shown in Program 7.1–3.

PROGRAM 7.1-3

```
/*******************************************************************************
* Title:        vector subtraction (revised)                                  *
* Filename:     vector2.c                                                      *
*                                                                             *
* Description: Compute the difference between two arrays and store the result in a *
*              third array.                                                    *
*                                                                             *
* Input:        logical array size, values for two arrays                      *
* Output:       computed difference between the input array values             *
* Process:      difference [ i ]  =  first [ i ] - second [ i ]                *
*                                                                             *
* Written by:  ...                                         Date: ...          *
*******************************************************************************/

#include <stdio.h>

#define  MAX_SIZE 100

main ( )
{

    int  first [ MAX_SIZE ], second [ MAX_SIZE ],  diff [ MAX_SIZE ],  i,  size;

    printf ( "\nHow many data items do you wish to enter (max = %d)?", MAX_SIZE );
    scanf ( "%d",   &size );

    while ( size < 1   ||   size > MAX_SIZE )   {                          /* Verify size */
      printf ( "\nError in array size...Must be 1-%d...Re-enter value:", MAX_SIZE );
      scanf ( "%d",   &size );
    }

    printf ( "\nEnter %d data items for first array>",  size );
    for (  i = 0;   i < size;   i++ )                          /* Input first array */
        scanf ( "%d",   &first [ i ] );
```

```
    printf ( "\nEnter %d data items for second array", size );
    for ( i = 0;  i < size;  i++ )                            /* Input second array */
        scanf ( "%d", &second [ i ] );

    for ( i = 0;  i < size;  i++ )                            /* Compute the differences */
        diff [ i ]  =  second [ i ]  -  first [ i ];

    printf ( "\n\nOutput the arrays:" );
    for ( i = 0;  i < size;  i++ )                            /* Output the arrays */
        printf ( "\n%5d %5d %5d",  first [ i ],  second [ i ],  diff [ i ] );

    return ( 0 );
}
```

Note the difference between **MAX_SIZE** and **size**. **MAX_SIZE** is the **physical size** of the declared array and must be a constant whose value is set at compile time. **size** is the **logical size** of the array. It is always a variable, it can be any value less than or equal to **MAX_SIZE**, and is usually determined by the user during the run of the program. The names **size** and **MAX_SIZE** were chosen for mnemonics, not syntax. Finally, note that in naming the physical size of an array you must use **#define** not **const**.

BEFORE YOU GO ON

Query: Why do you have to include the **while** loop after the value for **size** is read?

RESPONSE: The **while** loop detects whether the input value for **size** is out of the bounds of the array. This is important because there is no array-bounds error check in C.

7.1.3 Initializing Arrays

You can initialize arrays, like simple variables, in their declarations. Examples of this are as follows.

```
1. int    vector1 [ 5 ]   = { 12, -2, 33, 21, 13 };

2. float  rainfall [ 12 ] = {1.2, 2.3, 1.4, 3.2, 3.3, 2.3, 1.1, 0.8, 1.3, 2.3,
                             1.3, 1.9 };

3. double vector2 [  ]    = { 17.33333456,  -1.212121213,  222.191345 };

4. int    height [ 10 ]   = { 60, 70, 68, 72, 68 };
```

Example 1 declares **vector1** with five integer elements and is initialized as shown in Figure 7.1–3. Example 2 declares **rainfall** with 12 floating-point values. (The

Element	0	1	2	3	4
Value	12	−2	33	21	13

Figure 7.1–3   Initializing the `vector1` array

declaration can be split across two lines of the program.) Example 3 declares `vector2` without a size specification. In this case, the number of initializing values taken as the size (3). If the array is given an explicit size, the initializer list can be shorter than the size. The remaining cells of the array are set to 0. There is no mechanism for specifying a repeated initializer value.

BEFORE YOU GO ON

Query: How do we set all the cells of a 500-element array to 1?

RESPONSE: Assuming that the array `x` has been declared, use a `for` loop:

```
for ( index = 0; index < 500; index++ )
    x [ index ] = 1;
```

EXERCISES 7.1

Concept Check

Answer statements 1 through 4 with true *or* false.
1. Arrays provide storage for data during the execution of a program.
2. Arrays are called *structured* because they can hold various types of data.
3. The physical size of a declared array can be decided by the user of the program.
4. Bounds-checking on arrays is the responsibility of the programmer.

For statements 5 through 8 choose the answer that best completes the statement.
5. The following declares a `float` array whose elements are numbered 0 through 10:
   a. `float rainfall [ 10 ];`
   b. `float rainfall [ 11 ];`
   c. `float rainfall [ 9 ];`
   d. `float rainfall [ 0:10 ];`
6. Data structures
   a. are always heterogeneous
   b. are always homogeneous
   c. were mentioned, but none were covered in this section
   d. facilitate the storage and retrieval of a collection of data

7. A simple variable differs from a structured variable because a simple variable
   a. can have only one value during the entire execution of a program
   b. can have many values at one time during the execution of a program
   c. can have many values but only one value at any given time
   d. has a many-to-one relationship between the variable and its associated data

8. The following sets all cells of a five-element array to the value of 10.
   a. `int x    = { 10, 10, 10, 10, 10 };`
   b. `int x[ ] = { 5 * 10 };`
   c. `int x[5] = { 5 * 10 };`
   d. `int x[ ] = { 10, 10, 10, 10, 10 };`

For statements 9 through 12 fill in the blanks with the right word.

9. A 1D array is sometimes called a _____ or a _____.
10. All array elements have the same _____ and _____.
11. The _____ size of an array is set at compile time, whereas the _____ size is set during run time.
12. Individual elements of an array are referred to by means of a(n) _____.

Set A

Solve each of the following problems by writing one or more C statements.

13. Initialize a five-element array to the values $-10, 14, 22, -3, 12$.
14. Create a **for** loop to subtract 10 from all the elements in the array in Question 13.
15. Copy array **a** into array **b,** assuming the declaration

    ```
    int    a[10],  b[32];
    ```

16. Output the contents of a five-element array first on one line and then on five lines.

Set B

17. Output the odd elements of a 10-element array.
18. Input a list of 10 numbers into an array. Output the list backwards.
19. Input a list of numbers, letting the user decide how many. Output the list backwards, but only output numbers greater than 20.

Set C

20. Input a list of numbers, letting the user decide how many. Output the list backwards, but stop if the number 20 is found in the array.
21. Input up to 50 **float** numbers into an array, letting the user decide how many. Subtract **x** from each of each element, storing the results in a second array and letting the user specify **x**. Output the original array and the modified array side by side.
22. Output the sums of each nonoverlapping odd–even pair of a 10-element array.

7.2 ARRAYS AND FUNCTIONS

Introduction

Next, we cover some of the special requirements for passing arrays to functions. This section will also help you increase your skills for using arrays and functions.

7.2.1 Using Arrays with Functions

Passing an *individual* array element to a function is like passing any other variable. You list the array name, followed by a subscript reference to the desired element, as shown in Program 7.2–1.

PROGRAM 7.2–1

```
/*****************************************************************************
* Title:        array calculations                                         *
* Filename:     arraysum.c                                                  *
*                                                                           *
* Description: Compute the sum of the first three elements in an array.     *
*                                                                           *
* Input:        none (set within the program)                              *
* Output:       sum of array elements                                      *
* Process:      sum = x[0] + x[1] + x[2]                                    *
*                                                                           *
* Written by:   ...                                        Date: ...        *
*****************************************************************************/

#include <stdio.h>

int sum_elements ( int  a,   int  b,   int  c );        /* Function prototype */

main ( )
{

   int x [ 10 ],   total;

   x [ 0 ] = 10;                     /* Assign values to the first three elements */
   x [ 1 ] = 20;
   x [ 2 ] = 30;

   total =  sum_elements ( x [ 0 ], x [ 1 ], x [ 2 ] );   /* Compute the sum */

   printf ( "\nFor values: %d %d %d", x[0], x[1], x[2] ); /* Output the results */
   printf ( " the sum = %d",  total );
```

```
        return ( 0 );
}                                              /* End of main */



/*************************************************************************
 * Function name:    sum_elements                                        *
 * Description:      Add the values passed to the parameters.            *
 *                                                                       *
 * Input parameters: three integers                                      *
 * Output parameters: none                                               *
 * Return value:     sum                                                 *
 *************************************************************************/

int sum_elements ( int a,   int b,   int c )        /* Function header */
{
    int sum;
    sum = a + b + c;
    return ( sum );
}                                              /* End of sum_elements */
```

The parameters of **sum_elements** are listed as simple (nonarray) variables. This is because the data you are passing (the **arguments**) are not the array as a whole, just the individual array elements. Because each array element is by itself a simple integer, you list the parameters as integers.

This example is not typical of array problems. Usually a whole array, not just selected elements, is processed. Remember that since the purpose of an array is to hold a collection of logically related data items, it is reasonable to expect that an array-processing function needs all the elements—that is, the array itself. The following example shows how to pass a whole array to a function.

EXAMPLE 7.2–1

Problem
Read 12 numbers corresponding to rainfall amounts (in inches) for a period of one year. Compute the mean rainfall for the year. Print the mean rainfall. Then print the month number of all the dry months, or the months whose rainfall was less than the mean.

Reasoning
The problem needs an array to store the monthly rainfall amounts. You can compute the mean by summing all the data in the array and dividing by 12. Finding the dry months means reexamining each array element to determine whether it is less than the mean.

Formal Statement:

Input: rainfall data for one year
Output: mean, list of dry months
Process: mean = Σx_i / 12
              dry month = any month whose rainfall was < mean

Solution

The pseudocode for this problem is:

Step 1: LOOP all months
              INPUT rainfall[i]
Step 2: sum = 0
Step 3: LOOP all months
            sum = sum + rainfall[i]
Step 4: mean = sum / 12
Step 5: OUTPUT mean
Step 6: LOOP all months
              IF rainfall[i] < mean
                  OUTPUT i
Step 7: STOP

BEFORE YOU GO ON

Query: Why weren't Steps 1 through 3 combined into one loop?

RESPONSE: The loops at Steps 1 and 3 could have been combined in one loop but they were intentionally separated for modularity. The first loop concerns data input and the second loop concerns computing. As you can see in the C code, this problem readily lends itself to the use of functions.

Step 6 includes the test for dryness. If the amount of rain on the ith month is less than the mean, then output the month number (i). Now convert the algorithm to C as shown in Program 7.2–2. Each major step is written as a function.

PROGRAM 7.2–2

```
/******************************************************************************
* Title:      rainfall calculations                                          *
* Filename:   rainfall.c                                                      *
*                                                                            *
* Description: Compute the mean rainfall and produce a list of dry months--  *
*              that is, where the rainfall was less than the mean.           *
*                                                                            *
* Input:      rainfall data for one year                                     *
* Output:     mean rainfall, list of dry months                             *
* Process:    mean  =  sum(x[i]) / 12, where  dry month = rain was < mean     *
*                                                                            *
* Written by:  ...                                       Date: ...           *
******************************************************************************/
```

```c
#include <stdio.h>

void  input_rainfall             ( float   rainfall [ ]   );      /* Prototypes */
float calc_mean_rainfall         ( float   rainfall [ ]   );
void  output_mean_and_dry_months ( float   rainfall [ ],  float mean );

#define YEAR_LENGTH 12

main ( )
{

    float rainfall [ YEAR_LENGTH ],   mean;

    input_rainfall ( rainfall );                        /* Input the rainfall data */

    mean  =  calc_mean_rainfall ( rainfall );            /* Compute the mean */

    output_mean_and_dry_months ( rainfall, mean );       /* Output the results */

    return ( 0 );
}                                                        /* End of main */
```

```
/***************************************************************************
 * Function name:     input_rainfall                                       *
 * Description:       Input user values for yearly rainfall in inches.     *
 *                                                                         *
 * Input parameters:  none                                                 *
 * Output parameters: rainfall                                             *
 * Return value:      none                                                 *
 ***************************************************************************/

void input_rainfall ( float   rainfall [ ] )
{
    int month;

    printf (  "\nInput monthly rainfall amounts for one year"  );

    for ( month = 0;   month < YEAR_LENGTH;   month++ )
        scanf ( "%f",   &rainfall [ month ] );
}                                                /* End of input_rainfall */
```

```
/********************************************************************
 * Function name:      calc_mean_rainfall                          *
 * Description:        Compute the mean yearly rainfall in inches.  *
 *                                                                  *
 * Input parameters:  rainfall data                                *
 * Output parameters: none                                          *
 * Return value:       mean                                         *
 ********************************************************************/

float calc_mean_rainfall ( float   rainfall [ ] )
{
    int    month;
    float sum = 0.0;

    for ( month = 0;  month < YEAR_LENGTH;   month++ )
        sum += rainfall [ month ];

    return ( sum / YEAR_LENGTH );
}                                        /* End of calc_mean_rainfall */


/********************************************************************
 * Function name:      output_mean_and_dry_months                   *
 * Description:        Output the mean rainfall and list each of the dry months. *
 *                                                                  *
 * Input parameters:  rainfall data, mean rainfall                 *
 * Output parameters: none                                          *
 * Return value:       none                                         *
 ********************************************************************/

void output_mean_and_dry_months ( float rainfall [ ],  float mean )
{
    int month;

    printf ( "\nAverage annual rainfall = %5.2f",   mean );
    printf ( "\nList of dry months:" );

    for ( month = 0;  month < YEAR_LENGTH;   month++ )
        if ( rainfall [ month ] < mean )
            printf ( "\n%d",  month+1 );/* Add one to month to correspond */
                                        /* to normal month numbers 1 - 12 */

}                                        /* End of output_mean_and_dry_months */
```

Test

Supply a sample set of input to check that the mean is correctly computed and
the list of dry months correctly output.

Query: Why does the final output reference `month + 1` instead of just `month`?

RESPONSE: Remember, array subscripts are numbered from 0, so outputting `month` would look strange to the user (January would be displayed as month 0, etc.). Therefore, you compensate by adding 1 to the output.

The `input_rainfall` function has one parameter, `rainfall.` To call a function with an array, you simply list the name of the array as the argument. This passes the whole array. Note that it is really the *address* of the array that is passed, not the array itself. The advantage of doing so is that the data in the array does not need to be copied into the corresponding array parameter in the function. By contrast, if arrays were passed as simple arguments, copying the array data would take time. Also, a duplicate set of memory locations would have to be allocated. (This is discussed further in Chapter 9.)

Within the function the corresponding parameter is listed as the name of the array followed by a left and a right bracket. The brackets mean that the parameter is an array, not just a simple variable. Note that you can specify the size of the array within the brackets although this is not necessary.

The `input_rainfall` function treats the `rainfall` array as an output parameter. An **output parameter** is a variable whose value is determined in a function and returned through the corresponding argument to the calling function. `rainfall` has no legitimate data coming into the function so it is not an input parameter but instead gets its values within the function. These values are automatically returned to `main` for use in the remainder of the program. Because `rainfall` is a structured variable (it contains more than one value), its values cannot be returned via the `return` statement. Notice that the documentation header acknowledges the status of `rainfall` as an output parameter. (Using output parameters other than arrays is discussed in Chapter 9.)

PERSPECTIVE

Observe the use of the `month` variable as the subscript for `rainfall.` Some programmers use a generic name such as `i` or `j` for subscripts. However, in this case the mnemonic name `month` adds to the clarity of the program and is preferable.

The next array example revisits the histogram problem from the "Problem Situation" in Chapter 5. Here the user has to input the raw scores. The program compiles the histogram (**frequency count**) and outputs the corresponding bar graph. Compiling the histogram is keeping track of the number of occurrences of each grade. This is shown in Example 7.2–2.

EXAMPLE 7.2–2

Problem
Write a program to tally scores from an examination and output a histogram to produce a bar graph of the results. Also, output the mean of the data.

Reasoning
A histogram can be viewed as an array of counters in which each element of the histogram represents the number of occurrences of a particular data value. In other words, if **hist [80]** contains a 15, that means that 15 students received a score of 80 on the examination. Similarly, if no student received a 10 on the examination, **hist [10]** equals 0. The histogram is compiled by tallying each examination grade (adding 1) in the appropriate element of the array. Which is the appropriate element to add to? The element whose subscript equals the input grade. In pseudocode this might be

1. INPUT grade
2. hist[grade] = hist[grade] + 1

assuming that the grade is an appropriate subscript in the range of 0 to 100.

Formal Statement:
Input: number of grades, list of grades
Output: histogram, mean
Process: mean = $\Sigma x_i / n$

Solution

Step 1:   INPUT #grades
Step 2:   LOOP #grades
        a. INPUT grades[i]
Step 3:   LOOP grade range   /* Compile histogram */
        a. hist[i] = 0
Step 4:   LOOP #grades
        a. value = grades[i]
        b. hist[value] = hist[value] + 1
Step 5:   sum = 0   /* Compute mean */
Step 6:   LOOP #grades
        a. sum = sum + grades[i]
Step 7:   mean = sum / #grades
Step 8:   LOOP grades range   /* Output bar graph */
        a. OUTPUT i
        b. LOOP 1 to hist[i]
          i. OUTPUT '*'
Step 9:   OUTPUT mean
Step 10:   STOP

The C program for this example is shown in Program 7.2–3.

P R O G R A M   7 . 2 – 3

```
/******************************************************************************
* Title:        histogram of examination grades                              *
* Filename:     histo.c                                                       *
*                                                                             *
* Description: Compute a histogram (frequency distribution) for a set of      *
*              exam grades.  Also compute the mean.                           *
*                                                                             *
* Input:        number of grades and grade list                              *
* Output:       histogram (bar graph) and mean                               *
* Process:      hist[ i ] = frequency of each data value                     *
*               mean  =  sum ( x[i] )  /  n                                   *
*                                                                             *
* Written by:  ...                                         Date: ...          *
*******************************************************************************/

#include <stdio.h>
#include <math.h>


#define  MAX_NUM_GRADES   50                       /* Maximum class size */
#define  HIGH_GRADE      100                       /* Maximum exam grade */


                                                   /*  Prototypes */
int   get_num_grades ( void );
void  get_grades      ( int  grade_list [ ], int    num_grades                );
void  calc_histogram ( int  grade_list [ ], int    num_grades, int  hist [ ] );
float calc_mean       ( int  grade_list [ ], int    num_grades                );
void  put_histogram  ( int  hist [ ],        float mean                      );

main ()
{
   float mean;
   int   grade_list [ MAX_NUM_GRADES ],   hist [ HIGH_GRADE+1 ];
   int   num_grades;

   num_grades  =  get_num_grades ( );          /* Input number of exam grades */

   get_grades ( grade_list,  num_grades );            /* Input exam grades */

   calc_histogram ( grade_list, num_grades, hist );  /* Compile the histogram */

   mean = calc_mean ( grade_list,  num_grades );     /* Compute the mean */

   put_histogram ( hist,   mean );              /* Display histogram and mean */
```

```
   return ( 0 );
}                                                            /* End of main */



/***********************************************************************
* Function name:      get_num_grades                                   *
* Description:        Input and verify the number of grades to be entered. *
*                                                                      *
* Input parameters:   none                                             *
* Output parameters:  none                                             *
* Return value:       number of grades to be entered                   *
***********************************************************************/

int  get_num_grades ( void )
{
   int  num_grades;

   printf (  "\nInput number of grades > " );
   scanf (  "%d",   &num_grades );

                                            /* Verify number of grades */
   while (  num_grades < 1   ||   num_grades > MAX_NUM_GRADES  )   {
     printf (  "\nNumber of grades out of range. Must be 1-%d",
                                        MAX_NUM_GRADES );
     printf (  "\nPlease re-Input number of grades > "  );
     scanf (  "%d",   &num_grades  );
   }

   return ( num_grades );
}                                            /*  End of get_num_grades  */



/***********************************************************************
* Function name:      get_grades                                       *
* Description:        Input and verify the exam grades.                *
*                                                                      *
* Input parameters:   num_grades                                       *
* Output parameters:  grade_list                                       *
* Return value:       none                                             *
***********************************************************************/

void get_grades (  int   grade_list [ ],   int   num_grades  )
{
   int  grade_count;

   printf (  "\nNow input %d grades...\n",   num_grades  );
```

```
      for ( grade_count = 0;   grade_count < num_grades;   grade_count++ )  {
         scanf ( "%d",    &grade_list [ grade_count ] );

         while ( grade_list [ grade_count ] < 1   ||            /* Verify grade */
                  grade_list [ grade_count ] > HIGH_GRADE ) {
            printf ( "\nGrade out of range. Must be 0-%d", HIGH_GRADE ); ·
            printf ( "\nPlease re-Input grade > " );
            scanf ( "%d",   &grade_list [ grade_count ] );
         }
      }
   }                                                     /*  End of  get_grades  */




/****************************************************************************
* Function name:      calc_histogram                                        *
* Description:        Generate the histogram of grades.                     *
*                                                                           *
* Input parameters: grade_list,    num_grades                              *
* Output parameters: hist                                                   *
* Return value:       none                                                  *
****************************************************************************/

void calc_histogram ( int  grade_list [], int  num_grades,  int  hist [ ] )
{
   int  grade,  value;

   for ( grade = 0;  grade < HIGH_GRADE+1;  grade++ ) /*  Set histogram to 0s */
      hist [ grade ]  =  0;

   for ( grade = 0;  grade < num_grades;  grade++ ) { /*  Compute histogram  */
      value  =  grade_list [ grade ];
      hist [ value ]  +=  1;
   }
}                                                    /*  End of  calc_histogram  */




/****************************************************************************
* Function name:      calc_mean                                             *
* Description:        Compute the mean grade.                               *
*                                                                           *
* Input parameters: grade_list,    num_grades                              *
* Output parameters: none                                                   *
* Return value:       mean grade                                            *
****************************************************************************/
```

```
float calc_mean (   int   grade_list [ ],    int   num_grades  )
{
   int    grade;
   float sum = 0;

   for (   grade = 0;   grade < num_grades;   grade++ )
       sum += grade_list [ grade ];

   return (  sum / num_grades  );
}                                                    /* End of calc_mean */
```

```
/*************************************************************************
 * Function name:      put_histogram                                     *
 * Description:        Output the histogram and the mean.                *
 *                                                                       *
 * Input parameters:   grade_list,  mean                                 *
 * Output parameters:  none                                              *
 * Return value:       none                                              *
 *************************************************************************/

void put_histogram ( int   hist[],    float    mean  )
{
   #define MARKER '*'

   int  grade,   star;

   printf (  "\nGrade Frequency"  );

   for ( grade = 1;  grade < HIGH_GRADE+1;  grade++ ) {  /* For each grade ...*/

      printf (  "\n%4d ",   grade );

      for ( star = 0; star < hist[grade]; star++ )/* Output a row of stars  */
         printf (  "%c",   MARKER ); /* One for each exam with that grade  */
   }

   printf (  "\nMean grade = %5.2f",   mean );
}                                                 /*  End of put_histogram  */
```

Test

You can check this solution by entering a small set of data and checking the bar graph and the mean by hand.

EXERCISES 7.2

Concept Check

Answer statements 1 through 4 with true *or* false.
1. Individual array elements cannot be passed easily to a function.
2. To pass a whole array to a function, you specify the array name.
3. The parameter corresponding to a whole array must specify the array size.
4. An output parameter is defined as a value that is printed by a function.

For statements 5 through 8 choose the answer that best completes the statement.
5. To pass an individual element of an array to a function, you must specify
   a. the data type of the array, its name, and the element number
   b. the name of the array and the element number as two separate arguments
   c. the name of the array and the element number as one argument
   d. just the element number
6. Assuming the array declaration `float values [ MAX_VALUE ];`, which statement will pass the whole array to function `calc_max` ?
   a. `calc_max ( float values [ ] );`
   b. `calc_max ( values [ MAX_VALUE ] );`
   c. `calc_max ( float values [ MAX_VALUE ] );`
   d. `calc_max ( values );`
7. Given the declaration in Question 6, which statement will pass the third and fifth elements (from the beginning of the array) to a function called `pick_larger` ?
   a. `pick_larger ( values [ 3 ], values [ 5 ] );`
   b. `pick_larger ( values, 3, 5 );`
   c. `pick_larger ( values [ 2 ], values [ 4 ] );`
   d. `pick_larger ( float values [ 2 ], float values [ 4 ] );`
8. Given the declaration in Question 6, which statement is a possible prototype for `pick_larger` ?
   a. `float pick_larger ( float value1, float value2 );`
   b. `float pick_larger ( value1, value2 );`
   c. `float pick_larger ( float value[1], float value[2] );`
   d. `float pick_larger ( float value[2], float value[4] );`

For statements 9 through 12 fill in the blanks with the right word.
9. A(n) _____ is a value passed to a function from another function.
10. A(n) _____ is a value calculated within a function and passed back to the calling function.
11. A function is to receive a whole array as a parameter. The header should list the _____ and the _____ followed by a left and a right _____.
12. A function is to receive as a parameter a single element of an array. The header should list the _____ and the _____.

Set A

Solve each of the following problems by writing one or more C statements. See Example 7.2–1 as needed.

13. Write a prototype for a function `pick_min` that accepts the rainfall array and returns the minimum amount of rain. Also, write the function call.

14. Write a prototype for a function `summer_rain` that accepts the rainfall only from the summer months (assume June, July, and August) and returns the total amount of rain. Also, write the function call.

15. Write `summer_rain`.

Set B

16. Write a function called `find_max_rain` that locates and outputs the largest amount of rainfall of any month in the year.

17. Rewrite the answer to Question 16, but have the function return the value instead of outputting it.

18. Write a function that outputs the month number corresponding to the largest amount of rainfall.

19. Rewrite the answer to Question 18, but have the function return the value instead of outputting it.

Set C

When solving this set of problems, see Example 7.2–2 as needed.

20. The median or middle value is an important and easily calculated statistic. Its interpretation is like the mean because it is a single value that can be used to represent the whole data set. However, the median is less sensitive than the mean to extreme values called **outliers** because those data do not affect the location of the median.

    When there is an odd amount of data the median is taken as the middle value. When there is an even amount of data the median is computed as the average of the two midmost data items. Write a function to compute the median value of the examination grades. Note that for the median to be well defined the grades must be in sorted order. Be sure to instruct the user to input the data appropriately (or write a sort function).

21. The **standard deviation** is a measure of dispersion from the mean. We can think of it as a gauge of how accurately the mean represents the data. A data set in which all the values are the same has a standard deviation of 0 (no dispersion from the mean). Typically, if a set of data has a low standard deviation, the mean is probably an accurate reflection of the data. The standard deviation can be computed as

$$\text{standard dev} = \text{sqrt}(\Sigma(x_i - \text{mean})^2/n)$$

Thus the standard deviation is the sum of the squares of the deviations from the mean of each item in the data set. To keep the sum in the proper range, you **normalize,** or divide the sum by the number of items summed. You then take the square root to compensate for the squaring of each term in the calculation (before you take the square root the value is called the **variance**). Write a function to compute the standard deviation of the examination grades.

7.3   HIGHER-DIMENSIONAL ARRAYS

Introduction

Arrays of any type can be created in C, including **multidimensional (multi-D) arrays,** which are arrays of arrays. Whereas we can visualize a 1D array as a contiguous list or a vector, we usually visualize a 2D array as a **matrix** or table. You can also create higher-d arrays. Higher-d arrays are more complicated because the array references involve two or more subscripts.

7.3.1 Matrices

Figure 7.3–1 shows a 2D array, **x**, with four rows and six columns and the indexes for each cell. We create 2D arrays in the same way as 1D arrays through variable declarations. For instance, the following are all valid array declarations.

```
int    grades [100] [6];      /* 100 students, each having 6 grades */
float  rainfall [12] [31];             /* daily rain for one year */
double table [100] [200];   /* spreadsheet with 100 rows, 200 columns */
char   puzzle [25] [25];                    /* crossword puzzle */
```

In each case the declaration indicates the maximum number of rows followed by the maximum number of columns. As with 1D arrays, the indexing is zero-based. For the declaration above, the last element you can reference in the   **grades** array is **grades [99] [5].** Notice that you must specify each subscript separately, enclosed in its own set of brackets.

You can initialize 2D arrays when you declare them, as shown in Figure 7.3–2. The initializer list can be arranged by row, with each row enclosed in braces or arranged linearly, as shown.

```
int  x [3] [2] = { {17, 22},          /* Method 1 */
                   {-33,65},
                   {14,31} };

int  x [3] [2] = { 17, 22, -33, 65, 14, 31 };     /* Method 2 */
```

[0][0]	[0][1]	[0][2]	[0][3]	[0][4]	[0][5]
[1][0]	[1][1]	[1][2]	[1][3]	[1][4]	[1][5]
[2][0]	[2][1]	[2][2]	[2][3]	[2][4]	[2][5]
[3][0]	[3][1]	[3][2]	[3][3]	[3][4]	[3][5]

Figure 7.3–1   2D array, **x,** with four rows and six columns

```
int x[3][2] = { {17,22},
                {-33,65},
                {14, 31} };
```

17	22
−33	65
14	31

Figure 7.3–2   Initializing a 2D array

Regardless of the style you use, make sure that the data are listed in **row-major** or row-by-row order because that is how the data are inserted into the array. As with 1D arrays, if not enough data values are specified, the remaining elements of the array are set to 0.

Let's consider an elementary problem of **matrix addition:** adding the corresponding elements of two arrays and storing the sums in a third array. All three arrays must be **conformable:** They must have the same size and data type. We generally use a doubly nested **for** loop to add matrices. The first (outer) loop supplies the *row* index and the second (inner) loop supplies the *column* index. Assume that the input matrices are named **a** and **b** and the resulting output matrix is named **c**. The algorithm is as follows.

> Step 1:   LOOP rows
> >   a. LOOP columns
> > > c[row][column] = a[row][column] + b[row][column]
>
> Step 2:   STOP

The C code for this problem is shown in Program 7.3–1.

PROGRAM 7.3–1

```
/****************************************************************************
* Title:       matrix addition                                            *
* Filename:    matadd.c                                                    *
*                                                                          *
* Description: Add two compatible matrices and store the result in a third *
*              matrix.                                                     *
*                                                                          *
* Input:       none (data internal to the program)                        *
* Output:      sum of two matrices                                        *
* Process:     sum of corresponding elements of two matrices              *
*                                                                          *
* Written by:  ...                                         Date: ...      *
****************************************************************************/

#include <stdio.h>
```

```
#define  N_ROWS 3
#define  N_COLS 2

main ( )
{
    int  a [ N_ROWS ] [ N_COLS ]   =  {   {10, 20}, {22, 14}, {31, 17}  };
    int  b [ N_ROWS ] [ N_COLS ]   =  {   {20, 30}, {32, 28}, {19, 21}  };

    int  c [ N_ROWS ] [ N_COLS ];
    int  row,  col;

    for ( row = 0;  row < N_ROWS;  row++ )      /* Perform matrix addition */
        for ( col = 0;  col < N_COLS;  col++ )
            c [ row ] [ col ]  =  a [ row ] [ col ] + b [ row ] [ col ];

    printf ( "\n\nMatrix 1 + Matrix 2 = \n\n" );          /* Output a heading */

    for ( row = 0; row < N_ROWS;  row++ )  {  /* Output resulting matrix */
        printf ( "\nRow #%d:      ",  row+1 );
        for ( col = 0;  col < N_COLS;  col++ )
            printf ( "%4d",  c [ row ] [ col ] );
    }

    return ( 0 );
}
```

Use a desk check to verify that the output matrix is indeed the sum of the two input matrices.

EXAMPLE 7.3–1

Problem
A luxury-car dealer wants to keep a monthly log of the number of sales made for each of seven different luxury cars. The dealer wants a printout at the end of the year showing the total number of sales of each car and the best sales month for the year.

Reasoning
Because there are seven models of cars with sales over a period of 12 months, we use a 7 by 12 matrix. Let's call the matrix to store the sales data **sales**. A 1D array called **total [12]** is useful to store the totals for the monthly vehicle sales. To determine the best sales month we analyze the original matrix by finding the total monthly sales of all cars, comparing this total month by month, and keeping track of the best month. Before you try to solve the problem, visualize

SALES	JAN	FEB	MAR	APR	MAY	JUN	JULY	AUG	SEP	OCT	NOV	DEC	TOTAL
Ferrari	5	3	3	4	4	3	4	5	5	3	2	5	46
Porsche	6	7	8	5	4	3	1	3	2	3	4	11	57
Lexus	5	6	8	5	4	3	7	9	6	4	4	5	66
Mercedes	8	6	5	6	5	4	3	7	4	2	7	8	65
BMW	6	6	7	5	4	4	3	2	1	2	1	4	45
Rolls	2	3	4	3	2	1	2	2	3	3	1	4	30
Bentley	1	2	2	3	2	2	3	2	3	4	4	5	33

Figure 7.3–3   2D array of luxury-car sales arranged by month

the significant data structures. The rows and columns are numbered in C, but we can imagine that they are labeled according to the needs of the problem, as shown in Figure 7.3–3.

Solution

Formal Statement:
Input: sales data arranged by product for a one-year period
Output: yearly product totals, best month
Process: $total_i$ $= \Sigma_j \ sales_{ij}$
          $best\_month = MAX \ (\Sigma_j \ sales_{ij})$

Algorithm:
Step 1:   LOOP for each car model   /* Input the sales data */
              a. LOOP month
                 INPUT sales[car][month]

Step 2:   LOOP for each car model   /* Compute vehicle totals */
              a. total[car] = 0
              b. LOOP month
                 total[car] = total[car] + sales[car][month]

Step 3:   max_so_far = 0

Step 4:   LOOP for each month   /* Find best month */
              a. sum = 0
              b. LOOP for each car model
                 sum = sum + sales[car][month]
              c. IF sum > max_so_far
                 1. max_so_far = sum
                 2. best_month = month

Step 5:   LOOP for each car model
              OUTPUT total[car]

Step 6: OUTPUT best_month

Step 7: STOP

Step 2 computes the sum of each row of the **sales** matrix and stores the result in the corresponding element of the **total** array. Step 4 calculates the best month. The loop in Step 4b computes the total number of sales for the current month. Step 4c compares the total to the previous best-month sales. If the new total is better, this becomes the new best month. Program 7.3–2 shows the C code for the problem.

P R O G R A M   7 . 3 – 2

```
/*****************************************************************************
* Title:        luxury-car sales statistics                                 *
* Filename:     luxury.c                                                     *
*                                                                           *
* Description: Input sales data for several car models over a one-year period. *
*              Compute and output the statistics.                           *
*                                                                           *
* Input:        sales data arranged by product for a one-year period        *
* Output:       yearly product totals and best month                        *
* Process:      total_sales[car] = sum ( sales[car][month] )                *
*               best_month       = MAX ( sum ( sales[car][month] ) )        *
*                                                                           *
* Written by:  ...                                          Date: ...       *
*****************************************************************************/

#include <stdio.h>

#define  N_CARS    7
#define  N_MONTHS 12

main ( )
{
   int sales [ N_CARS ] [ N_MONTHS ];
   int total   [ N_CARS ];
   int car,  month,  max_so_far,  best_month,  sum;

   for ( car = 0;  car < N_CARS;  car++ )    {          /* Input monthly sales */
      printf ( "\nInput monthly sales for car model #%d",   car+1 );
      for ( month = 0;   month < N_MONTHS;   month++ )
          scanf ( "%d",   &sales [ car ] [ month ] );
   }
```

```
for ( car = 0; car < N_CARS; car++ ) {    /* Compute totals for each model */
    total [ car ] = 0;
    for ( month = 0;   month < N_MONTHS;   month++ )
        total [ car ] += sales [ car ] [ month ];
}

max_so_far = 0;

for ( month = 0; month < N_MONTHS; month++ ) {    /* Find best sales month */

    sum = 0;
    for ( car = 0;   car < N_CARS;   car++ ) /* Total sales for all models */
        sum += sales [ car ] [ month ];                /* on the given month */

    if  ( sum > max_so_far ) {                      /* Does this month */
        max_so_far = sum;                           /* have more sales than */
        best_month = month;                         /* best month so far */
    }
}


for ( car = 0; car < N_CARS; car++ )  /* Output total sales for each model */
    printf ( "\nTotal sales for car model #%d = %d", car + 1, total [ car ] );

printf ( "\nBest month for sales of all types was %d", best_month + 1 );

return ( 0 );

}                                                        /* End of main */
```

Test

Implementing this program and checking it with the data from Figure 7.3–3 verifies that the highest month for sales is December, with 42 cars. What should the program do if the total sales of all cars is the same on two different months?   ●

7.3.2 Passing Multidimensional Arrays

Passing a multi-d array is like passing a 1D array in that the argument is the name of the array. However, the corresponding parameter must include the physical sizes of all but the first dimension to enable computing the subscript references. As an example of how to do this, let's rewrite the luxury-car sales problem using functions, as shown in Program 7.3–3.

PROGRAM 7.3-3

```
/******************************************************************************
 * Title:       luxury car sales statistics (revised)                        *
 * Filename:    luxury2.c                                                     *
 *                                                                            *
 * Description: Input sales data for several car models over a one-year period. *
 *              Compute and output the statistics.                           *
 *                                                                            *
 * Input:       sales data arranged by product for a one-year period         *
 * Output:      yearly product totals and best month                         *
 * Process:     total_sales[car] = sum ( sales[car][month] )                 *
 *              best_month       = maximum of sum ( sales[car][month] )       *
 *                                                                            *
 * Written by:  ...                                      Date: ...            *
 ******************************************************************************/

#include <stdio.h>

#define  N_CARS    7
#define  N_MONTHS 12


                                                  /*  Function prototypes */
void get_sales_data   ( int   sales [ ] [ N_MONTHS ]                  );
void calc_total_sales ( int   sales [ ] [ N_MONTHS ], int total [ ]   );
int  find_best_month  ( int   sales [ ] [ N_MONTHS ]                  );
void put_sales_data   ( int   total [ ],              int   best_month );


main ( )
{

   int sales [ N_CARS ] [ N_MONTHS ];
   int total [ N_CARS ];
   int best_month;

   get_sales_data   ( sales );                         /* Read sales data */
   calc_total_sales ( sales,  total );              /* Compute the total sales */

   best_month = find_best_month ( sales );  /* Determine the best sales month */

   put_sales_data ( total, best_month );       /* Output the best sales month */

   return ( 0 );

}                                                      /*  End of main  */
```

```
/****************************************************************************
* Function name:    get_sales_data                                         *
* Description:      Input user values for monthly car sales, arranged by   *
*                   car model.                                             *
*                                                                          *
* Input parameters: none                                                   *
* Output parameters: sales                                                 *
* Return value:     none                                                   *
****************************************************************************/

void get_sales_data ( int   sales [ ] [ N_MONTHS ] )
{
    int  car,  month;

    for  (  car = 0;   car < N_CARS;   car++  )  {     /* For each model . . . */
        printf ( "\nInput monthly sales for car model #%d> ",    car+1  );
        for ( month = 0; month < N_MONTHS; month++ )        /* For each month, */
            scanf ( "%d", &sales [ car ] [ month ]  );    /* Input sales data */
    }
}                                              /*  End of  get_sales_data  */


/****************************************************************************
* Function name:    calc_total_sales                                       *
* Description:      Compute the total annual sales for each car model.     *
*                                                                          *
* Input parameters: sales [ car ][ month ]                                 *
* Output parameters: total [ car ]                                         *
* Return value:     none                                                   *
****************************************************************************/

void calc_total_sales ( int   sales [ ] [ N_MONTHS ], int total [ ]  )
{
    int  car,  month;

    for  (  car = 0;   car < N_CARS;   car++ )  {      /* For each model . . . */
        total [ car ] = 0;
        for ( month = 0;  month < N_MONTHS;   month++ )   /* For each month, */
            total [ car ] += sales [ car ] [ month ];    /* total sales for */
    }                                                    /*  each model */

}                                              /*  End of  calc_total_sales  */
```

```
/****************************************************************************
 * Function name:      find_best_month                                      *
 * Description:        Determine the best sales month for all car models.   *
 *                                                                          *
 * Input parameters:  sales [ car type ][ month ]                          *
 * Output parameters: none                                                  *
 * Return value:       best sales month for all car models                 *
 ****************************************************************************/

int  find_best_month ( int   sales [ ] [ N_MONTHS ]  )
{
   int car,  month,  sum,  best_month,  max_so_far = 0;

   for ( month = 0;   month < N_MONTHS;   month++ )    {

       sum = 0;
       for ( car = 0;  car < N_CARS;  car++  ) /* Total sales for all models */
           sum += sales [ car ] [ month ];              /* on the given month */

       if ( sum > max_so_far )   {                      /* Does this month */
          max_so_far =  sum;                         /* have more sales than */
          best_month =  month;                       /* best month so far? */
       }
   }
   return ( best_month );
}                                            /* End of  find_best_month */


/****************************************************************************
 * Function name:      put_sales_data                                       *
 * Description:        Output the total sales of each car and the best sales *
 *                     month.                                                *
 *                                                                          *
 * Input parameters:  total [ month ], best sales month                    *
 * Output parameters: none                                                  *
 * Return value:       none                                                 *
 ****************************************************************************/

void put_sales_data ( int   total [ ],    int   best_month )
{
   int car;

   for ( car = 0;   car < N_CARS;   car++  )
      printf ( "\n\nTotal sales for car model #%d = %d", car+1, total [ car ] );

   printf ( "\nBest month for sales of all models was %d", best_month + 1 );
}                                            /* End of  put_sales_data */
```

If **sales** were a 3D array as described by Figure 7.3–4, then the second and third dimensions would be necessary for each function that accessed the array. Assuming this data structure, we could revise **get_sales_data**, as shown in Program 7.3–4.

PROGRAM 7.3–4

```
/****************************************************************************
* Function name:       get_sales_data                                      *
* Description:         Input user values for each salesperson, arranged by car *
*                      model and sales month.                              *
*                                                                          *
* Input parameters:    none                                                *
* Output parameters:   sales                                               *
* Return value:        number of grades to be entered                      *
****************************************************************************/

void get_sales_data ( int   sales [ ] [ N_CARS ] [ N_MONTHS ]  )
{
   int  seller, car, month;

   for ( seller = 0; seller < N_SALESPERSONS; seller++ ) { /* For each seller */

       printf (  "\nInput sales data for seller # %d",   seller+1 );
       for ( car = 0;  car < N_CARS;  car++ )   {            /* For each model */

           printf (  "\nInput monthly sales for car model #%d> ",   car+1 );
           for ( month = 0;  month < N_MONTHS;  month++ )   /* For each month */
               scanf (  "%d",   &sales [ seller ] [ car ] [ month ]  );
       }
   }
}                                               /* End of  get_sales_data */
```

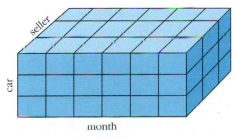

Figure 7.3–4   3D Array

EXERCISES 7.3

Concept Check

Answer statements 1 through 4 with true *or* false.
1. Multi-d arrays are sometimes called arrays of arrays.
2. Up to three dimensions for an array are allowed in C.
3. Multi-d arrays allow multiple data types.
4. In a 2D array, the first dimension always refers to the row and the second dimension always refers to the column.

For statements 5 through 8 choose the answer that best completes the statement.
5. The following declares a 2D `double` array with four rows and three columns:
   a. `double x [ 4, 3 ];`
   b. `double x [ 3, 4 ];`
   c. `double x [ 4 ] [ 3 ];`
   d. `double x [ 3 ] [ 4 ];`
6. The following initializes a 2D array to all ones:
   a. `int y [ 3 ] [ 2 ] = { 7 * 1 };`
   b. `int y [ 3 ] [ 2 ] = { 1, 1, 1, 1, 1, 1 };`
   c. `int y [ 3 ] [ 2 ] = { 1 };`
   d. `int y [ 3 ] [ 2 ] = { { 1, 1 } }, { { 1, 1 } }, { { 1, 1 } };`
7. Which statement initializes the array so that it looks like the picture?

7	7	6	6	6
7	6	6	6	6

   a. `x [ 5 ] [ 2 ] = { {7,7}, {7,6}, {6,6}, {6,6}, {6,6} };`
   b. `x [ 2 ] [ 5 ] = ( {7,7,6,6,6}, {7,6,6,6,6} );`
   c. `x [ 5 ] [ 2 ] = { {7,7,6,6,6}, {7,6,6,6,6} };`
   d. `x [ 2 ] [ 5 ] = { {7,7,6,6,6} {7,6,6,6,6} };`
8. Which loop sets all the elements of a five by seven integer array equal to 13?
   a. `for ( i=1; i<=7; ++i ) for ( j=1; j<=5; ++j ) matty [ i ] [ j ] = 13;`
   b. `for ( i=1; i<=5; ++i ) for ( j=1; j<=7; ++j ) matty [ i ] [ j ] = 13;`
   c. `for ( i=0; i<=6; ++i ) for ( j=0; j<=4; ++j ) matty [ i ] [ j ] = 13;`
   d. `for ( i=0; i<=4; ++i ) for ( j=0; j<=6; ++j ) matty [ i ] [ j ] = 13;`

For statements 9 through 12 fill in the blanks with the right word.
9. 2D arrays are sometimes called _____ or _____.
10. The last element in an *M* by *N* array called `x` would be referenced as _____.
11. When initializing a 2D array, you must ensure that the values are listed in _____ order.
12. When declaring a multi-d array as a function parameter, you must specify all but the _____ dimension.

Set A

Solve each of the following problems by writing one or more C statements.

13. Declare a `float` array called `x` with seven rows and 17 columns.
14. Initialize a 3 by 2 array to the integers 1 through 6.
15. Create a 4 by 7 array. Add the elements in column 1.

Set B

16. Create a 100 by 200 array. Compute the sum and the product of the elements in row 40.
17. Create a 3 by 2 by 4 array. Initialize the array to all zeros using `for` loops.
18. Multiply each element of a 7 by 5 by 3 array by a user-supplied value.

Set C

19. Create three 4 by 9 arrays. Subtract corresponding elements in the first two arrays and store the differences in a third array.
20. Create a 10 by 20 array. Add the elements in each row and store the sums in a 1D array.
21. Redesign the meteorology problem from Section 7.2 to incorporate a 2D array. The array should contain 12 rows and 31 columns so that daily rainfall can be stored (assume that each month has 31 days). Compute the mean daily rainfall for the whole year.
22. For Question 21, add a function that computes and stores (in a 1D array) the mean rainfall for each month. Output the means in `main`.

7.4   STRING PROCESSING

Introduction

Text processing, also called *string processing,* is common in computer software such as word processing programs and text editors. These are complex programs whose basic data unit is not numbers but characters and strings of characters. Next, we explore string processing in C. (Character- and string-processing functions are listed in Appendix A.)

7.4.1 Fundamentals of Strings

A **string constant** or **string** is any sequence of characters enclosed in double quotes. We have already used strings with the `print` and `scanf` functions, and strings can also be used with array variables. Although a string data type is not defined in C, we can think of a `char` array as a string. The C library of string-processing functions such as concatenation, text search, and character conversions can be used both for I/O operations and for general string processing. We look at some of these functions in this section.

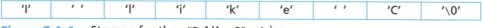

'I'	' '	'l'	'i'	'k'	'e'	' '	'C'	'\0'

Figure 7.4–1   Storage for the "I like C" string

Query: Is 'C' the same as "C" ?

RESPONSE: No! 'C' is a character constant and is not equal to the string constant "C".

Strings are stored as arrays of characters and have a special '\0' termination character called the **NUL** byte appended to them to signify the end of the string. Thus "I like C" is stored in memory as shown in Figure 7.4–1. This string can be associated with a nine-element array variable as in

```
char message[9]  =  "I like C";
```

Query: Where is the '\0' character in the last string?

RESPONSE: C supplies '\0' if you provide space for it in the array. The '\0' is important for string processing because it indicates the logical endpoint of a given string (as shown in Section 7.4.2).

A slightly simpler initialization is also allowed:

```
char message[] = "I like C";
```

In the absence of an explicit size constant, sufficient storage is allocated to hold the specified string, including the '\0' character.

7.4.2 String Input/Output

The easiest way to input strings is by using the C library function **gets** (for *get string*). The **gets** library function takes one argument, the string variable in which the data will be stored:

```
char    name [81];
printf (  "Input your name"  );
gets    ( name );
```

Notice that the string variable is declared as 81 characters so that a full 80-character line including the **NUL** byte can be stored.

The **gets** library function has an associated function for output called **puts** (for *put string*). The **puts** function also takes one string argument. Unlike **printf**, **puts** automatically advances the output to the following line after displaying it.

You can also use the `scanf` function for string input by means of the `%s` format specifier. Note these two caveats: First, the input string cannot have blanks because `scanf` interprets a blank to mean the end of a particular input value. As a result, you cannot conveniently input a person's first and last name with `scanf` unless you specify two string variables or use two `scanf` functions:

```
char    first[10],  last [10];

printf (  "\nEnter your first name:" );
scanf  (  "%s",  first );
printf (  "\nEnter your last name:" );
scanf  (  "%s",   last );
printf (  "\nYour full name is: %s %s",    first,  last );
```

Second, notice that the `&` *(address of)* operator is *not* used in the `scanf` function. This is because the name of a string variable, like the name of any array, is actually an address and is already in the correct form for `scanf`. (This is explained in greater detail in Chapter 9.)

BEFORE YOU GO ON

Query: In the last example, what happens if you enter the person's first or last name with more than nine characters?

RESPONSE: If you enter nine or fewer characters, the input name will be stored correctly as a string with the `'\0'` automatically appended. If you enter 10 characters, there is no room to append the `'\0'` and the data are not treated as a string, but as an array of characters. This means that you cannot use the string-processing functions with that variable. If you enter more than 10 characters you will be overwriting memory not associated with the array and the results will be unpredictable.

7.4.3 Built-In String Functions

A large collection of built-in string-processing functions that you can access through the `string.h` header are provided in C (see Appendix A–5 for a list). Let's consider a few of the most commonly used string functions.

In the descriptions that follow, references are made to string variables. All string variables must be legitimate strings terminated with the `'\0'` character, or the functions will not work properly.

1. `strcat ( string1, string2 )`

   The `strcat` function **concatenates** or joins `string1` and `string2`. A copy of `string2` is put at the end of `string1`. Make sure that `string1` is long enough to hold the resulting string.

PERSPECTIVE

If `string1` is not long enough to hold the result, the extra characters will be copied into the adjacent memory locations following those associated with `string1`. The extra characters will overwrite any legitimate data, causing unpredictable results!

```
char string1 [ 81 ] = "abc";
char string2 [  ]  = "def";

strcat ( string1, string2 );
puts   ( string1 );                        /* Outputs "abcdef" */
```

2. `strcpy ( string1, string2 )`

   The `strcpy` function copies `string2` into `string1`. Again, make sure that `string1` is long enough to hold the resulting string.

```
char string1 [ 81 ];
char string2 [  ]  = "memory";

strcpy ( string1, string2 );
puts   ( string1 );                        /* Outputs "memory" */
```

3. `strcmp ( string1, string2 )`

   The `strcmp` function compares `string1` to `string2` and returns an integer value to show the status of the comparison. If the function returns a 0, then the two strings are identical. A value of less than 0 shows that `string1` is lexicographically (according to its alphabetic ordering) less than `string2`. A value greater than 0 shows that `string1` is greater than `string2`.

```
char string1[ ]  = "John Doe";
char string2[ ]  = "John Doe";
char string3[ ]  = "Jane Doe";
char string4[ ]  = "John Does";

printf ( "%d %d %d", strcmp(string1,  string2),
                     strcmp(string1,  string3),
                     strcmp(string1,  string4) );
                            /* Outputs  0,  >0,   <0 */
```

Note that when the strings are not equal your concern is only whether the result is positive or negative and not the exact value of the function.

4. `strlen ( string1 )`

   The `strlen` function returns an integer equal to the length of the stored string, not including the termination character.

```
char string1[81];
char string2[ ]  = "Jane Doe";
```

```
printf ( "%d %d", strlen( string1 ), strlen( string2 ) );
                                          /* Outputs 0, 8 */
```

5. strchr (string, ch)

The **strchr** function searches **string** for the first occurrence of **ch**. We might expect this function to return the index of the search character in the string. Instead the function returns the *memory location* (address) of the character. Significantly, the address is set to the predefined value **NULL** if the character is *not* in the string.

```
char string[9] = "John Doe";
char search    = 'D';

if ( strchr ( string, search ) != NULL )
    printf ( "\nSearch character found" );/* Outputs this message */
else
    printf ( "\nSearch character not found" );
```

As with **strcmp,** your only concern is whether or not the character was found and not where in the string the character resides.

7.4.4 Examples of Character and String Processing

Now let's consider a few problems whose solutions incorporate string and character functions.

EXAMPLE 7.4–1

Problem
Write a function to convert a string of characters to lowercase.

Reasoning
Converting a string to lowercase requires replacing each uppercase character with its lowercase equivalent. You can do this by searching through the string for uppercase characters and converting them to lowercase as needed. Uppercase characters can be detected with the C **isupper** character function, which returns a 1 if its argument is an uppercase character. You can access the **isupper** function by including the **ctype.h** header file. (Appendix A–3 lists the common character functions in the **ctype.h** header file.) You can also *check* for uppercase with an **if** statement:

```
char ch;
scanf ( "%c", &ch );
if ( ch >= 'A' && ch <= 'Z' )
    printf ( "\n%c is uppercase!", ch );
```

You convert a character to lowercase by the **tolower** function, as in

```
ch = tolower ( 'D' );                      /* ch is set to 'd' */
```

We can understand **tolower** by first examining the ASCII collating sequence. (ASCII codes are listed in Appendix E.) There is a numerical relationship in and between the uppercase and lowercase characters: Each set of characters is in a contiguous sequence. Therefore, lowercase **'c'** is the same distance (numerically) from **'a'** as uppercase **'C'** is from **'A'**. The conversion from uppercase to lowercase with **tolower** applies a rule that might be written in pseudocode as

tolower (upper) = (upper − 'A') + 'a'

For example,

tolower ('C') = ('C' − 'A') + 'a'

= 2 + 'a'

= 'c'

The (upper − 'A') expression yields the numerical offset of any uppercase character from the first uppercase character **'A'**. This offset is then added to the first lowercase character **'a'**, yielding the equivalent lowercase character.

Solution
The C code for this function is as follows.

```
/****************************************************************************
 * Function name:       lower_str                                          *
 * Description:         Convert each uppercase character in a string       *
 *                      to its lowercase equivalent.                       *
 *                                                                         *
 * Input parameters:    string                                            *
 * Output parameters: string with uppercase characters converted to lowercase *
 * Return value:        none                                              *
 ****************************************************************************/

void lower_str ( char   str [ ]   )
{
   int i;
   for ( i = 0;   i < strlen ( str );    i++ )
      if ( isupper ( str [ i ] )  )              /* Is char uppercase? */
         str [ i ] = tolower ( str [ i ] );/* Yes, convert it to lowercase */
}
```

Test
Design and implement a full program to check this function.   •

Example 7.4–2, next, shows how arrays of strings are used. Note that because a single string is implemented as a 1D array of characters, it follows that an array of strings is a 2D array of characters.

EXAMPLE 7.4–2

Problem

For this problem, called *sentence generation* [1], write a program to compose sentences randomly, based on a limited, predetermined vocabulary of words. The word categories include article, noun, verb, and preposition. The program should randomly select a word from each category and add it to the growing sentence. The following rules apply.

1. Add the words in this order: Article, noun, verb, preposition, article, noun
2. Separate each word pair by a blank
3. Begin each sentence with a capital letter
4. End each sentence with a period

Reasoning

This is a more ambitious task than the previous example and uses the string arrays and string-processing functions we just described. The random-number generator (discussed later in this section) is also needed to create a variety of sentences.

Solution

The C code requires the creation of a string array—a 2D array of characters—for each word category. The arrays can be initialized to contain representative words such as the nouns *boy* and *girl*, etc., and the verbs *ran* and *drove*. For this example, the number of words is restricted to five in each category.

Selecting and adding a new word involves three steps. First, add a blank to the end of the growing sentence. Second, select a random number to use as the index to the next word category. Third, add a word from that category to the end of the sentence. Repeat this process for all the words to be generated. Now add a period to the end of the sentence and the resulting string is output.

The `stdlib.h` header file facilitates access to a **random-number generator** function called `rand` which can be used to generate random indexes in the arrays. (Appendix A–4 lists common functions in the `stdlib.h` file.) The `rand` function outputs random numbers between 0 and a predefined large number called `RAND_MAX`, as shown in the following statement. Note that most random-number generators output values between 0 and 1. To generate a number between 0 and n, you multiply the random number by n and either truncate or round to the nearest integer.

```
#include <stdlib.h>
    ...
x = rand ( );                    /* x is between 0 and RAND_MAX */
```

The value of `RAND_MAX` depends on the compiler, but according to the ANSI standard it must be at least 32,767. Assuming that there are five words in each word category, it makes sense to restrict the output of `rand` to numbers 0 through 4. You can do this by taking the result of `rand` modulo 5.

BEFORE YOU GO ON

Query: What is the output of `rand() % 5` ?

RESPONSE: Any number modulo 5 is in the range of 0 through 4.

Capitalizing the first word is tricky. Assume that the first word is always an article. As shown below, you have to copy the randomly chosen article into a temporary variable using **strcpy**. Then set the first character position of the word to uppercase using **toupper**. Finally, copy the changed article to the sentence.

```
index  =  rand() % NUM_WORD;                       /* Select random index   */
strcpy ( first_word, article[index] ); /* Copy "article" to temporary string */
first_word[0]  =  toupper( first_word[0] );        /* Capitalize first letter */
strcpy ( sentence, first_word );                   /* Put word into sentence  */
```

Program 7.4–1 shows how to do this.

PROGRAM 7.4-1

```
/*******************************************************************************
* Title:       sentence generator                                            *
* Filename:    sentence.c                                                     *
*                                                                            *
* Description: Generate random sentences of the form:  article,  noun,  verb, preposition, *
*              article,  noun.  The program randomly selects a word from a word list *
*              in a particular category and then concatenates the word to the growing *
*              sentence.  Several sentences are generated.                     *
*                                                                            *
* Input:       none                                                          *
* Output:      randomly generated sentence                                    *
* Process:     sentence is constructed by randomly extracting words from several *
*              categories (e.g., article, noun, verb, preposition) and concatenating *
*              them to the growing sentence.                                   *
*                                                                            *
* Written by:  ...                                          Date: ...        *
*******************************************************************************/

#include <stdio.h>
#include <string.h>                /* For access to string processing functions */
#include <stdlib.h>                  /* For access to random number generator   */
#include <ctype.h>                 /* For access to character processing functions */


#define  N_WORD     5
#define  N_SENTENCE 10
#define  BLANK      " "
#define  PERIOD     "."
#define  STR_LEN    81                     /* Allows extra space for NUL character */
```

```
main ( )
{
    char article [ N_WORD ][ STR_LEN ] = { "the", "a", "one", "some", "any" };
    char noun    [ N_WORD ][ STR_LEN ] = { "boy", "girl", "dog", "town", "car" };
    char verb    [ N_WORD ][ STR_LEN ] = { "drove", "jumped", "ran",
                                           "walked", "hopped" };
    char prep    [ N_WORD ][ STR_LEN ] = { "to", "from", "over", "under", "on" };

    char sentence [ STR_LEN ],    first_word [ STR_LEN ];
    int  i,  index;

    for ( i = 1;   i < N_SENTENCE;   i++ )   {

        index = rand() % N_WORD;
        strcpy ( first_word, article[index] );        /* First word must be capitalized */
        first_word [ 0 ] = toupper( first_word [ 0 ] );
        strcpy ( sentence, first_word );              /* And then copied into the sentence */

        strcat ( sentence, BLANK );
        index = rand ( ) % N_WORD;                                    /* Add a noun */
        strcat ( sentence, noun [ index ] );

        strcat ( sentence, BLANK );
        index = rand ( ) % N_WORD;                                    /* Add a verb */
        strcat ( sentence, verb [ index ] );

        strcat ( sentence, BLANK );
        index = rand ( ) % N_WORD;                               /* Add a preposition */
        strcat ( sentence, prep [ index ] );

        strcat ( sentence, BLANK );
        index = rand ( ) % N_WORD;                                  /* Add an article */
        strcat ( sentence, article [ index ] );


        strcat ( sentence, BLANK );
        index = rand ( ) % N_WORD;                                    /* Add a noun */
        strcat ( sentence, noun [ index ] );

        strcat ( sentence, PERIOD );              /* End the sentence with a period */

        puts ( sentence );

    }

    return( 0 );
}                                                                   /* End of main */
```

Test

The implementation and testing of this program are included in the exercises that
follow.   •

EXERCISES 7.4

Concept Check

Answer statements 1 through 4 with true *or* false.
1. C does not distinguish between `'C'` and `"C"`.
2. Strings are stored as arrays of characters.
3. The `gets` function is accessed through `string.h`.
4. The `strcmp` function returns a 0 if the two strings are equal.

For statements 5 through 8 choose the answer that best completes the statement.
5. The statement `strlen( string1 )`
   a. returns the length of the string including the null character
   b. returns the length of the string excluding the null character
   c. returns the length of the string as specified in its declaration
   d. returns the declared length of the string minus 1
6. The statement `strcpy( string1, string2 )`
   a. adds `string2` to the end of `string1`
   b. adds `string1` to the end of `string2`
   c. overwrites `string1` with `string2`
   d. overwrites `string2` with `string1`
7. The statement `strcmp( "Jill", "Jane" )`
   a. is not legal because `"Jill"` and `"Jane"` are not string variables
   b. returns the value 0 because the strings are not equal
   c. returns the value −1 because the strings are not equal
   d. returns a positive value because `"Jill"` is greater than `"Jane"`
8. The statement `strchr( "Jane", 'a' )`
   a. returns 0 because `'a'` is contained in `"Jane"`
   b. returns a negative value because `'a'` is contained in `"Jane"`
   c. returns a positive value because `'a'` is contained in `"Jane"`
   d. is a syntax error because `"Jane"` is not a string variable

For statements 9 through 12 fill in the blanks with the right word.
9. The string `"I like programming"` needs _____ memory cells.
10. The name of a string is actually a(n) _____.
11. String functions are accessible through the _____ header.
12. An array of strings is actually a _____ array.

Set A

Solve each of the following problems by writing one or more C statements.
13. Output the third character from an 80-character string.
14. Output the third string from an 80-string array of strings.
15. Copy the lexicographically smaller of two strings into the third position of a
    string array.

Set B

16. Copy the fifth string from an array of strings to a single string variable.
17. Copy the seventh string from an array of strings to the ninth string of a string array.

Set C

18. Input a series of strings into an array. Let the user specify how many strings are to be input.
19. Write a function to return the number of vowels in a string. Use the character function `isvowel`, which returns 1 if its argument is a vowel. Try writing the program two ways, with and without this function.
20. Output each word of a string on a separate line. Assume that the words are separated by a single blank with a period at the end of the string.
21. Implement and test the sentence generation program from this section.

ENDNOTE

1. Deitel, H. M., and Deitel, P. J. *C: How to Program*. Prentice Hall, Englewood Cliffs, N.J. (1992), p. 280.

8 Data Communications

Telephone switching room, Kansas City, Missouri, 1904.

After completing this chapter you should be able to do the following:

Learning Goals

- Identify terms related to data communications
- Distinguish between analog and digital transmission
- Characterize modulation methods for modems
- Classify the modes and media of data transmission
- Identify the layers of the OSI communications model
- Use parity for error detection
- Identify methods of error detection
- Construct methods for error correction
- Use the Hamming correction algorithm

Chapter Activity

The integrity of the information transmitted and received in data communications must be preserved at all levels from keyboard to computer to international satellite. Methods to detect and correct errors in data transfer have been in use for decades. One such method was developed in 1951 by R.W. Hamming.

Suppose an arbitrary number of information bits are represented by integers 0 and 1. The information is to be encoded in a Hamming single-bit error correction code. Construct a C program that encodes the information into a proper Hamming codeword and isolates and corrects the codeword if a single-bit error occurs.

8.1　COMMUNICATIONS OVERVIEW

Introduction

Data communications is the process of transmitting and receiving information. It is also the study and application of computer devices used to transmit and receive information. There are numerous applications for computers in data communications. In the microcosm of a PC, information is communicated among computer components such as keyboards, CPUs, monitors, disk drives, and printers. Computers communicate within a locale or region—for example, PCs on a network, which we discuss in Section 1.2.6. In the larger domain, information is exchanged among transmitting and receiving stations within a nation or among different nations, and along networks and satellites. All of these methods need a systematic technology that is friendly to users and compatible with a variety of communications devices.

8.1.1 Data Communications and Standards

Electronic communications first started in the latter part of the nineteenth century with the invention of the telegraph, the telephone, and the radio. These inventions set the pace for what was to come in the twentieth century: an explosion of electronic media. The first half of the twentieth century saw the birth of television and many sophisticated uses of electronic gadgets and instruments. These inventions operated in an environment relatively free of governmental controls, and how they worked and communicated was more often determined by manufacturers than by the ideal of common good.

PERSPECTIVE

The commercial use of electricity brought about three means of communications that revolutionized human culture. Although the concept was developed by others years before, the telephone was first patented by Alexander Graham Bell in 1876. Guglielmo Marconi invented the wireless radio in 1895 and patented it in 1896. Television, the transmission and reception of sound and images, was first proposed by Campbell Swinton in 1911 and demonstrated by Radio Corporation of America (RCA) in 1932.

In 1951 the first commercial electronic computer (the UNIVAC I) was installed. As computers became more accessible to ordinary people, the need arose for these machines to communicate with each other. Like other electronic devices of that era, the means by which computers interacted was largely determined by the manufacturer. Today, several independent groups contribute to the standardization of electronic machines and communications: The National Institute of Standards and Technology (NIST), formerly the National Bureau of Standards (NBS), a government research laboratory; and private organizations like the Institute of Electrical and Electronics

Engineers (IEEE), the American National Standards Institute (ANSI), and the National Information Standards Organization (NISO).

On the international scene, the International Standards Organization (ISO) has member organizations from almost 100 countries; the Conference of European Postal and Telecommunications (CEPT) has members among the European post, telephone, and telegraphy authorities (PTTs); and the Comité Consultatif Internationale de Telegraphique et Telephonique (CCITT) develops standards that are widely adopted for modems, switched interfaces, RS-232 connectors, and similar devices. The British BSI standards group is the equivalent of NISO.

Standards are rules acknowledged by participating members of an organization and the industry they represent. One of the challenges of any standards organization is to agree on what a standard should be. In the case of **computer networks** (systems of interconnected computers) there are hundreds of ways by which *any* computer could be connected and communicate with any other computer, any of which could serve as a standard.

Figure 8.1–1 is a diagram of a small network of different computers connected together in a ring. (Network topologies are covered in Section 1.2.6.) The computers on the network are called **hosts.** One of the computers on the network, a **file server,** has the primary function of holding files that can be used or shared

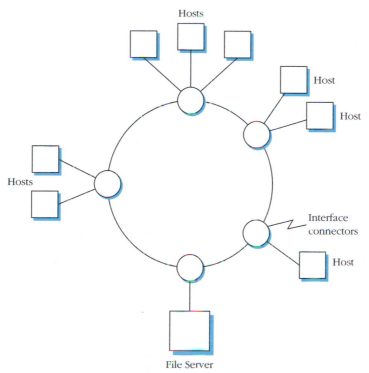

Figure 8.1–1   Local area network ring

by other machines on the network. A file server can also be used as a gateway to another network. File servers are generally more powerful than other machines on the network, both in processor speed and disk capacity.

A network of computers that communicate with each other and that are geographically dispersed, usually over a community, country, or continent, is a **long-haul network** or **wide area network (WAN).** Networks open to anyone are **public data networks (PDN).** WANs have been in use for about three decades and are becoming more popular, especially internationally, because they offer features such as online research, electronic mail (e-mail), and general communications. Examples of WANs are Internet, Telnet, and Bitnet. Networks can also serve a small region such as an office complex, a building, or a room. A small communications channel that connects computers and their peripherals is a **local area network (LAN).** LANs are becoming very popular, and many businesses, organizations, and agencies throughout the world install them for their own use.

The appeal of WANs and LANs is based on several factors. The first is simple economics; it costs less to install and use a network than to buy a mainframe with dumb terminals. For example, suppose a LAN serves 20 hosts. The LAN would need one expensive computer, the file server, and 19 inexpensive desktop computers. All 20 units on the LAN share the files and data provided by the file server so duplication of resources is minimized. Hardware, such as an expensive laser printer, can also be shared on the network.

The units on the LAN are often PCs that can be used as **smart terminals;** each PC is both a single-user machine and part of the LAN. They can also be more powerful computers like workstations. Networks allow information sharing and provide communications tools like e-mail to their users. Networks are also more flexible than mainframes because they allow incremental growth as needed and can easily be partitioned when appropriate.

Further, networks are generally more fault tolerant than mainframes. (**Fault tolerance** means a hardware system's ability to recover from a failure of one of its components.) If a mainframe CPU fails, the whole system and all user processes come to a halt. However, if one of the hosts on a LAN fails the rest of the network can continue working uninterrupted. For all these reasons, LANs are cheaper to install than a mainframe computer with terminals.

8.1.2 Digital and Analog Transmission

The past hundred years have witnessed revolutionary breakthroughs in electronic communications. The dominant influence in this revolution has been telephone companies throughout the world. Traditionally, telephone companies have concentrated on the transmission of voice.

Voice has a certain continuity and flow to it described as **sinusoidal,** meaning a pattern that resembles a sine wave. When we speak loudly, the **amplitude** of the sine wave increases and when we speak softly, the amplitude decreases. If we speak at a higher pitch (as when we sing), the **frequency** of the sine wave increases and when we speak at a lower pitch, the frequency decreases. Thus if the function $y = \sin(t)$ is considered normal, then a sound whose pitch

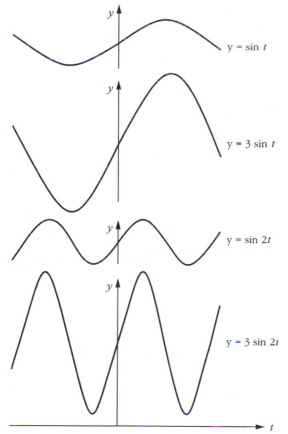

Figure 8.1–2   Graphs of sin t, 3 sin t, sin 2t, 3 sin 2t

(frequency) is twice as high as normal and three times as loud as normal is $y = 3\sin(2t)$. Figure 8.1–2 is a sketch of four sine waves, one that is normal, one that is three times the amplitude, one that is twice the frequency, and one that combines the two features of frequency and amplitude. Data communications that use a continuous mode of transmission or reception as a function of time, such as the sinusoid, are called **analog** transmissions.

When the information is transmitted as a discrete string of 0s and 1s, the mode of transmission is **digital.** Digital transmission can be synchronous or asynchronous. In **synchronous** transmission, bits are sent at a fixed rate for both receiver and transmitter. Special characters at the beginning of a message synchronize the data flow. Figure 8.1–3 is a sketch of information transmitted

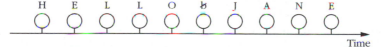

Figure 8.1–3   Synchronous transmission

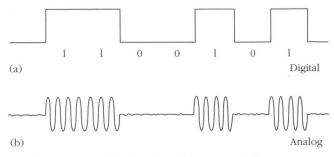

(a)   Digital

(b)   Analog

Figure 8.1–4   Digital and analog transmission

digitally in synchronous fashion. For asynchronous transmission, each character or data block has a start and stop bit preceding and following it. Synchronous and asynchronous transmissions have advantages. Synchronous transmission is suitable for high-speed transmissions when a computer clock and the data are precisely synchronized, and when sending and receiving devices are operating continuously. Asynchronous transmission is suitable when the transmission is irregular, as between a keyboard and a CPU.

PERSPECTIVE

A communications message can be broken into discrete **packets** at the originating host, sent in packets through a network of telecommunications switching systems, and reassembled at its destination. *Packetizing* a message breaks a big message into many small ones, which in turn makes it easier to process. [1]

Consider the transmission of the letter 'e', whose ASCII code is 1100101. Figure 8.1–4(a) shows the letter's pattern in a digital mode and Figure 8.1–4(b) shows the letter's pattern in analog mode. Digital signals can be checked for transmission errors, whereas analog signals cannot. In addition, when an analog signal is transmitted through a medium such as a wire, a loss of energy makes the signal weaker. This must be compensated for by periodically amplifying the signal along the transmission medium, a costly process. Analog transmission, however, has the potential for higher fidelity when transmitting information that was originally in a continuous mode, such as music or speech.

8.1.3 Modems

A **modem** (modulator-demodulator) is a communications device that converts a digital signal into an analog signal and an analog signal into a digital signal. The most common information carrier is the telephone line, usually an analog medium. When computer A wants to communicate with computer B over a telephone line, for example, the digital signal from A must be converted into an analog signal for the telephone line and then converted back to a digital signal at B. Figure 8.1–5 shows this process.

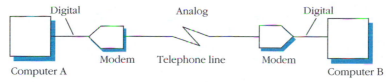

Figure 8.1–5 Modems and transmission

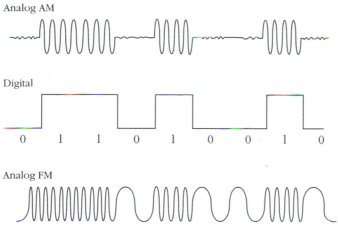

Figure 8.1–6 Amplitude and frequency modulation

Analog signals adjust a common signal called a **carrier,** which is basically a sinusoidal wave. When the carrier is adjusted, the signal is **modulated.** The modulation can be done in different ways. Two of the most common methods used are amplitude modulation and frequency modulation. **Amplitude modulation (AM)** changes the amplitude of the signal while keeping the frequency fixed. **Frequency modulation (FM)** changes the frequency of the signal while keeping the amplitude fixed. (AM and FM are used to designate common radio bands.) A modem modulates a carrier from a digital signal and demodulates a carrier to a digital signal. Figure 8.1–6 shows how a typical digital signal modulates a carrier to AM and FM waves. The performance of a modem is measured by its **baud,** or the maximum number of changes a signal can make each second. The *changes* in the bit state determine the baud, which is usually equivalent to bits-per-second. Common baud rates are 2,400, 4,800, 9,600, and 14,400.

8.1.4 Communications Media and Modalities

Information can be transmitted in a variety of ways. The traditional method was two insulated wires, usually made of copper, that were twisted along their length and called a **twisted pair.** Twisted pairs have been used by telephone companies around the world and are commonly found in homes, offices, and buildings. Rapidly replacing twisted pair for telephone lines is **fiber-optic cable,**

Twisted-pair

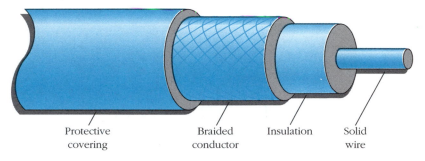

Protective   Braided   Insulation   Solid
covering   conductor   wire

Coaxial cable

Figure 8.1–7   Twisted-pair and coaxial media

which uses light transmitted along thin silica fibers. A **light-emitting diode (LED),** or sometimes a laser diode, is used as the transmitting source, converting electrical signals to light pulses. **Photodiodes** convert light to electrical signals. Fiber-optic cable is efficient and flexible, and capable of handling thousands of communications lines simultaneously.

Another medium is **coaxial cable,** an insulated solid copper wire encased in a braided outer conductor and covered by an insulated coating. Coaxial cable, also called *coax,* is best known for its protection against noise interference. Figure 8.1–7 shows a twisted pair and a coaxial cable.

When coaxial cable is used for digital transmission, it is called **baseband** and provides excellent transmission at high bit rates. It is not suitable, however, for very long-distance transmissions since there is an inverse relationship between the data rate (speed of transmission) and the distance. That is, the shorter the distance, the higher the data rate possible; the longer the distance, the lower the data rate.

When coaxial cable is used for analog transmission it is called **broadband.** Because broadband transmission is used for ordinary television transmission, it can accommodate very high carrier frequencies—up to 300 MHz—with a bandwidth as wide as 6 MHz. Coaxial cable can be used as broadband over relatively long distances, generally up to 100 km, making it suitable for communications between offices, buildings, and nearby towns and communities.

For transmissions over very long distances (over 50 miles) a variety of media are used. One is fiber-optic cable, and another is **wireless** communications. Wireless transmission and reception of information over the atmosphere is like

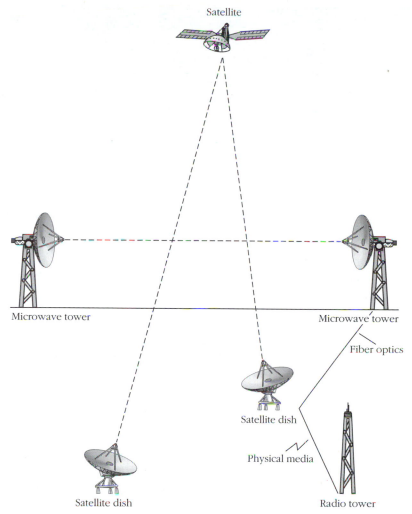

Figure 8.1–8 Radio communications system

broadband without the physical cables. **Radio** and **microwave** are examples of wireless communications between two or more towers for transmitting and receiving. **Cellular telephones** operating within a local area (cell) linked to other cells are another example. Other modes of wireless transmission include **laser** and **infrared** devices that transfer information through the atmosphere. Figure 8.1–8 shows a typical radio communications system.

Because microwave communications are restricted to distances of approximately 100 miles, intermediate radio boosters, microwave towers, and similar relay antennas are often put at reasonable distances so that transmission is not disrupted. For very long distances (intracontinental and intercontinental), **satellites** make data communications possible. Using today's communications technology computers can communicate with each other virtually anywhere on the planet.

8.1.5 Protocols

Computer networks interact according to specific rules called **protocols**. International standards for these protocols have been adopted by most countries, enabling data communications between devices all over the world. (Standards organizations are discussed in Section 8.1.1.)

One communications standard created by the ISO is called the Open Systems Interconnection (OSI) model that simulates the communications process using seven layers, each with its own set of protocols. The purpose of the OSI model is to enable any vendor's computer system to share data with any other vendor's system in an open networking environment. Figure 8.1–9 shows the structure of the OSI model. A description of each of the seven layers follows.

Layer 1. Physical Layer
The physical layer controls the electrical, mechanical, and functional transmission of bits over the data circuits.

Layer 2. Data Link Layer
The data link layer detects and compensates for transmission errors and ensures that information sent by high-speed transmitters is properly received by slow receivers.

Layer 3. Network Layer
The network layer determines how information is routed between computers and within and between individual networks. It also handles software interfaces between networks, including networks with different protocols.

Layer 4. Transport Layer
The transport layer specifies the rules for information exchange and manages end-to-end delivery of information within and between networks, including error recovery. It also controls information flow—for example, multiple data streams on a single channel.

Layer 5. Session Layer
The session layer controls the dialog between two computers, managing file transfers and putting checkpoints into a data stream to allow portions of files to be retransmitted as needed.

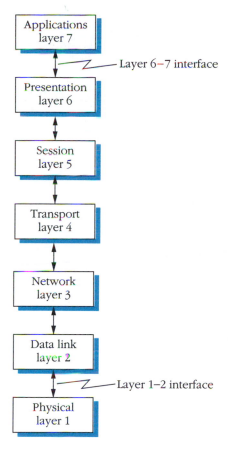

Figure 8.1–9 OSI model with interfaces

Layer 6. Presentation Layer

The presentation layer supplies transparent communications by masking the differences in unlike data formats such as the ASCII and EBCDIC character codes, and performs data compression and encryption.

Layer 7. Applications Layer

The applications layer supplies functions for particular applications such as file transfer, remote access, and virtual terminals.

When sending or receiving information according to the OSI model, the sender and receiver must use the seven-layer protocols and interfaces. The OSI model is an open system available on communications systems from many vendors. There are also proprietary systems such as IBM's System Network Architecture (SNA) and the Transmission Control Protocol/Internet (TCP/IP) used on the Internet. Figure 8.1–10 shows how the OSI model might be represented.

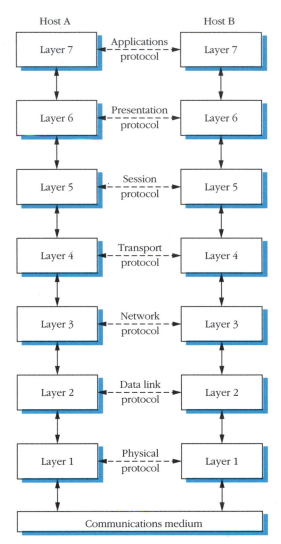

Figure 8.1–10 OSI model with protocols

It is not the intent of this chapter to present the details of the OSI model, but let's show how basic communications between two machines, called **hosts,** takes place. Suppose host A is sending information to host B. Both hosts have adopted the OSI model. At layer 7 host A begins to send information to B over a computer network. The information progresses to layer 6 and down through layer 1 at the site of A. From site A the physical transmission takes place along a medium such as cable or satellite to site B where the sequence of layers is reversed. At the site of B the information goes from layer 1 up through layer 7, where the information is received. Figure 8.1–11 shows the data path; in this case the corresponding layers of the two hosts are satisfied. Yet without the OSI model as a standard, it would

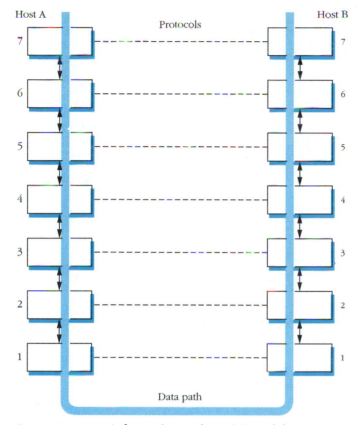

Figure 8.1–11 Information path on OSI model

be impossible for a computer on a network at a specific location to communicate with a computer on a different network at another location.

The three basic methods of transmission are called simplex, half-duplex, and full-duplex. **Simplex** allows information to travel in only one direction as in radio and television transmission. **Half-duplex** allows information to travel in both directions but *not* at the same time. A two-way radio is an example: each radio (*walkie-talkie*) can send and receive by alternating with the other. **Full-duplex** allows information to travel in both directions at the same time, such as on ordinary telephones.

EXERCISES 8.1

Concept Check
Answer statements 1 through 4 with true *or* false.
1. LANs are useful for satellite communications.
2. Analog transmission is more economical than digital transmission.
3. Both broadband and baseband transmission use coaxial cable as a medium.
4. The OSI protocol is an ANSI standard.

For statements 5 through 8 choose the answer that best completes the statement.

5. A mode of communications that allows information to travel in two directions but not simultaneously is called
   a. full-duplex
   b. half-duplex
   c. half-simplex
   d. simplex

6. In a communications network the unit that can act as a gateway to other networks is called a
   a. LAN
   b. host
   c. file server
   d. smart terminal

7. One method used to modulate signals from analog to digital or digital to analog is called
   a. baud modulation
   b. synchronous modulation
   c. asynchronous modulation
   d. frequency modulation

8. Rules acknowledged by members of organizations and industry are called
   a. laws
   b. agreements
   c. standards
   d. communications

For statements 9 through 12 fill in the blanks with the right word.

9. For a sinusoidal pattern, the height is called the _____ and the rapidity of the changes is called the _____.

10. A signal that is not transmitted at a fixed rate is called _____.

11. One wireless mode of transmission is _____.

12. In the OSI model, the transmission of data in bits takes place at the _____ layer.

Set A
13. Explain the difference between baseband and broadband.
14. Describe a coaxial cable.
15. Describe why synchronous transmission is better suited for parallel communications.
16. Explain the need to set standards in communication networks.
17. What are the advantages of fiber optics?
18. Identify several communications media that can be used over very long distances.

Set B
19. Describe the data link layer in the OSI model.
20. Describe how all the computers in a building might be connected to a main computer one mile away.

21. Describe how someone with a PC in Europe might communicate with someone else with a PC in Australia.

Set C

22. Research the American National Standards Institute (ANSI), including the details of its membership and its organizational structure. [Library activity]
23. Research the International Standards Organization (ISO), including its membership and organizational structure. [Library activity]

8.2   PARITY AND ERROR IN COMMUNICATIONS

Introduction

Section 8.1 was an overview of data communications and the International Standards Organization's OSI model. Next, we cover two aspects of data transmission: Error detection and correction, specifically, parity and Hamming codes. (The details of sending and receiving messages are not relevant to our discussion.)

As we saw in Section 8.1, the data link layer (layer 2) detects and compensates for transmission errors, ensuring the network layer (layer 3) that the information received is as free from error as possible. Layer 2 acts as a bridge between physical transmission (layer 1) and network protocols (layer 3).

8.2.1 Parity

A **parity** check determines whether a transmission is accurate. Parity is the evenness or oddness of a number and in this context, whether the sum of the bits in a message is even or odd. To achieve parity, we add an extra bit to the message. To make the parity either even or odd, we make the added bit a 0 or 1. This forces the extended message to have either even or odd parity. Symbolically, we let a message have h information bits. The extended message, which includes the parity bit, has $h + 1$ bits. Let i be a positive integer. If the sum of the bits is $2i$, the parity is even. Otherwise, if the sum of the bits is $2i - 1$, the parity is odd.

EXAMPLE 8.2–1

Problem
A message consists of the 7-bit ASCII character 1010001 for the letter 'Q'. Let the parity be even. Find the extended message code.

Reasoning
There are seven bits in the message ($h = 7$). The extended message must contain eight bits and the number of 1-bits must be even.

Solution
The sum of the bits in the message is

$$1 + 0 + 1 + 0 + 0 + 0 + 1 = 3$$

A single bit must be added to the message. Because the parity is even the bit must be a 1. Add this bit to the beginning of the message. The 8-bit extended message is now

11010001

Test
The sum of the bits in the extended message is

$$1 + 1 + 0 + 1 + 0 + 0 + 0 + 1 = 4$$

and it is even.   ●

Note that in Example 8.2–1 the added bit, called a *parity bit*, was appended to the front of the ASCII message. Depending on the transmission protocols (rules), it could also have been appended to the end of the message. Thus, how the parity bit is appended to a message must conform to the protocols that govern the transmission.

Let's say that the message *CAT* is to be sent on a network. Its ASCII code is

1000010   1000001   1010100

At the data link layer (layer 2) the message will be encoded with a parity bit appended to each ASCII code using odd parity. That is, the sum of the bits for each character must add up to an odd number. By appending to the front we get the new code

11000010   11000001   01010100

Each extended code now has eight bits and the sum of the bits for each code is an odd number (coincidentally, three in each case). At the physical layer (layer 1) the *extended message* for *CAT* is transmitted by the sending host. The receiving host accepts the message at the physical layer (layer 1) where it interfaces with the data link layer (layer 2) and parity is checked. Note again that layer 2 of the sending host and layer 2 of the receiving host must use the same protocol for parity checking. If parity is odd for each extended message, the receiving host sends the message to layer 3. If parity is not odd an error is detected.

Program 8.2–1 shows a simulation of how parity can be set for a 7-bit ASCII code. The code is simulated by the *byte* representation of the numbers 0 and 1 rather than by the actual bits. The program inserts the correct parity byte at the (right) end of the code to ensure parity. In addition, the program allows the user to set the parity to even or odd.

PROGRAM 8.2–1

```
/***************************************************************************
*    Title:        parity insertion                                       *
*    Filename:     prtynsrt.c                                             *
*                                                                         *
*    Description:  Read an array of characters 0 or 1 simulating a bit    *
*                  pattern for an ASCII character and then append a single *
*                  integer (bit) to ensure the selected parity.           *
```

```
*                                                                      *
*   Input:         integer digits of value  0  or  1  representing the bit   *
*                  pattern                                              *
*   Output:        bit pattern with parity bit appended                 *
*   Process:       sum simulated bit values to achieve parity           *
*                                                                      *
*   Written by:    ...                              Date: ...          *
***********************************************************************/

#include <stdio.h>

main ( )
{

    char parity,                            /* Even or odd parity variable */
        message[8];    /* String of eight ASCII characters representing bits */

    int  i,                                 /* Indexing variable */
        par,                        /* Integer variable used to test for parity */
        total;                              /* Sum of bits total */


    do {                                    /* Data filter for 0 or 1 only */
        printf ( "\nEnter 0 for even parity or 1 for odd parity: " );
        scanf ( "%c", &parity );
    } while ( parity != '0' && parity != '1' );

    if ( parity == '0' )                    /* Set parity integer variable */
        par = 0;
    else
        par = 1;

    printf ( "\n\n" );                             /* Skip two lines */


    total =  0;
    for ( i = 0; i < 7; i++ ) {                     /* Enter message string */
        do {                                /* Data filter for 0 or 1 only */
            printf ( "Enter binary digit for position %d: ", i );
            scanf ( "%c", &message[i] );
        } while ( message[i] != '0' && message[i] != '1' );

        if ( message[i] == '1' )                       /* Bit accumulator */
            total++;
    }
```

```
    if ( total % 2 == par )                      /*  Append 0 or 1 to end of message  */
       message[7] = '0';                          /* according to required parity  */
    else
       message[7] = '1';


    printf ( "\nThe 7-bit  input message is: " );              /*  Output  */
                                                               /*  original message  */
    for ( i = 0; i < 7; i++ )
       printf ( "%c", message[i] );


    printf ( "\nThe 8-bit output message is: " );              /*  Output  */
                                                               /*  encoded message  */
    for ( i = 0; i < 8; i++ )
       printf ( "%c", message[i] );


    return ( 0 );

}
```

8.2.2 Error Detection and Correction

Using a single bit to encode a message enables some errors to be detected. While this is an achievement, the use of a single parity bit has two flaws: (1) A defective code (say with two inverted bits) could trick the parity check, and (2) even if a defect in parity is found, it is not possible to correct it.

Consider the simple 1-character message e, whose 7-bit ASCII code is 1100101. To ensure even parity, we extend the code to 11001010. Suppose when this code is sent, however, two bits are changed during the transmission, yielding 11010010. The sum of the bits is even but the code is obviously wrong and the error would go undetected. This illustrates that a parity check only detects an odd number of incorrect bits.

What happens when a parity check results in an error being detected? There is no easy solution. One approach is to let the receiving host transmit a signal to the sending host to retransmit the defective signal. This is not always an option—for example, for simplex communications. Furthermore, would the sender transmit the message again? If the error were in one character of a million-byte message should the whole message be transmitted again? Another solution might be to transmit the message in duplicate so that an error in one version could be compared to the corresponding portion in the other version. However, this would increase the overhead of the network by 100 percent without assurance that the error would be corrected.

Other techniques used in error control include **framing,** in which the data link layer of the sending host partitions or **frames** a bit stream. One method of framing inserts a time gap—a time increment containing no data—between frames. This method is useful only when transmission is synchronous.

Another method is to count the number of ASCII characters in a frame and transmit this value along with the data. If a character is lost in transmission the receiving host detects and flags it as a transmission error, then signals the sending host to retransmit the message. The disadvantage is that numeric data and binary strings, for example, are not ASCII characters. Data link layers typically use the more accurate **cyclic redundancy check (CRC)** in which the transmitted data are read, a control character is calculated, and the value of the control character is compared to a control character already in the data. (This is an oversimplified description of a complex procedure best explained in an advanced text.)

8.2.3 Hamming Codes and Error Detection

In the late 1940s and early 1950s R.W. Hamming of Bell Labs developed his now famous algorithm for correcting transmission errors. Because of the efficiency of transmission technology today the algorithm is hardly used, but we present it here because of its prominence in computing and because of its clever construction.

Suppose data has a length of b bits and that k check bits are appended to the information bits. The total bits in the frame are m where $m = b + k$. The m bits in the frame make up a **codeword** for the transmission. There are 2^b possible data patterns and 2^m codewords. Because k ($k \geq 1$) check bits are present, it is clear that $2^b < 2^m$.

EXAMPLE 8.2–2

Problem
Suppose a 9-bit codeword contains two check bits. Find the number of possible codewords and the number of possible information patterns.

Reasoning
The number of codewords is 2^m. The number of information patterns is 2^b.

Solution

$$2^m = 2^9 = 512 \text{ codewords}$$
$$2^b = 2^7 = 128 \text{ information patterns}$$

Test
The number of information patterns is smaller than the number of codewords.

Consider, for example, a 6-bit codeword ($m = 6$) where two bits are check bits ($k = 2$). The remaining four bits ($b = 4$) are the information bits. This means that there are $2^4 = 16$ *legal* (according to the protocol used) information messages and we can determine the remaining legal codewords. Suppose a 5-bit

Table 8.2–1   Four-Bit Data with One Check Bit

0 *0* 0 0 0	0 *1* 0 0 1	0 *1* 0 1 0	0 0 0 1 1
0 *1* 1 0 0	0 0 1 0 1	0 0 1 1 0	0 *1* 1 1 1
1 *1* 0 0 0	1 0 0 0 1	1 0 0 1 0	1 *1* 0 1 1
1 0 1 0 0	1 *1* 1 0 1	1 *1* 1 1 0	1 0 1 1 1

codeword of *even* parity has a parity check bit in the second position. The codeword would be

iciii

for information bits *i* and check bit *c*. Now let the information represent the numbers 0 through 15 in binary. In this case there are 16 legal messages. The legal codewords (with the check bit in the second column and in italic) are shown in Table 8.2–1.

If only one bit is inverted in any of these 16 codewords, it could not produce a legal codeword. For example, if the lead bit of 00011 is inverted to produce 10011 this bit configuration is not a legal codeword. By inverting the first, second, fourth, and fifth bits of 11101 we would generate 00110, a legal codeword. In this case the *distance* between codewords is 4, and three inversions in any codeword would destroy parity. If two bits are inverted in any of the legal codewords, however, it produces another legal codeword. For example, if the third and fifth bits of 00110 are inverted, the resulting configuration of 00011 produces another legal codeword and the distance between the codewords is 2.

Hamming made the same observation and defined the distance between codewords as the smallest number of bit positions in which two codewords differ. We call this the **Hamming distance,** *d*. For example, the codewords 1111 and 1011 have a Hamming distance of $d = 1$. Hamming proposed that in a **complete code,** each codeword must have the same minimum distance from all other codewords; the Hamming distance. For the codewords in Table 8.2–1, the Hamming distance of $d = 2$ is a minimum so that the 16 codewords, each a distance 2 from each other, represent a complete code. From this Hamming concluded that a complete code of minimum distance *d* can detect *e* errors, where

$$e = d - 1$$

For the codewords in Table 8.2–1, $d = 2$ results in $e = 1$. Changing one bit in a code of distance 2 cannot produce another legal codeword, as we saw earlier. Although this gives us enough information to detect a 1-bit error, it does not give us enough information to correct it. For example, 10011 could have come from 00011, 10001, or 10010, all legal codewords.

8.2.4 Error-Correcting Codes

Hamming then showed that the error-detecting properties of a complete code can be expanded to correct a defective codeword. Consider a code having only two 6-bit legal codewords: 111011 and 001100. The minimum Hamming distance *d* is 5; that is, five bits must change to convert one codeword to the other. Suppose one of these legal codewords is transmitted but the codeword 110100 is received. Can we determine which legal codeword was transmitted? If the first codeword was transmitted, four single-bit errors were made—namely, the last four bits were inverted. If the second codeword was transmitted, three single-bit errors were made—namely, the first three bits were inverted. No conclusion can be made. Now suppose the codeword 101101 is received. If the first codeword was transmitted, three single-bit errors were made. However, if the second codeword was transmitted, only two single-bit errors were made. So what does this mean?

Hamming showed that to correct e errors in a complete code, we need the distance to be one more than twice the error. That is,

$$d = 2e + 1$$

In the previous problem, to correct four errors ($e = 4$) we need a distance-9 code. To correct three errors, we need a distance-7 code. To correct two errors, we need a distance-5 code. Because the problem is a distance-5 code, at most two single-bit errors can be corrected. Therefore, when the codeword 101101 is received, at most two bits can be changed to make a correction. If we invert the first and last bits of the codeword received we match the second of the legal codewords. We would have to invert the second, third, and fifth bit to match the first codeword.

The only way to determine whether the input words can be corrected is to assume that no more than the maximum number of errors occurred. That is, if the code has a Hamming distance of $d = 7$, not more than three single-bit errors occurred. The correction is based on the fact that the word received is closer to one legal information word than to any other. But if more bit errors occur than the maximum this scheme can handle, nothing can be done.

Program 8.2–2 simulates what might take place at the data link layer of a receiving host when the protocol requires identification of four legal codewords with an error-correcting scheme. The program's purpose is to determine the minimum Hamming distance given a 14-bit code with four legal codewords as constants. The user can then input other 14-bit words and the program will decide if the input words can be corrected. Codewords that can be corrected are changed to legal codewords. The Hamming distance is 7 so the maximum number of errors that can be corrected is 3: $2(3) + 1 = 7$. Improvements to the program are included in the exercises at the end of this section.

P R O G R A M   8 . 2 - 2

```
/*********************************************************************************
*   Title:       error-correcting algorithm on four codewords                  *
*   Filename:    errcoral.c                                                     *
*                                                                               *
*   Description: Given the legal codewords: 00000000000000 01010101010101       *
*                                           10101010101010 11111111111111       *
*                find the Hamming distance and determine the number of errors that can be *
*                corrected.  Input any 14-bit (integer) codeword. Determine if the        *
*                codeword is wrong and correct it if possible.                   *
*                                                                               *
```

```
*   Input:         data stream of 14-bit (integer) codewords                      *
*   Output:        Hamming distance, error detection, and correction where possible *
*   Process:       find Hamming distance, determine if correction is possible and make *
*                  correction                                                       *
*                                                                                   *
*   Written by:   ...                               Date: ...                       *
***********************************************************************************/


#include <stdio.h>
#include <ctype.h>                      /*  Special functions for alpha-numeric operations  */


#define  Z          '0'                                      /*  Define character for zero  */
#define  N          '1'                                      /*  Define character for one  */

#define  MAX_DIST    1000
#define  MAX_ERROR   3
#define  LEN         15          /*  Length of words including end of line character  */
#define  NUM_CW      4                              /*  Number of legal words  */

main ( )
{
   int  i, j, k,                                        /*  Indexing variables  */
        error[NUM_CW],                /*  Number of bit changes in compared to i-th  */
                                                         /*  legal word  */
        min_dist;                        /*  Minimum distance among legal codewords  */

   char ch,                                              /*  Character variable  */
        codeword[LEN];                                  /*  Entered codeword  */


   char legalword[NUM_CW][LEN] = {
              { Z, Z, Z, Z, Z, Z, Z, Z, Z, Z, Z, Z, Z, '\0' },
              { Z, N, Z, N, Z, N, Z, N, Z, N, Z, N, Z, N, '\0' },
              { N, Z, N, Z, N, Z, N, Z, N, Z, N, Z, N, Z, '\0' },
              { N, N, N, N, N, N, N, N, N, N, N, N, N, N, '\0' } };

   printf ( "\n\nThe Hamming Distance between any two legal codewords is 7. " );
   printf ( "\nTherefore, to perform an error correction on a codeword, " );
   printf ( "\nit can have at most 3 errors. ");

   do {

      printf ( "\n\n\nEnter a 14-bit codeword: " );
      scanf  ( "%s", &codeword );                        /*  Input test codeword  */
      min_dist = MAX_DIST;
```

```
     for ( i = 0; i < NUM_CW; i++ ) {              /* Calculate distance of test  */
                                                   /* codeword against each legal word */

         error[i] = 0;
         for ( j = 0; j < 14; j++ ) {
            if ( codeword[j] != legalword[i][j] )
            error[i]++;
         }

         printf ( "\n  Distance of codeword %s to legal codeword %s is %d",
                    codeword, legalword[ i ], error[ i ] );

         if ( error[ i ] < min_dist ) {            /* Find the Hamming distance  */
             min_dist =  error[ i ];
             k = i;
         }
     }



     if ( min_dist == 0 ) {                         /* Codeword is a legal word */
        printf ( "\n\nNumber of errors is %d. ", min_dist );
        printf ( "\n\nThe codeword %s is a legal codeword.", legalword[k] );
     }

     else if ( min_dist != 0  &&  min_dist <= MAX_ERROR ) {          /* Codeword is */
        printf ( "\n\nNumber of errors is %d. ", min_dist );          /* correctable */
        printf ( "\n\nCodeword can be corrected to legal codeword %s .",
                    legalword[ k ]  );
     }

     else if ( min_dist > MAX_ERROR )  {             /* Codeword cannot be corrected */
        printf ( "\n\nNumber of errors is %d.  ", min_dist );
        printf ( "\n\nCodeword %s has too many errors for a correction.", codeword );
     }

     printf ( "\n\nContinue?? [Y][N]: " );           /* Check sequence to continue */
     fflush ( stdin );
     scanf  (  "%s",  &ch );
     ch  =  toupper(ch);
     while  (  ch != 'Y'  &&  ch != 'N' )  {
        printf (  "Improper input! \n\nContinue?? [Y][N]: ");
        fflush ( stdin );
        scanf  (  "%c",  &ch );
        ch  =  toupper(ch);
     }
}  while  ( ch != 'N' );
```

```
printf ( "\n\n\tGood-bye!\n" );

    return (0);


}
```

Now we can generalize the process of correcting *single-bit* errors. As before, consider a set of m-bit codewords having h information bits and k check bits. Let the check bits be set (perhaps by parity) so that for each information pattern there is a corresponding legal codeword. The maximum number of information patterns on h bits is 2^h. The maximum number of possible codewords (not all legal) is 2^m. (See Figure 8.2–1.) Choose any one of the 2^h information patterns embedded in an m-bit codeword. Inverting any of the m bits produces another codeword. The generated codeword is not legal because the parity is wrong and it has a Hamming distance of 1 ($d = 1$). Therefore, each information word of h bits must have $m + 1$ patterns: the m patterns of distance 1 plus its own. The total legal patterns for all information words is $(m + 1)2^h$. This value can never exceed the total number of patterns for all codewords (legal or not), which is 2^m. This produces the expression

$$(m + 1)2^h \le 2^m$$

and because $m = h + k$,

$$(h + k + 1)2^h \le 2^{h+k} = 2^h2^k$$

or

$$h + k + 1 \le 2^k$$

The result is attributed to Hamming and gives the general condition needed for an error-correcting code.

We can use Hamming's relation ($h + k + 1 \le 2^k$) to find the number of check bits needed in a code for correcting single-bit errors. For example, suppose a code has eight information bits ($h = 8$). The number of check bits (k) needed must satisfy Hamming's relation. We can rewrite the relation as

$$k \le 2^k - h - 1$$

or

$$k \le 2^k - 9$$

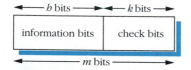

Figure 8.2–1 *m*-bit codeword

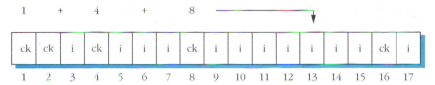

Figure 8.2–2   Twelve-bit information with five check bits

By substituting various integer values for k, we can find the minimum number of bits needed. Some trials are

$$
\begin{array}{ccccccl}
1 & \leq & 2^1 - 9 & = & -7 & \text{false} \\
2 & \leq & 2^2 - 9 & = & -5 & \text{false} \\
3 & \leq & 2^3 - 9 & = & -1 & \text{false} \\
4 & \leq & 2^4 - 9 & = & 7 & \text{true} \\
5 & \leq & 2^5 - 9 & = & 23 & \text{true} \\
6 & \leq & 2^6 - 9 & = & 55 & \text{true}
\end{array}
$$

Although five or six check bits would also work, a minimum of four check bits is needed.

Hamming not only gave the theoretical limits of an error-correcting code but also created an algorithm that can produce such a code for information words of any size. It works this way. First, make a codeword of m bits and label each bit position from left to right starting with the number 1. All labels that are powers of 2 (1, 2, 4, 8, 16, …) are the positions of the check bits. All other positions are information bits. Figure 8.2–2 shows the arrangement of the 12-bit information word together with the position of the check bits. Note that the labels of each position are formulated sums of powers of 2. For example, 13 = 8 + 4 + 1. After parity is assumed (odd or even), assign bit values to each check bit so that the sum of all bits it checks matches the established parity. Bit checking uses the method illustrated in Table 8.2–2.

The check bit at position 1 affects all odd-numbered bit positions, whereas the check bit at position 2 affects bit positions 2–3, 6–7, 10–11, 14–15, 18–19, etc. The check bit at position 4 affects bit positions 4–7, and 12–15, etc. The check bit at position 8 affects bit positions 8–15, etc. The check bit at position 16 affects bit positions 16–32, etc. The check bits act as pointers to the positions. For example, bit position 13 = 8 + 4 + 1 is identified by the three check bits 8, 4, and 1. Bit

Table 8.2–2   Check Bits and Bit Positions

CHK BIT	POSITION																		
	1	2	3	4	5	6	7	8	9	10	11	12	13	14	15	16	17	18	19
16																x	x	x	x
8								x	x	x	x	x	x	x	x				
4				x	x	x	x					x	x	x	x				
2		x	x			x	x			x	x			x	x			x	x
1	x		x		x		x		x		x		x	x	x		x		x

position 18 = 16 + 2 is identified by the two check bits 16 and 2. Note that the value of each check bit is determined completely by the data bits and *not* by any other check bit. Thus each is figured independently and the check-bit values can be evaluated in any order.

EXAMPLE 8.2–3

Problem

Use Hamming's algorithm to encode the 14-bit information word

10010010101010

using even parity.

Reasoning

The parity is even. Find the number of check bits needed using Hamming's relation $b + k + 1 \leq 2^k$. Calculate the value of each check bit according to the algorithm, starting at position 1.

Solution

The number of check bits must satisfy the relation

$$b + k + 1 \leq 2^k$$

where $b = 14$, so

$$k \leq 2^k - 15$$

the minimum value of k is 5 because

$$5 \leq 2^5 - 15 = 17$$

The codeword must then contain 19 (14 + 5) bits. Begin by setting up the 19 bits and labeling each position as in the following. Check-bit positions are emphasized and are identified by bit values $k1$ through $k5$.

$k1$	$k2$		$k3$				$k4$								$k5$			
1	2	3	4	5	6	7	8	9	10	11	12	13	14	15	16	17	18	19

Sequentially insert all information bits at positions that are not check bits as follows.

$k1$	$k2$	1	$k3$	0	0	1	$k4$	0	0	1	0	1	0	1	$k5$	0	1	0
1	2	3	4	5	6	7	8	9	10	11	12	13	14	15	16	17	18	19

Check-bit 1, indicated by $k1$, reflects all odd-number positions (including itself) and because of even parity,

$$k1 + 1 + 0 + 1 + 0 + 1 + 1 + 1 + 0 + 0 = \text{even number}$$

so

$$k1 + 5 = \text{even number}$$

Therefore, $k1$ must be 1. The codeword now becomes

1	*k2*	**1**	*k3*	0	0	**1**	*k4*	0	0	1	0	1	0	1	*k5*	0	1	0
1	2	3	4	5	6	7	8	9	10	11	12	13	14	15	16	17	18	19

Check-bit *k2* reflects positions 2, 3, 6, 7, 10, 11, 14, 15, 18, and 19, as shown in Table 8.2–2. Because of even parity,

$$k2 + 1 + 0 + 1 + 0 + 1 + 0 + 1 + 1 + 0 = \text{even number}$$

so

$$k2 + 5 = \text{even number}$$

Therefore, *k2* must be 1. The codeword now becomes

1	**1**	**1**	*k3*	0	0	**1**	*k4*	0	0	1	0	1	0	1	*k5*	0	1	0
1	2	3	4	5	6	7	8	9	10	11	12	13	14	15	16	17	18	19

Check-bit *k3* reflects positions 4, 5, 6, 7, 12, 13, 14, and 15, as shown in Table 8.2–2. Because of even parity,

$$k3 + 0 + 0 + 1 + 0 + 1 + 0 + 1 = \text{even number}$$

so

$$k3 + 3 = \text{even number}$$

Therefore, *k3* must be 1. The codeword now becomes

1	**1**	**1**	**1**	0	0	**1**	*k4*	0	0	1	0	1	0	1	*k5*	0	1	0
1	2	3	4	5	6	7	8	9	10	11	12	13	14	15	16	17	18	19

Similarly, we can determine that *k4* = 1 and *k5* = 1.

1	**1**	**1**	**1**	0	0	**1**	**1**	0	0	1	0	1	0	1	**1**	0	1	0
1	2	3	4	5	6	7	8	9	10	11	12	13	14	15	16	17	18	19

The 19-bit codeword that results from Hamming's algorithm is

1111001100101011010

Test

You can do a parity check on each of the code bits to ensure that the result is correct. ●

How does this code enable error correction? Consider the codeword from Example 8.2–3. Recall that we assumed even parity and that the assumption for this algorithm is that only one bit is wrong. Suppose one bit is inverted during transmission—for example, the thirteenth bit. Realize that the computer does not know which bit, if any, is inverted. The original and modified codewords with parity check bits identified are

⇓	⇓		⇓				⇓								⇓				[parity check bits]
1	1	1	1	0	0	1	1	0	0	1	0	1	0	1	1	0	1	0	[original codeword]
1	1	1	1	0	0	1	1	0	0	1	0	0	0	1	1	0	1	0	[modified codeword]
												↑							[incorrect bit]

Hamming showed that by calculating the parity bits you can identify the incorrect bit. Again, the assumption for this algorithm is that only one bit is wrong. The parity bits that are not correct are used in this identification as follows.

Parity bit 16 checks positions 16, 17, 18, and 19 of the modified codeword; the sum of the bits is

$$1 + 0 + 1 + 0 = 2$$

and it *is* even. Therefore, check-bit 16 *is not* involved in the correction process.

Parity bit 8 checks positions 8, 9, 10, 11, 12, 13, 14, and 15 of the modified codeword; the sum of the bits is

$$1 + 0 + 0 + 1 + 0 + 0 + 0 + 1 = 3$$

and it *is not* even. Therefore, check-bit 8 *is* involved in the correction process.

Parity bit 4 checks positions 4, 5, 6, 7, 12, 13, 14, and 15 of the modified codeword; the sum of the bits is

$$1 + 0 + 0 + 1 + 0 + 0 + 0 + 1 = 3$$

and it *is not* even. Therefore, check-bit 4 *is* involved in the correction process.

Parity bit 2 checks positions 2, 3, 6, 7, 10, 11, 14, 15, 18, and 19 of the modified codeword; the sum of the bits is

$$1 + 1 + 0 + 1 + 0 + 1 + 0 + 1 + 1 + 0 = 6$$

and it *is* even. Therefore, check-bit 2 *is not* involved in the correction process.

Finally, parity bit 1 checks positions 1, 3, 5, 7, 9, 11, 13, 15, 17, and 19 of the modified codeword; the sum of the bits is

$$1 + 1 + 0 + 1 + 0 + 1 + 0 + 1 + 0 + 0 = 5$$

and it *is not* even. Therefore, check bit 1 *is* involved in the correction process.

The digression from parity in the check process shows that parity bits 1, 4, and 8 were not correct. The algorithm locates the incorrect bit since

$$1 + 4 + 8 = 13$$

Therefore, the 13th bit must be inverted. The message is now corrected.

EXAMPLE 8.2–4

Problem

Information is transmitted in packets of four bits. The information string in one of these packets is 0110. Assume odd parity.

a. Encode this information so that a single-bit error can be detected and corrected.
b. Change one information bit and use Hamming's algorithm to correct it.

Reasoning

Before making the proper codeword, you must find the number of check bits needed. Using Hamming's inequality, we have

$$k \le 2^k - h - 1$$

and for $h = 6$,

$$k \le 2^k - 6 - 1$$

or

$$k \le 2^k - 5$$

leading to $k = 3$. The check bits are 1, 2, and 4.

Solution

a. The codeword has seven bits (4 parity, 3 information) and takes the following form with the information bits inserted.

k1	k2	0	k3	1	1	0
1	2	3	4	5	6	7

Parity bit $k1$ checks positions 1, 3, 5, and 7, so $k1 + 0 + 1 + 0 = k1 + 1 =$ odd, which implies that $k1$ is 0. Parity bit $k2$ checks positions 2, 3, 6, and 7, so $k2 + 0 + 1 + 0 = k2 + 1 =$ odd, which implies that $k2 = 0$. Parity bit $k3$ checks positions 4, 5, 6, and 7, so $k3 + 1 + 1 + 0 = k3 + 2 =$ odd, which implies that $k3 = 1$. The pattern becomes

0	0	0	1	1	1	0
1	2	3	4	5	6	7

and the codeword is 0001110.

b. Suppose during transmission one bit is inverted so that the modified codeword is now 0001100. By repeating the parity checks in (a) we find:

Parity bit 1 is correct because $0 + 0 + 1 + 0 = 1$ is odd.

Parity bit 2 is incorrect because $0 + 0 + 0 + 0 = 0$ is not odd.

Parity bit 4 is incorrect because $1 + 1 + 0 + 0 = 2$ is not odd.

Therefore, the algorithm tells us that the $(2 + 4)$ sixth bit in the codeword is not correct. The transmitted codeword is corrected by inverting the sixth bit with a result of 0001110, the original codeword.

Test

Change any other bit in the original codeword. The algorithm detects and corrects it.   •

It is clear that the overhead for error correction is very high and that retransmission is much easier. Consequently, error correction is used only when retransmission is not feasible, as in commands transmitted to distant space probes or in sensitive military communications. Nevertheless, Hamming's algorithm remains a landmark in the evolution of computer science.

EXERCISES 8.2

Concept Check

Answer statements 1 through 4 with true *or* false.

1. All transmission bit errors can be corrected.
2. Correcting errors is as easy as detecting them.

3. To detect three errors in a complete code, we need a Hamming distance equal to or greater than 2.

4. To correct three errors in a complete code, we need a Hamming distance that is greater than or equal to 7.

For statements 5 through 8 choose the answer that best completes the statement.

5. A Hamming single-bit correction code has 12 information bits. The minimum number of check bits needed is
   a. 1
   b. 3
   c. 5
   d. 7

6. Error detection and possible correction in the OSI protocol model is done at the
   a. data link layer
   b. applications layer
   c. physical layer
   d. presentation layer

7. A code with a Hamming distance of 5 can correct
   a. three errors
   b. two errors
   c. one error
   d. no error

8. Categorizing a pattern as odd or even is called
   a. framing
   b. error detection
   c. parity
   d. error correction

For statements 9 through 12 fill in the blanks with the right answer.

9. An error-detection scheme in which a time gap is inserted at fixed-time intervals is called _____.

10. A _____ bit is inserted in information to check if the aggregated bit count is odd or even.

11. A bit string consisting of both information and check bits is called a _____.

12. To correct six errors in a complete code, we need a Hamming distance that equals at least the value _____.

Set A

Solve each of the following problems.

13. There are four information bits in a complete code that corrects single-bit errors. How many check bits are needed?

14. There are 40 information bits in a complete code that corrects single-bit errors. How many check bits are needed?

15. A complete code can detect up to seven errors. Find the Hamming distance.

16. A complete code can correct up to seven errors. Find the Hamming distance.

17. A bit string is represented in hexadecimal as CFFE. Use a 6-bit framing pattern to encode the string for error detection and express the resulting code, left-justified, in hexadecimal.

18. A bit string is represented in hexadecimal as CFFE. Use a 9-bit framing pattern to encode the string for error detection and express the resulting code, left-justified, in hexadecimal.

Set B

19. Use the Hamming algorithm to encode with even parity the information-bit string 01101 and correct single-bit errors.

20. Use the Hamming algorithm to encode with odd parity the information-bit string 001010 and correct single-bit errors.

21. Given an information string in hexadecimal such as "FEED", encode it with odd parity so it can correct single-bit errors.

22. Given an information string in hexadecimal such as "CABBEE", encode it with even parity so it can correct single-bit errors.

23. The Hamming codeword 1011001000 written in binary has one incorrect bit. Correct the codeword and describe the information pattern. Assume even parity.

24. The Hamming codeword 00111010101 written in binary has one incorrect bit. Correct the codeword and describe the information pattern. Assume odd parity.

25. The Hamming codeword E2DB7 written in hexadecimal has one incorrect bit. Correct the codeword and describe the information pattern. Assume even parity.

26. The Hamming codeword FDD3BB written in hexadecimal has one incorrect bit. Correct the codeword and describe the information pattern. Assume odd parity.

Set C

27. Modify Program 8.2–1 so that the parity bit is always in the middle of the message bits. (Note that the number of message bits can be odd or even.)

28. Modify Program 8.2–1 so that it asks the user whether to continue to run the program or to terminate it.

29. Program 8.2–2 can be improved to better reflect the codeword checks.
    a. Modify the program so that it allows exactly 14 character representations for the bits in any codeword.
    b. Modify the program so that no character other than 0 or 1 can be used to represent a bit.

30. Modify and execute Program 8.2–2 for a variety of bit strings for six codewords of length 12 bits.

31. Write a C program with functional modularity using the Hamming correction algorithm for single-bit errors on a message string of 20 bits.

ENDNOTES

1. Hartmanis, J., and Lin, H., editors. *Computing the Future: A Broader Agenda for Computer Science and Engineering*. National Research Council, National Academy Press, Washington, D.C., 1992, p. 184.

2. "Prime Time Live," ABC Corporation, New York, 21 October 1993.

Pointers and Function Parameters

Road sign pointing to different locations around the world.

After completing this chapter you should be able to do the following:

Learning Goals

- Explain how to create and manipulate pointer variables
- Change the value of a variable without directly referring to its name
- Use the address-of (&) and dereference (*) operators
- Write a function using input and output parameters
- Distinguish between local variables and global variables
- Distinguish between arguments and parameters

Chapter Activity

Write a program that reads in a paragraph of text, one line at a time. Then analyze the text with a function whose output parameters include:

1. the number of occurrences of each vowel
2. the total number of letters
3. the total number of blank spaces
4. the total number of punctuation characters
5. the total number of words

9.1 POINTERS

Introduction

Consider the problem of writing a *swap* function that exchanges the values of its two parameters (as shown in Figure 9.1–1). What does this function return? A single number is not enough in this case because both parameters will be changed by the process and both the new values will be expected by the

Query: Why doesn't the following swap function solve the problem just described?

```
void swap ( int x,   int y )
{
    int temp;
    temp =  x;
    x    =  y;
    y    =  temp;
}
```

RESPONSE: Although the swap function does exchange the values of its parameters correctly, nothing is returned to the calling function. The changes to **x** and **y** are purely *local*—they exist only within the swap function and are not available to the calling function.

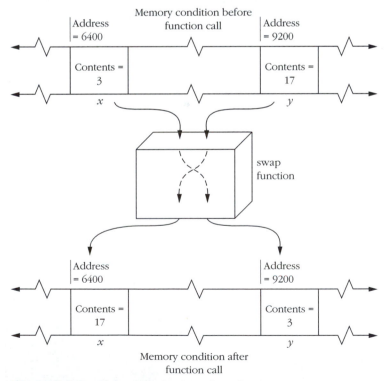

Figure 9.1–1 Behavior of **swap** function

calling function. The C `return` statement does not allow more than one value (a variable, constant, or expression) to be returned. Therefore, according to our definition of a function this problem cannot be solved!

What is needed in C is an *indirect* mechanism for returning values from a function. Pointer variables provide this mechanism. Because pointers are a difficult concept, we concentrate on them in this section and return to the swapping problem in Section 9.2.

9.1.1 An Overview of Pointer Variables

In programming, a *variable* is just a symbolic name associated with a physical address within the computer's memory. Thus the declarations

```
int    length,  width;
float area;
```

are requests to find a specific amount of memory (two bytes for an integer and four bytes for a float) and associate the particular names with the first byte of each memory area.

We can handle these declarations as shown in the following table. Note that ANSI C needs a minimum of two bytes for an `int` and four bytes for a `float` but that these values may be different depending on the compiler you are using.

length		width		area			
1000	1001	1002	1003	1004	1005	1006	1007

Arbitrarily starting with memory location 1000, we see that each variable is assigned the amount of storage needed. We also see that the address of `length` is 1000, the address of `width` is 1002, and the address of `area` is 1004.

The address of a variable is called its **lvalue** (for left-hand value because it is the address of the variable that is needed on the left side of the assignment operator). The associated data is called its **rvalue** (for right-hand value). A constant is an rvalue because it has no symbolic memory address. When an assignment statement such as `length = 10;` is analyzed, `length` is treated as an lvalue. Thus, the statement reads *store the rvalue 10 at the lvalue associated with* `length`. Yet `10 = length;` is a syntax error; 10 is not a valid lvalue. The assignment operator is defined as *lvalue = rvalue;*. The statement `area = length * width;` is valid because the left side is an lvalue, the address of `area`, and the right side has two rvalues, the data in `length` and `width`.

So far in our studies the distinction between lvalue and rvalue has been significant only for `scanf`, which needs the lvalue of each listed variable. The ampersand (`&`) means *supply the lvalue of the variable that follows*. Most beginning programmers think that a variable is synonymous with its rvalue and don't know what an lvalue is. As we see now, it is sometimes helpful to refer to the address (lvalue) of a variable. Knowing a variable's address gives us a second, indirect way to access the variable's rvalue.

A **pointer** is a memory address. It is a C data type whose legitimate range of values is the memory address space of the computer. A **pointer variable** can hold the address of (a pointer to) another variable. Pointer variables are usually associated with a specific data type. Thus, you can declare integer pointer variables, character pointer variables, and so on, in the variable declarations by prefixing the name of the variable with an asterisk. Examples of valid pointer variable declarations are

```
int   *x;
float *y,   *z;
```

The first statement reads: **x** *is declared to be a pointer to an integer variable.* Similarly, **y** and **z** are defined to be pointers to floating-point variables. In other words, the variables **x**, **y**, and **z** can hold the lvalues of other variables *of the appropriate data type.* Note that when you declare these variables they are not yet pointing to anything. This is true for most variables at declaration time. Although the data type and name are specified, nothing is known about their contents. We say that uninitialized variables hold **logical garbage** because their data are meaningless. The first exception is that when a variable is declared with the **static** qualifier, it is automatically initialized to 0. For example, **static int x[10];** declares a 10-element array of integers, all initialized to 0. The second exception is that variables declared outside a function are by default **extern** and are also initialized to 0.

How do we use pointer variables? The only legitimate data that a pointer variable can contain is the address (lvalue) of another variable of the appropriate data type. Assuming that **length** and **area** are declared as shown, and making use of the **&** address-of operator, the following statements are valid.

length		width		area			
1000	1001	1002	1003	1004	1005	1006	1007

```
x  =   &length;            /* x is assigned the address of length */
y  =   &area;              /* y is assigned the address of area */
printf ( "\nx = %p   y = %p",   x,  y );        /* Outputs x = 1000 */
                                                /*  y = 1004 */
```

The **&** address-of operator can be prefixed to any variable and returns its assigned memory location (lvalue). You can output an lvalue using the **%p** format although it is just an arbitrary memory location and is probably different each time the program executes.

We could say that **x** knows where **length** lives. Having access to its lvalue enables you to retrieve or alter the value of **length** through **x**, using the **dereference (indirection)** operator *****. An asterisk in front of a pointer variable (***x**) means *refer to the object that the pointer is pointing to.* A reference to ***x** is an indirect way of saying **length** because **length** is the data object that **x** is pointing to. Consider the following.

```
int  length, *x;
length = 10;
x = &length;                        /* x contains the address of length */
printf ( "\n length  =  %d",  *x );              /* Outputs 10 */
```

*x can be used wherever length can be used, and continuing from the previous code the following is acceptable.

```
*x   = 20;
printf (  "\nLength = %d", length );          /* Outputs 20 */
area = *x * 15;
printf (  "\nArea  = %d",   area );           /* Outputs 300 */
```

PERSPECTIVE

A pointer variable enables you to change the value of another variable without using that variable's name. In the preceding example, changing the value of *x changes the value of length. This is called **indirect addressing** and *x is sometimes called an **alias** for length.

PERSPECTIVE

For *any* variable v, *&v is equivalent to v itself. The expression reads *return the rvalue of the variable whose lvalue is* &v.

Although indirect addressing may seem strange at first, a little practice helps to demystify the concept. We suggest that you try all the exercises in this section. Next, we look at a useful application for indirection with function arguments. Pointers are discussed at length in Chapter 13.

EXERCISES 9.1

Concept Check
Answer statements 1 through 4 with true *or* false.
1. A function in C uses the return statement to indirectly return a value to the calling function.
2. An address can never be the data stored at a particular memory location.
3. An rvalue is the data value associated with a particular variable or constant.
4. When used with a pointer variable, the & operator gives the data that the pointer variable points to.

For statements 5 through 8 choose the answer that best completes the statement.
5. Assume that the following statements are made in a program.

```
int *x,  y;
x = &y;
```

What is the relationship between **x** and **y**?

a. ***y** is an alias for **x**.
b. ***x** is an alias for **y**.
c. **y** can change the value of **x**.
d. **x** can change the address of **y**.

6. Referring to the statements in Question 5, which of the following are true?
    a. **x**'s rvalue is the same as **y**'s lvalue.
    b. **x**'s lvalue is the same as **y**'s rvalue.
    c. ***x** is the same as **y**'s lvalue.
    d. **&y** is the same as **x**'s lvalue.

7. Which of the following are true?
    a. Literal constants and variables both have lvalues but only variables have rvalues too.
    b. Pointer variables can store either addresses or nonaddress data, such as integers and characters, as long as they are given the correct data type.
    c. The lvalue of a pointer variable might be the same as the rvalue of a nonpointer variable.
    d. The rvalue of a pointer variable might be the same as the lvalue of a nonpointer variable.

8. What is the outcome of the execution of the following statements?

    ```
    int *v, x;
    v = &x;
    *v  = 13;
    printf (  "\n%d %d",  *v, x  );
    ```

    a. The program prints 13 13.
    b. The program prints the value of the variable stored in memory location 13 followed by the value of **x**.
    c. The results are unpredictable since **v**'s rvalue is logical garbage.
    d. The results are unpredictable since **v**'s lvalue is logical garbage.

For statements 9 through 12 fill in the blanks with the right word.

9. Getting access to the object that a pointer variable points to is called _____.

10. Assigning the address of a variable to a pointer is done with the _____ operator.

11. To output the value of a pointer variable, use _____ ___ format.

12. At declaration time the value of most variables is _____.

Set A

Write a C statement or two to solve each of the following problems.

13. Declare **ch** as a character variable and **ch.ptr** as a pointer to a character variable.

14. Assign **ch** the value **'C'** and make **ch.ptr** point to **ch**.

15. Change the value of **ch** to **'X'** directly and indirectly.

16. Subtract `'A'` from the data pointed to by `ch_ptr` and add `'a'` to the result.
17. Output `ch_ptr` and the data it indirectly references.
18. Assuming that `ch` has been given the memory address 1234, determine the output of Question 17.

Set B

19. For each of the following, indicate whether the statement is correct. If not, explain the error. Assume the following declarations.

```
int    a, *i_pt1,  *i_pt2;
float b, *fl_pt1, *fl_pt2;
char   c, *c_pt1,  *c_pt2;
```

a. `fl_pt1 = &a;`

b. `c_pt1 = *c;`

c. `b = &fl_pt2;`

d. `fl_pt2 = &b;`

e. `*c_pt1 = 'c';`

f. `c_pt1 = &a;`

g. `fl_pt2 = 13.5;`

h. `*fl_pt1 = 13;`

i. `i_pt1 = &a;`

j. `*i_pt1 = *i_pt2;`

k. `&c_pt1 = *c;`

l. `i_pt2 = i_pt1;`

m. `i_pt2 = &i_pt1;`

n. `*i_pt1 = *i_pt2;`

o. `*i_pt1 = &i_pt2;`

p. `c_pt1 = *&c_pt2;`

q. `fl_pt2 = &a;`

r. `&fl_pt2 = 76.5;`

s. `b = *i_pt1;`

t. `a = *fl_pt1;`

20. Fill in the remaining rvalues, given the table of memory allocations and each of the following statements.

```
int  x = 23,  y,  z,  *a_pt, *b_pt, *c_pt;
a_pt =  &x;
b_pt =  &y;
c_pt =  &z;
*c_pt =  *a_pt + 17;
*b_pt =  *a_pt + *c_pt;
```

SYMBOLIC NAME	x	y	z	a_pt	b_pt	c_pt
Lvalue	1000	1002	1004	1006	1008	1010
Rvalue						

Set C

21. Write a program using only `main` to do the following: Create three integer variables `x`, `y`, and `temp`. Create two integer pointer variables `x_pt` and `y_pt`. Assign values to `x` and `y`. Swap their values directly using `x`, `y`, and `temp`. Swap their values again, indirectly, using `x_pt`, `y_pt`, and `temp`. Output the results, which should be the original values of `x` and `y`.

9.2   FUNCTIONS WITH OUTPUT PARAMETERS

Introduction

Next, we explore the use of pointers with functions. We see how passing the address of an argument and declaring the corresponding parameter as a pointer variable enable a function to change the value of the argument. In this way, functions can send back more than one value, increasing the power of a function to communicate with the rest of a program.

9.2.1 Input and Output Parameters

So far we have described functions as a series of zero or more parameters and zero or one return value. Now let's refine the terms we use for arguments and parameters. An **input argument** is a value that is passed to a function and assigned as the initial value of the corresponding **input parameter**. This is **call by value** because it is just the value (rvalue) of the argument that is passed to the function.

An **output argument** and the corresponding **output parameter** have values that are changed by the function and *indirectly* passed back to the calling function. We do this in the function call by specifying that the *address* (lvalue) of the output argument is to be passed, not the data itself (rvalue). On the receiving end, the corresponding parameters are declared as pointer variables. Each output parameter is initialized to the address of the corresponding argument, which enables the function to *alter the arguments by dereferencing the parameters*. Figure 9.2–1 shows how arguments correspond to their respective parameters.

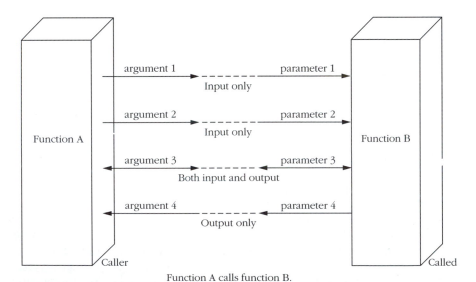

Function A calls function B.

Figure 9.2–1   Correspondence between input and output parameters (revisited)

PERSPECTIVE

C *always* passes arguments by value, regardless of whether the argument is input or output. With an input argument the rvalue is passed. With an output argument the lvalue is passed.

Consider Program 9.2–1, in which a function is used to compute both the area and the perimeter of a rectangle.

PROGRAM 9.2–1

```
/***************************************************************************
* Title:        rectangle calculations                                    *
* Filename:     rectangl.c                                                 *
*                                                                          *
* Description: Compute the perimeter and area of a rectangle based on values *
*              for the length and width.                                   *
*                                                                          *
* Input:        length,  width                                            *
* Output:       perimeter,  area                                          *
* Process:      perimeter = 2 * (length + width)                          *
*               area      = length * width                                *
*                                                                          *
* Written by:   ...                                   Date: ...            *
***************************************************************************/

#include  <stdio.h>

                                                        /*  Prototype  */
void calc_perim_and_area ( float length,     float width,
                           float *perim_ptr, float *area_ptr );

main ( )
{
   float length,  width,  perimeter,  area;

   printf ( "\nInput the length and width of a rectangle:" );
   scanf ( "%f %f", &length,  &width );            /* Input length and width */

   calc_perim_and_area ( length, width, &perimeter, &area ); /* Function call */

   printf ( "\nFor length =  %8.2f and width = %8.2f", length, width);
   printf ( "\nThe perimeter =  %8.2f",  perimeter );      /* Output results */
   printf ( "\nThe area =  %8.2f",  area );

 return ( 0 );
}                                                       /*  End of main  */
```

```
/*******************************************************************************
* Function name:     calc_perim_and_area                                      *
* Description:       Compute the perimeter and area of a rectangle with       *
*                    specified length and width.                              *
*                                                                             *
* Input parameters: length,  width                                           *
* Output parameters: perim_ptr,  area_ptr                                     *
* Return value:      none                                                     *
*******************************************************************************/

void calc_perim_and_area ( float length,     float width,
                           float *perim_ptr, float *area_ptr )
{

    *perim_ptr = 2 * ( length + width );    /* Indirect reference to perimeter */
    *area_ptr  = length * width;                /* Indirect reference to area  */

                                                /*    End of  calc_perim_and_area  */
}
```

calc_perim_and_area is called with two input arguments, length and width, and two output arguments, perimeter and area. The rvalues of length and width are passed to the corresponding parameters, and the lvalues of perimeter and area are passed to the function.

Let's see what happens in the function, starting with the header. The function return type is declared to be void since it does not use the return statement to communicate its results. The output parameters are listed as pointer variables of the appropriate type and their names have been changed slightly to reflect their status as pointers and to avoid giving them the same names as they have in main. After the function call, perim_ptr and area_ptr hold the respective addresses of perimeter and area from main, as shown in Figure 9.2–2.

The *calculation* of the perimeter looks the same as it might in main. However, assigning the result puts us in a quandary. Because perim_ptr is a pointer, it would be unacceptable to write

```
perim_ptr = 2 * ( length + width );          /* ERROR: Incorrect syntax */
```

in an attempt to assign a floating-point number to a pointer variable (they are incompatible data types). In any case it is not perim_ptr we want to change but the object that perim_ptr points to. It is not declared in the function so we cannot refer *directly* to perimeter. The following is also incorrect.

```
perimeter = 2 * ( length + width );          /* ERROR: Incorrect syntax */
```

This statement would result in a syntax error, indicating that perimeter is an undefined variable. We can, however, refer *indirectly* to perimeter via the address stored in perim_ptr. Thus, the statement

```
*perim_ptr = 2 * ( length + width );               /* Correct syntax */
```

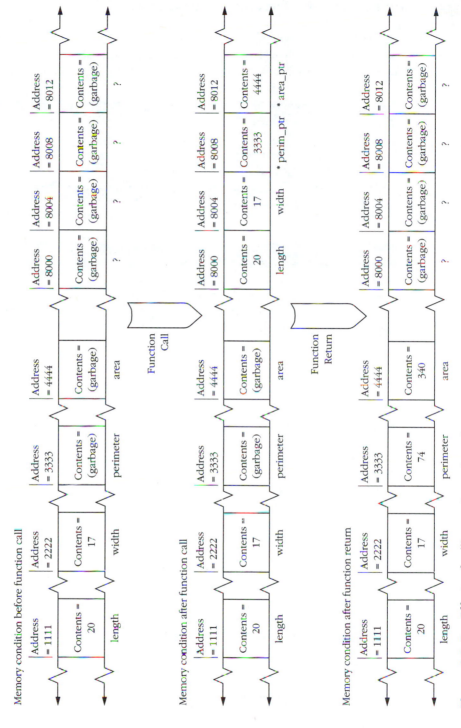

Figure 9.2-2 Effects of calling `calc_perim_and_area`

indirectly assigns the computed value to the variable `perimeter` in `main`. This works because `*perim_ptr` is an alias for `perimeter`. The `area` variable is changed in the same way with an indirect reference through `area_ptr`.

PERSPECTIVE

At last we solve the mystery of `scanf`! The `scanf` function accepts one input argument, the format string, and *many* output arguments—the list of variables to be read into. We use the `&`'s because each of these variables must have its address passed. `scanf` can therefore indirectly modify the arguments with the results appearing in the calling function.

PERSPECTIVE

You may have noticed that when a whole array is passed to a function, the array argument does not need the `&` even if the array is to be changed. This is because the name of an array is *already* a pointer: It is the address of its first element. (See Program 7.2–2.)

9.2.2 Inout Parameters

A given argument or parameter can be *both* input and output. This is the case with `swap` in Section 9.1. Recall that `swap` takes two variables and exchanges their values. Thus, valid data are assigned to the parameters when the function is called but these values will be different after the function executes. (Some programmers call these **inout** parameters.) Because the new values have to be passed back to the corresponding arguments, we define inout parameters as pointers. This is shown in Program 9.2–2.

PROGRAM 9.2–2

```
/****************************************************************************
* Title:      swap two numbers                                            *
* Filename:   swapvals.c                                                   *
*                                                                          *
* Description: Swap the values of two variables.                          *
*                                                                          *
* Input:      x, y                                                         *
* Output:     x, y (swapped)                                               *
* Process:    exchange the values of the two variables                    *
*                                                                          *
* Written by: ...                                        Date: ...         *
****************************************************************************/

#include <stdio.h>
```

```
void swap ( int  *x_ptr,   int *y_ptr );                    /*  Prototype */

main ( )
{

  int  x, y;

  printf ( "Input two numbers:" );
  scanf  ( "%d %d", &x,  &y );

  swap (  &x,  &y );                               /*  Passing the addresses */

  printf ( "\nAfter swapping, the values are:  %d %d",  x,  y );

  return ( 0 );
}                                                   /*  End of main */


/***********************************************************************
* Function name:      swap                                            *
* Description:        Exchange the values of the two arguments using pointers. *
*                                                                     *
* Input parameters:  x_ptr, y_ptr                                     *
* Output parameters: x_ptr, y_ptr                                     *
* Return value:       none                                           *
***********************************************************************/

void   swap ( int  *x_ptr,   int  *y_ptr )
{
   int temp;

   temp    = *x_ptr;
   *x_ptr  = *y_ptr;
   *y_ptr  = temp;
}                                                   /* End of swap */
```

Let's examine this carefully, looking at Figure 9.2–3. Assume that **swap** is called with **x** = 17 and **y** = 35.

Step 1: Inout parameters **x_ptr** and **y_ptr** are defined as integer pointers whose initial values are the addresses of the corresponding arguments **x** and **y** (Figure 9.2–3a).

Step 2: The local **temp** variable is given the dereferenced value of **x_ptr**. Because ***x_ptr** is an alias for **x**, **temp** now equals 17 (Figure 9.2–3b).

Step 3: The variable that **x_ptr** points to, **x**, is given the data that **y_ptr** points to, which is 35 (Figure 9.2–3c).

Step 4: The variable that **y_ptr** points to, **y**, is given the value of **temp**, which is now 17 (Figure 9.2–3d).

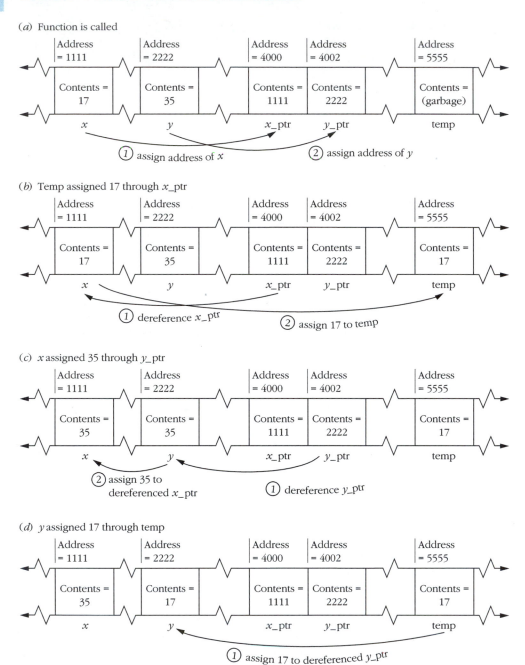

Figure 9.2–3 Detailed view of `swap` function

9.2.3 Variable Scope

When you write functions you often have to define variables within the function body. These variables (and constants) have **local scope** and are usually called **locals** because their existence begins and ends in the function. Their values are not known outside the function, as shown by the following program segment.

```
#include <stdio.h>

void silly ( void );                                       /* Prototype */

main ( )
{

    int  x;                                  /*  This  x  is local to main */
    x  =  14;
    printf ( "\nIn main, before the function,  x  =  %d",   x );
    silly ( );                                     /* Function call */

    printf ( "\nIn main, after the function,  x  =  %d",  x );

    return ( 0 );
}


void silly ( void )
{
    int x;                                 /*  This  x  is local to silly */
    x  =  -2;
    printf ( "\nIn the  function,  x  =   %d",  x );
}
```

The output of this program is:

In main, before the function, x = 14
In the function, x = −2
In main, after the function, x = 14

As you can see, **silly** changed a variable called **x**, which is a *different* variable from the **x** in **main**.

PERSPECTIVE

Remember that a function is sometimes called a miniprogram and in a sense exists in a world of its own. In this case the world of **silly** has its own variable called **x**.

Another scope, **global**, applies to any entity defined outside a function. Consider the following variation of the program we just analyzed.

```
#include <stdio.h>

void silly ( void );                                      /*  Prototype  */

int  x;                                    /*  x is declared globally  */

main ( )
{

    x = 14;
    printf ( "In main, before the function,  x  =  %d",   x );
    silly ( );                                /*  Function call  */

    printf ( "\nIn main, after the function,  x  =  %d", x );

    return ( 0 );
}


void silly ( void )
{
    x = -2;
    printf ( "\nIn the  function,  x  =   %d",  x );
}
```

The output of the revised program is:

In main, before the function, x = 14
In the function, x = −2
In main, after the function, x = −2

In this case both **main** and **silly** are using the same *global* variable called **x**. When **silly** changes **x**, it is also changing **x** in **main**.

An important principle of structured program design is to keep the number of global variables to an absolute minimum. It is hard to trace changes to global variables because any function can be written to change them. Beginning programmers often balk at this rule because it seems so much easier to make everything global and not have to deal with argument passing.

In response to this objection, let's imagine that a team of programmers has just finished a large programming project consisting of hundreds or even thousands of functions. Assume that the **x** variable is declared globally and used in many different functions without being passed as an argument. Each programmer changes **x** however he or she sees fit.

Now suppose there were a bug in the program that was related to **x** and you were given the job of debugging. Where would you look to find the source of the problem? The value of **x** is "out of control": *any* function could have changed **x** so you would have to examine the whole program. In a large program this could be a long and costly process.

Now let's consider the alternative. Assuming that **x** needs to be communicated between several functions, the better solution would be to pass it into functions as an argument. That way the person who is debugging knows exactly which functions are potentially at fault. Specifically, he or she must concentrate only on the functions for which **x** is an output parameter. In those cases the value of **x** can be tested on entry to and exit from the function until the problem is isolated and corrected.

Nevertheless, there are uses for global constants and prototypes. For instance, the information in **stdio.h** may be useful to the entire program, not to just one function. That is why we put **#include <stdio.h>** at the beginning of the program, outside of **main.** In addition, because constants cannot be altered, it is generally not a problem to place **#define** or **const** declarations globally.

Furthermore, programmers often build programs by combining files containing previously written functions. Thus, entire programs can extend beyond a single file. There is even a way for data to be shared between files by giving a variable the **extern** (external) scope declaration, which signifies the variable is global and can be found in two or more files of the overall program.

EXERCISES 9.2

Concept Check
Answer statements 1 through 4 with true *or* false.
1. An output parameter is one whose value is found in an output statement such as **printf**.
2. When an output argument is listed in a function call, there is always an ampersand (**&**) in front of it.
3. A variable declared outside of a function is called *global.*
4. C passes arguments to functions using call by value.

For statements 5 through 8 choose the answer that best completes the statement.
5. Assuming that **x** is an integer array and that this function call is made: **max = calc_max (x[0], x[1]);** which of the following would be a possible function header?
   a. **int calc_max (int x[0], int x[1])**
   b. **int calc_max (int *x[0], int *x[1])**
   c. **int calc_max (int x, int y)**
   d. **int calc_max (int *x, int *y)**
6. Assuming that **x** is an integer array and that the function call **square_elements (x, size);** is made, which of the following would be a possible function header?
   a. **int square_elements (int x, int size)**
   b. **void square_elements (int x[], int size)**
   c. **int square_elements (int &x, int size)**
   d. **void square_elements (int x, int size)**

7. Given the function call

    ```
    status = calc_volume ( radius, &volume );
    ```

    it is reasonable to expect that
    a. **radius** and **volume** are input arguments and **status** is the output argument
    b. **radius** is an input argument and **volume** is a **return** value
    c. **radius** is an input argument, **volume** is an output argument, and the **return** value is an **int**
    d. **radius** and **volume** are output arguments and **status** is the **return** value

8. An acceptable prototype for the function called in Question 7 would be
    a. **void calc_volume (float radius, float volume);**
    b. **void calc_volume (float radius, float *volume);**
    c. **int calc_volume (float radius, float volume);**
    d. **int calc_volume (float x, float *y);**

For statements 9 through 12 fill in the blanks with the right word.

9. A(n) _____ is a constant value passed to a function.
10. A(n) _____ is a value indirectly passed back to the associated argument.
11. A _____ is declared within a function and only known to that function.
12. A variable declared at the beginning of a program file has _____.

For the remaining exercises, assume the global declarations

```
#define FALSE 0
#define TRUE  1
```

Set A

Solve each of the following problems by writing one or more statements in C.

13. Call a **void** function **f** with two input arguments **a** and **b** and three output arguments **x, y,** and **z.**
14. Assuming that **a** and **b** are integers and **x, y,** and **z** are doubles, write the function header for the problem in Question 13.
15. Write a prototype for an **int** function called **check_status** that returns **TRUE** if all the elements in the **int** array (called **status**) passed to it are **TRUE.** Pass the logical size of the array also.
16. Write a function header for a **void** function called **set_status** that sets the elements in the above array to **FALSE.** Pass the logical size of the array also.
17. Write the function body for **set_status** in Question 16.

Set B

18. Assuming the **void f (int *x)** function header, write a statement in the body of this function that sets the calling argument to 17.

19. Given the same header as above, assume that **x** is an inout parameter. Write a statement in the body of this function that sets the calling argument to its incoming value times 17.
20. Assuming the `int f ( int a, int b, float *x )` function header, write a statement in the body of this function that sets the output parameter as equal to the product of the input parameters. Set the return value as equal to the sum of the input parameters times the current value of the output parameter.

Set C
21. Write a function with three integer input parameters and one output parameter. The output parameter should be set to the smallest of the input parameters.
22. Write a function with two floating-point input parameters and three output parameters. Set the output parameters to the sum, product, and quotient of the input parameters. If the second input parameter equals 0, do not compute the quotient. The function should return an **int** error status that is set to **TRUE** if the second input parameter is 0 and otherwise set to **FALSE**.
23. Write a function that takes an array and its size as input parameters and has an output parameter that is computed to be the product of all of the elements in the array.
24. Write a function that has a floating-point input parameter representing an amount of money and four output parameters that are computed as the number of quarters, dimes, nickels, and pennies in the original amount.

10 Software Engineering

Modular construction using Lego blocks.

After completing this chapter you should be able
to do the following:

Learning Goals

- Use the software engineering approach in software design and development
- Use software tools such as hierarchy charts and documentation consistently
- Explain the difference between top-down design and bottom-up design and know when to use each approach
- Write a formal statement for a software problem
- Apply the elements of the waterfall model to develop a software system
- Design, code, and maintain a small software system

Chapter Activity

A software system is needed to do the payroll for a company with no more than 50 employees. The project is complicated by the fact that income tax rates for both the state and federal governments are variable and can change at a moment's notice but are fixed to five wage categories for each agency. The project is further complicated by the fact that employees made concessions concerning holiday pay from three times the normal wage rate to two times the normal wage rate, but overtime is still time-and-a-half. Health costs are also variable with employee options at extra premiums. The maximum work week is 55 hours with a minimum wage rate of $5.25 per hour and a maximum wage rate of $45.50 per hour. A normal work week is 37.5 hours but this too can change. The union contract provides optional benefits such as payroll savings, pension, and vacation trusts. Design a software system in which a pay check is printed and a complete year-to-date payroll ledger is maintained for each employee, with year-to-date running totals calculated after each week. The system has a user manual so payroll department employees can use it easily.

10.1   THE SOFTWARE ENGINEERING APPROACH

Introduction

Sections 1 and 2 of Chapter 2 present problem solving from two points of view: the analytic and the algorithmic. These methods address problems that are specific, concise, and not too complicated. Solutions are attainable through analysis or a short algorithm, with answers that can be represented by specific, verifiable values.

Unfortunately, real-world problems are not always so simple. What is the answer to finding a cure for hypertension or AIDS? What is the solution to preventing earthquakes? How do you solve the problems of an air traffic control system in preventing accidents? Real-world problems that use computational software as a vehicle for their solution, come from a large-scale systems approach, require team work, or involve time measured in person-years, not hours, fall in the area of software engineering.

10.1.1 Tools for Algorithmic Design

By **software engineering** we mean the analysis and application of strategies to design, construct, and maintain large-scale software systems using certain common methods. A software design should have clear goals. Designing software (and hardware) to land an airplane using radar, for example, is no simple task because complex principles of aerodynamics, physics, and guidance systems are involved.

Consider the problem of designing software to issue payroll checks for employees of a company. One design tool for problems like this is a **hierarchy chart** that show the phases of the software design and execution in terms of levels. Each level describes the project according to the significant modules at that level, with the degree of detail increasing at each level. Figure 10.1–1 shows such a chart with three levels: 0, 1, and 2. The three levels in a chart like this typically consist of information such as the following.

Level 0 shows the purpose of the design and is labeled with the project title, here *Payroll*. Level 1 has three modules, generically equivalent to *input*, *process*,

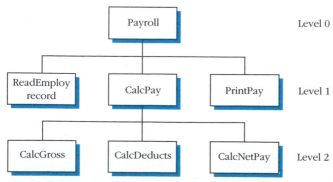

Figure 10.1–1   Hierarchy chart for payroll problem

and *output*. The *input* module is *ReadEmployeeRecord*, which means getting an employee record that includes each person's identification, rate of pay, and hours worked. Other data might be input such as a salary code or special deductions, but for the design it is enough to generalize and fill in the specifics later. This allows you to focus on the big picture without getting bogged down in details.

The *process* module is *CalcPay*, which calculates the net pay based on the data already input and on any other information needed such as a tax table. *CalcPay* is broken down into the three subparts shown in level 2: First calculate the gross pay, then calculate the deductions, and finally calculate the net pay. The *output* module (in level 1) is *PrintPayCheck* and is not subdivided.

Another tool is **program documentation,** which tells other programmers about the purpose and design of a software package. Program documentation is essential to all software design, especially large-scale systems. Documentation should also be written in the preliminary stages, such as algorithm development, because it is usually analyzed and modified before coding. Headers for the algorithms and inline comments are also part of the program documentation. Ideally, program documentation can be copied into the program modules as they are written. Realize that style is also important. You should include at least the title, description, formal statement, author, and date. This information should be boxed and offset by blank lines from the following code as we show throughout this text.

10.1.2 Design Strategies: Bottom-Up or Top-Down

One of the temptations to resist is what is called "the urge to program" before designing an algorithm. Busy students, when given a programming assignment, can't wait to get on the computer and ... and ... do what? Write C code? According to Henry Ledgard in his 1975 book, *Programming Proverbs*, "The sooner you start coding your program the longer it is going to take." Before writing any code, you should design the algorithm that will solve the problem. Unless the problem at hand is very simple, you cannot omit the design phase.

The two approaches to program design are bottom-up and top-down. The **bottom-up** approach looks at specific components needed, produces those components, then combines them to solve a larger problem. This approach has advantages in projects such as creating software module libraries but may not work for general problem solving.

Consider the following exaggeration of the bottom-up approach for building a house.

Go to construction site. Decide to lay the foundation. Forget to schedule the concrete and wait until next Tuesday for concrete mixer. How big was that house supposed to be anyway? Get dimensions and start pouring. Hire some carpenters. Buy some wood. However, the house is supposed to be a *brick* house. Buy some bricks. Find some masons. Learn from town inspector that building site is a protected wetland. Find a new parcel of land and start again.

This ridiculous scenario underscores the importance of proper planning at all levels. The bottom-up approach to problem solving is useful in certain circumstances, however, where starting with details leads to a more general result, as in scientific research. In these cases the result is motivated by a goal such as finding a cure for a disease or discovering a new atomic particle.

The **top-down** approach means much more preparatory work and much delayed gratification. First you look at the overall problem and then proceed to break the problem down into smaller units. You develop a plan of attack, which is carefully laid out, with specifications, hierarchy charts, and algorithms (written and rewritten). You must understand and draft all phases of the project *before* you write the first line of code. The formality of this method is the reason most beginners shun it and begin programming before solving the problem.

Let's recreate the scenario for building a house using a top-down approach.

You hire an architect. An architect's design tool is the blueprint. Blueprints are written in a hierarchical fashion and include an overview and secondary prints of each room. They can be drawn with computer aided design (CAD) and contain information such as standardized building practices, codes, and materials. Once the blueprints are completed, you can schedule all phases of the construction. You have building codes checked and get building permits, you hire workers and you order materials. Now that the job is coordinated, the foundation is laid and construction begins.

Naturally, the top-down approach does not always guarantee a satisfactory result. Things can still go wrong: delays, cost overruns, discrepancies between the owner's concept and the builder's practice, unavailability of materials, on-the-job changes. However, it should be clear that careful planning is better than hoping for the best or just winging it.

10.1.3 Formal Problem Statement

The most important step in the software life cycle comes right at the beginning when you analyze and understand the problem. Sometimes this phase is straightforward, particularly if you are experienced in the problem area. However, it can also be difficult, even for veteran programmers. For example, "Write a program to solve any quadratic equation" might be an easy problem to understand but "Develop an inertial guidance system for a space shuttle" would be hard even for a NASA scientist. Regardless of the scope, if you understand the problem and what you need to know to solve it, you have taken the first big step toward the solution.

BEFORE YOU GO ON

Query: The statement "Brass is an alloy composed of copper and zinc. Determine the amount of copper needed to form brass" is used to express a problem. Is this problem well-defined?

RESPONSE: No, it is not. It specifies neither the proportions of copper and zinc nor the amount of brass alloy that is to result from the mixture.

As discussed in Section 2.2, the problem statement can be formalized in three parts: Input, process, and output. *Input* is the information supplied to the algorithm by the user. *Process* is the algorithm and the information it manipulates. *Output* is the information produced by the algorithm for the benefit of the user.

10.1.4 The Waterfall Model

The **waterfall model** describes six phases in the software life cycle: Needs analysis, needs specification, algorithm design, software implementation, testing and integration, and delivery and operation. Figure 10.1–2 illustrates the waterfall model and how problem-solving *flows* from one phase to the next. The six phases are explained next.

The **needs analysis** determines the needs of the customer through a careful appraisal of the problem. The **needs specification** documents what the user expects from the software system in a formal statement showing input, process, and output. These two phases sometimes require the development of system testing and user manuals.

The **algorithm design** involves a give-and-take between *what* is needed and *how* it will be supplied. Because algorithms are not unique, there is room for different opinions. Even at this stage a well-designed system, using tools such as hierarchy charts to partition the problem into modules with an algorithm for each module, will make for a better product. The **software implementation** is the coding of the algorithm. This is generally the easiest part if the system is well-designed and a suitable programming language is used.

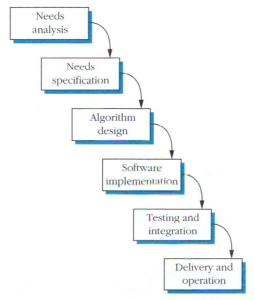

Figure 10.1–2   The waterfall model

Testing and integration are evaluation by the software vendor and, if the software will be embedded in other software or hardware systems, integration with those systems. For example, software that operates a robot must be tested from the standpoint of the whole hardware/software entity, not just the components, because of the many interactions within the total system. **Delivery and operation** are turning over the finished system to the customer. Once delivered, the system has to be maintained, as we shall see next.

10.1.5 Program Maintenance

Maintenance of a working system may include making changes resulting from the evolving needs of the customer, the redefinition of the original problem, or improvements suggested by the customer. In practice, waterfall models have feedback components that allow for such retooling and refining. Figure 10.1–3 is a seven-phase waterfall model showing the original six phases plus the maintenance phase. The feedback lines to earlier phases represent the changes needed when the system is in the maintenance phase. Sometimes the original problem changes even *before* the system is delivered, which also changes the needs specification.

Program maintenance is an almost continuous part of the software life cycle. Software engineers try to minimize this phase even if it does keep programmers

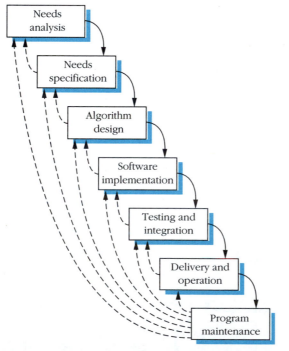

Figure 10.1–3   The waterfall model with feedback

occupied and accounts for approximately 80 percent of the total effort shown by the waterfall model. The goal, of course, is to develop the correct software once, although in practice this rarely happens.

EXERCISES 10.1

Concept Check

Answer statements 1 through 4 with true *or* false.

1. The analytic approach to problem solving is best for large, ill-defined problems.
2. A hierarchy chart always consists of three levels.
3. The top-down approach is like an architect trying to build a house without a blueprint.
4. The waterfall model consists of phases in software development.

For statements 5 through 8 choose the answer that best completes the statement.

5. The hierarchy chart does not
   a. graphically show the steps leading to the problem solution
   b. show the responsibility of each programmer on the project
   c. show the modules needed for the solution to the problem
   d. provide a structured programming tool
6. The bottom-up approach to problem solving
   a. is better than top-down since it is more intuitive
   b. is useful in scientific discovery methods
   c. goes hand-in-hand with structured programming
   d. is rarely used since there is so much preparatory work
7. In the payroll problem described, the employee record
   a. refers to the employee's performance on the job
   b. represents all the information gathered on that employee
   c. is the input needed to process the paycheck
   d. is left vague since it is just a design tool
8. Documentation of large- and small-scale designs
   a. is not necessary if the design is well formulated
   b. has a generally accepted format
   c. is not necessary for small-scale projects
   d. should be included at the beginning of every algorithm

For statements 9 through 12 fill in the blanks with the right word.

9. The analysis and application of strategies to design, construct, and maintain large-scale software systems is called _____.
10. Software upgrading is called _____.
11. Software implementation refers to _____ an algorithm.
12. The documentation statements in a program _____ executable.

Set A

Draw a hierarchy chart for each of the following problems.

13. Find a recipe in a cookbook for baking a cake and chart the steps for following it.
14. Chart the steps for getting to class in the morning, beginning with waking up to an alarm clock.
15. Compute the volume of a sphere ($\frac{4}{3}\pi r^3$). Check to make sure that the input value for the radius is greater than 0.
16. The monthly payment on a mortgage is calculated according to the following formula: $M = (P \times i \times (1 + i)^n)/((1 + i)^n - 1))$, where:

    > P represents the principal
    >
    > i represents the monthly interest (= yearly rate / 12)
    >
    > n represents the number of payments (= #years $\times$ 12)

    Input values for the principal, yearly interest rate, and term in years, and output the corresponding monthly payment.

Set B

Write a short essay for each of the following situations.

17. Write a brief scenario for a bottom-up approach to having a backyard barbecue.
18. Write a brief scenario for a top-down approach to having a backyard barbecue.
19. Bottom-up approaches to problems are often beneficial. Describe how this may be true in a game of chess.
20. Describe how chess would be played using a top-down approach. Contrast your response with your answer to Question 19.
21. How would a top-down approach differ from a bottom-up approach when you want to find a book in the public library?

Set C

22. Use the software engineering approach in a program to find the area of a circular ring with an internal radius of 3 cm and an external radius of 5 cm.
23. Use the software engineering approach to calculate the volume and surface area of a box 16.3 in. long, 12.4 in. wide, and 9.4 in. deep.
24. Items in a store are discounted at a certain rate. Use the software engineering approach in a program to compute the new price, given the original price and the discount rate.

10.2   THE SOFTWARE LIFE CYCLE: TWO APPLICATIONS

Introduction

Now let's integrate our understanding of C and software engineering to solve a problem. Recall that the software life cycle consists of the following seven phases (including maintenance):

Needs analysis:	Careful appraisal of the problem statement
Needs specification:	Formal statement showing input, process, output
Algorithm design:	Hierarchy chart showing significant modules
	Individual algorithms for each module
Software implementation:	Coding of algorithms into a programming language
Testing and integration:	Checking for correctness
	Incorporation into existing software (and hardware)
Delivery and operation:	Final installation and testing
Maintenance:	Refinement of existing features
	Addition of new features

10.2.1 First Application: Grading Problem

We begin with a relatively simple problem as follows.

> A professor wants to grade her students based on three exams. The exams are not of equal difficulty so it is only fair to weight them differentially. She chooses the following scheme:
>
> Exam1 is worth 20 percent of the final grade for the course.
> Exam2 is worth 35 percent of the final grade for the course.
> Exam3 is worth 45 percent of the final grade for the course.
>
> Write a program to compute the final weighted grade for any one student in the class.

Needs analysis

The problem calls for external information, namely the results of the three exams. The grade weights are preset and are not obtained from input. Their values are set as named constants. The output consists of a final weighted grade. The problem requires the calculation of a weighted sum based on the input values for the individual grades and the preset grade weights.

Needs specification

The simplicity of the problem allows us to write a formal statement at this point that summarizes our analysis.

Formal statement:	grading problem
Input:	student record: grade1, grade2, grade3
Output:	final grade
Process:	final grade = 20% grade1 + 35% grade2 + 45% grade3

What about the possibility of extra credit on an exam? Time to go back to the professor and ask for more information.

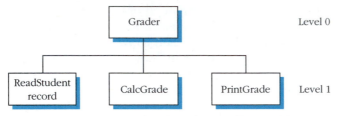

Figure 10.2–1 Hierarchy chart for grading problem

Algorithm design

The problem suggests a two-level hierarchy chart as shown in Figure 10.2–1. Level 0 is the main program. Level 1 is for input, process, and output. In this case the modules do not need further refinement.

Next, we design the algorithm. It is sequential, without any loops or decision structures:

Step 1.   INPUT grade1, grade2, grade3
Step 2.   finalGrade = 0.2 × grade1 + 0.35 × grade2 + 0.45 × grade3
Step 3.   OUTPUT finalGrade
Step 4.   STOP

Software implementation

In this step we code the algorithm in C, being sure to provide appropriate documentation. We also use an effective programming style that increases readability. Here is a version of the program.

P R O G R A M   1 0 . 2 – 1

```
/**************************************************************************
*    Title:        grading problem                                       *
*    Filename:     grader.c                                              *
*                                                                        *
*    Description:  This program computes a final grade for a student     *
*                  based on three test results.                          *
*                                                                        *
*    Input:        student record:  grade1, grade2, grade3              *
*    Output:       final_grade                                           *
*    Process:      final_grade = 20% grade1  +  35% grade2  +           *
*                                      45% grade3                        *
*                                                                        *
*    Written by:   ...                                    Date: ...      *
**************************************************************************/

#include   <stdio.h>                        /*  Global declarations  */

#define    WEIGHT1    0.20
#define    WEIGHT2    0.35
#define    WEIGHT3    0.45
```

```
main ( )
{
   int    grade1, grade2, grade3;                  /* Local declarations */
   float final_grade;

   printf ( "\n\nPlease input first exam result: " );
   scanf ( "%d",   &grade1 );                       /* Input sequence */

   printf ( "\nPlease input second exam result: " );
   scanf ( "%d",   &grade2 );

   printf ( "\nPlease input third exam result:  " );
   scanf ( "%d",   &grade3 );
                                                    /* Process statement */
   final_grade = grade1 * WEIGHT1 + grade2 * WEIGHT2 + grade3 * WEIGHT3;

   printf ( "\n\nfinal grade is %5.f",   final_grade );          /* Output */

   return ( 0 );
}
```

Testing and integration

The program is ready to be executed and tested. What values should you use? Try 100, 100, and 100 for the three grades. Next try 0, 0, and 0. What if the user enters values of less than 0? What if the user enters values of more than 100? Is that allowed? Can anyone score less than 0 on an examination? This solution has a flaw because it does not provide any means of verifying the input grades.

Delivery and operation

The program is turned over to the professor for *real-world* testing. The professor tries the program and everything seems to be OK until she types l00 (letter "l") instead of 100. Suddenly the program generates a strange result. What happened? This is a different and more subtle kind of input error. Here the data is simply out of range, it is the wrong data type—character instead of integer.

Some languages like Pascal catch this and generate a *run-time* error. Some C compilers catch it but most will not because the **scanf** function is not meant to be *smart*—it only converts the erroneous letter character "l" into a suitable integer representation. The program does not "know" that bad data has been introduced and computes the final grade anyway. Sometimes it is obvious that the answer is wrong, but this kind of error can be hard to detect. In any case, what should you do? One typical solution is to enter all data as characters and then convert it to integers or floats as needed. When a character does not have an equivalent numeric value, the program can issue a message asking that the input be reentered.

Program maintenance

Besides the correction of the input problems, what other features could be added to the solution? For starters, you could generate a letter grade as well as a numeric grade. This would involve a conversion scheme in which numeric bounds were set for A, B, C, etc., as in the sales commission problem from Chapters 2 and 5.

What about allowing for more than one student? The professor should not have to restart the program for each of, say, 60 students in a class. This is better handled by a loop structure in a program that repeats until all students have been processed. (Loop structures are covered in Chapter 5.)

What about generating class statistics like the minimum, maximum, mean, and the standard deviation of all of the grades? (To calculate statistics such as these, you might store each student's grades for later analysis using a data structure such as an array, as covered in Chapter 7.) How about grading on a curve? How about entering the class results in a database with other grade information? Or a direct link to the registrar to create a transcript? Or even generating the grades in various orders such as alphabetic, numeric, or grouped by letter (covered in Chapters 11 and 12)? The above solution is preliminary. By the end of this text, you will be able to add many useful features to this program to resolve some of these questions.

10.2.2 Second Application: Payroll Calculations

We begin with the problem statement.

A program is needed to calculate the gross and net pay of each employee of a small company. For any given pay period the total number of employees can vary. Provision is to be made for overtime. The program is to print the pay check on the last day of each work week. A recent union contract specified the following for all employees.

Federal income tax rate:	18 percent of gross wages per week
Social security rate:	8.8 percent of gross wages per week
Hospital insurance rate:	2.3 percent of gross wages per week
Union dues rate:	1.0 percent of gross wages per week
Minimum hours for overtime:	37.5 hours for each week
Overtime rate:	1.5 times regular rate
Minimum wage rate:	$4.25 per hour
Maximum wage rate:	$25.00 per hour
Minimum work week:	5.0 hours
Maximum work week:	60.0 hours

Needs analysis

The complexity of the problem does not allow for writing a complete formal statement immediately. First, the problem requires external information including: Employee identification, number of hours worked, and rate of pay. Conditions for overtime pay are set, as are authorized deductions such as federal and state taxes. A paycheck is to be printed each week. The input specific to each employee includes: Name, social security number, rate of pay for regular hours worked, and number of hours worked. The input for the payroll includes: Minimum number of working hours in a pay period required to receive overtime pay, the overtime rate, the federal tax rate on wages, the social security tax rate, the union rate for dues, and the rate for hospital insurance.

Needs specification

Now we can write a formal, although not complete, statement for the problem as follows:

Formal statement: payroll problem
         Input: employee name, rate of pay, hours worked
        Output: net pay and pay check
       Process: calculations according to needs specification and algorithm

Algorithm design

The problem suggests a multilevel hierarchy chart. Remember, algorithms are not unique so there are many ways to proceed. In this instance, it might be easier to completely process one employee at a time with a loop in which each employee record is obtained. An employee is processed by calculating her gross pay, deductions, and net pay, then printing the check. We also must calculate the conditions for the loop to determine the number of records to process. Figure 10.2–2 shows a possible hierarchy chart for this problem.

   Next, we can write a level-0 algorithm, as follows.

Algorithm: PAYROLL PROBLEM (main)
   Step 1.   READ_COMPANY_SIZE (...)
   Step 2.   LOOP for all employees in company
             a.   READ_AND_CHECK_EMPLOYEE_RECORD (...)
             b.   CALC_GROSS_PAY (...)
             c.   CALC_DEDUCTS_AND_NET (...)
             d.   PRINT_PAYCHECK
   Step 3.   STOP

As you can see, most of the solution details are omitted at this level but a foundation has been laid and we can develop the level-1 algorithms, as follows.

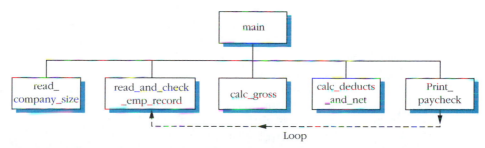

Figure 10.2–2   Hierarchy chart for payroll problem

Algorithm: READ_COMPANY_SIZE
    Description: input and verify the number of employees
    Input params: none
    Output params: none
    Return value: n_employees
      Step 1.   INPUT n_employees
      Step 2.   WHILE n_employees out of range
            a.   OUTPUT error message
            b.   INPUT n_employees
      Step 3.   RETURN n_employees

Algorithm: READ_AND_CHECK_EMP_RECORD
    Description: input and verify the employee record
    Input params: none
    Output params: name, wage, hours
    Return value: none
      Step 1.   INPUT name
      Step 2.   INPUT wage
      Step 3.   WHILE wage out of range
            a.   OUTPUT error message
            b.   INPUT wage
      Step 4.   INPUT hours
      Step 5.   WHILE hours out of range
            a.   OUTPUT error message
            b.   INPUT hours
      Step 6.   STOP

Algorithm: CALC_GROSS_PAY
    Description: calculate the gross pay, including overtime
    Input params: wage, hours
    Output params: gross
    Return value: none
      Step 1.   IF hours $<=$ REG_HOURS
              gross = wage $*$ hours
            ELSE
              reg_pay = wage $*$ REG_HOURS
              overtime_pay = OVERTIME_RATE $*$ (hours $-$ REG_HOURS) $*$ wage
            gross = reg_pay + overtime_pay
      Step 2.   STOP

Algorithm: CALC_DEDUCTS_AND_NET
    Description: calculate series of deductions and net pay
    Input params: gross
    Output params: fed_tax, soc_sec, hosp, union, net
    Return value: none
      Step 1.   fed_tax = gross $*$ FED_TAX_RATE
      Step 2.   soc_sec = gross $*$ SOC_SEC_RATE
      Step 3.   hosp = gross $*$ HOSP_RATE
      Step 4.   union = gross $*$ UNION_RATE

Step 5.   net = gross − (fed_tax + soc_sec + hosp + union)
Step 6.   STOP

Algorithm: PRINT_PAYCHECK
   Description: output the paycheck for each employee
   Input params: name, wage, hours, gross, fed_tax, soc_sec, hosp, union, net
   Output params: none
   Return value: none
      Step 1:   OUTPUT paycheck data
      Step 2:   STOP

Software implementation

In this step we convert the algorithm into the language of choice, in this case C.

PROGRAM 10.2-2

```
/************************************************************************
*    Title:       payroll                                               *
*    Filename:    payroll.c                                             *
*                                                                       *
*    Description: This program produces a payroll for a small company.  The program    *
*                 calculates the gross pay and a series of deductions for each employee.    *
*                                                                       *
*    Input:       employee record: name, wage rate, hours worked        *
*    Output:      pay check: gross pay, fed tax, social security, hospital, union dues,    *
*    Process:     net gross, deductions, net pay                        *
*                                                                       *
*    Written by:  ...                            Date: ...              *
************************************************************************/

                                                /*  GLOBAL DECLARATIONS  */
#include <stdio.h>

#define  MIN_WAGE            4.25
#define  MAX_WAGE            25.00

#define  FED_TAX_RATE        0.18
#define  SOC_SEC_RATE        0.088
#define  HOSP_RATE           0.023
#define  UNION_RATE          0.01

#define  MIN_HOURS           5.00
#define  MAX_HOURS           60.00

#define  REG_HOURS           37.5
#define  OVERTIME_RATE       1.50
#define  MIN_COMPANY_SIZE    1
#define  MAX_COMPANY_SIZE    99
```

```
#define  MAX_NAME_LEN       81


                                        /*  FUNCTION PROTOTYPES  */


int   read_company_size        ( void                );

void  read_and_check_emp_record ( char   name[ ],
                                  float  *wage,
                                  float  *hours      );

void  calc_gross               ( float  wage,
                                  float  hours,
                                  float  *gross      );


void  calc_deducts_and_net     ( float  gross,
                                  float  *fed_tax,
                                  float  *soc_sec,
                                  float  *hosp,
                                  float  *union_dues,
                                  float  *net        );

void  print_paycheck           ( char   name[ ],
                                  float  wage,
                                  float  hours,
                                  float  gross,
                                  float  fed_tax,
                                  float  soc_sec,
                                  float  hosp,
                                  float  union_dues,
                                  float  net         );


main ( )
{
   char   name [MAX_NAME_LEN];
   int    emp_count;
   int    n_employees;
   float  wage;
   float  hours;
   float  gross;
   float  fed_tax;
   float  soc_sec;
   float  hosp;
   float  union_dues;
   float  net;
```

```
    n_employees = read_company_size ();

    for ( emp_count = 1; emp_count <= n_employees; emp_count++) {

        read_and_check_emp_record( name,   &wage,        &hours    );

        calc_gross               ( wage,   hours,        &gross    );

        calc_deducts_and_net     ( gross, &fed_tax,      &soc_sec,
                                   &hosp, &union_dues, &net        );

        print_paycheck           ( name,   wage,         hours,
                                   gross, fed_tax,      soc_sec,
                                   hosp,  union_dues,   net        );
    }

    return ( 0 );

}                                                      /* End of payroll main */


/**************************************************************************
 *    Function name:      read_company_size                              *
 *    Description:        Input and verify the number of employees.      *
 *                                                                       *
 *    Input parameters:   none                                           *
 *    Output parameters:  none                                           *
 *    Return value:       n_employees                                    *
 **************************************************************************/

int read_company_size ( void )
{
    int    n_employees;

    printf ( "\nInput #employees to be paid for the week >" );
    scanf  ( "%d", &n_employees );

    while  ( n_employees < MIN_COMPANY_SIZE
                        || n_employees > MAX_COMPANY_SIZE) {
       printf ( "\n\nError in company size!!!!\n\n" );
       printf ( "\nMust be between:  %d  and  %d...Please re-enter value >",
                   MIN_COMPANY_SIZE, MAX_COMPANY_SIZE    );
       scanf  ( "%d",   &n_employees  );
    }

    return ( n_employees );

}                                            /* End of read_company_size */
```

```
/************************************************************************
 *   Function name:       read_and_check_emp_record                     *
 *   Description:         Input and verify the employee record.         *
 *                                                                      *
 *   Input parameters:    none                                          *
 *   Output parameters:   name, wage, hours                             *
 *   Return value:        none                                          *
 ************************************************************************/

void read_and_check_emp_record ( char name[ ], float *wage, float *hours )
{
   printf ( "\n\n\nInput employee name >" );
   scanf  ( "%s", name );

   printf ( "\nInput wage rate > " );
   scanf  ( "%f", wage );                    /* Recall that wage is a pointer!!  */

   while  ( *wage < MIN_WAGE || *wage > MAX_WAGE ) {
      printf ( "\nError in wage rate!!!!\n" );
      printf ( "\nMust be between: %.f - %.f...Please Re-enter >",
               MIN_WAGE, MAX_WAGE );
      scanf  ( "%f", wage );
   }

   printf ( "\nInput hours worked > " );
   scanf  ( "%f", hours );                   /* Note that hours is a pointer too!  */

   while  ( *hours < MIN_HOURS || *hours > MAX_HOURS ) {
      printf ( "\nError in hours worked!!!!\n" );
      printf ( "\nMust be between: %.f - %.f...Please Re-enter >",
               MIN_HOURS, MAX_HOURS );
      scanf  ( "%f", hours );
   }
}                                            /* End of read_and_check_emp_record */




/************************************************************************
 *   Function name:       calc_gross                                    *
 *   Description:         Calculate the gross pay, including overtime.   *
 *                                                                      *
 *   Input parameters:    wage, hours                                   *
 *   Output parameters:   gross                                         *
 *   Return value:        none                                          *
 ************************************************************************/
```

```
void calc_gross ( float wage, float hours, float *gross )
{

   float reg_pay, overtime_pay

   if ( hours <= REG_HOURS )
      *gross = wage * hours;
   else {
      reg_pay      = wage * REG_HOURS;
      overtime_pay = OVERTIME_RATE * (hours - REG_HOURS) * wage;
      *gross       = reg_pay + overtime_pay;
   }
}                                              /* End of calc_gross */
```

```
/**************************************************************************
*    Function name:      calc_deducts_and_net                            *
*    Description:        Calculate series of deductions and net pay.     *
*                                                                        *
*    Input parameters:   gross                                           *
*    Output parameters:  fed_tax, soc_sec, hosp, union, net             *
*    Return value:       none                                            *
**************************************************************************/

void calc_deducts_and_net ( float gross, float *fed_tax,    float *soc_sec,
                            float *hosp, float *union_dues, float *net      )
{
   *fed_tax    = gross * FED_TAX_RATE;
   *soc_sec    = gross * SOC_SEC_RATE;
   *hosp       = gross * HOSP_RATE;
   *union_dues = gross * UNION_RATE;
   *net        = gross - ( *fed_tax + *soc_sec + *hosp + *union_dues );

}                                          /* End of calc_deducts_and_net */
```

```
/**************************************************************************
*    Function name:      print_paycheck                                  *
*    Description:        Output the paycheck for each employee.          *
*                                                                        *
*    Input parameters:   name, wage, hours, gross, fed_tax, soc_sec,     *
*                        hosp, union_dues, net                           *
*    Output parameters:  none                                            *
*    Return value:       none                                            *
**************************************************************************/
```

```
void print_paycheck  ( char  name[ ],  float wage,      float hours,
                       float gross,   float fed_tax,   float soc_sec,
                       float hosp,    float union_dues, float net      )
{
   printf ( "\nPaycheck for: %s",            name     );
   printf ( "\nGross pay          = $%.f", gross    );
   printf ( "\nWage rate          = $%.f", wage     );
   printf ( "\nHours worked       =  %.f", hours    );
   printf ( "\nFederal tax        = $%.f", fed_tax  );
   printf ( "\nSocial security = $%.f", soc_sec  );
   printf ( "\nHospitalization = $%.f", hosp     );
   printf ( "\nUnion dues         = $%.f", union_dues );
   printf ( "\nNet pay            = $%.f", net      );


}                                           /* End of print_paycheck */
```

Testing and integration

The program is ready to be executed and tested. First, we consider reasonable and unreasonable responses to the input prompts. When prompted for hours worked, for example, we try reasonable numbers such as 0, 22.7, 37.5 (why?), and 48.2 as well as unreasonable numbers such as 735.2, −14.5, and 60.1. We should also respond with different data types—for example, try alphabetic characters when prompted for numerical values.

Remember that C puts the burden on the programmer to ensure that data is entered properly. Again, the scanf function simply converts an erroneous character into a suitable numerical representation. The program does not "know" that bad data has been introduced and proceeds according to the instructions given by the programmer. For example, suppose the program requires an integer input. The program issues a message requesting that the input be re-entered when an input character does not correspond to an integer between 0 through 9.

Delivery and operation

Software is delivered to the customer to use on hardware already in place at the customer site or on hardware provided by the software vendor. The software is tested in-house on the software/hardware integrated system by the vendor and by the customer. The job is complete when the software performs ? ...ording to specification and to the satisfaction of both customer and vendor.

Program maintenance

As with most software products, changes and updates are expected. A new union contract, for example, may require new dues rates, new insurance rates, options for group dental plans, payroll savings, or other related options. Federal and state taxes could change and FICA (social security) contributions might increase. A software vendor usually *maintains* the software according to an agreement with the customer. Over time, program maintenance can easily cost as much or more than the original program. Maintenance is covered in Set C of the following exercises.

EXERCISES 10.2

Concept Check

Answer statements 1 through 4 with true *or* false.

1. The software life cycle consists of three phases.
2. The formal statement is written in the needs analysis phase.
3. Final testing is done in the delivery phase.
4. The algorithm design includes writing the hierarchy chart.

For statements 5 through 8 choose the answer that best completes the statement.

5. In Program 10.2–1 the following statement would approximate the final grade with equal weight given to each grade.
   a. `final_grade = (0.33*grade1 + 0.33*grade2 + 0.33*grade3) / 3;`
   b. `final_grade = (0.333*grade1 + 0.333*grade2 + 0.333*grade3);`
   c. `final_grade = (grade1 + grade2 + grade3) / (grade1*grade2*grade3);`
   d. `final_grade = (grade1 + grade2 + grade3) / 3.33;`

6. In Program 10.2–2 the following statement could have been used to input the name of the employee.
   a. `scanf( "%c", &name );`
   b. `scanf( "%d", name );`
   c. `scanf( "%c", name );`
   d. None of these.

7. In Program 10.2–1 the following statement could have been used to output final_grade as an integer (rounded up).
   a. `printf( "\nfinal grade is %d", final_grade + 0.5 );`
   b. `printf( "\nfinal grade is %d", final_grade );`
   c. `printf( "\nfinal grade is %c", final_grade + 0.5 );`
   d. `printf( "\nfinal grade is %4.f", final_grade + 0.5 );`

8. Entering the characters L00 instead of numbers 100 will
   a. cause a run-time error
   b. not affect the output of the program
   c. have an unpredictable effect on the output
   d. cause a syntax error

For statements 9 through 12 fill in the blanks with the right word.

9. The _____ phase of the software life cycle refers to coding in some appropriate language.
10. A hierarchy chart is an element of the _____ phase of the software life cycle.
11. The grade weights for the grading problem are determined in the _____ phase of the software life cycle.
12. An ongoing phase of the software life cycle is _____.

Set A

13. Suppose the professor wants to have all examinations weighted equally. Describe the changes to be made to the grading program.

14. Give some reasons why the needs specification phase might change for the grading problem.

15. The hierarchy chart for the grading problem suggests three modules at level 1. Which program lines would correspond to these modules?

16. Why is the needs analysis phase considered the most important?

17. Why is hardware a consideration in the delivery phase? In this context, why is C useful?

18. Explain why in Program 10.2–2 in the `read_and_check_emp_record` function, the `*wage` and `*hours` parameters were used rather than simply `wage` and `hours`.

19. In the parameters of the `calc_gross` function of Program 10.2–2 explain why `gross` is declared as a pointer but `wage` and `hours` are not.

Set B

20. With reference to Program 10.2–1, write a segment of code to compute a final grade when four exams with equal weights are averaged.

21. Suppose seven exams were used to calculate a final grade. What can be said about the weights for each exam?

22. Give two examples of why a delivery and operation phase could fail.

23. Write a program segment that outputs a student's name along with the final grade.

24. In Program 10.2–1 what changes would need to be made if the professor gave 20 short exams rather than three?

25. In the `calc_gross` function of Program 10.2–2 explain the meaning of the `*gross = wage * hours` statement.

Set C

26. Rewrite the program for the grading program so that it includes six examinations: five having equal weight and the final exam worth 25 percent of the final grade.

27. The payroll problem needs changes due to a new union contract. Some of the new terms of the contract are

Hospital insurance rate:	2.9 percent of gross wages per week
Union dues rate:	1.2 percent of gross wages per week
Minimum hours for overtime:	35.0 hours for each week
Maximum union dues:	$600.00 per year
Minimum wage rate:	$4.75 per hour
Maximum wage rate:	$30.00 per hour
Maximum work week:	55.0 hours

Explain how you would modify all the phases of the life cycle as needed.

28. In the payroll problem the new union contract allows employees to have a fixed amount of money deducted from their pay check each week and held

by the company to buy savings bonds. An employee can have up to $100.00 in multiples of $20.00 saved each week. Additionally, employees can enroll in a group dental plan for $1/2$ of 1 percent of their gross pay or $5.00 each week, whichever is larger. Modify Program 10.2–2 to reflect these changes.

29. Congress has passed a new bill to tax gross income at the following weekly rates:

18 percent	on all weekly gross income up to and including $200.00
28 percent	on all weekly gross income of $200.00 or more but below or equal to $500.00
33 percent	on all weekly gross income of $500.00 or more but below or equal to $900.00
40 percent	on all weekly gross income of $900.00 or more

   Modify Program 10.2–2 to reflect these changes.

30. Social security and union dues usually have a maximum annual amount. For instance, social security payments stop after the year-to-date gross salary exceeds $57,000. Similarly, union dues might have a cap of $500. Assume that new input is included at the beginning of the program showing the current week of the year and that the weekly gross is always the same. Modify `calc_deducts_and_net` to include these maximum amounts.

11 Data Structures

A queue in New York City.

After completing this chapter you should be able to do the following:

Learning Goals

- Describe a data structure and an abstract data type (ADT)
- Construct an array as an ADT
- Describe datatypes with the `enum` declaration
- Create descriptive data-type names using the `typedef` declaration
- Use the `struct` declaration as an effective data-type tool
- Design and implement an ADT stack with arrays
- Implement postfix arithmetic with stacks
- Design and implement an ADT queue with arrays

Chapter Activity

Write a program to generate random drill-and-practice arithmetic problems. Problems that are incorrectly answered on the first try should be queued and asked again at the end of the session. The program should score the user as follows: One point if correctly answered on the first try, $1/2$ point if correctly answered on the second try, zero if both are misses.

Sample interaction (user input is underlined):

```
*****************************************************************

Problem #1:  87 + 50 = 117
Wrong.

More problems (Y/N)? Y

Problem #2: 56 - 33 = 23
Right!

More problems (Y/N)? Y

Problem #3:  256 * 8 = 1024
Wrong.

More problems (Y/N)? N

Now you have a chance to correct your mistakes:

Problem #1:  87 + 50 = 137
Right!
```

(continued)

```
Problem #3:   256 * 8 = 64
Wrong.

Your final score is 1.5 out of 3.   Please reread the chapter on arithmetic!!
***************************************************************
```

The program should use the random-number generator to generate random problems. Do this by calling the **rand()** function (access it through **stdlib.h**) for each of the two operands for each problem. Scale the output of **rand()** to range between, say, 1 and 1,000. Select the operators using any simple scheme. For example, the first problem is addition, the second problem is subtraction, and so on, and then repeat the sequence.

Here is a brief algorithm:

1. DO
   a. Randomly generate problem
   b. OUTPUT problem
   c. INPUT user answer
   d. IF answer = correct answer
        Add 1 to score
      ELSE
        enqueue (problem)
   e. Ask user to continue or not continue
   WHILE not done
2. WHILE NOT empty queue
   a. dequeue (problem)
   b. OUTPUT problem
   c. IF answer = correct answer
        Add .5 to score
3. OUTPUT final score

11.1   TOOLS FOR CREATING DATA STRUCTURES

Introduction

Up to this point our studies of problem solving have concentrated on algorithms. Now we turn to the other fundamental tool used in problem solving, the data structure. A **data structure** is any programming construction for representing and managing a collection of data. **Data management** in turn means storing and accessing data in a convenient way for a particular problem.

We use the **abstract data type** (**ADT**) to explore data structures. An ADT is a *nonimplemented* data structure together with a listing of the relevant accessing functions. The ADT specifies only the abstract or logical properties of the data structure and accessing functions, leaving the implementation of its physical properties and associated programming code to the programmer.

This chapter explores both the logical design and the physical implementation of two fundamental ADTs, the stack and the queue. Both are implemented using array-based structures. Additional ADTs and an alternative implementation of stacks and queues using dynamically linked lists are covered in Chapter 13.

11.1.1 The Array Revisited

As an example of the ADT approach, consider the array data structure but imagine that it is not directly available in C. First, as ADT designers we define an array abstractly:

> An **array** is a homogeneous collection of data in which individual elements can be directly accessed by supplying an index or subscript.

Next, we identify the relevant accessing functions—for example: Create, store, retrieve, and destroy. In C we might specify these functions and their arguments as:

```
create   (array_name, size, data_type)
store    (array_name, index, value)
retrieve(array_name, index, value)
destroy (array_name)
```

These four functions describe the interface to the ADT array. A programmer who wanted to incorporate an ADT array into a program would be given access to these functions (through a header file or by linking them), and be instructed on their use. The programmer does not need to know how the ADT array is represented in the computer.

The following example shows how the ADT array could be used. It creates an ADT array of integer type, stores data in the ADT array, then outputs the data.

```
/*  Example showing the use of an ADT array */

#include <stdio.h>
#include "array.h"                /*  header file for the ADT array package  */
#define SIZE 100                           /*  arbitrary array size  */

main( )
{
 ARRAY_TYPE  x;                       /*  ARRAY_TYPE  is defined in array.h  */
 int         index,  value;

 create_array ( x,  SIZE,  INT_TYPE ); /*  INT_TYPE  is defined in array.h */

 printf ( "\nEnter array data...\n" );
 for ( index = 0;  index < SIZE;  index++ ) {           /* Input user data */
  scanf ( "%d",  &value );
  store ( x,  index,  value );               /* Insert data into ADT array */
 }
```

```
for ( index = 0;  index < SIZE;  index++ ) {
  retrieve ( x,  index,  value );          /* Retrieve data from ADT array */
  printf ( "\n%d",  value );
}

destroy_array ( x );                        /* Dispose of ADT array */

return ( 0 );
}
```

This program shows that you can use an ADT without necessarily under-standing how that ADT is represented on the computer. It is usually a *different kind* of programmer who has to implement the code for the ADT array package, using whatever techniques are available. For instance, we might use dynamic memory allocation, the ability to request or relinquish a portion of memory while the program is executing. C provides the memory allocation and deallocation functions, **malloc** and **free**, which are discussed in Chapter 13. In addition, we would need to implement an indexing scheme to correctly interpret the array sub-script references. We would also make provisions for higher-dimensional arrays.

Before we can develop complex data structures it is useful to augment the existing methods for declaring data objects. The three tools to do this in C are: **enum**, **typedef**, and **struct**. Together, these tools allow the programmer to create a variety of data structures that are not directly available in C.

11.1.2 The enum Specifier

Using the first tool, **enum**, we can enumerate (specify) the values of a new data type. Enumerated data types clarify the meaning of a variable as it relates to a particular problem. The following are all valid enumerated-type definitions:

```
enum  boolean   { FALSE,  TRUE  };
enum  weekday   { MONDAY,  TUESDAY,  WEDNESDAY,
                  THURSDAY,  FRIDAY  };
enum  month     { JAN,  FEB,  MAR,  APR,  MAY,  JUN,
                  JUL,  AUG,  SEP,  OCT,  NOV,  DEC  };
```

The identifier given after the word **enum** is called the **tag** and distinguishes one enumerated data type from another. Variables declared to be an enumerated data type can have values in the range specified for that type. For example,

```
enum boolean  error_flag;
```

creates a variable called **error_flag** that is of the **enum boolean** type and can be assigned the values **FALSE** or **TRUE**, as shown next.

```
if ( wage < MIN_WAGE  ||  wage > MAX_WAGE )
  error_flag  =  TRUE;
else
  error_flag  =  FALSE;
```

Similarly, the following outputs an appropriate message according to the value of day.

```
enum weekday day;
  . . .
switch ( day )   {
  case MONDAY    : printf ( "\nToday is Monday"    );  break;
  case TUESDAY   : printf ( "\nToday is Tuesday"   );  break;
  case WEDNESDAY : printf ( "\nToday is Wednesday" );  break;
  case THURSDAY  : printf ( "\nToday is Thursday"  );  break;
  case FRIDAY    : printf ( "\nToday is Friday"    );  break;
}
```

Note that the values of enumerated data types are *identifier names*, not *character strings* (no quotation marks are placed around these names). Internally, integers starting with 0 are associated with each of the identifier names. Therefore, **FALSE** is assigned the value 0 and **TRUE** is assigned the value 1. If we try to print **error_flag**, the internal value according to its current assignment is displayed. Because the names are essentially constants many programmers capitalize them, although this is not a C requirement.

11.1.3 The typedef Specifier

Using the second tool, **typedef**, we can invent mnemonic names for the data structures we are developing—for example, the following declarations create synonyms for the simple data types **int** and **float**:

```
typedef int   INTEGER;
typedef float REAL;
```

These names can be used to declare variables. For instance, the declarations

```
INTEGER count;
REAL    temperature;
```

create an **int** variable called **count** and a **float** variable called **temperature**. Many programmers use the convention that **typedef** names should be in uppercase, although again this is not a requirement of C.

    typedefs are sometimes combined with **enums** as in the declaration

```
typedef enum boolean  { FALSE, TRUE } BOOLEAN;
```

The advantage of this **typedef** is that we can use the single-word identifier **BOOLEAN** to declare both variables and functions instead of the two words **enum boolean**:

```
BOOLEAN error_flag,  end_of_data;                        /* Variables */
BOOLEAN check_status ( int   value );                    /* Function prototype */
```

Note the awkward syntax of this `typedef`, which uses both the `enum boolean` tag and the `typedef BOOLEAN` name. Because the `enum` tag is optional we can omit it in this case and write

```
typedef enum { FALSE, TRUE } BOOLEAN;
```

In the next example the `GRADE_LIST` name is declared to be synonymous with an array of 10 integers

```
typedef int GRADE_LIST [ 10 ];
```

With this declaration the `grades` variable can be declared to be an array of 10 integers:

```
GRADE_LIST grades;
```

Next we create a `string` data type

```
typedef char STRING [ MAX_STRING_LENGTH + 1 ];
```

That is, any variable of the `STRING` type is a valid C string. It is simpler to use the `STRING` name than the underlying C syntax, especially with function parameters, as in the function header

```
void print_grades ( char name [ ], int grades [ ], char letter_grade [ ] )
```

versus the more mnemonic

```
void print_grades ( STRING name, GRADE_LIST grades, STRING letter_grade )
```

Query: Why is `STRING` declared to be of the length `MAX_STRING_LENGTH + 1`?

RESPONSE: Remember, C strings are just arrays of characters but we have to include an extra array location to hold the string termination character (`'\0'`).

11.1.4 The struct Specifier

One of the most powerful data typing tools in C is the `struct` (structure) specifier. Using `struct` we can create what are generically called **records**: Heterogeneous data structures containing logically related data. The `struct` declaration names the record's **fields** (members). The fields can be of any type, including programmer-defined types such as `BOOLEAN` or `INTEGER`. For instance, consider a medical record that includes a patient's blood pressure reading:

```
struct pressure_record {
    INTEGER  diastolic;
    INTEGER  systolic;
    BOOLEAN  danger_level;
};
```

This is a description of the record's configuration. The `pressure_record` name is the structure tag. Memory is not allocated until a variable is associated with `struct pressure_record`. Once a variable is declared, we can refer to the individual fields in the record through the member operator, also called the dot (`.`) operator. This is shown next, with the structure variable called `patient`:

```
struct pressure_record patient;          /* Declare the structure variable */

patient.diastolic    = 70;                      /* Set the diastolic field */
patient.systolic     = 120;                     /* Set the systolic field */
patient.danger_level = FALSE;                      /* Pressure is ok */
```

Records can be as complicated as necessary and can include other records such as

```
struct patient_record {                         /* Structure definition */
    float                   basal_temp;
    struct pressure_record pressure;             /* Nested structure */
};

struct   patient_record patient;                /* Variable declaration */

patient.basal_temp              = 98.6;     /* Assignment to the fields */
patient.pressure.diastolic      = 70;
patient.pressure.systolic       = 160;
patient.pressure.danger_level   = TRUE;
```

Because the `patient` declaration only allows for one patient, how would it be declared for an entire case load? In that instance `patient` can be declared an array of records such as

```
struct patient_record patient [ NUM_PATIENTS ];
```

An assignment to the first record in `patient` might look like this:

```
patient[0].basal_temp               = 98.6;
patient[0].pressure.diastolic       = 70;
patient[0].pressure.systolic        = 120;
patient[0].pressure.danger_level    = FALSE;
```

(Figure 11.1–1 shows this record's internal configuration.)
    If we use `typedef` with `struct`, we can omit the tag,

```
typedef   struct {
                    float                   basal_temp;
                    struct  pressure_record pressure;
                  } PATIENT_RECORD;             /* Name of the typedef */
```

and use the `PATIENT_RECORD` name to declare variables. This is the same as `struct patient_record` but easier to use because it is just one word.

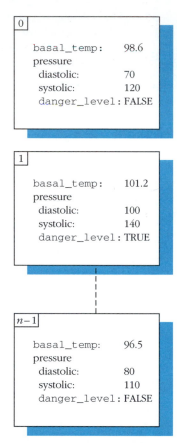

Figure 11.1–1 Configuration of a patient array with *n* elements

In general, we assign values to records field by field. But if two records have the same data type, we can assign a whole **struct** to another, as shown.

```
PATIENT_RECORD patient1, patient2;

patient1.basal_temp          = 98.6
patient1.pressure.diastolic  = 70;
patient1.pressure.systolic   = 120;
patient1.pressure.danger_level = FALSE;

patient2 = patient1;   /* Copy all fields of patient1 into patient2 */
```

The last statement is valid because **patient1** and **patient2** are **assignment compatible** (they have the same data type). Note that it is never permissible to compare two whole records. This must be done on a field-by-field basis. Thus the following is a syntax error.

```
if ( patient1 == patient2 )                    /* ERROR:  Cannot do this !!  */
    printf ( "\nSame info in both records!" );
```

Instead, we do this on a field-by-field basis:

```
if ( patient1.basal_temp       == patient2.basal_temp      &&
  patient1.pressure.diastolic  == patient2.pressure.diastolic &&
  patient1.pressure.systolic   == patient2.pressure.systolic  &&
  patient1.pressure.danger_level == patient2.pressure.danger_level )
 printf ( "\nSame info in both records!" );
```

Whole records can be passed as arguments to functions by naming them in the function call. Within the function, we can access the individual fields using the dot (.) operator, as we just saw. The syntax gets tricky, however, when a structure is used as an output parameter—that is, when the function changes the fields of a record. Like other nonarray variables, the structure must be passed using the **&** address-of operator. Within the function, the structure pointer has to be de-referenced so that values can be assigned to fields:

```
void check_pressure ( PATIENT_RECORD   *patient )
{
  if ( (*patient).pressure.systolic > 160 )
      (*patient).pressure.danger_level = TRUE;
  else
      (*patient).pressure.danger_level = FALSE;
}
```

The **(*patient).pressure.danger_level** notation needs some explanation. Within the function, we declare **patient** as a *pointer* to an object of the **PATIENT_RECORD** type. We do this because the function changes some of the data in the record. To refer to the record's fields we must de-reference the pointer using the ***** operator. However, the statement

```
*patient.pressure.danger_level  =  TRUE;                    /* Syntax error */
```

is actually a syntax error! Because higher priority is given to the dot operator than to the dereference operator, the statement is interpreted as *dereference the* **danger_level** *field of the* **pressure** *field of* **patient**. **patient** is just a pointer, not a structure, and does not have any fields to dereference. Therefore, to make the statement read correctly—*the* **danger_level** *field of the* **pressure** *field of the object pointed to by* **patient**—we change the precedence by using parentheses

```
(*patient).pressure.danger_level          /* Correct syntax */
```

This kind of reference is simplified by arrow (->) operator:

```
patient -> pressure.danger_level  =  TRUE;     /* Also correct */
```

patient-> means **(*patient).**, and is the convention used by most C programmers. Although the arrow is a single operator in C, we have to enter it as two characters: **-** followed by **>**.

White

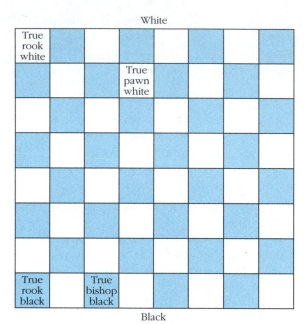

Black

Figure 11.1–2   A chess board

As a final example, consider a data structure to represent a chess board. A chess board is an 8 by 8 array of squares, each of which can hold a game piece (see Figure 11.1–2). What information needs to be stored in each of the game squares? At a minimum, we should record the kind of piece occupying the square (king, queen, bishop, knight, rook, pawn). But that is not enough to distinguish white pieces from black pieces. We need a second field to specify the owner (black, white). What if a square is unoccupied? We could add a third field to represent the status of the square (occupied, unoccupied).

Thus the game board is a 2D array of squares in which each square is a structure consisting of three fields. The fields can be simple integers (for example, 0 = unoccupied, 1 = occupied) but mnemonic names such as **FALSE** and **TRUE** are better. They are also a good use of enumerated data types:

```
typedef enum    { FALSE, TRUE }                 BOOLEAN;
typedef enum    { NONE, BLACK, WHITE }          OWNER_COLOR;
typedef enum    { EMPTY, PAWN, KNIGHT,
                  BISHOP, ROOK, QUEEN, KING }   PIECE_VALUE;

typedef struct {                                        /* Note: tag field omitted */
                BOOLEAN      occupied;
                PIECE_VALUE  piece;
                OWNER_COLOR  owner;
        } ONE_SQUARE;
```

Now we can describe the data type for the game board as

```
#define N_SQUARES  8
typedef ONE_SQUARE GAME_BOARD [ N_SQUARES ] [ N_SQUARES ];
```

A move from one square to another needs two steps: Copy the piece to the appropriate new square and delete the piece from its original square. We can do this in several different ways:

```
/* Example using the chess board data structure */

main ( )
{
  ONE_SQUARE current_move;
  GAME_BOARD board;

  initialize ( board );                                 /*  Set up the game board  */

                                              /*  Move king's pawn two spaces forward  */

  board[3][4]          = board [1][4];                   /*  First method:  */
                                                   /*  Copy the entire structure  */

  board[3][4].occupied = TRUE;                           /*  Second method:  */
  board[3][4].piece    = PAWN;             /*  Assign new values to each field  */
  board[3][4].owner    = WHITE;

  current_move.occupied = TRUE;                          /*  Third method:  */
  current_move.piece    = PAWN;              /*  Create a temporary structure  */
  current_move.owner    = WHITE;              /*  and assign it to the square  */
  board[3][4]           = current_move;


  clear_square( &board [1][4] );           /*  Must clear the original square  */

  return ( 0 );
}
```

Obviously, the first method is the easiest to use. The other two methods are shown for instructional purposes only. The `initialize ( board )` function needs a series of assignment statements to set up each of the 64 squares with the appropriate information. Here is a portion of this function:

```
void initialize ( GAME_BOARD board )
{
  ONE_SQUARE white_pawn = { TRUE, PAWN, WHITE };
  ONE_SQUARE black_pawn = { TRUE, PAWN, BLACK };

  board[0][0].occupied =  TRUE;              /* Set up white queen's rook  */
  board[0][0].piece    =  ROOK;
  board[0][0].owner    =  WHITE;

  for ( i = 0;  i < N_SQUARES;  i++ )        /* Set up row of white pawns  */
    board[1][i]  =  white_pawn;

}                        /*  NOTE:  Add remaining statements as necessary  */
```

The `clear_square` function takes a particular board position as an argument and correctly sets the corresponding fields to indicate an empty square:

```
void clear_square ( ONE_SQUARE  *square )
{
  ONE_SQUARE  empty_square  =  { FALSE, EMPTY, NONE };
  *square  =  empty_square;
}
```

BEFORE YOU GO ON

Query: The `board[1][4]` argument in the call to `clear_square` and the corresponding `square` parameter seem quite different from each other. Why isn't `board` the parameter?

RESPONSE: `board[1][4]` is a specific square on the board, whereas `board` is a 2D array of squares. Because `clear_square` is expecting only a single square and not the entire board, the argument correctly matches the parameter.

EXERCISES 11.1

Concept Check
Answer statements 1 through 4 with true *or* false.
1. A data structure is a tool for managing data.
2. An abstract data type combines the logical definition of a data structure with its physical implementation.
3. An enumerated data type is one whose values are specified by the programmer.
4. Two entire structures can be tested for equality as long as they are the same data type.

For statements 5 through 8 choose the answer that best completes the statement.

5. Assuming that `day` is the `enum weekday` type, what would be output by the following?

    ```
    day  =  TUESDAY;
    printf ( "\nDay = %d",  day );
    ```

    a. TUESDAY
    b. 1
    c. 2
    d. cannot output the values of `enum` variables

6. Assuming   the   `void check_pressure ( PATIENT_RECORD *patient )`   function header, which of the following is acceptable syntax

    a. `patient-> pressure-> danger_level = TRUE;`
    b. `patient.pressure.danger_level = TRUE;`
    c. `patient->pressure.danger_level = FALSE;`
    d. `patient->danger_level = TRUE;`

7. In the `enum weekday day` declaration, the word `weekday` is called a
    a. variable
    b. tag
    c. data structure
    d. constant

8. Given the declaration `struct PERSONNEL_RECORD person1, person2;`
    a. the two variables can be compared for equality since they are the same data type
    b. the two variables can be assigned to each other since they are the same data type
    c. the two variables cannot be assigned to each other or compared
    d. the two variables can either be assigned or compared

For statements 9 through 12 fill in the blanks with the right word.

9. An ADT is a(n) _____ data structure, together with a set of _____ .

10. An array is a _____ collection of data.

11. The _____ specifier allows us to create mnemonic names for complex data structures.

12. The _____ operator allows us to dereference a structure pointer.

Set A

Solve each of the following problems.

13. Write an `enum` declaration to declare the days Monday through Sunday.

14. Write an `enum` declaration to declare the summer months (June, July, and August).

15. Write an `enum` declaration to declare the names of your family members.

16. Write a `typedef` for the `enum` declaration in Question 13.

17. Write a `typedef` for the `enum` declaration in Question 14.

18. Write a `typedef` for the `enum` declaration in Question 15.

Set B

19. Declare a **struct** called **personnel_info** containing fields for your name, address, and social security number.
20. Declare a **struct** called **exam_rec** to represent the grades on your last three exams.
21. Modify the **personnel_info struct** to include a field for **exam_rec**.
22. Declare an array of **personnel_info structs**.

Set C

23. Implement a function called **assign_exams** that assigns arbitrary values to the fields of **exam_rec** (see Question 20). The function should pass the **struct** back to **main** as an output parameter.
24. Rewrite the answer to Question 23 but have the function **return** the **struct**.
25. Implement a function called **assign_personnel_data** that assigns arbitrary values to **personnel_rec** (see Question 22). The calling function should contain a loop that calls **assign_personnel_data** repeatedly, once for each student in a class. **assign_personnel_data** should **return** the value of the updated **struct**.
26. Rewrite the answer to Question 25 but have the function pass the **struct** back as an output parameter.

11.2   ADT STACKS

Introduction

As its name suggests, a stack is a collection of things arranged in a particular way. In a school cafeteria, trays are sometimes put on a holding device (stack) that has a spring to push the trays upward. Trays can be added and removed with this constraint: The last tray put onto the stack has to be removed first (see Figure 11.2–1). There is no other way to get at the trays because their access is strictly limited by the construction of the stack. Notice that the access restriction causes trays to be removed in the reverse order from how they are placed, a property called **last-in-first-out (LIFO)**.

The stack is a fundamental ADT in many computer programs, especially in system software such as compilers and operating systems. It is also the first data structure presented in this book for which there is no predefined data type in C (like **int** or **float**). Because it is not directly available, we must design and implement it ourselves rather than just describe it.

Before we talk about stacks, let's review the two kinds of software (discussed in Chapter 1) and the two kinds of programmers. First, there are **applications programmers** who use existing software tools to write special-purpose programs such as word processors and spreadsheets. Their typical audience is **end-users** who are usually not programmers. Second, there are **systems programmers** who write the software tools used by applications programmers. In the context of ADTs, the systems programmers design and write the ADT and the applications programmers use the ADT in their applications software.

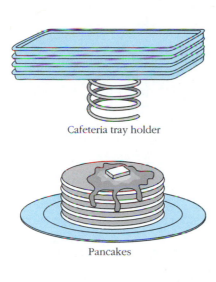

Cafeteria tray holder

Pancakes

Greatest Hits of 1990
Greatest Hits of 1980
Greatest Hits of 1970
Greatest Hits of 1960
Greatest Hits of 1950

Records

Figure 11.2–1   Some examples of stacks

These are usually two different job categories in the workplace, and the two kinds of programmers usually work independently of each other. The distinction is analogous to the principle of the ADT, which separates the logical properties (design) of a data structure from the physical properties (coded implementation).

PERSPECTIVE

Systems programmers sometimes need to change an ADT implementation when, for example, a more efficient algorithm is developed or a hardware change necessitates a corresponding software change. The ADT approach is consistent with the principle of **information hiding**—deliberately concealing the details of a data structure or function from another programmer. With information hiding, the systems programmer is free to change the implementation of an ADT without causing a problem for the applications programmer (user of the ADT). Note that the systems programmer cannot change the interface to the ADT because that would mean that all applications programs already in use would have to be rewritten.

11.2.1 The ADT Stack

An ADT **stack** is a homogeneous collection of items of any one type, arranged linearly with access at one end only, called the **top**. The following operations describe the applications programmer's interface of an ADT stack:

Operation	Meaning
`create_stack( stack )`	Make stack logically accessible
`destroy_stack( stack )`	Make stack logically inaccessible
`empty_stack( stack )`	True if stack is empty
`full_stack( stack )`	True if stack is full
`push( stack, item )`	Add item to the top of the stack
`pop( stack, item )`	Remove item from the top of the stack

The items can be simple or structured as long as each item is the same data type. Therefore, we might have a stack of characters or integers, or a series of personnel records, each containing many fields and substructures. Logically, it does not matter what is being stacked. The operations just listed behave the same way regardless of the item's data type.

According to the stack definition, each item is added to or removed from the same stack location: the top. The notion of a stack having a top is purely a descriptive device. In software it does not matter if the stack is accessed via its top or its bottom—the stack could be pictured as lying horizontally, vertically, or in any other orientation. For now, the cafeteria tray holder is a reasonable analogy. Later, when we implement the stack, we can reconsider the construction details.

Let's illustrate these concepts with a simple applications program called **string reversal**. The input to this program is a series of characters that are **pushed** (inserted at the top) onto an ADT stack one at a time. Then the stack is repeatedly **popped** (top item removed) and its items output, causing the original string to be displayed in reverse order. This is demonstrated in Program 11.2–1.

P R O G R A M   1 1 . 2 – 1

```
/***************************************************************************
* Title:       string reversal                                            *
* Filename:    strev.c                                                     *
*                                                                          *
* Description: Reverse the order of characters in an input string using a stack. *
*                                                                          *
* Input:       series of characters                                       *
* Output:      characters in reverse order                                *
* Process:     push each input character onto a stack; pop and output the stack *
*                                                                          *
* Written by:  ...                                               Date: ... *
***************************************************************************/
```

```
#include <stdio.h>

typedef enum { FALSE, TRUE }   BOOLEAN;

typedef char ITEM_TYPE;          /*  Stack user can define item type as needed  */

#include "stack.h"               /*  Definitions and prototypes for ADT stack  */

void input_stack ( STACK_TYPE *stack );               /*  Function prototypes */
void output_stack ( STACK_TYPE *stack );              /* for this application */

main ( )
{
  STACK_TYPE stack;                           /*  Local declaration of stack  */

  create_stack  ( &stack );
  input_stack   ( &stack );                     /* Push characters onto stack */
  output_stack  ( &stack );                    /* Pop and output the characters */
  destroy_stack ( &stack );

  return ( 0 );
}                                                         /*  End of main  */




/******************************************************************************
* Function name:       input_stack                                           *
* Description:         Load input characters onto stack.                     *
*                                                                            *
* Input parameters:  none                                                    *
* Output parameters: stack with input loaded                                 *
* Return value:        none                                                  *
******************************************************************************/

void input_stack ( STACK_TYPE *stack )
{
  ITEM_TYPE    in_value;

  printf ( "\nEnter a string of characters followed by a carriage return\n" );

  while ( ((in_value=getchar()) != '\n') && /* As long as there is more input */
           full_stack(stack) == FALSE )   /* and more room on the stack . . . */

      push ( stack,  in_value );                    /* Push character onto stack */

}                                              /*  End of input_stack  */
```

```
/*****************************************************************************
 * Function name:     output_stack                                          *
 * Description:       Pop and output each character from stack.             *
 *                                                                          *
 * Input parameters:  stack                                                 *
 * Output parameters: emptied stack                                         *
 * Return value:      none                                                  *
 *****************************************************************************/

void output_stack ( STACK_TYPE   *stack )
{
  ITEM_TYPE out_value;

  printf ( "\nString reversed...\n");

  while ( empty_stack ( stack ) == FALSE )  {   /* More characters on stack? */
    pop ( stack,  &out_value );                         /* Pop character */
    putchar ( out_value );                              /* Output character */
  }
}                                                /*  End of output_stack  */
```

This is a pure applications program: No reference is made to the stack implementation other than the **#include "stack.h"** statement, which gives access to a variety of stack definitions.

PERSPECTIVE

Note the use of double quotes with **#include "stack.h"** instead of angle brackets. Angle brackets are used only with standard headers such as **stdio.h** and **math.h** and mean that those files are in a system-defined directory. With a non–standard file, you must tell the preprocessor the **path** (the sequence of directories) to follow to find the file. In this case, a path is not indicated so the **stack.h** file is assumed to reside in a default directory.

In addition to **#include**, there is a **typedef** that describes the stack **ITEM_TYPE**. Since the ADT stack does not restrict the **ITEM_TYPE**, it is safe to let the applications programmer have control over this. If **ITEM_TYPE** were defined in the ADT implementation, the applications programmer would be restricted to one arbitrary type of stack!

BEFORE YOU GO ON

Query: **ITEM_TYPE** is defined before **#include "stack.h"**. Does the order of these statements matter?

RESPONSE: Yes, the order is critical. Many statements in **stack.h** refer to **ITEM_TYPE**. If it were not already defined, a syntax error would occur on each reference to **ITEM_TYPE** in **stack.h**.

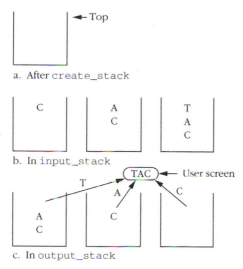

a. After `create_stack`

b. In `input_stack`

c. In `output_stack`

Figure 11.2–2   Stack contents for string-reversal program

Let's look at the contents of the stack, as shown in Figure 11.2–2. The **create_stack** function makes the stack accessible and initializes its contents. Don't worry if it is not yet clear what this means. For now, we can assume that the stack has no items in it. Any other details are irrelevant to the applications programmer, the stack user.

The program invokes a function (written by the applications programmer) called **input_stack**, which reads a series of characters and pushes them onto the stack. This is done with a complex **while** loop:

```
while( ( (in_value = getchar()) != '\n') && /* As long as there is more input */
        full_stack ( stack ) == FALSE )     /* and more room on the stack... */
```

The loop header reads a character using the **getchar** function and stores the value in **in_value**. The loop condition specifies that the input process is to continue as long as both

a. the end of line character (**'\n'**) has not been input
b. the stack is not full

As each character is input it is pushed onto the stack. The top of the stack always points to the last character that was input. Notice that before pushing any new characters, the programmer includes a test, `full_stack`. Without this test it might be possible to push onto an already full stack, a condition called **stack overflow**. Because the stack is not infinitely large, this check is necessary to ensure the integrity of the data structure.

The `output_stack` function (also written by the applications programmer) pops the stack contents one character at a time, then outputs each character. Again, a test is included that stops the process as soon as the stack is emptied. The `empty_stack` test prevents **stack underflow**—popping an already empty stack. Finally `destroy_stack` is called, which presumably makes the stack inaccessible.

11.2.2 Implementing the Stack as an Array

Now that we understand the logical picture of a stack and how it might be used in a program, let's assume the role of the systems programmer and write the code for the ADT stack. First, we describe the data structure itself. As we said earlier, there are many ways to represent the stack. We use a data structure consisting of an array to hold the stack items and an integer field to represent the stack top (see Figure 11.2–3).

We put these definitions in a header file called `stack.h`.

```
/* stack.h: definitions and prototypes for ADT stack package          */

#define MAX_STACK 100                    /*  Arbitrary size of the stack  */
```

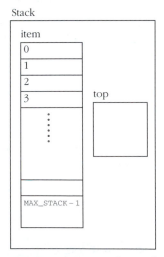

Figure 11.2–3 A stack implemented as an array-based structure

```
typedef struct stack_type {
        ITEM_TYPE item[MAX_STACK];
        int       top;
    }   STACK_TYPE;


                                              /* ADT Stack function prototypes */
void    create_stack  ( STACK_TYPE  *stack );
void    destroy_stack ( STACK_TYPE  *stack );
BOOLEAN empty_stack   ( STACK_TYPE  *stack );
BOOLEAN full_stack    ( STACK_TYPE  *stack );
void    push          ( STACK_TYPE  *stack,ITEM_TYPE  new_item );
void    pop           ( STACK_TYPE  *stack,ITEM_TYPE  *old_item );
```

The definition of ITEM_TYPE is unspecified and left to the stack user. The value of the MAX_STACK constant is arbitrary and could be set to any reasonable value.

PERSPECTIVE

The prototypes specify that the *address* of the stack rather than the stack itself is to be passed to all the functions. For the empty_stack and full_stack functions, this is done for reasons of efficiency rather than necessity. As shown below, these functions do not change the contents of the stack but only test its status (empty or full). Because the stack is potentially a large structure (depending on MAX_STACK and ITEM_TYPE), however, it is reasonable to pass the address rather than the contents. You can use the const qualifier to emphasize that a parameter is input-only, as in

```
BOOLEAN empty_stack ( const STACK_TYPE *stack )
```

Now consider the implementations of the stack functions. The purpose of create_stack is to make the stack logically accessible to the stack user. Although other possibilities exist, we set top to point to the next free spot in the stack, or location 0. This means that the first time an item is pushed onto the stack it goes into cell 0 of the array.

```
/**********************************************************************
 * Function name:      create_stack                                   *
 * Description:        Initialize stack.                              *
 *                                                                    *
 * Input parameters:   none                                          *
 * Output parameters:  initialized stack                             *
 * Return value:       none                                          *
 **********************************************************************/
```

```
void create_stack ( STACK_TYPE   *stack )
{
  stack->top = 0;
}
```

The function changes the stack so the stack's address is passed to the function. We have to dereference the local variable **stack** with the arrow operator **->** to change the stack argument in the calling function.

Query: In the **create_stack** function, what happens if we write **stack.top = 0;** ?

RESPONSE: This causes a syntax error! Within the function, **stack** is declared to be a *pointer* to a variable of **STACK_TYPE**. Because it is a pointer and not a structure, it does not have any subfields. Note that you could have written **(*stack).top**, which has the same meaning as **stack->top**.

In this implementation, **destroy_stack** uses the same processing as **create_stack**. The way we wrote it here, the stack can be made empty by setting the **top** to 0. We can write the function as

```
/***************************************************************************
 * Function name:      destroy_stack                                       *
 * Description:        Logically remove all stack contents.                *
 *                                                                         *
 * Input parameters:   none                                                *
 * Output parameters:  destroyed stack                                     *
 * Return value:       none                                                *
 ***************************************************************************/

void destroy_stack ( STACK_TYPE   *stack )
{
 stack->top = 0;
}
```

PERSPECTIVE

Query: Because **create_stack** and **destroy_stack** are the same, why not just have one function such as **create_destroy_stack**?

RESPONSE: The two functions are the same in *this* implementation but (as we see in Chapter 13) they are not the same when the stack is represented as a dynamically linked list. Having two or more interfaces to the stack depending on the implementation details would contradict the basic principle of the ADT approach!

The `empty_stack` function returns a `BOOLEAN` value if the stack is empty (if the `top` is 0) and the `full_stack` function checks whether `top` is set to `MAX_STACK` (beyond the last free location in the stack), as shown next.

```
/**************************************************************************
* Function name:     empty_stack                                         *
* Description:       Test whether any items are on stack.                *
*                                                                        *
* Input parameters:  stack, new_item                                     *
* Output parameters: none                                                *
* Return value:      TRUE if stack is empty; FALSE if stack not empty    *
**************************************************************************/

BOOLEAN empty_stack ( STACK_TYPE *stack )              /* Function header */
{
   return ( stack->top == 0  ?  TRUE  :  FALSE );
}
```

```
/**************************************************************************
* Function name:     full_stack                                          *
* Description:       Test whether stack is full.                         *
*                                                                        *
* Input parameters:  stack                                               *
* Output parameters: none                                                *
* Return value:      TRUE if stack is full; FALSE if stack not full      *
**************************************************************************/

BOOLEAN full_stack ( STACK_TYPE *stack )               /* Function header */
{
  return ( stack->top == MAX_STACK  ?  TRUE  :  FALSE );
}
```

Notice that both `empty_stack` and `full_stack` use the **conditional** `?` operator. The interpretation is:

1. If the expression preceding the `?` is true, then execute the expression immediately following the `?` operator.
2. If the expression preceding the `?` is false, then execute the expression immediately following the colon (`:`).

We could also say this using the more readable code

```
      if ( stack -> top == 0 )
        return ( TRUE );
      else
        return ( FALSE );
```

BEFORE YOU GO ON

Query: What is the output of the following code?

```
int  y = 5,  z = 6;
( y > z  ?  printf ( "%d",  y )  :  printf ( "%d",  z );
```

RESPONSE: Since `y > z` is false, the second `printf` is executed and the output is the value of `z`, which is 6.

The next two functions are the core of the ADT stack: `push` and `pop`.

```
/******************************************************************************
* Function name:      push                                                    *
* Description:        Add new item to top of stack.                           *
*                                                                             *
* Input parameters:   stack, new_item                                         *
* Output parameters:  stack with new top item                                 *
* Return value:       none                                                    *
*                                                                             *
* Precondition:       stack is not full                                       *
* Postcondition:      stack will contain new top item                         *
******************************************************************************/

void push ( STACK_TYPE *stack,   ITEM_TYPE  new_item )
{
 stack->item [ stack->top++ ]  =  new_item;        /* Top  increments after  */
}                                        /*    assignment statement executes! */


/******************************************************************************
* Function name:      pop                                                     *
* Description:        Remove item from top of stack.                          *
*                                                                             *
* Input parameters:   stack                                                   *
* Output parameters:  stack with top item removed, former top item           *
* Return value:       none                                                    *
*                                                                             *
* Precondition:       stack is not empty                                      *
* Postcondition:      stack will have top item removed                        *
******************************************************************************/

void pop ( STACK_TYPE  *stack,  ITEM_TYPE  *old_item )
{
*old_item =  stack->item [ --stack->top ];        /* Top decrements before  */
}                                       /* assignment statement executes!  */
```

`push` and `pop` complement each other. `push` adds `new_item` to the stack and then increments `top` to the next free location. Notice the use of the postfix increment operator. In this case top is incremented after the assignment statement executes. pop decrements top first and then returns old_item, which is the item top is pointing to. Because top is designed to point to the next free location on the stack, old_item has been logically removed from the stack.

PERSPECTIVE

Recall that the *postfix* increment/decrement operator increments/decrements the variable after the expression evaluates. In *prefix* form, the operator (increment or decrement) changes the variable before the expression evaluates.

Note the inclusion of a **precondition** and a **postcondition** in the documentation of these two functions. A precondition is a **logical assertion** (true or false statement) that must be true before a portion of a program executes. With push, the precondition states that there must be room on the stack before adding a new item. Similarly, at least one item must exist on the stack before attempting to pop.

A postcondition is a logical assertion that is true if the preconditions are met. Therefore, according to the postcondition for push, the stack is guaranteed to have a new top item if there is room for one when the function is called. Similarly for pop, the top item is removed but only if there *is* a top item when the function is called.

PERSPECTIVE

The top of the stack is actually the bottom of the array! The image of the stack having a fixed top with all the trays moving down or up is logically useful but in this case physically impractical. If the stack had a fixed top at location 0, pushing and popping would move all the stack items down or up one location. It is more efficient to increment or decrement the top than to move all the stack items.

You may have noticed that none of the functions listed above can prevent a stack user (an applications programmer) from making an unauthorized access to the stack. For instance, what prevents a programmer from putting the following statement into a function?

```
stack->item[2]  =  17;
```

Such a clear violation of the ADT stack can only occur if the applications programmer knows the implementation details; for example, that the stack is a **struct** containing an array. Using the ADT approach (separating the use of an ADT from its implementation), we reduce the chance that an unauthorized access can take place. Furthermore, if the systems programmer puts the code for the functions in a library (incorporating the principle of information hiding), another programmer cannot easily uncover the implementation of the stack.

11.2.3 Postfix Arithmetic Using a Stack

Next consider a practical use for a stack: The computer evaluation of arithmetic expressions. In a conventional arithmetic expression, the operator is between the operands. This is called **infix notation**. A drawback of this notation is the potential ambiguity in evaluating infix expressions. For example, what does $3 + 4 \times 5$ equal? In a simple left-to-right calculation, the answer is 35. However, according to the rules of algebra, the answer is 23. We resolve the ambiguity with a set of implied operator-precedence rules.

Putting each operator either before or after the operands to which it relates, called **prefix** or **postfix** notation respectively, makes the requirement of a precedence scheme unnecessary. Because the precedence is embedded in the expression rather than in an external table of precedence rules, these notations are more efficient for evaluating expressions. This efficiency is important when the expressions must be evaluated more than once as when they are used in a program loop. Because of the increased efficiency, infix expressions are converted to postfix notation by compilers before machine code is generated.

PERSPECTIVE

Postfix notation, also called reverse Polish notation, was named for its inventor, the logician Jan Lukasiewicz.

Consider the following expressions

Prefix	Infix	Postfix
* 3 4	3 * 4	3 4 *
+ 3 * 4 5	3 + 4 * 5	3 4 5 * +
* + 3 4 5	(3 + 4) * 5	3 4 + 5 *

In postfix notation the expression 3 4 5 * + is evaluated as follows. Find the first operator symbol, in this case *. The operands always come right *before* the operator. Now do the operation

4 5 *

which is the same as $4 \times 5 = 20$. The expression now reads

3 20 +

which is the same as

$3 + 20 = 23$.

Program 11.2–2 uses a stack to evaluate a well-formed postfix expression—one in which each pair of operands has an associated operator.

PROGRAM 11.2–2

```
/*****************************************************************************
 * Title:       postfix evaluate                                            *
 * Filename:    postfix.c                                                    *
 *                                                                          *
 * Description: Evaluate a well-formed postfix expression using a stack.     *
 *                                                                          *
 * Input:       well-formed postfix expression                              *
 * Output:      arithmetic evaluation of the input                          *
 * Process:     1) push operands onto the stack as they are input by the user *
 *              2) when an operator is input, pop the stack twice, perform the *
 *                 operation, and push the result onto the stack            *
 *              3) when the end-of-line character is input, pop the stack    *
 *                                                                          *
 * Written by:  ...                              Date: ...                  *
 *****************************************************************************/

#include <stdio.h>

#define BLANK   ' '
#define EOLN    '\n'                              /* Define the end-of-line character */

typedef int    ITEM_TYPE;

#include "stack.h"


main ( )
{
 char     in_char;
 ITEM_TYPE op1,  op2,  result;
 STACK_TYPE op_stack;

 create_stack ( &op_stack );

 while ( ( in_char = getchar ( ) )    !=   EOLN &&           /* Read characters until */
       full_stack ( &op_stack ) == FALSE ) {               /* carriage return */
                                                           /* or full stack */

     if ( in_char  !=  BLANK )                              /* Skip over blanks */

     if ( in_char >= '0'  &&   in_char <= '9' )             /* Is in_char an operand? */
          push ( &op_stack,  in_char - '0' );              /* Convert to numeric value */

        else   {
          pop ( &op_stack,  &op2 );                  /* Input was an operator . . .so, */
          pop ( &op_stack,  &op1 );                  /* retrieve last two operands */
```

```
        switch ( in_char )   {                                    /* Perform operation */
              case '+' : push ( &op_stack,  op1 + op2 ); break;
              case '-' : push ( &op_stack,  op1 - op2 ); break;
              case '*' : push ( &op_stack,  op1 * op2 ); break;
              case '/' : push ( &op_stack,  op1 / op2 ); break;
              default : printf ( "\nError in input" );
        }                                                         /* End switch */
     }                                                            /* End else */
}                                                                 /* End while */

pop ( &op_stack,  &result );                  /* Stack should only contain the final result */
printf ( "\nResult = %d\n\n",  result );

destroy_stack ( &op_stack );

return ( 0 );
}                                                                 /* End main */
```

EXERCISES 11.2

Concept Check

Answer statements 1 through 4 with true *or* false.

1. A stack is accessed in the same way as an array.
2. Stack items can be of any data type.
3. Items are added to the end of a stack and removed from the front.
4. It is the job of the applications programmer to implement the ADT stack.

For statements 5 through 8 choose the answer that best completes the statement.

5. The data type of the stack item is
   a. determined by the applications programmer
   b. determined by the systems programmer
   c. determined by the user
   d. determined by the C compiler
6. The **destroy_stack** function
   a. removes any existing stack items
   b. makes the stack items inaccessible
   c. deallocates the stack
   d. is not accessible to the applications programmer
7. The **full_stack** and **empty_stack** functions
   a. are not really necessary because **push** and **pop** always check for possible errors
   b. should always be used with **push** and **pop**, respectively, to maintain the integrity of the stack
   c. should always have identical implementations
   d. are used only by systems programmers to design the functions for accessing the stack

8. An expression in postfix form is evaluated more efficiently than the corresponding infix expression because
   a. infix expressions have more operands
   b. postfix expressions use parentheses instead of an operator precedence scheme
   c. postfix expressions are shorter than infix expressions
   d. infix needs an operator-precedence scheme and postfix does not.

For statements 9 through 12 fill in the blanks with the right word.

9. In this chapter the `create_stack` and `destroy_stack` functions are both implemented by setting _____.
10. Popping an empty stack can result in _____ and pushing onto a full stack can result in _____.
11. The practice of intentionally concealing the internal coding of a data structure or function is called _____.
12. According to the implementation specified in the text, the _____ of the stack is physically located at the _____ of the array.

Set A

Evaluate each of the following postfix expressions:

13. 7 3 /
14. 3 4 5 + *
15. 4 3 2 1 + * +
16. 4 3 2 1 * + +
17. 3 4 − 1 2 + /
18. 9 3 2 4 + 5 − * / 7 +

Set B

Convert each of the following infix expressions to postfix.

19. A + B * C
20. (A + B) * (C - D)
21. A ^ B * C − D + E / F / (G + H)
22. A − B / (C * D ^ E)
23. A * (B + C / (D − E))
24. (A / 2 / 4 + B * C) / (1 − 2)

Set C

25. Rewrite `pop` so that it uses a `return` statement for `old_item` instead of an output parameter.
26. Modify `push` so that it checks for stack overflow. One way to do this is to call a function such as `err_message (err_code)` from within `push` with an argument representing the error number. For instance, `err_message ( 1 );` might mean that the stack was about to overflow.
27. Modify `pop` so that it checks for stack underflow in the same way as is described in Question 26.
28. Add a new ADT function called `stack_top` that uses a `return` statement to return the item on the top of the stack without changing the stack.

29. Rewrite the answer to Question 28 so that instead of using a **return** statement, you return the top item as an output parameter.
30. The code for **postfix.c** is written as one large function. Rewrite it modularly by incorporating other functions where appropriate.
31. Modify **postfix.c** so that it can handle improperly formulated postfix expressions (such as 4 5 + − or 4 5 6 +).
32. Modify **postfix.c** so that it can handle multiple postfix expressions and stop when users indicate that they are finished.
33. Modify **postfix.c** so that it prevents division by 0.

11.3   ADT QUEUES

Introduction

Like an ADT stack, an ADT queue is a collection of objects. The difference between the two ADTs is how they are accessed. A stack is arranged as last-in-first-out (LIFO) and a queue is arranged as first-in-first-out (FIFO). A good analogy is people waiting in line, as shown in Figure 11.3–1. When they arrive at an airport gate people queue up to get on the plane. Each new arrival goes to the end of the line and each person at the front of the line is in turn given a boarding pass and allowed to get on the plane. Therefore, unlike a stack which has one access point (the top), the queue has two access points—the front and rear.

Like the stack, the queue is a basic data structure in many computer programs, especially in system software. For instance, one of the tasks of an operating system

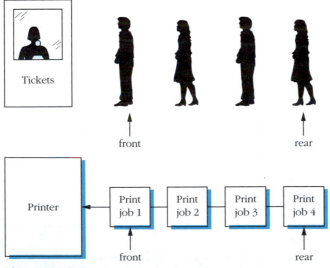

Figure 11.3–1   Some examples of queues

is resource scheduling. In a mainframe setting with many users, it is likely that more than one user will request a particular resource, such as the printer, while it is allocated to another user. To handle this situation the system puts the requests in a **print queue** and typically processes them as first-in-first-out. Alternatively, in a network setting with many nodes, the node designated as the file server handles multiple requests for the shared file system. These requests are queued and handled in the order received.

Let's first describe the ADT queue and then see how it works.

PERSPECTIVE

Stacks and queues are **time-ordered** ADTs because the placement of a given piece of information depends on its relative time of arrival. Chapter 13 presents other ADTs in which the data are arranged according to different protocols.

11.3.1 The ADT Queue

An ADT **queue** is a homogeneous collection of data items arranged linearly with access at both ends, called the front and rear. The following operations describe how the applications programmer interfaces with an ADT queue.

Operation	Meaning
create_queue(queue)	Make queue logically accessible
destroy_queue(queue)	Make queue logically inaccessible
empty_queue(queue)	True if queue is empty
full_queue(queue)	True if queue is full
enqueue(queue, item)	Add item to the rear of the queue
dequeue(queue, item)	Remove item from the front of the queue

The data items in an ADT queue can be simple or structured as long as all the items are the same data type. Logically, it does not matter what is being queued. The operations just listed are independent of the item's data type.

Here is an application in which a queue and a stack are used to detect whether an incoming string is a **palindrome** (reads the same way forward and backward). The input to this program is a series of characters that are both 1. pushed onto a stack and 2. enqueued onto a queue. Therefore, the string is in reverse order on the stack but in its original order on the queue. To check for a palindrome the program pops the top stack character and dequeues the front queue character. This process repeats as long as the two characters are equal. If the two characters are unequal, the processing stops and the program reports that the string is not a palindrome. Otherwise, if each character on the stack matches each character on the queue the program outputs a message that the string is a palindrome. This is shown in Program 11.3–1.

PROGRAM 11.3 – 1

```
/*************************************************************************
 * Title:        palindrome                                             *
 * Filename:     pal.c                                                  *
 *                                                                      *
 * Description: Determine whether a string is a palindrome; that is, whether *
 *              it reads the same way left-to-right as right-to-left.  The   *
 *              program is case and punctuation insensitive.            *
 *                                                                      *
 * Input:        string of characters                                  *
 * Output:       message indicating whether string is a palindrome or not *
 * Process:      Place each input character onto both the stack and the queue. *
 *              After all characters have been input, pop the stack and dequeue *
 *              the queue.  If all the characters from both data structures *
 *              agree, the string is reported to be a palindrome.       *
 *                                                                      *
 * Written by:  ...                                    Date: ...        *
 *************************************************************************/

#include <stdio.h>
#include <ctype.h>

#define EOLN  '\n'

typedef enum {FALSE, TRUE} BOOLEAN;

typedef char           ITEM_TYPE;                   /* For stack and queue */

#include "stack.h"            /*  Definitions and prototypes for ADT stack */
#include "queue.h"            /*  Definitions and prototypes for ADT queue */

                                       /*  Application function prototypes */
void   load_stack_and_queue ( STACK_TYPE *stack,  Q_TYPE  *queue );
BOOLEAN test_for_identity   ( STACK_TYPE *stack,  Q_TYPE  *queue );

main ( )
{

  STACK_TYPE stack;
  Q_TYPE     queue;

  create_stack ( &stack );
  create_queue ( &queue );

  load_stack_and_queue ( &stack,  &queue );   /* Put input on stack and queue */
```

```
    if ( test_for_identity( &stack,  &queue ) == TRUE )   /* Check for identity */
        printf ( " Is a palindrome.\n\n" );
    else
        printf ( " Is not a palindrome.\n\n" );



    destroy_stack ( &stack );
    destroy_queue ( &queue );
    return (0);
}                                                          /*  End of main  */



/****************************************************************************
* Function name:      load_stack_and_queue                                 *
* Description:        Push and enqueue each alphabetic input character.     *
*                                                                          *
* Input parameters:   none                                                 *
* Output parameters:  stack, queue                                         *
* Return value:       none                                                 *
****************************************************************************/

void load_stack_and_queue ( STACK_TYPE *stack,  Q_TYPE *queue )
{
  ITEM_TYPE item;

  printf ( "\nEnter a string to test for palindrome\n" );

  do   {
    scanf ( "%c",  &item );
    item  =  toupper ( item );
                                            /*  Restrict to alphabetics  */
    if ( isalpha ( item )  &&  full_queue( queue ) == FALSE )  {

        push ( stack,  item );                     /* Add character to stack */
        enqueue ( queue,  item );          /* Add character to queue, also */
    }

  }    while ( item  !=  EOLN );                              /*  End do  */


}                                             /* End of load_stack_and_queue */



/****************************************************************************
* Function name:      test_for_identity                                    *
* Description:        Compare each item on stack and queue.                *
*                                                                          *
```

```
* Input parameters:   stack, queue                                          *
* Output parameters:  stack, queue                                          *
* Return value:       TRUE if stack and queue contain same items            *
*****************************************************************************/

BOOLEAN test_for_identity ( STACK_TYPE  *stack,  Q_TYPE  *queue )
{

  ITEM_TYPE    stack_item,  q_item;
  BOOLEAN      stack_and_q_are_same  =  TRUE;      /* Assume they are the same */


  while ( ( stack_and_q_are_same == TRUE ) &&
          ( empty_queue ( queue )  == FALSE ) )   {

    pop ( stack, &stack_item );                        /* Remove top stack item */
    dequeue ( queue, &q_item );                        /* Remove front queue item */

    if ( stack_item == q_item )                            /* Are they the same? */
        stack_and_q_are_same  =  TRUE;
    else
        stack_and_q_are_same  =  FALSE;
  }


  return ( stack_and_q_are_same );
}                                               /* End of test_for_identity */
```

Let's analyze the program by examining the contents of the ADTs, as shown in Figure 11.3–2. **main** calls **create_stack** and **create_queue** to initialize each of the ADTs (Figure 11.3–2a). Next, **load_stack_and_queue** processes the user input. This function puts the data onto each of the ADTs, stopping at the end-of-line character. Notice the use of the **toupper** and **isalpha** functions. Together, they ensure that only uppercase, alphabetic characters are considered (Figure 11.3–2b). For example, the expression "Madam, I'm Adam" is a palindrome if we disregard punctuation and case.

Now the **BOOLEAN test_for_identity** function checks the contents of the ADTs. As long as the top stack character equals the front queue character the processing continues. When there is a mismatch or when there are no more items to check, the function returns (Figure 11.3–2c). The status of the return determines which message is output in **main**.

Finally, notice that the applications programmer has to check for underflow and overflow whenever a stack or queue is used (see **load_stack_and_queue** and **test_for_identity** in Program 11.3–1). Similarly, the **destroy_stack** and **destroy_queue** functions should be called once these ADTs are no longer needed by the program.

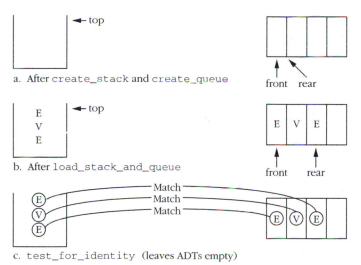

a. After `create_stack` and `create_queue`

b. After `load_stack_and_queue`

c. `test_for_identity` (leaves ADTs empty)

Figure 11.3–2   Queue and stack contents for palindrome program

11.3.2 Implementing the Queue as a Circular Array

Now that we understand the logical picture of a queue and how it might be incorporated into a program, let's consider the implementation of the queue software package, looking first at some of the subtleties of queue design.

Assume that the items are held in an array structure with a maximum of, say, six cells and that three items, A, B, and C, have already been enqueued. Furthermore, assume that **rear** always points to the next free slot for insertion on the queue and that **front** always points to the next available item for deletion.

Now, let's dequeue:

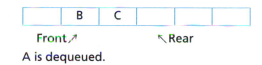

A is dequeued.

Next, enqueue D and E:

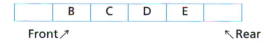

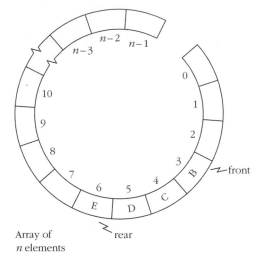

Figure 11.3–3   Circular queue design

Finally, dequeue B, C, D, and E:

Front↗ ↖Rear

What happens if F comes along? The linear structure of the array leaves F nowhere to go even though the six-element array is empty! It does not matter that the array is limited to a small number of cells. In a **volatile queue**, one with repeated calls to enqueue and dequeue, this problem eventually recurs. The most common solution is to describe the array circularly. That is, let the **front** and **rear** indexes wrap around to the physical beginning of the array whenever necessary. The result is that the queue can always accommodate as many items as there are unoccupied slots. (This is shown in Figure 11.3–3 and in the illustrations that follow.) Now we can enqueue F, as shown.

Enqueue F:

↖Rear   Front↗

In a circular queue, **rear** can be incremented modulo the size of the array to return the **rear** to the (physical) beginning. Continuing the process, enqueue G to advance **rear** to the next vacant slot while **front** remains unchanged.

Enqueue G:

↖Rear   Front↗

The **dequeue** operation allows **front** to be incremented modulo the array size. Dequeuing F results in **front** moving to the physical beginning of the queue.

Dequeue F:

G					

Front↗   ↖Rear

There is one further subtlety to the circular design. What happens if G is now dequeued?

Dequeue G:

Front↗ ↖Rear

The queue is empty, a condition we can test by finding out whether **front** equals **rear**.

Now consider what would happen if we were to enqueue six items:

Enqueue ABCDEF:

F	A	B	C	D	E

Front↗ ↖Rear

Hmm... with this design an empty queue is indistinguishable from a full queue! Of the several solutions to this problem, one is designing the queue structure to include an additional field called **queue_count** that always holds the number of items in the queue. **queue_count** is incremented at each **enqueue** operation and decremented for each **dequeue** operation. An empty queue has a **queue_count** of 0 and a full queue has a **queue_count** equal to the maximum number of elements allowed on the queue. This is a reasonable solution despite the disadvantage of having to manage the count field.

A more common solution is to leave a gap (an empty slot) that always precedes the logical beginning of the queue. **front** always points to this slot and is always positioned at the slot before the first item in the queue. **rear** is always positioned at the last item. This solution is shown next.

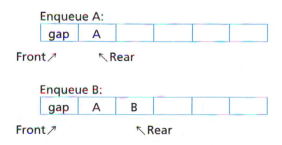

Enqueue A:

gap	A				

Front↗   ↖Rear

Enqueue B:

gap	A	B			

Front↗   ↖Rear

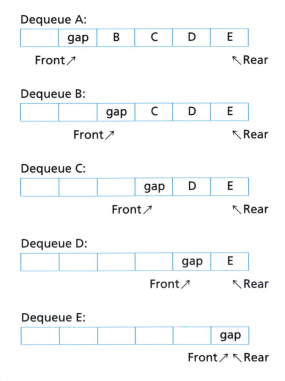

Enqueue C:

| gap | A | B | C | | |

Front ↗   ↖ Rear

Enqueue D:

| gap | A | B | C | D | |

Front ↗   ↖ Rear

Enqueue E:

| gap | A | B | C | D | E |

Front ↗   ↖ Rear

The queue is full because adding another item would close the gap. Thus, a full queue is one in which an *attempt* to enqueue causes **front** to equal **rear**.

What happens as the queue is emptied? Successive dequeues produce the following.

Dequeue A:

| | gap | B | C | D | E |

Front ↗   ↖ Rear

Dequeue B:

| | | gap | C | D | E |

Front ↗   ↖ Rear

Dequeue C:

| | | | gap | D | E |

Front ↗   ↖ Rear

Dequeue D:

| | | | | gap | E |

Front ↗   ↖ Rear

Dequeue E:

| | | | | | gap |

Front ↗ ↖ Rear

Thus, in an empty queue **front** equals **rear**, which is distinct from a full queue. We use this technique in the implementation that follows on the next few pages.

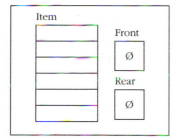

a. After `create_queue`

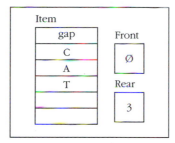

b. After enqueue "CAT"

Figure 11.3–4   A queue as
an array-based structure

Now that we understand how the queue is designed, we can describe the queue
data structure itself. Like the stack, the queue has many possible representations.
We use a data structure consisting of an array to hold the queue items and
integer fields to represent **front** and **rear** (see Figure 11.3–4). The following
definitions are contained in a header file called **queue.h**.

```
/* queue.h:  header for ADT queue package                       */

#define MAX_Q 100                    /*  Arbitrary size of the queue  */

typedef struct  q_type  {
        ITEM_TYPE item [ MAX_Q ];
        int     front;/* Always points to the item prior to the front */
        int     rear;                  /* Always points to the rear */
     }  Q_TYPE;

                                        /*  ADT Queue Prototypes  */
void    create_queue ( Q_TYPE *queue );
void    destroy_queue ( Q_TYPE *queue );
```

```
BOOLEAN empty_queue    ( Q_TYPE  *queue );
BOOLEAN full_queue     ( Q_TYPE  *queue );
void    enqueue        ( Q_TYPE  *queue,  ITEM_TYPE  new_item );
void    dequeue        ( Q_TYPE  *queue,  ITEM_TYPE  *old_item );
```

Consider the implementation of the queue functions. As we did with the stack, we store the queue data items in an array. The **create_queue** function does not actually allocate the queue; this is done at compile time. Instead, this function initializes the queue's indexes, **front** and **rear**.

```
/******************************************************************************
* Function name:     create_queue                                           *
* Description:       Initialize queue.                                       *
*                                                                           *
* Input parameters:  queue, new_item                                        *
* Output parameters: queue initialized                                      *
* Return value:      none                                                    *
******************************************************************************/

void create_queue ( Q_TYPE   *queue )
{
  queue->front  =  0;
  queue->rear   =  0;
}
```

In this implementation, the **destroy_queue** function cannot actually destroy the queue; all it can do is to reinitialize the **front** and **rear** indexes.

```
/******************************************************************************
* Function name:     destroy_queue                                          *
* Description:       Logically remove queue contents.                       *
*                                                                           *
* Input parameters:  queue                                                  *
* Output parameters: queue destroyed                                        *
* Return value:      none                                                    *
******************************************************************************/

void destroy_queue ( Q_TYPE   *queue )
{
  queue->front  =  0;
  queue->rear   =  0;
}
```

The **BOOLEAN** function **empty_queue** allows the applications programmer to prevent **queue underflow**. As we just saw, the queue is empty if **front** equals **rear**.

```
/***********************************************************************
 * Function name:     empty_queue                                      *
 * Description:       Test whether any items are on the queue.         *
 *                                                                     *
 * Input parameters:  queue                                            *
 * Output parameters: none                                             *
 * Return value:      TRUE if queue is empty; FALSE if any item is on queue *
 ***********************************************************************/

BOOLEAN empty_queue ( Q_TYPE  *queue )
{
  return ( queue->front  ==  queue->rear  ?  TRUE  :  FALSE );
}
```

As `empty_queue` does for queue underflow, the `BOOLEAN` function `full_queue` allows the applications programmer to prevent **queue overflow**. Recall that the queue is full if the next available rear position—modulo the size of the queue—is equal to the front of the queue.

```
/***********************************************************************
 * Function name:     full_queue                                       *
 * Description:       Test whether queue is full.                      *
 *                                                                     *
 * Input parameters:  queue                                            *
 * Output parameters: none                                             *
 * Return value:      TRUE if queue is full; FALSE if space is available *
 ***********************************************************************/

BOOLEAN full_queue ( Q_TYPE  *queue )
{
  return ( ( queue->rear + 1) % MAX_Q  ==  queue->front  ?  TRUE : FALSE );
}
```

Query: Assume that the queue holds the following items:

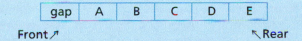

| gap | A | B | C | D | E |

Front ↗   ↖ Rear

Is the queue full?

RESPONSE: Yes. `rear` has index value 5, whereas `MAX_Q` equals 6. Thus (**(rear+1) % MAX_Q**) is the same as ((5 + 1) % 6), which equals 0. `front` now has index 0 so the queue is full.

The `enqueue` function works as follows. First, find the next position in which to make an insertion. Because `queue->rear` is the index of the current rear of the queue, increment it modulo `MAX_Q`. Then insert `new_item` at this new location, as shown next.

```
/*****************************************************************************
 * Function name:       enqueue                                              *
 * Description:         Insert item on rear of queue.                        *
 *                                                                           *
 * Input parameters:    queue, new_item                                      *
 * Output parameters:   queue with new item at rear                          *
 * Return value:        none                                                 *
 *                                                                           *
 * Preconditions:       queue not full                                       *
 * Postconditions:      queue will have new rear item                        *
 *****************************************************************************/

void enqueue ( Q_TYPE   *queue,  ITEM_TYPE   new_item )
{
   queue->rear   =   ++queue->rear % MAX_Q;              /*  Increment rear */
   queue->item [ queue->rear ]   =   new_item;           /*  Insert new_item */
}
```

To `dequeue`, first increment `front` by 1 (modulo `MAX_Q`). Then return as `old_item` the item indexed by `front`.

```
/*****************************************************************************
 * Function name:       dequeue                                              *
 * Description:         Remove item from front of queue.                     *
 *                                                                           *
 * Input parameters:    queue                                                *
 * Output parameters:   queue with front item removed, former front item     *
 * Return value:        none                                                 *
 *                                                                           *
 * Preconditions:       queue not empty                                      *
 * Postconditions:      queue will have front item removed                   *
 *****************************************************************************/

void dequeue ( Q_TYPE *queue,  ITEM_TYPE *old_item )
{
   queue->front   =   ++queue->front % MAX_Q;            /*  Increment front */
   *old_item    =   queue->item [ queue->front ];        /*  Pass front item */
}
```

PERSPECTIVE

Even though the empty_queue and full_queue functions are part of the ADT software package, systems programmers sometimes include an extra level of security to maintain the integrity of the ADT. This might be specific code to check for a full or empty queue in the enqueue and dequeue functions themselves, providing a fail-safe mechanism in case the applications programmer forgets to check the status of the ADT before changing it. These modifications are included in the exercises that follow.

EXERCISES 11.3

Concept Check

Answer statements 1 through 4 with true *or* false.

1. Like stack items, queue items must be the same data type.
2. Like stack items, queue items can be inserted at random locations.
3. A queue is a FIFO structure.
4. A queue can be efficiently implemented as a circular array.

For statements 5 through 8 choose the answer that best completes the statement.

5. According to the queue implementation in this section, checking for queue overflow is the responsibility of
   a. the systems programmer
   b. the applications programmer
   c. the end user
   d. the operating system
6. The purpose of the gap cell in the circular array implementation is
   a. to act as a spare cell in case the queue gets full
   b. to help to distinguish an empty queue from a full queue
   c. to store the current number of occupied queue cells
   d. to make sure that front is always ahead of rear
7. According to the text, an alternative to the gap cell is an explicit count field that always holds the number of queue items. Including this feature would require
   a. changing the data structure but not the queue functions
   b. changing the queue functions but not the data structure
   c. changing both the queue functions and the data structure
   d. changing enqueue and dequeue only
8. According to the implementation in this section, front and rear are always positioned using the scheme
   a. front points to the front item and rear is always just before the rear item
   b. front points to the front item and rear points to the rear item
   c. front is just before the front item and rear is just before the rear item
   d. front is just before the front item and rear points to the rear item

For statements 9 through 12 fill in the blanks with the right word.

9. _____ occurs when an attempt is made to put an item onto an already full queue.

10. _____ occurs when an attempt is made to remove an item from an empty queue.

11. According to the implementation in this section, an empty queue can be detected by checking whether _____.

12. According to the implementation in this section, a full queue can be detected by checking whether _____.

Set A

13. Redesign **struct q_type** to include a **queue_count** field.

14. Modify the palindrome program to allow characters and digits. For example, the string "123abba321" should be an acceptable palindrome. (Hint: Check the functions available through **ctype.h** and make a minor modification to **load_stack_and_queue**.)

15. Indicate the coding changes to the palindrome program needed to accept more than one user input string.

16. Discuss the relative merits of the gap technique and the **queue_count** technique.

Set B

17. Rewrite **dequeue** so that instead of using an output parameter, **old_item** is returned as the function's return value.

18. Rewrite **enqueue** so that it explicitly checks for overflow before attempting to add a new item. Output a warning message if there could be overflow.

19. Rewrite **dequeue** the same way—that is, output a warning message if there could be underflow.

20. Rewrite **enqueue** without using the modulo operator. When **rear** equals the end of the array, reset it to 0. Otherwise add 1. Also, remove the prefix increment operator.

21. Rewrite **dequeue** using the same techniques as in Question 20.

22. Rewrite **full_queue** so that it is more readable. For example, replace the conditional and modulo operators with more explicit code.

Set C

23. Implement any of the Set B problems on the computer.

24. Redesign and implement the queue data structure and functions to include a **queue_count** field instead of a gap as suggested in the text.

25. A **deque** (doubly ended queue) is a variant queue design that allows insertions or deletions at either end of the queue. Implementing a deque requires two additional access functions, **enqueue_front** and **dequeue_rear**. Write each of these functions.

Databases 12

Noncomputerized file management system for an insurance company.

After completing this chapter you should be able to do the following:

Learning Goals

- Distinguish between records, fields, and subfields
- Define an ADT file
- Know the difference between sequential files and random-access files and how they are used
- Establish an external file structure using the `fopen` and `fclose` functions
- Define an ADT database
- Differentiate among the functions of the layers of a database
- Distinguish between entities and attributes
- Identify a database schema and its related topics
- Distinguish between physical data models and logical data models
- Describe category and connection relationships
- Describe the entity-relationship model
- Use the elements of a relational database
- Create a simple database

Chapter Activity

Write a C program to generate a physical database for any number of people up to 100. The database should include each person's name, street address, city, state, zip code (zip+4), telephone number, and social security number. The user must be able to add, delete, and retrieve information from the database, and print its contents. Number entries must strictly conform to the following formats.

Zip code	xxxxx-xxxx
Telephone number	xxx-xxx-xxxx
Social security number	xxx-xx-xxxx

The program must also include full use of data filters.

12.1 AN OVERVIEW OF FILES AND DATABASES

Introduction

You have already been introduced to data structures including arrays, stacks, and queues. You have also learned about data types, some of which (such as `char` and `double`) are standard in C. Others are created by the applications programmer with the `struct`, `typedef`, and `enum` declarations.

You can organize items with similar data structures. However, how would you organize items of different structures? For example, how would you organize the academic records of all the students at your university? How would you look up an individual student? Who should have access to your student record? Who should have authorization to change a student record? An understanding of records, files, and databases will help you answer these questions.

12.1.1 Records

Before considering file organization, let's investigate a simple record. A **record** is a collection of related fields. Each field contains data items that can be as simple as an ASCII character or a floating-point number, or as complicated as an array or another record. Every record contains at least one field. Examples of records are academic records, employee records, inventory records, and sports records.

Figure 12.1–1 shows an employee record as an 80-column punched card (antiquated but visual). The first three fields (columns 1 through 12, columns 13 through 20, and columns 21 through 25) represent *last name*, *first name*, and *middle name*, respectively. The fourth field (columns 26 through 34) represents the *social security number*. The fifth, sixth, seventh, and eighth fields (columns 35 through 50, columns 51 through 60, columns 61 through 62, and columns 63 through 67) represent the *street address*, the *city*, the *state*, and the *zip code*, respectively. The ninth field (columns 68 through 72) represents the *rate of pay*. Columns 73 through 80 are for identification. Today such records are kept on disk, tape, or CD-ROM rather than punched cards.

A student record would look like the record shown in Figure 12.1–1. You could expect to find the student's name, address, and social security number, each as a separate field. Other information might include high school, SAT scores, major, minor, GPA, and honors status, each as a separate field. You might find a list of courses taken and grades by semester, and courses in progress. These last two fields are themselves records because courses taken by semester, for example, include the (sub)fields of course number, course name, and grade received.

We have already seen that in C records such as those above are created using the `struct` declaration. For the employee record in Figure 12.1–1, the C structure might look as follows (recall that C strings need an extra byte for the NULL character).

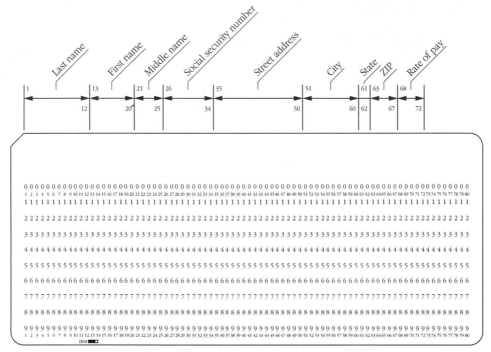

Figure 12.1–1 Employee record on a punched card

```
typedef    char   LAST_TYP[ 13 ];     /*  Define 12 characters: Cols  1-12  */
typedef    char   FIRST_TYP[ 9 ];     /*  Define 8 characters: Cols 13-20   */
typedef    char   MID_TYP[ 6 ];       /*  Define 5 characters: Cols 21-25   */
typedef    char   SS_TYP[ 10 ];       /*  Define 9 characters: Cols 26-34   */
typedef    char   STREET_TYP[ 17 ];   /*  Define 16 characters: Cols 35-50  */
typedef    char   CITY_TYP[ 11 ];     /*  Define 10 characters: Cols 51-60  */
typedef    char   STATE_TYP[ 3 ];     /*  Define 2 characters: Cols 61-62   */
typedef    char   ZIP_TYP[ 6 ];       /*  Define 5 characters: Cols 63-67   */

struct     employee     {                  /*  Define  employee  record  */
    LAST_TYP          lastname;
    FIRST_TYP         firstname;
    MID_TYP           midname;
    SS_TYP            ss_numb;
    STREET_TYP        street;
    CITY_TYP          city;
    STATE_TYP         state;
    ZIP_TYP           zip;
    float             pay_rate;
}
```

The declarations formed by `typedef char` have associated with them character strings of the lengths specified, which correspond to those shown in Figure 12.1–1, for last, first, and middle names, and for street, city, and state. The last field, `pay_rate`, must be declared as `float` because of the real-value calculations that are anticipated.

A student record could have a more complex C structure than an employee record because some of the record fields are themselves records. One structure for the student record might be the following, called `student1` for student record version 1.

```
typedef   char   NAME_TYP[ 26 ];         /* Define 25 chars for full name  */
typedef   char   ADDR_TYP[ 34 ];     /* Define 33 chars for full address  */
typedef   char   CRS_NUM_TYP[ 9 ];    /* Define 8 chars for course code  */
typedef   char   CRS_NAM_TYP[ 16 ];   /* Define 15 chars for course name  */
typedef   char   CRS_GRAD_TYP[ 3 ];   /* Define 2 chars for course grade  */

struct    course    {                        /* Define course  record  */
  CRS_NUM_TYP       crs_code;        /*  Field course code declared  */
  CRS_NAM_TYP       crs_name;        /*  Field course name declared  */
  CRS_GRAD_TYP      crs_grade;       /*  Field course grade declared  */
  float             sem_gpa;       /*  Field for semester gpa declared  */
}

struct    student1  {                        /*  Define  student  record #1  */
  NAME_TYP          name;                 /*  Field name declared  */
  ADDR_TYP          address;         /*  Field address declared  */
  SS_TYP            ss_numb;         /*  Field ss number declared  */
  float             gpa;          /*  Field gpa declared as float  */
  struct   course   course_past;         /*  Fields course past and  */
  struct   course   course_curr;    /*  current declared as structures  */
}
```

Note that the `student1` structure has six fields and the `course` structure has four fields that are really subfields of the two subfields of the `student1` structure. We use more detailed record structures later in this chapter.

12.1.2 Files

A declaration of student records including only one or two students presents no difficulty. Suppose that at Anytown College there are 8,000 student records. How should they be organized? One way is to make a list of records organized either randomly or according to a scheme and put the list in a file. A **file** is an abstract data type whose elements are its records. We can initialize it (go to its beginning), add to it, and retrieve and delete from it. A file organized in such a way that the records must be processed one by one from the beginning of the file to the end is called a **sequential file**.

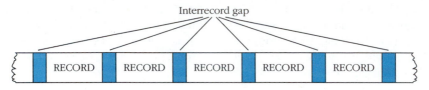

Figure 12.1–2 Records stored on magnetic tape

Figure 12.1–2 shows how five records are stored sequentially on magnetic tape. Between each record is an interrecord gap that separates one record from another. At the end of the sequence is an end-of-file (EOF) marker that indicates the conclusion of the file. The marker is in the form of a control character supplied by the system and does not affect the information the program manipulates.

In contrast to sequential files, **random-access files** (or direct-access files) enable the processing of one record without the review of other records. One of the record fields is set as a **key field** or **index:** a table of indexes holding access addresses. For example, for student records a key field might be the student's social security number, which gives you access to the record. An example of a random access structure with a built-in index table is an **array**. The index of the array both identifies a record and gives you access to it by its address. (Arrays are discussed in Chapter 7.) Figure 12.1–3 shows how an index can be used.

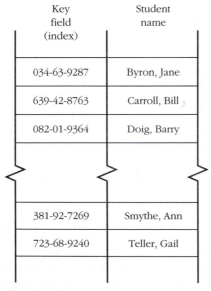

Figure 12.1–3 Random-access index table

A program may need one or more files to do its work. The **printf** and **scanf** functions in C are two examples of using files to write and read. The files are transparent to the applications programmer because by default they are, respectively, the monitor and the keyboard, which are automatically opened when a program starts running. You access these files by using the **#include <stdio.h>** directive, which includes declaration of the standard input and output files for C.

However, what happens when you need to access files that are not automatically opened by C? Such files are called **external files** and must be opened by the applications programmer before they are used. The function that opens an external file is **fopen**, which takes the form

```
fopen (   "filename",   "mode" )
```

where **filename** is the name of the file to be opened and **mode** specifies how the file is to be used. Some common modes are

> **r**   for reading
> **w**   for writing
> **a**   for appending

A **text file** is composed of bits representing ASCII characters; a **binary file** is just a sequence of bits. To specify the type of file to be opened, text or binary, you append a **t** or a **b** to the mode specifier. For example, **rt** opens a file to be read as a text file; **wb** opens a file to be written as a binary file. If the **t** or **b** are excluded, the default is text. The **fopen** function returns a pointer to data type **FILE**, which is declared in **stdio.h**. If the file cannot be opened, the **fopen** function returns **NULL**, a constant equivalent to a zero pointer. After you open a file and the processing is completed, you should close the file. To do this use

```
fclose ( file_pointer )
```

where **file_pointer** is the variable to which **fopen** points. Here is a code segment illustrating the sequence you need to open and close a file in C.

```
#include <stdio.h>                         /* For preprocessing FILE */
. . .                                      /* Ordinary processing   */
FILE   *tree;                 /* Declares tree as a pointer to FILE */
tree  =  fopen ( "treefile", "at" ); /* Opens file called treefile */
                                           /* for appending text    */
. . .                                      /* File processing       */
fclose ( tree );                     /* Close file called treefile */
```

In this case, the *treefile* file is opened as a text file to be appended to a file. If the file can not be opened, **fopen** returns **NULL**. If the file can be opened, **fopen** returns a pointer that is assigned to the **tree** variable. After the processing, the file called **treefile** is closed by the **fclose** function.

Query: Why is the following code sequence incorrect?

```
FILE x;
x = fopen ( "name", "wb" );
```

RESPONSE: `fopen` returns the address of the file so `x` must be declared as a pointer to a variable of the `FILE` type.

It is instructive to show the various uses of files in a single program. Program 12.1–1, a weight-reduction program, does this and uses two new functions: `fprintf` and `fscanf`. These are more general versions of `printf` and `scanf`. The `printf` and `scanf` functions assume that the respective files are `stdout` and `stdin`, which are the monitor and keyboard. The function forms are as follows.

```
fprintf ( file_pointer,"format", arguments )
fscanf ( file_pointer,"format", &arguments )
```

The `fprintf` function writes the values of its arguments in the specified format to the file indicated. The `fscanf` function reads the list of values of the arguments in the specified format from the

Program 12.1–1 uses some programmer-defined functions to create a file and to process information. Specifically, the program creates a file of strings (representing names) and corresponding floating-point values (representing body weights). It then retrieves the created file as an input file; reduces each value by some percent (say, 15%); and stores the name, the original weight, and the reduced weight in an output file.

PROGRAM 12.1–1

```
/**********************************************************************************
* Title:      weight reduction                                                  *
* Filename:   wghtrduc.c                                                         *
*                                                                               *
* Description: Creates two files consisting of records with names of individuals *
*              and their corresponding initial weights.  As part of a weight reduction *
*              plan, these individuals are to lose a percentage of the indicated weight. *
*              An output file is created that contains the name, initial weight, and *
*              goal weight of each individual, and this output file's contents are printed.*
*                                                                               *
* Input:      string of characters for name,  a number for weight               *
* Output:     file containing name, initial and goal weights,  printout of same  *
* Process:    create an initial data file for input, read file, calculate goal weights, *
*              save in output file, and print same                               *
*                                                                               *
* Written by: ...                                              Date: ...         *
**********************************************************************************/
```

```c
#include  <stdio.h>
#include  <string.h>

#define   NAME_LEN   12                                            /*  Length of name  */
#define   FACTOR     0.85                  /*  Reduction factor to achieve goal weight  */
                                           /*  Note: 15% loss implies FACTOR is 85%  */
                                                       /*  Global declarations  */


typedef   struct  {
    char       name[NAME_LEN];
    float      weight_curr;
    float      weight_goal;
} record;

FILE    *filein;
FILE    *fileout;

int     count;
char    flag[5] = "DONE\0";

                                                    /*  Function Prototypes  */
void  create_file  ( int  *total_ptr );
void  process_info ( int  total );
void  print_file   ( int  total );

main ( )
{                                                          /*  Begin main  */
    int   total;                             /*  The number of records in a file  */

    create_file ( &total );
    process_info ( total );
    print_file ( total );
    printf ( "\n\n\n\n\n\t\t\t\t\t\t\tGood-bye!\n" );
    return (0);
}                                                          /*  End main  */



/*************************************************************************
*   Function name:      create_file                                      *
*   Description:        Creates an initial file called  initfile.dat  containing the name  *
*                       (up to 12 characters) and current weight of any number of          *
*                       individuals.                                      *
*                                                                        *
*   Input parameters:   none                                             *
*   Output parameters:  total                                            *
*   Return value:       none                                             *
*************************************************************************/
```

```
void  create_file  (  int  *total_ptr  )                          /*  Function header  */
{

    record person;

    fileout  =  fopen  (  "initfile.dat",  "w"  );

    *total_ptr = 0;

    printf  (  "\n\nEnter name of person, or \n"  );
    printf  (  "DONE, in upper case, when data entry is complete! \n\n"  );
    printf  (  "\tEnter first name of person>: "  );
    scanf  (  "%s",  person.name  );

    while  (  strcmp( flag, person.name )  != 0  ) {
      printf  (  "\tEnter current weight>:  "  );
      scanf  (  "%f",  &person.weight_curr  );

      fprintf  (  fileout,  "%s\n%f\n",  person.name,  person.weight_curr  );

      printf  (  "\n\nEnter name of person, or \n"  );
      printf  (  "DONE, in upper case, when data entry is complete! \n\n"  );
      printf  (  "\tEnter name of person>: ");
      scanf  (  "%s",   person.name  );

      (*total_ptr)++;                                /*  Increment record number  */
    }

    fclose  (  fileout );
}                                                     /*  End function   create_file  */



/*****************************************************************************************
 *  Function name:      process_file                                                    *
 *  Description:        Reads information from  initfile.dat  and creates a new file     *
 *                      called  datafile.dat  containing name, current weight,           *
 *                      and goal weight of all individuals.                              *
 *                                                                                       *
 *  Input parameters:  total                                                            *
 *  Output parameters: none                                                             *
 *  Return value:      none                                                             *
 *****************************************************************************************/

void  process_info  (  int  total  )                             /*  Function header  */
{
    record           person;
```

```
    filein  =  fopen (  "initfile.dat",  "r" );
    fileout =  fopen (  "datafile.dat",  "w" );

    count   =  0;
    do  {
        fscanf( filein,  "%s\n%f\n",  person.name,  &person.weight_curr );

        person.weight_goal  =  FACTOR * person.weight_curr;

        fprintf   (  fileout, "%s\n%f\n%f\n", person.name, person.weight_curr,
                                     person.weight_goal  );
        count++;
    }   while ( count < total );

    fclose (  filein );
    fclose (  fileout );

}                                                          /* End function  process_info */

/*******************************************************************************
 *  Function name:       print_file                                           *
 *  Description:         Prints a table of all information in the file called  datafile.  *
 *                                                                            *
 *  Input parameters:  total                                                  *
 *  Output parameters: none                                                   *
 *  Return value:       none                                                  *
 *******************************************************************************/

void  print_file (  int  total )                            /*  Function header */
{
    record person;

    filein  =  fopen (  "datafile.dat",  "r" );

    printf(  "\n\n\n          Person Name\t Current Weight\t    Goal Weight" );
    printf(  "\n          -----------\t --------------\t    ----------" );

    count  =  0;
    fscanf( filein,  "%s\n%f\n%f\n",  &person.name,  &person.weight_curr,
                            &person.weight_goal  );
    while ( count < total )  {
        printf(  "\n\t%12s\t\t%7.1f\t\t%7.1f",   person.name,   person.weight_curr,
                            person.weight_goal );
        count++;
        fscanf( filein,  "%s\n%f\n%f\n",  &person.name,  &person.weight_curr,
                            &person.weight_goal  );
    }
```

```
printf (  "\n        ------------\t -------------\t     -----------\n" );

fclose (  filein );
```

```
}                                                /* End function   print_file */
```

12.1.3 Databases

What is a database? Is it just a collection of information? In Sections 12.1.1 and 12.1.2 we suggest that all the student records at Anytown College be put in a file with either sequential or random access. This is fine but very limiting. How do we access all the students taking History 101 or all the students living in Ohio? Although files are a valuable abstract data type (ADT), we need a different ADT that allows us not only to store, add, delete, and retrieve information, but to be selective in accessing it. (ADTs are discussed in Chapter 11.)

The **database** data type is needed for bulk storage of data because it provides the flexibility to accommodate user needs and applications. The student records at Anytown College must be stored so that each element of the student records is accessible for 1 student or for all 8,000 students. As an example, we should be able to determine which students at the college have a GPA of more than 3.5 or to select those students whose GPA is less than 2.0. What we need is not just a file but a database. Figure 12.1–4 illustrates this concept.

How do you create a database? There are several aspects to consider. The **physical database** is viewed as a data structure. The way information is stored in the physical database depends on the needs of its **end users** (or customers). The information retrieved from the physical database has to be meaningful to them. **Applications software** must be written to meet the end user's needs.

Suppose the physical database consists of the 8,000 student records at Anytown College. The registrar of the college needs access to the identifying information for each student (such as name and social security number) and to the student's

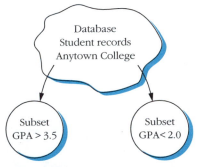

Figure 12.1–4 Selection from a database

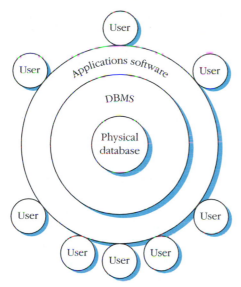

Figure 12.1–5   Layered concept of a database

academic record. You could write applications software that enables the registrar (the end user) to get this information from the physical database.

However, should the registrar be privy to each student's financial background and other personal information? Should an applications programmer have access to this information? Indeed there may be no control over the access to the physical database. For this reason, we have an intermediate software layer, the **database management system (DBMS)** (introduced in Section 1.1.1), which not only controls access to the physical database but also specifies how the information is to be managed. Thus the physical database is managed through a *software shell* (the DBMS) so that programmers can write applications software using the DBMS (not the physical database) for the end user. Figure 12.1–5 shows a layered conception of a database, allowing you to view its raw physical state, its management system, its applications software, and the user's perspective.

12.1.4 Database Entities and Attributes

As a repository of data to serve the needs of its users, a database must be accessible, accurate, and secure. The DBMS must provide an efficient and convenient environment for users to add, to retrieve, and to delete data to and from the database. The physical database is almost always on disk, magnetic tape, or CD-ROM, providing easy access by a computer.

A database represents a model in which an **entity**, abstract or concrete, is an object. An entity has **attributes** that are items of information, much as a structure has fields. With the STUDENT entity might be associated three attributes: social security number, name, and GPA. The entity might then be defined something like

STUDENT[768]
    012345678
    WILLIAM JAMESON
    3.46

The STUDENT[768] entity changes when William Jameson graduates and is replaced by another student.

The logical design of a database is called its **database schema** or simply its **schema**. For a relational database (see Section 12.2), a schema is essentially a logical set of tables of the data types used, giving the names of entities and attributes and the relationships among them, and supplying a framework for the values of the data items. Database schemas are classified as **internal** when they correspond to physical databases and **external** when they correspond to data in applications programs. A **conceptual** schema is an integrated view of data linking internal and external schemas.

The capability to change the internal schema as needed without affecting the external schema is called **data independence** and ideally exists at the physical as well as the logical level. Without data independence, a slight change of the schema would entail the redesigning of the entire schema. Schemas are generally written in a **data definition language**, which generates the schema tables stored in a file called a data dictionary. The **data dictionary** does not hold the physical data itself but instead holds information about the data. It is always accessed before any change to the physical data is made. Figure 12.1–6 illustrates some of these concepts.

PERSPECTIVE

In databases, distributed networks, and operating systems, any change in the state of the system caused by a transaction should have the **a**cid properties. These are **a**tomic (an all or nothing change), **c**onsistent (a correct state transformation), **i**solated (free of concurrency anomalies), and **d**urable (transaction results maintained in case of system failure). [1]

We encourage you to consult more advanced references on the topic of databases. You will find that given the complexities of databases, many creative schemas and logical models have been devised. (Section 2 of this chapter presents a sampling of these models.) It is left to the imagination of future computer scientists to create new database models that are even more comprehensive and efficient.

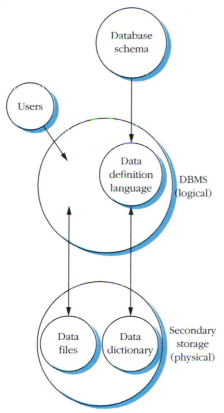

Figure 12.1–6   Database system showing data independence

Concept Check

Answer statements 1 through 4 with true *or* false.

1. A field in a structure is the same as an attribute of an entity.
2. A database management system is needed to make applications programming easier.
3. From the computing standpoint, a file is a database.
4. A data dictionary is a file of schema tables.

For statements 5 through 8 choose the answer that best completes the statement.

5. Logically, a file is a
   a. collection of records
   b. set of attributes
   c. collection of entities
   d. dynamically linked list of nodes

6. The overall logical design of a database is called a
   a. list
   b. logical database
   c. schema
   d. data set
7. A correct way to open a file named `happyfile` is the C statement
   a. `fopen( "happyfile", r );`
   b. `fopen( "wt", "happyfile" );`
   c. `fopen( "happyfile", "rb" );`
   d. `fopen( happyfile, wt );`
8. Attributes are associated with
   a. records
   b. databases
   c. data definition languages
   d. entities

For statements 9 through 12 fill in the blanks with the right word.
9. Two requirements of a database management system are _____ and _____.
10. Only the _____ of a database has access to the physical data.
11. A collection of records is called _____ .
12. Bulk data is associated with the _____ part of a database.

Set A
13. You need to open an external file named `data`. Write the C code to do this.
14. Close the file in Question 13.
15. Describe some advantages of sequential files.
16. Describe some advantages of random access files.
17. What is an index?
18. Describe the difference between a database and a database management system.

Set B
19. Explain how entities and their attributes can be modeled in C.
20. How might you develop a schema for a telephone directory database?
21. Given a physical database with defined fields, explain how you might access it.
22. Explain why the argument of the `fclose` function is a pointer.
23. What is the difference between `printf` and `fprintf`?
24. What is the difference between `scanf` and `fscanf`?

Set C
25. Write a program to create a text file containing the first 12 letters of the English alphabet.
26. Read the file generated in Question 25 and print it in reverse order.
27. Use Program 12.1–1 for at least 20 individuals.

Figure 12.2–1 Teacher-student entities

12.2 LOGICAL DATABASE MODELS

Introduction

A model highlights important aspects of a subject and obscures unimportant aspects of it. A model of a ship shows the hull, mast, and sails but not the frame of a porthole. A **data model** emphasizes features of interest to the user and makes its interaction with a database management system transparent. Data models can be physical or logical. **Physical data models** show how the data structures are organized so that their resources are optimized. **Logical data models** interpret the data in the context of the application. Databases are concerned with the data entities, their attributes, and the relationships among entities. Figure 12.2–1 shows two entities, a teacher and a student, and the relationship between them.

12.2.1 Overview of Logical Models

Logical data models can be used for documenting and integrating data resources, designing information systems, and designing and implementing a physical database. A good logical data model is independent of the database management system and can be moved from one management system to another. A data model should be detailed enough to do the job but not so detailed that it becomes hard to use.

A link or bond among two or more entities is called a **relationship**. The relationships among entities are of two types: Category and connection. **Category relationships** are relations among similar entities. **Connection relationships** are relations among dissimilar entities. Consider the following three entities: College, Student, ChemMajor. Because the ChemMajor is a particular Student there is a category relationship between them. Category relationships relate a generic entity (Student) to a subtype (ChemMajor). The attribute *major* must be associated with Student to distinguish ChemMajor from other majors. Figure 12.2–2 shows the category relationship between Student and ChemMajor. The circle shows the attribute that determines the subtype.

A connection relationship exists between Student and College, and between ChemMajor and College. Connection relationships have action names such as "College *enrolls* Student" or "ChemMajor *is enrolled in* College." Figure 12.2–3 shows how these two entity pairs are connected. The dot at the end of the connection lines shows the direction of the action.

There are many approaches to logical data modes. We explore a few of them next: the entity-relationship model, the network model, the hierarchical model, and the relational model.

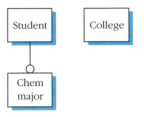

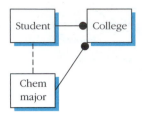

Figure 12.2–2 Example of a category relationship

Figure 12.2–3 Example of a connection relationship

12.2.2 The Entity-Relationship Model

Recall that a data entity is a real or abstract object described by a collection of attributes. A collection of entities is called an **entity set**. For example, the collection of all students taking a particular course forms an entity set. Recall also that a bond among different entities is a relationship. The collection of relationships forms a **relationship set**. The interaction of entity sets with relationship sets is the basis of the **entity-relationship (E–R)** model.

Consider two entity sets X and Y. Let $X = \{x_1, x_2, x_3, \ldots, x_n\}$ where each x_i represents an entity in set X. Let $Y = \{y_1, y_2, y_3, \ldots, y_m\}$ where each y_j represents an entity in set Y. If each x_i is related to exactly one y_j and each y_i is related to exactly one x_j, then a **one-to-one relationship** exists between entity sets X and Y. Figure 12.2–4 shows the one-to-one relationship between entity sets X and Y.

When viewed collectively, all the entities in set X form a relationship with the entities in set Y. Likewise, all the entities in set Y form a relationship with the entities in set X. This collection of relationships forms the relationship set between the two entity sets and is often illustrated by a diamond. Entity sets are customarily represented by rectangles with their attributes shown as ovals or circles. The lines show the category or connection. Figure 12.2–5 shows two entity sets, Student and Student_ID, with Identifier as the relationship set. The two arrows show that the relation is one-to-one.

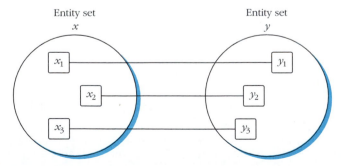

Figure 12.2–4 One-to-one entity relationship

Figure 12.2–5 Entities with identifier as relationship set

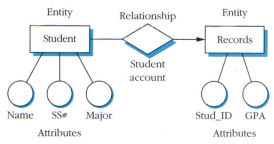

Figure 12.2–6 Many-to-one relationship

Relationships are not always one-to-one. They can be many-to-one, one-to-many, or many-to-many. This means that many entities can be related to one entity, one entity can be related to many entities, or an entity can be related to many entities and many entities can be related to it. Figure 12.2–6 shows a many-to-one relationship. In Figures 12.2–5 and 12.2–6 the relationships are assumed to be **binary relationships**—that is, confined to two entity sets. It is probable in the real world that relationships are ternary (three entities) or of even higher dimension. The relationship set must accommodate all the entities involved. Figure 12.2–7 shows a four-dimensional relationship among entities.

To implement E-R models, you must convert each relationship set and each entity set to a **data table**. The set of all data tables forms the database for the E-R model. Tables tagged as entity sets have the entities as their rows with the attributes in columns. Tables tagged as relationship sets have one or more common attributes identified as a **principal key** for each entity in the relationship. The rows of the table identify the entity and the columns specify the principal key attributes, as explained in Section 12.2–4.

12.2.3 The Hierarchical and Network Models

Recall that a record is a data structure whose information is found in its fields. An entity contains information in its attributes, and a **segment** contains information in its **data fields**. If two records are related, the relationship is represented by a **link** joining them. A database model in the form of a tree where the nodes of the tree are the segments and the branches of the tree are the links is called a **hierarchical data model**. Each child must have a link that points (shown by an arrow) to its parent. The tree has a hierarchical structure determined by a

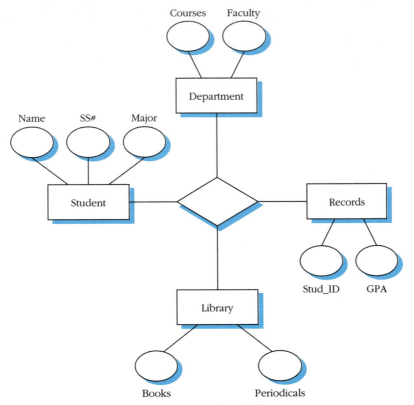

Figure 12.2–7 Four-dimensional relationship

sequence key that is part of the segment. A parent may or may not point to a child even though it is linked to it. Figure 12.2–8 illustrates the hierarchical model.

The hierarchical model is like the entity-relationship model. In each case entities (segments) are related (linked) to entities. For example, the E-R diagram of Figure 12.2–9(a) is equivalent to the hierarchical diagram of Figure 12.2–9(b). Connection relationships are formed by parent-to-child relationships in the tree structure, which form one-to-many relationships.

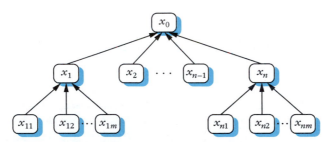

Figure 12.2–8 Hierarchical data model

(a)

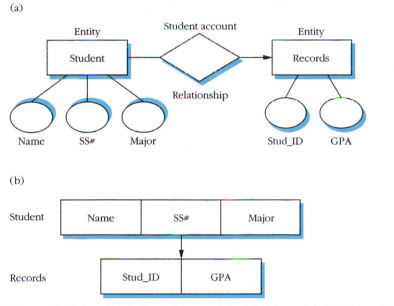

(b)

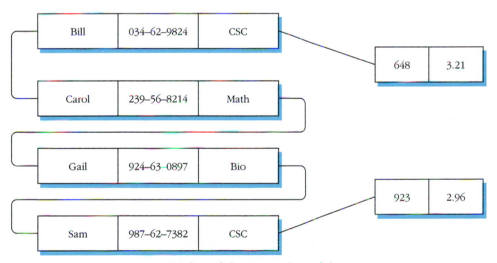

Figure 12.2–9   Equivalent data models: (a) E-R model; (b) hierarchical model

Figure 12.2–10   An organization of the network model

The **network data model** is like the hierarchical model with the exception that the relationships are not based on a tree structure. Instead, any segment can be related or linked to any other segment. Figure 12.2–10 shows how a network model can be visualized using six segments.

12.2.4 The Relational Model

The most popular logical data model in use today is the relational model, which is noted for its consistency, simplicity, and data independence. The **relational data model** is composed of relations, attributes, domains, keys, tuples, and the representation of these elements. A **relation** is a table of rows and columns. Each *column* of the table is an **attribute**. The **domain** of each attribute is the collection of values that can be assigned to a particular attribute. A **principal key** is one or more attribute values that uniquely identify an entity instance. A **tuple** is an ordered sequence of elements as in the ordered pair (x, y), the triple (x, y, z), or the 6-tuple (p, q, r, s, t, u). Each *row* is an entity instance represented by a tuple. Typically, relations have a **representation** when you name the relation followed by its attributes within parentheses with the principal key highlighted.

Consider a relation called Student that has four attributes: Name, Ident, Major, and Average. The domains are identified as follows.

Name: The set of all last names of students enrolled at a particular
               college
Ident: The set of all nine-digit social security numbers used to identify
               students
Major: The set of all possible majors at the college in which Student is
               enrolled, including undeclared
Average: The grade point average expressed as a decimal number between
               0.00 and 4.00, inclusive

The representation is described as

Student(NAME, Ident, Major, Average)

where the uppercase NAME signifies the principal key. Table 12.2–1 shows a typical relational data model for this information, called an **instance table**. The rows are 4-tuples that uniquely identify each student. There are six students (entity instances) each having four attributes: Name, Ident, Major, and Average. The entity Student (the table) defines the relation. Table 12.2–2 defines another relation for the entity Courses. There are five courses (entity instances) described with three attributes: CourseId, Teacher, and Core. These attributes represent

Table 12.2–1 Instance Table for Student

NAME	IDENT	MAJOR	AVERAGE
Elliot	258392943	History	3.94
Baker	934233236	Undecided	2.38
Wilson	035893828	Physics	2.84
Stevens	934562845	English	3.36
Maggiore	384572934	Physics	3.47
Smythe	648728383	History	2.74

Table 12.2–2 Instance Table for Courses

COURSEID	TEACHER	CORE
Engl204	Allen	No
Phys100	Strivsky	No
Hist150	Mullen	Yes
Engl100	Conte	No
Engl101	Allen	Yes

course identification, the instructor for the course, and an indication of whether the course is a core course required of *all* majors.

In a relational database you can form category relationships for relations such as Student and Course. The process can become complicated when it is difficult to distinguish entities from their attributes (subtypes). Connection relationships, however, are easier to establish. You can form them by having the principal key attribute of the parent transfer into the entity of the child, as viewed from a tree structure.

For example, let *must enroll in* be the connection relationship in which the parent is Student and the child is understood to be Course. Figure 12.2–11 shows this situation. Let Major be the principal key for Student in Table 12.2–1. In this case Course takes on an ancillary attribute (Major) from Student. This results in a new relation (table), which we call CourseRequirement. Table 12.2–3 shows one possible way to represent the new relationship.

Notice that in this case, because Engl 101 and Hist 150 are required for all majors, they are duplicated as appropriate for each of the three majors shown in Table 12.2–1. The Undecided major was intentionally not listed because we assume that it is not an actual major.

Relational data models contain relational operations so that new relations can be formed from existing relations. There are many such operations: Some are

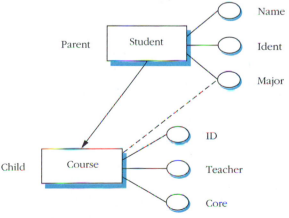

Figure 12.2–11 Parent-to-child connection relationship

Table 12.2–3 Instance Table for CourseRequirement

MAJOR	COURSEID	TEACHER	CORE
English	Engl100	Conte	No
English	Engl101	Allen	Yes
English	Engl204	Allen	No
English	Hist150	Mullen	Yes
History	Engl101	Allen	Yes
History	Hist150	Mullen	Yes
Physics	Engl101	Allen	Yes
Physics	Hist150	Mullen	Yes
Physics	Phys100	Strivsky	No

unary (one operand) and some are binary (two operands). The operands are always relations (tables). *Select* is one unary operation that chooses certain rows of a relation based on some condition. For example,

Select [from Student](Average > 3.00)

would produce a new relation as shown in Table 12.2–4. Another unary operation is *Project*, which chooses entities according to specified attributes with duplications eliminated. For example,

Project [from Student] (Major)

would produce a new relation, as shown in Table 12.2–5. Notice that duplications of Physics and History are removed in the resulting table.

A useful binary operation is *Join*, which combines two existing relations (tables) according to some condition to form a new relation. For example,

Join [Student] ((English Majors) and (Department Teacher)) [Course]

Table 12.2–4 Instance Table for Select Operation

NAME	IDENT	MAJOR	AVERAGE
Elliot	258392943	History	3.94
Stevens	934562845	English	3.36
Maggiore	384572934	Physics	3.47

Table 12.2–5 Instance Table for Project Operation

MAJOR
History
Undecided
Physics
English

Table 12.2–6 Instance Table from Join Operation (Student Teacher)

NAME	IDENT	MAJOR	AVERAGE	TEACHER
Stevens	934562845	English	3.36	Conte
Stevens	934562845	English	3.36	Allen

produces a new relation (table) with duplications removed, called StudentTeacher. Table 12.2–6 shows the result.

Of the various logical data models discussed here, the relational database model, which uses relations and relational operations, is the most popular version today and is found in many commercial database management systems. Databases need a great deal of memory. They are used extensively in the business world on systems powerful enough to accommodate them.

12.2.5 A Database Program

Program 12.2–1 shows how a simple database is constructed using arrays. It constructs a database with three fields: a key, a name, and an age. With this database we can add, delete, and retrieve an entry and we can also display the entire database. The program incorporates **general.h** and **dbheader.h** header files that declare several data types. These include the structures used for the database and the prototypes for the functions. The program also includes some **data filters** that force the user to enter input within the required bounds. (Check these features in the program.)

The program has some intentional defects. For example, it gives no warning that it does not accept an entry with a duplicate key until after the information is entered. Also, an input with the wrong data type can cause errors. Discussion of program modifications are included in the exercises at the end of this chapter.

P R O G R A M   1 2 . 2 – 1

```
/********************************************************************************
*    Title:       database manager                                            *
*    Filename:    database.c                                                   *
*                                                                             *
*    Description: Database management system. Maintains a set of records in    *
*                 ascending order according to a key field.  User can insert, delete, *
*                 and print database.                                         *
*                                                                             *
*    Input:       requests by the user for access to database                 *
*    Output:      database contents                                           *
*    Process:     insert in ascending order;  delete; print datbase           *
*                                                                             *
*    Written by:  ...                                            Date: ...     *
********************************************************************************/
```

```
#include   "general.h"                                        /*  Header files  */
#include   "dbheader.h"


main ( )
{

        BOOLEAN          error;                        /*  Types defined in header files  */
   static DATABASE        db;
        MENU_CHOICE      choice;

   db.size = 0;

   get_database ( &db );

   do  {
        choice = show_menu ( );


        switch ( choice )  {                             /*  Begin switch  */

          case QUIT:
               break;

          case INSERT:
               if ( db.size < MAX_SIZE ) {
                    error = insert_rec ( &db );
                    if ( error == TRUE )
                         printf ( "\nRecord already in database!!!" );
                    else
                         printf ("\nRecord inserted" );
                }
                else
                    printf ( "\nDataBase FULL!!!!\n");
                break;

          case DELETE:
               error = delete_rec (  &db );
               if ( error == TRUE )
                    printf ( "\nRecord not found!!!!!" );
               else
                    printf ( "\nRecord deleted" );
               break;
```

```
            case PRINT_ONE:
                error = print_one ( &db );
                if ( error == TRUE )
                    printf ( "\nRecord not found!!!!!" );
                else
                    printf ( "\nEnd of record" );
                break;

            case PRINT_ALL:
                if ( db.size == 0 )
                    printf ( "\nDatabase empty!!!!!" );
                else {
                    print_all ( &db );
                    printf ( "\n\nEnd of database" );
                }
                break;

    }                                                       /*  End switch  */

    }   while ( choice != QUIT );


    put_database ( &db );

    return ( 0 );
}                                                           /*  End of main  */




/*******************************************************************************
 *  Function name:     show_menu                                               *
 *  Description:       Display menu to user;  accept/verify user choice of     *
 *                     activity.                                               *
 *                                                                             *
 *  Input parameters:  none                                                    *
 *  Output parameters: none                                                    *
 *  Return value:      user choice of activity                                 *
 *******************************************************************************/

MENU_CHOICE show_menu ( void )
{

    MENU_CHOICE choice;
```

```
printf  ( "\n\nDataBase Management System\n" );
printf  ( "\nPlease select an activity from the following menu:\n\n" );
printf  ( "\n(0) Quit" );
printf  ( "\n(1) Add item" );
printf  ( "\n(2) Delete item" );
printf  ( "\n(3) Print one record" );
printf  ( "\n(4) Print entire database" );
printf  ( "\n\nChoice >" );


scanf   ( "%d", &choice );

while( !(  ( choice == QUIT)          ||
           ( choice == INSERT )       ||
           ( choice == DELETE )       ||
           ( choice == PRINT_ONE )    ||
           ( choice == PRINT_ALL )  )  ) {

       printf ( "\nError in choice...Re-enter value > " );
       scanf  ( "%d", &choice );
}

  return ( choice );
}                                                        /* End of show_menu */




/********************************************************************************
 *  Function name:     print_one                                               *
 *  Description:       Output one record to screen.                            *
 *                                                                             *
 *  Input parameters:  database                                                *
 *  Output parameters: none                                                    *
 *  Return value:      error = true if record not found                        *
 ********************************************************************************/

BOOLEAN    print_one ( DATABASE *db_ptr )
{
  BOOLEAN       error;
  int           user_key, pos_of_key, ignore;

  user_key = get_key ();                                   /* Ask user for key */

  find ( db_ptr, user_key, &pos_of_key, &ignore );       /* Is record in database? */

  if ( pos_of_key == NOT_FOUND )
       error = TRUE;
```

```
    else {                                              /*  Yes, so print it  */
        error = FALSE;

        printf ( "\nKey = %d \nName = %s \nAge = %d \n\n",
                                db_ptr->info[pos_of_key].key,
                                db_ptr->info[pos_of_key].name,
                                db_ptr->info[pos_of_key].age);

    }


    return ( error );
}                                                       /*  End of print_one  */




/******************************************************************************
 *  Function name:     print_all                                             *
 *  Description:       Output entire database to screen.                     *
 *                                                                           *
 *  Input parameters:  database                                             *
 *  Output parameters: none                                                 *
 *  Return value:      none                                                 *
 ******************************************************************************/

void  print_all ( DATABASE  *db_ptr )
{
    int i;

    printf( "\nAll items in database...\n\n\n" );
    printf( "\nITEM\tKEY\tNAME\t\t\tAGE\n" );

    for ( i = 0; i < db_ptr->size; i++ )
        printf ( "\n%d\t%d\t%s\t\t\t%d",i+1,
                                db_ptr->info[i].key,
                                db_ptr->info[i].name,
                                db_ptr->info[i].age);
}                                                       /*  End of print_all  */




/******************************************************************************
 *  Function name:     insert_rec                                            *
 *  Description:       Insert a record into the database in ascending order by key. *
 *                                                                           *
 *  Input parameters:  database                                             *
 *  Output parameters: updated database                                     *
 *  Return value:      error = true if record with same key already exists  *
 ******************************************************************************/
```

```
BOOLEAN    insert_rec( DATABASE *db_ptr )
{

  BOOLEAN    error;
  int        pos_of_key, pos_of_prev;
  int        i;
  INFO_REC   new_rec;

  new_rec = get_user_data ( );

  find  ( db_ptr, new_rec.key, &pos_of_key, & pos_of_prev );

  if ( pos_of_key != NOT_FOUND )          /* Error is true if record with this key was found */
      error = TRUE;

  else {                                                    /*  Key not found... */

     error = FALSE;

     for ( i = db_ptr->size; i > pos_of_prev+1; i-- )    /*  Push all records "down" to  */
         db_ptr->info [ i ] = db_ptr->info [ i-1 ];      /*  Create a gap for new record */

     db_ptr->info [ i ]  = new_rec;                       /*  Insert new record */
     db_ptr->size++;
  }

  return ( error );
}                                                          /*  End of insert_rec */




/***************************************************************************************
 * Function name:     delete_rec                                                       *
 * Description:       Delete a record from the database.                               *
 *                                                                                     *
 * Input parameters:  database                                                         *
 * Output parameters: updated database                                                *
 * Return value:      error = true if record with key not found                        *
 ***************************************************************************************/

BOOLEAN    delete_rec( DATABASE *db_ptr )
{

  BOOLEAN    error;
  int        user_key, pos_of_key, ignore;
  int        i;
```

```
user_key = get_key ( );

find ( db_ptr, user_key, &pos_of_key, &ignore );

if ( pos_of_key == NOT_FOUND )            /*  Error is true if record with key not found  */

    error = TRUE;

else {                                                      /*  Record with key was found  */

    error = FALSE;
                                                    /* Remove record by moving remaining  */
    for ( i = pos_of_key; i < db_ptr->size-1; i++ )        /* records "up" one position  */
        db_ptr->info [ i ] = db_ptr->info [ i+1 ];

    db_ptr->size--;
}

return ( error );
}                                                           /*  End of delete_rec  */


/*********************************************************************************
 *  Function name:      get_database                                             *
 *  Description:        Read database from file.                                 *
 *                                                                              *
 *  Input parameters:   none                                                    *
 *  Output parameters:  database with data form input file                      *
 *  Return value:       none                                                    *
 *********************************************************************************/

void    get_database    ( DATABASE *db_ptr)
{

    FILE    *in_ptr;
    int     i;

    in_ptr = fopen ( "db.dat", "r" );

    if ( in_ptr == NULL )
        printf ( "\nError....file not found\n" );
```

```
   else {
          for ( i = 0;  i < MAX_SIZE  &&  !feof ( in_ptr );  i++ )
              fscanf ( in_ptr, "%d %s %d\n",&db_ptr->info [ i ].key,
                                           db_ptr->info [ i ].name,
                                           &db_ptr->info [ i ].age  );

          db_ptr->size = i;

          fclose ( in_ptr );
  }
}                                                   /*  End of get_database  */


/******************************************************************************
*  Function name:      put_database                                          *
*  Description:        Write database to file.                               *
*                                                                            *
*  Input parameters:  database                                              *
*  Output parameters: none                                                   *
*  Return value:       none                                                  *
******************************************************************************/

void    put_database     ( DATABASE *db_ptr)
{

   FILE       *out_ptr;
   int        i;

   out_ptr = fopen ( "db.dat", "w" );

   for ( i = 0;  i < db_ptr->size;  i++ )
       fprintf ( out_ptr, "%d %s %d\n",db_ptr->info [ i ].key,
                                   db_ptr->info [ i ].name,
                                   db_ptr->info [ i ].age  );

   fclose ( out_ptr );
}                                                   /*  End of put_database  */


/******************************************************************************
*  Function name:      find                                                  *
*  Description:        Find location of user_key in database. Location is set *
*                      NOT_FOUND if no such record is found.  Location of logical *
*                      predecessor to key is also determined.                *
*                                                                            *
*  Input parameters:  database, user_key                                    *
*  Output parameters: pos of key, pos of previous key                        *
*  Return value:       none                                                  *
******************************************************************************/
```

```
void    find    ( DATABASE *db_ptr,      int  user_key,
                  int     *pos_of_key,   int *pos_of_prev )
{

    int    i;

    for ( i = 0; i < db_ptr->size && user_key > db_ptr->info[i].key;  i++ )
        ;                                              /*  Keep searching...  */

    *pos_of_prev = i-1;                        /*  Logical predecessor is just before i  */

    if ( i < db_ptr->size  &&  user_key == db_ptr->info[i].key )       /*  Found record  */
        *pos_of_key = i;

    else                                               /*  Record not found  */
        *pos_of_key = NOT_FOUND;

}                                                      /*  End of find  */


/*************************************************************************************
 *  Function name:      get_user_data                                               *
 *  Description:        Input user-specified record (key, name, age).               *
 *                                                                                   *
 *  Input parameters:  none                                                          *
 *  Output parameters: none                                                          *
 *  Return value:       record                                                       *
 *************************************************************************************/

INFO_REC    get_user_data    ( void )
{

    INFO_REC    new_rec;

    printf ( "\nPlease enter new data as follows:\n" );

    new_rec.key = get_key ( );

    printf ( "\nName: " );
    fflush ( stdin );
    gets   ( new_rec.name );

    new_rec.age  = get_age ( );

    return ( new_rec );

}                                                  /*  End of get_user_data  */
```

```
/******************************************************************************
 *  Function name:     get_key                                                *
 *  Description:       Input user-specified key.                              *
 *                                                                            *
 *  Input parameters:  none                                                   *
 *  Output parameters: none                                                   *
 *  Return value:      key                                                    *
 ******************************************************************************/

int get_key    ( void )
{
    intkey;

    printf  ( "\nKey ( %d to %d ): ", MIN_KEY, MAX_KEY );
    scanf   ( "%d", &key );
    while   ( key < MIN_KEY ||  key > MAX_KEY ) {
        printf ( "\nKey must be between %d and %d....Re-enter: ", MIN_KEY, MAX_KEY);
        scanf   ( "%d", &key );
    }

    return ( key );

}                                                          /*  End of get_key  */


/******************************************************************************
 *  Function name:     get_age                                                *
 *  Description:       Input user-specified age.                              *
 *                                                                            *
 *  Input parameters:  none                                                   *
 *  Output parameters: none                                                   *
 *  Return value:      age                                                    *
 ******************************************************************************/

int get_age    ( void )
{
    int age;

    printf ( "\nAge ( %d to %d ): ", MIN_AGE, MAX_AGE );
    scanf  ( "%d", &age );
    while  ( age < MIN_AGE ||  age > MAX_AGE ) {
        printf ( "\nAge must be between %d and %d....Re-enter: ", MIN_AGE, MAX_AGE);
        scanf  ( "%d", &age );
    }
    return ( age );
}                                                          /*  End of get_age  */
```

Following are the descriptions of the **general.h** and **dbheader.h** header files that are needed in Program 12.2–1. They must be included in separate files accessible to the **database.c** program.

```
/*****************************************************************************
* general.h    -    Header for   database.c                                 *
*****************************************************************************/

#include <stdio.h>
#include <ctype.h>

#define   MAX_STRING    80


typedef   enum { FALSE,  TRUE }    BOOLEAN;

typedef   char                     STRING[MAX_STRING + 1];



/*****************************************************************************
* dbheader.h    -    Header for   database.c                                 *
*****************************************************************************/

#define MAX_SIZE     100
#define NOT_FOUND     -1
#define MIN_KEY        0
#define MAX_KEY       99
#define MIN_AGE       10
#define MAX_AGE       80


typedef enum { QUIT, INSERT, DELETE, PRINT_ONE, PRINT_ALL }   MENU_CHOICE;


typedef   struct {
              int    key;
              STRING name;
              int    age;
          }  INFO_REC;

typedef   struct {
              int        size;
              INFO_REC   info [ MAX_SIZE ];
          }  DATABASE;
```

```
                                              /*  Level 1 Prototypes  */
void            get_database    ( DATABASE *db_ptr );
void            put_database    ( DATABASE *db_ptr );


MENU_CHOICE     show_menu       ( void           );
BOOLEAN         insert_rec      ( DATABASE *db_ptr );
BOOLEAN         delete_rec      ( DATABASE *db_ptr );
BOOLEAN         print_one       ( DATABASE *db_ptr );
void            print_all       ( DATABASE *db_ptr );


                                              /*  Level 2 Prototypes  */
void            find            ( DATABASE *db_ptr,
                                    int      user_key,
                                    int      *pos_of_key,
                                    int      *pos_of_prev );
INFO_REC        get_user_data   ( void );


                                              /*  Level 3 Prototypes  */
int             get_age         ( void );
int             get_key         ( void );
```

EXERCISES 12.2

Concept Check
Answer statements 1 through 4 with true *or* false.
1. Logical data models show how data structures are organized.
2. A collection of entities of the same representation is called a relationship set.
3. Relations usually have a representation denoted by naming the relation, followed by the attributes in parentheses.
4. Instance tables are used in all database models.

For statements 5 through 8 choose the answer that best completes the statement.
5. A link between two or more entities is called
    a. a database
    b. a connection
    c. a relationship
    d. a key
6. A data model composed of relations, attributes, domains, keys, tuples, and the representation of these elements is
    a. binary model
    b. relational model
    c. a network model
    d. hierarchical model

7. Relations among dissimilar entities are
   a. binary relationships
   b. networked relationships
   c. category relationships
   d. connection relationships
8. Relationships confined to two entity sets are called
   a. Boolean relations
   b. principal key relations
   c. binary relations
   d. data models

For statements 9 through 12 fill in the blanks with the right word.
9. A database model in which any segment can link to any other segment is called _____.
10. A collection of entities of the same representation is called _____.
11. The interaction of entity sets with relationship sets is the basis of the _____ model.
12. The _____ operation is a unary operation in a relational data model that chooses entities according to specific attributes with no duplications.

Set A

Write a short essay for the following questions.
13. Describe the difference between a physical data model and a logical data model.
14. How do category relationships differ from connection relationships?
15. What is a data table in the E-R model?
16. What is an instance table in a relational model?
17. Why can there be many instance tables in a relational model?
18. What is a tuple in a relational model?

Set B

19. Explain how an entity-relationship model provides a basic format for a database.
20. Explain how a hierarchical model provides a basic format for a database.
21. Explain how a network model provides a basic format for a database.
22. Explain how a relational model provides a basic format for a database.

Set C

23. Research database models and write a short essay on a model not covered in this section.
24. In the `get_database` function of Program 12.2–1, the `fscanf` function uses the `&db_ptr-> info[i].key` variable in one instance and the `db_ptr-> info[i].name` variable in another. Explain why the address operator `&` is used in one case but not the other.

25. When you run Program 12.2–1 and attempt to enter information that duplicates a key already in the database, the program first lets you enter the information and then displays the message *Record already in database*. Modify the program so that when a key is duplicated, a warning is given *before* the user attempts to add information to the database.

26. When you enter information in Program 12.2–1 using the wrong data type for Choice, Key, or Age, serious errors can occur. Discuss the reasons for such errors and suggest ways in which they could be corrected.

ENDNOTE

1. Hartmanis, J., and Lin, H., eds. *Computing the Future: A Broader Agenda for Computer Science and Engineering*. Washington, D.C.: National Research Council, National Academy Press, 1992, p. 187.

Dynamic Lists 13

Farm equipment linked on flatbed railroad cars.

After completing this chapter you should be able to do the following:

Learning Goals

- Use `malloc` to allocate memory during program execution
- Design a dynamically allocated data structure
- Implement a stack using dynamic memory allocation
- Design and implement a queue using dynamic memory allocation
- Describe the different kinds of linked lists
- Design and implement a dynamically allocated, linked list
- Explain what a header and trailer node are used for

Chapter Activity

One use of a queue is for computer simulation of real events. For instance, a bank might want to know how many tellers it should hire to reduce the average waiting time for its customers; a movie theater might want to know how many ticket takers to hire. Similarly, a computing center might want to know if buying an additional printer is justified, based on the average time each pending print job needs.

In each of these cases, a queue with its FIFO organization is a natural data structure to model the real-life situation. In this problem, we use a queue to simulate a waiting line at a bank. The queue items represent the time of arrival for each bank customer. For simplicity, we limit the simulation to one teller and create a single queue. The goal of the simulation is to find the average waiting time before a person is served.

The passage of time can be simulated by the iteration of a loop. That is, the value of the loop counter represents the time in minutes since the simulation began. The simulation can run as long as we want, but one possibility would be 480 iterations, the number of minutes in an 8-hour day.

We can assume that a customer arrives every fourth minute. Note that in a sophisticated simulation the customer arrival time would have to be carefully analyzed and accurately modeled. Each time a customer arrives, the arrival time is **enqueued**: The current iteration count of the timer loop is stored.

During each iteration if the ticket taker is free, the queue should be dequeued and the waiting time computed. This is the difference between the current iteration count and the dequeued arrival time. After dequeuing, an independent timer variable is set to, say, five minutes. This represents the average time it takes to serve one customer. This timer is decremented each time through the loop.

When the simulation time is over, the program should output statistics such as the number of clients served, the average wait time, the shortest wait time, and the longest wait time.

A partial algorithm for this problem is

1. LOOP time from 0 to length of simulation
   a. IF time is divisible by 4   /*customer arrived */
      enqueue(time)
   b. IF remaining_service_time = 0 and   /* serve customer */
      queue is not empty
      1. dequeue(entry_time)
      2. determine wait time
      3. add 1 to passengers served
      4. reset remaining_service_time to 5
   c. IF remaining_service_time > 0
      decrement remaining_service_time

2. OUTPUT statistics

13.1   MEMORY ALLOCATION AND DYNAMICALLY LINKED STACKS

Introduction

The Array Revisited

Chapter 11 shows that an array is an effective and convenient data structure for implementing the ADT stack and queue. First, the array provides an accessing scheme that is simple to learn and use. Instead of having to supply names for individual items, we can access the data with a single name and a variable index (subscript). Second, the array is directly supported by the compiler so we do not have to be concerned about the array's design or implementation other than to know how to use it.

The *declared* array, on the other hand, has several limitations. Its physical size must be fixed in advance. This can lead to problems if the physical size of an array does not correspond to its logical size. Consider an array used to store campus phone numbers. What size should the array be? If we set the array at the current enrollment level, we do not allow for additional students. However, if we set the size too large, some of the array space is wasted and memory may be unavailable for other data structures.

Note that until now array size is always determined at compile time. At the end of this section we show a technique for creating dynamically allocated arrays whose size and allocation can be determined while the program is executing. Yet even with this capability, the array size is still fixed at allocation time. It cannot expand or shrink to accommodate a given situation.

Continuing with the phone book problem, what happens when student information needs to be added or deleted? Assuming that the phone numbers are arranged alphabetically by student name, we have to insert and delete to maintain the right ordering. Inserting into an ordered array means finding the right location and then moving all the subsequent data down one position. Similarly, deleting

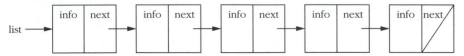

Figure 13.1–1 Generalized linked list

an entry means moving all the data up one position. With a large set of names and numbers such as in the Manhattan phone book this could be extremely time-consuming.

Because of these limitations, programmers often turn to a different structure for storing and accessing large quantities of related data. As we see in Section 13.3, a **generalized linked list** is an ADT that facilitates insertions and deletions. (See Figure 13.1–1.) A linked list is shown as a consecutive series of **nodes**, each consisting of an information-carrying field and a pointer to the next node on the list. When a linked list is designed to use **dynamic memory allocation**, the size of the list can grow or shrink while the program is running. Therefore, the phone book database can start with zero entries and grow or shrink dynamically as names are added and deleted.

Now we discuss dynamic memory allocation as it applies to stacks and queues. Note that although the stack and queue ADTs remain as they were originally described, their implementations are completely rewritten.

13.1.1 The ADT Stack Revisited

First, remember the ADT definition of a **stack** as a homogeneous collection of data items of any type arranged linearly with access at one end only, called the top. Items are stacked as last-in-first-out (LIFO). The following operations describe the applications programmer's interface to an ADT stack.

Operation		**Meaning**
create_stack	(stack)	Make stack logically accessible
destroy_stack	(stack)	Make stack logically inaccessible
empty_stack	(stack)	True if stack is empty
full_stack	(stack)	True if stack is full
push	(stack, item)	Add item to the top of the stack
pop	(stack, item)	Remove item from the top of the stack

In Chapter 11 the stack was implemented as a **struct** consisting of an array and an integer field to represent the top of the stack. The limitation of this representation is the need to predetermine the physical size of the array. We could create a stack that is either too small for a given application or too large and therefore wasteful of memory. By implementing the stack dynamically as a limited-access linked list, we allow it to grow and shrink dynamically, and thus we solve the problem of a predetermined stack size.

BEFORE YOU GO ON

Query: Why is the stack a limited-access linked list?

RESPONSE: A generalized linked list allows insertions and deletions anywhere in the structure. However, a stack has insertions and deletions made only in one location called the top. A queue is also limited access because insertions can be made only in the rear and deletions only at the front.

13.1.2 Tools for Dynamic Memory Allocation

Memory is allocated dynamically by means of standard C functions such as `malloc`, `calloc`, `farmalloc`. We limit this discussion to `malloc` (accessible through `<stdlib.h>`). This function allows us to request a specific amount of memory to be made available to the program at the time of the request. We indicate the number of bytes needed and `malloc` returns a pointer to an area of memory (called the **heap**) reserved for such requests. The pointer (memory address) that `malloc` returns has no data type associated with it and is termed a `void` pointer. To be useful, the pointer has to be forced to a particular data type, using the type cast operator. For instance, the following code segment enables us to request space dynamically for an integer and store a value there.

```
int       *int_ptr;              /*  Declare a pointer to an integer  */
int_ptr  = (int *) malloc ( 2 );     /* Allocate 2 bytes and give  */
                                     /*  the address to int_ptr  */

*int_ptr  = 17;              /*  Store the number 17 at the location  */
                                     /* pointed to by int_ptr  */
```

The `malloc` function has reserved 2 bytes on the heap and returned the address of (a pointer to) the first byte. The address is cast to an integer pointer (`int *`) and assigned to `int_ptr`. We then dereference `int_ptr` and store a 17 at the dynamically allocated address.

> **PERSPECTIVE**
>
> Notice that there is no specific, *named* variable associated with the 17 stored in the heap. This is sometimes called an **anonymous** or **dynamic** variable, and the 17 can only be accessed indirectly through `int_ptr`. In fact, if at a later time `int_ptr` is given the address of some other memory location, the 17 becomes a **lost object** with no way for us to reference it. It just takes up space and serves no purpose.

One problem with the call to `malloc` is that it does not work on computers that use a 4-byte integer or an 8-byte integer. To be safe, use the `sizeof` operator, which determines the number of bytes for the specified data type. On a machine with a 4-byte integer, `sizeof ( int )` is 4 and `malloc(sizeof (int))` reserves 4 bytes from the heap. `sizeof` is fully portable and is the method of choice when using `malloc`. Note that `sizeof` works for any data type, even programmer-defined ones.

Finally, when you no longer need a portion of dynamic memory you should return it to the heap using the `free` function. Thus `free ( int_ptr );` returns the bytes that were allocated by `malloc`. The revised code to allocate and deallocate an integer is

```
int          *int_ptr;
int_ptr      = (int *) malloc ( sizeof ( int )  );
*int_ptr     = 17;
free ( int_ptr );            /* return dynamic memory to the heap */
```

PERSPECTIVE

After a call to `free`, the associated pointer is no longer well defined and is called a **dangling pointer**. When using dynamic memory watch out for lost objects and dangling pointers!

13.1.3 The Dynamic Stack: An Informal Tour

Let's now consider the data structure and implementation for a dynamically allocated stack. Because this is our initial exposure to dynamic allocation and linking, we first walk through the steps and later formalize the processing.

For this implementation, envision the stack as a linked list. Unlike the array in which elements are unalterably linked to each other in contiguous memory locations, this structure consists of a series of **nodes** that are explicitly linked by pointers. Each node can be allocated and deallocated depending on whether the stack is being pushed or popped.

Looking back at Figure 13.1–1 we see that a node holds two fields:

1. An information field into which the (stack) data are placed
2. An explicit-link field, which is a pointer containing the address of the next node in the stack

We describe a node in C as follows.

```
typedef    struct node_type {
               ITEM_TYPE              info;              /* User's data */
               struct  node_type  *next;     /* Pointer to next node */
           } NODE_TYPE;
```

A node is a C `struct` holding two fields. We have called the first field `info`. Its data type is specified abstractly as `ITEM_TYPE`. Recall that the applications programmer who uses the stack decides what `ITEM_TYPE` is. It can be a simple integer or even a structure consisting of many fields and substructures. The second field's data type refers to the node itself! Therefore, `next` is a pointer to a `struct node_type`. This self-referencing definition is necessary because, according to the description of a linked list, nodes need to be able to point to each other.

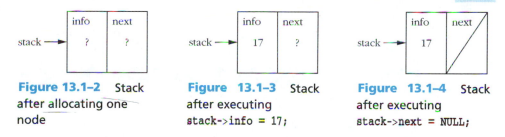

Figure 13.1–2 Stack after allocating one node

Figure 13.1–3 Stack after executing `stack->info = 17;`

Figure 13.1–4 Stack after executing `stack->next = NULL;`

To create a stack dynamically, we need a pointer containing the address of the first node on the stack (the top). We declare a **STACK_TYPE** as a pointer to a stack node. For example:

```
typedef   NODE_TYPE      *STACK_TYPE;
```

We declare the stack variable as

```
STACK_TYPE      stack;
```

With these declarations and variables we can allocate a stack node this way:

```
stack = ( STACK_TYPE ) malloc ( sizeof ( NODE_TYPE ) );
```

Accordingly, **stack** now contains the address of an area of memory large enough to hold one stack node, as shown in Figure 13.1–2.

Next, let's store something in that node. Assuming that the **ITEM_TYPE** is an integer, the following stores the value 17 in the node at the top of the stack.

```
stack->info   = 17;
```

Recall that the arrow operator **->** dereferences a pointer to a structure. In this case the **stack** pointer is dereferenced so that **stack->** means *the object that stack is pointing to* (a **struct** containing two fields). By specifying the **info** field we can make an assignment, as shown in Figure 13.1–3.

What should the other field of the node, the **next** field, point to? We have not stored anything there so it contains logical garbage, which is ill-defined data. Because the **next** field is a pointer but it doesn't have anywhere to point, we set it to a special pointer value called **NULL** and assign it as

```
stack->next = NULL;
```

We can think of **NULL** as a *specific* nowhere! A node whose **next** field holds the **NULL** address is usually interpreted as the last node in a linked list. As we see later, **NULL** signifies the end (or bottom) of the stack. The stack is pictured in Figure 13.1–4, with a diagonal line representing **NULL.**

If we need to push a second item, where should it come from? The top of the heap, of course. Where should it be placed? On top of the stack. Let's see how to do this.

First, we need to allocate a new node so we need a second pointer. If we use the same **stack** pointer, we lose track of the node **stack** was pointing to. So we declare a **NODE_PTR** in the same way that we declare a **STACK_TYPE:**

```
typedef    NODE_TYPE          *NODE_PTR;
NODE_PTR                      new_node; /* new_node can point to nodes */
```

Next, we allocate a node and assign new_node to point to it as

```
new_node = ( NODE_PTR ) malloc ( sizeof ( NODE_TYPE ) );
```

Now we put some data into the node, just as we did with the first node, and write

```
new_node->info  = 25;
```

The stack is pictured in Figure 13.1–5.

Something isn't quite right! The stack has two nodes but the nodes don't know about each other. They are just two pieces of unrelated memory. We need to link the nodes in stack-like order. Which node should stack point to? Remember that on a stack the last node added is the first node to be removed. Therefore, stack should point to the node that new_node is pointing to now and new_node should point to the node that stack is pointing to now. This can be done with two pointer assignments as

```
new_node->next   = stack;
stack            = new_node;
```

Now the stack is properly linked, as shown in Figure 13.1–6.

BEFORE YOU GO ON

Query: A student suggested that the statements

```
new_node->next   = stack;
stack            = new_node;
```

could be executed in reverse order. What would happen?   (ɔntinued)

Figure 13.1–5 Stack after allocating second node

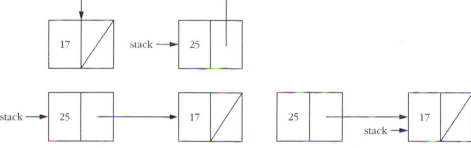

Figure 13.1–6 Stack after linking second node in front of first node

Figure 13.1–7 Stack after popping top node

RESPONSE: If we first assign `stack` the value of `new_node`, the node containing the data 17 would be unreferenced and lost in memory. Thus, when dealing with dynamic variables, the order of pointer assignments is critical.

How can a node be removed (popped) from the stack? We make `stack` point to the next node in the list, as in

```
stack          = stack->next;
```

As we see in Figure 13.1–7, the stack is correct but something is wrong with memory. The node holding the 25 is unreferenced but it is still allocated. To prevent such lost objects from proliferating, remember to return dynamic memory when it is no longer needed. We set a temporary pointer to the node to be deleted and call the `free` function to return the memory to the heap. This is shown below and in Figure 13.1–8.

```
NODE_PTR      temp_ptr;          /* Declare a temporary pointer */

temp_ptr   = stack;   /*   temp_ptr now points to the top node */

stack      = stack->next;   /* stack now points to the node */
                            /* following the top node */

free ( temp_ptr ); /* Return the memory that temp is pointing to */
```

Therefore now we see how to create and destroy nodes on a stack. Continuing with this line of thinking would enable us to generate a much larger stack but the code would become repetitive. What we need is a general method for adding and deleting (pushing and popping) stack nodes, as explained next.

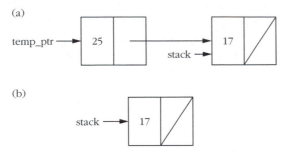

Figure 13.1–8 Correct way to pop a stack

13.1.4 Implementing the ADT Stack

Now let's implement the ADT stack. First, we use a header file called `stack.h` to describe the structure of nodes, the data type given to stacks and nodes, and the prototypes for the functions needed.

```
/* stack.h:   header file for linked-list implementation of an ADT stack      */

#include       <stdlib.h>                    /* Needed for malloc and free */

typedef        struct node_type {
                   ITEM_TYPE          info;                    /*  User's data  */
                   struct node_type *next;       /*  Pointer to next node  */
               } NODE_TYPE;

typedef        NODE_TYPE  *STACK_TYPE;               /*  STACK_TYPE is reserved  */
                                                     /*  for the stack pointer  */

typedef        NODE_TYPE  *NODE_PTR;         /*  NODE_PTR is used to allocate  */
                                             /*   additional stack nodes  */


                                                         /*  Function prototypes  */
void           create_stack    ( STACK_TYPE  *stack  );
void           destroy_stack   ( STACK_TYPE  *stack  );

BOOLEAN        empty_stack    ( STACK_TYPE  *stack  );
BOOLEAN        full_stack     ( STACK_TYPE  *stack  );

void           push           ( STACK_TYPE  *stack,  ITEM_TYPE  new_item  );
void           pop            ( STACK_TYPE  *stack,  ITEM_TYPE  *old_item  );
```

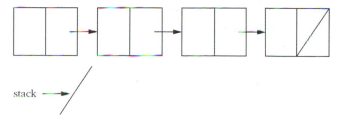

Figure 13.1–9   Incorrect way to destroy a stack

Next, consider the stack access functions. Notice in the prototypes listed above that the variable containing the address of the top node, the **stack** pointer, is passed as a pointer to all the functions. With the exception of **empty_stack** and **full_stack**, this variable is changed by these functions. Because the **stack** is itself a pointer, the function parameters are in fact pointers-to-pointers (**double indirection**). The reason for passing the **stack** address to **empty_stack** and **full_stack** is to maintain compatibility with the array-based implementation. (This is discussed in Chapter 11.)

The **create_stack** function creates the stack. Because there are no nodes yet, initialization is setting the stack pointer to **NULL**.

```
/****************************************************************************
*  Function name:      create_stack                                        *
*  Description:        Initialize stack to empty state.                     *
*                                                                          *
*  Input parameters:  none                                                 *
*  Output parameters: stack (initialized)                                  *
*  Return value:      none                                                 *
****************************************************************************/

void  create_stack ( STACK_TYPE  *stack )
{
    *stack = NULL;            /* Indirectly set the stack argument to NULL */
}                                               /* End of create_stack */
```

The **destroy_stack** function is more complicated in the linked-list implementation than in the array-based implementation. We can set the **stack** pointer to **NULL**, as shown in Figure 13.1–9, but this has the unwanted effect of leaving all the stack nodes allocated but not referenced. Instead, each node must be visited, a temporary pointer set, and the memory returned using the **free** function. This process repeats until the end of the stack is reached—that is, the stack pointer equals **NULL**.

```
/*****************************************************************************
 *  Function name:     destroy_stack                                         *
 *  Description:       Destroy all elements in stack, leaving stack empty.   *
 *                                                                           *
 *  Input parameters:  stack                                                 *
 *  Output parameters: stack (destroyed)                                     *
 *  Return value:      none                                                  *
 *****************************************************************************/

void destroy_stack ( STACK_TYPE *stack )
{
    NODE_PTR    temp_ptr;

    while ( *stack != NULL ) {
      temp_ptr = *stack;                   /* temp_ptr points to the node to free */
      *stack   = temp_ptr->next;             /* Unlink top node from stack */

      free ( temp_ptr );                    /* Free space from old top node */
    }
}                                           /* End of destroy_stack */
```

The `empty_stack` function is straightforward and just checks whether the stack pointer currently equals `NULL`.

```
/*****************************************************************************
 *  Function name:     empty_stack                                           *
 *  Description:       Test whether stack is empty.                          *
 *                                                                           *
 *  Input parameters:  stack                                                 *
 *  Output parameters: none                                                  *
 *  Return value:      TRUE if stack is empty; FALSE if any nodes on stack   *
 *****************************************************************************/

BOOLEAN  empty_stack ( STACK_TYPE *stack )
{
  return ( *stack == NULL  ?  TRUE : FALSE );
}                                           /* End of empty_stack */
```

BEFORE YOU GO ON

Query: When will `empty_stack` be `TRUE`?

RESPONSE: `empty_stack` returns `TRUE` after a call to `create_stack` or `destroy_stack`, or after popping all the stack nodes.

Because the `stack` is implemented dynamically, there is no fixed maximum size: It can grow and shrink as necessary. Therefore, the `full_stack` function returns `FALSE`. It is included only to maintain compatibility with the array-based stack implementation.

Note that because the stack pointer is neither referenced nor changed (it is not used at all in the function) the compiler may issue a warning message. This is one of the few warning messages that can safely be ignored.

```
/*****************************************************************************
*   Function name:     full_stack                                           *
*   Description:       Test whether stack is full.                          *
*                                                                           *
*   Input parameters:  stack                                                *
*   Output parameters: none                                                 *
*   Return value:      TRUE if stack is full;  FALSE if space available on stack*
*                                                                           *
*   NOTE:              since stack is neither referenced nor changed,       *
*                      a compiler warning may be issued.                    *
*****************************************************************************/

BOOLEAN  full_stack (  STACK_TYPE   *stack )
{
    return ( FALSE );
}                                                /*  End of full_stack  */
```

PERSPECTIVE

Memory on the heap is not infinite! It is possible to exhaust the available storage, in which case this implementation has a potential bug. Unfortunately, there is no convenient way to check whether dynamic memory is still available. If `malloc` cannot allocate the memory requested it returns a `NULL` pointer. We should check this before allowing any function that allocates memory to continue. (See the `push` function later in this section and Question 19 in the section exercises.)

The next functions, **push** and **pop**, are the core of the ADT stack. **push** is implemented this way: Allocate a new node, insert the new item, and reset the links so that **stack** points to the new item. Note that a check is included in case **malloc** cannot find any additional space on the heap.

```
/*****************************************************************************
*   Function name:     push                                                 *
*   Description:       Put an item on the top of the stack.                 *
*                                                                           *
*   Input parameters:  stack, new top item                                  *
*   Output parameters: stack with new top item                              *
*   Return value:      none                                                 *
*****************************************************************************/

void  push (  STACK_TYPE  *stack,
              ITEM_TYPE   item  )
{
    NODE_PTR  temp_ptr;
```

```
                                              /*  Allocate space for new item  */
    temp_ptr = ( NODE_PTR ) malloc ( sizeof ( NODE_TYPE ) );

    if ( temp_ptr != NULL) {            /* Assuming space was allocated...  */

        temp_ptr->info = item;              /* Put new item into info field   */
        temp_ptr->next = *stack;/*Link new node in front of current stack top*/

        *stack        = temp_ptr;      /* Reset stack pointer to new top    */
    }
}                                               /* End of push  */
```

pop is implemented this way: 1. Verify that the stack is not empty, 2. send the top item to the calling function (indirectly), 3. advance the stack pointer to the next node, and 4. free the former top node.

```
/***********************************************************************
 *  Function name:     pop                                            *
 *  Description:       Remove top element from stack and return its value. *
 *                                                                    *
 *  Input parameters:  stack                                          *
 *  Output parameters: stack with top item removed, old top item      *
 *  Return value:      none                                           *
 ***********************************************************************/

void pop (   STACK_TYPE   *stack,
             ITEM_TYPE    *old_item   )
{

    NODE_PTR  temp_ptr;

    if ( empty_stack ( stack ) == FALSE ) { /*  Is there something to pop... */

        temp_ptr  = *stack;                  /*  temp_ptr points to stack top */
        *old_item = temp_ptr->info; /*Put info from top into output parameter*/
        *stack    = temp_ptr->next; /* Advance stack pointer to next node */
        free ( temp_ptr );                       /* Dispose of old top node  */

    }

}                                               /*  End of pop  */
```

13.1.5 Dynamically Allocating Arrays

A useful application of dynamic memory allocation is to create an array while the program is executing. Arrays and pointers are very closely related in C. As we said in Chapter 7, the name of an array is a pointer constant — it is the address of the first element of the array. Moreover, no distinction is made in C between

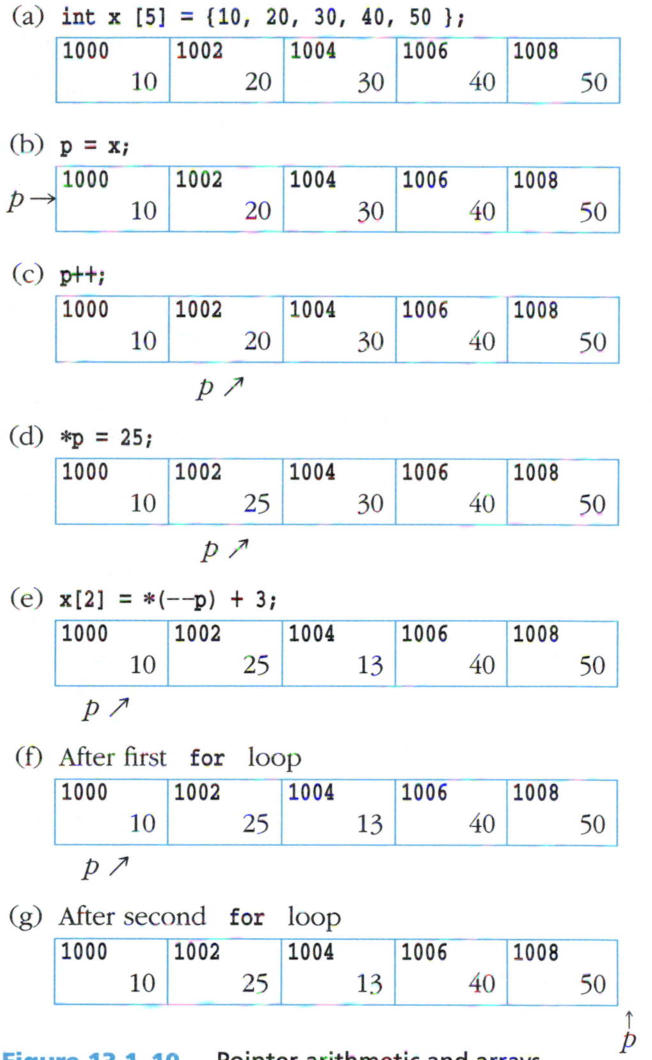

(a) `int x [5] = {10, 20, 30, 40, 50 };`

1000	1002	1004	1006	1008
10	20	30	40	50

(b) `p = x;`

$p \rightarrow$

1000	1002	1004	1006	1008
10	20	30	40	50

(c) `p++;`

1000	1002	1004	1006	1008
10	20	30	40	50

$p \nearrow$

(d) `*p = 25;`

1000	1002	1004	1006	1008
10	25	30	40	50

$p \nearrow$

(e) `x[2] = *(--p) + 3;`

1000	1002	1004	1006	1008
10	25	13	40	50

$p \nearrow$

(f) After first **for** loop

1000	1002	1004	1006	1008
10	25	13	40	50

$p \nearrow$

(g) After second **for** loop

1000	1002	1004	1006	1008
10	25	13	40	50

$\uparrow$
p

Figure 13.1–10   Pointer arithmetic and arrays

an array subscript and an appropriate pointer reference to the array. Thus, if the pointer variable `p` holds the address of the array `x`, then `p+1` is the address of the next element of `x` and `*(p+1)` is equivalent to `x[1]`. These concepts are shown in code next and in Figure 13.1–10.

```
/* Example showing the similarity between pointers and arrays */

#include <stdio.h>
#include <stdlib.h>

main ( )
{
    int i, *p, x [ 5 ] = { 10, 20, 30, 40, 50 };
```

```
p = x;                                    /* p holds the address of x[0] */
p++;                                      /* p holds the address of x[1] */
printf ( "\n%d", *p );                         /* Outputs 20 */

*p = 25;                                        /* x[1] = 25 */
printf ( "\n%d", x [ 1 ] );                     /* Outputs 25 */

x [ 2 ] = *( --p ) + 3;                         /* x[2] = 13 */

for ( i = 0; i < 5; i++ )             /* Outputs 10 25 13 40 50  and */
    printf ( "\n%d", *( p+i ) );      /* leaves p at the start of the array */

for ( i = 0; i < 5; i++ )                  /* same output as above, but */
    printf ( "\n%d", *p++ );           /* leaves p after the end of the array */

return ( 0 );
}
```

Let's assume that x is arbitrarily given the starting address 1000. After the declarations (see Figure 13.1–10a), the first assignment gives p the address of the array x (see Figure 13.1–10b). Thus p's rvalue is 1000. The expression p++ (see Figure 13.1–10c) means add 1 to the contents of p. Because this is our first example of pointer arithmetic we should explain that addition and subtraction of pointers is allowed in C, so expressions such as p+1, p-2, p++, p--, --p, ++p are syntactically correct.

We might think that p++ assigns the value 1001 to p. However, p has been declared as a *pointer to an integer*, that is, the base type associated with p is an object needing two bytes (this number is compiler-dependent). Adding 1 would give p address 1001, which happens to be the second byte of the first integer in the array! Instead, addition and subtraction of pointers is automatically *scaled* to the base type. Therefore, adding 1 to an integer pointer is really adding 2 (bytes). Similarly, adding 1 to a **float** pointer is really adding 4 (assuming a 4-byte floating-point data type). Therefore, p++ is calculated as 1000 + 2, giving p the address of the first byte of x[1]. After the addition, *p is the same as x[1], namely 20.

BEFORE YOU GO ON

Query: Because x and p are so closely related, why not just do the pointer arithmetic with x instead of p?

RESPONSE: x is a pointer constant—the address of the first element of the array. Because x is a constant it cannot be changed. p is a pointer variable that was initially given the value of x and then changed in various ways.

Assigning the value 25 to `*p` (see Figure 13.1–10d) is the same as writing `x [ 1 ] = 25;`. The next statement,

```
x [ 2 ] = *( --p ) + 3;
```

is evaluated as follows (see Figure 13.1–10e).

1. `--p` resets `p` to 1000 by subtracting one integer length or two bytes
2. `*( --p)` is the current contents of `x [ 0 ]`, namely 10
3. 10 + 3 = 13
4. 13 is assigned to `x [ 2 ]`

Next, the `for` loop (Figure 13.1–10f) shows an alternate way of traversing an array. The `printf` statement outputs the indirect contents of `p+i` where `i` is varying from 0–4. `p+i` is the same as `x [ i ]`. When the loop ends, `p` is still pointing to the beginning of the array. In the second `for` loop (Figure 13.1–10g), `p`'s value is changed by the increment operator `p++`. The resulting output is the same as in the previous loop but `p` itself has been changed so that it points to the first memory address after the end of the array (address 1010).

> **PERSPECTIVE**
>
> Although logically equivalent, a pointer used to traverse an array is computationally more efficient than a subscript. C programmers use pointer arithmetic to speed program execution time. Some might argue, however, that a penalty is paid in the readability of the resulting source code.

Now we turn to dynamic array allocation. Because array subscripting and pointer arithmetic are logically equivalent, we can dynamically allocate storage from the heap and treat that storage as if it were an array:

```
/* Example showing dynamic array allocation */

#include <stdio.h>
#include <stdlib.h>
main ( )
{
   int i, *p;

   p = (int *) malloc ( 5 * sizeof ( int ) ); /*  p holds the address of the 1st byte of  */
                                              /*  a block of memory for 5 integers  */

   *p = 10;                                    /*  the 1st integer is set to 10  */
   p++;
   *p = 20;                                    /*  the 2nd integer is set to 20  */

   *++ p = 30;                                 /*  advance p and set the 3rd integer to 30  */
```

```
    p [ 4 ] = 40;                 /*  C allows subscript notation to be used with pointers!!  */
    p [ 5 ] = 50;

    free ( p );                                   /*  Return the memory to the heap  */

    return ( 0 );
}
```

The first assignment allocates storage for five integers, type casts the returned address to an integer pointer, and gives that address to **p.** **∗p** is the same as **p [0]. p++** advances **p** to the second integer. **∗p = 20** sets that integer to 20. **∗++p** advances **p** to the third integer and indirectly references its contents. Next, we see that pointers and subscripts can be used interchangeably, allowing array-like references

```
    p[4] = 40;
```

and

```
    p[5] = 50;
```

Finally, using

```
    free ( p );
```

we return the memory to the heap.

PERSPECTIVE

Always remember to use **free** once you are finished with memory that was allocated by **malloc.**

A final comment on dynamic arrays. Because **malloc** allows a variable expression to be used as an argument, we could replace the expression **5∗ sizeof (int)** with **size ∗ sizeof (int)**, where **size** is a variable. We can get the value of **size** by an assignment or from the end user, as shown next.

```
/*  Example showing dynamic array allocation with the array size determined by the user  */

#include <stdio.h>
#include <stdlib.h>
main (  )
{
    int i, *p, size;

    printf ( "\nWhat size array would you like????" );
    scanf ( "%d", &size );

    p = (int *) malloc ( size * sizeof ( int ) );/*  p holds the address of the 1st byte  */
                                    /*  of a block of memory sufficient for "size" integers  */
```

```
      printf ( "\nNow input %d integers:", size );
      for ( i = 0; i < size; i++ )
          scanf ( "%d", &p [ i ] );                  /* ok to use array subscripting */

      free ( p );                                    /* Return the memory to the heap */
      return ( 0 );
}
```

EXERCISES 13.1

Concept Check

Answer statements 1 through 4 with true *or* false.

1. The applications programmer should be informed whether the array-based or the linked-list-based stack is in use.
2. A stack is an example of a general-purpose linked list.
3. Dynamic memory allocation allows a linked structure to grow and shrink in size during the execution of a program.
4. `malloc` returns an error message if no more memory can be allocated.

For statements 5 through 8 choose the selection that best completes the statement.

5. Assuming that `temp` is pointing to the first node of the stack (the top), the statement `free ( temp );`
   a. deallocates the pointer `temp`
   b. deallocates the entire stack
   c. deallocates the node pointed to by `temp`
   d. deallocates the data field of the node pointed to by `temp`
6. An anonymous variable
   a. is any pointer variable
   b. is any variable created with `malloc`
   c. is any named variable
   d. is any dynamic variable that is no longer pointed to
7. The following statement safely allocates a dynamic integer:
   a. `int_ptr = malloc ( sizeof ( int ) );`
   b. `int_ptr = malloc ( 4 );`
   c. `int_ptr = ( int ) malloc ( sizeof ( int) );`
   d. `int_ptr = ( int * ) malloc ( sizeof ( int ) );`
8. Assuming that the stack has been created and holds several items, the following statements would set `new_node` to the third item from the top:
   a. `new_node = stack->next->next->next;`
   b. `new_node = stack->next->next->next->next;`
   c. `new_node = stack->next->next;`
   d. `new_node = stack [3];`

For statements 9 through 12 fill in the blanks with the right word.

9. The _____ implementation requires setting the physical size of the stack at compile time.
10. `malloc` returns a _____ pointer to the allocated memory area.
11. The _____ function returns memory to the _____.

12. The declaration of a **struct node_type** names two fields called _____ and _____.

Set A

Each of the following problems can be solved with a single C statement.

13. Write an alternative to **destroy_stack** that loses the stack without freeing all the nodes.

14. Set **temp** to the second node in the stack.

15. Assuming that the stack has exactly three nodes, free the last node. Assume that **stack** is pointing to the top of the stack. Add a second statement to ensure that the new last node points to **NULL**.

Set B

16. Rewrite **pop** so that instead of using an output parameter it returns the item from the top of the stack.

17. Add a new ADT function called **stack_top** that returns the item on top of the stack without changing the stack.

18. Rewrite the answer to Question 17 so that the top item is passed back as an output parameter instead of a return value.

Set C

19. Rewrite **full_stack** so that it checks whether any memory is available. Recall that **malloc** returns **NULL** if it is unsuccessful in allocating memory. Therefore, the function can temporarily allocate a node. If **malloc** is successful, immediately free the node and return **FALSE** (since memory is available on the heap). If **malloc** is unsuccessful (returns **NULL**), **full_stack** should return **TRUE** (because memory *is not* available on the heap).

Implement the next three functions as applications functions, not systems functions. Do not make any direct references to the stack data type.

20. Write a function whose output parameter is the information field of the nth item from the top of the stack. The function should not change the stack in any way. Assume that the stack has at least n items.

21. Rewrite the function in Question 20 so that the nth item is *removed* from the stack. Assume that the stack has at least n items.

22. Rewrite the answers to Questions 20 and 21 but do not assume that the stack has n items. Each function should return a **BOOLEAN** value indicating whether the action was successful (whether the stack had at least n items).

13.2   DYNAMICALLY LINKED QUEUES

Introduction

Like the stack, the dynamically linked queue can be viewed as a limited-access, linked list. The same advantages apply: There is no need to preallocate the queue size and no need to move data when enqueueing or dequeueing. As an added bonus, because the queue can grow and shrink dynamically, there is no need to contrive the implementation of the data structure as circular. The linked-list queue is strictly linear.

13.2.1 The ADT Queue Revisited

Recall from Chapter 11 that a **queue** is a homogeneous collection of data items arranged linearly with access restricted to either end, called the front and rear. The following operations describe the applications programmer's interface to an ADT queue.

Operation		**Meaning**
create_queue	(queue)	Make queue logically accessible
destroy_queue	(queue)	Make queue logically inaccessible
empty_queue	(queue)	True if the queue is empty
full_queue	(queue)	True if the queue is full
enqueue	(queue, new_item)	Add a new item to the rear of the queue
dequeue	(queue, old_item)	Remove the item at the front of the queue

Consider a data structure to represent the queue. Figure 13.2–1 shows the queue as a linked list of nodes with two access pointers, front and rear.

As with stack nodes, a queue node consists of an information field and a field holding a pointer to the next node. We describe this as

```
typedef struct   node_type  {
                ITEM_TYPE        info;                    /* User's data */
                struct node_type *next;            /* ptr to next node */
          } NODE_TYPE;
```

The queue itself is a pair of pointers that always hold the addresses of the front and the rear of the dynamic queue. We describe it as

```
typedef struct  {
                NODE_TYPE *front;                  /* ptr to q front */
                NODE_TYPE *rear;                   /* ptr to q rear */
          }   Q_TYPE;
```

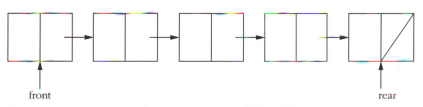

front   rear

Figure 13.2–1   Queue implemented as a linked list

The header file for the ADT queue package is shown next.

```
/* queue.h:  header file for linked-list implementation of an ADT queue     */

typedef struct  node_type  {
                ITEM_TYPE         info;                      /*  User's data  */
                struct node_type *next;                 /*  ptr to next node */
        } NODE_TYPE;

typedef NODE_TYPE  * NODE_PTR;                            /* Pointer to nodes */

typedef struct  {
                NODE_PTR front;                          /*  ptr to q front  */
                NODE_PTR rear;                           /*  ptr to q rear   */
        }   Q_TYPE;


                                                         /*  Function prototypes  */
void    create_queue  ( Q_TYPE    *queue  );
void    destroy_queue ( Q_TYPE    *queue  );

BOOLEAN empty_queue  ( Q_TYPE    *queue  );
BOOLEAN full_queue   ( Q_TYPE    *queue  );

void    enqueue      ( Q_TYPE    *queue,   ITEM_TYPE   new_item );
void    dequeue      ( Q_TYPE    *queue,   ITEM_TYPE   *old_item );
```

13.2.2 Implementing the ADT Queue

We now turn to the implementation of each of the queue access functions. As with the stack, `create_queue` does not have to allocate any storage. It just sets the queue pointers to `NULL`:

```
/****************************************************************************
* Function name:     create_queue                                          *
* Description:       Initialize queue.                                      *
*                                                                          *
* Input parameters:  none                                                  *
* Output parameters: queue initialized                                     *
* Return value:      none                                                  *
****************************************************************************/

void create_queue ( Q_TYPE    *queue )
{
   queue->front   =  NULL;
   queue->rear    =  NULL;
}                                                  /*  End of create_queue  */
```

The `destroy_queue` function traverses the queue, deallocating each node along the way. This means that you set a temporary pointer and then free the associated node. The process continues until the queue is empty.

```
/****************************************************************
* Function name:    destroy_queue                              *
* Description:      Destroy queue contents.                    *
*                                                              *
* Input parameters: queue                                      *
* Output parameters: queue destroyed                           *
* Return value:     none                                       *
****************************************************************/

void destroy_queue ( Q_TYPE  *queue )
{
   NODE_PTR  temp_ptr;

   while ( empty_queue ( queue ) == FALSE ) {        /* Any more nodes? */
      temp_ptr   = queue->front;              /* Set aside the front node */
      queue->front = queue->front->next;      /* Move on to the next node */
      free ( temp_ptr );                   /* Dispose of the old front node */
   }
   queue->rear = NULL;                             /* Reset rear to NULL */
}                                           /*  End of destroy_queue  */
```

The `empty_queue` function tests whether the front pointer equals `NULL`. Note that the function could test the rear pointer instead.

```
/****************************************************************/
* Function name:    empty_queue                                *
* Description:      Test whether any items on queue.           *
*                                                              *
* Input parameters: queue                                      *
* Output parameters: none                                      *
* Return value:     TRUE if queue is empty; FALSE if any item on queue  *
****************************************************************/

BOOLEAN empty_queue ( Q_TYPE *queue )
{
 return ( queue->front == NULL  ?  TRUE  :  FALSE );
}                                           /*  End of empty_queue  */
```

As with the stack, the `full_queue` function always returns `FALSE` (see Exercise 21 at the end of this section for a useful modification). Its inclusion is to maintain consistency with the array-based implementation, which *does* need to check for a full queue. The compiler may issue a warning because the queue pointer is not used in the function body.

```
/***************************************************************************/
* Function name:     full_queue                                          *
* Description:       Test whether queue is full.                         *
*                                                                        *
* Input parameters:  queue                                              *
* Output parameters: none                                               *
* Return value:      TRUE if queue is full; FALSE if space available    *
*                                                                        *
* NOTE:              since queue is neither referenced nor changed, a compiler *
*                    warning may be issued.                             *
***************************************************************************/

BOOLEAN full_queue ( Q_TYPE   *queue )
{
 return ( FALSE );
}                                                      /*  End of full_queue  */
```

The **enqueue** function (shown in Figure 13.2–2) first tries to allocate a new node. If memory is available, the data in **item** are inserted in the **info** field of the newly allocated node. Because the node is to be linked at the end of the queue, set its **next** field to **NULL**. If the queue is empty, update **queue->front** to point to the new node. Otherwise **queue->front** does not need to change. Instead, point the former rear node to the newly added node by putting the address of the new node in **queue->rear->next**. Finally, reset **queue->rear** to point to the new node.

```
/***************************************************************************/
* Function name:     enqueue                                             *
* Description:       Insert item on rear of queue.                       *
*                                                                        *
* Input parameters:  queue, new rear item                               *
* Output parameters: queue with new item at rear                        *
* Return value:      none                                               *
***************************************************************************/

void enqueue ( Q_TYPE  *queue,
               ITEM_TYPE item  )
{
    NODE_PTR new_node;

                                            /* Allocate space for new item  */
    new_node = ( NODE_PTR ) malloc ( sizeof ( NODE_TYPE ) );

    if ( new_node != NULL ) {              /* Assuming memory is available... */

        new_node->info = item;             /*  Put new item into info field  */
        new_node->next = NULL;/* This is the last node..it has no successor */
```

```
        if ( empty_queue ( queue ) == TRUE ) /*Inserting into an empty queue*/
            queue->front = new_node;     /* So, must change the front ptr */
        else
            queue->rear->next = new_node;/*Inserting into a non-empty queue*/

        queue->rear = new_node; /*  Rear needs the address of the new node  */
    }
}                                              /*  End of enqueue  */
```

The **dequeue** function is simpler (see Figure 13.2–3). Assuming that the queue is not empty, the function returns (as an output parameter) the information held

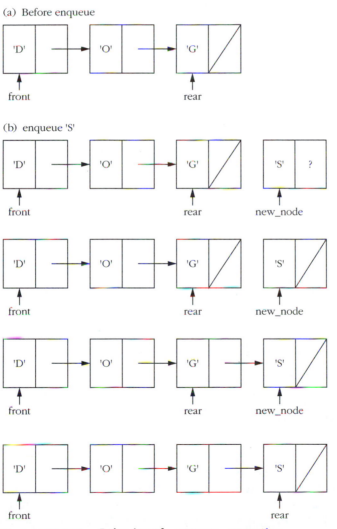

Figure 13.2–2 Behavior of enqueue operation

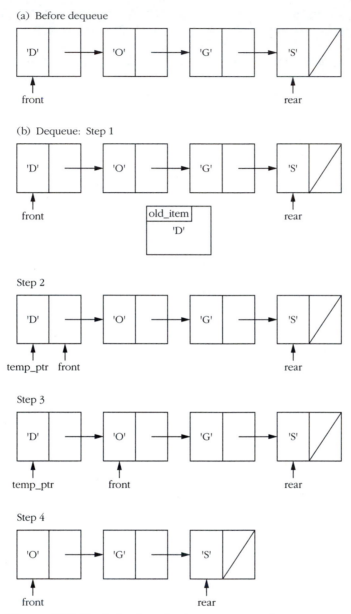

Figure 13.2–3 Behavior of `dequeue` operation

in the node at the front of the queue. Next, assign a temporary pointer to the node so that the node can later be freed, then update `queue->front` to the next node on the list. If the dequeued node is the only one present, the queue is empty. In that case, set `queue->rear` to `NULL` to ensure the integrity of the data structure. Finally, return the space associated with the dequeued node to the heap. The function is coded as follows.

```
/*****************************************************************************/
* Function name:     dequeue                                                *
* Description:       Remove item from front of queue.                       *
*                                                                           *
* Input parameters:  queue                                                  *
* Output parameters: queue with front item removed, old front item         *
* Return value:      none                                                   *
*****************************************************************************/

void dequeue ( Q_TYPE *queue,
               ITEM_TYPE *old_item )
{
   NODE_PTR  temp_ptr;

   if ( empty_queue ( queue ) == FALSE ) {  /* Is there a node on the queue */

        *old_item    = queue->front->info;/* Take info from front of queue */
        temp_ptr     = queue->front;               /* Save it for free( )  */
        queue->front = queue->front->next;/*     Update front to next node */

        if (  empty_queue ( queue ) == TRUE )    /*  If queue is now empty */
              queue->rear  =  NULL;          /* rear should point to NULL  */

        free ( temp_ptr );                   /* Dispose of former front item */
   }
}                                               /* End of dequeue  */
```

EXERCISES 13.2

Concept Check

Answer statements 1 through 4 with true *or* false.

1. Unlike the array-based implementation, dynamic queue items do not need to be the same data type.
2. Because of dynamic memory allocation, `empty_queue` does not serve any purpose beyond conformity with the array-based implementation.
3. The dynamic queue is a purely linear structure.
4. Before calling `dequeue`, the applications programmer should first check `full_queue`.

For statements 5 through 8 choose the answer that best completes the statement.

5. A variable of `Q_TYPE` is
   a. a set of linked nodes
   b. a pair of dynamically allocated pointers
   c. a pair of pointers to `Q_TYPE` variables
   d. a pair of pointers to `NODE_TYPE` variables

6. A variable is declared as `NODE_TYPE x`; Assuming `item` is `ITEM_TYPE`, which of the following is a legitimate assignment to `x`?
   a. `x->front.info = item;`
   b. `x->front->info = item;`
   c. `x.info = item;`
   d. `x.front.info = item;`

7. A variable is declared as follows: `Q_TYPE *x`; Assuming that `item` is `ITEM_TYPE`, which of the following is a legitimate assignment to `x`?
   a. `x->front->info = item;`
   b. `x->front.info = item;`
   c. `x.front->info = item;`
   d. `x.front.info = item;`

8. In the `enqueue` function the queue is declared as `Q_TYPE *queue`. This is an example of
   a. a pointer to a pointer (double indirection)
   b. a pointer to a node
   c. a pointer to a structure
   d. a pointer to the front of the queue

For statements 9 through 12 fill in the blanks with the right word.

9. If `malloc` is unable to allocate memory, it returns a value of _____.

10. A `NODE_TYPE` is a structure containing fields representing _____ and _____.

11. If dequeueing results in an empty queue, you must set `rear` to _____.

12. When enqueueing for the first time, you must set `front` to _____.

Set A

Solve each of the following problems.

13. Rewrite the `empty_queue` function to test the rear pointer instead of the front pointer.

14. Because `queue` is not changed by `empty_queue` it does not need to be passed as a pointer. Rewrite the function with `Q_TYPE queue` as an input parameter.

15. Rewrite `dequeue` so that instead of using an output parameter it returns the item from the front of the queue.

16. Set `temp` to the second node (from the front) in the queue.

Set B

17. Add a new ADT function called `get_q_front` that returns the first item on the queue without removing it.

18. A *doubly ended queue* is one that allows insertions and deletions at both ends. Add the ADT access function `enq_front`, allowing an item to be enqueued at the front of the queue. Note that including this function and the one below necessitates rewriting the ADT specifications!

19. Discuss how you would implement the ADT access function `deq_rear`, allowing an item to be removed from the rear of the queue.

Set C

20. Another way to handle potential queue overflow or underflow is to include an error field in the `Q_TYPE` structure. Rewrite both `enqueue` and `dequeue` to use such a field. Each function should return a `BOOLEAN` value showing the status of the operation.

21. Rewrite `full_queue` so that instead of just returning `FALSE` it checks whether memory is available for an additional queue node. Use the same technique outlined in Exercise 19, Section 13.1.

22. Write a function whose output parameter is the info field of the nth item from the front of the queue. The function should not change the queue in any way. Assume that the queue has at least n items.

23. Rewrite the function in Exercise 22 so that the nth item is *removed* from the queue. Assume that the queue has at least n items.

24. Rewrite the answers to Exercises 22 and 23 but do not assume that the queue has n items. Each function should return a `BOOLEAN` value showing whether the action was successful (whether the queue had at least n items).

13.3 GENERALIZED LINKED LISTS

Introduction

Now we turn to linked-list structures that have total accessibility, not just accessibility from either end. Such structures are often ordered based on the value of a data field present in each of the nodes. **Key-ordered** structures have a specially identified **key field** whose value determines the placement of each node. An example of a key field is a social security number or employee **id** number, both of which are *uniquely* determined. **Last name** may not be a good choice for a key field because of the high probability of duplicate key values. A secondary key can often disambiguate requests to access nodes.

13.3.1 ADT Linked Lists

A linked list is a linear sequence of zero or more homogeneous nodes together with a set of operations. A **key-ordered** list is one in which the nodes are ordered on the basis of the value of a specific field called the **key**. In a **unique key-ordered** list, no two nodes can have the same key value. The following operations provide a minimal set of accessing functions for a key-ordered linked list.

Operation		Meaning
create_list	(list)	Make list logically accessible
destroy_list	(list)	Make list logically inaccessible
empty_list	(list)	True if list is empty
full_list	(list)	True if list is full
insert	(list, new_item)	Add new_item to list
delete	(list, target_value)	Delete the node whose key matches the target key value

retrieve	(list, target_value, old_item, found)	If found, return the data in the node whose key matches the target key value
modify	(list, target_value)	Change the data in the node whose key matches the target key value
print_list	(list)	Print all the nodes in ascending key order

The first six functions are like the stack and queue functions: The only difference is in the placement of the items to be added or deleted. In the stack and queue the placement is at either end of the data structure. Here the placement is data or key ordered, meaning that insertions and deletions might be anywhere in the ADT as long as the key ordering is preserved.

The **retrieve** function is a nondestructive version of **dequeue** (or **pop**). **retrieve** finds a node in the list and returns its associated data *without* removing the node from the list. The **modify** function allows the information in a node to be changed, as in changing a person's address. Notice that **modify** could be written as an applications function using the ADT functions **retrieve**, **delete**, and **insert**.

The **print_list** function allows the end user to see the entire list contents. This function calls a second function, **print_item**, that does the actual printing of the information fields in each node. Both the structure of a node's **info** field and the implementation of **print_item** are the responsibility of the applications programmer and not the ADT systems programmer.

Let's now consider the list data structure.

```
/*llist.h: header file for ADT key-ordered singly linked list with header node*/

#include  <stdlib.h>

typedef  struct node_type   {
                ITEM_TYPE                   info;     /* List-user's data */
                struct  node_type           *next;    /* Pointer to next node */
         }   NODE_TYPE;

typedef  NODE_TYPE    * NODE_PTR;       /* This is used to add a new node */

typedef  NODE_TYPE    * LIST_TYPE; /* This is reserved for the list pointer */

                                         /* Function prototypes */
void    create_list   ( LIST_TYPE    *list );

BOOLEAN empty_list    ( LIST_TYPE    *list );

BOOLEAN full_list     ( LIST_TYPE    *list );

void    print_list    ( LIST_TYPE    *list );

void    insert        ( LIST_TYPE    *list,
                        ITEM_TYPE     new_item );
```

```
void      delete       ( LIST_TYPE   *list,
                          KEY_TYPE    target_value );
```

```
/*Prototypes for destroy_list, modify, and retrieve are left as exercises */
```

13.3.2 Implementing the ADT Linked-List Functions

Next we look at the implementations of several of the linked-list access functions. Others, such as `destroy_list`, `modify`, and `retrieve`, are included as exercises at the end of this section.

The `create_list` function is slightly more complicated to implement here than for the ADT stack and queue. A special node is placed at the head of the list. This node is usually called a **header** and serves no other purpose here than to mark the beginning of the list. Although this may surprise you, it turns out to be useful. By giving it a special key that is lower than all other keys, we make sure that the header is always present and the list is never empty. Doing so reduces the programming complexity of `insert` and `delete`, both of which must otherwise include special code for detecting an empty list.

PERSPECTIVE

A newly created list is logically empty but with a header node present it can never be physically empty.

Briefly stated, `create_list` allocates the header node and inserts `MIN_KEY` in the key field.

```
/****************************************************************************
*  Function name:      create_list                                        *
*  Description:        Allocate the header node and insert its special key value. *
*                                                                         *
*  Input parameters:  none                                                *
*  Output parameters: list with header node                               *
*  Return value:      none                                                *
****************************************************************************/

void  create_list    ( LIST_TYPE    *list )
{
                                                    /* Allocate header node */
    *list = ( LIST_TYPE ) malloc ( sizeof ( NODE_TYPE ) );

    ( *list ) -> info.key =  MIN_KEY;     /* MIN_KEY set by the applications programmer */
    ( *list ) -> next     =  NULL;             /* No other nodes to point to yet */
}                                                   /* End of create_list */
```

Notice the complex reference to the key field (*list) -> info.key. The `list` variable is a pointer to a `LIST_TYPE`, which is itself a pointer type. Therefore, to refer to the `info.key` field of the header node we need a *double* dereference. The parentheses are necessary around `*list` because the arrow operator `->` has a higher precedence than the dereference operator `*`. Without the parentheses, `*list->info.key` would be an indirect reference to the `info.key` field of `list`. However, `list` is a pointer (to a `LIST-TYPE`) and does not have such a field.

> ## PERSPECTIVE
>
> A header node is sometimes used for storing important information about the linked list. For instance, a header might contain the total number of nodes in the list. It might also contain a pointer to the last node in the list or to the last node accessed. A **trailer** node can also be used to mark the end of the list. The minimal overhead for headers and trailers is more than offset by the gain in programming simplicity.

Checking for an empty list involves examining the node after the header node, `(*list)->next`. Because of the header node, `list` itself never points to `NULL`. However, `(*list)->next` is `NULL` when the list is (logically) empty. For consistency with the other ADT packages developed in this book, `list` is passed as a pointer and therefore must be dereferenced twice.

```
/****************************************************************************
*  Functions name:     empty_list                                          *
*  Description:        Determine if list is empty.                         *
*                                                                          *
*  Input parameters:   list                                                *
*  Output parameters:  none                                                *
*  Return value:       TRUE if list is empty, FALSE if one or more nodes present *
****************************************************************************/

BOOLEAN    empty_list    ( LIST_TYPE *list )
{
  return ( (*list)->next == NULL  ?  TRUE : FALSE ); /* Is node after header NULL */
}                                                    /* End of empty_list */
```

Because of dynamic memory allocation, `full_list` returns `FALSE` and is included for compatibility with other implementations, such as an array-based list.

```
/****************************************************************************
*  Function name:      full_list                                           *
*  Description:        Test whether list is full.                          *
*                                                                          *
*  Input parameters:   list                                                *
*  Output parameters:  none                                                *
*  Return value:       TRUE if list is full, FALSE if not full             *
*                                                                          *
*  NOTE:               since list is neither referenced nor changed,       *
*                      a compiler warning may be issued                    *
****************************************************************************/
```

```
BOOLEAN    full_list    (  LIST_TYPE *list  )
{
  return ( FALSE );
}                                            /*  End of full_list  */
```

The `print_list` function traverses the linked list (starting after the header node) and calls `print_item` to do the actual printing. `print_item` can be as simple or complex as wanted, depending on the application.

```
/*****************************************************************************
 *  Function name:     print_list                                           *
 *  Description:       Output list items in order.                          *
 *                                                                          *
 *  Input parameters:  list                                                 *
 *  Output parameters: none                                                 *
 *  Return value:      none                                                 *
 *****************************************************************************/
void  print_list  (  LIST_TYPE *list  )
{
    NODE_PTR        ptr;                            /*  Traversing pointer  */

    ptr = (*list)->next;                /*  Initialize to node after header  */

    while ( ptr != NULL ) {             /*  Print until end of list reached  */
      print_item ( ptr->info );  /*  Applications programmer-defined routine  */
      ptr = ptr->next;                        /*  Advance to next node in list  */
    }
}                                            /*  End of print_list  */
```

The `delete` function (see Figure 13.3–1) uses a helper function, `find_node`, to locate the node to be deleted. `find_node` returns two pointers as output parameters: one holding the address of the node being searched for (`current`) and the other holding the address of the node that logically precedes the node being searched for (`previous`). After calling `find_node`, `delete` resets the links around the target node, removing it from the list. The memory taken up by the deleted node is then returned to the heap.

```
/*****************************************************************************
 *  Function name:     delete                                               *
 *  Description:       Remove node from list whose key matches the target key *
 *                     value.                                               *
 *                                                                          *
 *  Input parameters:  list, target key value of node to be deleted        *
 *  Output parameters: list with specified node removed                     *
 *  Return value:      none                                                 *
 *                                                                          *
 *  Preconditions:     node containing target_value must be present        *
 *  Postconditions:    list with target node deleted                        *
 *****************************************************************************/
```

```
void delete  (  LIST_TYPE *list,
                KEY_TYPE  target_value  )
{
    NODE_PTR    current;
    NODE_PTR    previous;

    find_node ( list,  target_value,  &previous,  &current ); /* Find node to */
                                                              /* delete      */
    previous->next  =  current->next;        /* Link around node to delete  */
    free ( current );                        /* Dispose of deleted node     */
}                                            /* End of delete               */
```

The **insert** function (see Figure 13.3–2) allows a new node to be inserted at the appropriate location in the list. First, a new node is allocated (if possible). Next, the user's data is inserted in the **info** field. **find_node** is then called to find the node that logically precedes the location where **new_node** is to be placed. In this case the last argument to **find_node** is not needed and is called

(a) Find the node to delete.

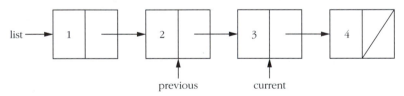

(b) Reset the pointers.

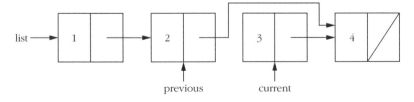

(c) Free the node.

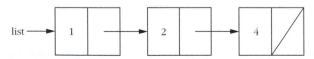

Figure 13.3–1   Deleting a node form a linked list

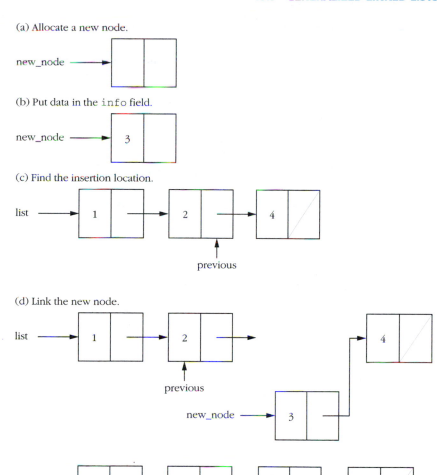

(a) Allocate a new node.

new_node

(b) Put data in the info field.

new_node → 3

(c) Find the insertion location.

list → 1 → 2 → 4

previous

(d) Link the new node.

list → 1 → 2

previous

new_node → 3

4

list → 1 → 2 → 3 → 4

Figure 13.3–2   Inserting a node into a linked list

ignore.   Once the insertion spot is found, the pointers are reset to include the newly allocated node.

Query: Why is the last argument to find_node not needed by insert?

RESPONSE: It is assumed that the node to be inserted does *not* already exist in the linked list. Therefore, find_node will not find its location and current has a meaningless value.

```
/*******************************************************************************
 * Function name:      insert                                                  *
 * Description:        Add new item to list, maintaining key-ordered structure.*
 *                                                                             *
 * Input parameters:  list, node to be inserted                               *
 * Output parameters: list with specified node added                          *
 * Return value:      none                                                    *
 *                                                                             *
 * Preconditions:     node containing key must not be present                 *
 * Postconditions:    list contains new node inserted by key                  *
 *                                                                             *
 * NOTE:              because ignore is not referenced or changed, a compiler warning *
 *                    may be issued                                           *
 *******************************************************************************/

void insert ( LIST_TYPE *list,
              ITEM_TYPE new_item )
{
    NODE_PTR    new_node;                              /* Pointer to the new node */
    NODE_PTR    previous;                     /* Pointer to node prior to insertion point */
    NODE_PTR    ignore;                          /* Extra pointer for call to find_node */

    new_node = ( NODE_PTR ) malloc ( sizeof ( NODE_TYPE ) );       /* Allocate node */

    if (new_node != NULL ) {                          /* Assuming there is space... */

        new_node->info = new_item;                              /* add the info */

        find_node ( list, new_item.key, &previous, &ignore );   /* Find insertion point */

        new_node->next = previous->next;                /* Insert new_node into list */
        previous->next = new_node;

    }

}                                                       /* End of insert */
```

The **find_node** function searches through the linked list for a node whose key value matches the input parameter called **target_value**. **previous** starts out pointing to the header node and **current** is always one node ahead. The loop continues to update the pointers as long as these conditions are met:

1. **current** is not pointing past the end of the list.
2. The key value of the node **current** is pointing to is less than the target key value.

Next, we test which of the two conditions stopped the loop. If **current**'s key value equals the target key value, the search was successful. However, if the node was not found (current's key does not equal the target key) we set current to NULL.

```
/****************************************************************************
*  Function name:      find_node                                           *
*  Description:        Locate node (and its predecessor) having key = target *
*                      value.                                              *
*                                                                          *
*  Input parameters:   list, target key value of node to search for        *
*  Output parameters:  previous (logical predecessor of target node)       *
*                      current (pointer to target node or NULL if node not  *
*                      found)                                              *
*  Return value:       none                                                *
****************************************************************************/

void  find_node (  LIST_TYPE  *list,
                   KEY_TYPE   target_value,
                   NODE_PTR   *previous,
                   NODE_PTR   *current        )
{

  *previous = *list;                       /* previous is placed at header node */
  *current  = (*list)->next;        /* current is placed at node after header */

                         /*  Traverse list as long as current has not reached */
                         /*  the end of the list ... or passed the target node */

  while ( ( *current  != NULL) && ( *current )->info.key  < target_value ) {
    *previous = *current;                       /* Update the traversing pointers */
    *current  = (*current)->next;
  }

                         /*  If node was not found, set current to NULL */
  if ( ( *current != NULL ) && ( *current )->info.key != target_value )
    *current  = NULL;
}
                                                       /*  End of find_node  */
```

PERSPECTIVE

It is important to check current for *not equal to* NULL as part of the while and if statements in find_node. If that portion of the tests is omitted and current does equal NULL, the second half of the test will cause a run-time error!

Query: Why isn't `find_node` listed as part of the applications programmer's ADT interface?

RESPONSE: `find_node` is an internal (systems programmer) function used to facilitate the implementation of several other ADT functions. Because it makes direct reference to the data structure, it is not intended for the applications programmer and is therefore not listed in the ADT interface.

We conclude this section by showing a simple driver package to partially test the ADT linked list.

```
/*****************************************************************************
*  File name:    llist.c                                                     *
*  Description: Partial driver for ADT singly linked list.                   *
*****************************************************************************/

#include <stdio.h>

#define  MIN_KEY 0;

typedef  int KEY_TYPE;

typedef  struct {
           KEY_TYPE key;
                        /*  Insert other fields according to the application  */
           }  ITEM_TYPE;

void  print_item ( ITEM_TYPE  item );              /* Prototype for print_item */

#include  "llist.h"

main ( )
{
   LIST_TYPE  list;
   ITEM_TYPE  item;

   create_list ( &list );

   item.key = 3;   insert ( &list,  item );
   item.key = 5;   insert ( &list,  item );
   item.key = 1;   insert ( &list,  item );
   item.key = 7;   insert ( &list,  item );
   print_list ( &list );                           /* Outputs 1 3 5 7 */

   delete ( &list, 3 );   delete ( &list, 5 );
   delete ( &list, 1 );   delete ( &list, 7 );
```

```
        if ( empty_list ( &list ) )
            printf (  "\nList empty...\n");              /* Outputs this message */
        else
            printf (  "\nList not empty...\n" );

        destroy_list ( &list );

        return ( 0 );
}
```

```
/*************************************************************************
 * Function name:     print_item                                        *
 * Description:       Print various fields from the item.               *
 *                                                                      *
 * Input parameters: list item                                         *
 * Output parameters: none                                             *
 * Return value:     none                                              *
 *************************************************************************/

void  print_item  ( ITEM_TYPE item )
{
    printf ( "Key = %d\n",  item.key );
                /* Add other print statements according to the application  */

}                                                       /* End of print_item */
```

13.3.3 Other Linked Structures

Although we do not explore them in detail here, other linked structures are also useful. One variation, the **circular linked list**, links the last node to the first, as shown in Figure 13.3–3. The list pointer is not fixed to the first node but can float and point to any node in the list. Another variation, the **doubly linked list**, has an extra link field called **previous** that points to the immediate

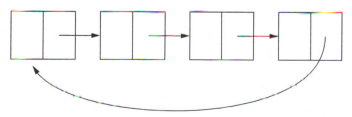

Figure 13.3–3   Circular linked list

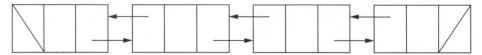

Figure 13.3–4   Doubly linked list

predecessor of a given node, as shown in Figure 13.3–4. This allows traversals in a forward or a reverse direction. Assuming that `current` points to a particular node, its immediate predecessor is `current->previous` and its immediate successor is `current->next`.

Other variations include a **multiply linked list,** or *list of lists*. This is roughly analogous to a 2D (or *n*-D) array. In a multiply linked list a node points to its successor (or predecessor) and to another list (shown in Figure 13.3–5 as an appointment calendar). The horizontal lists represent days of the week and the vertical lists represent appointments for a given time of day. Note that insertions

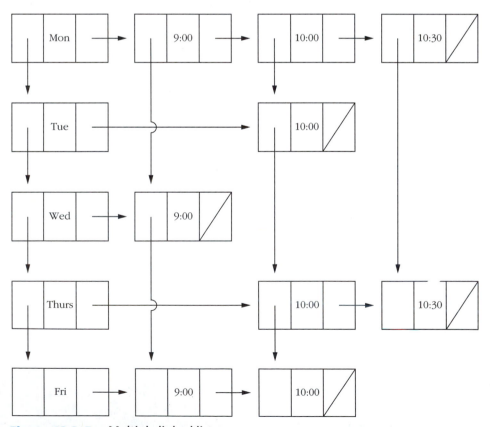

Figure 13.3–5   Multiply linked list

and deletions can become cumbersome because pointers must be updated in multiple lists.

A multiply linked list is potentially much more memory-efficient than a 2D array. Consider the following scenario: A large hardware distributor has 10,000 products and 5,000 salespeople. To track each person's sales would need a 5,000 × 10,000 or 50-million-element 2D array. However, suppose each salesperson handles only 100 different products. In that case, only 1 percent of this array would have data entered; the other 99 percent of the cells would be 0. This is called a **sparse matrix.** Implementing a multiply linked list requires allocating only as many nodes as are needed for each salesperson—for example, 5,000 × 100, or 500,000 nodes.

EXERCISES 13.3

Concept Check

Answer statements 1 through 4 with true *or* false.

1. In a unique key-ordered linked list, only one node has a key field.
2. A header node can be used to simplify the logic for list functions.
3. The `find_node` function is accessible to the applications programmer.
4. A doubly linked list is analogous to a 2D array.

For statements 5 through 8 choose the answer that best completes the statement.

5. A person's last name might not be a good choice for a key field because
   a. the name might change
   b. it is not unique
   c. key fields should be numeric, not alphabetic
   d. of potential privacy issues

6. The `print_item` function is not part of the ADT package because
   a. the ADT systems programmer does not know the structure of the `info` field
   b. the applications programmer does not know the structure of the `info` field
   c. the applications programmer shouldn't be given access to an implementation function
   d. the ADT systems programmer doesn't know which field will be the key

7. If `find_node` does not find the node with the key value requested, it
   a. returns `NULL`
   b. sets `previous` to `NULL`
   c. sets `current` to `NULL`
   d. sets both `previous` and `current` to `NULL`

8. The `insert` function calls `find_node` with a pointer argument called `ignore` because
   a. that argument is not used by any of the ADT functions and it is there in case a new feature is added to the ADT at a later time
   b. the presence of a header node means the argument is not important
   c. `find_node` does not need to know the value of that pointer
   d. it is assumed that `find_node` will not find a node with that key

For statements 9 through 12 fill in the blanks with the right word.

9. Deleting a node needs _____ pointer(s), called _____.
10. A _____ allows bidirectional traversals.
11. In a _____ the last node is linked to the first node.
12. A multiply linked list is sometimes called a _____.

Set A

Solve each of the following problems.

13. Rewrite `empty_list` assuming that a trailer node (containing `MAX_KEY`) is present in the list.
14. Discuss the changes needed for `find_node` to allow for a trailer node.
15. Design a structure for `ITEM_TYPE` that would be suitable for an address book. Include fields for name, address, and key. The key could be the phone number. Add other fields as wanted.

Set B

16. Rewrite `full_list` with checking for available memory.
17. Rewrite `insert` without calling `find_node` (but `insert` should produce the same results).
18. Rewrite `delete` without calling `find_node` (but `delete` should produce the same results).

Set C

19. Rewrite `create_list` but create a header and a trailer. The header should link to the trailer and the trailer should point to `NULL`.
20. Rewrite `find_node` on the assumption that the list has a trailer node. Remember that the trailer node has a key that is larger than any other key in the list so `current` can never advance beyond the trailer.
21. Implement the ADT `destroy_list` function. The function should traverse the list and free each node, including the header node, leaving `list` pointing to `NULL`.
22. Implement the ADT `retrieve` function. The function should request the key of the node to be retrieved. It should then call `find_node` to locate the node. Finally, use `print_item` to output all the information fields to the end user. Include an error message if the node to be modified is not currently in the list.
23. Implement `modify` as an applications function using the method suggested in the text.

Programming Languages 14

Tower of Babel (1563), by Pieter Bruegel, depicts a biblical story. The tower was never completed because the workers spoke in different languages.

After completing this chapter you should be able to do the following:

Learning Goals

- Differentiate between machine language and assembly language
- Know the purpose of languages such as FORTRAN, ALGOL, and COBOL
- Distinguish between syntax and semantics
- Know the elements of Backus–Naur Form and context-free grammars
- Explain the differences between the procedural, object-oriented, functional, and logic programming paradigms
- Identify the elements of imperative languages
- Identify the elements of object-oriented languages
- Identify the elements of applicative languages
- Identify the elements of declarative languages
- Identify languages relative to their paradigms

Chapter Activity

The derivation of a sentence generated by a grammar is as follows.

$$
\begin{array}{llll}
\langle\text{assign}\rangle \longrightarrow & \langle\text{id}\rangle & ::= & \langle\text{expr}\rangle \\
\longrightarrow & A & ::= & \langle\text{expr}\rangle \\
\longrightarrow & A & ::= & \langle\text{expr}\rangle + \langle\text{term}\rangle \\
\longrightarrow & A & ::= & \langle\text{term}\rangle + \langle\text{term}\rangle \\
\longrightarrow & A & ::= & \langle\text{factor}\rangle + \langle\text{term}\rangle \\
\longrightarrow & A & ::= & \langle\text{id}\rangle + \langle\text{term}\rangle \\
\longrightarrow & A & ::= & B + \langle\text{term}\rangle \\
\longrightarrow & A & ::= & B + \langle\text{term}\rangle * \langle\text{factor}\rangle \\
\longrightarrow & A & ::= & B + \langle\text{factor}\rangle * \langle\text{factor}\rangle \\
\longrightarrow & A & ::= & B + \langle\text{id}\rangle * \langle\text{factor}\rangle \\
\longrightarrow & A & ::= & B + C * \langle\text{factor}\rangle \\
\longrightarrow & A & ::= & B + C * \langle\text{id}\rangle \\
\longrightarrow & A & ::= & B + C * D \\
\end{array}
$$

Construct a parse tree for the sentence.

14.1 OVERVIEW OF PROGRAMMING LANGUAGES

Introduction

A **programming language** is used to represent an algorithm and provide a vehicle through which a computer and its users can communicate. Some languages allow the programmer to manipulate the machine's hardwired instruction set directly. These are called **low-level languages.** Other **high-level languages** are far removed from the hardware and must be translated by compilers to low-level instructions. Because it is easy to use, most software is written in high-level languages.

14.1.1 Historical Perspectives

Each computer has its own **machine language** based on its architecture. Machines with the Intel Pentium processor use a different machine language from machines with the Motorola 68040 processor. Before the development of low-level and high-level programming languages, all programming was done at the machine level. As you can imagine, programming in machine language was tedious because each transfer of information had to be handled in binary as an individual instruction. (See Chapter 1 for more on this kind of programming.)

Assembly language was developed to alleviate some of the difficulties of machine-language programming. In **assembly language** (also discussed in Chapter 1), mnemonics are used to write statements in a one-to-one correspondence with the machine language of the computer. This may not seem any different from machine language but the difference is in *how* it is presented.

Consider the following fictitious machine language sequence in octal; it has no intrinsic meaning as presented.

```
2463
3446
5457
```

However, suppose the first column represents an operation, the second column represents a register, and the third and fourth columns represent an address. In the first column let *2* identify *load,* let *3* identify *subtract,* and let *5* identify *store.* An assembly language equivalent could be

```
LOAD  4,X
SUBT  4,Y
STORE 4,Z
```

This translates as the following, which is easier to understand than its machine language equivalent.

Load the contents at address location 63 (octal) called **X** into register 4, subtract from the contents of register 4 the contents at address location 46 (octal) called **Y**, and store the new contents of register 4 at address location 57 (octal) called **Z**.

Assembly languages first became popular in the early 1950s and are still in use, particularly with special-purpose hardware or when execution speed is critical.

The example just cited of machine and assembly languages suggests that a value located at X is to have a value located at Y subtracted from it with the result stored at location Z. Restated algebraically,

```
Z = X - Y
```

The simplicity of this formulation led computer scientists to pursue languages that were more accessible to people. In 1954 IBM developed the first widely used high-level programming language, called **FORTRAN** (FORmula TRANslating system). The language was implemented in 1957 and, as its name suggests, it is best suited for numerical computation. (FORTRAN is included in the historical overview in Chapter 1.)

PERSPECTIVE

Estimates suggest that 18 people-years were needed to develop FORTRAN. Its originator and designer, IBM engineer John Warner Backus, is also credited with the feat of developing the first compiler.

FORTRAN is still a useful language, especially among scientists and engineers, and has been revised several times, as FORTRAN-II in 1958, FORTRAN-IV in 1962, FORTRAN-66 in 1966, FORTRAN-77 in 1977, and FORTRAN-90 in 1990. (FORTRAN-77 became an ANSI Standard in 1978.) Hundreds of other programming languages evolved from FORTRAN. Also, concepts such as program **modularity** (covered in Chapter 5) are the backbone of **procedural languages** (discussed in Section 14.2). Modularity in FORTRAN is a way of constructing a program in separate independent modules called **subroutines** or **subprograms.** FORTRAN's COMMON statement allows subroutines to share information as if the information were in a global environment. This and other features gave FORTRAN the prominence it has today.

FORTRAN's modular approach was also a basis for a new concept called **block structuring** that allowed modularity within a program. Block structuring coupled with recursion (covered in Chapter 15) led to the development of a new language called **ALGOL** (ALGOrithmic Language) in 1958. ALGOL-58 became ALGOL-60 in 1960, which evolved to a language that used some elements of ALGOL-60 and allowed the programmer to develop programs external to the ALGOL environment. This was a great achievement and the result was ALGOL-68. However, this independence of the language put many restrictions on the programmer and may have prevented ALGOL-68 from developing into a popular language. A few notions of ALGOL-68 survived, but not the essentials of the language.

We learned in Chapter 1 that computers have been an important tool for scientific computation since the early 1940s. Prompted by this success and the achievements of FORTRAN, Grace Murray Hopper initiated a movement in the mid 1950s to introduce computers to the business world as well. Activities such as doing payroll, taking inventory, billing, and accounting were labor-intensive, and more efficient systems were needed. The solution was **COBOL** (COmmon Business Oriented Language). COBOL facilitated the description of data with English-like commands and introduced data records—for example, an employee's name, address, salary, tax deductions—as a data structure. COBOL evolved into new versions that led to the COBOL-65 standard, the COBOL-74 ANSI Standard in 1974, and COBOL-85 in 1985. Even today, the language continues to change with the needs of the time. Because of its prominence in the commercial world, COBOL still enjoys a reputation as one of the most popular programming languages in use today.

FORTRAN, ALGOL, and COBOL are basically procedural languages in that you write procedures using information to get the results you want. Specifically, procedural languages are sequential and center on assignments. However, not all programming languages use this paradigm. Programming for artificial intelligence, for example, uses the functional representation of a problem. From 1956 to 1962, **LISP** (LISt Processing) was developed at MIT under the direction of John McCarthy. This language consists of a set of basic functions (**primitive functions**) from which other functions are developed. LISP uses **dynamically typed** data structures in which, at any given time, the value of a variable depends on the last function to be associated with it. This concept is a departure from the von Neumann philosophy of computers, which relies heavily on assignments, variables that have changing values, and transfer of control.

The combined features of FORTRAN, ALGOL, and COBOL were the genesis of a new IBM language called **PL/I** (Programming Language I) that was developed in 1964. PL/I was meant to replace a variety of languages in use at the time with a single language. However, its features—pointers, modularity, and recursion—were isolated characteristics that detracted from their usefulness and made the language overcomplicated. PL/I never took hold, and after two decades of modest use it is probably destined to become extinct.

Several of the many programming languages have more appeal than others and are more commonly used. For example, **BASIC** (Beginner's All-purpose Symbolic Instruction Code) was introduced in 1964 and became popular because of its simplicity, time-sharing capability, and interactive features. BASIC is still popular today. **BCPL** (Basic Combined Programming Language) was developed in 1969 as an experimental systems language and gave rise to the **C** language, developed at AT&T Bell Laboratories by D. Ritchie in 1974. C enjoys widespread use in business, education, and industry. **Pascal** was introduced in 1971 as an educational language and is used in many educational environments. C and Pascal are ALGOL-based languages.

Figure 14.1–1 is a chronology of programming languages, beginning with machine and assembly languages. The chronology can never be complete because new languages are born whenever they are needed. Nevertheless, this gives us a sense of language development over the past five decades.

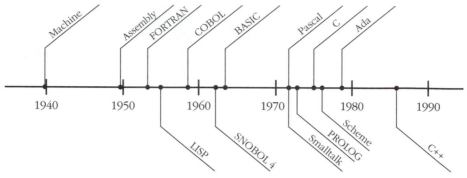

Figure 14.1–1 Chronology of programming languages

14.1.2 Grammars, Syntax, and Semantics

In any human language there are rules for forming sentences. In English, for example, letters of the alphabet form words. Words are combined to form sentences consisting of a subject and a predicate, and predicates are formed by combining a verb with an object. The form of the English sentence is dictated by its **syntactical** rules and its meaning is dictated by its **semantic** rules. Some of these rules are shown in the syntax diagram for a disjunction in Figure 14.1–2 and for a conditional in Figure 14.1–3.

For example, consider the sentence

Yllib syub spihc.

According to the structure of the English language, this sentence probably has a subject called *Yllib*, a verb called *syub*, and an object called *spihc*, but what about its meaning? None of the three words is in the English vocabulary. If each word is reversed, however, you can see that the sentence

Billy buys chips.

does indeed satisfy the syntax of the language. *Billy* is the subject, *buys* is the verb, and *chips* is the object. The sentence is also semantically correct because it expresses the intended meaning of the subject and predicate.

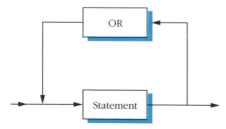

Figure 14.1–2 Syntax diagram for disjunction

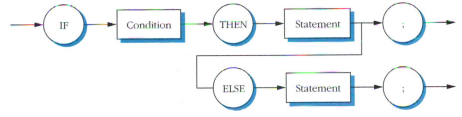

Figure 14.1–3 Syntax diagram for conditional

Programming languages are like human languages in that they both have syntax and semantics. The syntax and semantics of a programming language are described by a language vehicle called a **metalanguage**—a language describing other languages. For programming languages the metalanguage must be precise and unambiguous so that there is no possibility of misinterpretation. One such metalanguage is **Backus–Naur Form (BNF),** created by John Warner Backus of the United States and Peter Naur of Denmark. Backus and Naur's BNF is often considered the finest example of a programming metalanguage.

PERSPECTIVE

Noam Chomsky developed the concept of transformational grammar in computational linguistics and classified grammars using a four-tier hierarchy called the Chomsky Hierarchy.

To give you an idea of the BNF metalanguage, consider again the English sentence *Billy buys chips.* We can make a rule (in a metalanguage) that

```
sentence  ::= subject  predicate
```

We can even produce a set of such rules for an English grammar for the language. For example, the rules

```
subject ::= [ article ] noun
```

and

```
predicate ::= verb [ object ]
```

where bracketed items are optional, suggest that all sentences must contain a noun and a verb.

   Billy buys.

is a valid sentence even though it lacks an object.

   This example of a metalanguage illustrates the elements of a **BNF grammar,** which takes the form

```
A ::= B
```

where the metasymbol ::= is a production operator that stands for *is defined as*. Other metasymbols are

[ ]   for optional inclusions
{ }   for repetitions
| for choice

In addition to the ::= operator, there are terminal and nonterminal symbols. **Terminal symbols** have values that are explicitly represented and are symbols of the grammar. **Nonterminal symbols** represent other symbols of the grammar according to a BNF rule `A ::= B`. The symbol `A` is always a nonterminal. The symbol `B` represents a string of nonterminal and terminal symbols. Thus we can show a construct in a BNF grammar as

```
x ::= 758 [ .234 ] | λ
y ::= 345 | x
z ::= y | { x } | "cat"
```

Although there is no intrinsic meaning in this construct, it does illustrate the following. `x` is a nonterminal defined as a choice between a terminal (a number 758 with optional decimal .234) and λ (lambda) defined as a null string terminal. `y` is a nonterminal defined as a choice between a terminal (number 345) or a nonterminal `x`. `z` is defined as a choice among the nonterminal `y`, the repetition of the nonterminal `x`, and the terminal string "cat".

This is not a complete explanation of programming grammars and BNF, and we encourage you to plan some future study of these subjects. Still, this overview shows that languages such as C, designed according to rules like those of the BNF metagrammar, are **context-free grammars (CFG).** These grammars consist of a set of nonterminals with a symbol to specify the beginning of the grammar sequence, a set of terminals, and a set of production rules of the form `A ::= B` where `A` is a single nonterminal symbol. Nonprogramming languages are usually dependent on **context** because a nonterminal symbol is created by incorporating a previous meaning in the nonterminal. All programming languages are designed to be context-free.

As a final note on grammars, consider an expression composed of the nonterminal symbols `w`, `x`, `y`, and `z` and the ordinary arithmetic operations of * and +. Let the expression be described as

```
w ::= x * y + z
```

Without rules for the order of operations, this expression is ambiguous: We cannot tell whether addition precedes multiplication. What is needed is a structured hierarchy of syntax, called a **parse tree,** to interpret expressions based on the grammar of a language. One parse tree for the expression just described is shown in Figure 14.1–4, where it is interpreted as

```
w ::= x * ( y + z )
```

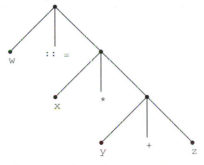

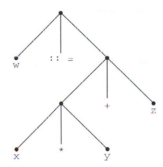

Figure 14.1–4   Parse tree for
w ::= x * (y + z)

Figure 14.1–5   Parse tree
for w ::= (x * y) + z

Another interpretation is

```
w ::= ( x * y ) + z
```

shown in Figure 14.1–5 and decidedly different from the interpretation in Figure 14.1–4. This situation is destined for problems. The grammar is *ambiguous* because it allows at least two different interpretations for the expression. The correct interpretation is w ::= (x * y) + z, which is a *statement* in the grammar of a language. Thus the statements generated by a programming language's grammar must be unambiguous for the language to be reliable.

14.1.3 What Makes a Language Tick?

"Which is the best programming language?" is a question often asked by programmers. This is like asking "What is the best boat?" or "What is the best car?" A van is best to transport a ski team, but a van is not best for a sports car driver.

The same is true for programming languages. One language is better for a particular application than another language. As we saw in Section 14.1.1, the attempt to create one language for all applications, PL/I, did not succeed. COBOL is good for processing business data, whereas FORTRAN is good for numerical computation. C is a good, general-purpose, structured language, but LISP and PROLOG are better for artificial intelligence applications. C does have the advantage of versatility, however, making it suitable for many applications, especially systems programming.

Now let's focus on what makes a programming language good. It should be clear, simple, and unambiguous with a predefined purpose. It should be flexible enough to program applications and its syntax should be easy to use. We would expect a language to be cost-effective for its users and compatible with a variety of computers. Serving a useful purpose, either practical or theoretical, is also an advantage. Ideally, we want a language to help the programmer in work that benefits both computer science and society.

EXERCISES 14.1

Concept Check

Answer statements 1 through 4 with true *or* false.
1. The first high-level programming language was COBOL.
2. Semantics deals with the meaning of a sentence.
3. A language about languages is called a grammar.
4. C is a good systems programming language.

For statements 5 through 8 choose the answer that best completes the statement.
5. A context-free grammar
   a. has `A ::= B + C` as its production rule
   b. only uses nonterminals
   c. has `A ::= B` as its production rule
   d. cannot be used in today's languages
6. The assumed grammar for the languages of the 1960s and 1970s is
   a. context-sensitive grammar
   b. BNF
   c. English grammar
   d. the class of metalanguages
7. PL/I is derived from
   a. FORTRAN
   b. COBOL
   c. ALGOL-60
   d. all of the above
8. Syntax refers to
   a. the form of a sentence
   b. the interpretation of a sentence
   c. the meaning of a sentence
   d. the grammar of a sentence

For statements 9 through 12 fill in the blanks with the right word.
9. COBOL was designed for the _____.
10. The language most closely associated with a computer is _____.
11. Backus–Naur Form describes the _____ of a language.
12. A language such as C is considered a _____ language because one instruction produces many machine-language instructions.

Set A

Write a short essay for each of the following.
13. Explain what is meant by an ALGOL-based language.
14. Explain some differences between FORTRAN and COBOL.
15. Explain what is meant by a context-free grammar.
16. Describe some advantages of high-level languages over low-level languages.

17. Describe some advantages of low-level languages over high-level languages.
18. Explain the difference between block structuring and subprograms.

Set B

19. Design a syntax diagram for a conjunction.
20. Describe the meaning of the BNF `a ::= b | {c} | d`.
21. Describe a parse tree and explain its significance.
22. Describe the difference between a grammar and a language and give an example of each.
23. Explain some of the features that make a programming language a good language.
24. Why is BNF considered a CFG?
25. What would make a grammar unambiguous?

Set C

26. The following code is written in FORTRAN-77.

```
      PROGRAM MAIN
      REAL array( 50 )
23    READ *, len
      IF ( len .LE. 0 .OR. len .GT. 50 )    STOP
      READ *, ( array( i ),  i = 1,len )
      PRINT *, ( array( i ),  i = 1,len )
      GOTO 23
      END
```

Reflect on its purpose and convert it to C.

27. The following code is written in ALGOL.

```
i := 4
for j := i - 1 step 3 until 99 do
     k := j * j
```

Reflect on its purpose and convert it to C.

28. The following code is written in COBOL.

```
input_module.
    read  input_data.
    add   x  to  sum.
    add   1  to  count.
    move  x  to  x_output.
    move  sum   to  sum_output.
    move  count to  count_output.
    write output_line.
    go to input_module.
```

Reflect on its purpose and convert it to C.

29. The following code is written in PL/I.

```
total  :  procedure ( array ) returns ( float );
         declare array( * ) float,
                 sum  float  initial( 0 );
         do i = 1  to  dim( array, 1 );
            sum  =  sum  +  array( i );
         end;
         return( sum );
      end  total;
```

Reflect on its purpose and convert it to C.

14.2   LANGUAGE PARADIGMS

Introduction

In Section 14.1 we suggested that no single language is capable of satisfying all computing needs. We said that some languages are better suited for numerical computation (FORTRAN), whereas others are better suited for processing business data (COBOL). Some are powerful for general-purpose and systems programming (C). These three languages are based on a procedural paradigm. By **paradigm** we mean a model, an approach, or a way of reasoning to solve a problem.

The paradigm for the most common classification of languages resembles the hardware structure of the computer. Memory location, assignment, and procedures (functions, in C) are central to this mode of programming, which is called the **procedural paradigm** and follows the fetch-decode-execute phases of an instruction cycle. Languages using the procedural paradigm are called procedural or **imperative languages.** C is an example of an imperative language.

Programming languages are not confined to processing data as input. Some languages form objects consisting of both the data and the routines to manipulate the data. We call this the **object-oriented paradigm** and languages using this paradigm are called **object-oriented languages.** C++ is an example of an object-oriented language.

Other languages follow a **functional paradigm** that treats programming as a set of functions, each doing its part to solve a problem. This paradigm does not depend on assignment and repetition but on data objects to which values are assigned according to a function's application and then passed to other functions. For this reason, languages using the functional paradigm are called **applicative languages.** LISP is an example of an applicative language.

There are also nonprocedural languages—languages that are not "data processors" in the strict sense. These programming languages are characterized less by problem solving and more by a logical development that results in a solution: They discover the nature of the problem rather than its solution. These nonprocedural languages are in the category of logic programming. They follow a **logic paradigm** and are called **declarative languages.** PROLOG (PROgramming LOGic) is an example of a declarative language.

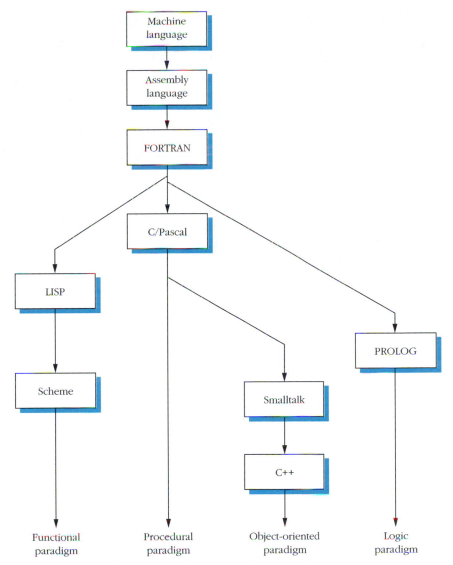

Figure 14.2–1   Genealogy of programming paradigms

We will now take a short "tour" of programming paradigms. Figure 14.2–1 shows a genealogy tree for several popular languages. Its root is in machine and assembly languages. It has four branches that represent four language paradigms: procedural, functional, logic, and object-oriented. Needless to say, many of the details cannot be covered here. However, this sampling of language paradigms highlights the importance of different ways of using programming tools.

14.2.1 Imperative Languages

By now you are familiar with C, an imperative language that uses the procedural fetch-decode-execute paradigm. This paradigm is based on variables, assignments

Table 14.2–1 Languages Using the Procedural Paradigm

IMPERATIVE LANGUAGES	DATE DEVELOPED	PROGRAMMING APPLICATIONS
FORTRAN	1954	Numerical computations
COBOL	1959	Data and file processing
BASIC	1963	Interactive, educational
PL/I	1963	Multipurpose
Pascal	1971	General-purpose, educational
C	1974	General-purpose, systems
Ada	1979	General-purpose, real-time

to these variables through statements, and the repetition of statements. Program statements look for an instruction, learn what the instruction is, and then execute it. Most programming as we know it follows this mode of operation. For example, consider the C function `fscanf` in the following example.

```
fscanf ( "payroll.dat", %f, &wage );
```

The program statement looks for the `fscanf` function, decodes an instruction to read a floating-point number from a file called `payroll.dat`, and executes it by reading the number.

The procedural paradigm is modeled on machine functions that include memory allocation, assignments, control structures, and processing. It does data typing, distinguishes variables from constants, and separates memory contents from memory locations. Each of these processes is isolated in a program module. In FORTRAN the modules are subroutines; in C they are functions. Table 14.2–1 lists some imperative languages and their programming applications.

14.2.2 Object-Oriented Languages

A popular view of programming is that we take passive information and use program statements to manipulate it. Consider a floating-point number `radius` that must be squared. In C we could write

```
radius =  7.94;
exp    =  2.0;
new    =  pow ( radius,  exp );
```

The program statement looks for `radius` and `exp`, decodes the `pow` function, acts on it, places the result in `new`, and moves on to the next instruction. The **object-oriented paradigm** treats data and the routines that act on it as a single object or data structure. So the `radius` and `exp` variables and the `pow` function are treated as a single object that, when invoked, automatically squares `radius`.

Object-oriented programming (called **OOP** colloquially) is based on the data structure rather than the process or the subprogram. It also has dynamic binding: An abstract data type called an **object** can be associated with different data types at run time. Programming is thus simplified because instead of rewriting an existing object for a different data type and a different purpose, we modify the object when it is invoked. In addition, when we create an object we are also creating its function as part of the object.

Also, because one object can be used (inherited) by more than one programmer on a system, the object has multiple applications. The ability to generate required abstract data types and the features of dynamic binding and usability by others make the object-oriented paradigm attractive.

The first OOP language, **Smalltalk,** was developed in 1968 by Alan Kay at the University of Utah and is the model for the OOP paradigm we use today. Smalltalk creates an environment that combines an operating system, compiler, and editor all programmed in the language of the environment, Smalltalk. This is a departure from the procedural paradigm that separates the program from the compiler and the operating system. It enables programmers to take the whole environment—operating system, compiler, and editor—and adapt it for their own purpose.

Smalltalk is simple but powerful, as shown in the following sample calculating the average of the average of the first N numbers with the result expressed as an integer.

```
num <- 0.
sum <- 0.
[ num <= N ]
   whileTrue;
       [ sum <- sum + num.
         num <- num + 1.
       ]
avg <- sum // num.
```

Despite its soundness, Smalltalk does have at least one drawback, namely, that the language is inefficient. Perhaps the increased speed and storage capacity of today's computers will put Smalltalk in a more positive light.

C++ (C plus plus) is a newer object-oriented language that was developed at AT&T Bell Laboratories and publicized in 1985. It is not a "pure" object-oriented language as is Smalltalk but it fits the paradigm in that its data structures are objects. In fact, C++ is really a superset of C, incorporating all the elements of ANSI C. C++ has recently had a surge of popularity, mainly because it enhances the already popular C with the OOP paradigm.

In C++ an object is represented by a **class** that encapsulates both the data used to describe the object and a set of functions called **methods** to manipulate the data. Notice its difference from the examples in Chapter 11, which use the `struct` definition in C without using objects. Following is an example of a stack class in C++. (Stacks are discussed in Chapters 11 and 13.)

```
class  stack                            // Begin object
{
  private:                    // Private means that there is no direct
                              //  access to these data or functions.

    int *top;               // Therefore, no stack user can access these.
    int *bot;
```

```
protected:                      // Protected means that access to data and functions
                                //  is only for special "derived classes."
                                //  It is not used with this object.


public:                          // Direct access to data and procedures


   stack ( )
   {                                                  // Function stack is a
     top = bot = new int [ MAX_STACK ];    // dynamically allocated array
   }                                                  // pointed to by top  and  bot


   void push ( int  c )
   {
     if (  ( top - bot ) <  MAX_STACK )
       *top++ = c;
   }


   int  pop ( )
   {
     if (  --top  >=  bot )
       return( *top );
   }


};                                              // End object
```

The object class is partitioned into three sections: Private, protected, and public. The *public* portion describes three functions that initialize, push, and pop a stack. The **top** and **bot** pointers encapsulated in the class are in the *private* portion of the class. The object does not make use of the possible *protected* portion in this case.

Object-oriented programming has excited new levels of interest, particularly because of features such as the ability to "inherit" objects in a system. It is not yet clear, however, whether this programming paradigm will become a mainstay of computing. Table 14.2–2 lists some object-oriented languages and

Table 14.2–2 Languages Using the Object-Oriented Paradigm

OBJECT-ORIENTED LANGUAGE	DATE DEVELOPED	PROGRAMMING APPLICATION
SIMULA67	1968	Simulation
Smalltalk	1971	Integrated environment, personal use
C++	1985	General-purpose, systems programming
Object Pascal	1986	General-purpose, educational
Eiffel	1988	General-purpose

their programming applications. Note that although Smalltalk was the first truly object-oriented programming language, SIMULA67 had some features of the object-oriented paradigm.

14.2.3 Applicative Languages

Consider a function that acts on a list of names. The function is to read a person's first and last names, reverse the last name and the first, add to or delete from a list of existing names in a file, sort the list by last name, and then write the result back to the file. We can call this whole process a single "black-box" operation with an input and an output. Inside this black-box function are four other black-box functions, each with an input and output, that read, interchange, sort, and write, as shown in Figure 14.2–2. This programming approach using a set of basic functions (called primitives) with a defined collection of data objects describes the **functional paradigm.** Functional paradigms are more efficient and dynamic when the functions operate in parallel. As an analogy, consider evaluating the function

$$f(x) = 2.3x^2 - 7.4 \sin x + \cos(3.4x)$$

The single black box is really the algebraic sum of three other functions: $2.3x^2$, $7.4 \sin x$, and $\cos(3.4x)$. Each of these functions is a function of other functions, namely,

$2.3x^2$	is a function consisting of the product of the square of the variable x, which is itself a function, and the floating-point number 2.3;
$-7.4 \sin x$	is a function consisting of the negative product of the trigonometric sine function of the variable x and the floating-point number 7.4;
$\cos(3.4x)$	is the trigonometric cosine function of the function that is the product of the floating-point number 3.4 and the variable x.

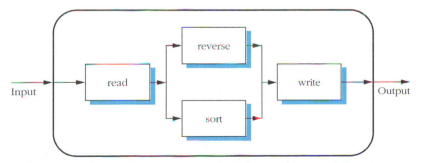

Figure 14.2–2   Black-box illustration of functional paradigm

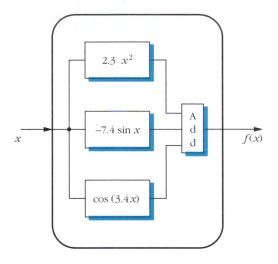

$$f(x) = 2.3\ x^2 - 7.4 \sin x + \cos (3.4x)$$

Figure 14.2–3   Parallel functions in functional paradigm

Primitive functions consist of the three floating-point constants and the variable x. Figure 14.2–3 shows how the parallel functions produce one single function, called f.

Programming languages derived from the functional paradigm are called **applicative languages** because of the way they apply functions. A set of primitive functions including arithmetic, logical operations, and special functions is described by the language. Another set consists of rules for formatting the functions. To produce a value we can use several data types and a predefined method called **application operation** that applies a function to its arguments. Some applicative languages are **LISP** and **APL** (A Programming Language).

Following is an example of a factorial function in LISP that calculates $k!$, using the predefined **sub1** and **times** functions. **sub1** subtracts 1 from its parameter and **times** calculates the product of parameters that follow it. The "words" **defun**, **cond**, and **zerop** are endogenous to the LISP language. Even without knowing details about LISP, we know that factorials are calculated by forming a function from a function of itself. (This is called *recursion* and is discussed further in Chapter 16.)

```
*( defun  factorial( k )
      ( cond
          ( ( zerop  k )   1   )
          ( t ( times   k   ( factorial( sub1   k  ) )))
  ))
```

The function calculates 0! as 1 and $k!$ as $k * (k - 1)!$ for $k > 0$ (for integer k). Notice that in this factorial example there is no assignment of a variable as in imperative languages. Notice also that

```
( times   k   ( factorial( sub1   k  )  ))
```

uses *preorder arithmetic* where the operands follow the operation **times**.

Scheme, developed by Sussman and Steele in 1975, is another applicative language derived from LISP. The intent was to create a simple, learnable language in the functional paradigm. A sample of Scheme to find *k*! is

```
(define ( fact  k )
    (  cond
        (  ( zero ?  k )  1 )
        (  else  ( * k  ( fact  ( - k  1 )
)))))
```

This example shows the general similarity of Scheme to LISP. Note also the preorder operations in the **else** clause.

Applicative languages use mathematical-styled functions, conditional expressions, and recursion. Values generated by functions are used as input to other functions. The extensive use of recursion makes looping structures such as **while** and **for** loops unnecessary.

Because imperative languages reflect machine operations and applicative languages use functions, we might expect applicative languages to be less efficient. Yet languages based on the functional paradigm are generally more elegant and closer to nonprogramming (higher-level) languages than imperative languages. This ease of use versus machine efficiency is always a trade-off when using applicative languages. In fact, efficiency should not be the only criterion for choosing a language. Ease of use and the applications it is suited for are far more important. Table 14.2–3 shows some applicative languages and their programming applications.

14.2.4 Declarative Languages

Some languages are used to describe a problem as a set of facts and relationships rather than to write a procedure for solving it. They are concerned with "what" to do as opposed to "how" to do it. This mode of reasoning is called the **logic paradigm.** Languages following the logic paradigm are nonprocedural languages and are called **declarative languages.** The declarative language form first appeared in the 1960s and evolved into an association with formal logic. We now call declarative languages **logic programming** because they are modeled on the logic paradigm.

Table 14.2–3 Some Languages Using the Functional Paradigm

APPLICATIVE LANGUAGE	DATE DEVELOPED	PROGRAMMING APPLICATION
LISP	1956	Artificial intelligence
APL	1959	Mathematical expressions
Scheme	1975	General-purpose
Common LISP	1984	Dialect of LISP

Some declarative languages simulate events. One such language is SIMULA67 (SIMUlation LAnguage 1967). Another is GPSS (General Purpose Simulation System) language (earlier called General Purpose System Simulation), developed in 1961. Simulation languages follow the "what if" scenario: for example, simulating the motion of a wheel on a car as the contour of the road interacts with the car's springs and shock absorbers.

By contrast, languages based on the procedural paradigm are not suited for simulation—problems that generate a response to a situation over a period of time instead of number crunching. In these problems, calculations at one moment are predicated on the response of the previous moment. That is,

$$\text{response}(t + 1) = f(\text{response}(t))$$

or the response at time $t + 1$ is a function of the response at time t. The *response* function is the simulation for the problem.

By simulating a situation over time, languages such as GPSS V solve queuing, mechanical, electrical, environmental, and economic problems. Using GPSS V, for example, we describe the relationships among the problem's parameters. The language generates a repetitive process in which each repetition simulates the passage of time. Figure 14.2–4 is a block diagram of a problem in GPSS.

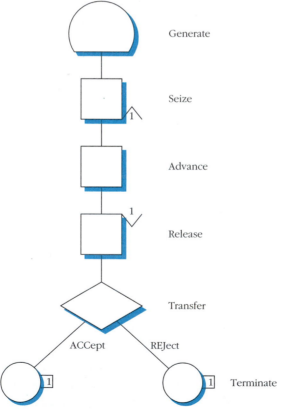

Figure 14.2–4   Block diagram of GPSS problem

Table 14.2–4   Languages Using the Logic Paradigm

DECLARATIVE LANGUAGE	DATE DEVELOPED	PROGRAMMING APPLICATION
GPSS	1961	General-purpose simulation
SNOBOL4	1962	String manipulation and processing
SIMULA67	1967	General-purpose simulation
PROLOG	1972	Artificial intelligence and expert systems

One well-known declarative language is SNOBOL4 (StriNg Oriented symBOlic Language), developed at Bell Laboratories in the early 1960s. SNOBOL4 has an extensive set of primitives, many data types, and the capability of manipulating character strings. Two features of SNOBOL4 are pattern matching on character strings and the interrelatedness of its subprograms.

Declarative (as opposed to simulation) languages are particularly suitable for database management systems. **SQL** (Structured Query Language) developed by IBM is a complete data-manipulation language. **QUEL** (QUEry Language) is another data-manipulation language.

Perhaps the most popular declarative language is **PROLOG** (PROgramming in LOGic). PROLOG has wide appeal in artificial intelligence and expert systems and was a prime element in the Japanese fifth-generation computer project. PROLOG is also one reason why the declarative paradigm is called a **logic paradigm.** First used in 1972 at the University of Aix-Marseille and later at the University of Edinburgh, PROLOG specifies facts about objects and the relationships among objects to model the problem. A set of rules for using the model is derived from a knowledge base about the problem. Whereas a query language searches a database for retrievable information, a PROLOG program holds information from which it can draw inferences about what is true or false.

Languages based on logic paradigms were once viewed with skepticism because they did not offer algorithms for solving problems. Declarative languages such as PROLOG were considered experimental. However, recent interest in formal mathematical logic has spread to declarative languages because logical schemes do in fact produce an algorithmic solution. It remains to be seen whether the path of mathematical logic to algorithmic problem solving will also lead to the use of declarative languages in general-purpose computing. Table 14.2–4 lists some declarative languages and their programming applications. Although SNOBOL4, GPSS, and SIMULA67 use the logic paradigm, they are not considered logic languages.

14.2.5 Reflections

The procedural paradigm is one of many ways to approach programming. Applications such as the simulation of forestation, epidemiological patterns, or automated highways, however, call for paradigms other than the procedural paradigm's assignment to memory locations. For this reason, an appreciation of the diversity of programming applications and an understanding of language paradigms is essential for all computer professionals.

EXERCISES 14.2

Concept Check

Answer statements 1 through 4 with true *or* false.

1. Applicative languages use the object-oriented paradigm.
2. PROLOG is an example of a declarative language.
3. Imperative languages use the logic paradigm.
4. The first language to use the functional paradigm was LISP.

For statements 5 through 8 choose the answer that best completes the statement.

5. SNOBOL4 is
   a. an object-oriented language
   b. a declarative language
   c. an imperative language
   d. an applicative language
6. The procedural paradigm is best identified by
   a. module processing
   b. logic programming
   c. the use of objects
   d. embedded functions
7. Two languages that are best associated with artificial intelligence are
   a. Ada and LISP
   b. COBOL and Pascal
   c. PROLOG and LISP
   d. Smalltalk and PROLOG
8. Which of the following is a procedural language?
   a. LISP
   b. Ada
   c. Smalltalk
   d. Scheme

For statements 9 through 12 fill in the blanks with the right word.

9. The language best known for its early use of the object-oriented paradigm is
   _____.
10. The paradigm that best describes simulation languages is _____.
11. The _____ paradigm is best suited for expressing languages as composite functions.
12. The earliest language used for business applications was _____.

Set A

13. State two features that best describe the procedural paradigm.
14. State two features that best describe the object-oriented paradigm.
15. State two features that best describe the functional paradigm.
16. State two features that best describe the logic paradigm.
17. How do declarative languages differ from imperative languages?
18. State the relationship between C and C++.

Set B

19. Describe how assembly language was an improvement over machine language.
20. Explain the meaning of objects in an object-oriented language.
21. How would an object in the object-oriented paradigm be used in a database?
22. Explain why the Japanese fifth-generation computer project would adopt the principles of PROLOG as its foundation.
23. Express reasons why artificial intelligence would use the principles of non-procedural languages.
24. Why do you think that imperative languages have had great popularity over four decades?
25. SIMULA67 is sometimes considered a functional language as well as a declarative language. Speculate on why this is so.
26. Some computer scientists think that object-oriented languages are just a fad, whereas others believe they are the wave of the future. Comment on this observation.
27. Speculate on why nonprocedural languages might achieve greater popularity than procedural languages.

Set C

28. Fibonacci numbers are generated by the statement $F(n) = F(n-1) + F(n-2)$ for integer $n \geq 2$ initialized by $F(0)$ and $F(1)$. Using the information for the factorial function for LISP shown in Section 14.2.3, rewrite the function in pseudo-LISP so that it calculates the Fibonacci numbers.
29. Using the information in the factorial function for LISP, rewrite the function in pseudo-Scheme so that it calculates the Fibonacci numbers.
30. Use the example of the stack shown in C++ and construct an object for a queue in pseudo-C++.

15 Recursive Algorithms

Still life showing reflected images.

After completing this chapter you should be able
to do the following:

Learning Goals

- Distinguish between recursive and iterative solutions to a problem
- Detect runaway (infinite) recursion
- Explain how recursion can be used to reverse the order of a process
- Distinguish between static and dynamic memory allocation
- Describe an activation record
- Describe a binary tree
- Explain inorder, preorder, and postorder tree traversals
- Use recursion to solve a complex problem in medical image processing
- Discuss the merits and drawbacks of recursive versus iterative solutions

Chapter Activity

Write a *recursive* program to find out if an input string is a palindrome (reads the same way forwards and backwards). The function takes three arguments: The string, the index of the head of the string, and the index of the tail of the string. On each recursive call, the head is incremented by 1 and the tail is decremented by 1.

15.1   THINKING RECURSIVELY

Introduction

Throughout this text we have seen examples of functions that, in the process of solving a task, call on other functions for help. Logically, the number of calls that can be *nested* is boundless. The solutions to some problems, however, are expressible in terms of simpler versions of themselves. For them, a function might call on *itself* to help. Such a call is **recursive** or self-referencing. Although at first this seems mysterious, recursive solutions can sometimes be simpler to write (and to read) than iterative solutions.

15.1.1 Examples of Recursive Functions

As a first example of recursion, consider the factorial function. One way to describe the calculation of n factorial (**$n!$**) is to spell out all the individual calculations: $n! = n * (n - 1) * (n - 2) * \ldots * 2 * 1$. However, you can see that $n! = n * (n - 1)!$ That is, the calculation of $n!$ is simply a larger instance of the calculation of $(n - 1)!$, which is itself a larger instance of $(n - 2)!$. To solve $n!$ we need only to solve $(n - 1)!$, which in turn needs only to solve $(n - 2)!$, etc. Thus the calculation of $n!$ is a self-referencing process.

What happens if the process is allowed to continue?

$$n! = n * (n - 1)!$$
$$(n - 1)! = (n - 1) * (n - 2)!$$
$$(n - 2)! = (n - 2) * (n - 3)!$$
$$(n - 3)! = (n - 3) * (n - 4)!$$
$$\vdots$$

Let's give a value to n, say 4:

$$4! = 4 * 3!$$
$$3! = 3 * 2!$$
$$2! = 2 * 1!$$
$$1! = 1 * 0!$$
$$0! = 0 * (-1)!$$
$$-1! = -1 * (-2)!$$
$$\ldots$$

We seem to have a runaway situation. Just as a **while** loop or a **for** loop needs a limiting condition to prevent an infinite loop, a recursive solution needs a stopping condition to prevent infinite recursion. A recursive solution consists of two parts: A *general* (recursive) step and a step called the *base case*. For $n!$ the base case is $0! = 1$. To summarize, define $n!$ as follows:

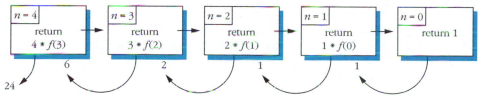

Figure 15.1–1   Evaluation of N factorial for *n* = 4

$$n! = \begin{cases} 1 & \text{for } n = 0 \quad \text{(base case)} \\ n*(n-1)! & \text{for } n > 0 \quad \text{(general case)} \end{cases}$$

The following function captures this idea in C (see Figure 15.1–1).

```
/**************************************************************************
* Function name:     n_fact                                              *
* Description:       Compute n factorial (n!) recursively.               *
*                                                                        *
* Input parameters:  n                                                   *
* Output parameters: none                                                *
* Return value:      n!                                                  *
**************************************************************************/

int n_fact ( int   n )
{
    if ( n == 0 )                              /*  Base case  */
        return ( 1 );
    else
        return ( n * n_fact ( n-1 ) );      /*  General (recursive) case  */

}                                              /* End of n_fact */
```

When **n** is positive, the function computes **n** *times the result of the next lower value of* **n** *factorial.* Each successive call diminishes the value of *n* until it reaches 0. At that point the function stops the **recursive descent** and returns 1. As it would with any chain of unfinished function calls, the computer retraces its steps and completes the processing, filling in the missing values. At the final retrace, the function returns the value of **n!**.

Query: What happens if the user calls **n_fact** with a negative argument?

RESPONSE: The function goes into infinite recursion if the argument **n** is negative since the base case is never reached. (See Question 18 at the end of this section.)

n! can also be solved iteratively, without recursion, as follows.

```
/************************************************************************
* Function name:     n_fact_it                                         *
* Description:       Compute n factorial (n!) iteratively.             *
*                                                                      *
* Input parameters:  n                                                 *
* Output parameters: none                                              *
* Return value:      n!                                                *
*************************************************************************/

int n_fact_it ( int  n )
{
    int count, nfactorial;

    nfactorial  =  n;
    for ( count = n-1;  count > 0;  count--  )
        nfactorial  =  nfactorial * count;

    return ( nfactorial );

}                                                       /* End of n_fact_it */
```

As a second example, let's implement the power function recursively. First, we analyze the definition of $base^{exp}$. One way to do the calculation is:

$$base^{exp} = base * base * base * \cdots * base$$

for *exp* repetitions. A more compact way is:

$$base^{exp} = base * base^{exp-1}$$

In this case the solution to $base^{exp}$ is a larger case of solving $base^{exp-1}$. The stopping condition (the base case) occurs when exp = 0. Since any number raised to the 0 power is 1, we have the following situation.

$$base^{exp} = \begin{cases} 1 & \text{for exp = 0} \\ base * base^{exp-1} & \text{for exp > 0} \end{cases}$$

This can be expressed in C as follows.

```
/************************************************************************
* Function name:     power                                             *
* Description:       Recursive computation of base raised to the exponent *
*                    power for integer base and power.                 *
*                                                                      *
* Input parameters:  base, exponent                                    *
* Output parameters: none                                              *
* Return value:      base raised to the exponent power                 *
*************************************************************************/
```

```
int power ( int   base,    int   exp )
{
    if ( exp  ==  0 )                                    /*  Base case  */
        return ( 1 );
    else
        return ( base * power ( base, exp - 1 ) );      /*  Recursive case  */

}                                                        /* End of power */
```

Note that there is no check for a negative exponent (see Question 19 at the end of this section). Now contrast the slightly more cumbersome iterative solution:

```
/***************************************************************************
 * Function name:     power_it                                            *
 * Description:       Iterative computation of base raised to the exponent *
 *                    power for integer base and power.                    *
 *                                                                         *
 * Input parameters:  base, exponent                                       *
 * Output parameters: none                                                 *
 * Return value:      base raised to the exponent power                    *
 ***************************************************************************/

int power_it ( int   base,    int   exp )
{
  int count, product;

  product  =   base;
  for (  count = exp-1;    count > 0;   count--  )
     product  =   product * base;

  return ( product );
}                                                        /* End of power_it */
```

PERSPECTIVE

As we have just seen, recursive solutions are often like iterative ones, with the iterative loop structure replaced by an if statement that selects between the recursive case and the base case(s).

15.1.2 Recursion and Reversal

An interesting aspect of recursion is its ability to reverse a process. The output from the following program is the reversal of the input string of characters.

```
/******************************************************************************
 * Title:       string reversal (revisited)                                  *
 * Filename:    strev2.c                                                      *
 *                                                                            *
 * Description: Reverse the order of characters in an input string using      *
 *              recursion.                                                    *
 *                                                                            *
 * Input:       series of characters                                          *
 * Output:      characters in reverse order                                   *
 * Process:     input characters and output them in reverse order using       *
 *              recursion                                                      *
 *                                                                            *
 * Written by:  ...                                        Date: ...          *
 ******************************************************************************/

#include <stdio.h>

void reverse_string ( void );              /*  prototype for reverse_string  */

main ( )
{
   printf ( "\nEnter a string:\n" );
   reverse_string ( );
   return ( 0 );
}                                                            /* End of main */


/******************************************************************************
 * Function name:     reverse_string                                          *
 * Description:       Output a string of characters in reverse order using     *
 *                    recursion.                                              *
 *                                                                            *
 * Input parameters:  none                                                    *
 * Output parameters: none                                                    *
 * Return value:      none                                                    *
 ******************************************************************************/

void reverse_string ( void )
{
    char    ch;

    scanf ( "%c", &ch );                              /*  Input a character */

    if ( ch != '\n' )                     /*  Is it carriage return?? */
        reverse_string ( );                       /*  No: Recursive case */

    printf ( "%c", ch );                              /*  Base case */
}                                               /* End of reverse_string */
```

This program reads a string input by the user, one character at a time. As each character is read it is checked for end of line (`'\n'`) and if it is not that character the function is called recursively. Notice that the `printf` statement has not executed by the time of the recursive call. The statement is said to be **pending**. When *does* the `printf` statement get executed? Not until the function finishes calling itself.

When the user enters a carriage return, the recursive process stops and the `printf` statement executes for the first time. Which character is output? The *last* one entered by the user. At that point the function finishes. But what about all the pending `printf` statements? They execute now, starting with the most recent one, followed by the next most recent one. The output is therefore the reverse of the input.

As we see next, recursion relies on an internal (usually hardware) **run-time stack** to store the information for keeping track of the recursive calls. When the recursive process finishes (when the base case is encountered), the stack is popped. Because the stack stores information as LIFO, the effect is to reverse the order of any pending statements such as `printf` in the problem we just discussed. We can show this by using an ADT stack to simulate recursion. Here is an iterative version of the string-reversal program using an ADT stack:

```
/****************************************************************************
 * Function name:      reverse_string_with_stack                           *
 * Description:        Output a string of characters in reverse order using a *
 *                     stack to simulate recursion.                        *
 *                                                                         *
 * Input parameters:   none                                                *
 * Output parameters:  none                                                *
 * Return value:       none                                                *
 ****************************************************************************/

void reverse_string_with_stack ( void )
{
    ITEM_TYPE  ch;
    STACK_TYPE stack;

    create_stack ( &stack );

    scanf ( "%c", &ch );                              /* Input a character */
    while ( ch != '\n'  &&  full_stack ( &stack ) == FALSE ) {
        push ( &stack, ch );                /* Push it for later retrieval */
        scanf ( "%c", &ch );                  /* Input the next character */
    }
```

```
    while ( empty_stack ( &stack ) == FALSE )  {
       pop ( &stack,  &ch );                        /* Pop the top character */
       printf ( "%c",  ch );                              /* Output it */
    }

    destroy_stack ( &stack );
}                                            /* End of reverse_string_with_stack */
```

In this example, each character is placed on top of the stack as it is input. Once the input completes, the stack is popped and the contents are printed. We could say that the output statement is pending the completion of the input. When we look at the string-reversal program this way, we understand the secret of recursion: The internal run-time stack is pushed with each recursive call and then popped once the recursive process completes. Because the run-time stack is hidden, it seems that something magical is taking place. In fact, there is a stack hidden "up the computer's sleeve."

15.1.3 How Recursion Works: The Run-Time Stack

Let's put recursion aside for the moment and consider ordinary (nonrecursive) function calls. When a function calls another function, the computer needs to keep track of the **state** of the caller function just before making the call. The following information is stored for later reference.

1. the address of the instruction following the call
2. the values of all local variables and output

The first item is needed so that the program knows where to return once the called function completes. The second item is needed to reassign the variables of the original function as they were at the time of the second call. Note that the function body is a constant and is kept in the **code segment**, a portion of memory reserved for program instructions.

Except when recursion is involved, we can create and allocate storage for this information during compilation. At that time the compiler can readily determine where in the program each function is called (to establish a return address) and exactly how much storage has to be set aside to hold local variables and parameters. Because this can be done before the program runs, it is called **static storage allocation** and is used in languages such as FORTRAN and BASIC that do not allow recursion.

An alternative called **dynamic storage allocation** generates the memory addresses for variables and parameters at run time. With each function call, an **activation record** (AR) holding the necessary information is created and pushed onto the run-time stack. The stack, which resides in a separate memory area, grows or shrinks as each AR is pushed or popped (shown in Figure 15.1–2).

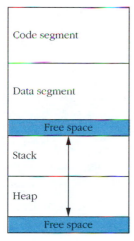

Figure 15.1–2 Dynamic memory allocation model

Dynamic memory allocation is needed for recursion since the depth of the recursive calls cannot be predicted at compile time. Thus, we cannot preallocate enough storage for each of the potential ARs.

The handling of recursive calls proceeds as follows (and as illustrated in Figure 15.1–3). An AR is created and pushed each time the function calls itself. Once the base case is reached, the run-time stack is popped and the next-to-last instance

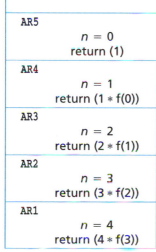

Figure 15.1–3 Activation records

of the function is reconstructed and concluded. The stack is again popped and the next-to-next-to-last instance is reconstructed and completed. The process continues until the stack is empty and the recursive function has finished its original task.

PERSPECTIVE

Note that although the run-time stack is allocated dynamically it is not infinitely large! Thus a recursive function can cause a run-time stack-overflow error. This happens, for instance, if the local variables in each AR happen to be large data structures, if the depth of recursion is great, or if the programmer forgets to include a base case.

EXERCISES 15.1

Concept Check

Answer statements 1 through 4 with true *or* false.
1. Recursive solutions consist of a base case, a recursive case, and a non-recursive case.
2. In a recursive solution an **if** statement is often replaced by a **while** statement.
3. Recursive solutions can be simulated by incorporating a queue into an iterative solution.
4. Recursion needs a dynamic memory model for storage allocation.

For statements 5 through 8 choose the answer that best completes the statement.
5. To prevent runaway recursion, be sure to include a(n)
    a. recursive case
    b. base case
    c. iterative case
    d. stop flag
6. In the **reverse_string** function, what happens if the recursive call is placed after **printf**, as shown next?

```
void reverse_string ( void )
{
    char  ch;
    scanf ( "%c",  &ch );                /* Input a character */
    if ( ch != '\n' )                 /* Is it carriage return?? */
        printf ( "%c",  ch );                    /* Base case */

    reverse_string ( );                        /* Recursive case */
}
```

    a. The string still prints in reverse order.
    b. The string prints in normal order.
    c. `reverse_string` goes into infinite recursion.
    d. Only the first character in the string is output.
7. In the static model of storage allocation,
    a. addresses for variables and code are established at run time.
    b. addresses for variables and code are established at compile time.
    c. addresses for variables are established at run time and addresses for code are established at compile time.
    d. addresses for variables are established at compile time and addresses for code are established at run time.
8. Dynamic memory allocation is needed for recursion because
    a. it is not known at compile time whether runaway recursion will result.
    b. it is not known at run time whether runaway recursion will result.
    c. it is not known at compile time how many recursive calls will be invoked.
    d. it is not known at run time how many recursive calls will be invoked.

For statements 9 through 12 fill in the blanks with the right word.
9. When writing a recursive solution we call the nonrecursive step the _____.
10. To get the effect of reversal, the nonrecursive step is said to be _____.
11. A(n) _____ is pushed on the _____ for each recursive call.
12. The _____ is a portion of memory reserved for program instructions.

Set A
Solve each of the following problems.
13. What is wrong with the following function?

```
void f ( void )
{
    printf ( "Help\n" );
    f ( );
}
```

14. The following function is supposed to compute the sum of the squares of the integers from 1 to *n*, where *n* is supplied in the initial function call. Find three errors.

```
int sum_of_sq ( int n )
{
    if ( n = 1 )
        return ( 0 );
    else
        return ( n * n + sum_of_sq ( n+1 ) );
}
```

15. Assuming that the following function is called with the arguments 3 and 32, what is the final returned value?

```
int    weird ( int  one,    int  two )
{
    if ( one == 0 )
        return ( two );
    else
        return (  weird ( one-1,    two / 2 )  );
}
```

Set B

16. Write a recursive function that prints Help exactly n times.
17. Write a recursive function that prints the numbers n down to 1.
18. Rewrite the recursive factorial function so that it does not allow negative numbers to be evaluated.
19. Rewrite the recursive power function so that it does not allow a negative exponent.

Set C

20. Write a recursive function to print the elements of an array of integers in reverse order.
21. Write a recursive function to print all the uppercase letters in reverse order. Hint: If an integer variable is printed with **%c** format, it displays as a character. The ASCII values of "A" through "Z" are 65 through 90.
22. Write a recursive function to compute the sum of the integers from 1 to n.

15.2 APPLYING RECURSION

Introduction

In Section 15.1 we examined a few elementary examples of recursion and its implementation. Now let's turn to some more interesting applications. We first consider the use of recursion with ADTs and conclude with an application in medical imaging.

15.2.1 Applications of Recursion with ADTs

The following function revisits the dynamically linked list ADT from Chapter 13. Recursion is used here to process the data in a list in reverse order:

```
/*****************************************************************************
* Function name:    traverse                                                *
* Description:      Traverse a linked list recursively.                     *
```

```
 *                                                                      *
 * Input parameters:  list                                             *
 * Output parameters: none                                             *
 * Return value:      none                                             *
 ****************************************************************************/

void traverse ( LIST_TYPE list )
{
    if ( list  !=  NULL ) {
        traverse ( list->next );                  /* Recursive traversal */
        process ( list );/*Process could be any function needing a list node */
    }                                             /* Base case...do nothing */

}                                                 /* End of traverse */
```

At each recursive call, the argument is the **next** field of whatever node **list** is now pointing to. The **next** field becomes the new parameter **list** in the succeeding call. The calls to **process** are pending completion of the recursive descent. Because the recursion stops when **list** is **NULL**, the first node passed to **process** is the last one in the list. We have thus traversed (and processed) the linked list in reverse order.

BEFORE YOU GO ON

Query: In this example, what happens if the recursive call is placed after the call to process?

RESPONSE: When we switch the two statements, the processing occurs *before* the recursive call. The effect is to traverse the list in its natural (unreversed) order. This could be a substitute for the iterative version in Section 13.3.2.

process could be any function that needs access to a list node. What if **process** is replaced by a call to **print_item**? (See Section 13.3.) This causes the list to print backward. Without recursion, such a task would be clumsy, as shown next in a nonrecursive solution using a stack. The stack is used here to store the information in each list node. Once the whole list has been traversed, the stack is popped, yielding the information in reverse order.

```
/****************************************************************************
 * Function name:      reverse_print                                   *
 * Description:        Output nodes from a linked list (with a header node) *
 *                     in reverse order, using simulated recursion via a stack. *
 *                                                                      *
 * Input parameters:   list                                            *
 * Output parameters:  none                                            *
 * Return value:       none                                            *
 ****************************************************************************/
```

```
void reverse_print ( LIST_TYPE *list )
{
    STACK_TYPE  stack;
    ITEM_TYPE   item;
    NODE_PTR    ptr = (*list)->next;/*Initialize ptr to node after list header*/

    create_stack ( &stack );

    while ( ptr != NULL  &&  full_stack ( &stack )  == FALSE )  {
        push ( &stack, ptr->info );       /* Push the info field on the stack */
        ptr = ptr->next;                  /* Advance to the next node */
    }

    while ( empty_stack ( &stack )  ==  FALSE )  {
        pop ( &stack, &item );                         /* Pop the item */
        print_item ( item );                           /* Output the item */
    }

    destroy_stack ( &stack );
}                                              /* End of reverse_print */
```

An interesting example of recursion is with an ADT called a *binary tree*. We briefly explore the binary tree and show a few examples of the power of recursion to simplify the algorithms for accessing this ADT.

A **binary tree** is a set of nodes that either is empty or consists of a root and one or two disjoint binary trees called the left and right **subtrees**. Figure 15.2–1

(a)

(b)

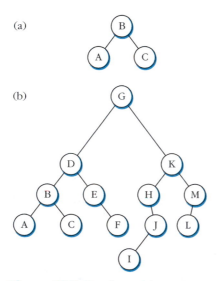

Figure 15.2–1   Some binary trees

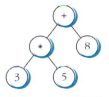

Figure   15.2–2
Expression   tree
for $3 * 5 + 8$

shows some examples of binary trees. A node that has no parent is called a **root** (node "G" in Figure 15.2–1b); a node that has no child is called a **leaf** (nodes "A", "C", "F", "I", and "L" in Figure 15.2–1b). A child is either a single node or a binary subtree. Note that our previous concept of a node must be expanded to include *two* pointers (plus an **info** field), one for the left child and one for the right child, as shown in Figure 15.2–1.

Notice that the definition itself is recursive in that a tree is defined as consisting of trees. We can use binary trees to represent arithmetic expressions before their evaluation by the compiler. Thus, the expression $3 * 5 + 8$ could be represented by the **expression tree** shown in Figure 15.2–2. Although we do not attempt to explain how this type of tree is generated, note how easy it is to traverse and output the contents of this data structure.

The three ways to traverse such a tree are inorder, preorder, and postorder. An **inorder traversal** uses the algorithm

1. Search the left tree recursively.
2. OUTPUT the node.
3. Search the right tree recursively.

The process continues until all nodes have been visited. Applying the algorithm to the expression tree of Figure 15.2–2 yields the sequence

   3   *   5   +   8

A **postorder traversal** uses the algorithm

1. Search the left tree recursively.
2. Search the right tree recursively.
3. OUTPUT the node.

and yields the sequence

   3   5   *   8   +

A **preorder traversal** uses the algorithm

1. OUTPUT the node.
2. Search the left tree recursively.
3. Search the right tree recursively.

and yields the sequence

```
+  *  3  5  8
```

In each instance, the traversal path corresponds to one of the arithmetic evaluation schemes discussed in Chapter 11: infix, postfix, and prefix. Using recursion, these schemes can be written with surprising simplicity. First, let's declare a tree node as a C structure consisting of an `info` field and two pointer fields, `left` and `right`.

```
typedef struct node_type {
        ITEM_TYPE        info;
        struct node_type *left; /* Pointers to left and right subtree */
        struct node_type *right;
     } NODE_TYPE;

typedef NODE_TYPE *TREE_TYPE;
```

Next, let's translate the traversal algorithms into C. In each instance, the base case is when no nodes are left to process. The functions are as follows:

```
/****************************************************************************
 * Function name:      inorder                                              *
 * Description:        Inorder recursive tree traversal.                    *
 *                                                                          *
 * Input parameters:   root                                                 *
 * Output parameters:  none                                                 *
 * Return value:       none                                                 *
 ****************************************************************************/

void inorder ( TREE_TYPE root )
{
   if ( root != NULL ) {
       inorder ( root->left );                      /* Look left . . . */
       printf ( "%d\n", root->info );               /* Output leaf node */
       inorder ( root->right );                     /* Look right . . . */
   }
}                                                    /* End of inorder */



/****************************************************************************
 * Function name:      postorder                                            *
 * Description:        Postorder recursive tree traversal.                  *
 *                                                                          *
 * Input parameters:   root                                                 *
 * Output parameters:  none                                                 *
 * Return value:       none                                                 *
 ****************************************************************************/
```

```
void postorder ( TREE_TYPE root )
{
    if ( root != NULL ) {
        postorder ( root->left );              /* Look left . . . */
        postorder ( root->right );             /* Look right . . . */
        printf ( "%d\n", root->info );         /* Output leaf node */
    }
}                                              /* End of postorder */


/***************************************************************************
* Function name:     preorder                                             *
* Description:       Preorder recursive tree traversal.                   *
*                                                                         *
* Input parameters: root                                                  *
* Output parameters: none                                                 *
* Return value:      none                                                 *
***************************************************************************/

void preorder ( TREE_TYPE root )
{
    if ( root != NULL ) {
        printf ( "%d\n", root->info );         /* Output node */
        preorder ( root->left );               /* Look left . . . */
        preorder ( root->right );              /* Look right . . . */
    }
}                                              /* End of preorder */
```

By contrast, the next program shows an inorder traversal using an ADT stack (simulating recursion). The stack stores the pointer to the current tree node. The algorithm says to traverse the tree to its leftmost leaf node, which is then output. Next, move to the right subtree and repeat the process.

```
/***************************************************************************
* Function name:     inorder_it                                           *
* Description:       Inorder tree traversal with simulated recursion via  *
*                    a stack.                                             *
*                                                                         *
* Input parameters: root                                                  *
* Output parameters: none                                                 *
* Return value:      none                                                 *
***************************************************************************/

void inorder_it ( TREE_TYPE root )
{
    STACK_TYPE stack;
    TREE_TYPE  ptr;
```

```
        create_stack ( &stack );

    ptr  =  root;


    do  {
            while ( ptr != NULL ) {            /*  Push the tree-node pointer  */
               push ( &stack, ptr );           /*  until left-most leaf node  */
               ptr  =  ptr->left;
            }

            if ( empty_stack ( &stack ) == FALSE ) {/*  Pop, print, and move  */
               pop ( &stack, &ptr );               /*  to the right subtree  */
               print_item ( ptr->info );
               ptr  =  ptr->right;
            }

    }  while ( ptr != NULL  ||  empty_stack ( &stack ) == FALSE );

    destroy_stack ( &stack );
}                                              /* End of inorder_it */
```

The recursive solution is surely simpler to design, implement, and read (see Question 17 at the end of this section).

15.2.2 An Application from Medical Imaging

Medical image processing (discussed in Chapter 19) is the automated analysis of medical imagery. Examples include a computerized analysis of microscopic slides, X-ray, CAT scan, or MRI images. In each case the data for the computer are a 2D array of numbers representing the degrees of brightness or the different colors of the objects under scrutiny. For the following example, let's assume that the data consist of a series of "blob-like" cells such as red or white blood cells that are in various configurations across a 2D grid, as shown in Figure 15.2–3. Each element of the grid is either occupied or not occupied. We can see in the figure that the occupied areas take on a variety of sizes and shapes. By *blob* we mean a set of connected, occupied grid elements. *Connected* means that for any pair of grid elements within a blob, an unbroken path of occupied grid elements can be found between them.

For any identified blob, we might ask, for example: What is its size? What is its shape? What is its location relative to the other blobs? These **features**, or measurable properties of an object, can be used to classify the blobs into clinically meaningful categories. For instance, if the blobs happen to be white blood cells, this differential classification can be used to determine the nature of a particular infection. For now, let's concentrate on finding the size of a blob.

Look at Figure 15.2–3 again and see if you can figure out an algorithm for finding blob size. To appreciate the complexity of the task, keep in mind that the

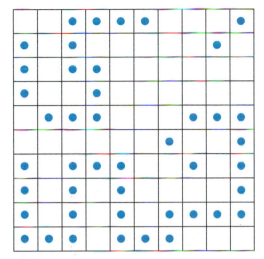

Figure 15.2–3 Grid with blobs

computer cannot "see" the extent of the blob as we can. It only knows that for any given grid element there are eight elements immediately connected to it, some of which are occupied and some not. Given an arbitrary starting point, the goal is to locate and count the total number of grid elements that are connected to it, no matter how far away they may be and no matter how circuitous the path.

If the starting point happens to be empty or outside the bounds of the grid, the blob size is 0. However, if the starting point is within a blob, our algorithm must scan in all directions and count all the immediate, nonempty neighbors of the point. So far so good, but what happens next? We apply the same rule to each of the neighbors, counting all their nonempty neighbors. We continue counting each of the neighbors' neighbors and their neighbors' neighbors. As soon as we hit a dead end in any given direction (an empty grid element) we continue in another direction, counting neighbors and neighbors' neighbors.

From the description, the task sounds like a bookkeeping nightmare—which indeed it is (imagine tracking a tapeworm!). It should also be apparent that this is a self-referencing process and is, therefore, amenable to a recursive solution.

Program 15.2–1 declares a **grid** as a 2D array whose elements are either **EMPTY** or **FILLED**. A **load_grid** function is called to fill the array with a variety of blobs. (The implementation of this function is given as an exercise at the end of this section.) The user is asked to input a particular row and column from which to start counting the blobs. **blob_cnt** is a recursive function with two base cases:

1. If the current grid element is unoccupied, return 0.
2. If the current row or column is outside the borders of the grid, return 0.

If neither of the base cases is chosen, the grid element must be part of a blob and should be counted. To ensure that the element is not counted again, it is set to **EMPTY**. The function then calls itself, adding 1 for the current element to the result of the recursive check of each of the immediate eight neighbors.

P R O G R A M   1 5 . 2 – 1

```
/**************************************************************************
 * Title:        recursive blob counter                                   *
 * Filename:     blob.c                                                    *
 *                                                                        *
 * Description: Locate and count all contiguous neighbors emanating from a *
 *              user-specified starting point.                            *
 *                                                                        *
 * Input:        grid with blobs indicated, user specified (row, col) start*
 *              point.                                                     *
 * Output:       size of specified blob.                                   *
 * Process:      recursively count all connected, occupied neighbors of    *
 *              original point.                                           *
 *                                                                        *
 * Written by:  ...                                    Date: ...          *
 **************************************************************************/

#include <stdio.h>
#include <stdlib.h>

#define  MAX_ROW 20
#define  MAX_COL 20

typedef  enum  { EMPTY, FILLED } STATUS;
typedef  STATUS                  GRID_TYPE[ MAX_ROW ][ MAX_COL ];


                                                        /* Prototypes */
void     load_grid ( GRID_TYPE  grid );
int      blob_cnt  ( GRID_TYPE  grid,   int  row,   int  col );


main ( )
{
   GRID_TYPE grid;
   int       row, col;

   load_grid ( grid );                          /* Fill the grid with blobs */

   printf ( "\nEnter row, col> " );               /* Input blob coordinates */
   scanf ( "%d %d", &row, &col );

   printf ( "\nBlob emanating from row=%d...col=%d..is connected to
            %d elements\n", row, col, blob_cnt ( grid, row, col ) );
```

```
        return ( 0 );
}                                                        /*  End of main  */



/**************************************************************************
 * Function name:     blob_cnt                                           *
 * Description:       Recursively count all neighbors of a given cell.   *
 *                                                                       *
 * Input parameters:  grid array, row, col to search from               *
 * Output parameters: none                                              *
 * Return value:      count of touching cells                           *
 **************************************************************************/

int blob_cnt ( GRID_TYPE grid,   int  row,   int  col )
{
                                     /*  Base case 1: check for grid border  */
    if ( row < 0  ||  row > MAX_ROW-1 ||  col < 0  ||  col > MAX_COL-1 )
        return ( 0 );

    else if ( grid[row][col] == EMPTY )  /*  Base case 2: empty grid element  */
        return ( 0 );

    else {                                  /*  Found an occupied element . . .  */
        grid[row][col]  =  EMPTY;                   /*  don't count it twice  */

                        /*  Add 1 to the results of checking all neighbors  */
        return ( 1 + blob_cnt ( grid, row+1, col-1 )
                   + blob_cnt ( grid, row+1, col   )
                   + blob_cnt ( grid, row+1, col+1 )
                   + blob_cnt ( grid, row,   col+1 )
                   + blob_cnt ( grid, row,   col-1 )
                   + blob_cnt ( grid, row-1, col+1 )
                   + blob_cnt ( grid, row-1, col   )
                   + blob_cnt ( grid, row-1, col-1 )       );
    }
}                                                      /*  End of blob_cnt  */
```

Note that when the size of a blob is counted, the relevant grid elements are set to **EMPTY**, destroying the original data. If the initial grid is needed, make a copy before calling this function.

15.2.3 Final Comments on Recursion

As these examples show, recursion can be a powerful tool for algorithm simplification. There are, however, some drawbacks to recursion. Certain problems, such as computing $n!$, are safer and more efficient if coded iteratively. The computation of $n!$ can need a huge number of recursive calls, depending on the value of n. At some point there is sure to be a stack overflow. This is not so for iteration, although **integer overflow** (when the result is too large to fit into an integer data type) is still a potential problem in both recursion and iteration.

As we just said, stack overflow can result depending on the memory requirements of each AR and the number of recursive calls. For this reason, design recursive functions to have as few local variables and parameters as possible. If a complex structure is needed as a parameter, pass its address. This way the AR needs storage for only a pointer and not for a copy of the structure itself.

EXERCISES 15.2

Concept Check
Answer statements 1 through 4 with true *or* false.
1. A binary tree is designed to process binary numbers.
2. A leaf node is one whose right and left subtrees are empty.
3. An inorder traversal of an expression tree lists the expression in infix order.
4. To prevent stack overflow, we should limit the number of local variables in recursive functions.

For statements 5 through 8 choose the answer that best completes the statement.
5. Assuming that a list is declared with a header node, the call to the recursive function traverse would be
   a. `traverse ( list->info );`
   b. `traverse ( list );`
   c. `traverse ( list->next );`
   d. `traverse ( list.next );`
6. The sequence to print an expression tree with a preorder traversal is
   a. left tree, print, right tree
   b. right tree, print, left tree
   c. print, left tree, right tree
   d. left tree, right tree, print
7. The sequence to print an expression tree with a postorder traversal is
   a. left tree, print, right tree
   b. right tree, print, left tree
   c. print, left tree, right tree
   d. left tree, right tree, print
8. To find the size of an arbitrary blob, `blob_cnt`
   a. recursively checks the left and right neighbors of each element
   b. recursively checks all neighbors, stopping a particular path only if an empty grid element is found

c. recursively checks all neighbors, stopping a particular path when either the grid border is reached or an empty element is found

d. looks at all neighbors in increasingly larger circles around the original (user-specified) element

For statements 9 through 12 fill in the blanks with the right word.

9. A **NODE_TYPE** for a tree is declared as structure consisting of an **ITEM_TYPE** and _____ pointer fields called _____.

10. A **GRID_TYPE** is declared as _____ of data type _____.

11. In image processing, a measurable property of an object is called a _____ of that object.

12. The **blob_cnt** function needs _____ recursive calls per grid element.

Set A

Solve each of the following problems.

13. Assuming that a linked list is declared with a trailer node, rewrite the recursive list-traversal function.

14. Discuss nonrecursive techniques for printing a linked list in reverse order.

Set B

15. Write a **load_grid** function that (1) sets all grid elements to empty, and (2) reads in a series of coordinates representing the grid elements that are to be filled.

16. Write **destroy_list (LIST_TYPE list)** to free all the nodes in a linked list recursively.

Set C

17. Write nonrecursive versions of postorder and preorder tree traversals.

18. Rewrite **main** for the blob-counting program so that the user has the option of counting *all* blobs. This means calling **blob_cnt** repeatedly, once for each x,y coordinate in the grid. Note that we cannot by accident repeatedly count a given blob since **blob_cnt** scts each occupied grid element to **EMPTY** after checking its status.

The next two questions involve a substantial programming effort.

19. Design a nonrecursive version of **blob_cnt** using a stack.

20. Design a nonrecursive version of **blob_cnt** without using a stack.

16 **Searching and Sorting Algorithms**

Card player using an insertion sort to arrange a hand.

After completing this chapter you should be able to do the following:

Learning Goals

- Explain how response time is measured for various searching algorithms
- Discuss the merits of the various sorting algorithms
- Distinguish between internal and external searching
- Implement iterative and recursive linear searches for array-based and linked structures
- Implement iterative and recursive binary searches for array-based structures
- Evaluate the efficiency of binary search
- Implement iterative and recursive selection sorts for array-based and linked structures
- Implement iterative and recursive insertion sorts for array-based and linked structures
- Implement a Shell sort
- Describe Quicksort
- Implement a bucket sort
- Define hashing

Chapter Activity

Section 2 of this chapter discusses a few sorting functions. Implement as many of them as you can and test them as best you can. Testing a sort function involves at least three sets of data: ordered, reverse-ordered, and random-ordered. Create integer arrays with each kind of data (the first two sets can be generated from a **for**-loop control variable; the third set needs the random-number generator). Make the arrays as large as you can without causing a compiler error. Use the system clock function to test the sorts. Call this function before and after each sort is applied to each set of data. Store the time difference in an array and output the results.

16.1   LINEAR AND BINARY SEARCH

Introduction

In addition to number crunching, the arithmetic manipulation of large quantities of data, a common use of computers is information retrieval. We discuss this in Chapter 12 and see it daily throughout the computer-oriented world. One aspect of information retrieval is **searching** or scanning through a list to find a particular record. Searching usually needs a key field such as a name or social security number. In a key-ordered list, each record has a key field and the list is always maintained in key order. A request for information requires the user to specify a particular target key value. If the record holding this key is found, the associated information is displayed. If the record is not found, an informative message is generated. An issue in processing a search request is response time. Apart from differences in hardware speed, response time depends on considerations including:

1. the size of the list; the number of records and the record size
2. the data structure used; array, linked list, binary tree
3. the organization of the data; random, key ordered
4. the search strategy; linear, binary (for ordered lists)
5. the location of the list; **external** on a disk or **internal** in primary memory

Notice the range of scenarios that you might face. For instance, linear search of a large, randomly ordered, linked list and binary search of a small, key-ordered array are some possibilities. We confine this discussion to two internal search strategies: linear and binary for key-ordered arrays and linked lists. (See Chapter 13 for more on linked lists.)

16.1.1 Linear Search: Unordered Data Structures

First consider a linear search of an array-based list whose algorithm is

Traverse the list as long as

1. the last logical record in the list has not been reached
2. the value of the current item in the list doesn't equal the target value

If the target item is found its index is returned. Otherwise a flag such as -1 is returned.

To implement this in C we first make the following declarations.

```
typedef   struct  {
               long int       ss_num;     /* long int has more bits than int */
                                          /* Other fields as desired */
          }  ITEM_TYPE;



typedef   struct   list_type  {
               ITEM_TYPE          info [MAX_SIZE];
               int                current_size;
          }   LIST_TYPE;
```

Accordingly, a **LIST_TYPE** variable consists of an array of structures (records) and a separate field holding the current number of structures in the list (its logical size). The base type of the array, **ITEM_TYPE**, is declared to hold at least one field, which in this case is the social security number. Other fields could be added depending on the application. For instance, a student-information database might contain information such as name, campus address, home address, major field, class standing, or GPA. There might also be a field for the current transcript, which could be another array or even a linked list of some sort. Figure 16.1–1 shows some possibilities.

The C code for this algorithm, given as a function called **lin_search1**, is found in Program 16.1–1.

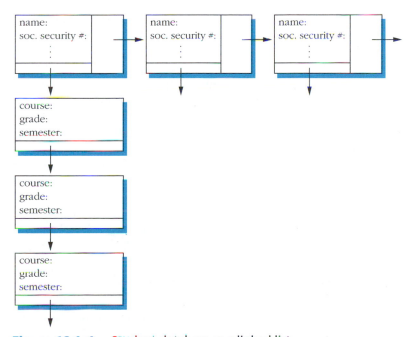

Figure 16.1–1   Student database as a linked list

PROGRAM 16.1-1

```
/*********************************************************************************
 * Function name:     lin_search1   (array-based, iterative version)            *
 * Description:       Perform a linear search through an unordered list,        *
 *                    returning the location of the target item (or -1 if not found). *
 *                                                                              *
 * Input parameters:  list,  target value (social security #)                  *
 * Output parameters: none                                                      *
 * Return value:      location of item containing target value, or -1 if item not found *
 *********************************************************************************/
int  lin_search1 ( LIST_TYPE    *list,
                   long int     target_value )
{

    int    loc;                                    /* Location of an item in the list */

    for (loc = 0;  loc < list->current_size &&
                  list->info[loc].ss_num != target_value;
                  loc++                                 )
        ;                              /* Keep searching as long as the list has not */
                                       /* been exceeded and no match has been found */

    if ( list->info[loc].ss_num == target_value )          /* Found target item? */
        return ( loc );                             /* Yes, return the loc of the item */
    else
        return ( -1 );                               /* No, set function to  -1 */
}                                                    /* End of lin_search1 */
```

The program solves the search problem iteratively according to the algorithm. Alternative implementations are possible. For instance, the function can be designed so that **loc** is an output parameter and the function itself returns a **BOOLEAN** representing the status of the search: found the item or didn't find the item. (See the Set C exercises at the end of this section.)

Now consider a linear search of a dynamically linked list structure beginning with some declarations:

```
typedef   struct node_type   {
                  ITEM_TYPE           info;
                  struct node_type    *next;
          }   NODE_TYPE;


typedef   NODE_TYPE       *NODE_PTR;
typedef   NODE_TYPE       LIST_TYPE;
```

Notice that we can use the same **ITEM_TYPE** as in the array-based implementation. The implementation of this algorithm, called **lin_search2**, is shown in Program 16.1–2.

PROGRAM 16.1-2

```
/******************************************************************************
 * Function name:      lin_search2   (linked list-based, iterative version)   *
 * Description:        Perform a linear search through an unordered list,      *
 *                     returning the location of the target item.  If the item is not *
 *                     found, the function returns NULL.                       *
 *                                                                            *
 * Input parameters:   list,target value (social security #)                  *
 * Output parameters:  none                                                    *
 * Return value:       location of item containing target value, or NULL      *
 *                     if not found                                            *
 ******************************************************************************/

NODE_PTR    lin_search2  (LIST_TYPE      *list,
                          long int       target_value )
{
  NODE_PTR      loc;

  for ( loc = *list;  loc != NULL  &&
                      loc->info.ss_num != target_value;
                      loc = loc->next)
     ;                                      /* Keep searching as long as the list has not */
                                            /* been exceeded and no match has been found */

  if ( loc->info.ss_num == target_value)                /* Found target item? */
      return(loc);                                      /* Yes, return its address */

  else                                                  /* No,return NULL */
     return ( NULL );
}                                                       /* End of lin_search2 */
```

Finally, for comparison, consider the recursive version as a function called lin_search3 and shown in Program 16.1–3.

PROGRAM 16.1-3

```
/******************************************************************************
 * Function name:      lin_search3   (linked list-based, recursive version)   *
 * Description:        Perform a linear search through an unordered list, returning the *
 *                     location of the target item.  If the item is not found, the *
 *                     function returns NULL.                                  *
 *                                                                            *
 * Input parameters:   list,target value (social security #)                  *
 * Output parameters:  none                                                    *
 * Return value:       location of item containing target value. or NULL if not found *
 ******************************************************************************/
```

```
NODE_PTR     lin_search3 ( LIST_TYPE    list,
                           long int     target_value )
{
  if ( list == NULL )                                   /* Base case 1: item not in list */
     return ( NULL );

  else if ( list->info.ss_num  ==  target_value )   /* Base case 2:  found target item */
     return ( list );                               /* Yes, return pointer to the item */

  else                                                    /* Not found yet */
     return ( lin_search3 ( list->next,  target_value ));    /* Keep searching */

}                                                       /* End of lin_search3 */
```

The recursive version has two base cases, *item not found* and *item found*. The general case calls the function with the list pointer advanced by one node. Note that we pass **list** as an input argument so that the sequence of recursive calls does not change its original value.

16.1.2 Binary Search: Ordered Data Structures

If there are n names in a list, a linear search would need approximately $n/2$ checks to find out whether an item with a particular target key value is present. This figure takes into account the best-case search when the target item is the first one in the list and the worst-case search when the target item is the last. We would have to search through approximately half the list to find any given item. (Algorithm performance and complexity are discussed further in Chapter 18.)

On the other hand, if someone asks you to look up the word *zebra* in a dictionary or find the phone number of *ZZZ Cleaners*, you would probably not use a linear search! Because a dictionary or phone book is ordered, there is no point in starting at the very beginning and checking every record. When searching an ordered list, a better strategy is expressed by the following algorithm for **binary search**.

Jump to the middle of the list. There are three possibilities:

   a. The target item was found.
   b. The target item was overshot.
       Apply the algorithm to the lower half of the list.
   c. The target item was undershot.
       Apply the algorithm to the upper half of the list.

For case a the searching is done. For case b the target must be in the lower half of the list, whereas for case c the target must be in the upper half. In either case b or case c, *half the list can be excluded from the remainder of the search process.* Apply the algorithm again using the remaining half of the list.

Program 16.1–4 is an iterative binary search for an array-based list. Notice that instead of social security number we use the designated key field as the basis for the search. Remember that binary search can be used only when the list is ordered. Because we assume that the ordering is based on the key field, the key must be included as a parameter.

The `low` and `high` parameters delineate the bounds of the search. To search the entire list, we set `low` to 0 and `high` to the current size of the list, less one. Alternatively, we can specify any desired subrange of the list.

P R O G R A M   1 6 . 1 – 4

```
/********************************************************************************
*   Function name:       bin_search1(array-based, key-ordered, iterative version)  *
*   Description:         Perform a binary search through a key-ordered list,        *
*                        returning the location of the target item.  If the item is not  *
*                        found, the function returns a value of -1.                 *
*                                                                                  *
*   Input parameters:    list, target_value, indexes of lowest and highest items to consider *
*   Output parameters:   none                                                      *
*   Return value:        location of item containing target_value, or -1 if not found  *
********************************************************************************/

int     bin_search1 ( LIST_TYPE    *list,
                      KEY_TYPE      target_value,
                      int           low,
                      int           high        )
{
   int     middle;

   while ( low <= high)  {                       /* Stop searching when low overtakes high */

      middle = ( low + high ) / 2;

      if ( list->info[middle].key  ==  target_value )
          return ( middle );                      /* Item found, return its location */

      else if ( list->info[middle].key  <  target_value )
          low  =  middle + 1;                     /* Item is in "upper" half of list */

      else
          high  =  middle - 1;                    /* Item is in "lower" half of list */
   }

   return ( -1 );                                 /* Item not found */

}                                                 /* End of bin_search1 */
```

The recursive version of binary search, called `bin_search2,` is shown in Program 16.1–5.

PROGRAM 16.1–5

```
/*******************************************************************************
* Function name:      bin_search2 (array-based, key-ordered, recursive version) *
* Description:        Perform a binary search through a key-ordered list,        *
*                     returning the location of the target item.  If the item is not *
*                     found, the function returns a value of -1.                 *
*                                                                                *
* Input parameters:   list, target_value, indexes of lowest and highest items to consider *
* Output parameters:  none                                                       *
* Return value:       location of item containing target_value, or -1 if not found *
*******************************************************************************/

int    bin_search2 ( LIST_TYPE   *list,
                     KEY_TYPE    target_value,
                     int         low,
                     int         high            )
{
      int middle;

      if ( low > high )                             /* Base case 1:  item not found */
          return ( -1 );                            /* Stop searching when low overtakes high */


      middle  =  ( low + high ) / 2;

      if (  list->info[middle].key  ==  target_value )     /* Base case 2:  item found */
          return ( middle );                              /* Return its location */

      else if ( list->info[middle].key  <  target_value ) /* Item is in "upper" half */
          return ( bin_search2 ( list, target_value, middle + 1, high ));

      else                                          /* Item is in "lower" half */
          return ( bin_search2 ( list, target_value, low, middle - 1 ));
}
                                                    /* End of bin_search2 */
```

Assuming that the data are ordered, binary search is far more efficient than linear search, as we see in Chapter 18. If we successively halve the number of records to scan, we can show that binary search is logarithmic: It needs $\log_2(n)$ checks to find the target record. This means that in a list of, say, 1000 items, binary search needs no more than 10 steps to find the target because $\log_2(1000) \cong 10$. Compare this to a linear search needing approximately 500 steps to find the same item. The more the list grows, the more dramatic the difference becomes. When n is 1,000,000 (think of a phone book), binary search needs approximately 20 steps, whereas linear search needs approximately 500,000 steps!

Because binary search is so much more efficient, why not always use it? Unfortunately, there are two catches to using binary search. First, the data must be ordered by a sorting process (see Section 16.2) and so we incur an overhead before using the search. Second, a binary search cannot be applied to linear, dynamically linked lists. Because the items are explicitly linked, there is no convenient way to find the middle of the list without linearly searching for it. The solution is to create an alternative, dynamically linked list structure such as a binary tree that when properly balanced has a $\log_2(n)$ search time.

EXERCISES 16.1

Concept Check

Answer statements 1 through 4 with true *or* false.

1. As they are described in this section, all search algorithms assume the presence of a key field.
2. External searching can be done only with a binary search algorithm.
3. With a linked structure, finding the kth element takes one step.
4. Binary search is not possible unless the list is ordered.

For statements 5 through 8 choose the answer that best completes the statement.

5. For a large list the most important factor in determining response time is the
   a. size of each record
   b. presence of a key field
   c. use of recursion versus iteration
   d. search strategy used
6. Binary search is preferable to linear search as long as the following conditions can be met:
   a. the data are ordered and the data structure is not a linear-linked list
   b. the data are unordered but the data structure is an array or binary tree
   c. the list is very large to warrant the complexity of the binary search algorithm
   d. the programming language allows recursion because binary search is most efficient when written recursively
7. Because binary search needs $\log_2(n)$ steps, a search through a sorted list containing 1 billion records needs
   a. about 500,000,000 steps
   b. 1 step
   c. 30 steps
   d. 1000 steps

8. For a linear search of the list in Question 7, the best-case scenario needs
   a. about 500,000,000 steps
   b. 1 step
   c. 30 steps
   d. impossible to predict the number of steps

For statements 9 through 12 fill in the blanks with the right word.

9. The arithmetic manipulation of large quantities of data is called

   _____.

10. When a list is too large to be stored in memory, the retrieval of information
    is called _____.

11. In a recursive linear search the two base cases are labeled

    _____ and _____.

12. Since each step of a binary search reduces the remaining number of records
    to search in half, the processing is called _____.

Set A

Solve each of the following problems.

13. Rewrite the **for** loop for the array-based, iterative linear search using a
    while loop.
14. Rewrite the **for** loop for the linked-list, iterative linear search the same
    way as in Question 13.

Set B

15. The C code for linear search has two **return** statements. Some programmers
    consider this a violation of the structured programming principle that there
    should only be one way into a function or control structure and one way out.
    Rewrite the iterative, array-based **lin_search1** function so that there is only
    one **return** statement.
16. Rewrite the iterative, linked version of **lin_search2** with one **return**.
17. Rewrite the iterative **bin_search1** with one **return**. Comment on the
    practicality of adhering to the one way in, one way out principle.

Set C

18. Write a linear search in which the location of the item is an output parameter
    instead of a **return** value. The data type of the function should be **BOOLEAN**
    and should represent the status of the search: found item, did not find item.
19. Write an iterative linear search of a key-ordered, array-based structure.
20. Write a recursive version of Question 19.

16.2 SORTING FUNCTIONS

Introduction

Sorting is a common activity when we process collections of data. Even when a
list is maintained in key order, sorting might be needed for a different field. For

instance, because it is unique, a social security number is a good choice for a key. However, if the user wants an alphabetized listing by *last name*, the social security field is useless. Instead, we would need to sort lexicographically (alphabetically) by name before output. Because it takes so much processing time, sorting is a serious topic of inquiry in computer science, about which many volumes have been written.

There is to date no single, *perfect* sorting algorithm. No single sorting algorithm is guaranteed to be the fastest without qualifications and regardless of the organization of the data. Sorting functions take more or less time depending on factors that include the initial arrangement of the data (random, partially sorted, totally sorted, reverse-sorted) and the data structure used to represent the data (array, linked list, tree). Available memory is also a concern, as we see at the end of this section.

Of course, the amount of data plays a role in the total execution time. However, we can evaluate the performance of sorting functions by letting the number of data records be a parameter. (This idea is introduced in Section 16.1 on the binary search algorithm needing $\log_2 n$ steps. We make a mathematical assessment of algorithm complexity in Chapter 18.) For now, we concentrate on a few of the so-called simple sorts followed by some of the more complex ones.

16.2.1 Simple Sorts: Selection and Insertion

All sorting routines are alike in that they involve rearranging either data or, in the case of linked structures, the pointers to data. Many "intuitive" sorts, also called **simple sorts**, do some variation of **selection sort** (illustrated in Figure 16.2–1). This method includes the following steps.

1. Find the smallest (or largest) item in the data.
2. Place this item at the beginning of the list.
3. Repeat Steps 1 and 2 starting at the beginning of the remaining list.

Let's look at both an iterative and a recursive version of selection sort. For simplicity, we assume an array-based structure without a key field and with all possible elements filled (the logical size equals the physical size). This is shown as a function in Program 16.2–1.

PROGRAM 16.2–1

```
/********************************************************************************
 * Function name:      sel_sort1    (iterative, array-based)                    *
 * Description:        Perform a selection sort on an array of integers.        *
 *                                                                              *
 * Input parameters:   array of integers                                       *
 * Output parameters:  sorted array                                            *
 * Return value:       none                                                     *
 ********************************************************************************/
```

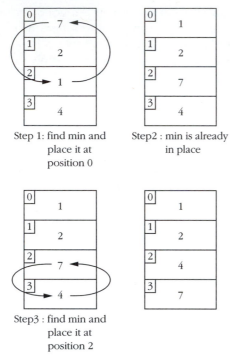

Step 1: find min and
place it at
position 0

Step2 : min is already
in place

Step3 : find min and
place it at
position 2

Figure 16.2–1   Selection sort

```
void   sel_sort1  (  int  list [ ]  )
{
    int    min_pos,  start_pos;

    for (  start_pos = 0;   start_pos  <  MAX_SIZE -1;   start_pos++  )    {
        min_pos = find_pos_min1 ( list, start_pos );          /*  Find smallest item */
        swap1 ( list,  start_pos,  min_pos );             /* Swap it with the current */
                                                          /* beginning item */

    }

}                                                         /* End of sel_sort1 */
```

The two helper functions are straightforward:

```
/****************************************************************************
*  Function name:       find_pos_min1                                       *
*  Description:         Find the position of the smallest item, starting from *
*                       start_pos+1.                                        *
*                                                                           *
*  Input parameters:    array of integers, starting position to search from  *
*  Output parameters:   none                                                *
*  Return value:        position of smallest integer                        *
****************************************************************************/
```

```
int    find_pos_min1 (  int  list [ ],
                        int  start_pos  )
{
    int   i,  pos_min = start_pos;

    for (  i = start_pos+1;   i <  MAX_SIZE;    i++  )
        if (  list [ i ]  <  list [ pos_min ]  )          /* Is ith item < pos_min item? */
            pos_min  =  i;                                /* Yes, so update pos_min */

    return ( pos_min );
}                                                          /* End of find_pos_min1 */
```

```
/********************************************************************************
*   Function name:      swap1                                                   *
*   Description:        Swap value at position 1 with value at position 2.      *
*                                                                               *
*   Input parameters:   array of integers, indexes of values to swap           *
*   Output parameters:  updated array                                          *
*   Return value:       none                                                    *
********************************************************************************/

void    swap1 (  int list [ ],
                 int pos1,
                 int pos2  )
{
    int   temp;

    temp        =  list[ pos1 ];
    list[ pos1 ] =  list[ pos2 ];
    list[ pos2 ] =  temp;
}                                                          /* End of swap1 */
```

The recursive version is only slightly different. **start_pos** has been changed to a parameter since it determines when the recursive calls are finished. The function is shown in Program 16.2–2 with no changes needed for the helper functions.

PROGRAM 16.2-2

```
/*******************************************************************************
*  Function name:      sel_sort2    (recursive, array-based)                 *
*  Description:        Perform a selection sort on an array of integers.      *
*                                                                            *
*  Input parameters:   array of integers, starting position for sort         *
*  Output parameters:  sorted array                                          *
*  Return value:       none                                                  *
*******************************************************************************/

void   sel_sort2 (    int list [ ],
                      int start_pos  )
{
   int    min_pos;

   if ( start_pos < MAX_SIZE -1 )    {
       min_pos = find_pos_min1 ( list, start_pos );         /* Find smallest item */
       swap1 ( list, start_pos, min_pos ); /* Swap it with the item at the beginning */
       sel_sort2 ( list, start_pos+1 );    /* Repeat..with the remainder of the list */
   }
}                                                           /* End of sel_sort2 */
```

Selection sort for a dynamically linked, key-ordered structure (shown in Program 16.2–3) is like the array-based implementation. Note that this version swaps the data, not the pointers to the data. Swapping the pointers is much more efficient because it reroutes pointers instead of copying the whole **info** field. The pointer-swapping version and a recursive version are included in the exercises at the end of this section. Assume these global declarations:

```
typedef   struct node_type   {
                  ITEM_TYPE          info;
                  struct node_type  *next;
          }  NODE_TYPE;

typedef   NODE_TYPE      *NODE_PTR;
typedef   NODE_TYPE      LIST_TYPE;
```

PROGRAM 16.2-3

```
/*******************************************************************************
*  Function name:      sel_sort3    (iterative, key-ordered linked-list)     *
*  Description:        Perform a selection sort on a list of records.         *
*                                                                            *
*  Input parameters:   list of records                                       *
*  Output parameters:  sorted list                                           *
*  Return value:       none                                                  *
*******************************************************************************/
```

```
void   sel_sort3 ( LIST_TYPE *list  )
{
    NODE_PTR          min_pos, ptr = *list;

    while ( ptr != NULL )   {
       min_pos = find_pos_min2 ( ptr );              /* Find position of smallest item */
       swap2 ( ptr,  min_pos );            /* Swap its info with the current beginning node */
       ptr = ptr->next;                              /* Advance to next node  */
     }
}                                                     /* End of sel_sort3 */


/*************************************************************************************
 * Function name:      find_pos_min2                                                *
 * Description:        Find the position of the smallest item,                      *
 *                     starting from position "start".                             *
 *                                                                                  *
 * Input parameters:   pointer to node to start searching from                      *
 * Output parameters:  none                                                         *
 * Return value:       pointer to node with smallest key value                      *
 *************************************************************************************/

NODE_PTR   find_pos_min2 (  NODE_PTR   start  )
{
  NODE_PTR     pos_min = ptr = start;                /* ptr is used to traverse the list */
                                                     /* pos_min is updated to the position */
                                          /* of the node found with the smallest key value */

  while ( ptr != NULL )   {
    if ( pos_min->info.key  > ptr->info.key  )        /* Is ptr's key less than */
        pos_min = ptr;                                /* smallest key seen so far */
                                                      /* Yes . . . so save it */

    ptr = ptr->next;                                  /* Advance to next node */
  }

  return ( pos_min );
}                                                     /* End of find_pos_min2 */


/*************************************************************************************
 * Function name:      swap2                                                        *
 * Description:        Swap value at position 1 with value at position 2.           *
 *                                                                                  *
 * Input parameters:   pointers to nodes whose info fields are to be swapped        *
 * Output parameters:  none (list contents will be changed!!)                       *
 * Return value:       none                                                         *
 *************************************************************************************/
```

```
void  swap2 (    NODE_PTR    pos1,
                 NODE_PTR    pos2  )
{

   ITEM_TYPE    temp;

   temp        =  pos1->info;                            /* Save pos1's info */
   pos1->info  =  pos2->info;                                  /* Now swap */
   pos2->info  =  temp;

}                                                           /* End of swap2 */
```

Selection sort has the advantage of simplicity and is an adequate method for relatively small lists of a few hundred records. The processing time for even a small list depends on the size of each record and the speed of the hardware. The problem with selection sort becomes apparent when the list gets large. The main loop in **sel_sort** executes approximately n (the number of records) times. However, at each iteration it has to search the rest of the array to find the position of the smallest element. Because there are n passes, each with about n subpasses, selection sort needs a total of approximately n^2 steps. For this reason we call it a **quadratic sorting method**. If $n = 100$, this means about 10,000 operations on the data; if $n = 1000$, then about 1,000,000 operations must be done. Note that these are very crude underestimates that do not take into account the extent of the operations. For instance, each time a swap is performed, three assignment statements are executed, so a 1000-item list needs closer to 3,000,000 processing steps.

PERSPECTIVE

Because the algorithm always scans the whole list looking for the smallest item, the performance of selection sort is always basically the same even if the original data happen to be in order.

A second quadratic sorting method called **insertion sort** has an advantage over selection sort under certain circumstances. Insertion sort handles an *ordered* list in linear time. That is, it discovers in one pass across the n items that the data are in order and then stops. Insertion sort works in nearly linear time when the initial data configuration is close to being sorted and in this particular situation it is the fastest possible sorting method. Otherwise, for random- or reverse-order data its performance is about the same as that of selection sort.

Insertion sort is like a card player trying to arrange a hand as it is being dealt. (See Figure 16.2–2.) Assuming that the first i cards are already in order, the card player does something like this each time a card is dealt:

1. Starting from the end of the hand, scans the new card for its proper insertion point.

2. Once found, moves aside the cards following it and places the new card.
3. Repeats the process until all remaining cards have been dealt and correctly inserted.

Note that if the hand happens to be dealt in the *correct order*, inserting in the partially sorted hand reduces to adding each new card to the end instead of searching for an insertion spot (linear time).

The algorithm works the same way. It first sets aside a copy of the ith item (equivalent to the last card dealt) and proceeds to search backward through the first $i - 1$ items (already presumed to be sorted) to find the correct insertion point. As it searches, it moves the items down one position, creating a gap into which the ith item can be placed. When the correct point is found, the held item is inserted into the gap.

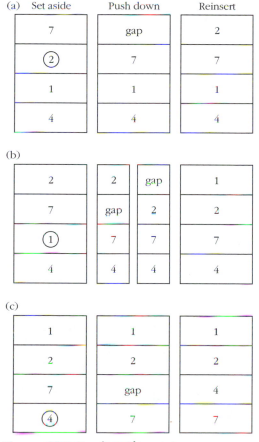

Figure 16.2–2   Insertion sort

The code for insertion sort is shown in Program 16.2–4. Note that since a *single* item is inserted in its correct location, the function begins with the second item (i is initialized to 1 rather than to 0 in the **for** loop).

PROGRAM 16.2–4

```
/***************************************************************************
*  Function name:      ins_sort       (iterative, array-based)            *
*  Description:        Perform an insertion sort on an array of integers.  *
*                                                                          *
*  Input parameters:   array of integers                                  *
*  Output parameters:  sorted array                                       *
*  Return value:       none                                               *
***************************************************************************/

void  ins_sort ( int  list [ ]  )
{
    int    i, j, hold;

    for ( i = 1;  i < MAX_SIZE;  i++ ) {

        hold  = list [ i ];                        /* Set aside the ith element */
        j     = i;

        while ( ( j-1 >= 0 ) && list [ j-1 ] > hold ) {    /* Now check all the */
            list [ j ] = list [ j-1 ];             /* preceding elements and move them */
            j          = j-1;                      /* forward until a smaller element is found */
        }

        list [ j ] = hold;             /* Reinsert the held item into the gap created */
    }
}                                                  /* End of ins_sort */
```

BEFORE YOU GO ON

Query: What is the purpose of checking for j–1 >= 0 in the while loop?

RESPONSE: If the item to be inserted happens to belong in the very first location of the structure (when j equals 0), the list [j–1] > hold test would cause an array-bounds problem.

16.2.2 Advanced Sorting: Shell Sort and Quicksort

A simple variation of insertion sort, called **Shell sort** (named for its inventor, Donald Shell, in 1959), can dramatically improve processing time.

The problem with insertion sort is that for any given item it looks only locally— at items directly adjacent—to find an insertion spot. An item that happens to be a great distance from its correct location is constantly moved back to make room for new items.

By contrast, the Shell sort algorithm first looks at items that are d apart, where d is, for example, $\frac{1}{2}$ or $\frac{1}{3}$ the size of the list. On succeeding passes d is reduced by some factor and the sort reapplied. Items that are greatly out of order are quickly placed in the approximately correct portion of the list. Figure 16.2–3 shows Shell sort on a small data set using arbitrary increments of 5, 2, and 1.

Although we do not explore it here, much work has been done on a scheme for generating successive values of d. In Program 16.2–5, d is represented by the `incr` (increment) variable. `incr` is initialized to the size of the list and then successively divided by 3. When `incr` reduces to 1 the data are guaranteed to be nearly sorted with no item more than two positions from its correct insertion point. Because the data are almost sorted, the last call runs in nearly linear time.

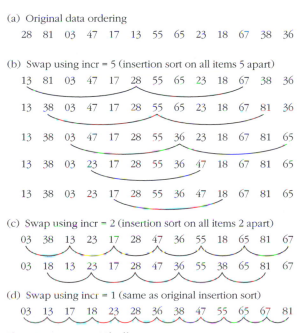

(a) Original data ordering

    28   81   03   47   17   13   55   65   23   18   67   38   36

(b) Swap using incr = 5 (insertion sort on all items 5 apart)

    13   81   03   47   17   28   55   65   23   18   67   38   36

    13   38   03   47   17   28   55   65   23   18   67   81   36

    13   38   03   47   17   28   55   36   23   18   67   81   65

    13   38   03   23   17   28   55   36   47   18   67   81   65

    13   38   03   23   17   28   55   36   47   18   67   81   65

(c) Swap using incr = 2 (insertion sort on all items 2 apart)

    03   38   13   23   17   28   47   36   55   18   65   81   67

    03   18   13   23   17   28   47   36   55   38   65   81   67

(d) Swap using incr = 1 (same as original insertion sort)

    03   13   17   18   23   28   36   38   47   55   65   67   81

Figure 16.2–3   Shell sort

PROGRAM 16.2-5

```
/*****************************************************************************
 * Function name:        shell_sort(iterative, array-based)                 *
 * Description:          Perform a Shell sort on an array of integers.      *
 *                                                                          *
 * Input parameters:     array of integers                                 *
 * Output parameters:    sorted array                                      *
 * Return value:         none                                              *
 *****************************************************************************/

void    shell_sort ( int    list[ ]  )
{
    int  incr = MAX_SIZE;

    do {
            incr = incr / 3 + 1;
            ins_sort_2 ( list,  incr );

    }   while ( incr > 1 );
}                                                       /* End of shell_sort */
```

Note that **ins_sort_2** is the same as in insertion sort (Program 16.2–4), with the added **incr** parameter representing the distance between successive elements. In insertion sort the distance between elements is always 1 and here it is determined by **incr**.

```
/*****************************************************************************
 * Function name:        ins_sort_2                                         *
 * Description:          Perform an insertion sort on a set of records.     *
 *                                                                          *
 * Input parameters:     array of integers, increment value                *
 * Output parameters:    sorted array                                      *
 * Return value:         none                                              *
 *****************************************************************************/

void    ins_sort_2 (    int list [ ],
                        int incr   )
{
    int    i,  j,  hold;
```

```
   for (  i = incr;   i < MAX_SIZE;   i++  )    {

      hold   = list [ i ];                          /*  Set aside the ith element  */
      j      = i;

      while (  ( j-incr  >= 0)  &&  list [ j-incr ]  >  hold  )  {        /*  Now check  */
         list [ j ]    = list [ j-incr ];                /*  preceding elements and moving  */
         j             = j-incr;           /*  forward until a smaller element is found  */
      }

      list [ j ]  = hold;               /*  Reinsert the held item into the gap created  */
   }
}                                                            /* End of ins_sort2 */
```

PERSPECTIVE

On an array of 25,000 reverse-ordered integers, Shell sort was clocked as 250 times faster than insertion sort!

Another efficient algorithm, **quicksort**, was developed by C. A. R. Hoare and works by partitioning the data at some pivot point. The partitioning consists of putting all items that are less than the pivot value (*to the left of it*) in one partition and putting all items that are greater than the pivot (*to the right of it*) in another partition. Once the left and right halves have been sorted they can be concatenated (joined end-to-end) to make the completely sorted list. Applying the partitioning process recursively (with successively smaller partitions) leads to partitions of size 1, at which point all items have been correctly sorted.

To give you an idea of the process, here is the code for the main function plus a simple partitioning function:

```
/*******************************************************************************
 * Function name:     quicksort                                                *
 * Description:       Perform a quicksort on an array of integers.             *
 *                                                                             *
 * Input parameters:  array of integers, left and right indexes of partition   *
 * Output parameters: sorted array                                             *
 * Return value:      none                                                     *
 *******************************************************************************/

void   quicksort (   int list [ ],
                     int left,
                     int right   )
{
   int pivot;
```

```
      if (  left < right  )  {                            /*  If left doesn't exceed right */
          pivot = partition ( list,  left,     right);         /* Partition the data */
          quicksort        ( list,  left,     pivot-1);     /* Sort the left partition */
          quicksort        ( list,  pivot+1,  right);      /* Sort the right partition */
      }
}                                                         /* End of quicksort */
```

The following partitioning scheme uses the middle location of the data as the pivot point and then swaps all items that are less than the pivot with all items that are greater than the pivot.

```
/**************************************************************************************
 *  Function name:      partition                                                   *
 *  Description:        For the given partition, place all values that are less than *
 *                      the value at the pivot point into the left half of the array;*
 *                      place all values greater than the pivot value into the       *
 *                      right half.                                                 *
 *                                                                                  *
 *  Input parameters:   array of integers, left and right indexes of partition      *
 *  Output parameters:  partially sorted array                                      *
 *  Return value:       index of pivot value                                        *
 **************************************************************************************/

int     partition ( int list [ ],
                    int left,
                    int right   )
{
   int    i, pivot_value, pivot_loc;

   swap1 ( list,  left,  (left+right)/2  );          /*  Temporarily place pivot value into */
                                                     /* leftmost location of current partition */
   pivot_value     = list [ left ];                      /* Set aside pivot value */
   pivot_loc       = left;                            /* Set aside index of pivot value */

   for (  i = left+1;   i <= right;   i++  )          /*  All items which are < pivot value */
       if ( list [ i ]  <  pivot_value )   /* are swapped into left half of partition. */
           swap1 ( list,  ++pivot_loc,  i );      /* Items > pivot value are therefore */
                                                      /* placed into right half */

   swap1 ( list,  left,  pivot_loc );                    /*  Return pivot to middle */

   return ( pivot_loc );
}                                                      /* End of partition */
```

In theory, quicksort is a very efficient algorithm needing $n \log n$ steps. For example, for $n = 1024$ (1k) quicksort should need only 10 K steps (1024 * 10) compared with approximately 1,000,000 steps for insertion sort or selection sort. In practice, however, its performance depends on the pivot, which is ideally the median of the data. However, finding the median means sorting the data! Various heuristics (rules of thumb) have been explored for finding pivots but the farther we get from the median, the more lopsided the partitions and the greater the depth of recursion. In its worst case quicksort takes as long as insertion or selection. Worse yet, the program can cause a stack overflow and crash. Insertion sort works best with nearly ordered data; quicksort works best with random data and sometimes crashes with either ordered or reverse-ordered data.

16.2.3 The Best Sort of All?

As a final word on sorting we present a sorting method that is interesting regardless of the data organization: **Bucket sort** is one of the fastest possible sorts since it does not depend on comparing keys. It is also extremely simple to understand and code. Unfortunately, as it will be shown, it can be used only within certain limitations.

To do a bucket sort, we distribute the records by key in a local array. As shown in Figure 16.2–4, we make an association between the local array indexes and the key values of the records. This process needs only *one pass* through the original array. An optional second pass can be added in which the data are returned to the original array. Because there may be gaps in the local array— representing keys not present at the time of the sort—the return to the original array allows the data to be compacted, leaving no gaps. Distributing n records takes about n steps, so bucket sort is called **linear**. The code for bucket sort is shown in Program 16.2–6 and needs this global declaration

```
typedef    struct  list_type {
                   ITEM_TYPE           info [ MAX_KEY ];
                   int                 current_size;
           }   LIST_TYPE;
```

PROGRAM 16.2-6

```
/************************************************************************
*  Function name:        bucket_sort                                    *
*  Description:          Perform a bucket sort on a structure holding an array of records.  *
*                                                                       *
*  Input parameters:     structure holding an array of records          *
*  Output parameters:    structure with sorted array items              *
*  Return value:         none                                           *
*************************************************************************/
```

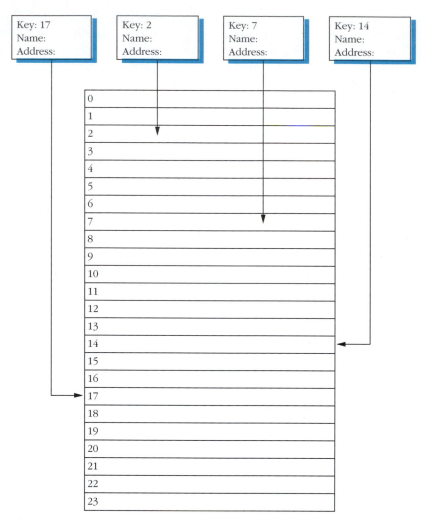

Figure 16.2–4   Bucket sort

```
void   bucket_sort ( LIST_TYPE   *list )
{
    LIST_TYPE   local_list;
    int   i,  j;

    for ( i = 0;   i < MAX_KEY;   i++ )                       /*  Initialize local list  */
        local_list.info[ i ].key = -1;

    for ( i = 0;  i < list->current_size;  i++ )   /*  Distribute data into local list  */
        local_list.info[ list->info[ i ].key ]  =  list->info[ i ];
```

```
      j = 0;
      for (  i = 0;   i < MAX_KEY;   i++  )              /* Copy back to original list  */
         if (  local_list.info[ i ].key != -1  )         /*  compacting as we go  */
            list->info[ j++ ]  =  local_list.info[ i ];
}                                                        /* End of bucket_sort */
```

The first loop initializes the key field of each record of the local array to an arbitrary marker value that is outside the range of the key. Cells in the local array in which data are not inserted (because no record has that key) are therefore detectable.

The second loop does the actual sorting. The `list->info[i].key` key field from the original array is used as an index to the local array. The whole `info` field is inserted in the local array at that key-determined index. Because the loop searches through the original list, it uses `i < list->current_size;` as the continuation condition rather than `i < MAX_KEY;`, which is used for searching through the local array.

Finally, the local list is copied back into the original array. The last loop checks whether the *i*th record has anything in it (its key is not −1) and, if so, copies the `info` field into the next free location in the original array.

The catch to bucket sort is that it can be used only as follows. First, the key must be a unique, positive integer and not a string or a floating-point or even a negative-integer value. Second, the range of key values must be relatively small or the local array might be impossibly huge. For instance, if the key happens to be social security numbers, `MAX_KEY`, which is used to dimension the local array, would be 999999999. This creates an array too large to fit into memory. But if the key range is not too large, bucket sort is highly efficient.

Note that if the key value happens to be something other than a positive integer, it still might be possible to use bucket sort. For instance, a key in the range of −100 to +100 could be arithmetically manipulated (by adding 100) to put it in a usable range. Similarly, a real-valued key might be convertible to an integer by multiplying each key by a constant to remove the fractional portion (for example, multiplying 50.34 by 100 gives an integer key, 5034). Remapping the keys is called **hashing** and is a standard technique for designing and accessing lists.

EXERCISES 16.2

Concept Check

Answer statements 1 through 4 with true *or* false.

1. No perfect sorting algorithm exists.
2. The complexity of an algorithm means the degree of difficulty in converting it to a program.

3. The performance of most sorting routines is independent of the original organization of the data.
4. Bucket sort allows keys of any data type as long as there are no duplicate values.

For statements 5 through 8 choose the answer that best completes the statement.

5. Best case for selection sort is when the data are
   a. in order
   b. in reverse order
   c. in random order
   d. none of the above: selection sort works the same way regardless of the data ordering

6. Best case for insertion sort is when the data are
   a. in order
   b. in reverse order
   c. in random order
   d. none of the above: insertion sort works the same way regardless of the data ordering

7. Quicksort works most efficiently when
   a. the pivot point is the mean of all the data
   b. the pivot point is the median of all the data
   c. the data is already ordered
   d. the data is reverse-ordered

8. The performance of bucket sort is
   a. logarithmic since the number of steps is about $\log_2(n)$
   b. quadratic since the number of steps is about n^2
   c. linear since the number of steps is about n
   d. difficult to characterize

For statements 9 through 12 fill in the blanks with the right word.

9. Regarding its complexity, selection sort is called a _____ sorting method.

10. For use with Shell sort, insertion sort is modified to include an extra parameter `incr` representing _____.

11. Taking all factors into account, the best overall sort method appears to be

   _____.

12. Converting a noninteger key to an integer range is called

   _____.

Set A

Solve each of the following problems.

13. Rewrite `find_pos_min` so that `pos_min` is an output parameter instead of a return value.

14. Identify the base case for recursive selection sort.

15. Assume that a list contains about 1000 records in random order. Discuss which sorting method you would choose.

Set B

16. Write a hashing function that accepts a character key and returns a unique integer value.
17. Write a hashing function that accepts a floating-point value guaranteed to be between 0.00 and 99.99 and returns a unique integer.
18. A key is specified as a two-character string. Discuss various ways to convert the string to a unique-integer representation.

Set C

19. Another quadratic sorting method is called **bubble sort**. With this method the list is scanned from beginning to end and whenever an adjacent pair of items is found to be out of order, they are swapped. After one pass, the element with the largest key has been "bubbled" to the end of the list. The procedure continues by successively increasing the starting point in the list by 1. Write a bubble sort program in C.
20. Rewrite bubble sort recursively.
21. Rewrite selection sort recursively for a linked-list implementation.
22. Rewrite selection sort for a linked-list implementation but swap the pointers to the nodes when needed, not the data in those nodes. Hint: Node swapping needs a pointer to the previous node and to the node itself. Swapping with the first node in the list is a special case because the list pointer itself must be changed. You can avoid this by using a header node.

17 Numerical Algorithms

Trajectory after rocket launch.

After completing this chapter you should be able to do the following:

Learning Goals

- Solve both linear and quadratic equations using closed-form methods
- Apply the bisection algorithm to solve any equation in one variable for which a root exists
- Apply the secant algorithm to solve any equation in one variable for which a root exists
- Apply the Newton-Raphson algorithm to find the zeros of any function in one variable that is a polynomial of degree 3 or less or that involves sine and cosine functions for which a root exists
- Solve any n-by-n system of equations manually for n less than or equal to 3 using Gaussian elimination
- Apply the Gaussian elimination with backward substitution algorithm to solve any system of linear equations
- Apply the Gauss-Seidel algorithm to solve any system of linear equations by iteration
- Using either the forward-difference or the forward-backward-difference algorithm, find the numerical derivative of any function having a sufficient number of points
- Apply the algorithms of integration to any region defined by a suitable function over a real interval; the algorithms include rectangular, trapezoidal, and parabolic methods

Chapter Activity

A satellite is launched from a space shuttle and an experiment is performed starting at a relative time in seconds. The velocity, measured in miles per second, is tracked and recorded from the initial point in time $t_0 = 35$ seconds to some other point in time t_n in increments of 0.5 seconds. The data are presented in the form of ordered pairs (t_i, v_i) for $i = 0, 1, 2, \ldots, n$ where t_i is the time at the ith data point and v_i is the velocity at time t_i. That is, the velocity $v_i = v(t_i)$. Figure 17.0–1 is a printout of the data acquired over

TIME (SECONDS)	VELOCITY (MILES PER SECOND)
t0 = 35.0	0.07595
t1 = 35.5	0.07814
t2 = 36.0	0.08035
t3 = 36.5	0.08260
t4 = 37.0	0.08488
t5 = 37.5	0.08719
t6 = 38.0	0.08953
t7 = 38.5	0.09190
t8 = 39.0	0.09430
t9 = 39.5	0.09674
t10 = 40.0	0.09920

Figure 17.0–1 Velocity data from space satellite

a period of five seconds. Write a program to calculate simultaneously the acceleration of the satellite and the distance it traveled over this time period where the distance already traveled at t_0 is 2.658 miles.

17.1 ZEROS OF FUNCTIONS

Introduction

One of the first uses of computers was to calculate mathematical formulas. As we learned in Chapters 1 and 14, this application was so vital that in the early 1950s the first of the third generation of programming languages was invented: FORTRAN (FORmula TRANslating system).

The solution of mathematical equations and the representation of functions have been studied for centuries. In the early 1700s Brook Taylor showed how any function satisfying certain conditions could be represented by an infinite series of polynomials. Over the last three centuries there have been numerous attempts to solve differential equations, with only a moderate degree of success. Iterative (numerical) methods, although known, were tedious and lacked the precision to actually "solve" the problem at hand. With the invention of the computer iterative methods became automated. Solutions to problems were not only possible, but the speed at which the problems could be solved was far greater than if the task were performed by humans.

> ### PERSPECTIVE
>
> Did you know that before the time of computers (from the 1940s) people executed the algorithms for finding zeros of functions, finding derivatives and integrals, and solving systems of equations manually? For example, to process a system of 10 equations in 10 unknowns could take weeks of work. Modern PCs can do the same problem in just a few seconds.

In this section we look at some numerical ways to find the zeros of a function. The methods are not unique and have been known for many years. What makes the methods important today is the fact that a computer has the power to do high-speed calculations with a precision that was unimaginable just a few decades ago. Problems that were once computationally unfeasible are now solved in seconds.

17.1.1 Functions and Their Zeros

Mathematical functions can be described in many ways. Any set of ordered pairs is called a **relation**. We define a **function** by a set of ordered pairs (x, y) where for each element x there exists a unique element y. Thus, every function is a relation. The set of all values x satisfying the function is called the **domain** of the function. The set of all values of y generated by the function is called the **range** of the function. For example, let the set $\{(2.96, -3.17), (3.58, 4.27), (-0.72, 4.27)\}$ describe function F. The domain of function F is $\{2.96, 3.58, -0.72\}$. The range of function F is $\{-3.17, 4.27\}$.

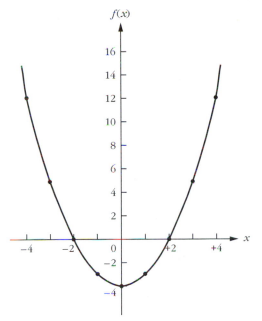

Figure 17.1–1   Graph of f(x) = x² – 4

Relations are often represented by mathematical equations. As an example, the set

$$\{(x, y) : y = x^2 - 4 \text{ where } x \text{ is an integer}\}$$

describes a function. The notation reads: The set of all ordered pairs (x, y) so that for all integers x, $x^2 - 4$ equals y. In this case we can abbreviate the set by writing

$$y = f(x) = x^2 - 4$$

Some elements of this set are $(3, 5), (-2, 0), (0, -4), (-3, 5)$, and $(2, 0)$. When two different ordered pairs have the same value for x, the set of ordered pairs is not a function. For example, the set $\{(2, 3), (3, 4), (3, 5), (4, 6)\}$ is not a function. Given the input 3, there is no way to know for sure if the correct output is 4 or 5.

Relations are also described by graphs that are generated by the ordered pairs. The graph of function $y = f(x) = x^2 - 4$ for real values of x in Figure 17.1–1 is recognized as a parabola. The graph in Figure 17.1–2, however, is not a function because for all values of x greater than -9, there are two different values for y, such as $(7, 4)$ and $(7, -4)$. In general, if one value of x corresponds to more than one value of y, the relation is not a function. Therefore, even though the graph in Figure 17.1–2 is not a function, it does represent a relation.

The graph of the function in Figure 17.1–1 shows two ordered pairs where the value of y is zero: $(-2, 0)$ and $(2, 0)$. This condition can also be described by

$$f(-2) = 0 \quad \text{and} \quad f(2) = 0$$

since $(-2)^2 - 4 = 0$ and $(2)^2 - 4 = 0$, respectively. We call values -2 and 2 zeros of the function f. For a given function f, any value of x that makes $f(x) = 0$ is called a **zero of the function**.

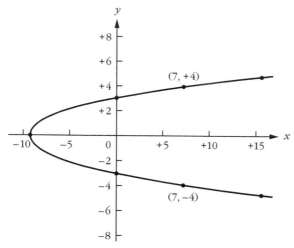

Figure 17.1–2   Relation that is not a function

Functions of the $f(x) = ax + b$ form for real constant coefficients a and b with $a \neq 0$ are called **linear functions** because the graph of the function is a straight line. The zero of a linear function is easily calculated as

$$x = -\frac{b}{a}$$

EXAMPLE 17.1–1

Problem
Find the zero of $f(x) = 3.1x - 26.35$.

Reasoning
To find the value of x that makes the function equal to 0, set the function equal to 0 and solve for x.

Solution
Let $f(x) = 0$. Then

$$3.1x - 26.35 = 0$$

Solving for x results in

$$3.1x = 26.35$$
$$x = 8.5$$

Test
Substitution into the function shows that

$$f(8.5) = 3.1(8.5) - 26.35 = 0$$

and solves the problem.   ●

Not every function has a zero over the domain for which it is defined. In Example 17.1–1 we assume, perhaps incorrectly, that the domain of the function is the set of all real (floating-point) numbers. If we assume that the domain is the set of all *integers*, then there is no solution and the function has no zeros.

BEFORE YOU GO ON

Query: A function is defined as $f(x) = 2x + 5$ over the integers. What are the zeros of the function, if any?

RESPONSE: Setting $f(x) = 0$ yields $x = -5/2$, which is not an integer. Therefore, the function has no zeros.

Zeros of functions are closely related to roots of equations. Suppose we are given an equation in one variable, say x, written so that all terms of the equation are on the left of the equal sign and zero is on the right. The **root of the equation** is the set of all values of x that satisfy the equation. For example, suppose an equation in x is given as

$$x^2 - 4 = 3x$$

We have to put all terms on the left of the equation. This results in

$$x^2 - 3x - 4 = 0$$

We recognize this as an example of a quadratic equation. The values of x that satisfy or **solve** this equation are its roots. Note that this equation factors into

$$(x - 4)(x + 1) = 0$$

resulting in two roots: $x = 4$ and $x = -1$.

A function is **quadratic** if it takes the form

$$f(x) = ax^2 + bx + c$$

where the constant coefficients a, b, and c are real numbers and $a \neq 0$. Setting the function equal to zero results in the quadratic equation

$$ax^2 + bx + c = 0$$

Notice that the *roots* of the quadratic equation become the *zeros* of the quadratic function. A convenient way to solve this equation is by using the **quadratic formula** derived to be

$$x = \frac{-b \pm \sqrt{b^2 - 4ac}}{2a}$$

This formulation enables a quick calculation using the coefficients to get the result needed. Over the domain of real numbers, there are three possibilities for the zeros of f, based on the **discriminant** $b^2 - 4ac$. There are two zeros if the discriminant is positive, one zero if the discriminant is zero, and no zero if the

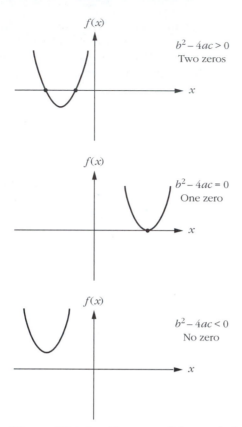

Figure 17.1–3   Three possible parabolas

discriminant is negative. Figure 17.1–3 shows the three possibilities for a typical parabola.

BEFORE YOU GO ON

Query: Find the zeros of $f(x) = x^2 - 3x$.

RESPONSE: In this case $a = 1$, $b = -3$, and $c = 0$. The discriminant is $(-3)^2 - 4(1)(0) = +9$ so there are two zeros calculated to be $x_1 = 0$ and $x_2 = 3$.

17.1.2 The Bisection Method

We do not mean to give the impression that we can always do a mathematical manipulation to find the zero of a function. Consider the trigonometric function

$$f(x) = x - \cos x$$

for all real numbers x on the interval $[-\pi, \pi]$. There is no **closed-form solution** (a solution that can be obtained by a formula) like the quadratic formula to calculate the zeros of this function. The graph in Figure 17.1–4 suggests, however,

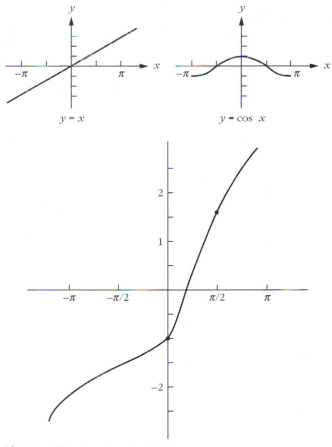

Figure 17.1–4 Graph of $f(x) = x - \cos x$

that one zero does exist. We can *guess* at what an answer might be, but this is not very scientific. A better approach is to find an algorithm—for example, the bisection algorithm—that gives a close approximation of the true answer.

Figure 17.1–4 shows that the zero of the f function lies on the real number interval $0 \le x \le \pi/2$ where $\pi/2 = 1.57079632\ldots \approx 1.57$, approximately. That is, for some x between 0 and 1.57

$$f(x) = 0$$

or

$$x - \cos x = 0$$

We begin by testing the endpoints of the interval: $a = 0$ and $b = 1.57$. Thus

$$f(a) = f(0) = -1$$

and

$$f(b) = f(1.57) = 1.57, \text{ approximately}$$

so $f(a) < 0$ (negative) and $f(b) > 0$ (positive), implying that a zero of f exists between 0 and 1.57. Another way to test for this is to find the product $f(a) * f(b)$. If this product is negative, a zero exists between a and b; that is, the graph of the function crosses the x-axis. If the product is positive, we cannot assume that the graph of the function crosses the x-axis. If the product is zero, then $f(a)$ or $f(b)$ equals zero, implying that the zero of the function is $x = a$ or $x = b$.

Using the bisection algorithm we find the midpoint mp of the current interval $[a, b]$ by calculating $mp = (a + b)/2$ and evaluating the function at that midpoint by finding $f(mp)$. Then we find the test product between $f(mp)$ and the endpoints. The following conditions hold.

1. If $f(\text{mp}) * f(b) < 0$, then establish a new interval $[a', b]$ where $a' = $ mp.
2. If $f(a) * f(\text{mp}) < 0$, then establish a new interval $[a, b']$ where $b' = $ mp.
3. If $f(\text{mp}) * f(b) = 0$ or $f(a) * f(\text{mp}) = 0$, then mp is a zero of function f.

Case 3 ends the algorithm because it suggests that the zero of f was found. In cases 1 and 2 the algorithm does another iteration using the newly created interval and continues until the zero is found, or until the difference between two successive midpoints is less than a tolerance prescribed by the user.

EXAMPLE 17.1–2

Problem
Use three iterations of the bisection algorithm to approximate the zero of $f(x) = x - \cos x$ on the $[0, \pi/2]$ interval.

Reasoning
Before we can use the algorithm, we have to confirm that the function is continuous on the interval and that the endpoints of the interval bracket the zero. The terms of the function, x and $\cos x$, are each continuous so the f function is continuous. For $a = 0$ and $b = \pi/2$,

$$f(a) * f(b) = f(0) * f(1.57) = (-1)(1.57) = -1.57 < 0$$

That is, $f(a) * f(b)$ is negative ($f(a)$ and $f(b)$ on opposite sides of the x-axis) so there is a zero between a and b. This tells us that we can use the bisection algorithm.

Solution
The bisection algorithm begins with initial endpoints $a_0 = 0$ and $b_0 = 1.57$. From these values calculate $\text{mp}_1 = (a_0 + b_0)/2 = (0 + 1.57)/2 = 0.785$ and evaluate the $f(x) = x - \cos x$ function as

$$\begin{aligned} f(\text{mp}_1) = \text{mp}_1 - \cos \text{mp}_1 &= 0.785 - \cos 0.785 \\ &= 0.785 - 0.70739 \\ &= 0.07761 \end{aligned}$$

Note that the angle of the cosine is a real number (radian measure). Now we must check $f(a_0) * f(\text{mp}_1)$ and $f(\text{mp}_1) * f(b_0)$ to find where the graph of the function crosses the x-axis. Thus

$$f(a_0) * f(\text{mp}_1) = -1 * 0.07761 = -0.07761 < 0$$

so it does cross the x-axis. But

$$f(mp_1) * f(b_0) = 0.07761 * 1.57 = +0.12185 > 0$$

so it does not necessarily cross the x-axis. Therefore, set the new value of b to equal mp_1 and let the new value of a be the same as the previous value of a. Therefore, the new interval $[a_1, b_1]$ becomes $[0, 0.785]$. Now we repeat the iterative cycle. Calculate $mp_2 = (a_1 + b_1)/2 = (0 + 0.785)/2 = 0.3925$ and evaluate the function $f(x) = x - \cos x$ as

$$f(mp_2) = mp_2 - \cos mp_2 = 0.3925 - \cos 0.3925$$
$$= 0.3925 - 0.92396$$
$$= -0.53146$$

Next, we check $f(a_1) * f(mp_2)$ and $f(mp_2) * f(b_1)$ to find out if the graph of the function crosses the x-axis. Because

$$f(mp_2) * f(b_1) = -0.53146 * 0.785 = -0.41719 < 0$$

it does cross the x-axis. Therefore, set the new value of a equal to mp_2 and let the new value of b be the same as the previous value of b so the new interval $[a_2, b_2]$ becomes $[0.3925, 0.785]$. Now we repeat the iterative cycle. Calculate $mp_3 = (a_2 + b_2)/2 = (0.3925 + 0.785)/2 = 0.58875$ and evaluate the $f(x) = x - \cos x$ function as

$$f(mp_3) = mp_3 - \cos mp_3 = 0.58875 - \cos 0.58875$$
$$= 0.58875 - 0.83163$$
$$= -0.24288$$

Then check $f(a_2) * f(mp_3)$ and $f(mp_3) * f(b_2)$ to find out if the graph of the function crosses the x-axis. Since

$$f(mp_3) * f(b_2) = -0.24288 * 0.07761 = -0.01885 < 0$$

it does cross the x-axis, so set the new value of a to equal mp_3 and let the new value of b be the same as the previous value of b. The new interval $[a_3, b_3]$ becomes $[0.58875, 0.785]$ and we calculate $mp_4 = (a_3 + b_3)/2 = (0.58875 + 0.785)/2 = 0.686875$. Now we can repeat the iterative cycle.

Note the differences in the midpoints in absolute value.

$$|mp_2 - mp_1| = |0.39250 - 0.78500| = 0.39250$$

and

$$|mp_3 - mp_2| = |0.58875 - 0.39250| = 0.19625$$

and

$$|mp_4 - mp_3| = |0.68687 - 0.58875| = 0.09812$$

They appear to *converge* toward zero and they do converge toward zero if the algorithm continues through its iterative cycles. After three iterations, a best approximation to the zero of $f(x) = x - \cos x$ is $mp_4 = 0.686875$.

Test

Substituting mp_4 into $f(x)$ results in

$$f(mp_4) = mp_4 - \cos mp_4 = 0.686875 - \cos 0.686875$$
$$= 0.686875 - 0.773231$$
$$= -0.086356$$

That is, $x = 0.686875$ is a close approximation to the zero of f. Further iterations would result in a closer approximation. •

Figure 17.1–5 shows how the bisection algorithm causes intervals to converge and to bracket the desired zero or root for the $f(x) = x - \cos x$ function of Example 17.1–2.

The beauty of the bisection algorithm is that once we know that a zero of a function exists on a certain interval, the algorithm converges within a prescribed tolerance to the zero of the function. After each iteration, the interval in which the zero lies is divided by 2. Thus, if I_0 is the initial interval, then $I_1 = I_0/2$, $I_2 = I_1/2$, $I_3 = I_2/2$, $I_4 = I_3/2$, and so on. We can write, for example,

$$I_4 = I_3/2 = I_2/4 = I_1/8 = I_0/16$$

or after n iterations (n is an integer)

$$I_n = I_0/2^n$$

leading to

$$2^n = I_0/I_n$$

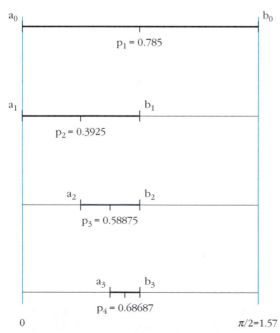

Figure 17.1–5 labels:

a_0 .... b_0

$p_1 = 0.785$

a_1 .... b_1

$p_2 = 0.3925$

a_2 ... b_2

$p_3 = 0.58875$

a_3 . b_3

$p_4 = 0.68687$

0 .... $\pi/2 = 1.57$

Figure 17.1–5   Example of bisection

or

$$n = \log_2(I_0 / I_n)$$

Although n must be an integer, $\log_2(I_0 / I_n)$ is not necessarily an integer, so we have to round its value *up* to the nearest integer. Therefore, if I_n is the desired ending tolerance and I_0 is the initial interval width, then n is the number of iterations needed for the result wanted.

BEFORE YOU GO ON

Query: How many iterations are needed to find the zero of a function by the bisection method if the interval [*a*, *b*] is [3, 9] and the tolerance wanted is $1/4096$?

RESPONSE: Since $1/4096 = 2^{-12} = I_n$ and $9 - 3 = 6 \le 8 = 2^3$, then the number of iterations is $n = \log_2(2^3/2^{-12}) = \log_2 2^{15} = 15$. That is, 15 iterations are needed.

Program 17.1–1 is a function that implements the bisection algorithm. A driver for this function is given in Program 17.1–3. The logic is similar to the logic of Example 17.1–1.

PROGRAM 17.1–1

```
/*****************************************************************************
*  Function name:      bisect                                               *
*  Description:        This is a function to find the zero of any           *
*                      single-argument float function FUN using             *
*                      bisection.  The user must supply the range (low,      *
*                      high) where zero is known to lie and the             *
*                      number of iterations maxiter.  The zero is           *
*                      refined until its accuracy falls within a            *
*                      TOLERANCE  provided by the driving program.          *
*                                                                           *
*  Input parameters:   low, high, maxiter                                   *
*  Output parameters:  root_bisect,  iter_ptr                               *
*  Return value:       status                                               *
*****************************************************************************/

                              /*  Assumes information from driver program  */

BOOLEAN bisect ( float low, float high, int maxiter,
                 float *root_bisect, int *iter_ptr  )
{
   float mid,                              /*  Midpoint of interval  */
         ylow, yhigh, ymid;       /*  Function values at low, high, and mid  */

   int    iter;                            /*  Loop iteration index  */
```

```
for ( iter = 0; iter < maxiter; iter++ ) {
    mid  = low + (high - low) / 2.0;
    ymid = FUN(mid);

    if ( ymid == ZERO || (high - low)/2.0 < TOLERANCE ) {
        *iter_ptr    = iter;      /* Check if interval within tolerance */
        *root_bisect = mid;
      return (true);
    }

    ylow = FUN(low);                          /* Reevaluate function */
    ymid = FUN(mid);

    if ( ylow * ymid > ZERO )                 /* Adjust interval */
        low  = mid;
    else
        high = mid;

}

*iter_ptr = iter;                         /* Zero of function not found */
return (false);
}
```

17.1.3 The Secant Method

One deficiency of the bisection algorithm is that it is slow to converge to the result wanted. An improvement on this method is to form a secant line between the two initial points and then calculate where the *secant* crosses the x-axis. Although the secant line is not the graph of the function, it is a first step to approximating the zero of the function. The idea is that the slope of the secant line between two initial points is the same as the slope of the segment of the line between one of the points and the point at which it crosses the x-axis. We can write this as

$$\text{Slope}_{\text{secant}} = \text{Slope}_{\text{segment}}$$

or for initial points, say A and B, having coordinates $(a, f(a))$ and $(b, f(b))$, we can write the slopes as

$$\frac{f(b) - f(a)}{b - a} = \frac{f(b) - 0}{b - c}$$

in which c is the *new* value of x where the secant crosses the x-axis, as shown in Figure 17.1–6. We can rewrite this as

$$\frac{b - c}{1} = \frac{f(b) * (b - a)}{f(b) - f(a)}$$

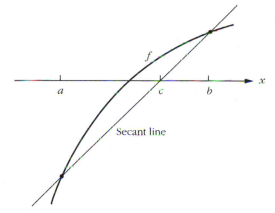

Figure 17.1–6   The secant method

or

$$c = b - \frac{f(b) * (b - a)}{f(b) - f(a)}$$

In terms of x we can rewrite this equation with obvious substitutions for a, b, and c as

$$x_n = x_{n-1} - \frac{f(x_{n-1}) * (x_{n-1} - x_{n-2})}{f(x_{n-1}) - f(x_{n-2})}$$

The algorithm of the secant method is implemented in Program 17.1–2. It follows the reasoning just discussed where x_1 and x_2 are the initial values for x.

PROGRAM 17.1-2

```
/**********************************************************************
*  Function name:        secant                                       *
*  Description:          This program contains a function named secant.  It finds the zero  *
*                        of a function FUN using the secant algorithm where the zero is   *
*                        thought to lie between the values low and high after a number    *
*                        of iterations maxiter.  The zero is refined until its accuracy   *
*                        falls within a TOLERANCE supplied by the driving program.        *
*                                                                     *
*  Input parameters:     low, high, maxiter                           *
*  Output parameters:    root_secant,  iter_ptr                       *
*  Return value:         status                                       *
**********************************************************************/

                              /* Assumes information from driver program */
```

```
BOOLEAN secant ( float low, float high, int maxiter,
                 float *root_secant, int *iter_ptr )
{

    float answer,                           /* Value of proposed zero of function */
          ylow, yhigh, yanswer,             /* Function evaluations at low, high, answer */
          diffquot;                                     /* Difference quotient */

    int    iter;                                      /* Loop iteration index */

    float delx,                             /* Difference in x  values */
          dely;                             /* Difference in y  values */


    ylow  = FUN(low);                                   /* Initialize values */
    yhigh = FUN(high);
    answer = high;


    for ( iter = 0; iter < maxiter; iter++ ) {          /* Begin iteration loop */

        delx = fabs ( low - answer );
        if ( delx == ZERO ) {                           /* Zero of function found */
            *root_secant = answer;
            *iter_ptr    = iter;
          return (true);
        }


        diffquot = (yhigh - ylow) / ( high - low);      /* Find difference quotient */

        if ( diffquot == ZERO )                         /* Adjust answer */
            answer  =  high;
        else
            answer  =  high - yhigh / diffquot;


        yanswer = FUN(answer);                          /* Reevaluate function */
        dely    = fabs(yanswer);
        if ( (dely == ZERO) || (delx < TOLERANCE && dely < TOLERANCE ) ) {


            *root_secant = answer;                              /* Check for */
            *iter_ptr    = iter;                                /* convergence */
          return (true);
        }
```

```
    low   = high;                                      /*  Reset interval  */
    ylow  = yhigh;

    high  = answer;
    yhigh = FUN(answer);


}                                                      /*  End iteration loop  */


*iter_ptr = iter;                                      /*  Zero of function not found  */
return (false);
}
```

A driver for the bisection and secant algorithms is given in Program 17.1–3.

PROGRAM 17.1-3

```
/****************************************************************************
 *  Title:        zeros of functions - bisection and secant               *
 *  Filename:     bisecant.c                                              *
 *                                                                        *
 *  Description: This program finds the zero of a function FUN using the  *
 *               bisection and secant algorithms where the zero is thought*
 *               to lie between the values low and high up to a maximum   *
 *               number of iterations maxiter.  The zero is refined until *
 *               its accuracy falls within a TOLERANCE supplied by the    *
 *               driving program.                                         *
 *                                                                        *
 *  Input:        low,  high,  maxiter                                    *
 *  Output:       the zero of FUN                                         *
 *  Process:      bisection and secant algorithms                        *
 *                                                                        *
 *  Written by:  ...                                      Date: ...        *
 ****************************************************************************/

#include <stdio.h>
#include <math.h>
#include <stdlib.h>

#define  FUN(x)    0.5 - cos(x)       /*  <<< Arbitrary function defined here  */

#define  TOLERANCE 0.0001                            /*  Tolerance value  */
#define  ZERO      0.0

typedef  enum { false, true } BOOLEAN;
```

```
                                         /* Function prototypes */
BOOLEAN bisect ( float low, float high, int maxiter,
                 float *root_bisect, int *iter );

BOOLEAN secant ( float low, float high, int maxiter,
                 float *root_secant, int *iter );


main ( )                                          /* Begin main */
{

    int    maxiter,                   /* Maximum number of iterations */
           iter;                          /* Number of iterations */

    float  low, high,                   /* Limits of interval on x-axis */
           ylow, yhigh,        /* Evaluation of function at low and high */
           root_bisect, root_secant;     /* Zero of function by algorithm */

    BOOLEAN status;


    printf ( "\nEnter the lower value of the domain of the function>:  " );
    scanf ( "%f",   &low );
    printf ( "\nEnter the upper value of the domain of the function>:  " );
    scanf ( "%f",   &high );


    if ( low >= high ) {                     /* Check for correct interval */
        printf ( "\n\n\tERROR:  Wrong interval.  Algorithms fail!!\n" );
        printf ( "\n\n\t\tGood-bye! " );
        return (0);
    }


    printf ( "\n\nEnter maximum number of iterations>:  " );   /* Get maximum */
    scanf ( "%d",   &maxiter );                    /* number of iterations */


    if ( maxiter <= 0 ) {                    /* Check for non-positive */
        printf ( "\n\n\tERROR:  Number of iterations must be positive.\n" );
        printf ( "\n\n\t\tGood-bye! " );
        return (0);
    }


    ylow  = FUN(low);
    yhigh = FUN(high);
```

```
if ( ylow * yhigh > ZERO ) {              /*  Check if function crosses x-axis  */
    printf ( "\n\n\tERROR:  For the interval described," );
    printf ( "\n\t\tthe evaluations of the function at low and high" );
    printf ( "\n\t\tdo not differ in sign. " );
    printf ( "\n\n\t\tAlgorithms FAIL!!\n " );
    printf ( "\n\n\t\tGood-bye! " );
    return (0);
}


status = bisect ( low, high, maxiter, &root_bisect, &iter );      /*  Call  */
                                                        /*  bisection algorithm  */
if ( status == false )
    printf ( "\n\n\tERROR! - Bisection method fails. \n" );
else {
    printf ( "\n\n\nThe zero of the function between  x = %4.1f ",  low );
    printf ( "and  x = %4.1f", high );
    printf ( "\nwith %d iterations using the BISECTION method,\n ",  iter );
    printf ( "\n\t is approximately: %12.6f\n\n", root_bisect  );
}


status = secant ( low, high, maxiter, &root_secant, &iter );      /*  Call  */
                                                        /*  secant algorithm  */

if ( status == false )
    printf ( "\n\n\tERROR! - Secant method fails. \n"  );

else {
    printf ( "\n\n\nThe zero of the function between  x = %4.1f ",  low );
    printf ( "and  x = %4.1f",   high );
    printf ( "\nwith  %d  iterations using the SECANT method,\n ",  iter );
    printf ( "\n\t is approximately: %12.6f\n\n",  root_secant  );
}

printf (  "\n\n\t\tGood-bye! " );
return(0);

}                                                      /*  End main  */
```

17.1.4 The Newton-Raphson Algorithm, Abbreviated

The Newton-Raphson algorithm, derived from the calculus, improves the secant algorithm for finding zeros of functions. For our purposes, we consider one result of this algorithm called the **Newton-Raphson formula**, which says that

$$x_{n+1} = x_n - \frac{f(x_n)}{f'(x_n)}$$

where f is the given function and f' is the **derivative** of f. Knowledge of calculus is not assumed in this text, so you are not expected to calculate the derivative of a given function. The derivative represents the rate of change of a function and is discussed further in Section 17.3. For some functions, we can get the derivative from a table of derivatives. Table 17.1–1 shows, for constants a and b, four polynomial and two trigonometric functions in variable x with their respective derivatives. Therefore, we can use the Newton-Raphson algorithm to find the zeros of these special functions.

EXAMPLE 17.1–3

Problem
Let $f(x) = 5 \sin 3x$ where $\pi/4 \le x \le \pi/2$. Use the Newton-Raphson algorithm to find the approximate value of x for which $f(x) = 0$.

Reasoning
First find out if a zero of the function exists on the interval. For $x = \pi/4$, $f(\pi/4) = 5 \sin 2.3562 = 5(0.7071) = 3.5356$ (positive). For $x = \pi/2, f(\pi/2) = 5 \sin 3\pi/2 = 5(-1) = -5$ (negative). Therefore, f has a zero on the interval. We can make a first guess that the answer is an average of the two extremities of the interval. That is, to four-place accuracy

$$x_0 = (\pi/4 + \pi/2)/2 = (0.7854 + 1.5708)/2 = 1.1781$$

Using Table 17.1–1, the derivative of the function is

$$f'(x) = 5(3) \cos 3x = 15 \cos 3x$$

Solution
The Newton-Raphson algorithm says that

$$x_{n+1} = x_n - \frac{f(x_n)}{f'(x_n)}$$

Table 17.1–1 Some Functions and Their Derivatives

FUNCTION $f(x)$	DERIVATIVE $f'(x)$
a	0
ax	a
ax^2	$2ax$
ax^3	$3ax^2$
$a \sin(bx)$	$ab \cos(bx)$
$a \cos(bx)$	$-ab \sin(bx)$

and for the given function and its derivative, after simplification we have

$$x_{n+1} = x_n - \frac{\sin 3x_n}{3\cos 3x_n}$$

For $n = 0$,

$$x_1 = x_0 - \frac{\sin 3x_0}{3\cos 3x_0} = 1.1781 - \frac{\sin 3(1.1781)}{3\cos 3(1.1781)}$$

$$= 1.1781 - 0.1381 = 1.0400$$

Iterate once more using $x_1 = 1.0400$ to calculate x_2 by

$$x_2 = x_1 - \frac{\sin 3x_1}{3\cos 3x_1} = 1.0400 - \frac{\sin 3(1.0400)}{3\cos 3(1.0400)}$$

$$= 1.0400 - (-0.0072) = 1.0472$$

Iterate once more using $x_2 = 1.0472$ to calculate x_3 by

$$x_3 = x_2 - \frac{\sin 3x_2}{3\cos 3x_2} = 1.0472 - \frac{\sin 3(1.0472)}{3\cos 3(1.0472)}$$

$$= 1.0472 - (-0.0000) = 1.0472$$

Because the difference between x_3 and x_2 is negligible, x_3 represents the solution. Note that one of the salient features of the Newton-Raphson algorithm is the rapidity of the convergence.

Test
Substitution of x_3 into the function yields

$$
\begin{aligned}
f(x_3) &= 5\sin 3x_3 &&= 5\sin 3(1.0472) \\
&= 5\sin 3.1416 &&= 5(-0.000007346) \\
&= -0.0000367
\end{aligned}
$$

and is certainly the result to three-place accuracy.   ●

Program 17.1–4 shows the Newton-Raphson algorithm. Notice that the algorithm takes the approach described in Example 17.1–3 and follows the Newton-Raphson formula. The algorithm also keeps the calculation within the initial boundaries of x.

P R O G R A M   1 7 . 1 – 4

```
/*******************************************************************************
*  Title:      newton-raphson algorithm                                        *
*  Filename:   newtraph.c                                                       *
*                                                                              *
*  Description: This program contains a function named newton.  It finds the zero of *
*               a function named FUN1 using the Newton-Raphson algorithm where the *
*               zero is known to lie on the closed interval between the low and high *
*               values.  The zero is refined until its accuracy falls within a *
*               TOLERANCE.  The FUN2 function is a corresponding function       *
*               representing the derivative of FUN1 as a function of x.  The    *
*               functions to be used for FUN1 and FUN2 are taken from those found *
*               in Table 17.1-1.  The number of iterations is limited by the   *
*               value maxiter.                                                   *
*                                                                              *
*  Input:      low, high, maxiter                                              *
*  Output:     zero of function                                                *
*  Process:    implementation of Newton-Raphson algorithm                      *
*                                                                              *
*  Written by: ...                                 Date: ...                   *
*******************************************************************************/

#include <stdio.h>
#include <math.h>
#include <stdlib.h>

#define  FUN1(x)    x * x * x  - 4.0              /* <<<<Define function here */
#define  FUN2(x)    3.0 * x * x                   /* <<<< Corresponding derivative */

#define  TOLERANCE 0.0001                                    /* Tolerance */
#define  ZERO       0.0

typedef  enum { false, true } BOOLEAN;

                                                  /* Function prototype */
BOOLEAN newton ( float old, float new, int maxiter,
                 float *root_newton, int *iter_ptr );


main ( )                                          /* Begin main */
{

   int     maxiter,                    /* Maximum number of iterations */
           iter;                        /* Number of iterations */
```

```
float    low, high, answer,                    /* Values of low, high, and answer on x-axis */
         root_newton;

BOOLEAN status;

printf ( "\nEnter the left value of the interval>:  " );          /* Input interval */
scanf ( "%f",   &low );
printf ( "\nEnter the right value of the interval>:  " );
scanf ( "%f",   &high );

if ( low >= high ) {                                              /* Input check */
    printf ( "\n\n\tERROR!:  Interval not correct! " );
    printf ( "\n\n\t\tGood-bye! " );
    return (0);
}


printf ( "\n\nEnter the maximum number of iterations>:  " );
scanf ( "%d",   &maxiter );

if ( maxiter <= 0 ) {                                            /* Input check */
    printf ( "\n\n\tERROR:  Number of iterations must be positive.\n" );
    printf ( "\n\n\t\tGood-bye! " );
    return (0);
}


status = newton ( low, high, maxiter, &root_newton, &iter );     /* Function call */

if ( status == false ) {
    printf ( "\n\n\tAlgorithm FAILS!\n" );                       /* Algorithm fails */
}
else {                                                           /* Print zero */
    printf ( "\n\n\nFor interval values x= %4.1f  and  x=%4.1f",   low,  high );
    printf ( "\nwith %d  iterations using the NEWTON method,\n",   iter );
    printf ( "\nthe zero of the function is: %12.6f\n\n",   root_newton );
}

printf ( "\n\n\t\tGood-bye! " );
return (0);

}                                                                /* End main */
```

```
/******************************************************************************
*  Function name:        newton                                               *
*  Description:          Finds the zero of a function using the               *
*                        newton-raphson algorithm.                            *
*                                                                             *
*  Input parameters:     old, new, maxiter                                    *
*  Output parameters:    root_newton, iter_ptr                                *
*  Return value:         status                                               *
******************************************************************************/

BOOLEAN newton ( float old, float new, int maxiter,
                 float *root_newton, int *iter_ptr )
{

   int   iter;                                    /*  Loop iteration index  */

   float yold, ynew,                   /*  Function evaluation at  old  and  new  */
         derivfun,                     /*  Evaluation of derivative function  */
         delx, dely,                        /*  Differences in  x  and  y  */
         left, right;                       /*  Interval boundary variables  */


   left  = old;                                   /*  Establish interval  */
   right = new;

   iter  = 0;
   old   = ( old + new ) /2.0;                     /*  Initial approximation  */
   yold  = FUN1(old);                               /*  Evaluate function  */

   if ( yold == ZERO ) {                  /*  Check if zero of function found  */
        *root_newton = old;
        *iter_ptr    = iter;
        return (true);
   }


   for  ( iter = 1; iter <= maxiter; iter++ ) {            /*  Begin iteration  */


      yold     = FUN1 (old);                           /*  Evaluate function  */
      derivfun = FUN2 (old);                         /*  Evaluate derivative  */
```

```
    if ( derivfun == ZERO ) {
        printf ( "\n\n\tERROR! - Division by zero" );
        *iter_ptr = iter;
        return (false);
    }
    else
        new = old - yold / derivfun;                    /*  Update approximation  */


    if ( (left - new) * (new - right) < ZERO ) {        /*  Check if new result  */
        printf ( "\n\n\tERROR:  Result exceeds interval" );    /*  is in interval  */
        return (false);
    }

    printf ( "\n\tAfter %3d iterations, the approximate zero is %10.6f  ",  iter,  new );


    ynew = FUN1(new);                                   /*  Reevaluate function  */

    delx = fabs (old - new);
    dely = fabs (ynew);

    if ( (dely == ZERO) ||
         (delx < TOLERANCE && dely < TOLERANCE) ) {
        *root_newton = new;
        *iter_ptr    = iter;
        return (true);
    }


    old  = new;                                         /*  Establish next starting point  */
    yold =  ynew;

}

    return (false);                                     /*  Maximum number of iterations exceeded  */

}
```

To execute this algorithm we have to define a function and its derivative in the **newton** function.

17.1.5 Reflections

Although the Newton-Raphson algorithm is faster to converge to the solution of the zeros of the function than the bisection algorithm, it is not necessarily better than bisection. Which is better also depends on the function and the user's knowledge of its derivative. The third algorithm, the secant, is a discrete version of the Newton-Raphson algorithm that does not need the derivative of the function because it is approximated by the $[f(x_{n-1}) - f(x_{n-2})]/[x_{n-1} - x_{n-2}]$ quotient. In terms of convergence, to find zeros of "well-behaved" functions, the Newton-Raphson algorithm is faster than the secant algorithm, which, in turn, is faster than the bisection algorithm. Again, which algorithm is better depends on the function at hand. We compare these methods in the exercises that follow and leave the theory of these algorithms' convergence for a more advanced course.

EXERCISES 17.1

Concept Check
Answer statements 1 through 4 with true *or* false.
1. The domain of any function is the set of real numbers.
2. The quadratic formula is used to find the range of a quadratic function.
3. The Newton-Raphson algorithm can be used to find the root of all functions whose derivative is known.
4. The secant algorithm is generally superior to the bisection algorithm when used to find roots of equations.

For statements 5 through 8 choose the answer that best completes the statement.
5. The secant algorithm more closely resembles
   a. the bisection algorithm
   b. the quadratic formula
   c. the Newton-Raphson algorithm
   d. none of these
6. The best way to find the zero of a linear function is
   a. the bisection algorithm
   b. the Newton-Raphson algorithm
   c. the secant algorithm
   d. direct calculation
7. The root of an equation is
   a. always the zero of a function
   b. never the zero of a function
   c. sometimes the zero of a function
   d. needed in applications
8. A relation is
   a. a function
   b. a domain and a range
   c. a set of ordered pairs
   d. a graph

For statements 9 through 12 fill in the blanks with the right word.
9. The secant algorithm is a discrete form of the _____ algorithm.
10. The set of values that result when a function evaluates all elements for which it is defined is called the _____ of the function.

11. Every function is a _____.
12. To use the Newton-Raphson algorithm properly, we need the _____ of a function.

Set A

Solve each of the following problems.

13. Find the domain of $\{(2, 5), (6, 3), (8, 4), (1, 7)\}$.
14. Using Table 17.1–1, find the derivative of $7 \cos 5t + 13$.
15. Calculate the zero(s) of $f(x) = x^2 - 8x + 3$, if any.
16. Find the first iterative root of $x^3 - x^2 + 3x - 4 = 0$ on the $[1, 2]$ interval using the bisection algorithm.
17. For the information in Question 16, do the same using the secant algorithm.
18. For the information in Question 16, do the same using the Newton-Raphson algorithm.

Set B

Solve Questions 19 through 22 using a calculator.

19. Given that $f(x) = x^3 - 3x - 2$ with $[0, 3]$ as its domain, find the approximate zero of f after four iterations using the bisection algorithm.
20. Given that $f(x) = x^3 - 3x - 2$ with $[0, 3]$ as its domain, find the approximate zero of f after four iterations using the secant algorithm.
21. Use the Newton-Raphson algorithm to find the zero to three decimal places of the $g(x) = \sin 3x + 2x - 1$ function.
22. Use the secant method to find the zero to three decimal places of the $h(x) = x - \tan x$ function on the $[0.5, 1.5]$ interval.
23. Explain how the bisection algorithm resembles the binary search algorithm.

Set C

24. Execute the bisection and secant algorithms for the following functions.
    a. $f(x) = 3x - 4$ on the interval $[0, 2]$
    b. $g(x) = x^2 - 9$ on the interval $[-4, 0]$
25. The driver program for the **bisect** and **secant** functions forces an exit from the program when the evaluation of the function at the extremities of the interval does not produce opposite signs. Rewrite this portion of the program so that it allows reentry of interval values.
26. For the $f(x) = 3.5 \cos 1.9x$ function defined on the $[0, \pi/2]$ interval, use the bisection algorithm (Program 17.1–1) to find the zero of f to six decimal places.
27. For the $g(x) = e^{-3x} - 0.5$ function defined on the $[-1.0, 3.0]$ interval, use the secant algorithm (Program 17.1–2) to find the zero of g to six decimal places.
28. For the $h(x) = \sin 3x \cos 3x - 0.5$ function defined on the $[0.0, \pi/12]$ interval, use the Newton-Raphson algorithm (Program 17.1–3) to find the zero of g to seven decimal places.
29. The driver program for the **newton** function forces an exit from the program when the interval is not correct or when the number of iterations is not positive. Rewrite this portion of the program so that it allows reentry of interval values and the number of iterations.

17.2 SOLVING SYSTEMS OF EQUATIONS

Introduction

One of the important tasks in computer science and mathematics is finding a solution to a problem by solving one or more equations (called a **system of equations**) related to the problem. This is especially true for simulation problems and other computer applications. One of the simplest of equations to solve is a single linear equation in one unknown. **Linear** means that all variables are to the first power. The linear equation

$$ax + b = 0$$

for real number constants a and b where $a \neq 0$, has as a solution

$$x = -\frac{b}{a}$$

However, not all problems can be resolved by linear equations in one variable. Nonlinear equations in one variable have countless variations such as the ordinary seventh-degree polynomial equation

$$ax^7 + bx^6 + cx^5 + dx^4 + ex^3 + fx^2 + gx^1 + hx^0 = 0$$

or the nondescriptive transcendental (nonalgebraic) equation

$$x^4 \cos(x^2 + \log(1 - x^3) - 5) + \tan(1 + e^x) = 0$$

Neither of these equations has a closed-form solution, which is a solution we can find by a formula. It is not our purpose here to look for closed-form solutions to all problems but instead to find solutions by approximation. In particular we seek algorithmic solutions to systems of linear equations.

17.2.1 Two Equations in Two Unknowns

Before embarking on a journey through systems of equations, let's begin by considering two linear equations in two unknowns. Consider the system

$$2x + 3y = 6$$
$$4x - y = 5$$

If we assume that a solution exists, one way to solve the system is by guessing all the possible ordered pairs (x, y) to substitute in the equations until *both* equations are true. For example, the ordered pair $(3, 0)$ causes the first equation to be true but not the second; the ordered pair $(2, 3)$ causes the second equation to be true but not the first; and the ordered pair $(7, 4)$ satisfies neither equation. Obviously, the guessing game is not the right approach here.

A more systematic approach is a procedure that *isolates* each variable so it can then be used to solve the problem, as shown in the following steps.

Multiply the first equation by -2. The system becomes

$$-4x + -6y = -12$$
$$4x - y = 5$$

Notice that $(3, 0)$ still satisfies the first equation and $(2, 3)$ still satisfies the second equation.

Add the first equation to the second. The system becomes

$$-4x - 6y = -12$$
$$0 - 7y = 7$$

Notice that $(3, 0)$ still satisfies the first equation but $(2, 3)$ no longer satisfies the second equation. Why?

Multiply each equation by -1. The system becomes

$$4x + 6y = 12$$
$$7y = -7$$

Notice that $(3, 0)$ still satisfies the first equation.

Multiply the first equation by $\frac{1}{2}$ *and the second equation by* $\frac{1}{7}$. The system becomes

$$2x + 3y = 6$$
$$y = -1$$

Notice that $(3, 0)$ still satisfies the first equation. Also, now we have succeeded in solving for one of the variables, namely, $y = -1$.

Substitute the answer to the second equation back into the first equation. The system becomes

$$2x + 3(-1) = 6$$
$$y = -1$$

or

$$2x - 3 = 6$$
$$y = -1$$

or

$$2x = 9$$
$$y = -1$$

Notice that $(3, 0)$ no longer satisfies the first equation.

BEFORE YOU GO ON

Situation: Before the last step in the problem we just did, $(3, 0)$ satisfied the first equation. Why does it no longer do so?

EXPLANATION: The ordered pair $(3, 0)$ means $x = 3$ and $y = 0$. However, when $y = -1$ was substituted back into the first equation, the value of y was no longer 0.

Multiply the first equation by $\frac{1}{2}$. The system becomes

$$x = 9/2$$
$$y = -1$$

And the solution to the system is $(9/2, -1)$; that is, $x = 4.5$ and $y = -1$.

17.2.2 Gaussian Elimination

There are several ways to solve a generalized system of linear equations. One of these is **Gaussian elimination with backward substitution,** which can process n linear equations in n unknowns, as we see next.

EXAMPLE 17.2–1

Problem
Use Gaussian elimination to solve the $2.9x - 4.1y = 5.2$ and $3.7x + 7.4y = 2.3$ system of linear equations.

Reasoning
We begin by aligning common variables for the two equations. It makes no difference which equation is written first. The method used is similar to that discussed in subsection 17.2.1. The system to be solved is

$$3.7x + 7.4y = 2.3 \tag{1}$$

$$2.9x - 4.1y = 5.2 \tag{2}$$

where each equation is appropriately labeled. Notice also that the numbers in each of these original equations are precise to one decimal place value.

Solution
First we make the coefficient of x for each equation the same value. For convenience, choose the least common multiple of 3.7 and 2.9, which is 10.73. Multiply the first equation by 2.9 and the second equation by 3.7. The system becomes

$$10.73x + 21.46y = 6.67 \tag{1}$$

$$10.73x - 15.17y = 19.24 \tag{2}$$

Now to eliminate the x in the second equation, multiply the first equation by -1 and add the first equation to the second. The system becomes

$$10.73x + 21.46y = 6.67 \tag{1}$$

$$-36.63y = 12.57 \tag{2}$$

To solve for y, multiply the second equation by $-1/36.63$. The system now becomes

$$10.73x + 21.46y = 6.67 \tag{1}$$

$$y = -0.3431613 \tag{2}$$

where the result of the division is rounded off to seven significant digits. This value for y is now *back substituted* in the first equation to produce the system

$$10.73x - 7.3642424 = 6.67 \tag{1}$$

$$y = -0.3431613 \tag{2}$$

or

$$10.73x = 14.0342424 \tag{1}$$

$$y = -0.3431613 \tag{2}$$

Multiplying the first equation by $1/10.73$ yields

$$x = 1.3079443 \tag{1}$$

$$y = -0.3431613 \tag{2}$$

so the proposed answer is $(1.3079443, -0.3431613)$. Note that since the precision of the numbers in the original problem is only to the tenths place value, it is customary in applied problems to provide an answer with the same precision. The practical answer would be rounded off to $(1.3, -0.3)$.

Test

To show that the proposed answer solves the system, substitute the values for x and y in the *original* equations:

$$3.7(1.3079443) + 7.4(-0.3431613) = 4.8393939 - 2.5393936$$

$$= 2.3000003 \tag{1}$$

$$2.9(1.3079443) - 4.1(-0.3431613) = 3.7930385 + 1.4069613$$

$$= 5.1999998 \tag{2}$$

An error in rounding off limits the precision of the verification. Still, the first equation yields approximately 2.3 and the second equation yields approximately 5.2, as we anticipated. Figure 17.2–1 illustrates the solution.

PERSPECTIVE

The great German mathematician Carl Friedrich Gauss (1777–1855) was also a physicist and an astronomer. Among his many accomplishments were the invention (with W. Weber) of the electric telegraph and the development of a theory of planetary motion. Gauss's work in non-Euclidean geometry was the foundation of Einstein's theory of relativity.

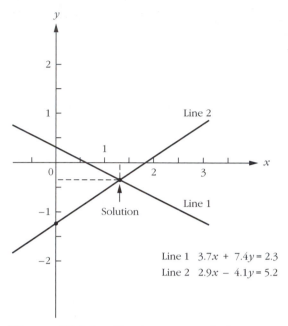

Line 1 $3.7x + 7.4y = 2.3$
Line 2 $2.9x - 4.1y = 5.2$

Figure 17.2–1 Simultaneous solution: two equations in two unknowns

17.2.3 Matrix Reduction of Equations

We can formalize the solution to a system of equations by representing the system with matrices and using operations on these matrices. The method allows for the solution of n linear equations in n unknowns.

Consider a generalized system of three linear equations in three unknowns. We can write the system as

$$
\begin{aligned}
a_{11}x_1 &+ a_{12}x_2 &+ a_{13}x_3 &= b_1 \\
a_{21}x_1 &+ a_{22}x_2 &+ a_{23}x_3 &= b_2 \\
a_{31}x_1 &+ a_{32}x_2 &+ a_{33}x_3 &= b_3
\end{aligned}
$$

where the three variables are represented by x_j (x_1, x_2, and x_3), the coefficients of these variables for each row are represented by the real numbers a_{ij} positioned in the ith row and jth column, and the b_i are real constants. Essentially, we can represent this system by the matrix equation

$$AX = B$$

where the coefficient matrix A, the variable matrix X, and the constant matrix B are, respectively,

$$
A = \begin{bmatrix} a_{11} & a_{12} & a_{13} \\ a_{21} & a_{22} & a_{23} \\ a_{31} & a_{32} & a_{33} \end{bmatrix} \qquad X = \begin{bmatrix} x_1 \\ x_2 \\ x_3 \end{bmatrix} \qquad \text{and} \qquad B = \begin{bmatrix} b_1 \\ b_2 \\ b_3 \end{bmatrix}
$$

The matrices X and B are called **column matrices** because they have only one column. We can also write the system as

$$\begin{bmatrix} a_{11} & a_{12} & a_{13} \\ a_{21} & a_{22} & a_{23} \\ a_{31} & a_{32} & a_{33} \end{bmatrix} \begin{bmatrix} x_1 \\ x_2 \\ x_3 \end{bmatrix} = \begin{bmatrix} b_1 \\ b_2 \\ b_3 \end{bmatrix}$$

where ordinary matrix multiplication produces the original expression.

| **BEFORE YOU GO ON** | Query: Consider the matrix equation |

Query: Consider the matrix equation

$$\begin{bmatrix} 2 & 3 \\ -1 & 4 \end{bmatrix} \begin{bmatrix} x \\ y \end{bmatrix} = \begin{bmatrix} 4 \\ 2 \end{bmatrix}$$

and find the resulting system.

RESPONSE: The system becomes

$2x + 3y = 4$

$-x + 4y = 2$

Using elementary row operations on matrices makes matrix manipulations simpler. An **elementary row operation** is any one of the three following operations on a given matrix.

1. Interchange any two rows of the matrix
2. Multiply any row of the matrix by a constant (real number)
3. Add to any row of the matrix a multiple of any other row

Observe that these operations are the same ones that we used in subsection 17.2.1 and Example 17.2–1 with two linear equations in two unknowns. Row operations used on a matrix cause construction of an **equivalent matrix** (not necessarily equal).

EXAMPLE 17.2–2

Problem
Find equivalent matrices by using each of the elementary row operations on the given matrix

$$\begin{bmatrix} a_{11} & a_{12} & a_{13} \\ a_{21} & a_{22} & a_{23} \end{bmatrix}$$

Reasoning
Find three different but equivalent matrices for the given matrix by using each of the elementary row operations.

Solution

1. Interchange any two rows of the matrix.

   Since there are only two rows, an equivalent matrix is

   $$\begin{bmatrix} a_{21} & a_{22} & a_{23} \\ a_{11} & a_{12} & a_{13} \end{bmatrix}$$

2. Multiply any row of the matrix by a constant.

   Choose any arbitrary real number as a constant, say 7, and multiply the first row by this value. The equivalent matrix is

   $$\begin{bmatrix} 7a_{11} & 7a_{12} & 7a_{13} \\ a_{21} & a_{22} & a_{23} \end{bmatrix}$$

3. Add to any row of the matrix a multiple of any other row.

   Suppose we add 3 times the second row to the first row. The equivalent matrix becomes

   $$\begin{bmatrix} a_{11} + 3a_{21} & a_{12} + 3a_{22} & a_{13} + 3a_{23} \\ a_{21} & a_{22} & a_{23} \end{bmatrix}$$

   Note that the second row remains unchanged.

Test

Verify these easily using the three definitions of elementary row operations.   ●

Now we use elementary row operations to solve a system of equations. We augment the coefficient matrix A by adding an extra column—column B—which contains the constants. Symbolically, we write the augmented matrix as

$[A|B]$

Next, we use elementary row operations to transform the augmented matrix into one that takes the form of an n–by–$(n + 1)$ matrix

$$\begin{bmatrix} 1 & 0 & 0 & \cdots & 0 & b_1 \\ 0 & 1 & 0 & \cdots & 0 & b_2 \\ 0 & 0 & 1 & \cdots & 0 & b_3 \\ -- & -- & -- & \cdots & -- & -- \\ 0 & 0 & 0 & \cdots & 1 & b_n \end{bmatrix}$$

where the values of b_i are the transformation of the original constants through the row operations. The matrix of n rows and n columns of the form

$$\begin{bmatrix} 1 & 0 & 0 & \cdots & 0 \\ 0 & 1 & 0 & \cdots & 0 \\ 0 & 0 & 1 & \cdots & 0 \\ -- & -- & -- & \cdots & -- \\ 0 & 0 & 0 & \cdots & 1 \end{bmatrix}$$

is the **identity matrix** of order n.

Let's illustrate the process of solving systems of equations. Suppose there are three equations in three unknowns x, y, and z given as follows.

$$3x + 3y + 3z = 6$$
$$2x - y + 3z = 1$$
$$x + 3y - 4z = 3$$

The augmented matrix for the system becomes

$$\begin{bmatrix} 3 & 3 & 3 & 6 \\ 2 & -1 & 3 & 1 \\ 1 & 3 & -4 & 3 \end{bmatrix}$$

To solve the system of equations using matrices, manipulate the *first column* so that the coefficient of x in the first row is 1. This now becomes the **pivot element** of the first row. Use row operations to make the coefficients of the remaining rows of the first column 0. Multiply the first row by $\frac{1}{3}$ to get

$$\begin{bmatrix} 1 & 1 & 1 & 2 \\ 2 & -1 & 3 & 1 \\ 1 & 3 & -4 & 3 \end{bmatrix}$$

Then do these steps: 1. multiply the first row by -2 and add the result to the second row and 2. multiply the first row by -1 and add the result to the third row. This gives you

$$\begin{bmatrix} 1 & 1 & 1 & 2 \\ 0 & -3 & 1 & -3 \\ 0 & 2 & -5 & 1 \end{bmatrix}$$

Now manipulate the *second column*. Make the second row, second column entry equal to 1 and make the first and third row elements of the second column 0. The pivot element here is -3. To do this, first multiply the second row by $-\frac{1}{3}$ to get

$$\begin{bmatrix} 1 & 1 & 1 & 2 \\ 0 & 1 & -\frac{1}{3} & 1 \\ 0 & 2 & -5 & 1 \end{bmatrix}$$

To make the remaining second-column entries in the first and third row equal to 0, do these steps: 1. multiply the second row by -1 and add the result to the first row, and 2. multiply the second row by -2 and add the result to the third row. This gives you the matrix

$$\begin{bmatrix} 1 & 0 & \frac{4}{3} & 1 \\ 0 & 1 & -\frac{1}{3} & 1 \\ 0 & 0 & -\frac{13}{3} & -1 \end{bmatrix}$$

Finally, manipulate the *third column*. The pivot element $-\frac{13}{3}$ is the third row, third column entry. To make it equal to 1, multiply the third row by $-\frac{3}{13}$ to get

$$\begin{bmatrix} 1 & 0 & \frac{4}{3} & 1 \\ 0 & 1 & -\frac{1}{3} & 1 \\ 0 & 0 & 1 & \frac{3}{13} \end{bmatrix}$$

To make the first and second entries of the third column equal to 0, do these steps: 1. multiply the third row by $-\frac{4}{3}$ and add the result to the first row, and 2. multiply the third row by $\frac{1}{3}$ and add the result to the second row. This gives you the matrix

$$\begin{bmatrix} 1 & 0 & 0 & \frac{9}{13} \\ 0 & 1 & 0 & \frac{14}{13} \\ 0 & 0 & 1 & \frac{3}{13} \end{bmatrix}$$

This matrix corresponds to the *new* system of equations that is equivalent to the original system and has the same solution set. Note the identity matrix of order 3 as the new coefficient matrix. The new system is

$$\begin{aligned} x & & & = \frac{9}{13} \\ & y & & = \frac{14}{13} \\ & & z & = \frac{3}{13} \end{aligned}$$

We verify that this is the solution by substituting these values in the *original* system of equations. That is,

$$\begin{aligned} 3(\tfrac{9}{13}) & + 3(\tfrac{14}{13}) + 3(\tfrac{3}{13}) = \tfrac{78}{13} = 6 \\ 2(\tfrac{9}{13}) & - (\tfrac{14}{13}) + 3(\tfrac{3}{13}) = \tfrac{13}{13} = 1 \\ (\tfrac{9}{13}) & + 3(\tfrac{14}{13}) - 4(\tfrac{3}{13}) = \tfrac{39}{13} = 3 \end{aligned}$$

Note that the pivot element does not *always* occur along the main diagonal. Consider the augmented matrix

$$\begin{bmatrix} 1 & 1 & 1 & 2 \\ 1 & 1 & 3 & 4 \\ 0 & 3 & 0 & 9 \end{bmatrix}$$

Making the second row, first column entry equal to zero simultaneously makes the second-row, second-column entry 0, which can create difficulties in the solution. In fact, this may cause no solution to exist and make the system of equations **inconsistent**. The algorithm presented in Program 17.2–1 accounts for such possibilities.

BEFORE YOU GO ON

Query: Given the $2x + 3y = 4$ and $x - y = 7$ system of equations, find the solution using matrices and row operations.

RESPONSE: When we write $x - y = 7$ as the first equation and $2x + 3y = 4$ as the second equation, the augmented matrix becomes

$$\begin{bmatrix} 1 & -1 & 7 \\ 2 & 3 & 4 \end{bmatrix} \rightarrow \begin{bmatrix} 1 & -1 & 7 \\ 0 & 5 & -10 \end{bmatrix} \rightarrow \begin{bmatrix} 1 & -1 & 7 \\ 0 & 1 & -2 \end{bmatrix} \rightarrow \begin{bmatrix} 1 & 0 & 5 \\ 0 & 1 & -2 \end{bmatrix}$$

The solution is $x = 5$ and $y = -2$.

17.2.4 Gaussian Elimination with Backward Substitution

We can expand the process of row reduction using matrices to any system of n equations in n unknowns. However, it becomes tedious when the system increases to four or more equations. For the generalized system, an algorithm is more efficient. As we learned in subsection 17.2.3, Gaussian elimination resembles row reduction using matrices. We use that algorithm here with one major feature added: the ability to find a proper pivot element that is not necessarily the diagonal pivot. This is essential when the system of equations is not presented so that after you use row operations, all diagonal elements are nonzero. Program 17.2–1, called **gauselim**, parallels matrix reduction except that instead of producing an identity matrix, we use backward substitution and row operations only, as we did in matrix reduction.

The n-by-n coefficient matrix A is augmented by the column matrix B, whose values we provide individually. If a pivot position (on the main diagonal) is zero, we interchange rows until we find a nonzero pivot element or an error message says that a unique solution is not possible. The algorithm produces a transformed n-by-$(n+1)$ augmented matrix and reverse substitution produces the solution set.

For example, the illustration in subsection 17.2.4 shows the system

$$3x + 3y + 3z = 6$$
$$2x - y + 3z = 1$$
$$x + 3y - 4z = 3$$

that is represented by the augmented matrix

$$\begin{bmatrix} 3 & 3 & 3 & 6 \\ 2 & -1 & 3 & 1 \\ 1 & 3 & -4 & 3 \end{bmatrix}$$

In upper triangular form, the augmented matrix becomes

$$\begin{bmatrix} 1 & 1 & 1 & 2 \\ 0 & 3 & -1 & 3 \\ 0 & 0 & \frac{13}{3} & 1 \end{bmatrix}$$

This leads to the solution of $z = \frac{3}{13}$ in the third row, which is substituted back into the second row to give

$$3y - (\tfrac{3}{13}) = 3 \qquad \text{or} \qquad y = \tfrac{14}{13}$$

Now z and y are substituted back into the first row to produce

$$x + (\tfrac{14}{13}) + (\tfrac{3}{13}) = 2 \qquad \text{or} \qquad x = \tfrac{9}{13}$$

These results confirm the results found in subsection 17.2.3.

Program 17.2–1 implements the Gaussian elimination with backward substitution algorithm for solving a system of equations. The program is similar to methods found in standard references in the area of numerical methods. This implementation, however, traces how the algorithm works through row operations.

PROGRAM 17.2-1

```
/******************************************************************************
*  Title:       gaussian elimination - backward substitution              *
*  Filename:    gauselim.c                                                *
*                                                                         *
*  Description: Solution of a system of n equations in n unknowns where n <= 5. Starting *
*               with the first column, place the largest element in the first row *
*               position. ·All remaining first column elements are set to 0. Continue *
*               with remaining columns until the matrix is upper triangular.  Back *
*               substitute until all values of x are resolved.            *
*                                                                         *
*  Input:       coefficients of system                                    *
*  Output:      solution, or error message if algorithm fails             *
*  Process:     Transform the augmented matrix to upper-diagonal form. Solve for x[n]. *
*               Use this solution to find x[n-1]. Continue process until all x values *
*               are found.                                                *
*  Written by:  ...                              Date: ...                *
******************************************************************************/


#include <stdio.h>
#include <stdlib.h>

#define  MAX    5                                   /*  Maximum dimension of system  */


main ( void )
{

    float a[MAX][MAX+1],                       /*  Augmented matrix for system  */
          b[MAX][MAX+1],                  /*  Copy of original augmented matrix  */
          x[MAX],                               /*  Solution column matrix  */
          current, pivot,             /*  Current and pivot column element  */
          sum,                                 /*  Partial sum variable  */
          ratio;              /*  Column element divided by column position element  */

    int   i, j, k, c,                           /*  Row and column indices  */
          n,                          /*  Dimension of system of equations  */
          p,                                   /*  Positional index  */
          r[MAX],                             /*  Row operation index matrix  */
          temp;                           /*  Temporary storage variable  */

    char  dummy;                              /*  Dummy variable for program delay  */
```

```
do {                                                    /*  Input matrix size  */
   printf ( "\n\nEnter size of system of " );
   printf ( "\n  n equations in n unknowns, where n < %1d:    ",  MAX  );
   scanf ( "%d",   &n );
}  while   ( n >= MAX );


for ( i = 1; i <= n; i++ ) {                            /*  Input matrix information  */
   printf ( "\n\nEnter the coefficients of  x  for equation %d: \n",   i  );
   for ( j = 1; j <= n; j++ )
      scanf ( "%f",    &a[ i ][ j ]  );
   printf (  "\nEnter the constant for equation  %d\n",   i  );
   scanf ( "%f",   &a[ i ][ n+1 ]  );
}


                                                        /*  Print out system  */
printf ( "\n\n\nThe system of equations is:\n\n");
for ( i = 1; i <= n; i++ ) {
   printf( "\t" );
   for ( j = 1; j <= n; j++ ) {
      b[ i ][ j ] = a[ i ][ j ];
      printf ( "%5.1f X[%1d]",   a[ i ][ j ],   j   );
      if ( j <= n-1 )
      printf ( " + " );
   }
   b[ i ][ n+1 ] = a[ i ][ n+1 ];
   printf ( "  = %5.1f\n",  a[ i ][ n+1 ]  );
}


                                                        /*  Print out augmented matrix  */
printf ( "\n\n\nThe corresponding augmented matrix is:\n"  );
for ( i = 1; i <= n; i++ ) {
   printf ( "\nRow %d:\t\t",   i  );
   for ( j = 1; j <= n+1; j++ )
      printf ( "%10.2f",  a[ i ][ j ]  );
}


fflush ( stdin );                                       /*  Pause sequence  */
printf ( "\n\n\n\tTo continue, press <return>:  "  );
scanf ( "%c",  &dummy  );
```

```
                                                         /*  Gaussian Elimination begins  */

  for ( i = 1; i <= n; i++ )                        /*  Initialize pivot row indicator  */
     r[ i ]  =  i;


  for ( p = 1; p <= n-1; p++ ) {                              /*  Begin positional loop  */

       printf ( "\n\n\n\nPOSITION %d: The augmented matrix is:\n", p );
       for ( i = 1; i <= n; i++ ) {               /*  Begin display of intermediate step  */
          printf ( "\nRow %d:\t\t", i );
          for ( j = 1; j <= n+1; j++ )
             printf ( "%10.2f", a[ r[ i ] ][ j ] );
       }



       fflush ( stdin );                                          /*  Pause sequence  */
       printf ( "\n\n\tTo continue, press <return>:  " );
       scanf ( "%c", &dummy );                /*  End display of intermediate step  */


       for ( k = p+1; k <= n; k++ ) {
          current = abs( a[ r[k] ][ p ] );
          pivot   = abs( a[ r[p] ][ p ] );
          if ( current > pivot ) {
              temp   = r[ p ];
              r[ p ] = r[ k ];
              r[ k ] = temp;
          }
       }


       if ( a[ r[ p ] ][ p ]  ==  0 ) {
          printf ( "\n\n\n\tERROR-1! -  Singular matrix.  Algorithm FAILS.\n" );
          printf (  "\n\n\n\t\t\t\tGood-bye! \n" );
          return (0);
       }



     for ( k = p+1; k <= n; k++ ) {
        ratio = a[ r[ k ] ][ p ] / a[ r[ p ] ][ p ];

        for ( c = 1; c <= p; c++ )
           a[ r[ k ] ][ c ] = 0.0;

           for ( c = p+1;  c <= n+1;  c++ ) {
              a[ r[ k ] ][ c ] = a[ r[ k ] ][ c ] - ratio * a[ r[ p ] ][ c ];
```

```
              printf ( "\n\n\nPOSITION %d: Row %d,  Col %d ", p, k, c );
              printf ( "\nThe augmented matrix is:\n" );
              for ( i = 1; i <= n; i++ ) {    /* Begin display of intermediate step  */
                  printf ( "\nRow %d:\t\t", i );
                  for ( j = 1; j <= n+1; j++ )
                      printf ( "%10.2f",   a[ r[ i ] ][ j ] );
              }                                /* End display of intermediate  */

              fflush ( stdin );                           /* Pause sequence  */
              printf ( "\n\n\n\tTo continue, press <return>:  " );
              scanf ( "%c", &dummy );

          }                                             /* End  for - c  loop  */
      }                                                 /* End  for - k  loop  */
  }                                                     /* End positional loop  */

                                                /* Backward substitution begins  */

  if ( a[ r[ n ] ][ n ] == 0 ) {                /* Check if last row element is zero  */
      printf ( "\n\n\n\tERROR-2! -  Singular matrix.  Algorithm FAILS.\n" );
      printf ( "\n\n\n\t\t\tGood-bye! \n" );
      return (0);
  }


  x[ n ] = a[ r[ n ] ][ n+1 ] / a[ r[ n ] ][ n ];        /* Calculate last  x  value  */


  for ( k = n-1; k >= 1; k-- ) {
      sum = 0.0;
      for ( c = k+1; c <= n; c++ )
          sum = sum + a[ r[ k ] ][ c ] * x[ c ];

      x[ k ] = ( a[ r[ k ] ][ n+1 ] - sum ) / a[ r[ k ] ][ k ];/* Calculate next x value */
  }
                                                /* Backward substitution ends  */

                                                /* Display original system  */
  printf ( "\n\n\nThe original system of equations is :\n\n");
  for ( i = 1; i <= n; i++ ) {
      printf ( "\t" );
      for ( j = 1; j <= n; j++ ) {
          printf ( "%5.1f X[%1d]",  b[ i ][ j ],   j  );
          if ( j <= n-1 )
          printf ( " + " );
      }
```

```
            printf ( "  = %5.1f\n",  b[ i ][ n+1 ] );

      }


   printf ( "\n\n\nThe solutions are:  \n" );                    /* Display solutions */
   for ( i = 1; i <= n; i++ )
        printf ( "\n\t\tX[%d]  = %10.4f",    i,   x[ i ] );


   printf ( "\n\n\n\t\t\t\tGood-bye! \n" );                      /* Exit */
   return (0);
}
```

17.2.5 Gauss-Seidel Iteration

Another way to solve a system of equations algorithmically is by iteration. To do this, consider the generalized system of three linear equations in three unknowns. We can write the system as

$$a_{11}x_1 \; + \; a_{12}x_2 \; + \; a_{13}x_3 \; = \; b_1$$
$$a_{21}x_1 \; + \; a_{22}x_2 \; + \; a_{23}x_3 \; = \; b_2$$
$$a_{31}x_1 \; + \; a_{32}x_2 \; + \; a_{33}x_3 \; = \; b_3$$

where the three variables are represented by x_j ($x_1, x_2,$ and x_3), the coefficients of these variables for each row are represented by the real numbers a_{ij} positioned in the ith row and jth column, and where the b_i are real constants. Rewrite the system so that in the first equation x_1 is isolated on the left, in the second equation x_2 is isolated on the left, and in the first equation x_3 is isolated on the left. The system now becomes

$$a_{11}x_1 \; = \; b_1 \; - \; a_{12}x_2 \; - \; a_{13}x_3$$
$$a_{22}x_2 \; = \; b_2 \; - \; a_{21}x_1 \; - \; a_{23}x_3$$
$$a_{33}x_3 \; = \; b_3 \; - \; a_{31}x_1 \; - \; a_{32}x_2$$

or

$$x_1 = (b_1 - a_{12}x_2 - a_{13}x_3)/a_{11} \qquad\qquad (1)$$
$$x_2 = (b_2 - a_{21}x_1 - a_{23}x_3)/a_{22}$$
$$x_3 = (b_3 - a_{31}x_1 - a_{32}x_2)/a_{33}$$

Each variable x_i is written in terms of the other variables, provided each of the coefficients $a_{11}, a_{22},$ and a_{33} is not zero. We begin by initializing the variables on the *right* side of the system of equations (1) with a guess. Typically, the guess is $x_1 = 0$, $x_2 = 0$, and $x_3 = 0$, which makes the first iterative approximation for the three values equal to

$$x_1 = \frac{b_1}{a_{11}} \qquad x_2 = \frac{b_2}{a_{22}} \qquad x_3 = \frac{b_3}{a_{33}}$$

We now take these values and substitute them in the right side of system (1) to get a second iterative approximation. We continue the process, called **Gauss-Seidel iteration,** until all variables converge to a stabilized result or until there are a fixed number of iterations. Program 17.2–2 shows a version of the method that can solve a system of equations of up to four equations in four unknowns. The method is guaranteed to converge if the coefficient matrix is **diagonally dominant.** This means that the elements on the main diagonal of the matrix must be greater than the sum of the remaining elements in the corresponding row. When implementing this program use values in the coefficient matrix that make the matrix diagonally dominant and also values that do not.

P R O G R A M   1 7 . 2 – 2

```
/***********************************************************************
*  Title:      gauss-seidel iteration on system of equations         *
*  Filename:   gausseid.c                                            *
*                                                                    *
*  Description: This program uses iterative methods to solve for a system of four *
*              equations in four unknowns by the Gauss-Seidel approach.  The *
*              coefficients a[i][j] and the constant b[i] are entered manually. The *
*              solution is given as x[i] where                        *
*                    x[i] = ( b[i] - Sumj [a[ij] * x[j] ] ) / a[ii]   *
*              for all j ≠ i.                                         *
*                                                                    *
*  Input:      coefficients of system                                *
*  Output:     solution, or error message if algorithm fails         *
*  Process:    Iteration with null solution as an initial case        *
*                                                                    *
*  Written by:  ...                              Date: ...           *
***********************************************************************/

#include <stdio.h>
#include <stdlib.h>

#define  MAX        4              /* Maximum dimension of system */
#define  ITERATION  16             /* Maximum number of iterations */


main ( void )
{
    float a[ MAX ][ MAX ],                    /* Coefficient matrix */
          b[ MAX ],                      /* Constant column matrix */
          x[ MAX ],                          /* Solution matrix */
          sum;                           /* Partial sum variable */
```

```
int    i, j,                                        /* Matrix index loop variables  */
       n,                                           /*  Dimension of system  */
       iter,                                        /*  Iteration loop variable  */
       diagdom;                                     /*  Diagonally dominant check variable  */

char   dummy;


do {                                                /*  Input dimension of system  */
    printf ( "\n\nEnter size of system of  \n  n   equations " );
    printf ( "in  n   unknowns, where  n <= %1d:   ",    MAX );
    scanf ( "%d",  &n );
} while ( n > MAX );


for ( i = 0; i < n; i++ ) {                         /*  Input module for system  */
    printf ( "\n\nEnter the coefficients of  x  for equation %d: \n", i+1 );
    for ( j = 0; j < n; j++ )
        scanf ( "%f",  &a[ i ][ j ] );              /*  Input coefficient matrix  */
    printf ( "\nEnter the constant for equation  %d\n",  i+1 );
        scanf ( "%f",   &b[ i ] );                  /*  Input constant matrix  */
}


printf ( "\n\n\nThe system of equations is as follows:\n\n");
for ( i = 0; i < n; i++ ) {                         /*  Display system  */
    for ( j = 0; j < n; j++ ) {                     /*  of equations  */
        printf( "%6.1f X[%1d]",   a[ i ][ j ],  j+1 );
        if ( j < n-1 )
        printf ( "  +  " );
    }
    printf ( "  = %6.1f\n",  b[ i ]  );
}


diagdom = 0;                                        /*  Check if system is diagonal dominant  */
for ( i = 0; i < n; i++ ) {
    sum = 0.0;
    for ( j = 0; j < n; j++ )
      if ( j != i )
        sum =  sum  + abs( a[ i ][ j ] );
      if (  a[ i ][ i ] <= sum  )
        diagdom++;
}
```

```
if ( diagdom == 0 ) {                                   /*  Display results of diagonal  */
    printf ( "\n\n\tMatrix is diagonally dominant.  " );           /*  dominant test  */
    printf ( "\n\tGauss-Seidel method may be applied to the system.\n\n" );
}
else {
    printf ( "\n\n\tCAUTION: Matrix is not diagonally dominant.  " );
    printf ( "\n\tGauss-Seidel method MAY NOT converge.\n\n" );
}


printf ( "\n\n\tChecking for stability ...\n" );       /*  Check for system stability  */
for ( i = 0; i < n; i++ ) {
    if ( a[ i ][ i ] == 0.0 ) {
        printf ( "\n\t\tERROR!:  Equation %d causes division by zero", i+1 );
        printf ( "\n\t\t\tMethod FAILS!\n" );
        printf ( "\n\n\n\t\t\tGood-bye!\n" );
        return ( 0 );
    }
    else if ( a[ i ][ i ] < 0.0 )
        printf ( "\n\t\tCAUTION: Equation %d may not cause convergence. ", i+1 );
    else
        printf ( "\n\t\tCLEARED: Equation %d is OK.", i+1 );
}


fflush ( stdin );                                       /*  Ready to go  */
printf ( "\n\n\nTo execute the algorithm, press <return>:  " );
scanf ( "%c",  &dummy );

for ( i = 0; i < MAX; i++ )                             /*  Initialize solution  */
   x[ i ] = 0.0;

printf ( "\n\n\nIteration\t   X[1]\t    X[2]\t   X[3]\t   X[4]\n" );      /*  Set up  */
  printf ( "---------\t -------\t -------\t -------\t -------" ); /* table headers */

iter  =  0;
while  ( iter <= ITERATION ) {                          /*  Begin iteration  */
   printf ( "\n%5d\t\t%9.4f\t%9.4f\t%9.4f\t%9.4f",   iter,  x[0],  x[1],  x[2],  x[3]  );

   for ( i = 0; i < n; i++ ) {
      sum = 0.0;
      for ( j = 0; j < n ; j++ )
         if ( j != i )
            sum = sum + a[ i ][ j ] * x[ j ];
      x[ i ] = ( b[ i ] - sum ) / a[ i ][ i ];
   }
```

```
    iter++;
}

printf ( "\n\n\n\t\tGood-bye! " );
return (0);

}
```

EXERCISES 17.2

Concept Check

Answer statements 1 through 4 with true *or* false.

1. A system of linear equations must have a solution.
2. The equation $ax + by = c$ for constants a, b, and c has a unique solution.
3. Use of matrices generally makes the solution of a system of linear equations easier.
4. Gaussian elimination is not a useful algorithm for solving systems of linear equations.

For statements 5 through 8 choose the answer that best completes the statement.

5. A matrix is
   a. a box of numbers
   b. equations represented by symbols
   c. a rectangular array of elements
   d. a vector
6. Which of the following is a nonlinear equation?
   a. $3x - 4y - 7 = 0$
   b. $x = 3y - z$
   c. $4x = 3/y$
   d. $y = 3x + 4$
7. Gaussian elimination is a useful algorithm to solve
   a. systems of several equations in several unknowns
   b. any system of equations
   c. only systems of linear equations
   d. nonlinear equations
8. Which of the following is not an elementary row operation?
   a. interchange any two rows
   b. add to any row a multiple of another row
   c. interchange rows and columns
   d. multiply the last row by π

For statements 9 through 12 fill in the blanks with the right word.

9. A matrix with only one column is called _____.
10. The Gauss-Seidel algorithm uses _____ on a system of equations after assuming an initial solution for the system.

11. A system of equations with no solution is often called _____.
12. The equation $e^x = \sin x + 7x^3$ can best be described as a _____ equation.

Set A

Solve each of the following problems.

13. Find a value of x that solves $7.3x - 4.7 = 8.2$.
14. If $3t - 7.4 = 2.4t$, find t.
15. If $x = 2y$ and $y + x = 7$, find x and y.
16. If $x = 3y$ and $2y - 3x = 4$, find x and y.
17. If $x - y = 7$ and $3x + 2y = 1$, find x and y.
18. If $2u + v = 6$ and $u - v = 5$, find u and v.

Set B

19. Use Gaussian elimination with backward substitution (not Program 17.2–1) to solve the $3x - 4y = 7$ and $5y + 2z = 3$ system of equations.
20. Use Gaussian elimination with backward substitution (not Program 17.2–1) to solve the $x + 3y = 1$ and $3x - y = 5$ system of equations.
21. Use the Gauss-Seidel algorithm (not Program 17.2–2) to solve the $y = 3x + 4$ and $x = 2y - 7$ system of equations.
22. Use the Gauss-Seidel algorithm (not Program 17.2–2) to solve the $3x - y = 4$ and $4x + 3y = 2$ system of equations.

Set C

23. Walk through Program 17.2–1 to solve $5x + 4y - 7 = 0$ and $x + y = 5$.
24. Rewrite Program 17.2–1 to solve n equations in n unknowns.
25. Rewrite a portion of Program 17.2–1 and call another function to input the system of equations.
26. Rewrite a portion of Program 17.2–1 and call another function to print out the solution to the system of equations.
27. Use Program 17.2–1 to solve the $4x - 5y - 5z = 2$ and $x + 4y = 7$ system of equations.
28. Use Program 17.2–1 to solve the $3x - 2y + 4z = 5$, $6x - 4y - z = 3$ and $3x + 2y - 5z = 4$ system of equations.
29. Use Program 17.2–2 on the $8x - 4y + 2z = 12$, $x + 3y - 4z = 5$ and $4x - 2y + z = 6$ system of equations.
30. Use Program 17.2–2 on the system

$$8x - 4y + 2z = 12$$
$$x + 3y - 4z = 5$$
$$4x - 2y + z = 6$$

31. Use Program 17.2–1 on the system

$$8x - 4y + 2z = 7$$
$$x + 3y - 4z = -4$$
$$4x - 2y + z = 2$$

32. Use Program 17.2–2 on the system

$$8x - 4y + 2z = -3$$
$$x + 3y - 4z = 13$$
$$4x - 2y + z = 4$$

17.3 DIFFERENTIATION AND INTEGRATION

Introduction

The concept of the differentiation of functions and the related concept of integration have a rich mathematical background in the calculus, spanning three centuries. Computer scientists need to be familiar with these methodologies to help solve application problems, such as the computerized stability of a moving vehicle. Differentiation and integration have been incorporated into almost every branch of science and engineering. Both are based on the mathematical notion of limit. The **limit of a function** $f(x)$ is a number that is *reached* by the function as *x approaches* a value in the domain of the function. We write this as

$$\lim_{x \to a} f(x) = L$$

and read it as: The limit of the function f as x approaches a is L.

The concept of the limit is based on the understanding that although x is never equal to a, the limit actually equals L. For example,

$$\lim_{x \to 5} (x^2 - 3x + 4) = 14$$

That is, as *x approaches* the value 5 (without bound), the function *achieves* the value of 14. Leaving the details of this subject to the study of mathematics, we can say, however, that limits and their uses have had an impact in many fields such as applied and theoretical mathematics, physics, and engineering.

PERSPECTIVE

The *concept* of the calculus was developed by Galileo Galilei in the early 1600s when he measured motion over increments of time, especially in his famous Leaning Tower of Pisa experiments. In 1687 Sir Isaac Newton formulated the calculus in his grand work, *Principia Mathematica*, a literary landmark in mathematics and physics. Shortly thereafter, Gottfried Leibniz developed the calculus in the symbolic form much as we know it today.

With the advent of computers the notion of limits in the computational sciences has become less important. This is because computer-generated numbers are in a discrete domain rather than a continuous domain as limits must be. A **continuous**

domain is an interval of the set of real numbers. For example, the $3 < x \le 7$ interval is the set of *every decimal* greater than 3 but less than or equal to 7. Between any two points on this interval, no matter how close, there is an infinite number of decimals. This is *not* the case with numbers that can be represented on computers. As we learned in Section 4.3, all floating-point or *real* computer numbers are confined to *finite* register lengths, usually 32 bits or 64 bits, making every interval of numbers discontinuous.

With their speed and precision, computers have complemented the applications of limits in the calculus. Problems once considered unapproachable can now be solved within a prescribed tolerance. We saw this in Section 17.1 with zeros of functions. Now we show how computer algorithms can be used to solve some problems from the calculus.

17.3.1 The Meaning of Differentiation

Consider the function described as $f(x) = x^3 - 3x - 2$ for $-2 \le x \le 4$. At *even* integer values of x, the function attains the following values.

$$f(-2) = -4, \quad f(0) = -2, \quad f(2) = 0, \quad f(4) = 50$$

Between $x = -2$ and $x = 0$, the value of the function increases from -4 to -2. Between $x = 0$ and $x = 2$, the value of the function increases from -2 to 0. Between $x = 2$ and $x = 4$, the value of the function increases from 0 to 50. We can use these three situations to show three secant lines. Designate these lines by L_1, L_2, and L_3 with respective slopes m_1, m_2, and m_3 defined by

$$m_1 = \frac{f(0) - f(-2)}{0 - (-2)} = \frac{(-2) - (-4)}{2} = \frac{2}{2} = +1$$

$$m_2 = \frac{f(2) - f(0)}{2 - 0} = \frac{(0) - (-2)}{2} = \frac{2}{2} = +1$$

and

$$m_3 = \frac{f(4) - f(2)}{4 - 2} = \frac{50 - 0}{2} = \frac{50}{2} = +25$$

The function with its secant lines is shown in Figure 17.3–1.

At *all* integer values of x on the $-2 \le x \le 4$ interval, the $f(x) = x^3 - 3x - 2$ function attains the following values.

$$f(-2) = -4, \quad f(-1) = 0, \quad f(0) = -2, \quad f(1) = -4$$
$$f(2) = 0, \quad f(3) = 16, \quad f(4) = 50$$

Between $x = -2$ and $x = -1$, the value of the function increases from -4 to 0. Between $x = -1$ and $x = 0$, the value of the function decreases from 0 to -2. Between $x = 0$ and $x = 1$, the value of the function decreases from -2 to -4. Between $x = 1$ and $x = 2$, the value of the function increases from -4 to 0. Between $x = 2$ and $x = 3$, the value of the function increases from 0 to 16, and between $x = 3$ and $x = 4$, the value of the function increases from 16 to 50. We

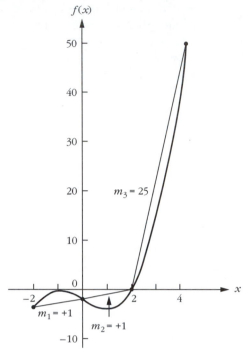

Figure 17.3–1 Three secant lines for
$f(x) = x^3 - 3x - 2$

can use these six situations to show six secant lines designated by $L_1, L_2, \ldots, L_6$ with respective slopes $m_1, m_2, \ldots, m_6$. We calculate these slopes as in the problem we just did to take on the values

$$m_1 = +4 \quad m_2 = -2 \quad m_3 = -2$$
$$m_4 = +4 \quad m_5 = +16 \quad m_6 = +34$$

The six secant lines with their slopes are shown in Figure 17.3–2.

BEFORE YOU GO ON

Query: How do we calculate the values of the slopes? Verify these values.

RESPONSE: We do this by calculating the quotients of the change in the function values, divided by the change in the x values. For example, the value of $m_6 = [f(4) - f(3)]/[4 - 3] = 50 - 16 = +34$.

Table 17.3–1 shows the same $f(x) = x^3 - 3x - 2$ function evaluated at increments of 0.5 in x. The quotient of the differences in the function to the differences in x is called the **difference quotient** and is used to calculate new values of the slope. Notice that when we calculate the slope between successive values of x, we form differences in the numerator by evaluating the function at the larger value of x and subtracting from it the evaluation of the function at the lower value

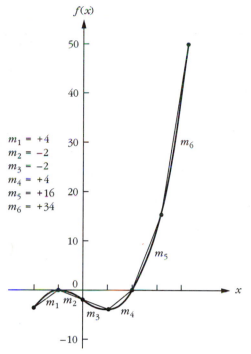

Figure 17.3–2 Six secant lines of $f(x) = x^3 - 3x - 2$

of x. The slope cannot be calculated at $x = +4$ because 4.5 is not in the domain of the function.

The meaning of this operation is the following. In the first phase with four points and three slopes, the slopes are always positive. In the second phase with seven points and six slopes, the slopes are positive, then they become negative, and then they become positive again. Table 17.3–1 is a further refinement of the changing slope from positive to negative to positive. Continued refinement of this process shows that the values of m begin to describe a new function related to

Table 17.3–1

x	$f(x)$	m
−2.0	− 4.000	+ 6.250
−1.5	− 0.875	+ 1.750
−1.0	0.000	− 1.250
−0.5	− 0.625	− 1.375
0.0	− 2.000	− 2.750
+0.5	− 3.375	− 1.250
+1.0	− 4.000	− 1.750
+1.5	− 3.125	+ 6.250
+2.0	0.000	+12.250
+2.5	+ 6.125	+19.750
+3.0	+16.000	+28.750
+3.5	+30.375	+39.250
+4.0	+50.000	—

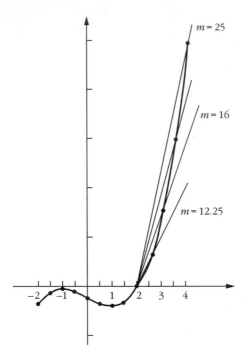

Figure 17.3–3   Successive secants at $x = 2$

f. This new function is called the **derivative of f**, denoted f', and is formally defined by the limit

$$f'(x_1) = \lim_{x_2 \to x_1} \frac{f(x_2) - f(x_1)}{x_2 - x_1}$$

This limit of the difference quotient as x_2 approaches x_1 is a way of formalizing the refinement that results from partitioning the domain of the function $(-2 \le x \le 4$ in the problem we just did) into smaller and smaller parts. This refinement causes the secant line to continue to approach the tangent line at the point when $x = x_1$, as shown in Figure 17.3–3. In fact, the slope of the tangent line is approximated by the successive secant lines. That is, numbers in the column labeled m in Table 17.3–1 represent the slopes of the secant lines but they are really an approximation of the slopes of the *tangent* lines at the respective points.

Our purpose here is not to study the derivative function but instead to stimulate some thought about the derivative of a function as a measure of the rate of change of a function. It describes "how fast" the function is changing between two successive values of x.

EXAMPLE 17.3–1

Problem

Suppose a function f represents the distance s that an object moves as a function of time t. What is the meaning of $f'(t)$? What is the meaning of $f''(t)$, the derivative of the derivative?

Reasoning

Because distance is a function of time, we can write $s = f(t)$. **Distance** can be measured in miles, feet, or centimeters. Time can be measured in hours, minutes, or seconds.

Solution

The time rate of change of s can be *the number of feet traveled in a given number of minutes* or *the centimeters an object moved in t seconds* or *the number of miles traveled in an hour*. Each of these descriptions suggests that the time rate of change for distance is **velocity**. Therefore, the meaning of $f'(t)$ is velocity when $f(t)$ is distance.

The time rate of change of velocity is called **acceleration**. Acceleration is physically experienced when driving a car, riding a bicycle, or moving on a ride at an amusement park. In this context $f''(t)$ means acceleration when $f'(t)$ is velocity and when $f(t)$ is distance. That is, acceleration measures the rate of change of the rate of change of a function.

Test

If you compare them to the definitions in a physics textbook, you will find that these definitions are consistent with the scientific interpretation of distance, velocity, and acceleration.   •

17.3.2 Algorithms for Approximating Derivatives

Theories of the calculus suggest many examples for finding the derivative of a function. The only ones that can be solved, however, are those in which we can find the *limit* for the derivative, a subject best studied in the context of mathematics.

Although theoretical limits for the derivatives of functions are important, we can find an approximation to the derivative of almost any function by numerical means. Consider the $f(x) = x^2 + 3$ function defined on the *discrete* interval $0 \leq x < 2$ where x can vary only in increments of 0.25. That is, a value such as $x = 1.6$ is *not* on the interval. We discuss two of several algorithms here. The first parallels the method we just explained (shown in Table 17.3–1). The slope of the secant line goes through the point at which the derivative is to be found and another point is calculated from the function an x increment away. The slope of this secant line *approximates* the slope of the tangent line. We confined the approximation for the derivative by changing the limit definition of the derivative to read

$$f'(x_1) \approx \frac{f(x_1 + h) - f(x_1)}{h}$$

where h is the discrete distance between two adjacent values of x (x_1 and $x_1 + h$), and where x_1 is the x value of the point $(x_1, f(x_1))$ where the derivative is to be approximated. (This is shown in Figure 17.3–4.)

For the $f(x) = x^2 + 3$ function the derivative of f is approximated by

$$f'(x_1) \approx \frac{f(x_1 + h) - f(x_1)}{h} = \frac{[(x_1 + h)^2 + 3] - [x_1^2 + 3]}{h}$$

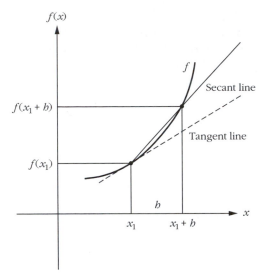

Figure 17.3–4 The derivative at $x = x_1$

If we were computing this manually we could simplify this expression. But since the computation is to be made by computer, simplification is unnecessary. All we need is the description of the function, the initial value of x, the terminal value for x, and the number of partitions n in the defined interval. Note that initial and terminal values a and b, respectively, are found by the x variable. In this problem $a = 0$ and $b = 1.75$, not 2. (Why?)

Because the value of the x variable is incremented positively by h, the process of finding the derivative is called the **forward-difference** algorithm. Program 17.3–1 is a function that implements this algorithm. The program assumes information from a driver program given as an exercise.

PROGRAM 17.3–1

```
/****************************************************************************
 * Function name:      derivfn1                                            *
 * Description:        This function finds the derivative of a function FUN *
 *                     supplied by a driver program on an interval from low *
 *                     to high using a forward-difference algorithm.  The   *
 *                     number of increments on the interval is input as     *
 *                     increments.                                          *
 *                                                                          *
 * Input parameters:   low,  high,  increments                             *
 * Output parameters:  none                                                 *
 * Return value:       the derivative at a point                           *
 ****************************************************************************/

                        /* Assumes information from driver program */
float derivfn1( float x, float width )
{
```

```
   float x1, x2,                         /*  Incremental boundaries  */
         y1, y2,                 /*  Corresponding function values  */
         deriv;                         /*  The derivative at  x  */

   x1 = x;                        /*  Coordinates of first point  */
   y1 = FUN(x1);                 /*  Function FUN defined in driver  */

   x2 = x+width;                   /*  Coordinates of second point  */
   y2 = FUN(x2);

   deriv = ( y2 - y1 ) / width;    /*  Calculation of derivative at  x  */

   return (deriv);
}
```

Another algorithm for finding the derivative of a function at a point brackets the point where the derivative is to be found. The idea behind this is to make the secant line that is created from the three points almost parallel to the tangent line at the point where the derivative is to be found. For example, if the point in question is x_i, then the two values of x that bracket x_i are the left value $x_i - h$ and the right value $x_i + h$. Notice that the increment between these two values of x is $2h$, not h. The evaluation of the function at these two points is $f(x_i - h)$ and $f(x_i + h)$, respectively. Now we can write the difference quotient to approximate the derivative of the function as

$$f'(x_i) \approx \frac{f(x_i + h) - f(x_i - h)}{2h}$$

Observe that this algorithm (illustrated in Figure 17.3–5) is useful only for internal values of the defined interval since both a forward difference $x_i + h$ and a backward difference $x_i - h$ are needed to calculate the derivative at x_i. Because of this, calculating derivatives this way is called the **forward-backward-difference** algorithm. Program 17.3–2 is a function that implements this algorithm and is similar to Program 17.3–1. The program assumes information from a driver program given as an exercise.

PROGRAM 17.3–2

```
/******************************************************************************
*  Function name:       derivfn2                                             *
*  Description:         This function finds the derivative of a function FUN  *
*                       supplied by a driver program on an interval from low  *
*                       to high using a forward-backward-difference algorithm. *
*                       The number of increments on the interval is input as  *
*                       increments.                                           *
*                                                                            *
*  Input parameters:    low,  high,  increments                              *
*  Output parameters:   none                                                 *
*  Return value:        the derivative at a point                            *
******************************************************************************/
```

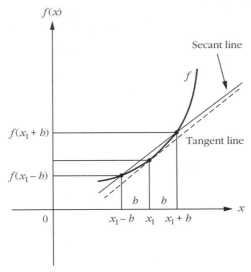

Figure 17.3–5   Forward-backward difference for $f'(x_1)$

```
                              /*  Assumes information from driver program  */
float derivfn2 ( float x, float width )
{

     float x1, x2,                          /*  Incremental boundaries  */
           y1, y2,                     /*  Corresponding function values  */
           deriv;                             /*  The derivative at  x  */

     x1 = x - width;                     /*  Coordinates of first point  */
     y1 = FUN(x1);                  /*  Function FUN defined in driver  */

     x2 = x + width;                    /*  Coordinates of second point  */
     y2 = FUN(x2);

     deriv = ( y2 - y1 ) / (2*width);    /*  Calculation of derivative at  x  */

     return (deriv);
}
```

To use this program, we need a function specified as a C definition, input for the initial value a and the final value b for the variable x, and the number n of partitions to be used on the interval from a to b. The program outputs calculations for the derivative for all discrete values of x between $a + h$ and $b - h$.

17.3.3 The Meaning of Integration

Consider the $f(x) = x^2 + 2$ function for $1 \leq x \leq 3$. Suppose we have to find the area of the region bounded by the graph of the function and the x-axis over the given interval. (The area is shown in Figure 17.3–6.) The area is not a conventional geometric shape: it is not a square, trapezoid, circle, or other shape for which a formula for the area is known. Therefore, because we cannot use a closed-form formula to find the area, we use an approximation algorithm instead.

One way to approximate the area of the region is to divide the region into rectangles. The height of each rectangle is the evaluation of the function at some x value in or on the rectangle. We calculate the product of the height of each rectangle with its width to give subareas for each rectangle under the graph of the function. The summation of the subareas gives an approximation of the area of the region. For example, suppose the region is divided into four rectangles each having the same width. For the $1 \leq x \leq 3$ interval each width equals $(3 - 1)/4 = 0.5$. Let the height of each rectangle be calculated by evaluating the $f(x) = x^2 + 2$ function at the left edge of each rectangle and let A_k be the area of the kth rectangle. The area of the region is approximated by

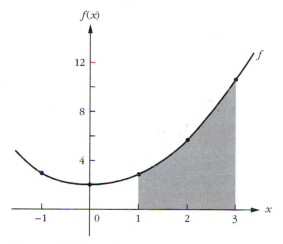

Figure 17.3–6   Area under curve on interval [1, 3]

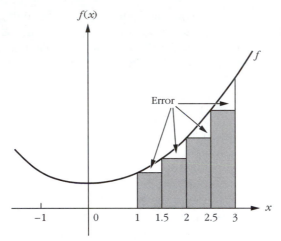

Figure 17.3–7 Rectangular approximation of area, $n = 4$

$$\text{Area} = A_1 + A_2 + A_3 + A_4$$

$$= f(1) * 0.5 + f(1.5) * 0.5 + f(2) * 0.5 + f(2.5) * 0.5$$

$$= 0.5[f(1) + f(1.5) + f(2) + f(2.5)]$$

$$= 0.5[(1^2 + 2) + (1.5^2 + 2) + (2^2 + 2) + (2.5^2 + 2)]$$

$$= 0.5[3 + 4.25 + 6 + 8.25]$$

$$= 21.5/2$$

$$= 10.75$$

Figure 17.3–7 shows the designated region and its rectangular approximation: the approximated area is less than the actual area and the difference is the error made in the approximation.

If we use more rectangles in the subdivision, the error is diminished. Figure 17.3–8 shows a rectangular subdivision of 16 units. We calculate the width of each rectangle to be $(3 - 1)/16 = 1/8 = 0.125$. We find the height of each rectangle by evaluating the $f(x) = x^2 + 2$ function at the left edge of each rectangle from $x = 1$ to $x = 2.875$. Using the same strategy as in the 4-rectangle subdivision, we calculate the area with 16 subdivisions to be approximately 12.1719. We see how this is done in the exercises at the end of this section.

The 4-rectangle and 16-rectangle problems show that we get the best answer by approximating as the number of subdivisions increases, preferably without bound. Thus increasing the number of partitions and summing up the rectangular areas provide the most precise area. As the number of partitions increases, the

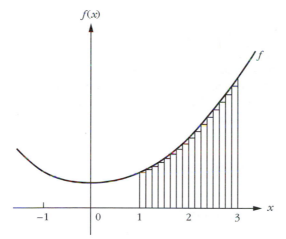

Figure 17.3–8   Rectangular area approximation, $n = 16$

width of the partitions decreases. If we let h denote the width of a partition, then h can be calculated as $h = (b - a)/n$ where n is the number of partitions, a is the left-most value of x for the region, and b is the right-most value of x for the region. For each x_i on the interval, $a \leq x_i < b$, $f(x_i)$ represents the left-edge height of the rectangles. The area of the ith rectangle (height times base) is simply

$$A_i = f(x_i)h = f(x_i)(b - a)/n$$

The total area A can be expressed as the limit of a summation, Σ, written as

$$A = \lim_{n \to \infty} \sum_{i=1}^{n} f(x_i)h = \int f(x)dx$$

for $i = 1, 2, \ldots, n$. This limit is called the **integral**, denoted by the $\int$ symbol, of the function from a to b. As with derivatives, we leave the theoretical details to the study of mathematics and concentrate on the summation, which is easily calculated by computer.

17.3.4 Algorithms for Integrals

Many algorithms can be used to evaluate integrals. We base the algorithm on the approach we take to the problem. Of the three methods we look at here, the first parallels the algorithm using rectangles in subsection 17.3.3. It assumes that the function to be integrated is defined in the algorithm. It also assumes that we know the interval of integration a to b and the number of partitions n. The algorithm is shown in Program 17.3–3.

PROGRAM 17.3-3

```
/*****************************************************************************
 * Function name:       rectrule                                             *
 * Description:         This function finds an approximate                   *
 *                      integral of a function FUN on the interval           *
 *                      from low to high using the method of                 *
 *                      approximating rectangles.  There are num_part        *
 *                      such rectangles.                                     *
 *                                                                           *
 * Input parameters:    low,  high,  num_part                                *
 * Output parameters:   none                                                 *
 * Return value:        area                                                 *
 *****************************************************************************/

float rectrule ( float low, float high, int num_part )
{
                                 /*  Assumes information from driver program */

   int   j;                                            /*  Loop index */

   float width,                           /*  Partition width */
         sum, area,                       /*  Partial sum and area */
         x;                               /*  Domain value of function */


   width = ( high - low ) / num_part;     /*  Calculate interval width */

   x    = low;                            /*  Initialize  x  and  sum */
   sum  = 0.0;

   for ( j=1; j <= num_part; j++ ) {      /*  Sum up partition areas */
      sum += FUN( x );
      x   += width;
   }

   area = sum * width;                              /*  Calculate area */

   return ( area );
}
```

The evaluation of integrals using the rectangular algorithm is simple but the resulting error lessens its appeal. One way to reduce the error is to form straight-line edges between points on the curve. These points are simply the evaluation of the function at the partition values given by x. Again, consider the $f(x) = x^2 + 2$ function for $1 \le x \le 3$ with four partitions. Instead of forming rectangles, form

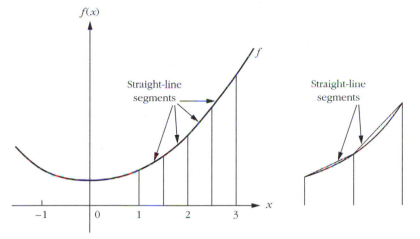

Figure 17.3–9 Trapezoidal approximation of area, $n = 4$

trapezoids using the straight-line segments along the curve. (Recall that a **trapezoid** is a four-sided figure in which two of its sides are parallel.) In this case, the parallel sides (bases) are the partition lines. Figure 17.3–9 shows how the trapezoids are formed over four partitions and compares them to rectangles.

We calculate the area of the region using trapezoids in the same way as with rectangles. Suppose we divide the region into four trapezoids. The height of each partition is the evaluation of the function at the respective x value. The area of a trapezoid is *one-half the product of the distance between the two parallel lines times the sum of the two bases.* That is, if h is the distance between the two bases, and b_1 and b_2 are the lengths of the two bases, then

$$\text{Area}_{\text{trap}} = \left(\tfrac{1}{2}\right)(b_1 + b_2)h$$

The summation of the subareas gives an approximation of the area of the region. Because the region is divided into four trapezoids, each having the same width on the $1 \le x \le 3$ interval, then each width equals $(3 - 1)/4 = 0.5$. Let the bases of each trapezoid be calculated by evaluating the $f(x) = x^2 + 2$ function and let A_k be the area of the kth rectangle. The area of the region is approximated by

$$
\begin{aligned}
\text{Area} &= A_1 + A_2 + A_3 + A_4 \\
&= \tfrac{1}{2}[(f(1.0) + f(1.5)) * 0.5] + \tfrac{1}{2}[(f(1.5) + f(2.0)) * 0.5] \\
&\quad + \tfrac{1}{2}[(f(2.0) + f(2.5)) * 0.5] + \tfrac{1}{2}[(f(2.5) + f(3.0)) * 0.5] \\
&= \tfrac{1}{2}[(f(1.0) + f(1.5)) + (f(1.5) + f(2.0)) + (f(2.0) + f(2.5)) \\
&\quad + (f(2.5) + f(3.0))] * 0.5 \\
&= \tfrac{1}{2}[f(1.0) + (f(1.5) + f(1.5)) + (f(2.0) + f(2.0)) \\
&\quad + (f(2.5) + f(2.5)) + f(3.0)] * 0.5 \\
&= \tfrac{1}{2}[f(1.0) + 2f(1.5) + 2f(2.0) + 2f(2.5) + f(3.0)] * 0.5
\end{aligned}
$$

At this point it is helpful to remember these facts about the trapezoidal algorithm of integration: The $\frac{1}{2}$ value is from the trapezoid formula, the 0.5 value is the partition width h, and the end points of the region have partition heights $f(1)$ and $f(3)$. Note that the internal partition heights are each doubled.

Continuing with our calculations, we find that

$$
\begin{aligned}
\text{Area} &= \tfrac{1}{2}[f(1.0) + 2f(1.5) + 2f(2.0) + 2f(2.5) + f(3.0)] * 0.5 \\
&= \tfrac{1}{2}[f(1.0) + 2[f(1.5) + f(2.0) + f(2.5)] + f(3.0)] * 0.5 \\
&= \tfrac{1}{2}[(1.0^2 + 2) + 2[(1.5^2 + 2) + (2.0^2 + 2) + (2.5^2 + 2)] + (3.0^2 + 2)] * 0.5 \\
&= \tfrac{1}{2}[(3.00) + 2[(4.25) + (6) + (8.25)] + (11)] * 0.5 \\
&= \tfrac{1}{2}[(3.00) + 2(18.5) + (11)] * 0.5 \\
&= \tfrac{1}{2}[51.00] * 0.5 \\
&= 12.75
\end{aligned}
$$

We can easily expand this operation on four partitions to many partitions, allowing increased accuracy in the answer. A generalization of this operation calculating the area under the curve generated by the $f(x)$ function between $x = a$ and $x = b$ is called the **trapezoidal rule** and is expressed as

$$
\text{Area} = \tfrac{1}{2}[f(x_0) + 2\sum f(x_i) + f(x_n)]h
$$

where $h = (b - a)/n$, $x_0 = a$, $x_n = b$ and where the summation is over $i = 1, 2, \ldots, n - 1$. Program 17.3–4 uses the algorithm of the trapezoidal rule and assumes that the function to be integrated is defined in the algorithm and that we know the limits of the interval, a and b, and the number of partitions, n.

PROGRAM 17.3–4

```
/****************************************************************************
 *  Function name:       traprule                                           *
 *  Description:         This function finds the approximate                *
 *                       area under the curve of a function FUN defined     *
 *                       on the interval from low to high using the         *
 *                       method of approximating trapezoids.  There are     *
 *                       num_part such trapezoids.                          *
 *                                                                          *
 *  Input parameters:    low,  high,  num_part                              *
 *  Output parameters:   none                                               *
 *  Return value:        area                                               *
 ****************************************************************************/

float traprule ( float low, float high, int num_part )
{
                                    /*  Assumes information from driver program  */
```

```
float x,                                    /*  Domain value of function  */
      area, sum, width;     /*  Variables for area, partial sum, and width  */

int   j;                                            /*  Loop index  */


if ( num_part == 1 ) {                  /*  Special case for one partition  */
    area = 0.5 * ( high - low ) * ( FUN( low ) + FUN( high ) );
    return ( area );
}

else {                                              /*  General case  */
    width = ( high - low ) / num_part;
    x     = low + width;
    sum   = 0.0;
    for ( j=1; j <= num_part - 1; j++ ) {          /*  Calculate summation  */
        sum += FUN( x );
        x   += width;
    }
                                                    /*  Calculate area  */
    area = 0.5 * ( FUN( low ) + FUN( high ) + 2.0 * sum ) * width;
    return ( area );
}

}
```

Approximating integrals with accuracy may be an eternal mission. We have already seen interval partitioning by a constant (rectangular) and by linear (trapezoidal) line segments. Suppose we approximate a subregion by a quadratic function—for example, a parabola? In this case three points are needed rather than two, forcing two partitions for each subregion. (See Figure 17.3–10.) This implies that an *even* number of partitions, n, is needed. For a given $f(x)$ function bounded by $x = a$, $x = b$, and the x-axis, we can find the area of the region by

$$\text{Area} = \left(\frac{h}{3}\right) * \left[f(x_0) + 2\sum f(x_j) + 4\sum f(x_k) + f(x_n)\right]$$

In this expression j is even with $2 \leq j \leq (n-2)$, k is odd with $1 \leq k \leq (n-1)$, $x_0 = a$, $x_n = b$, $h = (b-a)/n$, and n is a positive *even* integer. This is called **Simpson's 1/3 rule** or the **parabolic rule**. (See Appendix F for more on this rule.)

Figure 17.3–10 shows the familiar $f(x) = x^2 + 2$ function for $1 \leq x \leq 3$ with four (an even number) partitions. We calculate the area of the region by Simpson's rule as follows.

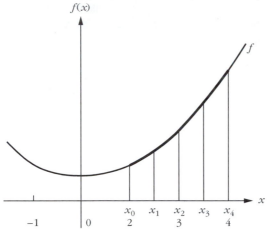

Figure 17.3–10 Parabolic approximation of area, $n = 4$

$$\text{Area} = \left(\frac{b}{3}\right)[f(x_0) + 2[f(x_2)] + 4[f(x_1) + f(x_3)] + f(x_4)]$$

where $b = (3 - 1)/4 = 0.5$ then

$$\text{Area} = \left(\frac{0.5}{3}\right)[f(1) + 2[f(2)] + 4[f(1.5) + f(2.5)] + f(3)]$$

$$= \left(\frac{0.5}{3}\right)[(3) + 2(6) + 4[(4.25) + (8.25)] + (11)]$$

$$= \left(\frac{0.5}{3}\right)[14 + 12 + 50]$$

$$= \left(\frac{0.5}{3}\right)[76]$$

$$= 12.666$$

Program 17.3–5 uses the parabolic algorithm for approximating integrals. It assumes that the function integrated is defined in the algorithm and that the values of a, b, and n are known.

P R O G R A M   1 7 . 3 – 5

```
/*********************************************************************
*    Function name:     simprule                                    *
*    Description:       This function finds an approximate area under the *
*                       curve of a function FUN defined on the interval from *
*                       low to high using the method of approximating *
*                       parabolas.  There are num_part / 2 such parabolas. *
```

```
*                                                                     *
*   Input parameters:   low,  high,  num_part                         *
*   Output parameters:  none                                          *
*   Return value:       area,  or  error value if any                 *
*********************************************************************/

float simprule ( float low, float high, int num_part )
{
                                  /*  Assumes information from driver program  */

    int   j;                                              /*  Loop index  */

    float x,                              /*  Domain value of function  */
          sum1, sum2,                              /*  Partial sums  */
          width, area;                     /*  Partition width and area  */


                                    /*  Check conditions for Simpson's rule  */
    if ( num_part % 2 != 0 || num_part == 0 ) {
       printf ( "\n\n\tERROR:  Condition for Simpson's rule is that\n " );
       printf ( "\t\tnumber of partitions must be even but not zero." );
       printf ( "\n\n\t\tSimpson's Rule FAILS!!\n\n\n" );
       return ( ERROR );
    }


    width = ( high - low ) / num_part;         /*  Calculate increment width  */

    sum1  = 0.0;
    x     = low + 2.0 * width;
    for ( j=2; j<=num_part - 2; j=j+2 ) {  /*  Calculate sum on even indices  */
       sum1 += FUN( x );
       x    += 2.0 * width;
    }

    sum2  = 0.0;
    x     = low + width;
    for ( j=1; j <= num_part - 1; j=j+2 ) { /*  Calculate sum on odd indices  */
       sum2 += FUN( x );
       x    += 2.0 * width;
    }

                                              /*  Calculate area  */
    area = ( width/3.0 ) * ( FUN(low) + FUN(high) + 2.0 * sum1 + 4.0 * sum2 );

    return ( area );
}
```

A driver for **rectrule**, **traprule**, and **simprule** is given in Program 17.3–6.

PROGRAM 17.3–6

```
/*********************************************************************
*  Title:      numerical integration                               *
*  Filename:   integrat.c                                          *
*                                                                   *
*  Description: Find the integral of a defined function  FUN  for   *
*               incremental values of x on the interval from low to *
*               high using the rectangular, trapezoidal, and parabolic *
*               rules.                                              *
*                                                                   *
*  Input:      low, high, num_part                                 *
*  Output:     the integral of FUN(x)                              *
*  Process:    algorithm functions for  rectrule,  traprule,  and   *
*              simprule.                                            *
*                                                                   *
*  Written by: ...                            Date: ...            *
*********************************************************************/

#include <stdio.h>
#include <math.h>

#define  FUN(x) 3.0*x*x + 4              /*  <<<<  Function defined here */

#define  ERROR  -999.0                   /*  Error value on function return */


                                          /*  Function prototypes */
float rectrule ( float low, float high, int num_part );
float traprule ( float low, float high, int num_part );
float simprule ( float low, float high, int num_part );

main ( )                                  /*  Begin main */
{
   int    num_part;                       /*  Number of partitions */

   float low, high,                       /*  Interval of integration */
         width,                           /*  Size of partition */
         rect, trap, simp;                /*  Integral values for 3 algorithms */


   printf ( "\nEnter the lower value of the domain of the function>:  " );  /*  Input */
   scanf ( "%f",  &low );                                              /*  limits */
   printf ( "\nEnter the upper value of the domain of the function>:  " );  /*  of */
   scanf ( "%f",  &high );                                            /*  integration */
```

```
while  ( low == high ) {                              /*  Check for null interval  */
   printf ( "\n\n\tCAUTION:  Interval is null." );
   printf ( "\n\n\tThe integral (all methods) is zero!\n\n " );
   printf ( "\nEnter the lower value of the domain of the function>:  " );
   scanf ( "%f",   &low );                            /*  Reenter limits  */
   printf ( "\nEnter the upper value of the domain of the function>:  " );
   scanf ( "%f",   &high );
}


printf ( "\n\nEnter the number of partitions>:  " );    /*  Input number of partition  */
scanf ( "%d",   &num_part );

while  ( num_part <= 0.0 ) {                           /*  Check for nonpositive  */
   printf ( "\n\n\tERROR:  Number of partitions must be positive" );
   printf ( "\n\nEnter the number of partitions>:  " );    /*  Reenter  num_part  */
   scanf ( "%d",   &num_part );
}


rect = rectrule ( low, high, num_part );              /*  Call to functions  */
trap = traprule ( low, high, num_part );
simp = simprule ( low, high, num_part );


if (simp != ERROR ) {                                 /*  Output results  */
   printf ( "\n\tIntegral by Rectangular Rule is %10.4f",   rect );
   printf ( "\n\tIntegral by Trapezoidal Rule is %10.4f",   trap );
   printf ( "\n\tIntegral by Simpson's   Rule is %10.4f",   simp );
}
else {
   printf ( "\n\tIntegral by Rectangular Rule is %10.4f",   rect );
   printf ( "\n\tIntegral by Trapezoidal Rule is %10.4f",   trap );
}

return (0);
                                                      /*  End main  */
}
```

17.3.5 Reflections

When we use numerical algorithms we have to consider the error in the method and how that error affects the problem we are solving. The forward-backward-difference algorithm might be better than the forward-difference algorithm for finding derivatives because it creates secant lines, which more closely parallel tangent lines. Let's review the $f(x) = x^3 - 3x - 2$ function for $-2 \leq x \leq 4$. Table 17.3–2 shows the first derivative of the function f represented by the slope m for values of x in increments of 0.5. This is repeated in Table 17.3–2 with

Table 17.3–2 Calculation for the Derivative of $f(x) = x^3 - 3x - 2$

x	$f(x)$	$f'(x)_{\text{forward-difference}}$	$f'(x)_{\text{forward-backward-difference}}$	$f'(x)_{\text{true}}$
−2.0	− 4.000	+ 6.250	—	+ 9.00
−1.5	− 0.875	+ 1.750	+ 4.00	+ 3.75
−1.0	0.000	− 1.250	+ 0.25	0.00
−0.5	− 0.625	− 1.375	− 2.00	− 2.25
0.0	− 2.000	− 2.750	− 2.75	− 3.00
+0.5	− 3.375	− 1.250	− 2.00	− 2.25
+1.0	− 4.000	− 1.750	+ 0.25	0.00
+1.5	− 3.125	+ 6.250	+ 4.00	+ 3.75
+2.0	0.000	+12.250	+ 9.25	+ 9.00
+2.5	+ 6.125	+19.750	+16.00	+15.75
+3.0	+16.000	+28.750	+24.25	+24.00
+3.5	+30.375	+39.250	+34.00	+33.75
+4.0	+50.000	—	—	+45.00

the column heading $f'(x)_{\text{forward-difference}}$ together with x and $f(x)$. In addition, Table 17.3–2 shows two other columns: $f'(x)_{\text{forward-backward-difference}}$, which we discussed in this section, and $f'(x)_{\text{true}}$, which we get from the calculus. We verify the $f'(x)_{\text{forward-backward-difference}}$ entries in the exercises at the end of this section. Notice that the values of $f'(x)_{\text{forward-difference}}$ and $f'(x)_{\text{forward-backward-difference}}$ vary from $f'(x)_{\text{true}}$ and that the entries found with the forward-backward-difference algorithm are closer to the true values.

Error is also a prime consideration when we approximate integrals. If we use the $f(x) = x^2 + 2$ function for $1 \leq x \leq 3$ with each of the three algorithms (rectangular, trapezoidal, and parabolic), we get different results. The three algorithms with four partitions result in Area$_{\text{rect}}$ = 10.75, Area$_{\text{trap}}$ = 12.75 and Area$_{\text{parab}}$ = 12.6666. The true area obtained from the calculus is $\frac{38}{3} = 12\frac{2}{3}$, which tells us that the parabolic rule might be superior to the other two methods.

BEFORE YOU GO ON

Query: Why is Area$_{\text{parab}}$ the same as the true area?

RESPONSE: The original $f(x) = x^2 + 2$ function is quadratic and it graphs as a parabola. Because Simpson's rule uses quadratic approximations, we expect it to produce the exact result. This would not be so for any arbitrary function other than a quadratic one.

EXERCISES 17.3

Concept Check
Answer statements 1 through 4 with true *or* false.
1. Derivatives of functions are the same as integrals.
2. Derivatives approximated by the forward-backward-difference algorithm are not usually better than those approximated by the forward-difference algorithm.

3. Integration of functions measures their rate of change.
4. Simpson's rule for finding integrals is generally a poor method for finding integrals.

For statements 5 through 8 choose the answer that best completes the statement.

5. An integral of a function is best described as
   a. finding the rate of change of the function
   b. summing all functions derived from the original function
   c. finding the area under the curve of the function
   d. finding a geometric region for study
6. The trapezoidal rule is generally
   a. better than Simpson's rule
   b. inferior to the rectangular rule
   c. of some interest in determining particle speeds
   d. easier to calculate than Simpson's rule
7. The derivative of a function is generally
   a. needed to find areas of regions
   b. important to find the distance traveled by an object
   c. not important in mathematics
   d. none of these
8. The rectangular method
   a. is of no interest to mathematicians
   b. can be used to find integrals
   c. is generally superior to the parabolic method
   d. would be used to find derivatives

For statements 9 through 12 fill in the blanks with the right word.

9. Finding the area of a region is called _____.
10. The ratio of $f(x + h) - f(x)$ to h is called the _____.
11. The _____ can be used to find the speed of an object.
12. A consideration for all numerical algorithms is the _____ generated by the particular algorithm.

Set A
Solve each of the following problems using a scientific calculator.

13. Calculate the area of the region formed by $f(x) = x^2 + 2$ and the x-axis over the interval $1 \leq x \leq 3$ by the rectangular method using 8 partitions. This should verify the result given in subsection 17.3.3.
14. Calculate the area of the region formed by $f(x) = x^2 + 2$ and the x-axis over the interval $1 \leq x \leq 3$ by the trapezoidal method using 8 partitions.
15. Let $f(x) = x^3 - 3x - 2$. Find the derivative of the function at $x = -1, 0, 1, 2, 3$ using the forward-backward difference method for $h = 1.0$.
16. Repeat Question 15 but now use $h = 0.5$. Compare results to those of Question 15 and the values shown in Tables 17.3–1 and 17.3–2.
17. Use Simpson's rule to evaluate the integral of $f(x) = x - \sin x$ on the interval $0 \leq x \leq 4$ using eight partitions.
18. Use Simpson's rule to evaluate the integral of $f(x) = \cos x - x$ on the interval $0 \leq x \leq 4$ using 12 partitions.

Set B

19. Research the subject of physics and comment on three problems that involve distance, velocity, and acceleration.

20. Use the forward-difference algorithm to find the derivative of the $f(x) = x^3 - \cos 3x$ function on the interval $[0, 2]$ with increment $h = 0.1$.

21. Use the forward-backward-difference algorithm to find the derivative of the $f(x) = x^3 - \cos 3x$ function on the interval $[0, 2]$ with increment $h = 0.1$.

22. The theoretical derivative of the function in Questions 20 and 21 is $f'(x) = 3x^2 + 3\sin 3x$. Use this to calculate the error made by using both the forward-difference algorithm and the forward-backward difference algorithm to find the derivative of the function. Hint: for each value of x on the interval, calculate $f(x)$ and the three representations of $f'(x)$ for the true results, the forward-difference results, and the forward-backward-difference results.

23. Use the **rect** algorithm with 20 partitions to integrate the $f(x) = 3\sin 2x$ function on the $[0, \pi/2]$ interval. The true answer from the calculus is 3. Find the error made by using the **rect** algorithm.

24. Use the **trap** algorithm with 20 partitions to integrate the $f(x) = 3\sin 2x$ function on the $[0, \pi/2]$ interval. The true answer from the calculus is 3. Find the error made by using the **trap** algorithm.

25. Use the **simp** algorithm with 20 partitions to integrate the $f(x) = 3\sin 2x$ function on the $[0, \pi/2]$ interval. The true answer from the calculus is 3. Find the error made by using the **simp** algorithm.

26. Given the $g(x) = e^{-x}\sin x$ function defined on the $[0, 6]$ interval, find the numerical integral for 24 partitions using the following algorithms:
    a. **rectrule**
    b. **traprule**
    c. **simprule**

27. Given the $g(x) = e^{-x}\sin x$ function defined on the $[0, 6]$ interval, find the numerical derivative for 24 partitions using the following algorithms:
    a. **derivfn1**
    b. **derivfn2**

28. A particle moves with a velocity described by the $V(t) = 6t + 19t^2 - \cos t$ function on the time $[0, 3]$ interval.
    a. Using 60 partitions, calculate the acceleration using a numerical algorithm.
    b. Find numerically the distance traveled by the particle.

Set C

29. In subsection 17.3.3 we considered the $f(x) = x^2 + 2$ function defined on the $1 \le x \le 3$ interval. Divide the region into 16 partitions and find the area by Simpson's rule using a calculator.

30. Write a C main program that drives both **derivfn1** and **derivfn2** functions. The program should compute and compare the approximate derivative for the $f(x) = 2\sin 3x + 3\cos 2x$ function for $1 \le x \le 3$ in increments of 0.1.

31. Write a C main program to find the approximate integral of $f(x) = 3x - \cos 7x + 5$ for $0 \le x \le 8$.

32. Instead of using a closed-form function, modify the forward-backward-difference algorithm to accept an array of function values for data input and compute the derivative of this data.

33. Instead of using a closed-form function, modify the Simpson's rule algorithm to accept an array of function values for data input and compute the integral of this data.

34. Write a C program to read distance represented by 41 data points from a keyboard using the array index as the time subscript. Calculate and place the velocity data in an array indexed from 0 (for t_0) to 40 (for t_{40}).

18 Theoretical Perspectives in Computing

Do these clockwork gears know how to tell time?

After completing this chapter you should be able to do the following:

Learning Goals

- Define a finite-state machine
- Find the output of a finite-state machine for a given input string
- Construct a state table
- Construct a state graph
- Define a Turing machine
- Find the output of a given Turing machine based on an initial tape input
- Distinguish between a computable function and a Turing-computable function
- State the Church–Turing thesis
- Distinguish between solvable and unsolvable decision problems
- Describe the meaning of the halting problem
- Find Big-O expressions for algorithmic complexity
- Describe the complexities of linear and binary search
- Draw comparison trees for simple problems
- Distinguish between category P and category NP problems
- Describe the meaning of NP-complete problems

Chapter Activity

Design and write a C program to measure the computational complexity of several of the sorting schemes discussed in Chapter 16. The program generates a set of 5,000 random floating-point numbers and puts them in an array. The sorting algorithms include selection sort, insertion sort, quick sort, and bucket sort. Each method is a function that calculates the CPU time (in seconds) needed to do the sort, which is to be passed through the function by reference. A delay mechanism is included for each method to adjust the timing of a loop as needed to obtain a meaningful output for time. The results are produced by a single program execution.

18.1   FINITE-STATE AND TURING MACHINES

Introduction

Topics of theoretical computing parallel areas of computer science such as algorithm efficiency and complexity, programming languages, databases, and data communications. The foundations of computing center on the theory of computation, formal models of computation, and computational complexity. The fundamental question is: Which problems are computationally solvable?

You might be surprised to learn that computational solvability was conjectured and shown long before computers, as we know them, existed. Two mathematicians, the German Kurt Gödel and the British Alan Turing, had an impact on the question of solvability. In 1931 Gödel proved the existence of statements that are neither provable nor disprovable in any mathematical system that includes whole numbers and the operations of addition and multiplication. In 1936 Turing developed an abstract concept of the computers we use today. These two events in the 1930s were the beginning of the discipline called computer science and remain its theoretical basis.

PERSPECTIVE

A contemporary definition of theory in computer science and engineering must include the theory of computation, computational complexity, the analysis and synthesis of algorithms, formal languages, the syntax and semantics of programming languages, mechanical theorem proving, and the theory of numerical analysis and scientific computation.[1]

18.1.1 Finite-State Machines

Before investigating some of the details of the Gödel and Turing contributions to computer science, let's look at what is meant by a machine. Consider an ordinary vending machine, say, for postage stamps. The machine is in a waiting state when we approach it. It prompts us to deposit a certain amount of money, in this case $5.80 for a booklet of stamps. We insert the money and the item is dispensed, with change if necessary. During this sequence in our purchasing of a stamp booklet, we might hear the vending machine make various sounds as it goes through its operations and see information displayed such as "Deposit 35 cents more." After the transaction, the vending machine goes back to its waiting state until approached by the next customer, or possibly shuts off after a certain period of time.

In our example, the input consists of our selection of the stamp booklet and the money we deposit. The output consists of the stamp booklet (or no booklet) and possibly change. Furthermore, the machine has different states, determined by the customer's selection, the amount of money deposited, and the internal states of the machine. A deposit of $1.50 and a selection of a $4.00 booklet produce no booklet and either a prompt for more money or a return of $1.50. A deposit of $6.00 and a selection of a $4.00 booklet produce a booklet plus $2.00 change. Thus *Dispensing $4.00 booklet, Waiting, Off,* and *Quiescent* are some possible states.

Based on this example we see that the behavior of the vending machine could be represented by the following:

1. a finite number of predictable states
2. a set of inputs
3. a set of outputs

In addition, we see that the output at any point is a function of one of the states. Also, a new state of the machine is determined not only by the input but by the current state of the machine. That is,

$$\text{output} = f(\text{curr\_state})$$

and

$$\text{next\_state} = g(\text{curr\_state, input})$$

where f and g are functions and input, output, curr_state, and next_state are variables. These two functions, together with the set of possible inputs I, the set of possible outputs O, and the set of finite states S are part of the definition of a **finite-state machine**. Thus, specifying the sets I, O, and S together with the functions f and g fully describes a finite-state machine.

EXAMPLE 18.1–1

Problem

Let a finite-state machine be described according to the following: $I = \{0, 1\}$, $O = \{2, 3, 4\}$, and $S = \{x, y, z\}$. In addition,

$$f(x) = 3 \quad g(x, 0) = z \quad g(x, 1) = x$$
$$f(y) = 4 \quad g(y, 0) = x \quad g(y, 1) = z$$
$$f(z) = 2 \quad g(z, 0) = y \quad g(z, 1) = y$$

Let the initial state be y. Find the output for the input string 01101.

Reasoning

To find the solution, we create a new state based on the current state and input value. The initial state is y and the first input value from the string 01101 is 0. The output for the initial state is $f(y) = 4$.

Solution

The initial current state is y and the input is 0 from 01101. The output is

$$\text{output} \quad = f(y) \quad = 4$$

and the new state value is

$$\text{next\_state} \quad = g(y, 0) = x$$

The current state is now x and the new input value is 1 from 0*1*101. The output is

output = $f(x) = 3$

and the new state value is

next_state = $g(x, 1) = x$

The current state is now x and the new input value is 1 from 01*1*01. The output is

output = $f(x) = 3$

and the new state value is

next_state = $g(x, 1) = x$

The current state is now x and the new input value is 0 from 011*0*1. The output is

output = $f(x) = 3$

and the new state value is

next_state = $g(x, 0) = z$

The current state is now z and the new input value is 1 from 0110*1*. The output is

output = $f(z) = 2$

and the new state value is

next_state = $g(z, 1) = y$

The curr_state variable is now y but there is no further input value so the next_state variable cannot be calculated, the possible output of 4 is ignored, and the process ends. Thus for the given finite-state machine with input string 01101, the resulting output is 43332.

Test
Reconstruct these steps to confirm that the output is correct.

The finite-state machine in Example 18.1–1 can be described efficiently by a **state table**, as shown in Table 18.1–1.

Using Table 18.1–1, which is equivalent to Example 18.1–1, we can calculate the output function f and the new state function g for any input value from a string. •

Table 18.1–1 A Finite-State Machine

CURR_STATE VALUE	OUTPUT VALUE	NEXT_STATE VALUES INPUT VALUES	
		0	1
x	3	z	x
y	4	x	z
z	2	y	y

EXAMPLE 18.1–2

Problem

Use Table 18.1–1 to calculate the output for the input string 1010. The initial state is z.

Reasoning

We use Table 18.1–1 exclusively to calculate output values for the stated input. The results are given in an abbreviated form. We use a fictitious, discrete time base to distinguish the cycles. Note that the value of next_state at time t is the same as the value of curr_state at time $t + 1$.

Solution

Time $t = 0$ (initial state)

	curr_state:	z	and	input:	1
yields	output:	2	and	next_state:	y

Time $t = 1$

	curr_state:	y	and	input:	0
yields	output:	4	and	next_state:	x

Time $t = 2$

	curr_state:	x	and	input:	1
yields	output:	3	and	next_state:	x

Time $t = 3$

	curr_state:	x	and	input:	0
yields	output:	3	and	next_state:	z

Time $t = 4$

	curr_state:	z	and	input:	–
yields	output:	–	and	next_state:	–

Thus for an input string 1010, the output string becomes 2433.

Test

Duplicate these steps to confirm that the output is correct.   ●

18.1.2 Graphs and Finite-State Machines

We can construct a visual representation of a state table by means of a directed graph. A **graph** consists of a set of **nodes** (dots or circles) together with a set of **edges** (arcs or lines) so that each edge connects two nodes. A **directed graph** consists of a set of nodes (dots or circles) together with a set of edges (arcs or lines) so that each edge is connected in a direction *from* one node *to* another node. The direction is shown by an arrow. Figure 18.1–1 is a typical five-node directed graph with four edges. Note that a node need not have any edges connected to it.

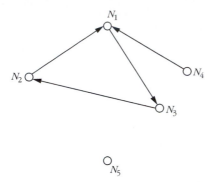

Figure 18.1–1 Directed graph of five nodes

A finite-state machine can be represented by a directed graph. One way to do this is to represent each state by a node. Recall that each state specifies an output value by its output function, $output = f(\text{curr\_state})$, so it is convenient to represent the output value for each state within the node. Each current state can be associated with the possible input values. Using this idea, we can draw an edge from a current state to a next state based on the particular input value. The resulting graph is called a **state graph**. For the finite-state machine described in Example 18.1–1, the two input values are 0 and 1 with three states x, y, and z. Putting these ideas together, we can design a directed graph of three nodes in which each node has at least one edge (one for each input value) drawn from it. This is shown in Figure 18.1–2. Notice that each node has an identification in the form of $state\backslash output$ that describes the relationship between a state and its corresponding output.

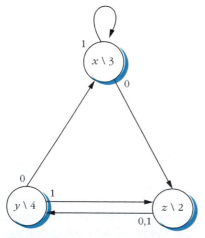

Figure 18.1–2 State graph from Table 18.1–1

EXAMPLE 18.1–3

Problem

Use the directed graph in Figure 18.1–2 to calculate the output of the finite-state machine for the input string 00110. Assume that the initial state is x.

Reasoning

The calculation begins at the node labeled x and we follow the directed graph for each current state and input.

Solution

The initial state is x, which has an output of 3.

Use x as the state. For input equal to 0 from the string **0**0110, the next state is z, which has an output of 2.

Use z as the state. For input equal to 0 from the string 0**0**110, the next state is y, which has an output of 4.

Use y as the state. For input equal to 1 from the string 00**1**10, the next state is z, which has an output of 2.

Use z as the state. For input equal to 1 from the string 001**1**0, the next state is y, which has an output of 4.

Use y as the state. For input equal to 0 from the string 0011**0** the next state is x. Because there is no input value left, the normal output of state x is not output, and the process terminates.

Therefore, the bit string 00110 produces an output of 32424.

Test

Check the result by using the state graph or the state table.   ●

As we have seen, there are several representations of a finite-state machine. We began with a functional definition that is equivalent to a state table. The state table, in turn, is equivalent to the state graph. The five components (input, output, states, output function, and state function) describe a unique finite-state machine. A change in any one of the five components defines a different machine.

When a machine is confined to only an input set, a state set, and the state transfer function,

$$\text{next\_state} = g(\text{curr\_state}, \text{input})$$

with no output function, it is called a **finite-state automaton** (pronounced aw-TOM-a-ton). We call more than one such machine **finite-state automata** (pronounced aw-TOM-a-tah).

18.1.3 Turing Machines

Although finite-state machines can direct action based on input and current state, they lack one important element that would make them useful as a calculating device—memory. Also, a finite-state machine cannot reread its input. As we saw in Section 18.1.2, input is presented as a data stream and, once read, there is no way to jump back to previous input information. In 1936 Alan Turing proposed a finite-state machine with infinite memory that had the additional capability of

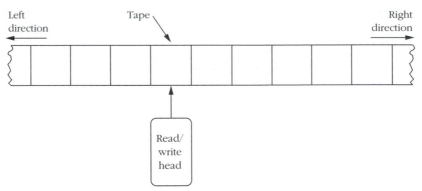

Figure 18.1–3   Turing Machine

rereading, overwriting, and erasing its input. This theoretical machine became known as a **Turing machine** and it embodies a finite-state machine together with an infinitely long tape. The tape is partitioned into equal-sized cells of which each cell can contain a single character. The characters are elements of a finite set that includes a blank and forms an **alphabet** for the machine.

We can imagine a Turing machine as a finite-state machine with a read/write sensor attached to it. This sensor can read from or write to the infinite tape one cell at a time, as shown in Figure 18.1–3. At any given time the tape holds a finite number of cells that are not blank. Here is how the Turing machine works. At a relative time t, we assume that the machine is in a current state; the sensor reads one cell. At time $t + 1$ the sensor writes an alphabetic character to the cell that was read, the machine transfers control to the next state, and the sensor moves to an adjacent (left or right) cell on the tape. The process continues until nothing happens and the machine halts.

A Turing machine can read and write characters of an alphabet (which must include a blank), have a current state and a next state, and move in a direction (left or right). This allows us to represent the possible actions by a 5-tuple. We generalize this as

$$(\ sc, rd, wr, sn, dr\ )$$

where sc is the current state, rd is read, wr is write, sn is the next state, and dr indicates the direction of the tape. A set of possible 5-tuples defines a Turing machine. Recall the finite-state machine described in Table 18.1–1. The three states are given as x, y, and z with possible input (read) values of 0 and 1. The output (write) values are 2, 3, and 4. If a blank is included as a possible read value, we can construct a Turing machine analogous to the machine in Table 18.1–1. This will generate at most nine (three read values for each of the three states) possible 5-tuples. Let b' denote a blank character. We describe this Turing machine as

$$(\ x, 0, 3, z, L\ )\quad (\ x, 1, 3, x, L\ )\quad (\ x, b', b', x, R\ )$$
$$(\ y, 0, 4, x, L\ )\quad (\ y, 1, 4, z, L\ )\quad (\ y, b', b', y, R\ )$$
$$(\ z, 0, 2, y, L\ )\quad (\ z, 1, 2, y, L\ )\quad (\ z, b', b', z, R\ )$$

It should be clear that the character set is $\{b, 0, 1, 2, 3, 4\}$, which constitutes the alphabet for this Turing machine. Also, the machine halts and establishes a **final state** when it encounters a state and a read value (sc and rd) that do not conform to one of the 5-tuples (nine patterns in this case) that describe the Turing machine. As with finite-state machines, an input string is converted to an output string. We illustrate this in the next example.

EXAMPLE 18.1−4

Problem

A Turing machine is described according to the nine 5-tuples we just discussed. Determine the final state of the machine for an initial tape configuration of

$$\ldots b\, b\, 1\, 0\, 1\, 0\, b\, b \ldots$$

when the initial state is z.

Reasoning

We begin reading from the left with an initial state of z and initial input 1. The arrow shows the sensor. The rules of the machine are determined by the nine 5-tuples just mentioned.

Solution

We begin with the initial tape.

..	..	b	b	1	0	1	0	b	b	..
				↑						

Initial cycle ($t = 0$): The symbol 1 is read at state z.

Next cycle ($t = 1$): According to the machine definition, write a 2 on the tape, jump to state y, and move the tape to the left. This results in an updated tape and sensor position.

..	..	b	b	2	0	1	0	b	b	..
					↑					

The symbol 0 is read at state y.

Next cycle ($t = 2$): According to the machine definition, write a 4 on the tape, jump to state x, and move the tape to the left. This results in an updated tape and sensor position.

..	..	b	b	2	4	1	0	b	b	..
						↑				

The symbol 1 is read at state x.

Next cycle ($t = 3$): According to the machine definition, write a 3 on the tape, retain state x, and move the tape to the left. This results in an updated tape and sensor position.

The symbol 0 is read at state x.

Next cycle ($t = 4$): According to the machine definition, write a 3 on the tape, jump to state z, and move the tape to the left. This results in an updated tape and sensor position.

The symbol $b̸$ is read at state z.

Next cycle ($t = 5$): According to the machine definition, write a $b̸$ on the tape, stay at state z, and move to the *right*. This results in an updated tape and sensor position.

The symbol 3 is read at state z. Since 3 is not in the input set of any of the 5-tuples, the process halts. Therefore, the final state is

Test
Reconstruct the preceding steps using the nine 5-tuples or the information from Table 18.1–1 to show that the final state is correct.   •

Note that the result of the Turing machine of Example 18.1–4 is the same as the finite-state machine of Example 18.1–2.

18.1.4 Turing Machines and Computability

We can think of a Turing machine as a finite-state machine used to compute a function. Let u and v each represent a string of symbols for the alphabet of the machine. Let a Turing machine be the function τ (Greek lowercase tau) so that

$$v = \tau(u)$$

where u is an input string and v is the resulting output string. When elements of u and v can be taken exclusively from a subset of the natural numbers $\{0, 1, 2, 3, \ldots\}$, τ is a **discrete numerical function**. If there is a method with which we can calculate the output of a function for a given input, the function is called a **computable function**. When elements are restricted to the binary set $\{0, 1\}$, τ is a **binary function**. When a discrete numerical function is evaluated by a Turing machine, the function is called a **Turing-computable function**. The terms *Turing-computable* and *computable* are synonymous.

An infinite number of different Turing machines can evaluate the function τ. All that is needed for each is to specify the current and next states, the read and write function, and the direction associated with the specific machine. The question arises, however, whether a single machine exists that can be used to represent all Turing machines capable of evaluating any Turing-computable function. Computer scientists have shown that yes, such a machine is possible. One machine can be designed to hold the parameters of all other possible Turing machines so that for *any* given input, this machine can evaluate *any* computable function. We call this machine the **universal Turing machine** and give it the symbol T (Greek uppercase tau). Thus Turing-computable functions can be represented as

$$v = \mathrm{T}(u)$$

where u is the input string and v is the output string. Although not as efficient, the universal Turing machine equals the calculating ability of any computer, including the most sophisticated computers to date. Anything a modern computer can do, a Turing machine can also do. Likewise, anything a Turing machine cannot do, a modern computer cannot do either. The universal Turing machine is essential to the theory of computation and we leave it for more advanced studies of this subject.

PERSPECTIVE

The concept of the universal Turing machine underlies much of computing. It is basic to the interchangeability of hardware and software, the existence of high-level computer languages, and the ubiquity of mistakes in programs.[2]

A Turing machine exemplifies a set of rules based on the five components of its 5-tuple (*sc, rd, sn, wr, dr*). These rules describe an *algorithm* that is used to evaluate Turing-computable functions. In 1937 mathematician Alonzo Church proposed that a necessary and sufficient condition for an algorithm to compute a discrete numerical function is that it be a Turing-computable function. This claim, called **Church's thesis** or the **Church–Turing thesis,** is a basis for the equivalence of algorithmic procedures and computing machines. The thesis conjectures that the set of computable functions includes all functions that can be computed by some formal machine (a Turing machine) and includes all functions that can be computed by an algorithm. For this reason, words such as *computable, mechanical,* and *algorithmic* can be considered equivalent in the context of Church's thesis. And it follows that all programming languages compute the same set of functions.

Because of the Church–Turing thesis, we can determine whether a function is computable by finding an algorithm to evaluate it. If an algorithm does not exist (cannot be executed by a Turing machine), the function is not computable. Problems formulated to find an algorithm that computes such functions are called **decision problems** and they may or may not have solutions. If we can prove that an algorithm exists to solve a particular decision problem, then the problem is **solvable**. If we can prove that no algorithm exists to solve the decision problem, then the problem is **unsolvable**. If neither of these two proofs can be shown, the decision problem is **undecidable**.

In terms of computability theory, we try to group similar forms of decision problems into classes so that the solvability of a category or set of problems can be determined by a single proof. For example, suppose we are given *any* Turing machine and *any* string *u* so that the tape of the Turing machine contains *u*. Is there an algorithm that can decide whether or not the Turing machine halts? This is the classic **halting problem** that has been proven to be *unsolvable.*

The significance of the halting problem is that it asks the question whether one algorithm exists that solves all problems in that category of problems. This is unsolvable. Consequently, all discrete numerical functions categorized by this decision problem are not computable. Whereas an individual problem (a specific Turing machine and a specific string) may have a solution, the set of all such problems does not.

EXERCISES 18.1

Concept Check
Answer statements 1 through 4 with true *or* false.
1. An edge of a graph always joins two nodes.
2. A Turing machine is an example of one of the first digital computers.
3. The output of a binary function is restricted to the set $\{0, 1\}$.
4. The Church–Turing thesis is one of the important theorems in mathematical computing.

For statements 5 through 8 choose the answer that best completes the statement.
5. Sets of input, output, current states, with output and next_state functions describe
   a. a Turing machine
   b. a finite-state machine
   c. an automaton
   d. a state graph
6. A response to a Turing machine is
   a. next_state and direction
   b. output and next_state
   c. output, next_state, and direction
   d. input and output

7. Decision problems
    a. may never be solved
    b. can always be solved
    c. remain undecided
    d. are indeterminate
8. The search for an algorithm to determine whether a Turing machine halts is called
    a. automata theory
    b. the halting problem
    c. graph theory
    d. computability

For statements 9 through 12 fill in the blanks with the right word.

9. Problems formulated to determine whether an algorithm exists to solve them are called _____.
10. Turing-computable functions and their relationship to computing a discrete numerical function are the basis of _____.
11. The elements of a finite-state machine are _____.
12. The question of whether an algorithm exists that halts a Turing machine is called the _____.

Set A

Solve each of the following problems.

13. For the finite-state machine in Example 18.1–1, calculate the output bit stream when the input data stream is 010.
14. Repeat Question 13 when the input data stream is 101101.
15. For the finite-state machine in the state table of Table 18.1–1, calculate the output bit stream when the input data stream is 011.
16. Repeat Question 15 when the input data stream is 01101101.
17. For the finite-state machine in Figure 18.1–2, calculate the output bit stream when the input data stream is 110.
18. Repeat Question 17 when the input data stream is 10101011.

Set B

19. Consider the Turing machine described by the set of 5-tuples in subsection 18.1.3. Determine the final state (tape status) when the initial tape configuration is . . . b́ b́ 0 0 b́ b́. . . , the initial state is x, and the initial input is the first nonblank symbol from the left.
20. Repeat Question 19 when the initial tape configuration of the Turing machine is . . . b́ b́ 0 1 0 1 b́ b́. . . .
21. Repeat question 19 when the initial tape configuration of the Turing machine is . . . b́ b́ 0 1 1 0 1 b́ b́. . . and the initial state is y.
22. Repeat question 19 when the initial tape configuration of the Turing machine is . . . b́ b́ 1 1 0 1 0 0 1 b́ b́. . . and the initial state is z.
23. Repeat question 19 when the initial tape configuration of the Turing machine is . . . b́ b́ 1 1 0 1 0 0 1 b́ b́. . . , the initial state is z, but the first symbol read is the first blank on the left.

24. Repeat question 19 when the initial tape configuration of the Turing machine is . . . b̸ b̸ 1 1 0 1 0 0 1 b̸ b̸. . . , the initial state is z, but the first symbol read is the first blank on the right.
25. Describe the difference between a computable function and a Turing-computable function.
26. Explain the meaning of a decision problem.
27. Explain how algorithms relate to computable functions.

Set C

28. Consider the Church–Turing thesis. What does it mean?
29. Again consider the Church–Turing thesis. Is it a mathematical theorem; that is, is it a provable statement? If so, who proved it and when? If it is not a theorem, why is so much credence given to it?
30. Write a C program to emulate the state table of Table 18.1–1.
31. Write a C program to emulate the Turing machine in subsection 18.1.3.

18.2   ALGORITHMIC EFFICIENCY AND COMPLEXITY

Introduction

In Section 18.1 we investigate the solvability of problems. Specifically, if an algorithm can be found to solve a problem or a category of problems, the problem is solvable and functions associated with the problem are computable. The universal Turing machine is the most general computational device and is at least as good, but not as efficient, as all possible computers. In the context of the Church–Turing thesis, terms such as *computable functions, algorithmic solutions,* and *mechanical processes* have the same meaning.

The fact that there is an algorithm to solve a problem does not mean that it is the most effective, the most efficient, or the best solution. Instead there may be many, perhaps an infinite number of algorithms to solve the same problem. A simple algorithm may not be efficient. A complex algorithm can be highly efficient. Next, we explore some of the concepts underlying algorithm efficiency and their effect on the problems they are intended to solve.

18.2.1 Two Search Algorithms

In Section 16.1 we discussed two algorithms for linear search and binary search, respectively, to find a specific item in a list of items based on a comparison of their keys. The answer to the question, "Does an algorithm exist that solves the problem?" is yes: The functions that represent the problem are computable by a universal Turing machine. As a result, these functions are computable by any computer.

We might ask which of the two different algorithms is better. Recall that the problem of finding an element in a list is immediately complicated by the fact that for the binary search algorithm, all elements in the list must be ordered according to a specified key. The linear search algorithm has no such requirement. For example, suppose we show that the binary search algorithm is faster than the linear search algorithm when the ordered list is large enough. Does this suggest that the binary search algorithm is better? Not necessarily. We said that a binary search needs an *ordered* list. If we have a random list of elements, the binary search algorithm is not even applicable. Therefore, in this case the linear search algorithm would be better. The point is that there is at least one algorithm that makes the generalized search problem solvable or computable. From a decidability perspective, a solution exists. From a complexity perspective, we must find out which is more efficient.

We discussed array-based, iterative algorithms for the linear and binary search algorithms in Section 16.1. Suppose we have an ordered list of a large number (say 12,000 maximum) of elements in an array called listinfo. We want to test both these algorithms for the time each algorithm needs to find a target value. To do this we modify the linear and binary search algorithms so that we find the time to do the search by clocking the relative time at the start of each process and the relative time at the end of each process. The difference between the start time and the end time is the absolute time it takes for each algorithm to do the search. We add a time delay to each search loop to exaggerate the time so that it is measurable in seconds. This is shown in Program 18.2–1.

PROGRAM 18.2–1

```
/***********************************************************************
*  Title:        time comparisons of search algorithms               *
*  Filename:     comptime.c                                          *
*                                                                    *
*  Description: This program generates an ordered list of elements. A search by comparison *
*               of keys is performed using linear search and binary search methods.  A     *
*               time delay is placed in the search loop to exaggerate the time needed      *
*               to execute the algorithm.                            *
*                                                                    *
*  Input:        value of target                                     *
*  Output:       location of target key in a successful search, execution time  *
*  Process:      generate list, do linear search, do binary search   *
*                                                                    *
*  Written  by: ...                              Date:  ...          *
***********************************************************************/

#include  <stdio.h>
#include  <time.h>

#define  MAX    12000                /*  Maximum number of elements in list  */

#define  DELAY 100000                /*  <<<<  Delay time ... a function of hardware  */
                                     /*  NOTE:  To be adjusted by user  */

long int    listinfo[MAX];           /*  Global declaration of listinfo  */
int         size;                    /*  Logical size of list  */
```

```
int generate_list        ( void );                              /*  Function prototypes  */
int linear_search_time ( int   target,   double  *timeptr );
int binary_search_time ( int   target,   int  low,   int  high,   double  *timeptr );


int main ( )                                                     /*  Begin main  */
{
  int    target,                              /*  Value of target sought in list  */
         low,  high;                          /*  Low and high bounds on interval  */

  int    location;                        /*  Index location where target is found  */
  double time1;                                    /*  Time to do search  */

  size  =  generate_list( );          /*  Function call to generate list of elements  */

  printf (  "\n\nEnter target value>:  " );                      /*  Get target value  */
  scanf (  "%d",   &target );


  location  =  linear_search_time (  target,  &time1 );      /*  Function call for  */
                                                             /*  linear search  */


  if ( location != -1 )
      printf ( "\n\nThe location of linear search is: %6d",   location  );
  else
      printf ( "\n\tTarget not found in list. " );

  printf ( "\n\nThe time for a  linear search is: %6.2f", time1 );     /*  Print time  */


  low = 0;
  location  =  binary_search_time ( target, low, size-1, &time1 );   /*  Function call  */
                                                               /*  to binary search  */
  if ( location != -1 )
      printf ( "\n\nThe location of binary search is: %6d", location  );
  else
      printf ( "\n\tTarget not found in list. " );

  printf ( "\n\nThe time for a  binary search is: %6.2f", time1 );     /*  Print time  */

  printf (  "\n\n\n\t\t\t\tGood-Bye!\n");

  return ( 0 );
}                                                               /*  End main  */
```

```
/**************************************************************************
*   Function name:      generate_list                                    *
*   Description:        Generate an ordered list of elements by an arbitrary formula where  *
*                       the size is chosen by the user.                  *
*                                                                        *
*   Input parameters:  none                                              *
*   Output parameters: none                                              *
*   Return value:       size                                             *
***************************************************************************/

int  generate_list ( void )
{
    int  i;

    printf ( "\nEnter size of list for size less than %6d>:  ", MAX );
    scanf ( "%d",  &size );
    while ( size < 1  ||  size > MAX )  {
       printf ( "\n\n\t\tERROR: size incorrect! \n" );
       printf ( " \nEnter size of list for size less than %6d>:  ",  MAX );
       scanf ( "%d", &size );
    }

    for (  i=0;  i < size;  ++ i )
        listinfo[ i ]  =  5*i + 3;              /* <<< Arbitrary formula to initialize list */

    return ( size );
}


/**************************************************************************
*   Function name:      linear_search_time                               *
*   Description:        Perform a linear search through an unordered list, returning the  *
*                       location of the target item.  If the item is not found, the function *
*                       returns a value of -1.  Calculate the time required to do the   *
*                       execution.                                       *
*                                                                        *
*   Input parameters:  target                                           *
*   Output parameters: CPU time                                         *
*   Return value:       location of item containing target key, or -1 if item not found *
***************************************************************************/

int linear_search_time ( int target, double *timeptr )
{
    int      loc;                                           /* Location of item in list */
    long int i;
    time_t   start,  end;          /* Time type variables for library header file  time.h */

    printf ( "\n\n\tDoing linear search.  Please wait ... " );
```

```
    start  =  time ( NULL );                          /* Function  time  from  time.h  file  */
    for (  loc  =  0;
           loc  <  size   &&   listinfo[ loc ]  != target;
           loc++  )

       for ( i=0;  i < DELAY;  i++ ) ;                         /* Delay loop  */
    ;                                                    /* Just keep searching  */

    end  =  time ( NULL );                          /* Function  time  from  time.h  file  */
    *timeptr  =  difftime ( end,  start );  /* Time difference function in  time.h file  */

    if (  listinfo[ loc ]   ==  target )                   /* Found target item?  */
        return ( loc );                          /* Yes, return the loc of the item  */
    else
        return ( -1 );                                /* No, set function to  -1  */
}




/**********************************************************************************************
 * Function name:       binary_search_time                                                   *
 * Description:         Perform a binary search through an ordered list, returning the       *
 *                      location of the target item.  If the item is not found, the function *
 *                      returns a value of -1.  Calculate the time needed to do the search.  *
 *                                                                                           *
 * Input parameters:    target, low and high values                                         *
 * Output parameters:   CPU time                                                             *
 * Return value:        location of item containing key, or -1 if item not found            *
 **********************************************************************************************/

int binary_search_time ( int target, int low, int high, double *timeptr )
{
    int      middle;
    long int i;
    time_t   start, end;          /* Time type variables for library header file  time.h  */

    printf ( "\n\n\n\tDoing binary search.  Please wait ... " );

    start  =  time ( NULL );                          /* Function  time  from  time.h  file  */
    while ( low  <=  high )   {           /* Stop searching when low overtakes high  */

      for ( i=0; i < DELAY; i++ ) ;                              /* Delay loop  */

      middle  =  ( low + high ) / 2;
```

```
    if ( listinfo[ middle ]  ==  target  ) {
        end      = time ( NULL );
        *timeptr = difftime ( end,  start );
        return ( middle );                    /* Item found, return its location  */
    }
    else if (  listinfo[middle] < target )
        low  = middle + 1;                    /* Item is in "upper" half of list  */
    else
        high  = middle - 1;                   /* Item is in "lower" half of list  */
}                                             /*  End while  */

end      = time ( NULL );                     /* Function time  from  time.h  file  */
*timeptr = difftime ( end, start );   /* Time difference function in  time.h  file  */

return ( -1 );                                /* Item not found  */
}
```

When Program 18.2–1 is run on a 486/33 computer with n = 8000 elements, target key = 2003, and DELAY = 1,000,000, the *delayed* execution times are 174 seconds for linear search and six seconds for binary search. For an unsuccessful search on 8000 elements with DELAY = 100,000, the *delayed* execution times are 392 seconds for linear search and one second for binary search. Based on a comparison of keys, the binary search algorithm is clearly superior to the linear search algorithm.

18.2.2 Big-O Notation

It is hard to judge the relative efficiency of algorithms accurately based on a computer's speed of execution. Some algorithms work differently on different machines. Therefore, instead of basing our judgment on a particular computer's speed of execution, we look at the number of steps needed to do the job. This makes algorithmic efficiency independent of the computer used to execute the algorithm.

The data set of Program 18.2–1 uses 8000 elements and binary search appears to be better than linear search. Would we reach the same conclusion if the list had only four elements? How about if it had 40,000,000 elements? The purpose of any computer is to simplify human tasks. For lists as small as four items, a child can find out if an item is on the list. As the lists become longer, however, our (human) efficiency diminishes and computational devices become more important.

One way to measure the behavior of algorithms is by calculating the number of steps needed on a given data set and then increasing without bounds the number of items in the set. In essence, we represent the number of steps for a particular algorithm to operate on n items as a function f of n. That is, for n items, the evaluation of $f(n)$ is the number of steps needed. The behavior of the algorithm is now represented by the function. For example,

$$f(n) = n^2/4 + n/2 - 3$$

might represent the behavior of an algorithm; we recognize function f as a quadratic function defined for integers $n \geq 1$. Notice that for small values of n, the linear and constant terms have more effect on the function than for large values of n.

EXAMPLE 18.2–1

Problem
Evaluate $f(n) = n2/4 + n/2 - 3$ for $n = 4, 40, 400$, and 4000.

Reasoning
We substitute each value of n in the function and then evaluate $f(n)$ for the given numbers.

Solution
Substitute for n and calculate $f(n)$.

$$
\begin{aligned}
f(4) &= 4^2/4 &+ 4/2 &- 3 &= 16/4 &+ 2 &- 3 &= 3 \\
f(40) &= 40^2/4 &+ 40/2 &- 3 &= 1600/4 &+ 20 &- 3 &= 417 \\
f(400) &= 400^2/4 &+ 400/2 &- 3 &= 160000/4 &+ 200 &- 3 &= 40197 \\
f(4000) &= 4000^2/4 &+ 4000/2 &- 3 &= 16000000/4 &+ 2000 &- 3 &= 4001997
\end{aligned}
$$

Test
Recalculate function f for each n.

The significance of Example 18.2–1 is that as the value of n becomes larger, the linear term $+n/2$ and the constant term -3 have a negligible effect on the value of the function. The function behaves more like the quadratic term n^2. If we create a function $g(n) = n^2$, we can then say that $f(n)$ behaves like $g(n)$ as n becomes very large. Here is a description of this idea.

Let functions f and g each be functions of positive integers n, and let c be any *positive* real number. If the absolute value of the ratio $f(n)/g(n)$ approaches some constant c as n increases without bound, then f is the same **order of magnitude** as g.

The order of magnitude of functions is usually represented in what is called **Big-O** notation by writing $\boldsymbol{f(n) = O(g(n))}$, which reads "function $f(n)$ is of the order of function $g(n)$." When applying this concept to a specific algorithm, we refer to the order of magnitude as the **complexity** of the algorithm and say that the complexity of the algorithm is of order $g(n)$.

EXAMPLE 18.2–2

Problem
Prove that the order of magnitude of the function $f(n) = n^2/4 + n/2 - 3$ from Example 18.2–1 is $g(n) = n^2$.

Reasoning

We use both functions for the definition of order of magnitude in this example.

Solution

First, find the absolute value of the ratio of $f(n)/g(n)$ and then simplify where possible. This results in

$$|f(n)/g(n)| = \left| \frac{(n^2/4 + n/2 - 3)}{n^2} \right|$$

$$= |\tfrac{1}{4} + 1/2n - 3/n^2|$$

Now let n increase without bound. As n becomes very large (approaches infinity), the term $\frac{1}{4}$ does not change, the term $1/2n$ approaches 0, and the term $3/n^2$ also approaches 0. Therefore, for very large n values,

$$\left| \frac{f(n)}{g(n)} \right| = |\tfrac{1}{4} + 0 - 0| = |\tfrac{1}{4}| = \tfrac{1}{4}$$

Because $\frac{1}{4}$ is a positive real number, the description is satisfied and the function $f(n) = n^2/4 + n/2 - 3$ is the same order of magnitude as $g(n) = n^2$. That is, $f = O(g)$.

Test

Example 18.2–1 shows how the concept of Big O can be verified for this example.

Note that if in Example 18.2–2 the function f represents an algorithm, we would say that the complexity of the algorithm is $O(n^2)$.

A comment about Example 18.2–2: We asked to show that function f was $O(g)$ when we were given function g. Function g is usually not given. In these cases we often try appropriate functions that satisfy the definition. Also, there is no guarantee that such a function can be found. We illustrate this next.

BEFORE YOU GO ON	**Query:** What is the meaning of $O(1)$?
	RESPONSE: For a function f to be $O(1)$ implies that $g(n) = 1$, meaning that $|f(n)/g(n)| = |f(n)/1| = $ constant. Therefore, $f(n)$ is a constant.

EXAMPLE 18.2–3

Problem

Find the order of magnitude of $f(n) = 5 * \lg n - 4 * n^3 + 7 * 2^n - 6 * \cos(n^2)$ where $\lg n$ means $log_2 n$.

Reasoning

In this case we are not given $g(n)$. The problem is to find a function g so that function f is approximately the "same size" as function g when n becomes very large. To do this, first observe that for any n, the magnitude of the cosine function of n never exceeds unity. Also, either by familiarity with functions or by calculation we know that logarithms of positive integers n are always less than powers of n and less than any exponential of n. Still, we may not know how the power of these numbers and the exponential of these numbers compare with each other. We guess that for a sufficiently large n, 2^n will become larger than n^3. Therefore, we try $g(n) = 2^n$.

Solution
First find the ratio of the given $f(n)$ to the assumed $g(n)$. In absolute value

$$\left|\frac{f(n)}{g(n)}\right| = |[5 * \lg n - 4 * n^3 + 7 * 2^n - 6 * \cos(n^2)]/[2^n]|$$

$$= \left|5\left(\frac{\lg n}{2^n}\right) - 4\left(\frac{n^3}{2^n}\right) + 7\left(\frac{2^n}{2^n}\right) - 6\left(\frac{\cos(n^2)}{2^n}\right)\right|$$

To compute the ratio we let n be an arbitrary number, say 8. Then $2^8 = 256, \lg 8 = 3, 8^3 = 512$, and $\cos(8^2) = 0.391857$. Therefore,

$$\left|\frac{f(8)}{g(8)}\right| = \left|5\left(\frac{\lg 8}{2^8}\right) - 4\left(\frac{8^3}{2^8}\right) + 7\left(\frac{2^8}{2^8}\right) - 6\left(\frac{\cos(8^2)}{2^8}\right)\right|$$

$$= \left|5\left(\frac{3}{256}\right) - 4\left(\frac{512}{256}\right) + 7\left(\frac{256}{256}\right) - 6\left(\frac{0.391857}{256}\right)\right|$$

The numerical evaluation of this expression is not important. The *ratios,* shown inside the parentheses are important. Observe that the first and fourth ratios are relatively small, and the third ratio is 1. But the second ratio is greater than 1. Does n^3 overpower 2^n? Let's see what happens for larger values of n.

Suppose we double the value of n to 16. Then $2^{16} = 65536, \lg 16 = 4, 16^3 = 4096$, and $\cos(16^2) = -0.039791$. Therefore,

$$\left|\frac{f(16)}{g(16)}\right| = \left|5\left(\frac{\lg 16}{2^{16}}\right) - 4\left(\frac{16^3}{2^{16}}\right) + 7\left(\frac{2^{16}}{2^{16}}\right) - 6\left(\frac{\cos(16^2)}{2^{16}}\right)\right|$$

$$= \left|5\left(\frac{4}{65536}\right) - 4\left(\frac{4096}{65536}\right) + 7\left(\frac{65536}{65536}\right) - 6\left(\frac{-0.039791}{65536}\right)\right|$$

Observe that the first and fourth ratios are now very small, and the third ratio is still 1. The second ratio, however, is now *less than* 1, leading us to believe that n^3 does *not* overpower 2^n. Thus as n increases without bound, we have

$$\left|\left(\frac{f(n)}{g(n)}\right)\right| = \left|5\left(\frac{\lg n}{2^n}\right) - 4\left(\frac{n^3}{2^n}\right) + 7\left(\frac{2^n}{2^n}\right) - 6\left(\frac{\cos(n^2)}{2^n}\right)\right|$$

$$= |0 - 0 + 7 - 0|$$

$$= |7| = 7$$

which is a positive real number. Therefore, $f = O(g)$ and the function $f(n) = 5 * \lg n - 4 * n^3 + 7 * 2^n - 6 * \cos(n^2)$ behaves like $g(n) = 2^n$ for very large values of n.

Test
Further calculation tells us that this result is correct. Thus any algorithm whose steps are described by the function

$$f(n) = 5 * \lg n - 4 * n^3 + 7 * 2^n - 6 * \cos(n^2)$$

would have a complexity of order 2^n.   •

18.2.3 Analysis of Search Algorithms

It is often hard to find a function that exactly describes the number of steps needed to solve a problem. One way is to count all comparisons and all assignments related to the algorithm for one item, then two items, then three items, ..., until *n* items. We can then create a function by describing the ordered pairs in the table. Table 18.2–1 is such an example for a fictitious algorithm.

We interpret this table by looking at ordered pairs. For example, the ordered pair (4,7) shows that to process four items we need seven comparisons, whereas the ordered pair (12,19) shows that to process 12 items we need 19 assignments. It may be impossible to predict the complexity of an algorithm based solely on this method.

Before investigating the details of complexity for linear and binary search, let's consider how comparisons are made for an iterative linear search. The algorithm starts at the beginning of the list and systematically visits each node or element to determine if the key of the node matches the target. If a match is found, the algorithm ends with the node identified. If no match is found, the algorithm proceeds to the next node. The process is repeated until one of two things happens: (1) the target is found, the node is identified, and the algorithm terminates, or (2) the search exhausts the list, the target is not found, and the algorithm ends with an appropriate indication. Note that for both cases, the algorithm *halts*.

Figure 18.2–1 illustrates the search process with a graph called a **comparison tree**. The nodes of the graph represent the values of each key. Here we label these nodes randomly as 4, 8, 6, and 2 since linear search does not need an ordered structure. Assuming that 4 is the first key value, it becomes the root of the

Table 18.2–1 Functions for a
Fictitious Algorithm's Complexity

n	COMPARISONS	ASSIGNMENTS
1	1	2
2	4	6
4	7	9
8	12	14
12	18	19
16	24	73

Root

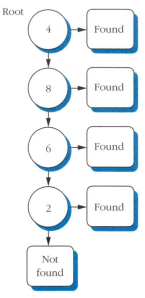

Figure 18.2–1 Comparison tree for linear search with four elements

tree and the beginning of the list. The leaves represent the end of the algorithm. The leaves to the right of each node represent the match of the key with the target and are labeled accordingly. The final leaf indicates that a match was not found and so is labeled NF.

Now we can see from Figure 18.2–1 that a linear search can be successful after 1, 2, 3, or 4 comparisons. When we analyze linear search, we find that the best case with success is one comparison, when the key matching the target is the first element, 4. The worst case with success is four comparisons when the key matching the target is the last element, 2. The average number of comparisons for a successful linear search is

$$\frac{1 + 2 + 3 + 4}{4} = \frac{10}{4} = 2.5$$

comparisons.

The only way to make a linear search unsuccessful is by traversing all nodes and ending at leaf NF. For this search there are four comparisons. Until now we have ignored the comparisons made inside the loop structure. If we consider the loop structure, a comparison is made before each node's key value is compared to the target. In these cases the number of comparisons for a successful search doubles. Therefore, the number of comparisons for the best case is 2, the worst case is 8, and the average case is 5. For an unsuccessful search the number of comparisons doubles to 8.

How we find the number of assignments needed for linear search parallels how we find the number of comparisons. No assignment is made outside the

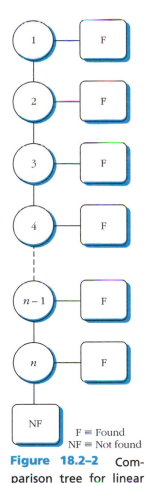

$F \equiv$ Found
$NF \equiv$ Not found

Figure 18.2–2 Comparison tree for linear search with n elements

loop structure. Inside the loop structure are the initialization assignment and the increment assignment. Consequently, the best case needs only the initialization assignment. The worst case needs the initialization plus three increments. The average case is again 2.5 assignments. For an unsuccessful search, the loop structure needs an initial assignment plus four increment assignments to bring the search to a null node. This gives a total of five assignments.

Figure 18.2–2 shows a comparison tree for an n-element linear search like the one we just discussed. For a successful linear search without the loop structure, the best case needs one comparison with no assignment and the worst case needs n comparisons with no assignment. The average number of comparisons can be calculated by

$$\frac{1 + 2 + 3 + \cdots + n - 2 + n - 1 + n}{n}$$

We recognize the numerator as the sum of the first n integers, which can be written as

$$\sum_{i=1}^{n} i = \frac{n(n+1)}{2}$$

Therefore, we can write the average as

$$\left[\frac{n(n+1)}{2}\right]\left[\frac{1}{n}\right]$$

which reduces to

$$\frac{(n+1)}{2}$$

The average case for a successful search has no assignment (without the loop structure). For an unsuccessful search without the loop structure, n comparisons are needed with no assignment.

The general results for a linear search of an n-element list without a loop structure are summarized in Table 18.2–2. The table also shows the results when the loop structure is included. Specifics of these results are covered in the exercises at the end of this section.

From Table 18.2–2 we observe that based on the number of comparisons in each of the average cases, the linear search algorithm is an order n algorithm. This is O(n) in Big-O notation, meaning that its complexity is proportional to the size of the list. If the list triples in size, the complexity triples. The results are not the same for assignments, however. Without the loop structure, the complexity is O(1); but with the loop structure, the complexity is O(n). The proofs of these statements are included in the exercises at the end of this section.

For binary search the problem is more complicated. From the comparison tree for eight elements in a binary search in Figure 18.2–3, note that each internal node represents a possible key value. All leaves represent failure, showing that the target was not found. Values of less than the value of a particular node fall to the left of the node; larger values fall to the right. If the key matches the target

Table 18.2–2 Summary of Linear Search Results

			COMPARISONS	ASSIGNMENTS
Loop excluded	Successful search	Best	1	0
		Worst	n	0
		Average	$(n+1)/2$	0
	Unsuccessful search		n	0
Loop included	Successful search	Best	2	1
		Worst	$2n$	n
		Average	$n+1$	$(n+1)/2$
	Unsuccessful search		$2n$	$n+1$

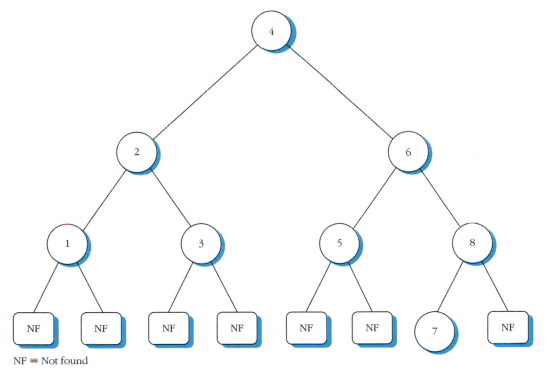

NF = Not found

Figure 18.2–3   Comparison tree for binary search with eight elements

value, the location is shown and the algorithm terminates. If no match is found, the algorithm proceeds to one of the leaves and again terminates.

Notice the "bushyness" of this tree compared to the tree for a linear search in Figure 18.2–2. This causes the **depth** of the tree—the largest number of edges from the root to a leaf—to be relatively shallow compared to the size of the list. A list of eight elements can be accommodated in a tree with a depth of 3. A list of 16 can be accommodated in a tree with a depth of 4. Recalling that $n = 2^d$ implies that $d = \log_2 n$, we can expect a list of n elements to be accommodated by a tree with a depth of at least $\log_2 n$.

How we determine the complexity of the binary search algorithm belongs in a separate study of search algorithms. Table 18.2–3 summarizes some of the results for binary search complexity without the loop structure comparisons and assignments.

Table 18.2–3   Summary of Binary Search Results

		ORDER OF COMPLEXITY	
		COMPARISONS	ASSIGNMENTS
	Best	1	1
Successful search	Worst	$\log_2 n$	$\log_2 n$
	Average	$\log_2 n$	$\log_2 n$
Unsuccessful search		$\log_2 n$	$\log_2 n$

Note that for a large number of elements, the average number of comparisons for a successful search approximates $\log_2 n$. In Big-O notation, we can describe binary search as a $O(\log_2 n)$ algorithm for both comparisons and assignments. The same order of complexity is true for an unsuccessful search. Best and worst cases, which occur only in special situations, are not as important as the average case.

We usually compare an algorithm's complexity for average cases. The order of complexity for the linear search is $O(n)$, whereas the order of complexity for the binary search is $O(\log_2 n)$. Thus

$$\log_2 n < n$$

for all $n \geq 1$ and binary search algorithms are more efficient than linear search algorithms provided that the keys of the elements are ordered. For example, in an ordered list of 4,096 elements,

$$\log_2 4{,}096 = 12 < 4{,}096$$

In fact, in the stated condition, binary search is significantly better than linear search. A graph comparing the two orders of complexity is shown in Figure 18.2–4.

PERSPECTIVE

When alphabetizing a list of 1000 names, a straightforward algorithm (insertion sort) takes approximately 1,000,000 comparisons of names in the worst case. A more clever algorithm (heap sort) takes just 10,000 comparisons in the worst case. Even this is the best possible result because sorting a list of items needs $n \log_2 n$ comparisons in the worst case, no matter what algorithm is used.[3]

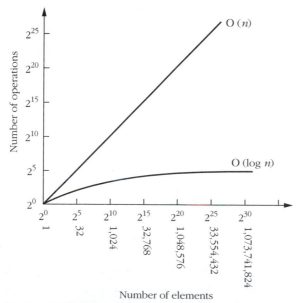

Figure 18.2–4   Graphical comparison of linear and binary search

18.2.4 Further Thoughts About Complexity

We have observed two orders of complexity in linear and binary search—linear and logarithmic; that is, complexities of $O(n)$ and of $O(\log_2 n)$, respectively. We use these two orders for categorizing certain algorithms. In addition to these categories for related search algorithms, there are many other categories for different algorithms. Some of these are quadratic for $O(n^2)$, cubic for $O(n^3)$, constant for $O(1)$, exponential for $O(2^n)$, and combinations of these such as $O(n \log_2 n)$ for sorting algorithms. Comparisons of these categories are shown in Figure 18.2–5.

Observe in Figure 18.2–5 that the category of exponential order overpowers all polynomial $(1, n, n^2, n^3)$ categories. For this reason we sometimes put all polynomial categories in a single category called **P** to represent all algorithms with polynomial complexity. Given the choice between an algorithm with polynomial complexity and an algorithm with exponential complexity, the former is the natural choice except in special cases. The Church–Turing thesis assures us of the equivalence between algorithms and computing machines that makes algorithmic complexity and computational complexity equivalent.

Turing machines as we have studied them are **deterministic:** Given a current state and input value, the next state, output, and direction are uniquely determined. However, suppose we allow the machine to choose *its own* performance at each step of the operation. We can no longer predict the behavior of the machine for

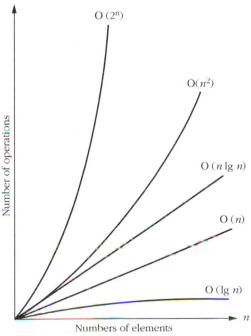

Figure 18.2–5 Relative comparisons of some orders of complexity

a given input and state, even though the machine still gives a next state, output, and direction, meaning that the machine still computes. This is the description of a **nondeterministic** Turing machine.

A nondeterministic Turing machine can be used to solve problems of polynomial complexity by introducing a new category of problems with their accompanying algorithms. We call this category of all algorithms with nondeterministic polynomial complexity **NP**. Category P is a subset of the NP category. It has yet to be determined whether or not category NP is a subset of category P. If this were true it would imply that P = NP and that all nondeterministic polynomial problems have polynomial complexity. However, there are NP problems for which no one has yet found a deterministic algorithm of polynomial complexity. Therefore, we cannot say that the complexities of categories P and NP are equal.

The quest for closure on P and NP equivalence has led to a category of **NP-hard** problems that are at least as hard to solve as any other NP problem. Any problem that is both NP and NP-hard is categorized as **NP-complete**. NP-complete problems are as hard to solve efficiently as any problem in the NP category. A classical NP-complete problem is the traveling salesman problem (TSP), which is to find, for a given set of cities and the distances between them, the salesman's shortest route to visit all cities.

If we could find even one problem in the class of NP-complete problems that had polynomial complexity, the P and NP categories would be equal. This would mean that if a deterministic algorithm of polynomial complexity can be found for one NP-complete problem, an algorithm would exist for all problems in the category. To date, no such algorithm has been found.

PERSPECTIVE

Theoretically, the traveling salesman problem has many useful applications. One is the routing of vehicles in a parcel delivery service. Another is the manufacture of complex circuit chips that can have well over 10,000 junctions that must be "visited" by a manufacturing tool.

Algorithms and machine complexity are important in theoretical computing. We encourage you to pursue more advanced study in this area.

EXERCISES 18.2

Concept Check
Answer statements 1 through 4 with true *or* false.
1. Big-O notation is used to measure the efficiency of a Turing machine.
2. Algorithm complexity measures how complicated an algorithm is to write.
3. A comparison tree is helpful for determining the complexity of an algorithm.
4. When a problem is in category NP, it can be solved in nonpolynomial time.

For statements 5 through 8 choose the answer that best completes the statement.

5. The complexity of linear search for a successful search is
   a. $O(\log_2 n)$
   b. $O(n^2)$
   c. $O(2^n)$
   d. $O(n)$
6. The complexity of binary search for an unsuccessful search is
   a. $O(\log_2 n)$
   b. $O(n^2)$
   c. $O(2^n)$
   d. $O(n)$
7. An algorithm of complexity $O(n \log_2 n)$ is not as efficient as one of order
   a. $O(\log_2 n)$
   b. $O(n^2)$
   c. $O(2^n)$
   d. $O(n \sqrt{n})$
8. A problem that is both NP and NP-hard
   a. cannot be solved
   b. is NP-complete
   c. is completely solvable
   d. can be solved only by a Turing machine

For statements 9 through 12 fill in the blanks with the right word.

9. The evaluation of Σi^2 for $i = 1$ to $i = 6$ is _____.
10. A problem categorized as _____ is at least as difficult to solve as any other NP problem.
11. An algorithm with complexity $(n + 1)/2 - 7$ has an order of magnitude of _____.
12. An algorithm with complexity $6n^3 - 5n^2 + 4n$ has an order of magnitude of _____.

Set A

Solve each of the following problems.

13. An algorithm with complexity $7(1 + 1/n) * \log_2(n + 1) - 4$ has an order of magnitude of _____.
14. An algorithm with complexity $3(n + 1/n) * \log_2(n + 47) - 8$ has an order of magnitude of _____.
15. An algorithm with complexity $(n^2 - n) * \log_2(n - 5) + 3$ has an order of magnitude of _____.
16. An algorithm with complexity $(2^n + n) * \log_2(n + 5) + n^2$ has an order of magnitude of _____.
17. Why does it take twice as many steps to perform an unsuccessful linear search as a successful one?
18. What is the order of complexity for each result of question 17?
19. Why do successful and unsuccessful binary searches take approximately the same time even though they have different formulations?
20. What is the order of complexity for each result of question 19?

Set B

21. Consider the comparison trees for both linear and binary search and give a rationale for why binary search is a better algorithm.
22. Why do you think that $O(2^n)$ can overpower any polynomial order?
23. Explain the difference between a deterministic and a nondeterministic Turing machine.
24. Give two examples of problems that are considered deterministic.
25. Give two examples of problems that are considered nondeterministic.
26. Explain the difference between categories P and NP.
27. Why do you think that category P is always a subset of category NP?
28. What is the difference between an NP-hard problem and an NP-complete problem?

Set C

29. Research the traveling salesman problem. What is the significance of this problem? How would you classify such a problem?
30. Write a short essay on what effect it would have on computational complexity studies if someone proved that P = NP.
31. Implement Program 18.2–1 for the intended data.
32. Show that for linear search, the results of Table 18.2–2 are correct when the loop structure is included.
33. Prove that the order of complexity for assignments using a linear search algorithm is $O(n)$ when the loop structure is included but $O(1)$ when the loop is not included.
34. Research the area of NP-complete problems. Describe two classic problems that are NP-complete.

ENDNOTES

1. Hartmanis, J., and Lin, H., eds. *Computing the Future: A Broader Agenda for Computer Science and Engineering*. Washington, D.C.: National Research Council, National Academy Press, 1992, p. 194.
2. Hartmanis, and Lin, eds., p. 172.
3. Hartmanis, and Lin, eds., p. 168.

Artificial Intelligence 19

Domestic robot doing household chores.

After completing this chapter you should be able to do the following:

Learning Goals

- Define artificial intelligence
- Define the subtopics of artificial intelligence
- Explain the concept of an expert system
- Explain the meaning of fuzzy logic and how it is used in artificial intelligence
- Distinguish between computer vision and computer graphics
- Distinguish between the roles of the low-level and high-level modules in vision processing

Chapter Activity

Computer vision, the machine interpretation of visual information, is an important application of artificial intelligence. The raw data consist of an image that has been *digitized*—converted into a 2D array of numbers using optical and electronic devices. Each cell of the array is called a **pixel** (picture element). The number associated with a pixel is proportional to the brightness level from the same location in the original visual scene. For programming convenience, pixels are generally stored as a 1-byte quantity with 0 representing black and 255 representing white.

Noise is sometimes introduced into this analog-to-digital process, causing blemishes in the visual appearance of the digitized image. A technique for reducing noise is **median filtering,** which calls for an examination of every pixel in the image, one at a time. At each pixel the median of all the eight neighbors (adjacent pixels), including the pixel under consideration, is computed and stored in an output image. (Recall that the median is the middle value in a sorted list of data.)

Write a program to do a median filter on a small, 2D array of numbers. Initialize the array to any numbers you want and then process it as we just described. Be sure to consider the edges of the image since the neighborhood will not always contain all eight pixels.

19.1   AREAS OF INQUIRY

Introduction

Artificial intelligence (AI) is perhaps the most promising, most misrepresented, and least understood field of computer science. It is certainly the most controversial. Academics from many disciplines—computer science, psychology, philosophy, neurophysiology, mathematics—are involved in the debates over AI. This question remains unanswered: Is it possible for a nonbiological entity, a product purely of human invention, a few (million) scratches in a piece of sand (silicon from which computer chips are made) to display intelligent behavior? Some people take the question a step further and ask: Would we even want such a device? Are the risks too great of machines becoming our superiors?

In over 20 years of teaching computer science we have discovered that many students, both majors and nonmajors, believe that AI has already arrived and that intelligent, thinking machines exist in one form or another. Yet the realization of true AI, although intriguing, is still a long way off. Much progress has been made in the field, however, especially with the advent of high-speed, highly parallel computer architectures. In this chapter we explore the foundations of AI and highlight some of the current research areas.

19.1.1 Basic Issues

So, what is AI? To some it is the development of machines that simulate intelligent human behavior. For these performance-oriented researchers, true AI will be attained when computers act and think as we do—or better than we do. These researchers take an engineering approach in which the world of intelligence (animal or machine) is viewed as a collection of discrete modules such as problem-solving ability, learning, language processing, and visual perception. As each of these subareas is implemented on a computer, it is to be added to the growing arsenal of AI modules whose sum will be an intelligent machine. Some researchers want more than just a smart PC; they want a mobile robot that can interact with the environment. A mobile robot could take an active role in the world, learn new ideas directly, and evolve at a higher rate than one confined to a desktop.

Some people consider the ultimate proof of the existence of performance-oriented AI to be the so-called Turing test, named for the mathematician Alan Turing in 1950. He proposed a scenario such as the following.

Give a human (called the *interrogator*) a computer terminal that is in communication with either a human or a program at the other end. The interrogator is allowed to ask any sequence of questions such as: How is the weather over there? What is the square root of π? What do you think of the designated hitter rule? In the end, if the interrogator thinks that he/she is communicating with another human when in fact he/she is communicating with a program, then that program shows true AI.

One of the limitations of this test is the presupposition that human intelligence can be evaluated through verbal communication. The ability to communicate verbally (or via computer) is taken as a sign of intelligence by some segments of some societies. However, it is surely not the only sign. Musicians, artists, and inventors all have other, nonverbal skills that are just as suggestive of intelligence. The underlying problem is that there is no scientific definition of intelligence, although researchers in different fields have working theories.

PERSPECTIVE

An annual Turing contest is held in Boston. To date no program has been able to fool a person after a reasonable amount of interaction.

For other researchers, AI is a tool to study the human brain. For these cognitive scientists and neuroscientists, the computer provides a controlled environment with which to model and test (simulate) theories of brain functions. The use of a computer model has the potential to provide feedback and insight into our own mental world. At present the tool for many brain researchers is the neural network. An **artificial neural network (ANN)** is a graph in which the nodes represent neurons and the arcs represent axons (the interneuronal connections), as shown in Figure 19.1–1a. The figure shows an *input layer* to which we give a pattern; for instance, two binary numbers to be added or a binary representation of a handwritten character. This layer is connected to one or more *hidden layers* that manipulate the bits and send results to the *output layer*.

Input layer   Hidden layers   Output layer

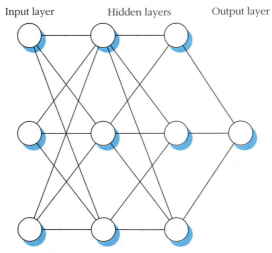

0	0	0	0	0	0	0	0	0	0
0	0	0	0	0	0	0	0	0	0
0	0	0	1	1	1	1	0	0	0
0	0	1	0	0	0	0	1	0	0
0	0	1	0	0	0	0	1	0	0
0	0	1	0	0	0	0	1	0	0
0	0	1	0	1	0	0	1	0	0
0	0	1	1	1	1	1	0	0	0
0	0	0	0	0	0	1	0	0	0
0	0	0	0	0	0	0	1	0	0

Figure 19.1–1a Artificial neural network

Figure 19.1–1b Digitized letter 'Q'

As we assume to be true for biological neurons, the nodes in the ANN get weighted input from other nodes according to the pattern of connectivity expressed in the graph. The weights represent the importance of the interconnections and in the ANN are initially assigned random values. When the sum of all the weights on a given node exceeds a threshold, the node *fires* and an output value is propagated through the preset interconnections of the graph.

An ANN can be *trained* to recognize specific patterns by **back propagation**. For example, we can train an ANN to recognize digitized handwritten images of the letter 'Q' (see Figure 19.1–1b) by first deciding what the correct answer is, say the ASCII code for 'Q.' Then we present the data (the pattern of 1's and 0's) to the input layer and execute the ANN. A pattern of bits emerges at the output layer and is evaluated by computing an *error factor,* the difference between the output layer and the correct answer. The error factor is sent through the ANN, starting at the output layer and working backwards, adjusting the weights in the process. Similar input data are then applied and executed by the newly adjusted network, a revised error factor is computed, and the error is back propagated. This cycle is repeated hundreds or thousands of times until the ANN adjusts itself to always produce the right answer. This process approximates the behavior of real neural networks and offers an insight into both human mental activity and the possibilities of AI.

PERSPECTIVE

Neural networks are typically explored in software. However, new ANN chips are on the market that have a few hundred neurons built into the circuitry. (No doubt the capacities of such chips will expand greatly as interest increases.) By comparison, the human brain has about 10^{11} neurons and a total of about 10^{16} interconnections, roughly equivalent to the number of characters in 10 billion 350-page books.

The difficulties of achieving true AI are staggering, especially since intelligence and perception are so poorly understood in biological creatures. Most AI researchers direct their energies to a particular subtopic. These include expert systems, natural-language processing, general problem solving, learning, robotics, and vision. We discuss expert systems and natural-language processing next and expand on computer vision in Section 19.2.

19.1.2 Expert Systems

Perhaps the greatest success of AI is in expert systems. An **expert system** tries to embody the knowledge of a human expert in a particular field. The software consists of a **knowledge base** of information and an **inference engine** that can draw conclusions based on hardcoded knowledge and on user responses to questioning. Anyone who has access to such a program has the equivalent of an in-house expert even when a human expert is not available.

For example, MYCIN, developed by E. H. Shortliffe at Stanford University in 1976, is a program designed to help treat bacterial infections. In a case of acute bacterial infection there may not be time to wait for laboratory tests to find the type of organism present—critical information for choosing an antibiotic. MYCIN tries to deduce the type of organism by asking the physician specific questions. Initially, these might include obvious demographics such as the age and sex of the patient. However, as MYCIN's understanding of the situation grows, its questions become more specific: What is the gram stain of the organism? Does the organism grow aerobically?

As with all expert systems, the sequence of questions depends on inferences and deductions from the answers given to previous questions. After a question and answer session, MYCIN may ask for additional information or give a recommendation—for instance, the probable identity of the organism and a suggested antibiotic.

To create an expert system, information must be taken from one or more human experts called **domain experts**. This process is usually long and often frustrating for both the **knowledge engineer**—the computer scientist developing the expert system—and the domain expert. Most experts are not aware of the totality of their knowledge and are sometimes unable to express themselves simply and logically.

Once the information has been taken it must be suitably coded for the computer. During the initial runs of the program the domain expert is available to test the system and help refine its knowledge. This is repeated until the program seems to have the level of performance wanted. Because expert systems are generally used in complex situations and may have a direct impact on human lives (such as automated medical diagnosis, air traffic control, or weapons control), the painstaking process of program verification is extremely important.

Most expert systems express knowledge in the form of a series of **IF** statements, as the following pseudocode illustrates.

```
IF ( temperature(x) > 101°F    and                    /* Antecedent */
     body_rash(x) == TRUE    and
     history(x) != chicken_pox    )
   diagnosis(x) = chicken_pox                          /* Consequent */
```

These statements are called **production rules** and consist of an **antecedent** (the conditions of the IF statement) and a **consequent** (the assignment). To activate the statement the inference engine requests relevant information from the user (such as temperature, presence of a rash, or history) and decides if the responses warrant the conclusion drawn from the production rules.

Note that the consequent of a production rule can be expressed discretely as it is in this case or as a confidence level meaning a degree of belief. In a discrete classification, the patient either has chicken pox or does not have chicken pox. In a *fuzzy* system the degree of belief in a particular consequent could be encoded in a range of, say, -1 to $+1$. In this case the diagnosis would be considered fuzzy because it is not all-or-nothing.

Fuzzy logic belongs to a relatively new and exciting branch of mathematics. Using fuzzy logic, computer systems can maintain multiple analyses of a given situation, postponing a final decision until enough information has filtered through. In this example the expert system does not have to be pinned down to a diagnosis of chicken pox. Instead it can allow for multiple diagnoses, each confirmed or refuted as new information is entered by the user. At any given moment, a physician can choose the single highest-confidence-level diagnosis or settle on the two or three most likely choices. As new patient information is obtained over the course of treatment, the expert system can update its analysis until the correct diagnosis is found. (We return to fuzzy logic in Section 19.2.)

Expert systems generally use forward chaining or backward chaining. In a **forward chaining** system, which is also called *data-driven,* the system has no one goal in mind but simply starts asking the user questions. Depending on the pattern of responses, the system settles on the set of conclusions that best fits the incoming information. In a **backward chaining** system, which is also called *goal-driven,* the system begins with one hypothesis and tries to either confirm or deny it, again by asking the user questions. If the responses do not fit the expectations, a new hypothesis is generated and is tested using any inputs already obtained. This process is sometimes called **hypothesis and test**. The sequence of questions is designed to remove the most uncertainty as quickly as possible so the most important questions are asked first.

Although much faith is placed in the potential of expert systems, many problems still remain, including

1. lack of deep knowledge of a given situation
2. lack of flexibility
3. difficulty of verification

As an example of lack of knowledge, consider the INTERNIST expert system developed by H. E. Pople and J. Meyers at Carnegie-Mellon University in 1975. This program was designed to make medical diagnoses based on a set of input symptoms. INTERNIST is reasonably successful at this but it has no understanding of anatomy, physiology, or biochemistry. These are critical knowledge areas for doctors when assessing their patients. INTERNIST's inadequate knowledge of the body could lead it to *unacceptable* mistakes in reasoning—like asking the sex of a pregnant patient—with potentially disastrous consequences for patients.

As examples of lack of flexibility, human experts can usually adapt their knowledge to unforeseen situations, whereas expert systems lack even a rudimentary ability to reason about a situation for which no rule can be derived. And no expert system to date has the ability to learn new facts or rules without direct reprogramming.

We said earlier that verification is critical. Yet as all programmers who have worked on large-scale systems know, true verification is virtually impossible. How do we test all possible outcomes of a system with 10,000 rules? This difficulty of verification leaves much to be explored in expert systems.

19.1.3 Natural-Language Processing

Another area of AI that has achieved modest success is natural-language processing (NLP). Applications of NLP include

1. machine translation of one human-language text to another
2. comprehension of human-language text with the resulting capability for summarizing and drawing conclusions
3. generation of human-language text such as product descriptions, user manuals, and fiction
4. software interfaces such as robotic systems and a database management system front end that allow users to make English-like queries

Note that the input to an NLP is assumed to be typed material: NLP research is separate from areas such as voice recognition or handwriting analysis, two other subtopics of AI. Output from those systems might ultimately become input for an NLP.

The first and by far the easiest task for an NLP is to parse a sentence and reveal its **syntax**. This means examining the surface structure of the sentence to identify nouns and verbs, and subjects and objects, according to the rules of syntax for the language. To date much progress has been made in this area although no existing program fully recognizes all English grammar.

After syntax, NLP deals with the more difficult task of semantics or meaning. **Semantic analysis** tries to identify the meaning of each word in a sentence, what the key actions are, and who is doing what to whom. The most difficult task is **contextual analysis** to assess *true* meaning. Contextual analysis considers semantic ambiguities in the broader context of the material.

To understand some of these difficulties consider the following example:

John lifted the weight.

A grammatical analysis of this sentence is straightforward and reveals, for instance, that *John* is a proper noun, *lifted* is a verb, *the* is an article, and *weight* is a noun. A semantic analysis might reveal that *John* is the agent controlling the *lifting* activity. When we put the sentence in the context of a story, we might guess that *John* is an Olympic hopeful and that this act is the turning point of his career with implications for his personal and professional life.

On the other hand, consider this slight modification:

John lifted the necklace.

Although the syntactic and semantic analyses are similar, there is an entirely new meaning to this simple statement. John is no longer a national hero but perhaps a miserable thief engaged in a felony. To derive this, the NLP would have to know that *lifting a necklace* in the sense of *picking it up to test its weight* is not something that people do routinely. Where would the program get this information? To work in the human world, AI needs everyday, commonsense knowledge. In other words, the program has to know things about the world and when to apply them to a given event. This is called the *background problem* and is the most difficult for contextual analysis.

PERSPECTIVE

One of the largest efforts to create a commonsense database is the CYC (for "encyclopedic") project started in 1984 under the direction of Douglas Lenat at the Microelectronics and Computer Technology Corporation. The project's goal is to give background knowledge of the human world to a computer. This ambitious undertaking stores millions of commonsense ideas such as *a child is never older than its parents, people usually cannot see through walls,* and *locomotives cannot be bought at drugstores.* Such ideas are known to most people but cannot be found in any reference book!

EXERCISES 19.1

Concept Check

Answer statements 1 through 4 with true *or* false.
1. One goal of AI is to mimic human behaviors and actions.
2. Researchers in expert systems have generated self-adapting systems that adapt to new situations the way human experts do.
3. One of the goals of NLP systems is to understand the spoken word.
4. Although the software is still under development, neural network chips have come close to the level of interconnectedness of the human brain.

For statements 5 through 8 choose the answer that best completes the statement.
5. In an artificial neural network
   a. nodes represent intellectual capabilities such as problem solving and visual perception
   b. nodes represent neurons and arcs represent the interconnections
   c. information about the world is stored in the nodes, whereas possible actions are indicated by the arcs
   d. neurons fire when the sum of the inputs is below a certain threshold
6. The major problems facing expert systems include:
   a. when to use backward versus forward chaining
   b. whether to use discrete or fuzzy logic
   c. depth of knowledge, flexibility, and program verification
   d. displacement of human experts
7. The stages of analysis for an NLP are
   a. context, syntax, and semantics
   b. syntax, semantics, and context
   c. backward chaining and forward chaining
   d. voice recognition, handwriting analysis, and semantic interpretation

8. Finding the meaning of a sentence is called
   a. recognition
   b. semantics
   c. syntax
   d. chaining

For statements 9 through 12 fill in the blanks with the right word.
9. The ultimate test for performance-oriented AI is called _____.
10. In _____ expert systems a goal is hypothesized and the sequence of questions tries to verify that goal.
11. The hardest task for NLP systems is called _____.
12. Using _____, information is encoded as confidences or probabilities instead of all-or-nothing answers.

Set A
Solve each of the following problems.
13. Comment on the feasibility of AI.
14. Criticize the Turing test for AI (for example, what aspects of intelligence does it fail to measure?). Create your own test for an intelligent machine.
15. Comment on the morality of AI (for example, some researchers believe that AI is dangerous because humans will put too much faith in machines).
16. Cite several potentially negative effects of AI on society.

Set B
17. Comment on the difference between a program choosing to act based on a complex sequence of IF statements and a human choosing to do one activity over another (the notion of free will).
18. Arthur Samuels developed a checkers program in the 1950s that is a landmark achievement in AI. At first the program was an amateur player but over time it was able to beat its inventor and virtually all other humans. And it was designed to improve with experience without being reprogrammed. Comment on this example of machine learning.

19.2   CASE STUDY: COMPUTER VISION

Introduction

Computer vision is considered one of the more difficult problems of AI and possibly one of the most difficult problems under scientific investigation. The goal is machine interpretation and complete understanding of any visual pattern. The domain is the entire visual world including features such as color, three-dimensionality, and motion.

Computer vision (CV) is sometimes confused with **computer graphics (CG)** although the two fields are complementary. CV is concerned with the *analysis* (breaking down) of a visual image. CG is concerned with the *synthesis* (building up) of a visual image. Whereas CV starts with an image, CG ends with an image. The mistake is made because both disciplines deal with images, but they use very different algorithms.

The human vision system evolved over millions of years into a highly complex component of the brain. It is so good at what it does that visual perception seems effortless. We just open our eyes and the visual world apparently identifies itself to us. Out of the billions of bits of information that come flying by us every second, we are somehow able to extract and symbolize a wealth of information in a fraction of a second, even while driving a car at 60 mph in a rainstorm on an unknown road while carrying on a conversation.

There are no identifying markers in the world that say, for instance, *This is a tree...it touches the sky and is rooted in the ground. In the summer its leaves are green but in the fall its leaves start to die—after turning several shades of color—and in the winter it has no leaves at all.* Much mental processing is done in the retina (the photoreceptive layer in the eye) and along the neural pathways leading to the visual cortex where a large percentage of our neural tissue resides. It is in the visual cortex that most of the processing called visual perception takes place. Neuroscientists are only beginning to understand some of the complexities of this most refined of our senses.

PERSPECTIVE

In his book *The Mind of a Mnemonist* (Harvard University Press, 1968), psychologist A. R. Luria tells the story of a man with an astonishing photographic memory. His capacity to store and recall sensory details was virtually unlimited, both in level of detail and length of retention. His gift nearly drove him insane. He was so completely overwhelmed by the infinite details of the visual (and nonvisual) world that he could not perceive *gestalts* (whole entities) such as a tree. He was compelled to pay attention to—and memorize—every bit of minutia that he encountered. The visual world literally bombarded him to the point where he was unable to function normally. Ironically, his therapy consisted of training him to suppress his memory for details, to learn how to forget, and to appreciate larger visual constructs. From this we might conclude that our brains have this capacity for details but its functioning is inhibited.

Research into **computer vision systems (CVS)** has been advancing for the past 30 years and focuses on the development of two modules: a low-level module that processes the raw sensory data and a high-level module that interprets the results of the low-level module. To date much progress has been made at the low level, with a modest amount of reliable information extracted for a number of applications. These include the Autonomous Land Vehicle, a computer-controlled Volkswagen that can drive at 60 mph on the autobahns using visual guidance; the cruise missile that uses visual guidance for target acquisition; medical imaging packages for analysis of CAT, MRI, and PET image scans; and visually guided industrial robots for use on assembly lines. Relatively inexpensive off-the-shelf software is commercially available that handles various low-level imaging tasks such as enhancement, transmission, compression, and image-database management. Research on the high-level module is still in its infancy and only one or two packages are available for high-level image interpretation.

19.2.1 The Digital Image

Before discussing the role of the low-level module, let's first define an image as a 2D intensity map whose coordinates represent the locations of discrete picture elements called **pixels** or *pels*. Aside from its location, a pixel has one or more intensity values representing its brightness or gray level (for a monochrome image) or its color. Standard color images are usually represented by three values indicating the red, green, and blue (RGB) intensities of the pixel. Nonstandard color images such as satellite photos may have more or fewer intensity values depending on the spectral characteristics of the raw data and the camera used to acquire the data. Figure 19.2–1 is a simple block diagram of a typical imaging system.

During the scanning phase, a visual input device such as a video camera is used to acquire the visual scene. The output of a video camera is an analog voltage signal whose amplitudes are proportional to the brightnesses present in the original scene. Through a sampling process called **digitization** the analog signal is converted to a digital signal suitable for storage in computer memory. (See Figure 19.2–2.)

A **digitizer** is a circuit designed to read an analog signal at a prespecified time interval (about every 77 nanoseconds for a video signal) and then convert the amplitude of the signal to a numeric value, as shown in Figures 19.2–2d and 19.2–2e. This assigns each pixel its gray level. The greater the sampling frequency, the greater the **spatial resolution** or sharpness of the resulting image. The more bits available, the finer the gray-level scale or **quantization** of the image. A typical video scan yields an image with a spatial resolution of about 512-by-512 pixels, each quantized to 8 bits (256 shades of gray). For color images, a color camera can be used with 3 digitizing chips.

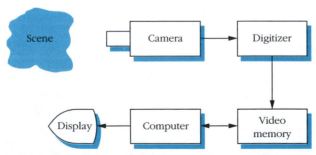

Figure 19.2–1   Block diagram of an image-processing system

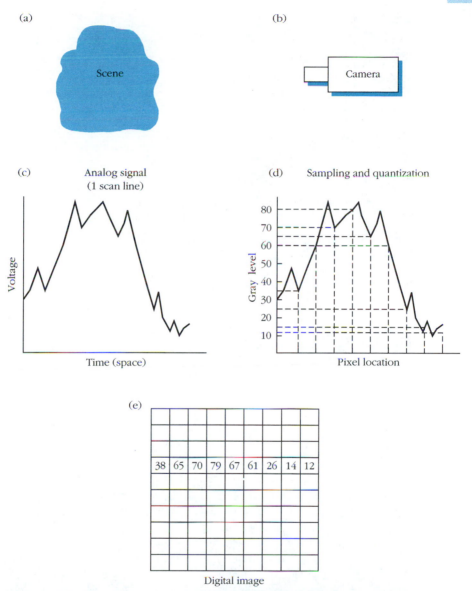

Figure 19.2–2   Digitization of an analog signal

Figure 19.2–3a   Digitized image of a house

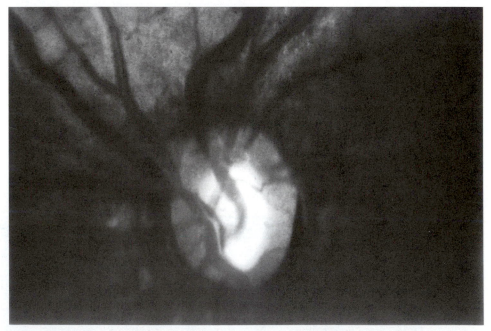

Figure 19.2–3b   Digitized image of an optic nerve and surrounding retina

Figure 19.2–3 shows two examples of digitized images. It is useful to study these images to get a flavor of the complexity and richness of the visual world. What properties stand out to distinguish a tree from a bush? A vein from an artery?

19.2.2 The Low-Level Module

The goal of the **low-level module** is to process the raw sensory data and reduce its overall complexity. This module locates features in the image data such as regions (connected areas), edges, and boundaries (connected edges). Once located, regions are assigned numeric values for color, size, shape, location, and texture. Similarly, edges are assigned orientation and strength (magnitude) values. Thus, a region or boundary is transformed into a **feature vector,** a series of measurements that summarizes the associated image data.

Transforming the mass of raw data into a small set of feature vectors means a tremendous degree of data reduction. Even a high-resolution image might only contain a few hundred regions of interest, each of whose feature vectors might hold only a few bytes of data. Therefore, an effective low-level module can reduce a 50-megabyte image to a (few) thousand-byte description. The challenge for this low-level module, however, is to identify only the **significant** regions and edges from the many thousands or millions of possibilities.

Let's first consider the meaning of a region. A **region** is a connected set of pixels that are invariant with respect to some feature of themselves. **Connected** means that a path exists from any pixel in the region to any other pixel in the region. A region is distinguishable from other regions by a consistent (invariant) attribute that can be measured at each pixel. This attribute might be color. For example, sky pixels would form one region and grass pixels might form another. Figure 19.2–4 shows the images from Figure 19.2–3 with their regions delineated by a region-growing program.

The problem is that it is rare to find an area of an image that is strictly invariant. If you carefully examine even a relatively uncomplicated object like a wall or ceiling, you find that there is a great deal of visual activity: numerous surface imperfections such as scratches, dents, scuff marks, brush strokes, etc. Any of these are potential problems for a program designed to group pixels based on visual invariance.

In practice this criterion can be relaxed and a tolerance factor or **threshold** of variability can be applied. Setting the threshold conservatively (at a low tolerance for pixel-to-pixel differences) tends to break up or fragment the image into many small regions. Setting the threshold liberally tends to merge areas that should be left as distinct regions. Various postprocessing steps have been devised to deal with each of these situations.

Whereas a region grower tries to join pixels based on local continuities, an **edge detector** applies the reverse process. An **edge** is any local discontinuity. An edge exists in an image whenever two adjacent pixels are not identical in value. If we look at digital data closely, it is immediately obvious that there are hundreds of thousands of edges, depending on the resolution and variability of the image. For this reason, edges are usually selected or **filtered** based on some

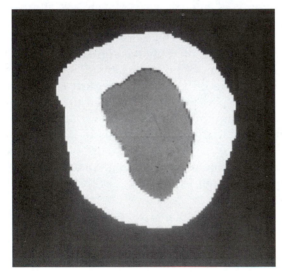

Figure 19.2–4   Results of region processing

preset criteria. A simple filtering algorithm allows only edges whose strength is above a certain threshold value and suppresses all weak edges. Figure 19.2–5 shows the edge-filtered images from Figure 19.2–3 with the edges superimposed over the raw data. Finding the right threshold is something of an art and can have dramatic consequences. As with setting the region threshold, setting the edge threshold too low (keeping edges whose pixel-to-pixel difference is very small) means many unwanted edges and setting it too high means allowing only strong edges, thus missing subtle edges that may be important.

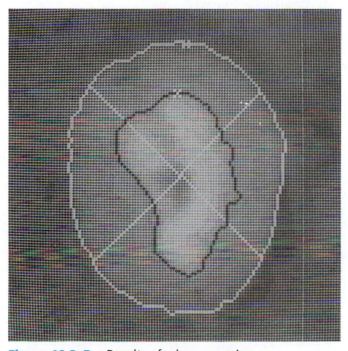

Figure 19.2–5   Results of edge processing

A more serious problem for the low-level module is with boundaries. A **boundary** is a connected set of edges that encloses a region. Thus, edges are not the same as boundaries. To be useful, edges must be part of something larger. Remember, the goal is to generate a compact description, not to find the hundred thousand strongest edges! Unfortunately, edge information is usually incomplete or inconsistent, and joining edges to form a boundary is a process that has not yet been completely mastered.

19.2.3 An Example of Low-Level Processing

A common technique used by a low-level module is **convolution,** which consists of a family of processes that can be applied to each pixel. The output depends in part on the information in a small area immediately surrounding the pixel, called the **neighborhood** of that pixel. Every pixel has a neighborhood, except for those immediately adjacent to the border of the image, where the neighborhood is *incomplete*. In a convolution, each pixel in a neighborhood is multiplied by a predetermined set of weights. The output is the sum of the products of each neighbor pixel with its corresponding weight. The final sum is then **normalized** or brought back into the original gray-level range. These ideas are shown in Figure 19.2–6 and discussed next.

The weights are usually stored in a small array of the same size as the neighborhood. This array is called a **mask** or **convolution kernel.** The following equation defines a convolution operator.

$$new_{xy} = \left(\sum_{k=x-1}^{x+1} \sum_{l=y-1}^{y+1} old_{k,l} * mask_{x-k,y-l} \right) \Big/ norm \qquad (1)$$

Assuming a 3-by-3 neighborhood immediately surrounding the pixel at location xy, old_{kl} (as k varies from $x-1$ to $x+1$ and l varies from $y-1$ to $y+1$) represents

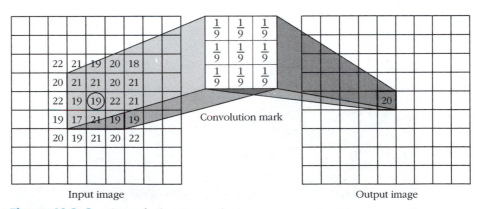

Input image   Convolution mark   Output image

Figure 19.2–6 Convolution processing

all nine pixels in its neighborhood (including the pixel itself). The weights can be any decimal or integer values although they are often kept as integers to reduce computation time. When the weights are all positive, the effect is to smooth the local image detail (analogous to integration) and when some of the weights are negative, the effect is to sharpen image detail (analogous to differentiation).

As an example, consider the following set of weights, collectively called a **smoothing filter.** Note that for this particular mask, all weights are the same. In general, they can be any suitable values.

Smoothing Filter:
Normalization = 1

$\frac{1}{9}$	$\frac{1}{9}$	$\frac{1}{9}$
$\frac{1}{9}$	$\frac{1}{9}$	$\frac{1}{9}$
$\frac{1}{9}$	$\frac{1}{9}$	$\frac{1}{9}$

Looking at the subimage shown next, we can apply the smoothing filter to the 3-by-3 image neighborhood immediately surrounding the shaded value 19, starting with the upper-left neighbor (21) and moving row by row to the lower-right neighbor (19).

22	21	19	20	18
20	21	21	20	21
22	19	19	22	21
19	17	21	19	19
20	19	21	20	22

The convolution operator computes the output value as

$$[(21 * \tfrac{1}{9}) + (21 * \tfrac{1}{9}) + (20 * \tfrac{1}{9}) +$$
$$(19 * \tfrac{1}{9}) + (19 * \tfrac{1}{9}) + (22 * \tfrac{1}{9}) +$$
$$(17 * \tfrac{1}{9}) + (21 * \tfrac{1}{9}) + (19 * \tfrac{1}{9})]/1 = 20$$

The computed value (20) is put in an output image and the convolution processor moves to the right adjacent pixel (22). Again the output is 20. We conclude that this convolution has the effect of smoothing over slight gray-level variations or reducing unwanted noise in the digitized image. The variability (or noise) can be caused by artifacts in the digitization since both the scanner and the digitizer have a limited degree of precision. The variability might also be real—a true reflection of changes in the visual data. In either case the variability seems random; it is therefore of no particular value to the CVS and might as well be smoothed over.

On the other hand, consider what happens when the smoothing filter is applied to a different subimage with a sharp boundary between two regions:

21	22	19	20	18
22	21	21	20	21
22	19	19	22	21
61	59	60	60	59
62	61	60	62	59

Note the contrast of numbers between the third row and the fourth row representing an edge. The convolution of the shaded cell (value 19) produces the output

$$[(21 * \tfrac{1}{9}) + (21 * \tfrac{1}{9}) + (20 * \tfrac{1}{9}) +$$
$$(19 * \tfrac{1}{9}) + (19 * \tfrac{1}{9}) + (22 * \tfrac{1}{9}) +$$
$$(59 * \tfrac{1}{9}) + (60 * \tfrac{1}{9}) + (60 * \tfrac{1}{9})]/1 = 33$$

In this case the output value is a **hybrid** or **alias** that is not representative of either the top region or the bottom region. Therefore, although the smoothing filter can reduce noise it can also blur legitimate edges. This is a typical dilemma in image processing: An operation that works well in one part of an image can be destructive in another part.

PERSPECTIVE

One solution to the problem of aliasing is to design algorithms that adapt to the characteristics of each subimage. For instance, the smoothing operator might be applied *conditionally*, as in *smooth the data only if the neighborhood variability appears to be random. Do not smooth the data if the neighborhood appears to have a strong edge or is part of a boundary.*

EXAMPLE 19.2–1

Problem
Implement a convolution operator according to Equation (1).

Reasoning
This is an array-processing task that needs a 2D array representing an image of gray levels and a small array containing the weights (the mask). The processing uses Equation (1) to calculate new_{xy}. Note that the output at each pixel must be sent to an output array. Otherwise, subsequent processing of neighboring pixels is (incorrectly) affected by the processing at previous pixels.

Formal statement:

Input: gray-level image, convolution mask
Output: image convolved with mask
Process: apply mask to each 3-by-3 neighborhood within the image; calculate the convolution formula and output the transformed pixels to an output array

Solution

For simplicity, we assign gray levels to the image using the random-number generator. We also assign the mask weights internally. Either of these variables could be input by the user (or from a file) to increase the program's usefulness.

ALGORITHM: main

1. Assign values to image and mask
2. LOOP for each image row
   a. LOOP for each image column
      1. new[row][col] = convolve(image, mask, row, col)

ALGORITHM: convolve

1. sum = 0
2. LOOP for each mask row $(0 - 2)$
   a. LOOP for each mask column $(0 - 2)$
      sum = sum + image[row − 1 + mask row]
      [col − 1 + mask column]*
      mask[mask row][mask column]
3. RETURN (sum / NORMALIZATION)

Program 19.2–1 implements this algorithm in C. Note that the weights have been changed from floating-point values $\frac{1}{9}, \frac{1}{9}, \ldots$ to integers 1, 1,... with a corresponding change in the normalization factor from 1 to 9. This yields the same result but greatly increases the computational efficiency.

PROGRAM 19.2-1

```
/************************************************************************
* Title:       convolution processor                                  *
* Filename:    conproc.c                                              *
*                                                                      *
* Description: Perform a convolution process on an image.              *
*                                                                      *
* Input:       none (image and mask are assigned values internally)   *
* Output:      image after convolution applied                        *
* Process:     1. assign random gray levels to image pixels           *
*                 2. apply convolution mask to each pixel neighborhood, *
*                    avoiding image border                             *
*                                                                      *
* Written by:  ...                                   Date: ...        *
************************************************************************/
```

```
#include <stdio.h>
#include <stdlib.h>                    /*  These two headers are needed  */
#include <time.h>                        /*  for the random function  */


#define IMG_SIZE    100                 /*  Length (or width) of image  */
#define N_GRAY      16                   /*  # gray levels per pixel  */
#define MASK_SIZE   3                     /*  Mask or Neighborhood size  */
#define NORMAL      9                 /*  Normalization factor for convolution  */


typedef int IMAGE_TYPE [ IMG_SIZE  ] [ IMG_SIZE ];
typedef int MASK_TYPE  [ MASK_SIZE ] [ MASK_SIZE ];


                                 /*  Prototype for convolution function  */
int  convolve ( IMAGE_TYPE  image,  MASK_TYPE  mask,  int  row,  int  col );


main ( )
{

   IMAGE_TYPE image, out_image;
   MASK_TYPE  mask = { 1,1,1,  1,1,1,  1,1,1 };     /*  Convolution mask for  */
                                              /*  smoothing filter  */
                                              /*  with integer weights  */
   int  row,  col;

   randomize ( );                       /*  Seed the random-number generator  */

   for ( row = 0;  row < IMG_SIZE;  row++ ) /*  Insert random data into image  */
      for ( col = 0;  col < IMG_SIZE;  col++ )
         image[ row ][ col ]  =  random ( N_GRAY );

   for ( row = 0;  row < IMG_SIZE;  row++ )/*  set up row and column indexes  */
      for ( col = 0;  col < IMG_SIZE;  col++ )

            if ( row == 0  ||  row == IMG_SIZE-1  ||   /*  Avoid image border  */
               col ==  0     ||    col ==  IMG_SIZE-1  )
                 out_image[ row ][ col ]  =  image[ row ][ col ];

            else                                        /*  Call convolve  */
                 out_image[ row ][ col ]  =  convolve ( image, mask, row, col );

   printf ( "\n\n\n" );
```

```
      for ( row = 0;  row < IMG_SIZE;  row++ ){        /*  Display output image  */
         printf ( "\nRow %2d:  ",  row+1 );
         for ( col = 0;  col < IMG_SIZE;  col++ )
            printf ( "%4d",  out_image[ row ][ col ] );
   }

   return ( 0 );
}                                                       /*  End of main  */


/**************************************************************************
 * Function name:    convolve                                            *
 * Description:      Convolve a neighborhood with mask.                  *
 *                                                                       *
 * Input parameters: image, mask, image row and column to process       *
 * Output parameters: none                                              *
 * Return value:     sum of the products of each neighbor pixel with the *
 *                   corresponding weight                                *
 **************************************************************************/

int  convolve ( IMAGE_TYPE image,  MASK_TYPE mask,  int row,  int col )

{
   int  sum,  mask_row,  mask_col;

   sum  =  0;

   for ( mask_row = 0;  mask_row < MASK_SIZE;  mask_row++ )
       for ( mask_col = 0;  mask_col < MASK_SIZE;  mask_col++ )

           sum +=    image [ row-1 + mask_row ][ col-1 + mask_col ]
                    * mask [        mask_row ][        mask_col ];

   return (  sum / NORMAL  );
}                                                       /*  End of convolve  */
```

Test
Enter the program and observe the output image. The mask chosen reduces the pixel-to-pixel variability. If displayed graphically, the output image would have a smoother appearance than the input image. Note that a smoothing filter can be applied repeatedly to an image. Try redesigning the program to include a loop just before the loops that call **convolve**. Be sure to copy the output image back to the input image before starting the next iteration of the loop. What happens if you apply smoothing 10, 20, or 100 times?   ●

19.2.4 High-Level Module

The goal of the **high-level module** is to interpret the low-level information. This is hard since there are so many possible interpretations for any given collection of information. We can often do this successfully, however, if we constrain the domain. For instance, an industrial robot might be needed to identify and grab a bolt or a screwdriver. This machine does not need knowledge of trees or houses or people, just bolts and screwdrivers. In such a constrained world it is easy to create an appropriate **discriminant function**—a formula that can be used to discriminate among a small set of possibilities. The process of discriminating among or *classifying* objects such as bolts and screwdrivers is sometimes called **pattern recognition** because it is used to recognize an object's pattern of distinctive visual characteristics.

PERSPECTIVE

The principles of pattern recognition (PR) or classification of objects present in a signal can be applied to many other kinds of problems, too. For instance, in **speech recognition** a waveform representing acoustic pressure variations in a person's speech can be analyzed to find distinct phoneme patterns and, ultimately, to find recognizable words.

Let's assume that an image containing a large set of bolts and screwdrivers is to be analyzed by the CVS. Using region-detecting algorithms, the low-level module tries to find all the regions. Next, it measures features of these regions such as size, shape, and position. This information is then sent to the high-level module for interpretation. The feature that best distinguishes bolts from screwdrivers is size. An appropriate discriminant function might therefore be the following pseudocode.

```
IF size(region_x) > threshold
    region_x is a screwdriver
ELSE
    region_x is a bolt
```

All we need is a value for the threshold that satisfies some criterion of accuracy. One way to find this value is by examining a histogram of the region sizes (recall the exam grades histogram from Program 7.2–2). As shown in Figure 19.2–7, the *x*-axis represents *region size* and the *y*-axis represents *the number of regions with a given size.*

The histogram reveals two distinct populations, each with its own mean and degree of variability. As you might have guessed, the left curve represents the bolts and the right curve the screwdrivers. The point where the two curves meet (a local minimum of the overall function) seems like an ideal value for the

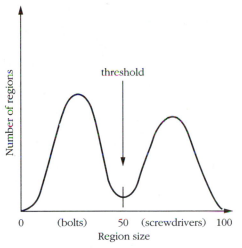

Figure 19.2–7   Histogram of sizes of bolts and screwdrivers

threshold, 50 in this case. Although we extracted this value by visual inspection of the histogram, techniques that exist for automatically selecting the threshold from a given histogram would be a standard part of the robot's control programs. After selecting the threshold value, the robot can apply the discriminant function to a particular region and be reasonably sure that it is grabbing the right part.

The process just described is adequate for images that are known to contain a small number of distinct objects. However, in an unconstrained image domain there may be hundreds of detectable objects. Histograms of such images do not reveal distinct subcurves for each object; the distributions of individual objects tend to overlap each other. The result could be a histogram with no distinct curves at all!

The high-level module needs a much more sophisticated approach to handle complex imagery. In **model-based** vision, a description of the expected objects and their spatial interrelationships is created by the programmer. The model specifies a set of **constraints** that must be satisfied by the low-level module's feature vectors for a particular model to be valid. A model of an outdoor scene might include constraints such as the fact that *objects in the distance appear smaller and bluer than those close up,* or *parallel lines appear to converge over distances.* In addition, object-specific knowledge might be included, as shown in Table 19.2–1.

Table 19.2–1   Object-Specific Knowledge

OBJECT	COLOR	TEXTURE	RELATIVE LOCATION
grass	green	smooth	below
tree	green	irregular	between
sky	blue	smooth	above

Table 19.2–2 Weighted Descriptors

OBJECT	COLOR	TEXTURE	RELATIVE LOCATION
grass	green (0.8) red (0.1) blue (0.1)	smooth (0.8) irregular (0.2)	below (0.9) between (0.1) above (0.0)
tree	green (0.8) red (0.1) blue (0.1)	smooth (0.2) irregular (0.8)	below (0.0) between (0.5) above (0.5)
sky	blue (0.8) red (0.2) green (0.0)	smooth (0.8) irregular (0.2)	below (0.0) between (0.1) above (0.9)

The information in Table 19.2–1 could be quantified using **fuzzy logic:** Instead of an all-or-nothing classification, relative weights could be assigned to the descriptors, as shown in Table 19.2–2.

As you can see, the weights give more flexibility to the model and allow for the possibility of, for instance, a reddish cloudy sky peeking through trees. Note that since the weights represent probabilities, the sum in each box is 1.

Vision processing can proceed either from the bottom up or from the top down. A **bottom-up** or *data-driven* approach starts with the raw data and uses the low-level module to obtain a set of feature vectors. This information is then passed to the high-level module for interpretation. Based on the feature vectors, the high-level module tries to find the model that best explains the data. Conversely, a **top-down** or *model-driven* approach starts with a particular model and tries to verify it by looking for confirmation in the raw image data. For example, given a model of the outdoor world, the high-level module might try to find blue sky at the top of the image, green grass at the bottom, and trees in between. Depending on the level of confirmation, more refined submodels might be applied or an entirely new model explored.

EXERCISES 19.2

Concept Check

Answer statements 1 through 4 with true *or* false.

1. The goal of computer vision is like the goal of computer graphics: the machine interpretation and complete understanding of any visual pattern.
2. A region is a connected set of pixels that are invariant with respect to some feature of themselves.
3. An edge is the same as a boundary.
4. Using fuzzy logic, objects are classified as all-or-nothing.

For statements 5 through 8 choose the answer that best completes the statement.

5. Digitization of an analog signal determines
   a. the spatial resolution of the resulting image
   b. the quantization of the resulting image
   c. both the resolution and the quantization of the resulting image
   d. the number of regions in the resulting image

6. Region and edge detection
   a. are essentially the same
   b. are complementary
   c. are used by the high-level module
   d. are no longer considered difficult for CV

7. The effect on a given image of applying a convolution process
   a. depends on the mask used
   b. depends on the normalization factor
   c. depends on the neighborhood data around each pixel
   d. depends on all the above factors

8. A model is
   a. the goal of the low-level module
   b. a set of region and edge feature vectors
   c. an idealized picture that is compared to the real image
   d. a set of constraints indicating expected properties and interrelationships between objects

For statements 9 through 12 fill in the blanks with the right word.

9. _____ is the process of synthesizing an image from a set of elementary visual entities such as circles or lines.

10. A _____ can enable the computer to distinguish among a small class of objects.

11. In a _____, each pixel neighborhood is processed with a mask to produce a new pixel value.

12. In _____, a model of the world is proposed that is either verified or rejected according to the incoming data.

Set A

Solve each of the following problems.

13. Discuss some of the difficulties created by digital imagery.

14. Discuss some of the difficulties in applying convolution masks.

15. Compute the output of the following masks on the subimages shown in Section 19.2.3:

-1	-1	-1		1	0	-1
	0	0		1	0	-1
1	1	1		1	0	-1

Mask 1   Mask 2

What would be appropriate names for these masks?

Set B

16. A 24-hour-a-day television station transmits about two terabytes of data per day (2,000,000,000,000 bytes). Verify this observation given the amount of data (mentioned in the text) in a single, color-video image and the fact that TV broadcasts 30 frames (images) per second.

17. Create an algorithm for automatically analyzing a histogram to find a threshold value.

18. What would happen to the algorithm in Question 17 if the histogram contained n curves? Revise the algorithm to handle an arbitrary number of thresholds.

Set C

19. Run the convolution program with the following mask and observe the output.

```
1    2    1
2    4    2
1    2    1
Normalization factor = 16
```

This mask is called a **Gaussian** because its weights approximate a 2D Gaussian distribution.

20. Run the convolution program with the following mask and observe the output.

```
−1   −1   −1
−1    8   −1
−1   −1   −1
Normalization factor = 1
```

This mask is called a **Laplacian** and its weights approximate the second derivative of a function.

21. Find a text on image processing and implement other masks.

22. Depending on the makeup of the input image, thresholding can sometimes do a good job of separating an image into regions. The processing consists of checking the gray level of each pixel against the threshold value. If the pixel is above the threshold, set the output to 1; otherwise, set the output to 0. Write a function to threshold the image. The input parameters are the threshold value and the image. The output is the thresholded image.

Appendixes

Common Functions in stdio.h File

| FUNCTION NAME | FUNCTION TYPE | PARAMETERS | | FUNCTION DESCRIPTION |
		NO.	TYPE	
fclose	int	1	FILE *	File close
fgets	char *	3	char * int FILE *	String input from a file
fopen	FILE *	2	char *	File open
fprintf	int	v	FILE * const char *	Text file output
fread	unsigned	4	void * unsigned unsigned FILE *	Binary file input
fscanf	int	v	FILE * const char *	Text file input
fwrite	unsigned	4	void * unsigned unsigned FILE *	Binary file output
getc	int	1	FILE *	Input character from text file
getchar	int	0		Character from stdin input
printf	int	v	const char *	Output (formatted) to stdout
putc	int	2	int FILE *	Output character to text file
putchar	int	1	int	Output character to stdout
scanf	int	v	const char *	Input from stdin
sprintf	int	v	const char *	Conversion (formatted) to string
sscanf	int	v	const char *	Conversion (formatted) from string

v = variable number

Common Functions in math.h File

FUNCTION NAME	FUNCTION TYPE	PARAMETERS		FUNCTION DESCRIPTION
		NO.	TYPE	
acos	double	1	double	Arc cosine
asin	double	1	double	Arc sine
atan	double	1	double	Arc tangent
atan2	double	2	double	Arc tangent
ceil	double	1	double	Smallest integer greater than or equal
cos	double	1	double	Cosine
cosh	double	1	double	Hyperbolic cosine
exp	double	1	double	Exponential (base-e)
fabs	double	1	double	Absolute value (double)
floor	double	1	double	Largest integer less than or equal
log	double	1	double	Logarithm (base-e)
log10	double	1	double	Logarithm (base-10)
pow	double	2	double	Exponential (general)
sin	double	1	double	Sine
sinh	double	1	double	Hyperbolic sine
sqrt	double	1	double	Square root
tan	double	1	double	Tangent
tanh	double	1	double	Hyperbolic tangent

Common Functions in ctype.h File

FUNCTION NAME	FUNCTION TYPE	PARAMETERS		FUNCTION DESCRIPTION
		NO.	TYPE	
isalpha	int	1	int	Alphabetic character check
isdigit	int	1	int	Digit(base-10)-character check
islower	int	1	int	Lowercase-letter check
ispunct	int	1	int	Punctuation-character check
isspace	int	1	int	Space-character check
isupper	int	1	int	Uppercase-letter check
tolower	int	1	int	Uppercase-to-lowercase conversion
toupper	int	1	int	Lowercase-to-uppercase conversion

Note: Parameter type can be either `int` or `char`.

Common Functions in stdlib.h File

| FUNCTION NAME | FUNCTION TYPE | PARAMETERS | | FUNCTION DESCRIPTION |
		NO.	TYPE	
abs	int	1	int	Absolute value
calloc	void *	2	unsigned	Allocate dynamic array
exit	void	1	int	Terminate program
free	void	1	void *	Deallocate dynamic memory
malloc	void *	1	unsigned	Allocate dynamic memory
rand	int	0		Random integer
system	int	1	const char *	Call operating system

Common Functions in string.h File

| FUNCTION NAME | FUNCTION TYPE | PARAMETERS | | FUNCTION DESCRIPTION |
		NO.	TYPE	
memmove	void *	3	void * const void * unsigned	Copies a specific number of bytes
strcat	char *	2	char * const char *	Concatenates two strings
strcmp	int	2	const char *	Compares strings
strcpy	char *	2	char * const char *	Copies a string
strlen	unsigned	1	const char *	Shows length of string (excluding the \0 character)
strncat	char *	3	char * const char * unsigned	Concatenates two strings up to a specific number of characters
strncpy	char *	3	char * const char * unsigned	Copies a string up to a specific number of characters

Escape Sequences

Escape sequence	Description	ASCII value
\0	Nul	000
\a	Bell	007
\b	Backspace	008
\f	Form feed	012
\n	New line (line feed)	010
\r	Carriage return	013
\t	Horizontal tab	009
\v	Vertical tab	011
\"	Quotation mark	034
\'	Apostrophe	039
\?	Question mark	063
\\	Backslash	092
\ooo	Octal number	—

Keywords in C

auto Modifies the duration of a variable so that it is created on entry to a block of code and is destroyed on exit from it. Local variables are **auto** by default.

Temporary variable created in a **while** *block.*

```
while (x != 3) {
    auto int j;
    j = x;
    printf("%d", j);
}
```

break Exits from a control structure (**if**, **for**, **while**, **do**, or **switch**).

Exit from a **for** *statement if a negative value is entered.*

```
for (i=0; i<10; i++ {
    printf ("Input value.");
    scanf ("%d", &val);
    if (val < 0)
        break;
    printf("Value = %d", val);
}
```

case Denotes a selector in a **switch** statement.

Selection in a **switch** *statement.*

```
switch (n) {
    case 5:  printf("Hi");
             break;
    case 9:  printf("Bye");
}
```

char Declares a character variable.

Specify a **char** *variable named* **letter**.

```
char letter;
```

const Prevents the value of a variable from changing.

Specify a `float` *variable named* `PI` *whose value cannot be changed.*

```
const float PI = 3.1416;
```

default Denotes the selector of a `switch` statement that executes when no match is found.

(See `switch`.)

do Creates a posttest loop in which the condition is put at the end of the loop.

Continuously read as long as positive decimal numbers are input.

```
do {
     printf ("Input a positive value - 0 or negative to stop");
     scanf ("%f",&x);
} while (x>0.0);
```

double Declares a double-precision `float` variable.

Specify a `double` *variable named* `dbl`.

```
double dbl;
```

else Allows execution of a statement block when an `if` expression is false.

Output `Sorry` *when* `x` *equals 5.*

```
x = 5;
if (x!=5)
   printf("OK");
else
   printf("Sorry");
```

enum Creates a programmer-defined data type whose values are explicitly stated (enumerated).

Declare data type `enum weekend` *with values* `Saturday` *and* `Sunday`.

```
enum weekend {Saturday, Sunday};             /* data type declaration */
enum weekend day;                            /* variable declaration */
```

extern Alters the scope of a variable so that it can be referenced across a program's files.

`float` *variable* `carry` *can be used in any program file.*

```
extern float carry;
```

float Declares a floating-point variable.

Declare a single precision, `float` *variable called* `y`.

```
float y;
```

for Creates an iterative loop by specifying initialization, condition, and increment.

Output the first five positive integers and their squares.

```
for ( i=1; i<=5; i++ )
   printf("%d%d", i, i*i);
```

goto Causes program execution to transfer to another location of the program identified by a label.

Transfer execution to location labeled `flag`.

```
goto flag;
   . . .
flag:
   print("New place");
```

if Allows execution of a statement block when the expression is true. Often used with `else`.

Output the message `Roast` *when the variable* `ch` *equals lowercase letter* `r`.

```
if (ch == 'r')
   printf("Roast");
```

int Declares an integer variable.

Declare the `int` *variable* `k`.

```
int k;
```

long Increases the storage for an integer variable.

Declare the `long int` *variable* `tree`.

```
long int tree;
```

register Requests that a variable be allocated to a CPU register for rapid execution. Register variables do not have an lvalue.

Declare the `register float` *variable* `smile`.

```
register float smile;
```

return Exits a function and sends the specified result to the caller.

Return the sum of `x` *and* `y`.

```
double sum  (double x, double y)
{
    return (x+y);
}
```

short Reduces the storage for an int variable.

Declare the short int *variable* count.

```
short int count;
```

signed Declares a signed integer data type (same as int).

Declare the signed int *variable* quotient.

```
signed int quotient;
```

sizeof Returns the storage in bytes of a data type.

Return the byte length of data type double.

```
sizeof(double);
```

static Modifies the duration of a variable so that it has permanent storage (in contrast to auto). Initializes the variable to 0.

Declare and initialize to 0 the static float *variable* area.

```
static float area;
```

struct Declares structures of one or more fields, usually of different data types.

Declare a struct *called* personnel *with three fields.*

```
struct personnel {
    char      name[80];
    long int  soc_security;
    int       age;
};
```

switch Creates a multibranched decision statement that uses case, break, and default.

Output depends on current value of in_value.

```
switch (in_value) {
    case 0:  printf ("Zero");
             break;
    case 1:  printf ("One");
             break;
   default:  printf ("Bye");
}
```

typedef Creates a new identifier name for a data type.

Define the symbol `BIG_INT` *as a* `static long int` *type.*

```
typedef  static long int  BIG_INT;
```

union Assigns two or more variables to the same memory location.

Declare two fields `area1` *and* `area2` *of the* `union` *that share the same memory location where* `space` *is the* `union` *tag and* `area` *is its variable name.*

```
union space {
   float area1;
   float area2;
} area;
```

unsigned Declares an integer variable without sign bits that allows only nonnegative integer values.

Declare the `unsigned int` *variable* `count`.

```
unsigned int count;
```

void Declares a no-data type. Usually associated with functions that either have no parameters or do not return a result.

Declare function `out` *to have neither an input parameter nor a return value.*

```
void out(void)
{
   . . .
}
```

volatile Allows a variable to be altered by an external event such as an interrupt.

Declare the variable `alarm` *as a* `volatile float`.

```
volatile float alarm;
```

while Creates a pretest loop in which the condition is placed at the beginning of the loop.

Print the first ten nonnegative integers.

```
x = 1;
while(x<=10) {
   printf("%d", x);
   ++ x;
}
```

Operator	Description	Associativity
() [] -> .	Function call Array element Structure member pointer reference Structure member reference	Left-to-right
++ -- - ! ~ (type) sizeof & *	Unary increment Unary decrement Unary negation Unary logical negation Unary one's complement Type conversion (cast) Storage size Address of Indirection	Right-to-left
* / %	Multiplication Division Modulus (remainder)	Left-to-right
+ -	Addition Subtraction	Left-to-right
<< >>	Left shift Right shift	Left-to-right
< <= > >=	Less than Less than or equal to Greater than Greater than or equal to	Left-to-right
== !=	Equal to Not equal to	Left-to-right
&	AND – bitwise	Left-to-right
^	Exclusive OR – bitwise	Left-to-right
|	Inclusive OR – bitwise	Left-to-right
&&	AND – Logical	Left-to-right
||	OR – Logical	Left-to-right
? :	Conditional expression	Right-to-left
= += -= *= /= %= &= ^= |= <<= >>=	Assignment and Compound Assignment	Right-to-left
,	Comma	Left-to-right

Note 1: Operators in each category have the same precedence and associativity.

Note 2: Operators toward the top of the table have higher priority than those toward the bottom.

ASCII / EBCDIC Character Codes

BINARY	BASE-10	BASE-16	ASCII 8-BIT	EBCDIC
00000000	0	00	NUL	NUL
00000001	1	01	SOH	SOH
00000010	2	02	STX	STX
00000011	3	03	ETX	ETX
00000100	4	04	EOT	PF
00000101	5	05	ENQ	HT
00000110	6	06	ACK	LC
00000111	7	07	BEL	DEL
00001000	8	08	BS	
00001001	9	09	HT	
00001010	10	0A	LF	SMM
00001011	11	0B	VT	VT
00001100	12	0C	FF	FF
00001101	13	0D	CR	CR
00001110	14	0E	SO	SO
00001111	15	0F	SI	SI
00010000	16	10	DLE	DLE
00010001	17	11	DC1	DC1
00010010	18	12	DC2	DC2
00010011	19	13	DC3	TM
00010100	20	14	DC4	RES
00010101	21	15	NAK	NL
00010110	22	16	SYN	BS
00010111	23	17	ETB	IL
00011000	24	18	CAN	CAN
00011001	25	19	EM	EM
00011010	26	1A	SUB	CC
00011011	27	1B	ESC	CU1
00011100	28	1C	FS	IFS
00011101	29	1D	GS	IGS
00011110	30	1E	RS	IRS
00011111	31	1F	US	IUS

BINARY	BASE-10	BASE-16	ASCII 8-BIT	EBCDIC
00100000	32	20	space	DS
00100001	33	21	!	SOS
00100010	34	22	"	FS
00100011	35	23	#	
00100100	36	24	$	BYP
00100101	37	25	%	LF
00100110	38	26	&	ETB
00100111	39	27	'	ESC
00101000	40	28	(	
00101001	41	29	)	
00101010	42	2A	*	SM
00101011	43	2B	+	CU2
00101100	44	2C	,	
00101101	45	2D	-	ENQ
00101110	46	2E	.	ACK
00101111	47	2F	/	BEL
00110000	48	30	0	
00110001	49	31	1	
00110010	50	32	2	SYN
00110011	51	33	3	
00110100	52	34	4	PN
00110101	53	35	5	RS
00110110	54	36	6	UC
00110111	55	37	7	EOT
00111000	56	38	8	
00111001	57	39	9	
00111010	58	3A	:	
00111011	59	3B	;	CU3
00111100	60	3C	<	DC4
00111101	61	3D	=	NAK
00111110	62	3E	>	
00111111	63	3F	?	SUB

BINARY	BASE-10	BASE-16	ASCII 8-BIT	EBCDIC
01000000	64	40	@	SP
01000001	65	41	A	
01000010	66	42	B	
01000011	67	43	C	
01000100	68	44	D	
01000101	69	45	E	
01000110	70	46	F	
01000111	71	47	G	
01001000	72	48	H	
01001001	73	49	I	
01001010	74	4A	J	¢
01001011	75	4B	K	
01001100	76	4C	L	<
01001101	77	4D	M	(
01001110	78	4E	N	+
01001111	79	4F	O	|
01010000	80	50	P	&
01010001	81	51	Q	
01010010	82	52	R	
01010011	83	53	S	
01010100	84	54	T	
01010101	85	55	U	
01010110	86	56	V	
01010111	87	57	W	
01011000	88	58	X	
01011001	89	59	Y	
01011010	90	5A	Z	!
01011011	91	5B	[	$
01011100	92	5C	\	*
01011101	93	5D	]	)
01011110	94	5E	^	;
01011111	95	5F	_	not

BINARY	BASE-10	BASE-16	ASCII 8-BIT	EBCDIC
01100000	96	60	'	-
01100001	97	61	a	/
01100010	98	62	b	
01100011	99	63	c	
01100100	100	64	d	
01100101	101	65	e	
01100110	102	66	f	
01100111	103	67	g	
01101000	104	68	h	
01101001	105	69	i	
01101010	106	6A	j	
01101011	107	6B	k	,
01101100	108	6C	l	%
01101101	109	6D	m	_
01101110	110	6E	n	>
01101111	111	6F	o	?
01110000	112	70	p	
01110001	113	71	q	
01110010	114	72	r	
01110011	115	73	s	
01110100	116	74	t	
01110101	117	75	u	
01110110	118	76	v	
01110111	119	77	w	
01111000	120	78	x	
01111001	121	79	y	
01111010	122	7A	z	:
01111011	123	7B	{	#
01111100	124	7C			@
01111101	125	7D	]	'
01111110	126	7E	~	=
01111111	127	7F	DEL	"

BINARY	BASE-10	BASE-16	ASCII 8-BIT	EBCDIC
10000000	128	80		
10000001	129	81		a
10000010	130	82		b
10000011	131	83		c
10000100	132	84		d
10000101	133	85		e
10000110	134	86		f
10000111	135	87		g
10001000	136	88		h
10001001	137	89		i
10001010	138	8A		
10001011	139	8B		
10001100	140	8C		
10001101	141	8D		
10001110	142	8E		
10001111	143	8F		
10010000	144	90		
10010001	145	91		j
10010010	146	92		k
10010011	147	93		l
10010100	148	94		m
10010101	149	95		n
10010110	150	96		o
10010111	151	97		p
10011000	152	98		q
10011001	153	99		r
10011010	154	9A		
10011011	155	9B		
10011100	156	9C		
10011101	157	9D		
10011110	158	9E		
10011111	159	9F		

BINARY	BASE-10	BASE-16	ASCII 8-BIT	EBCDIC
10100000	160	A0		
10100001	161	A1		
10100010	162	A2		s
10100011	163	A3		t
10100100	164	A4		u
10100101	165	A5		v
10100110	166	A6		w
10100111	167	A7		x
10101000	168	A8		y
10101001	169	A9		z
10101010	170	AA		
10101011	171	AB		
10101100	172	AC		
10101101	173	AD		
10101110	174	AE		
10101111	175	AF		
10110000	176	B0		
10110001	177	B1		
10110010	178	B2		
10110011	179	B3		
10110100	180	B4		
10110101	181	B5		
10110110	182	B6		
10110111	183	B7		
10111000	184	B8		
10111001	185	B9		
10111010	186	BA		
10111011	187	BB		
10111100	188	BC		
10111101	189	BD		
10111110	190	BE		
10111111	191	BF		

BINARY	BASE-10	BASE-16	ASCII 8-BIT	EBCDIC
11000000	192	C0		
11000001	193	C1		A
11000010	194	C2		B
11000011	195	C3		C
11000100	196	C4		D
11000101	197	C5		E
11000110	198	C6		F
11000111	199	C7		G
11001000	200	C8		H
11001001	201	C9		I
11001010	202	CA		
11001011	203	CB		
11001100	204	CC		
11001101	205	CD		
11001110	206	CE		
11001111	207	CF		
11010000	208	D0		
11010001	209	D1		J
11010010	210	D2		K
11010011	211	D3		L
11010100	212	D4		M
11010101	213	D5		N
11010110	214	D6		O
11010111	215	D7		P
11011000	216	D8		Q
11011001	217	D9		R
11011010	218	DA		
11011011	219	DB		
11011100	220	DC		
11011101	221	DD		
11011110	222	DE		
11011111	223	DF		

BINARY	BASE-10	BASE-16	ASCII 8-BIT	EBCDIC
11100000	224	E0		
11100001	225	E1		
11100010	226	E2		S
11100011	227	E3		T
11100100	228	E4		U
11100101	229	E5		V
11100110	230	E6		W
11100111	231	E7		X
11101000	232	E8		Y
11101001	233	E9		Z
11101010	234	EA		
11101011	235	EB		
11101100	236	EC		
11101101	237	ED		
11101110	238	EE		
11101111	239	EF		
11110000	240	F0		0
11110001	241	F1		1
11110010	242	F2		2
11110011	243	F3		3
11110100	244	F4		4
11110101	245	F5		5
11110110	246	F6		6
11110111	247	F7		7
11111000	248	F8		8
11111001	249	F9		9
11111010	250	FA		
11111011	251	FB		
11111100	252	FC		
11111101	253	FD		
11111110	254	FE		
11111111	255	FF		

Derivation of Simpson's Rule

The strategy for Simpson's rule is to approximate the graph of a function using parabolas. Consider the generalized parabola represented by the function

$$y = p(x) = Ax^2 + Bx + C$$

where A, B, and C are real numbers. Let $p(x)$ be defined for all x on the interval $-h \le x \le +h$ where h is a fixed increment. The integral of $p(x)$ is represented by Intg, which becomes

$$\text{Intg} = \int_{-h}^{+h} p(x)\,dx = \int_{-h}^{+h} (Ax^2 + Bx + C)\,dx$$

$$= [Ax^3/3 + Bx^2/2 + Cx \,|_{-h}^{+h}$$

$$= [A(+h)^3/3 + B(+h)^2/2 + (C + h)] - [A(-h)^3/3 + B(-h)^2/2 + C(-h)]$$

$$= +A(+h^3)/3 + B(+h^2)/2 + C(+h)$$

$$\quad - A(-h^3)/3 - B(+h^2)/2 - C(-h)$$

$$= A(2h^3)/3 \qquad\qquad + C(2h)$$

$$= (2Ah^2 + 6Ch)(h/3)$$

The parabola passes through the following three points: $(-h, p(-h))$, $(0, p(0))$, and $(+h, p(+h))$. Let $y_0 = p(-h)$, $y_1 = p(0)$, and $y_2 = p(+h)$. Then,

$$y_0 = p(-h) = Ah^2 - Bh + C$$
$$y_1 = p(0) = C$$
$$y_2 = p(+h) = Ah^2 + Bh + C$$

Now,

$$y_0 - y_1 = Ah^2 - Bh + C - C = Ah^2 - Bh$$
$$y_2 - y_1 = Ah^2 + Bh + C - C = Ah^2 + Bh$$

And,

$$y_0 - 2y_1 + y_2 = 2Ah^2$$

Therefore,

$$\text{Intg} = (2Ah^2 + 6Ch)(h/3) = [(y_0 - 2y_1 + y_2) + 6y_1](h/3)$$
$$= [y_0 + 4y_1 + y_2](h/3)$$

For an area partitioned into $2n$ segments, each of width h, the total area, *Area,* is calculated as follows:

$$\text{Area} = (h/3)[y_0 + 4y_1 + y_2$$
$$+ y_2 + 4y_3 + y_4$$
$$+ y_4 + 4y_5 + y_6$$
$$\cdots$$
$$+ y_{2n-4} + 4y_{2n-3} + y_{2n-2}$$
$$+ y_{2n-2} + 4y_{2n-1} + y_{2n}$$

$$\text{Area} = (h/3)[y_0 + 4y_1 + 2y_2 + 4y_3 + 2y_4 + \ldots + 2y_{2n-2} + 4y_{2n-1} + y_{2n}]$$
$$= (h/3)[y_0 + 4\Sigma y_{\text{odd}} + 2\Sigma y_{\text{even}} + y_{2n}]$$

Answers to Selected Exercises

(Headers to programs and functions are omitted, except for some cases in the Chapter 3 exercises.)

SECTION 1.1

1. True
3. False
5. C
7. C
9. Computer graphics
11. Protection
13. The Denning Report suggests the study of computing as a whole in the first stages of the discipline coupled with laboratory experiences. It also proposes knowledge units rather than prescribed courses. Previous curricula recommendations promoted depth in the beginning of the curriculum by the early study and concentration on programming.
15. The nine areas of computing are algorithms and data structures; programming languages; architecture; numerical and symbolic computing; operating systems; software methodology and engineering; database and information retrieval; artificial intelligence and robotics; and human-computer communication.
18. Pro: Provides the same user interface for each of its components. Con: Is restricted to the quality of the integrated package.
20. Computer graphics falls under the topics of symbolic computing, software engineering, and human-computer communication.
21. Programming falls under broader category of *programming languages.*
25. A LAN would be used by a company that has one or two offices in the same building. A WAN would be used by a company to connect offices that are in more than one city.

SECTION 1.2

1. True
3. True

5. D

7. B

9. Star, ring

11. Registers

13. An analog computer processes continuous quantities, while a digital computer processes discrete quantities.

15. The prefix *kilo* as used in *kilometer* means 1000. The prefix *kilo* as used in *kilobyte* means $1024 = 2^{10}$.

18. A serial port is an addressable interface that exchanges data one bit at a time. A parallel port is an addressable interface that exchanges data many bits at a time.

20. Two computers usually communicate on a network without a modem. A modem is required when transmission is over the telephone lines.

22. *MHz* refers to the clock speed of the computer. The instruction speed is indicated by *MIPS* (millions of instructions per second), which could potentially be different for each architecture.

24. A multiuser system operates on the concept of time sharing, dividing the processor time among the users. A multitasking computer can perform more than one task at a time.

SECTION 1.3

1. False

3. True

5. C

7. C

9. Assembly language

11. FORTRAN

13. Machine language is written in binary form. Assembly language made the programming of computers easier because it was a symbolic representation of machine language.

16. Each program would require hardwired instructions.

17. An integrated circuit has many components (usually between 10 and 10,000) contained within a single unit. A chip has tens of thousands to millions of components contained within a single unit.

20. Computers are not capable of learning, thinking, or being creative.

22. The fetch, decode, and execute process is simple to understand and design. However, parallel processing and RISC architectures are making inroads into the classical way of viewing computers.

24. Programmers write and modify computer programs. Computer scientists deal with the phenomena of computing and are well versed in the various topics of computing.

SECTION 2.1

1. False

3. False

5. C

7. D

9. At least $3,000

11. Sometimes/often

13. $20 [$130,000/(65 · 100) = $20 per chip]

16. 22 and 23

18. 8 and 12 [8 · 12 = 96 and 8 + 12 = 20]

19. $6000 [$195000 − $45000 = $150000; $150000/25 = $6000]

21. 22 (rounded up)

22. 8280 MB minimum

24. 5.2 [(3.2 + 5.6 + 3.9 + 8.1 + 7.3 + 2.9 + 5.2)/7 = 36.2/7 = 5.17]

SECTION 2.2

1. False

3. False

5. A

7. D

9. Inputs, outputs

11. Input, output, process

13. Step 1. INPUT side
    Step 2. area = side * side
    Step 3. OUTPUT area
    Step 4. STOP

16. Step 1. INPUT radius
    Step 2. area = 3.14159 * radius * radius
    Step 3. OUTPUT area
    Step 4. STOP

17. Step 1. INPUT radius
    Step 2. WHILE radius > 0
            a. volume = (4/3) * (3.14159) * (radius * radius * radius)
            b. OUTPUT volume
    Step 3. STOP

20. Step 1. LOOP many times
       a. INPUT p
       b. WHILE p < 50000 OR p > 500000
          1. OUTPUT error message
          2. INPUT p
       c. INPUT yearly_rate
       d. WHILE yearly_rate < 0.05 OR yearly_rate > 0.15
          1. OUTPUT error message
          2. INPUT yearly_rate
       e. INPUT num_years
       f. WHILE num_years < 10 OR num_years > 40
          1. OUTPUT error message
          2. INPUT num_years
       g. i = yearly_rate/12
       h. n = years * 12
       i. m = (p * i * (1 + i)^n)/((1 + i)^n- 1)
       j. OUTPUT m
    Step 2. STOP

22. Step 1. INPUT principal
    Step 2. INPUT time
    Step 3. IF time ≤ 1
              rate = 0.06
            ELSE IF time < 6
              rate = 0.07
            ELSE IF time ≥ 6 AND time ≤ 10
              rate = 0.08
            ELSE
              rate = 0.09
    Step 4. interest = principal * rate * time
    Step 5. OUTPUT interest
    Step 6. STOP

26. Step 1. i = 0
    Step 2. j = 1
    Step 3. WHILE i < 13
       a. WHILE j < 11
          1. result = i * j
          2. OUTPUT result
          3. j = j + 1
       b. i = i + 1
    Step 4. STOP

SECTION 3.1

1. False

3. False

5. B

7. C

9. Function

11. Those reading the program

13. `printf("C is fun");`

15. `float volume;`

18. `scanf("%d", &sales);`

20.
```
/*********************************************************************
 * Title:        area of trapezoid                                   *
 * Filename:     areatrap.c                                          *
 *                                                                   *
 * Description: Compute the area of a trapezoid.  Input two values   *
 *              representing the length and width of the base of the *
 *              figure, and a value for the height.  Then compute    *
 *              the corresponding area using:                        *
 *                   area = (base_1 + base_2) * height / 2           *
 *              Output the area.                                     *
 *                                                                   *
 * Input:       base_1, base_2, height                              *
 * Output:      area                                                 *
 * Process:     area = (base_1 + base_2) * height / 2               *
 *                                                                   *
 * Written by:  ...                            Date: ...             *
 *********************************************************************/
#include <stdio.h>

main()
{
   float base_1, base_2, basesum, height, area;

   printf("\nInput value for base 1 ->");          /* Input base_1 */
   scanf ("%f", &base_1);
   printf("\nInput value for base 2 ->");          /* Input base_2 */
   scanf ("%f", &base_2);
   printf("\nInput value for height ->");          /* Input height */
   scanf ("%f", &height);

   basesum = base_1 + base_2;                            /* Process */
   area    = basesum * height / 2;

   printf("\nThe area = %6.2f", area);           /* Output result */

   return(0);
}
```

23.
```c
#include <stdio.h>

main()
{
   int    inches;
   float centimeters;

   printf("\nEnter a value in inches->");
   scanf ("%d", &inches);

   centimeters = inches * 2.54
   printf("\n%d inches is equivalent to %6.2f centimeters",
                 inches, centimeters);

   return(0);
}
```

28.
```c
/*********************************************************************
* Title:       find quotient                                        *
* Filename:    divide.c                                             *
*                                                                   *
* Description: Compute the quotient of two numbers entered by the   *
*              user.  Output the result.                            *
*                                                                   *
* Input:       num_1, num_2                                         *
* Output:      quotient                                            *
* Process:     quotient = num_1 / num_2                             *
*                                                                   *
* Written by:  ...                                Date: ...          *
*********************************************************************/
#include <stdio.h>

main()
{
   double num_1, num_2, quotient;

   printf( "\nInput two numbers>" );
   scanf ( " %lf %lf ", &num_1, &num_2 );

   quotient = num_1 / num_2;

   printf("\nThe result of %8.2f / %8.2f is %8.2f",
             num_1, num_2, quotient);

   return(0);
}
```

SECTION 3.2

1. False

3. False

5. B

7. C

9. Two

11. Special

13. `float volume;`

15. `scanf("%f", &volume );`

17. `const int BASE = 2;`
    `const int HEIGHT = 5;`

19.
```
/************************************************************
 * Title:      display characters in ASCII and integer     *
 * Filename:   display.c                                    *
 *                                                          *
 * Description: Display a character to the screen, using both the *
 *              %c and the %d formats.  Using %c in the printf *
 *              statement causes the character to print to the *
 *              screen.  Using the %d format outputs the ASCII *
 *              value of that character.                    *
 *                                                          *
 * Input:      character                                    *
 * Output:     character                                    *
 * Process:    none                                         *
 *                                                          *
 * Written by: ...                          Date: ...       *
 ************************************************************/
#include <stdio.h>

main()
{
  char ch;

    printf("\nEnter a character->");
    scanf ("%d", &ch);

    printf("\nThis is the value using the character output> %c", ch );
    printf("\nThis is the value using the integer output> %d", ch );

    return(0);
}
```

26.
```
/*************************************************************
 * Title:        find square and cube                        *
 * Filename:     cube.c                                      *
 *                                                           *
 * Description: Compute the square and the cube of an input number. *
 *              Output the result.                           *
 *                                                           *
 * Input:        num                                         *
 * Output:       sqr_num, cube_num                           *
 * Process:      sqr_num  = num * num                        *
 *               cube_num = sqr_num * num                     *
 *                                                           *
 * Written by:  ...                           Date: ...      *
 *************************************************************/
#include <stdio.h>

main()
{
   int    num;
   double sqr_num, cube_num;

   printf("\nEnter a number->");
   scanf ("%d", &num);

   sqr_num  = num * num;
   cube_num = sqr_num * num;

   printf("\nThe squared value of %d is %8.2f", num, sqr_num);
   printf("\nThe cubed value of %d is %8.2f", num, cube_num);

   return(0);
}
```

27.
```
/*************************************************************
 * Title:        distance traveled                           *
 * Filename:     distanc.c                                   *
 *                                                           *
 * Description: Compute the distance traveled by a free-falling object. *
 *              The value for the time is input by the user. *
 *              Output the result.                           *
 *                                                           *
 * Input:        time                                        *
 * Output:       distance                                    *
 * Process:      distance = GRAV*pow(time,2)/2               *
 *                                                           *
 * Written by:  ...                           Date: ...      *
 *************************************************************/
```

```
#include <stdio.h>

main()
{
    const int GRAV = 32;

    int   time;                              /* in seconds */
    float dist;                              /* in feet */

    printf("\nEnter the time of fall>");
    scanf ("%d", &time);

    dist = GRAV * pow(time,2) / 2;

    printf("\nThe object fell %8.2f feet in %d seconds", dist, time );

    return(0);
}
```

SECTION 3.3

1. False

3. False

5. B

7. D

9. Highest precedence

11. Integer

13. 40

15. 14

17. 1.1286565971

19. 4

21. 25

23. 6

25. 11.50

27. 0

30. $x = 5$, $y = -5$, $z = 2$

SECTION 4.1

1. False

3. False

5. C

7. B

9. Negative

11. ASCII

13. 8644

15. 011101000110

17. 93

19. 0101000001101

21. 0110000110001111

23. 010100101110

25. 01001000 01100001 01110000 01110000 01111001

26. 6023572

29. 1101101110100010

31. 11000111 10000101 10010110 10011001 10000111 10001001 10000001

33. 175,976,270

34. 10E6E (hexadecimal) = 69230 (decimal)

SECTION 4.2

1. False

3. True

5. C

7. B

9. Conjunction

11. The negation

13. 0

15. 1

17. 0

19. (1, 0, 0, 1)

23. $g(x, y) =$ NOT y

25.

x	y	z	NOT x	NOT z	NOT x OR NOT z	x OR y	NOT(x OR y)	(NOT x OR NOT y) AND (NOT(x OR y))
0	0	0	1	1	1	0	1	1
0	0	1	1	0	1	0	1	1
0	1	0	1	1	1	1	0	0
0	1	1	1	0	1	1	0	0
1	0	0	0	1	1	1	0	0
1	0	1	0	0	0	1	0	0
1	1	0	0	1	1	1	0	0
1	1	1	0	0	0	1	0	0

27.

x	y	x AND y	NOT (x AND y)	NOT x	NOT y	(NOT x) OR (NOT y)
0	0	0	1	1	1	1
0	1	0	1	1	0	1
1	0	0	1	0	1	1
1	1	1	0	0	0	0

29. 0

31. 1

33. 0

SECTION 4.3

1. False

3. False

5. A

7. B

9. Mantissa

11. Characteristic

13. 94AE6DBF

15. Signature 1 signifies a negative number. Characteristic 10101001110 signifies that the exponent is $+344$.

17. 3, 3.1, 3.14, 3.142

19. $-[13 * 16^{-1} + 15 * 16^{-2} + 4 * 16^{-3} + 14 * 16^{-4}] * 16^3 = -3572.875$

21. -41

23. $-[12 * 16^{-1} + 4 * 16^{-2}] * 16^{-3} = -0.00018692$

SECTION 5.1

1. False

3. True

5. B

7. B

9. Input, return

11. Function prototype, function header

13. `double sqrt(double number);`

15. `net_pay = calc_net_pay(25.0, 40, 10);`
    `double calc_net_pay(double wage, int hours, int ot_hours);`

17. Add more `printf` statements

19.
```
float fahr_to_cels( float fahrenheit )
{
    float celsius;
    celsius = 5.0/9.0 * (fahrenheit - 32);
    return(celsius);
}
```

SECTION 5.2

1. True

3. False

5. B

7. D

9. Short circuit

11. `switch`

13.
```c
void check(char answer)
{
    if (answer == 'T')
        printf("\nThe answer is TRUE.");
    else if (answer == 'F')
        printf("\nThe answer is FALSE.");
    else
        printf("\nThere is an error in the answer!");
}
```

15.
```c
void test_letter(char test)
{
    if ( ch >= 'A' && ch <= 'M' )
        printf( "\nIt is in the first half of the alphabet.");
    else if ( ch > 'M' && ch <= 'Z' )
        printf("\nIt is in the second half of the alphabet.");
}
```

17.
```c
void test_char(char ch)
{
    if ( ch == 'A' || ch=='E' || ch == 'I' || ch == 'O' || ch == 'U' )
        printf("\nIt's a vowel.");
    else
        printf("\nIt's not a vowel.");
}
```

19.
```c
int find_val(int val_one,  int val_two)
{
    if ( (val_two % val_one) == 0 )
        return(0);
    else
        return(1);
}
```

SECTION 5.3

1. False

3. False

5. B

7. D

9. `for`

11. `float, double, int`

13. While an infinite loop, increment exterior to loop

15. Remove increment after `printf`

17. Initialize **x** to 1 not 0.

19. `k = 180`

21.
```c
#include <stdio.h>
main()
{
    int i, low_range, high_range;
    int sum = 0;
    printf("\nPlease enter the lower bound for your summation >");
    scanf ("%d", &low_range);
    printf("\nPlease enter the upper bound for your summation >");
    scanf ("%d", &high_range);
    for ( i=low_range; i<=high_range; i++ )
        sum += i;
    printf("\nThe sum is %d", sum);
    return(0);
}
```

22.
```c
int  factorial ( int  n )
{
    int    i, product = 1;
    for ( i=1; i<=n; i++ )
        product *= i;
    return ( product );
}
```

SECTION 6.1

1. False

3. False

5. C

7. B

9. Time-sharing

11. Interactive processing

13. $0.006/8 = 0.00075$

15. The simplest is FIFO: The first job on the scheduling queue is the first job to be executed. Another is SJF: The shortest job on the queue is the one that is executed first.

17. Due to priorities, a program on a queue might never complete execution because it or those before it are preempted or bumped. If a job queue is never emptied, a program can stay on it forever.

21. When $p = 1$, $T(n + 1) = t(n)$. This means that the predicted time is the same as the actual burst time. In this case prediction is nullified.

23. $T(n + 1) = 0.25(8.4) + 0.75(8.4) = 8.4 \mu s$

SECTION 6.2

1. False

3. False

5. C

7. D

9. Cache

11. Text editor

15. $(16 * 2^{10}) * 8192 = 134{,}217{,}728$ bytes $= 128$ MB

17. When a program is larger than physical memory, some portion of the program is loaded in memory while the other is placed into secondary memory. Pages are swapped into memory as needed.

19. $AT = 0 * FT + (1 - 0) * 2 \mu s = 2 \mu s$

21. $35 * 4096 = 143{,}360$ bytes $= 140$ KB

23. $AT = 0.84(400 \mu s) + 0.16(12 \mu s) = 337.92 \mu s$

SECTION 7.1

1. True

3. False

5. B

7. C

9. Vector, contiguous list

11. Physical, logical

13. `int x[] = {-10, 14, 22, -3, 12};`

15.
```
for ( i=0; i<10; i++ )
      b[i] = a[i];
```

17.
```
for ( i=0; i<10; i++ )
      if ( (i%2) != 0 )
          printf(" %d ", x[i] );
```

```
19. int  x[1000];
    scanf ( "%d", &size );
    for ( i=0; i<size; i++ )
       scanf ("%d", &x[i] );
    for ( i=size-1; i>=0; i-- )
       if ( x[i]>20 )
          printf("%d", x[i] );

21. float a[50], b[50];
    int    size, x;
    scanf ("%d", &size );
    scanf ("%d", &x );
    for ( i=0; i<size; i++ )
       scanf ("%f", &a[i] );
    for ( i=0; i<size; i++ )
       b[i] = a[i] - x;
    for ( i=0; i<size; i++ )
       printf("\n  %f   %f", a[i], b[i]);
```

SECTION 7.2

1. False

3. False

5. C

7. C

9. Input parameter

11. Data type, variable name, bracket

13.
```
float pick_min( float rainfall[])
min = pick_min(rainfall);
```

15.
```
float summer_rain( float june, float july, float august)
{
    float total=0;
    total = june + july + august;
    return(total);
}
```

17.
```
float find_max_rain( float rainfall[] )
{
    int i;
    float max = 0;
    for ( i=0, i<YEAR_LENGTH; i++ )
       if ( rainfall[i] > max )
          max = rainfall[i];
    return(max);
}
```

19.
```
int find_max_rain_month( float rainfall[] )
{
   int i, max_month, max=0;
   for ( i=0, i<YEAR_LENGTH; i++ )
      if ( rainfall[i] > max )  {
         max = rainfall[i];
         max_month = i;
      }
   return( max_month );
}
```

21.
```
double calc_std_dev( int grade_list[], int num_grades )
{
   int     i;
   double  sum, mean, sum_sq, var, std_dev;

   sum    = 0.0;
   for ( i=0; i<num_grades; i++ );
      sum += grade_list[i];
   mean   = sum / num_grades;

   sum_sq  = 0.0;
   for ( i=0; i<num_grades; i++ )
      sum_sq += pow( mean - grade_list[i], 2 );
   var     = sum_sq / num_grades;
   std_dev = sqrt( var );

   return( std_dev );
}
```

SECTION 7.3

1. True

3. False

5. C

7. D

9. Matrixes, tables

11. Row major

13. `float x[7][17];`

15.
```
sum_1 = 0;
for ( i=0; i<4; i++ );
   sum_1 += x[i][1];
```

```
17. for ( i=0; i<3; i++ )
        for (j=0; j<2; j++ )
            for ( k=0; k<4; k++ )
                x[i][j][k] = 0;

19. int a[4][9], b[4][9], c[4][9];
    int row, col;
    for ( row=0; row<4; row++ )  {
        for ( col=0; col<9; col++ )
            c[row][col] = a[row][col] - b[row][col];
    }

22. void month_means( float rainfall[][NUM_DAYS], float means[] )
    {
        float   sum;
        int     month, day;
        for ( month=0; month<NUM_MONTHS; month++ )  {
            sum = 0.0;
            for (day=0; day<NUM_DAYS; day++ )
                sum += rainfall[month][day];
            means[month] = sum / NUM_DAYS;
        }
    }
```

SECTION 7.4

1. False

3. False

5. B

7. D

9. 19

11. `string.h`

13. `printf("\n%c", name[2]);`

15. `if ( strcmp(string_one, string_two) > 0)`
    `    strcpy(all_strings[2], string_two);`
    `else`
    `    strcpy(all_strings[2], string_one);`

17. `strcpy( strings[8], strings[6] );`

```
20. void put_words( char str[] )
    {
        int   i;
        for ( i=0; i<strlen(str); i++ )
            if ( str[i]!=' ' && str[i]!='.' )      /* No punctuation, so */
                printf("%c", str[i] );             /* output character. */
            else                                   /* Punctuation, so skip */
                printf("\n");                      /* to new line. */
    }
```

SECTION 8.1

1. False
3. True
5. B
7. D
9. Amplitude, frequency (pitch)
11. Radio (or television, cellular phones, and so on)
13. A baseband medium is coaxial cable used to transmit digital signals; a broadband medium is coaxial cable used for analog transmissions.
15. Signals would be timed so that parallel information transmissions would arrive at their destinations at the same time.
17. Fiber optics converts electrical signals into light pulses. It works well over short distances because communication is fast and efficient.

SECTION 8.2

1. False
3. False
5. C
7. B
9. Framing
11. Codeword
13. $3 \leq 2^3 - 4 - 1 = 3$
15. $7 = d - 1; d = 8$
17. One possible answer is CCFCE0 that assumes a two-bit insertion of 00 after six-bit patterns.
19. 010011011
21. 001011111110111001101 (base-2) = 2FEE68 (base-16)
23. Codeword should be 0011001000. Information string is 100100.
25. Fifteenth bit of codeword inverted. Codeword should be E2D97.

SECTION 9.1

1. False

3. True

5. B

7. D

9. Indirection/dereferencing

11. `%p`

13. `char ch;`
    `char *ch_ptr;`

15. `ch = 'X';`
    `*ch_ptr = 'X';`

17. `printf("\n%p %c", ch_ptr,*ch_ptr);`

19.   a. Incompatible
      c. Incorrect. Possible solution: `b = *fl_pt2;`
      e. Correct
      g. Incorrect. Possible solution: `*fl_pt2 = 13.5;`
      i. Correct
      k. Incorrect. Possible solution: `c_pt1 = &c;`
      m. Incorrect. Possible solution: `i_pt2 = i_pt1;`
      o. Incorrect. Possible solution: `i_pt1 = i_pt2;`
      q. Incorrect. Possible solution: `fl_pt2 = &b;`
      s. Correct

SECTION 9.2

1. False

3. True

5. C

7. C

9. Input argument

11. Local variable

13. `f( a, b, &x, &y, &z );`

15. `int check_status( int status[], size );`

17. `void set_status( int status[], size )`
    ```
    {
        int count;
        for( count=0; count<size; count++ )
            status[count] = FALSE;
    }
    ```

19. `*x *= 17;`
21.
```
void find_smallest(int a, int b, int c, int *smallest)
{
    if ( (a<b) && (b<c) )
        *smallest = a;
    else if ( (b<a) && (a<c) )
        *smallest = b;
    else
        *smallest = c;
}
```

SECTION 10.1

1. False
3. False
5. B
7. C
9. Software engineering
11. Coding
18. Decide to have the barbecue. Make a list of who I'm inviting. Call people and invite them. Make list of food and supplies. Go to supermarket and get food. Come home. Prepare food. Greet guests. Serve food.
19. Use the Four Knight's Defense to allow me a cautious response to a strong opening. From there I will proceed to shape my attack toward his Queen's side. I will draw him into a passed pawn situation while at the same time work on my castling....The bottom-up approach works toward shorter goals that will lead you to checkmate. The bottom-up approach looks at individual situations and works its way to the top.
21. A top-down approach: Decide to get a book from the library. I go to the library. Look in the card or online catalog. Find where the book is. Take it out and read it.

    A bottom-up approach: Want to read a book but do not know which one. Go to the library to get the book. Book is on a shelf, but which shelf? Walk through library book stacks and pick a book.

SECTION 10.2

1. False
3. True
5. B
7. A
9. Software implementation
11. Needs analysis

13. We could make the constant weight be a variable entered at run-time. This would allow the professor to use whatever weight to apply equally to each of the three grades by doing this:

```
final_grade = (weight*grade1 + weight*grade2 + weight*grade3);
```

15. `ReadStudentRecord` = three corresponding `printf` and `scanf` statements that read in the student grades
    `CalcGrade` = `final_grade` assignment statement
    `PrintGrade` = final `printf` statement printing `final_grade`

17. It is important to know the hardware platform on which a program will run; otherwise, the software will not be compatible. C is useful because of its inherent portability between systems.

19. Only `gross` needs to be altered; `wage` and `hours` do not.

20. `final_grade = (grade1 + grade2 + grade3 + grade4) / 4;`

21. It depends on the situation. If all grades are of equal weight, a simple average is required. Otherwise, each grade requires a weight factor.

23. `printf("\n%s has a final grade of %d", name, final_grade);`

25. The address that `*gross` points to is assigned the content value of `wage*hours`.

SECTION 11.1

1. True

3. True

5. B

7. B

9. Nonimplemented, specifications for the relevant accessing functions

11. `typedef`

13. `enum weekdays {  MONDAY, TUESDAY, WEDNESDAY, THURSDAY,`
    `                FRIDAY, SATURDAY, SUNDAY  };`

15. `enum family { EDWARD, JACKIE, ERIC };`

17. `typedef enum summer_months SUMMER_MONTHS;`

19. ```
struct personnel_info {
                         STRING   name;
                         STRING   address;
                         long int soc_sec;
                       }
```
```

21.
```
struct personnel_info {
                        STRING          name;
                        STRING          address;
                        long int        soc_sec;
                        struct exam_record  test_result;
            }
```

23.
```
void assign_grades( struct exam_record *student )
{
    student->grade1 = 80;
    student->grade2 = 90;
    student->grade3 = 90;
}
```

SECTION 11.2

1. False
3. False
5. A
7. B
9. `stack->top = 0;`
11. Information hiding
13. $7/3 = 2$ (assuming C's rules for division)
15. $4 + 3 * (2 + 1) = 13$
17. $-1/3$
19. A B C * +
21. A B^C * D E F / G H + / −
23. A B C D E − / + *
25.
```
ITEM_TYPE   pop( STACK_TYPE *stack )
{
    return( stack->item[ --stack->top ] );
}
```

SECTION 11.3

1. True
3. True
5. B
7. C
9. Queue overflow

11. The front and rear indexes are equal.

13.
```
typedef struct q_type {
                          ITEM_TYPE item[ MAX_Q ];
                          int queue_count;
                          int front;
                          int rear;
                       } Q_TYPE;
```

15. Add a loop in **main**.

17.
```
ITEM_TYPE dequeue( Q_TYPE *queue )
{
    queue->front = ++queue->front%MAX_Q;
    return( queue->item[queue->front] );
}
```

20.
```
void  enqueue( Q_TYPE *queue,  ITEM_TYPE new_item )
{
    queue->rear = queue->rear + 1
    if ( queue->rear == MAX_Q )
       queue->rear = 0;
    queue->item[queue->rear] = new_item;
}
```

SECTION 12.1

1. True

3. False

5. A

7. C

9. Access to a physical database, managing information

11. File

13. **fopen ("data", "r");** is one way.

15. Sequential files are good if the data that you access most frequently are in the front of the file or if the information is in sequence.

17. An index is some key to a database that is easily incremented or decremented. To search for an item by an index, an array is loaded into main memory and searched according to the index. Without an index, each record must be retrieved into main memory; such retrieval is a great deal slower than loading a single array into memory once and searching it.

19. Through **struct** by associating records with their fields.

21. The applications programmer would use a DBMS (an intermediate software layer) to manipulate the physical database.

23. **printf** outputs to a standard output file (monitor). **fprintf** outputs to a designated file.

SECTION 12.2

1. False
3. True
5. C
7. D
9. Network data model
11. Entity-relationship (E-R)
13. The physical data model shows how the underlying data structures are organized so that their resources are optimized. Logical data models interpret the data in the context of a particular application.
15. A data table organizes a relationship set with an entity set. The set of all data tables in the E-R model forms the database for the E-R model.
17. Because you may want a variety of different ways you would like to represent your information.
19. Entity sets and relationship sets are organized so that relations are formed between entities.
21. A segment is related to any other segment without a tree structure. The links among the segments form the database.

SECTION 13.1

1. False
3. True
5. C
7. D
9. Declared array
11. **free**, heap
13. ***stack = NULL;**
15. **free ((*stack)->next->next);**
    (*stack)->next->next = NULL;
17. ```
    ITEM_TYPE stack_top( STACK_TYPE *stack)
    {
        return((*stack)->info);
    }
    ```
18. ```
    void stack_top( STACK_TYPE *stack, ITEM_TYPE *new_item)
    {
        *new_item =(*stack)->info);
    }
    ```

SECTION 13.2

1. False

3. True

5. D

7. A

9. `NULL`

11. `NULL`

13.
```
BOOLEAN empty_queue ( Q_TYPE *queue )
{
    return ( queue->rear == NULL ? TRUE : FALSE );
}
```

17.
```
NODE_TYPE get_q_front( Q_TYPE *queue )
{
    NODE_PTR temp_ptr;

    if ( empty_queue ( queue ) == FALSE )
        return ( queue->front->info );
    else
        return ( NULL );
}
```

21.
```
BOOLEAN full_queue( Q_TYPE *queue )
{
    temp_ptr = (NODE_PTR)malloc( sizeof(NODE_TYPE) );

    if ( temp_ptr == NULL )
        return( TRUE );
    else {
        free( temp_ptr );
        return( FALSE );
    }
}
```

SECTION 13.3

1. False

3. False

5. B

7. C

9. 2, `previous` and `current`

11. Circular-linked list

13. ```
BOOLEAN empty_list(LIST_TYPE *list)
{
    return((*list)->next->info.key == MAX_KEY ? FALSE : TRUE);
}
```

15. ```
typedef struct item_type {
                            char first_name[12];
                            char last_name[18];
                            char address[80];
                            char city[15];
                            char state[2];
                            KEY_TYPE phone_number[10];
                          } ITEM_TYPE;
```

16. ```
BOOLEAN full_list (LIST_TYPE *list)
{
    LIST_TYPE temp_ptr;
    temp_ptr = (LIST_TYPE)malloc(sizeof(NODE_TYPE));
    if (temp_ptr == NULL)
       return(TRUE);
    else {
       free(temp_ptr);
       return (FALSE);
    }
}
```

# SECTION 14.1

1. False

3. False

5. C

7. D

9. Business community

11. Syntax

13. A block-structured language that allows modularization within the program.

15. These grammars consist of a set of nonterminals with a symbol to specify the beginning of the grammar sequence and a set of terminals. They also include a set of production rules of the form  `A ::= B`  where  `A`  is a single nonterminal symbol.
```

17. A low-level language allows you to closely plan where and what goes into and out of memory. Instructions work almost directly with the hardware.

21. A parse tree is a structured hierarchy of syntax used to interpret expressions based on the grammar of a language. It allows you to see how a statement would be interpreted using the given grammar.

25. No string in the grammar could have two (or more) distinct parse trees.

SECTION 14.2

1. False

3. False

5. B

7. C

9. Smalltalk

11. Functional

13. The procedural paradigm follows the fetch-decode-execute phases of the instruction cycle and focuses on memory location, assignment, and functions.

15. The functional paradigm uses primitive functions from which other functions can be formed, and the use of recursion is a natural aspect of the method.

17. Imperative languages follow the procedural paradigm; declarative languages follow the logic paradigm.

19. Assembly language uses English-like mnemonics instead of straight binary, octal, or hexadecimal code.

21. The object would contain not only the data types but also the data that are to be executed.

23. Associations are identified at run time and then executed. Procedural languages could only execute data through a predefined process.

25. It is designed as a functional language, but its simulation characteristics are closely related to the logic paradigm.

27. The future of computing may not be number-crunching intensive as it is now, making nonprocedural languages very appealing.

SECTION 15.1

1. False

3. False

5. B

7. B

9. Base case

11. Activation record, run-time stack

13. The recursion is endless. It prints the word *help* until you fill the run-time stack with too many activation records.

15. 4

17.
```
void   count_back( int counter )
{
    if ( counter > 0 ) {
       printf("\n%d", counter );
       count_back( counter - 1 );
    }
}
```

19.
```
int power( int base,  int exp )
{
    if ( exp < 0 ) {                        /* Check for negative exponent */
       printf("\nNegative exponents not allowed.  Function terminated.");
       return( 0 );
    }
    else if ( exp == 0 )                         /* Base case */
       return( 1 );
    else                              /* Recursive case */
       return( base * power( base, exp-1 ) );
}
```

SECTION 15.2

1. False

3. True

5. C

7. D

9. Two (2), **left** and **right**

11. Feature

13.
```
void traverse ( LIST_TYPE list )
{
    if ( list->next->info.key != MAX_KEY ) {
       traverse( list->next );                  /* Recursive traversal */
       process ( list );                  /* Any process function */
    }
}
```

```
15. void  load_grid( GRID_TYPE grid )
    {
        int   row, col;
        char  response;
        for ( row=0; row<MAX_ROW; row++ )              /* For each row */
            for ( col=0; col<MAX_COL; col++ )          /* For each col in row */
                grid[row][col] = EMPTY;                /* Set status to EMPTY */
        printf("\n Input blob coordinate pairs.");
        printf("\n Enter -1 -1 to stop.");
        scanf ("%d %d", &row, &col);
        while ( row != -1 && col != -1){
            grid[row][col] = FILLED;
            scanf("%d %d", &row, &col);
        }
    }
```

SECTION 16.1

1. False
3. False
5. D
7. C
9. Number crunching
11. Item not in list, found target item
13.
```
    loc = 0;
    while ( loc < list->current_size  &&
            list->info[loc].ss_num != target_value  )
        loc++;
```
14.
```
    loc = *list;
    while ( loc != NULL   &&
            loc->info.ss_num != target_value  )
        loc = loc->next;
```

SECTION 16.2

1. True
3. False
5. D
7. B
9. Quadratic
11. Quicksort

```
13. void find_pos_min( int list[], int start_pos, int *pos_min )
    {
        int    index;
        *pos_min = start_pos;

        for ( index=start_pos+1; index<MAX_SIZE; index++ ) {
            if ( list[index] < list[*pos_min] )      /* Is item < pos_min item */
                *pos_min = index;                     /* If yes, update pos_min */
        }
    }
```

15. Quicksort

```
17. int hash_it( float x )
    {
        return( (int) 100*x );
    }
```

SECTION 17.1

1. False

3. True

5. C

7. C

9. Newton-Raphson

11. Relation

13. $\{ 1, 2, 6, 8 \}$

15. $4 + \sqrt{13} \approx 7.60555$ and $4 - \sqrt{13} \approx 0.39445$

17. 1.1429

19. 1.96875

21. 0.207935 (after three iterations)

23. In each case the algorithm divides in half the interval of interest.

SECTION 17.2

1. False

3. True

5. C

7. C

9. Column matrix (vector)

11. Inconsistent

13. $x = 1.76712$

15. $x = 14/3 = 4.66666, y = 7/3 = 2.33333$

17. $x = 3, y = -4$

19. $x = (47 - 8z)/15, y = (3 - 2z)/5$

21. Converges to $(-0.1428571, 3.5714285)$

SECTION 17.3

1. False

3. False

5. C

7. D

9. Integration

11. Derivative

13. Area $= 11.6875$ using 8 partitions.

15. $f'(-1) = 1, f'(0) = -2, f'(1) = 1, f'(2) = 10, f'(3) = 25$

17. 6.345765

29. Area of $f(x) = x^2 + 2$ using 16 partitions is
    12.17190 using the rectangular rule
    12.86719 using the trapezoidal rule
    12.65547 using Simpson's rule

SECTION 18.1

1. True

3. True

5. B

7. C

9. Decision problems

11. Current state, next state, input, output

13. 433

15. 433

17. 424

19. $\ldots \not{b} \not{b} \, 3 \, 2 \, \not{b} \, \not{b} \ldots$

21. $\ldots \not{b} \not{b} \, 4 \, 3 \, 3 \, 3 \, 2 \, \not{b} \, \not{b} \ldots$

23. $\ldots \not{b} \, \not{b} \, \not{b} \, \not{b} \, \not{b} \, \not{b} \, \not{b} \, \not{b} \ldots$

25. Computable functions are discrete numerical functions such that for a given input, the function produces an output. Turing computable functions are discrete numerical functions evaluated by a Turing machine.

27. If there is a method (an algorithm) with which we can calculate the output of a function for a given input, the function is called a computable function.

SECTION 18.2

1. False

3. True

5. D

7. A

9. 91

11. $O(n)$

13. $\log_2 n$

15. $n^2 \log_2 n$

17. The average number of steps for a successful search in a list of n items is $(n + 1)/2$. For an unsuccessful search the number of steps is n.

19. They have the same order of complexity.

22. Because 2^n is of exponential order. (For any positive integer k there exists a value of n large enough such that $2^n > n^k$.)

23. A deterministic Turing machine gives a unique output for a given input string. For a nondeterministic Turing machine the output is not predictable for a given input string.

25. Nondeterministic:
    1. Starting at Buffalo, New York, find the shortest route to visit each city in the state of New York.
    2. Find from a weather satellite's reading what the weather will be for the next week.

27. Deterministic polynomial problems are a subset of nondeterministic polynomial problems because each is of polynomial complexity.

SECTION 19.1

1. True

3. False

5. B

7. B

9. Turing test

11. Background problem

13. Feasibility of AI: Scientists lack theories of cognition.

15. Morality of AI: People tend to believe in computers too much.

SECTION 19.2

1. False

3. False

5. C

7. D

9. Computer graphics

11. Convolution process

13. Huge quantity of data; incomplete information; complex textures; 3D; motion

15. Mask1: horizontal edge detection; Mask2: vertical edge detection

16. number of seconds per day $= 86,400$
    number of bytes per color image $= 0.75$ MB
    number of frames per second $= 30$
    number of bytes per day $= 86,400 * 0.75\text{MB} * 30$
    $ = 1,944,000,000$ bytes
    $ \sim 2$ TB (terabytes)

18. Find all local maxima: $P_1, P_2, P_3, \ldots$. Find all local minima: $V_1, V_2, V_3, \ldots$. The values for the V_i are the thresholds.

22.
```
for ( row=0; row<IMG_SIZE; row++ )
    for ( col=0; col<IMG_SIZE; col++ )
        if ( image[row][col] > theta )
            out_image[row][col] = 1;
        else
            out_image[row][col] = 0;
```

Photo Credits

Chapter 1 *Opener:* Courtesy Moore School Computer Museum, University of Pennsylvania. **Figure 1.3–4:** Courtesy Intel. **Chapter 2** *Opener:* Art Resource. **Chapter 3** *Opener:* Courtesy the Cleveland Indians. **Chapter 4** *Opener:* Courtesy Intel. **Chapter 5** *Opener:* Ed Pritchard/Tony Stone Images. **Chapter 6** *Opener:* © Sun Microsystems. **Chapter 7** *Opener:* Joe Sherschel/Life Magazine © 1958 Time Inc. **Chapter 8** *Opener:* Permission of AT&T Archives. **Chapter 9** *Opener:* Peter Menzel/Stock, Boston. **Chapter 10** *Opener:* Courtesy LEGO Systems, Inc. **Chapter 11** *Opener:* Barbara Rios/Photo Researchers. **Chapter 12** *Opener:* UPI/Bettman. **Chapter 13** *Opener:* Union Pacific Railroad Photo. **Chapter 14** *Opener:* Erich Lessing/Art Resource. **Chapter 15** *Opener:* John W. Banagan/The Image Bank. **Chapter 16** *Opener:* Will Ryan/The Stock Market. **Chapter 17** *Opener:* Courtesy The U.S. Air Force. **Chapter 18** *Opener:* COMSTOCK, Inc. **Chapter 19** *Opener:* Shahn Kermani/Gamma Liaison. **Figures 19.2–3, 19.2–4, & 19.2–5:** Paul Nagin.

Index

An italicized page number indicates where the term is defined.